Contents

KT-527-071

About the Author

John O'Leary is a freelance journalist and education consultant. He was the Editor of *The Times Higher Education Supplement* from 2002 to 2007 and was previously Education Editor of *The Times*, having joined the paper in 1990 as Higher Education Correspondent. He has been writing on higher education for more than 30 years and is a member of the executive board of the QS World University Rankings. He is a member of the Higher Education Commission and the author of *Higher Education in England,* published in 2009 by the Higher Education Funding Council for England. He has a degree in politics from the University of Sheffield.

Acknowledgements
We would like to thank the many individuals who have helped with this edition of *The Times and Sunday Times and Sunday Times Good University Guide*, particularly Greg Hurst, Education Editor of *The Times*, Alastair McCall, Editor of *The Sunday Times University Guide*, and Patrick Kennedy, the lead consultant with Andrew Farquhar, for UoE Consulting Limited, which has compiled the main university league table and the individual subject tables for this *Guide* on behalf of *The Times*, *The Sunday Times* and HarperCollins Publishers.

To the members of *The Times and Sunday Times Good University Guide* Advisory Group for their time and expertise: Patrick Kennedy, Consultant, Collective Intelligence Limited; Christine Couper, Head of Planning and Statistics, University of Greenwich; James Galbraith, Senior Strategic Planner, University of Edinburgh; Alison Hartrey, Head of Planning, SOAS, London; Mark Langer-Crame, Senior Planning Officer, Cardiff University; Daniel Monnery, Head of Corporate Strategy, Northumbria University; Aaron Morrison, Principal Planning Officer, De Montfort University; Jackie Njoroge, Head of Strategic Planning, Manchester Metropolitan University; Komal Patel, Strategic Planning Officer, Imperial College, London; Dr Sarah Taylor, Head of Strategy Development, Aberystwyth University; David Totten, Head of Planning, Queen's University, Belfast; Jenny Walker, Planning Officer, Loughborough University; to James McLaren, Denise Jones and Pip Day of HESA for their technical advice; to Alice Hancock, Gurpreet Narwan and Adam O'Leary for their contributions to the book.

We also wish to thank all the university staff who assisted in providing information for this edition.

THE TIMES
THE SUNDAY TIMES

Good University Guide

2018

John O'Leary

378.4

Published in 2017 by Times Books

An imprint of HarperCollins Publishers
Westerhill Road
Bishopbriggs
Glasgow G64 2QT
www.harpercollins.co.uk
times.books@harpercollins.co.uk

First published in 1993. Twenty-third edition 2017

© Times Newspapers Ltd 2017

The Times is a registered trademark of Times Newspapers Ltd

ISBN 978-0-00-821346-6

Patrick Kennedy was the lead consultant with Andrew Farquhar for UoE Consulting Limited, which has compiled the main university league table and the individual subject tables for this *Guide* on behalf of *The Times*, *The Sunday Times* and HarperCollins Publishers.

Please see chapters 1 and 12 for a full explanation of the sources of data used in the ranking tables. The data providers do not necessarily agree with the data aggregations or manipulations appearing in this book and are also not responsible for any inference or conclusions thereby derived.

Project editor: Christopher Riches
Design, editorial and additional research: Edenside Computing Services Ltd

A catalogue record for this book is available from the British Library.

Printed and bound in Great Britain by Clays Ltd, St Ives plc.

MIX
Paper from
responsible sources
FSC **FSC™ C007454**
www.fsc.org

FSC™ is a non-profit international organisation established to promote the responsible management of the world's forests. Products carrying the FSC label are independently certified to assure consumers that they come from forests that are managed to meet the social, economic and ecological needs of present and future generations, and other controlled sources.

Find out more about HarperCollins and the environment at
www.harpercollins.co.uk/green

Timeline to a University Place

This book is designed to help you find a university place in September 2018. That may seem a long time away, but a decision that can change your life needs a lot of consideration. Add to that the fact that the application process is somewhat long-winded and there is less time than you might think – for example, if you want to study medicine starting in September 2018 you will have had to have some practical experience of helping to care for people, have taken an aptitude test during the summer of 2017 and completed your application by 15 October 2017, almost a year before your studies will start. Planning well ahead of application and decision deadlines will always give you greater flexibility and choice. The less time you give yourself, the more limited will become your choices.

So where to start? The dates below indicate the key staging points along the way to a university place.

Key dates
February to July 2017
This is the time to develop your thoughts on the subject you would like to study and on where you would like to be at university. See overleaf for where to find advice in this book on choosing a subject and a university.

March 2017 onwards
Attend university open days. Open Days are a good way to gain a personal impression of what a university feels like, where it is located, and what studying in a particular department or faculty would be like. You will only have the time and resources to attend a small number of Open Days, so careful planning is necessary, not least because Open Days at different universities can often clash – there are at least 16 Open Days on 1 July 2017, for example. A list of Open Days for 2017 (as announced by the end of November 2016) appears at the back of this book.

July 2017
Registration starts for UCAS Apply, the online application system through which you will make your application. You will have a maximum of five choices when you come to complete your application form.

September 2017
UCAS will begin to accept completed applications.

15 October 2017
Deadline for applications to Oxford or Cambridge (you can only apply to one of them), and for applications to any university to study medicine, dentistry and veterinary science. Note that for some courses you will need to have completed a pre-application assessment test by this date.

15 January 2018
Deadline for applications for all other universities and subjects (excluding a few art and

design courses with a deadline of 24 March 2018). It is advisable to get your application in ahead of this deadline; aim for the end of November 2017.

End of March 2018
Universities should have given you decisions on your applications by now if you submitted them by 15 January 2018.

April onwards
Apply for student loans to cover tuition fees and living costs.

Early May 2018
You will need to have responded to all university decisions. You have to select first choice, if your first offer is conditional, a second choice, and reject all other offers. Once you have accepted an offer, apply for university accommodation.

7 August 2018
Scottish examination results. If your results meet the offer from your first choice (or, failing that, your second choice), your place at university will be confirmed. If not, you can enter Clearing for Scottish universities in order to find a place on another course offered by a Scottish university.

16 August 2018
A-level results announced. If your results meet the offer from your first choice (or, failing that, your second choice), your place at university will be confirmed. If not, you can enter Clearing to find a place on another course offered by any university.

Mid to late September 2018
Arrive at university for Freshers' Week.

How This Book Can Help You

The process of making a successful application to university has many stages. Fundamental to the whole process are your decisions on which subject to pick and where to study it.

How do I choose a course?

As you will be taking a course that will last three and sometimes four years, you will need to enthusiasm for, and some aptitude in, the subject. The options of studying full-time or part-time also need to be considered.

» The first half of chapter 2 provides advice on choosing a subject area and selecting relevant courses within that subject.

» Chapter 12 provides details for 67 different subject areas (as listed on page 136). For each subject there is specific advice and a league table that provides our assessment of the quality of universities offering courses.

How will my choice of subject affect my employment prospects?

As the course you chose will also influence your job prospects at its conclusion, your initial subject decision will have an impact on your life long after you complete your degree.

» The employment prospects and average starting salaries for the main subject groups are given in chapter 3.

» The subject tables in chapter 12 give the employment prospects for each university offering a course.

» Universities are now doing more to increase the employability of their graduates. Some examples are given in chapter 3.

How do I choose a university?

While choosing your subject comes first, the place where you study will also play a major role. You will need to decide upon what type of university you wish to go to: campus, city or smaller town? How well does the university perform? How far is the university from home? Is it large or small? Is it specialist or general? Do you want to study abroad?

» Central is the main *Times and Sunday Times* league table in chapter 1. This ranks the universities by assessing their performance not just according to teaching quality and the student experience but also through seven other factors, including research quality, the spending on services and facilities, and graduate employment prospects.

» The second half of chapter 2 provides advice on the factors to consider when choosing a university.

» The second half of the book contains two pages on each university, giving a general overview of the institution as well as data on student numbers, contact details, accommodation provision, and the fees for 2017–18. Note that fees for 2018–19 will not be fixed until August 2017, and you must check these before applying.

» For those considering Oxford or Cambridge, details of admission processes and of all the undergraduate colleges can be found in chapter 13.

» If you are considering studying abroad, chapter 4 provides guidance and practical information.

» Specific advice for international students coming to study in the UK is given in chapter 11.

How do I apply?

» Chapter 6 outlines the application procedure for university entry. It starts by advising you on how to complete the UCAS application, and then takes you through the process that we hope will lead to your university place for autumn 2018.

Can I afford it?

Note that all information in chapters 5 and 7 refers to 2017 and there will be changes for 2018, which you will need to check.

» Chapter 5 describes how the system of tuition fees works and what you are likely to be charged, depending upon where in the UK you plan to study.

» Chapter 7 provides advice on the tuition fee loans and maintenance loans that are available, depending upon where you live in the UK, other forms of financial support (including university scholarships and bursaries), and how to plan your budget.

» Chapter 8 provides advice on where to live while you are at university. University accommodation charges for each university are given in chapter 14.

How do I find out more?

The Times and Sunday Times Good University Guide website at **http://extras.thetimes.co.uk/ web/2016/bespoke/university-guide/index.html** will keep you up to date with developments throughout the year and contains further information and online tables.

You can also find much practical advice on the UCAS website (**www.ucas.com**), and on individual university websites. There is also a wealth of official statistical information on the Unistats website (**www.unistats.ac.uk**).

Introduction

Universities have coped with their share of turmoil in the 23 years that this *Guide* has been published. But seldom have they faced uncertainty on such a variety of fronts as they will in the run-up to 2018, when the UK is scheduled to leave the European Union and the impact of higher fees and new teaching assessments will be felt for the first time. Already, applications for courses starting in 2017 are falling at many universities, although this may yet prove to be a seasonal blip. Students have been tending to apply for degree courses later in the year than their predecessors did, and it would be no surprise if this trend continued.

As in previous years, however, conditions that test university managers can work to the advantage of applicants. Since universities were obliged to rely much more on fee income, university entrance has been a buyer's market, beyond a select few institutions. If demand falls, particularly among EU and other international students because of real or perceived barriers to a UK education, 2017 and 2018 may prove to be golden years for those seeking a place on a degree course. There is already a decline in the number of 18-year-olds to work in applicants' favour.

This *Guide* is designed to help you make the most of those conditions and find a place at the best possible university. For the first time, it is published in February to fit in with the way schools and colleges approach university applications. A timeline of the process is published on pages 5–6. The new publication date also allows for additional features, such as a calendar of Open Days and a composite table of the top universities in the world from the three main international rankings.

After small but important changes last year to the way our tables are compiled, the methodology for the new edition remains stable. The *Guide* has always put a premium on consistency in the way that it uses the statistics published by universities and presents the results. The overriding aim is to inform potential students and their parents and advisors, not to make judgments on the performance of universities. As such, it will differ from the Government's proposed Teaching Excellence Framework (TEF), which will use some of the same statistics but make allowance for the prior qualifications of students and use an expert panel to place the results in context. Our tables use the raw data produced by universities to reflect the undergraduate experience, whatever advantages or disadvantages those institutions might face.

The TEF represents the first official intervention in this area since the Quality Assurance

Agency's assessments of teaching quality were abolished more than a decade ago. Scores in those reports correlated closely with research grades, and the first discussions on the framework in the Coalition Government envisaged one comparison taking account of both teaching and research. This remains our approach, to look at a broad range of factors (including the presence of excellent researchers on the academic staff) that will impact on undergraduates. While some elements of the tables may have changed over the years, their role in the process of choosing a university and a course has not. There will be many considerations in coming to a final decision, but this *Guide* may help to narrow down the options and give reassurance.

An era of change

Although £9,000 fees have hardly been popular and are back on the political agenda for a Jeremy Corbyn-led Labour Party, they have not led to the protracted slump in the demand for higher education that many critics predicted. Although part-time enrolments have been hit hard, so far, the numbers coming from low-income families and areas of low participation in higher education have held up, or even increased. If there is a decline now, it is unlikely that the extra £250 to be charged in 2017 will be the main cause.

What has changed with higher fees, however, is the pattern of applications and enrolments. Students are plainly opting in larger numbers for subjects that they think will lead to well-paid jobs. While there has been a recovery in some arts and social science subjects, the trend towards the sciences and some vocational degrees is unmistakeable. Languages have suffered particularly – perhaps partly because they tend to be four-year degrees – and so have courses associated with parts of the economy that were hardest hit in the recession. Building is one example, where numbers are still well down even though the subject is in the top ten for employment prospects, with four out of five graduates going straight into a professional job.

The vast majority of students take a degree primarily to improve their career prospects, so some second-guessing of the employment market is inevitable. But most graduate jobs are not subject-specific and the best brains in the country are hard-pressed to predict employment hotspots four or five years ahead, when today's applicants will be looking for jobs. Computer science is a good example of the pitfalls. Demand for the subject plummeted when the "dotcom bubble" burst and courses closed. Now parts of the IT industry are booming again and there is a skills shortage. Applications for the subject have shot up, but no one can be certain of market conditions in such a fast-moving industry so far ahead.

Just as it may be unwise to second-guess employment prospects, the same goes for the competition for places in different subjects. Universities may close or reduce the intake to courses that have low numbers of applicants while some of the more selective institutions may make more places available, especially to candidates who achieve good grades at A level. Bristol, Birmingham, Exeter and University College London have all taken hundreds more students than usual since the restrictions were relaxed for high-grade candidates. Now universities such as Sussex and Essex have announced that they intend to grow substantially, while the University of St Mark and St John plans to double in size to achieve economies of scale and become more secure.

Even before the increase to £9,250 fees in 2017, it seems that universities of all types saw the expansion of undergraduate provision as a sensible strategy. But even those that are expanding may do so only in areas where they are strong and extra students can be taught at reasonable cost. In the absence of clear announcements, applicants are still best advised to go for the courses and universities that meet their requirements, rather than trying to play the system.

Certainly, fee levels are unlikely to play a significant part in applicants' choices of university in 2017 and 2018 – other than in Scotland and Northern Ireland, where there are big financial incentives to study at a home university. The continuing absence of fees north of the border has been particularly influential in dissuading Scottish students from studying elsewhere, although the cap on recruitment there led to more coming south in 2015 and 2016. Most candidates were not swayed by differences of a few hundred pounds in the fees charged by universities in England. Even those differences have now practically disappeared: only two – the University of St Mark and St John and University College Birmingham – will charge less than the maximum for any Honours degrees in 2017–18.

Using this *Guide*

The merger of *The Times and Sunday Times* university guides three years ago began a new chapter in the ranking of higher education institutions in the UK. The two guides had 35 editions between them and, in their new form, provide the most comprehensive and authoritative assessments of undergraduate education at UK universities.

There is one new institution in the main table this year following the award of independent university status to the University of Suffolk, previously a joint enterprise by Essex and East Anglia universities.

Like last year, only three public universities with a focus on full-time undergraduate education are absent. For different reasons, University College Birmingham, Trinity Saint David and Wolverhampton have all instructed the Higher Education Statistics Agency not to release data on their performance and are missing from the institutional and subject tables. Private universities such as the University of Law, Regent's University and BPP University, do not currently have the necessary data to be included.

Some famous names in UK higher education have never been ranked because they do not fit the parameters of a system that is intended mainly to guide full-time undergraduates. The Open University, for example, operates entirely through distance learning, while the London and Manchester business schools have no undergraduates. Birkbeck, University of London, focuses predominantly on part-time education, although growth in the number of full-time students may bring it into the main table before long. Other specialist institutions, including a number of university colleges, appear in relevant subject tables.

There are now 67 subject tables, since the addition this year of criminology. Other subject tables will be added in due course because there is growing demand for information at this level. Successive surveys have found that international students are more influenced by subject rankings than those for whole institutions, and there is no reason to believe that domestic applicants think differently.

Since the separation of NSS scores, outlined above, there has been no change in the basic methodology behind the tables, however. The eight elements of the main table are the same, with the approach to scores in the 2014 Research Excellence Framework mirroring as closely as possible those for previous assessments. In order to reflect the likelihood of undergraduates coming into contact with outstanding researchers, the proportion of eligible academics entered for assessment is part of the calculation, as well as the average grades achieved.

This year's tables

This year's results show more movement than usual, perhaps reflecting the increased level of competition for undergraduates. The division of NSS scores continues to have an effect, with the three sections of the survey categorised as "Teaching Quality" given more weight than the remaining four. But, unlike last year, changes in universities' positions cannot be attributed to methodology. The graduate labour market continued to improve in 2015 – the year in which the latest available employment survey took place – and some universities had shared in the recovery more than others. There was more variation than usual in the amounts spent on student facilities and some universities (but by no means all) saw spectacular increases in student satisfaction.

It seems, however, that nothing can shake the dominance of Cambridge and Oxford at the head of the main table – and the majority of the subject tables. Cambridge has maintained a clear lead over its ancient rival, although the gap has narrowed slightly. St Andrews is now the nearest challenger and, even at almost 40 points, the gap between second and third is half what it has been in recent years. Cambridge also tops 31 of the subject tables, compared with five each for Oxford and St Andrews. Throughout all the years of the *Guide*, Oxford and Cambridge have seldom been challenged, especially in terms of the undergraduate education they offer. It will be interesting to see whether the TEF reaches to same conclusion.

St Andrews remains easily Scotland's top university in the table and Queen's, Belfast the same in Northern Ireland, while for the first time Swansea is the leader in Wales. Other movements in the upper reaches of the table have seen University College London move up four places to sixth and Lancaster re-enter the top ten. Leeds has made progress for the third year in a row and was rewarded with the title of *The Sunday Times* University of the Year, while Nottingham is back in the top 20 after a rise of five places.

Further down the table, Harper Adams has recorded its second big increase in succession (13 places) and is now the leading post-1992 university. Aberystwyth, Bournemouth and Liverpool Hope have all gone up at least 20 places, but the biggest rise of all is 37 places by West London. Those going in the other direction include York St John (21 places), St George's (22 places) and Norwich University of the Arts (27 places). A number of modern universities continue to feature above some older foundations. The first edition of *The Times Good University Guide* predicted the development of a new pecking order in an era of growing competition between universities, many of which had just acquired that title. It has taken longer than many expected and the top third of the table is still monopolised by old universities, but the previous binary division is breaking down.

Guide Award Winners

University of the Year	**Leeds**
Runner-up	**St Andrews**
Shortlisted	**Dundee**
	Loughborough
	Nottingham
Scottish University of the Year	**Dundee**
Welsh University of the Year	**Swansea**
Modern University of the Year	**Harper Adams**
Sports University of the Year	**Loughborough**
University of the Year for	
Teaching Quality	**St Andrews**
Student Experience	**Keele**
Graduate Employment	**Nottingham**
Student Retention	**Chichester**

Making the right choices

Anyone hoping to embark on a degree in 2018 will be well advised to tread carefully and muster as much comparative information as possible before making their choices. This

Guide is intended as a starting point, a tool to help navigate the statistical minefield that will face applicants, as universities present their performance in the best possible light. There is a chapter on the impact of the fee changes, as well as one focusing on all-important employment issues along with the usual ranking of universities and 67 subject tables.

Whatever their appetite for expansion, most of the leading universities will remain highly selective, particularly in popular subjects. Even when the demand for places dropped in 2012, there were between five and six applications (not applicants) to the place across the whole higher education system. The figure was almost double that at the most popular universities. The demand for places is far from uniform, however; even within the same university the level of competition will vary between subjects. The entry scores quoted in the subject tables in chapter 12 offer a reliable guide to the relative levels of selectivity, but the figures are for entrants' actual qualifications. The standard offers made by departments will invariably be lower.

Making the right choice for 2018 will require a mixture of realism and ambition. Most sixth-formers and college students have a fair idea of the grades they are capable of attaining, within a certain margin for error. Even with five choices of course to make, there is no point in applying to a course where the standard offer is so far from your predicted grades that rejection is virtually certain. If your results do turn out to be much better than predicted, there will be an opportunity through the Adjustment system, or simply through Clearing, to trade up to an alternative university.

With the relaxation of recruitment restrictions, universities that once took pride in their absence from Clearing are now continuing to recruit after A-level results day. As a result, the use of insurance choices – the inclusion of at least one university with lower entrance standards than your main targets – is likely to decline further. It is still a dangerous strategy, but there is now more chance of picking up a place at a leading university if you aimed too high with all your first-round choices. Oxford and Cambridge will not be appearing in the Clearing lists and the appearance of courses in medicine at St George's in 2016 was so rare that it made national headlines, but there is now a wider range of universities to choose from than ever before. Some may even come to you if you sign up for the new arrangements introduced by UCAS last year, which allow universities to approach unplaced candidates on Results Day if their grades are similar to other entrants'.

The Adjustment Period that runs for five days after results have been published is reserved for those with better grades than the offer they have accepted to approach other universities. Although only 1,100 students found places this way in 2015, the numbers may rise as the system offers a valuable safety net for those in this happy position. Universities at the very top of the table may be full, but there should be more opportunities elsewhere.

The long view

School-leavers who enter higher education in 2018 were not born when our first league table was published and most will never have heard of polytechnics, even if they attend a university that once carried that title. But it was the award of university status to the 34 polytechnics, a quarter of a century ago, that was the inspiration for the first edition of *The Times Good University Guide*. The original poly, the Polytechnic of Central London, had become the University of Westminster, Bristol Polytechnic was now the University of the West of England and – most mysteriously of all – Leicester Polytechnic had morphed into De Montfort University. The new *Guide* charted the lineage of the new universities and offered the first-ever comparison of institutional performance in UK higher education.

The university establishment did not welcome the initiative. The vice-chancellors described the table as "wrong in principle, flawed in execution and constructed upon data which are not uniform, are ill-defined and in places demonstrably false." The league table has changed considerably since then, although even then Oxford and Cambridge have reigned supreme. While consistency has been a priority for the *Guide* throughout its 23 years, only six of the original 14 measures have survived. Some of the current components – notably the National Student Survey – did not exist in 1992, while others have been modified or dropped at the behest of the expert group of planning officers from different types of universities that meets annually to review the methodology and make recommendations for the future.

While ranking is hardly popular with academics, the relationship with universities has changed radically, and this *Guide* is quoted on numerous university websites. As Sir David Eastwood, now vice-chancellor of the University of Birmingham, said in launching an official report on university league tables that he commissioned as Chief Executive of the Higher Education Funding Council for England: "We deplore league tables one day and deploy them the next."

Most universities have had their ups and downs over the years, although Oxford and Cambridge have tended to pull away from the rest. Both benefited from the introduction of student satisfaction ratings and from the extra credit given to the top research grades – the two measures that carry an extra weighting in our table. They also have famously high entry standards, much the largest proportions of Firsts and 2:1 degrees and consistently good scores on every other measure. Several other famous names have been among the chasing pack throughout. The London School of Economics, Imperial College and University College London have seldom been out of the top five, while Warwick and, in recent years, Durham and St Andrews have all been fixtures in the top ten.

There have been spectacular rises, however. Exeter, for example, was 36th in the inaugural table and only one place better off in the 2003 *Guide*, but is now enjoying its sixth year in the top ten. Perhaps even more impressively, Coventry was only 12 places off the bottom a decade ago and is now inside the top 50, having reached the highest position ever for a modern university two years ago. Harper Adams, which now enjoys that distinction, was not even a university until 2012.

Higher education has changed enormously since this book was first published. The number of universities has increased by another third and the full-time student population has rocketed. Individual institutions are almost unrecognisable from their 1993 forms. Nottingham, for example, had less than 10,000 students then, compared with more than 30,000 now. Manchester Metropolitan, the largest of the former polys, has experienced similar growth. Yet there are universities now which would have been too small and too specialist to qualify for the title in 1992. The diversity of UK higher education is celebrated as one of its greatest strengths, and the modern universities are neither encouraged nor anxious to compete with the older foundations on some of the measures in our table.

The coming years, let alone the next 20, may see another transformation in the higher education landscape, with the private sector competing strongly with established universities in some fields and distance learning becoming more popular as there is greater investment in Massive Open Online Courses (MOOCs) and the cost of full-time degrees rises. There may, indeed, be university closures and mergers, although they have been predicted before and seldom come about. Universities are among the most enduring of the UK's institutions, and will take some shifting.

Why university?

Particularly if the UK economy continues its recovery, more young people will be tempted to write off higher education, once the cost of living has been added to the growing fees burden and the attractions of university life balanced against loss of potential earnings. There are plenty of self-made millionaires who still swear by the University of Life as the only training ground for success, and commentators who believe that the expansion of higher education has gone too far. Yet even by narrow financial criteria, it would be rash to dismiss an opportunity to go to university. With so many more competing for jobs, a degree will never again be an automatic passport to a fast-track career. But graduates' financial prospects remain much brighter than school leavers', as are their prospects in other important areas, such as health.

Even for those who cannot or do not wish to afford the costs associated with three or more years of full-time education when they leave school, university remains a possibility. Degree apprenticeships are an attractive new option, while the modular courses adopted by some universities enable students to work through even a traditional degree at their own pace, dropping out for a time if necessary, or switching to part-time attendance. Distance learning is another option, and advances in information technology now mean that some nominally full-time courses are delivered mainly online.

For many – perhaps most – students, the university experience is not what it was in their parents' day. There is more assessment, more crowding, more pressure to get the best possible degree while also finding gainful employment for at least part of the year. The proportion of students achieving first-class degrees has risen significantly, while a 2:1 (rather than the previously ubiquitous 2:2) has become the norm. Research shows that the classification has a real impact in the labour market.

Most graduates do not regret their decision to go to university, however. Students from all over the world flock to British universities, and they offer a valuable resource for those on their doorstep. No league table can determine which is the right university for any candidate, but this *Guide* should provide some of the information necessary to draw up a shortlist for further investigation and make the right choice in the end.

1 The University League Table

Universities publish reams of statistics about themselves – more than ever now that the Government insists on greater transparency. But even some of the official attempts to provide prospective students with better information can leave the reader more confused, rather than less. The forthcoming Teaching Excellence Framework may fall into this category, with its use of benchmarks to allow for students' prior qualifications and an expert panel to put the results in context. Our main table has been developed over 23 years to focus on the fundamentals of undergraduate education and make meaningful comparisons in an accessible way.

What distinguishes a top university? And who is to say that one course is better than another – especially when the university system has been so reluctant to make any such comparison? Critics of league tables insist that this is because every university has different priorities, and every course has a different ways of approaching a subject. Students must choose the one that suits them best. So they must. Not everyone would find the top universities to their taste, even if they were able to secure a place. But that does not mean that there are not important differences in the quality of universities and the courses they offer. These, in turn, can have a crucial bearing on future employment prospects.

The table in this chapter offers applicants and others with an interest in higher education a means to assess the standing of UK universities with undergraduate education in mind. The institutions will have their own ideas about what should go into comparisons of this type, but ours has stood the test of time because it uses the statistics that universities themselves employ to measure their own performance and combines them in a straightforward way that generations of students have found revealing.

Every element of the table in this chapter has been chosen for the light it shines on the undergraduate experience and a student's future prospects. The selection of these measures and the way in which they are combined give a particular view of universities' overall strengths, and it is one that has stood the test of time. Unlike some others, *The Times and Sunday Times Good University Guide* has placed a premium on consistency, confident that the measures are the best available for the task. Some changes have been forced upon us. Universities stopped assessing teaching quality by subject, when this was the most heavily weighted measure in the table, for example. However, the arrival of the National Student Survey (NSS) 11 years ago has enabled the student experience to be reflected in the table.

The NSS is an initiative of the Funding Councils for England, Northern Ireland and Wales. Scottish universities are not automatically included in the survey, although all 15 opted to take part in the latest survey. It is designed, as an element of the quality assurance for higher education, to inform prospective students and their advisers in choosing what and where to study. It gives the views of final-year students on the quality of their courses.

Last year we split the student satisfaction measure in two while keeping the overall contribution of the NSS to the table ranking unchanged, and we have retained this approach. The new "teaching quality" indicator reflects the average scores of the teaching, assessment and feedback, and academic support sections of the NSS, while the "student experience" indicator is drawn from the average of organisation and management, learning resources, and personal development sections and the overall satisfaction question in the survey. Teaching quality is favoured over student experience and accounts for 67 per cent of the overall student satisfaction score, with student experience making up the remaining 33 per cent.

The basic information that applicants need, however, in order to judge universities and their courses does not change. A university's entry standards, staffing levels, completion rates, degree classifications and graduate employment rates are all vital pieces of intelligence for anyone deciding where to study. Research grades, while not directly involving undergraduates, bring with them considerable funds and enable a university to attract top academics.

Any of these measures can be discounted by an individual, but the package has struck a chord with readers. The ranking is the most-quoted of its type both in Britain and overseas, and has built a reputation as the most authoritative arbiter of changing fortunes in higher education. The measures used are kept under review by a group of university administrators and statisticians, which meets annually. The raw data that go into the table in this chapter and the 67 subject tables in chapter 12 are all in the public domain and are sent to universities for checking before any scores are calculated.

Indeed, while the various official bodies concerned with higher education do not publish league tables, several produce system-wide statistics in a format that invites comparisons. The Higher Education Funding Councils' Research Excellence Framework is one example of this. The Higher Education Statistics Agency (HESA), which supplies most of the figures used in our tables, also publishes annual "performance indicators" on everything from completion rates to research output at each university.

Any scrutiny of league table positions is best carried out in conjunction with an examination of the relevant subject table – it is the course, after all, that will dominate your undergraduate years and influence your subsequent career.

How *The Times and Sunday Times* league table works

The table is presented in a format that displays the raw data, wherever possible. In building the table, scores for student satisfaction (combining the teaching quality and student experience scores) and research quality were weighted by 1.5; all other measures were weighted by 1.

For entry standards, student–staff ratio, good honours and graduate prospects, the score was adjusted for subject mix. For example, it is accepted that engineering, law and medicine graduates will tend to have better graduate prospects than their peers from English, psychology and sociology courses. Comparing results in the main subject groupings helps to iron out differences attributable simply to the range of degrees on offer. This subject-mix adjustment means that it is not possible to replicate the scores in the table from the published indicators because the calculation requires access to the entire dataset.

The indicators were combined using a common statistical technique known as Z-scores, to ensure that no indicator has a disproportionate effect on the overall total for each university, and the totals were transformed to a scale with 1,000 for the top score. The Z-score technique makes it impossible to compare universities' total scores from one year to the next, although their relative positions in the table are comparable. Individual scores are dependent on the top performer: a university might drop from 60 per cent of the top score to 58 per cent but still have improved, depending on the relative performance of other universities.

Only where data are not available from HESA are figures sourced directly from universities. Where this is not possible, scores are generated according to a university's average performance on other indicators, apart from the measures for research quality, student–staff ratio and services and facilities spend, where no score is created.

The organisations providing the raw data for the tables are not involved in the process of aggregation, so are not responsible for any inferences or conclusions we have made. Every care has been taken to ensure the accuracy of the tables and accompanying information, but no responsibility can be taken for errors or omissions.

The Times and Sunday Times league table uses nine important indicators of university activity, based on the most recent data available at the time of compilation:

» Teaching quality
» Student experience
» Research quality
» Entry standards
» Student–staff ratio

» Services and facilities spend
» Completion
» Good honours
» Graduate prospects

Teaching quality and student experience

This year the student satisfaction measure has been split into two components which give the views of final-year students on the quality of their courses. The National Student Survey was the source of this data. Data from the survey published in 2016 were used.

» The National Student Survey covers six aspects of a course, with an additional question gauging overall satisfaction. Students answer on a scale from 1 (bottom) to 5 (top) and the score in the table is the percentage of positive responses (4 and 5) in each section.
» The teaching quality indicator reflects the average scores of the teaching, assessment and feedback, and academic support sections.
» The student experience indicator is drawn from the average scores of the organisation and management, learning resources, and personal development sections and the additional question on overall satisfaction.
» Teaching quality is favoured over student experience and accounts for 67 per cent of the overall score covering student satisfaction score, with student experience making up the remaining 33 per cent.
» The survey is based on the opinion of final-year students rather than directly assessing teaching quality. Most undergraduates have no experience of other universities, or different courses, to inform their judgements. Although all the questions relate to courses, rather than the broader student experience, some types of university – notably medium-sized campus universities – tend to do better than others.

Research quality

This is a measure of the quality of the research undertaken in each university. The information was sourced from the 2014 Research Excellence Framework (REF), a peer-review exercise used to evaluate the quality of research in UK higher education institutions undertaken by the UK Higher Education funding bodies. Additionally, academic staffing data for 2013–14 from the Higher Education Statistics Agency have been used.

» A research quality profile was given to every university department that took part. This profile used the following categories: 4* world-leading; 3* internationally excellent; 2* internationally recognised; 1* nationally recognised; and unclassified. The Funding Bodies have directed more funds to the very best research by applying weightings, and for the 2015 *Guide* we used the weightings adopted by HEFCE (the funding council for England) for funding in 2013–14: 4* is weighted by a factor of 3 and 3* is weighted by a factor of 1. Outputs of 2* and 1* carry zero weight. This means a maximum score of 3. In the interests of consistency, the above weightings continue to be applied this year.

» The scores in the table are presented as a percentage of the maximum score. To achieve the maximum score all staff would need to be at 4* world-leading level.

» Universities could choose which staff to include in the REF, so, to factor in the depth of the research quality, each quality profile score has been multiplied by the number of staff returned in the REF as a proportion of all eligible staff.

Entry standards

This is the average score, using the old UCAS tariff (see page 31), of new students under the age of 21 who took A and AS Levels, Scottish Highers and Advanced Highers and other equivalent qualifications (eg, International Baccalaureate). It measures what new students actually achieved rather than the entry requirements suggested by the universities. The data comes from HESA for 2014–15. The original sources of data for this measure are data returns made by the universities themselves to HESA.

» Using the UCAS tariff, each student's examination results were converted to a numerical score. HESA then calculated an average for all students at the university. The results have then been adjusted to take account of the subject mix at the university.

» A score of 360 represents three As at A level. Although all but seven of the top 50 universities in the table have entry standards of at least 360, it does not mean that everyone achieved such results – let alone that this was the standard offer. Courses will not demand more than three subjects at A level and offers are pitched accordingly. You will need to reach the entry requirements set by the university, rather than these scores.

Student–staff ratio

This is a measure of the average number of students to each member of the academic staff, apart from those purely engaged in research. In this measure a low value is better than a high value. The data comes from HESA for 2014–15. The original sources of data for this measure are data returns made by the universities themselves to HESA.

» The figures, as calculated by HESA, allow for variation in employment patterns at different universities. A low value means that there are a small number of students for each academic member of staff, but this does not, of course, ensure good teaching quality or contact time with academics.

» Student–staff ratios vary by subject, for example the ratio is usually low for medicine. In building the table, the score is adjusted for the subject mix taught by each university.

» Adjustments are also made for students who are on industrial placements, either for a full year or for part of a year.

Services and facilities spend

The expenditure per student on staff and student facilities, including library and computing facilities. The data comes from HESA for 2013–14 and 2014–15. The original data sources for this measure are data returns made by the universities to HESA.

» This is a measure calculated by taking the expenditure on student facilities (sports, grants to student societies, careers services, health services, counselling, etc.) and library and computing facilities (books, journals, staff, central computers and computer networks, but not buildings) and dividing this by the number of full-time-equivalent students. Expenditure is averaged over two years to even out the figures (for example, a computer upgrade undertaken in a single year).

Completion

This measure gives the percentage of students expected to complete their studies (or transfer to another institution) for each university. The data comes from the HESA performance indicators, based on data for 2014–15 and earlier years.

» This measure is a projection, liable to statistical fluctuations.

Good honours

This measure is the percentage of graduates achieving a first or upper second class degree. The results have been adjusted to take account of the subject mix at the university. The data comes from HESA for 2014–15. The original sources of data for this measure are data returns made by the universities themselves to HESA.

» Four-year first degrees, such as an MChem, are treated as equivalent to a first or upper second.
» Scottish Ordinary degrees (awarded after three years of study) are excluded.
» Universities control degree classification, with some oversight from external examiners. There have been suggestions that since universities have increased the numbers of good honours degrees they award, this measure may not be as objective as it should be. However, it remains the key measure of a student's success and employability.

Graduate prospects

This measure is the percentage of the total number of graduates undertaking further study or in a professional job. The results have been adjusted for subject mix. The data come from HESA for 2015 graduates.

» HESA surveys graduates six months after graduation to find out what they are doing and the data are based on this survey.

2017 rank	2016 rank		Teaching quality (%)	Student experience (%)	Research quality (%)	Entry standards	Student–staff ratio	Services and facilities spend per student (£)	Completion (%)	Good honours (%)	Graduate prospects (%)	Total
1	1	Cambridge	82.9	85.5	57.3	600	11	3,446	98.5	91.0	88.3	1000
2	2	Oxford	82.0	86.5	53.1	577	10.5	3,130	97.7	92.4	84.3	968
3	4	St Andrews	88.4	91.0	40.4	524	11.6	2,671	95.5	90.7	83.3	929
4	5	Durham	82.1	86.4	39.0	526	14.7	2,683	95.6	89.4	83.3	857
5	3	Imperial College	74.8	83.2	56.2	567	11.1	3,170	96.4	86.5	90.5	840
6	10	University College London	75.5	81.9	51.0	506	10.2	2,727	95.7	89.0	87.2	838
7	6	Warwick	80.1	84.4	44.6	490	12.5	2,566	94.9	82.7	80.4	813
8	9	London School of Economics	68.5	73.1	52.8	540	11.6	2,858	97.6	86.6	84.6	808
=9	7	Exeter	83.3	87.9	38.0	471	15.8	2,537	96.0	84.8	80.2	807
=9	11	Lancaster	82.3	87.8	39.1	421	13.4	2,827	92.8	76.8	82.5	807
11	13	Loughborough	81.9	87.9	36.3	411	14.6	2,582	94.9	81.7	85.3	793
12	12	Bath	81.6	85.1	37.3	481	15.5	2,210	96.3	84.5	85.4	786
13	14	Leeds	82.7	87.8	36.8	436	13.5	2,604	93.5	83.3	81.4	780
14	8	Surrey	83.7	87.3	29.7	424	13.9	2,697	91.6	80.7	81.1	774
15	18	East Anglia	83.0	87.4	35.8	423	13.2	2,653	92.2	83.4	74.2	769
16	17	Birmingham	80.8	84.4	37.1	429	14	2,531	94.8	86.1	85.3	761
17	15	York	83.8	87.5	38.3	431	14.5	2,144	93.3	80.5	77.0	758
18	19	Sussex	79.7	86.0	31.8	375	15.3	2,722	91.1	79.1	86.2	744
19	20	Bristol	78.8	84.0	47.3	479	13.8	2,032	95.0	87.9	79.0	741
20	25	Nottingham	81.2	86.0	37.8	425	13.2	2,180	93.7	80.5	82.7	738
21	16	Southampton	78.8	84.7	44.9	417	12	2,268	91.7	80.1	78.4	737
22	=23	Newcastle	82.9	87.8	37.7	432	15.5	1,894	94.9	81.3	82.6	728
23	=23	Kent	80.9	85.9	35.2	361	12.7	1,666	91.6	80.1	80.6	723
24	21	Sheffield	80.7	86.7	37.6	420	14.6	2,142	94.4	79.5	81.3	716

25	=28	Leicester	80.5	85.8	3?.8	390	12.9	2,742	91.8	77.2	75.3	713
26	31	Queen's, Belfast	82.8	88.7	33.7	388	15.1	2,151	92.6	78.3	80.3	710
27	27	King's College London	74.9	80.3	44.0	464	11.7	2,127	94.0	83.4	88.0	709
28	37	Dundee	85.9	88.8	31.2	413	12.6	1,705	86.4	77.8	80.9	706
29	26	Glasgow	79.4	85.6	39.9	478	14.5	2,292	88.4	79.3	81.8	704
30	35	Essex	82.4	87.2	37.2	313	16.5	2,945	88.3	74.3	73.4	701
31	32	Reading	80.2	84.8	36.5	372	14.7	2,175	92.2	80.6	73.6	696
32	=28	Manchester	77.3	83.4	39.8	439	13.4	2,283	92.9	76.2	82.2	694
33	30	Aston	81.9	86.8	25.8	365	19	2,177	93.7	86.2	82.3	693
34	36	Royal Holloway	81.9	83.9	36.3	400	15.3	1,941	93.8	75.6	69.3	688
35	44	SOAS London	79.5	83.1	27.9	410	11.1	2,206	84.3	79.9	70.8	687
36	49	Harper Adams	85.1	89.8	5.7	342	15.4	2,877	88.6	63.2	72.8	681
=37	22	Edinburgh	71.8	79.6	43.8	487	12	2,067	91.3	84.5	73.0	676
=37	=38	Heriot-Watt	80.0	85.3	36.7	407	15.6	2,375	84.4	75.5	79.7	676
39	=38	Liverpool	79.7	84.4	31.5	395	11.8	2,237	91.9	75.8	76.9	672
40	34	Queen Mary, London	76.7	80.7	37.9	417	11.9	2,512	90.5	74.3	79.8	665
41	=38	Buckingham	90.2	91.5	-	319	9.6	2,008	85.1	54.7	71.4	661
42	43	Keele	87.2	90.4	22.1	352	13.2	1,740	89.1	67.2	79.5	657
43	50	Stirling	80.4	83.7	30.5	377	14.9	1,811	86.1	83.7	77.5	656
=44	45	Aberdeen	78.1	84.4	29.9	443	13.5	2,300	84.3	77.9	78.5	653
=44	=41	Swansea	81.2	84.6	33.7	326	14.7	2,055	90.1	76.1	80.5	653
46	33	Cardiff	79.0	84.8	35.0	405	13.7	1,938	92.6	76.0	73.9	642
47	47	Coventry	87.6	89.8	3.8	317	14.6	2,116	84.4	70.1	79.9	639
48	46	Strathclyde	76.3	84.7	37.7	476	19.4	1,846	87.2	77.8	77.2	629
49	=79	Liverpool Hope	89.9	89.6	9.2	305	16.2	1,856	79.6	66.2	78.0	622
50	=41	City	80.1	84.3	21.4	375	16.6	2,469	85.4	71.8	82.6	620
51	=62	Lincoln	85.1	88.5	10.3	340	15.7	1,755	89.3	67.7	71.9	619
52	56	Falmouth	83.6	83.7	4.6	318	18.9	1,434	88.6	74.8	79.3	593

2017 rank	2016 rank		Teaching quality (%)	Student experience (%)	Research quality (%)	Entry standards	Student-staff ratio	Services and facilities spend per student (£)	Completion (%)	Good honours (%)	Graduate prospects (%)	Total
53	=62	University for the Creative Arts	84.4	83.5	3.4	321	12.1	2,647	84.9	63.4	53.6	591
=54	60	Brunel	78.6	83.2	25.4	349	15.7	1,979	87.4	72.2	71.2	588
=54	66	Goldsmiths, London	77.4	76.8	33.4	358	13.8	1,895	84.0	80.6	59.8	588
56	=79	Aberystwyth	85.0	87.0	28.1	299	19.1	1,694	88.6	66.9	68.2	583
57	54	Nottingham Trent	84.6	85.7	6.5	306	16.7	1,891	85.8	71.4	73.1	580
58	68	Edge Hill	85.0	86.0	4.9	328	14.8	1,968	84.6	69.8	71.5	579
59	59	Portsmouth	82.7	85.4	8.6	323	15.4	1,952	85.8	71.2	72.0	575
60	73	West of England	83.0	86.2	8.8	324	18.5	2,118	82.9	73.3	76.4	565
61	52	Bangor	84.8	86.4	27.2	344	16.9	1,528	82.3	64.2	66.3	557
62	=82	Bournemouth	78.2	82.1	9.0	322	17.3	2,112	85.5	77.9	71.6	555
63	51	Royal Agricultural University	77.2	83.9	1.1	303	20.8	2,811	93.8	62.2	74.7	551
64	81	Arts University, Bournemouth	80.7	81.2	2.4	324	14.9	1,214	91.5	62.2	73.9	546
=65	67	Hull	78.9	84.1	16.7	344	16.2	1,971	84.0	70.4	72.7	543
=65	=64	Northumbria	81.2	83.8	9.0	364	17.1	1,543	87.5	69.7	71.9	543
67	53	De Montfort	79.9	83.1	8.9	293	18.6	2,101	86.6	70.1	75.5	541
68	57	Ulster	81.5	86.9	31.8	307	17.1	1,799	81.0	65.9	65.6	539
69	55	Oxford Brookes	81.3	84.0	11.4	338	18.3	1,301	90.0	74.9	70.9	537
70	48	St George's, London	72.7	77.2	22.2	435	12.8	2,733	94.8	74.4	95.1	536
71	88	Gloucestershire	82.9	84.9	3.8	326	18.3	1,789	86.4	69.0	63.9	532
=72	77	Manchester Metropolitan	80.0	82.7	7.5	348	15.6	1,741	83.6	70.4	66.5	527
=72	=64	Winchester	81.7	83.3	5.8	295	16.7	1,344	88.7	77.3	61.2	527
74	=85	Middlesex	79.3	82.3	9.7	301	16.3	3,049	74.7	62.2	70.3	522
75	58	Bath Spa	81.4	81.6	7.9	322	18.5	1,677	87.2	72.8	61.0	521
76	75	Bradford	76.9	83.0	9.2	321	16	2,004	84.0	75.4	78.8	520

77	=69	Huddersfield	83.6	84.8	9.4	332	20.6	1,789	81.7	65.1	73.4	519
78	78	Roehampton	77.4	79.8	24.5	276	14.9	2,171	78.7	70.3	64.2	517
79	72	Sheffield Hallam	80.0	83.4	5.4	306	16.5	2,068	86.3	66.0	68.6	515
80	=85	Plymouth	81.1	83.2	15.9	314	16.4	1,555	84.9	69.9	69.8	514
81	87	Chester	82.9	81.6	41	304	14	2,148	80.4	63.8	64.3	513
82	=69	Chichester	82.9	84.9	6.4	305	16	1,255	89.1	69.0	58.5	511
83	84	Derby	83.5	83.9	2.5	305	14.8	1,798	81.8	66.1	64.0	507
84	121	West London	81.9	84.4	1.5	300	15.6	2,600	74.9	61.3	68.9	499
85	97	Abertay	83.0	84.5	51	346	19.3	1,657	77.2	70.9	68.4	498
=86	74	Liverpool John Moores	80.5	84.1	8.9	345	18.1	1,374	84.4	73.0	67.0	497
=86	=69	Robert Gordon	78.8	82.3	4.0	392	18.4	1,396	83.1	70.5	77.5	497
88	61	Norwich University of the Arts	79.3	79.1	5.6	378	17.8	1,349	88.5	67.9	57.7	491
89	103	Cardiff Metropolitan	77.2	81.3	3.9	318	17.9	2,162	82.3	67.5	70.4	490
90	=100	Worcester	82.5	84.1	4.3	303	17.3	1,315	85.7	65.8	68.0	486
91	76	Hertfordshire	78.2	81.8	5.6	301	17.5	2,142	82.1	65.0	77.5	483
92	95	Staffordshire	82.5	83.2	15.5	284	15.7	1,663	77.4	67.3	56.9	480
=93	105	Birmingham City	81.4	81.5	4.3	316	19.1	1,788	86.5	65.2	69.1	479
=93	93	Edinburgh Napier	80.1	83.3	4.6	350	20.1	1,290	82.5	73.9	72.3	479
95	=112	Bishop Grosseteste	86.3	86.2	2.1	287	25.1	1,031	90.0	67.9	67.1	477
96	91	Leeds Trinity	79.7	79.7	2.0	287	21.6	1,630	85.0	74.7	70.6	468
97	=82	Northampton	80.4	82.1	3.2	281	18.6	2,250	85.8	66.3	56.8	466
98	98	Salford	80.2	81.6	8.3	335	16.7	1,641	79.8	71.3	61.5	465
99	94	Glasgow Caledonian	75.7	81.8	7.0	387	21.1	1,523	83.3	73.0	71.2	460
100	104	Sunderland	80.5	83.1	5.8	290	16.3	1,770	80.3	54.6	66.8	459
=101	92	Central Lancashire	79.7	82.3	5.6	323	16.7	2,067	78.1	62.0	64.5	457
=101	96	Queen Margaret, Edinburgh	80.6	83.3	6.6	352	18.3	1,399	79.7	73.2	57.8	457
=101	102	Teesside	83.1	84.8	3.6	306	17.4	1,863	80.6	57.5	66.4	457
104	90	Brighton	77.6	79.5	7.9	305	17.4	1,426	84.1	66.9	71.3	454

2017 rank	2016 rank		Teaching quality (%)	Student experience (%)	Research quality (%)	Entry standards	Student-staff ratio	Services and facilities spend per student (£)	Completion (%)	Good honours (%)	Graduate prospects (%)	Total
105	=123	St Mark and St John	82.9	85.4	..	290	21.5	1,814	82.1	60.6	63.0	451
106	118	West of Scotland	82.1	83.6	4.3	327	19.8	1,365	79.0	65.5	69.9	445
107	106	Greenwich	77.3	80.4	4.9	337	18.6	1,763	83.2	65.0	66.0	442
108	108	Anglia Ruskin	83.5	84.0	5.4	257	17.3	1,676	80.6	64.8	56.8	439
109	99	University of the Arts London	76.4	73.9	8.0	322	17	1,686	83.7	62.7	61.2	437
=110	=115	Southampton Solent	79.3	81.8	0.5	279	16.9	1,695	78.5	67.7	57.0	431
=110	89	York St John	79.9	81.1	4.1	302	18.5	1,463	86.9	59.2	61.7	431
=112	114	Leeds Beckett	79.2	83.8	4.1	292	20.7	1,522	78.7	65.3	66.1	429
=112	=115	Newman	80.9	80.9	2.8	300	16.9	1,561	79.3	59.1	67.7	429
114	107	Canterbury Christ Church	79.8	80.8	4.5	276	16	1,323	80.8	66.8	61.0	427
115	=112	South Wales	78.4	79.4	4.0	321	17.4	1,661	82.3	64.9	56.4	418
116	=100	St Mary's, Twickenham	79.0	83.3	4.0	293	20.2	1,175	81.3	59.4	70.1	415
117	=115	Westminster	73.5	81.3	9.8	318	19.8	1,675	81.5	68.6	58.1	407
118	109	Buckinghamshire New	81.2	81.9	1.5	260	17.6	1,947	79.7	55.3	61.4	403
119	119	Cumbria	80.0	78.8	1.2	292	19.7	1,349	84.3	61.6	66.3	402
120	120	London South Bank	77.1	81.2	9.0	256	17.2	1,995	73.2	60.4	75.4	400
121	110	Bedfordshire	80.1	82.5	7.0	239	17.4	1,969	76.3	50.4	61.7	393
122	111	Kingston	75.2	79.7	5.1	291	19.3	1,781	81.3	64.3	64.6	383
123	127	East London	79.9	82.6	7.2	278	20	1,933	73.3	59.1	52.3	370
124	=123	Bolton	82.4	81.6	2.9	290	15.9	1,136	71.0	55.0	59.1	369
125	122	Wrexham Glyndŵr	83.5	82.4	2.3	250	22.1	1,533	74.2	55.6	58.9	358
126	...	Suffolk	77.8	79.4	..	309	20	..	76.2	51.6	61.0	320
127	125	London Metropolitan	77.3	81.4	3.5	251	17.4	1,210	71.1	52.6	59.2	313
128	126	Highlands and Islands	78.6	74.1	..	293	..	543	67.7	55.1	51.1	240

Notes on the Table

The University of Suffolk is the one newcomer this year.

University College Birmingham, Trinity St David, University of Wales, and Wolverhampton have refused the release of their data and so no not appear in this year's league table.

The following universities provided replacement data or requested modifications as follows:
» Entry standards: Aberystwyth, Essex, Staffordshire.
» Student–staff ratio: Bangor, Central Lancashire, Exeter, Liverpool, Queen Mary, London.
» Services and facilities spend: Central Lancashire, Exeter.
» Good honours: Bangor.
» Graduate prospects: Liverpool John Moores, Manchester.

2 Choosing What and Where to Study

To read the comments of many politicians and media pundits, it would appear that there is only one reason to go to university: to earn as much as possible when you graduate. Indeed, this will be one of the main measures by which universities will be judged in the Government's Teaching Excellence Framework. It is a big part of the motivation for many students, but there should be more to it than that when you come to choose a university and a course. It is a potentially life-changing decision. Many graduates end up living and working near their university; they often make their closest friends in their student days and may even meet their future partner there. And then there is the little matter of the three or four years you will spend as an undergraduate, which should develop your intellect and shape you as a person.

Of course, with fees now exceeding £9,000, no one is suggesting that you should ignore career prospects – although it is dangerous to read too much into employment statistics that are collected only six months after graduation. Whatever else they want out of a degree course, students all over the world are seeking an advantage in the labour market more than anything. This chapter will suggest some of the signs to take into account in selecting the course that is right for you, if indeed you are certain that your immediate future should be in higher education at all.

Most young people with the necessary qualifications to go to university do decide that it is right for them. But applications and enrolments since the introduction of much higher fees are beginning to show clear patterns that favour particular subjects and universities – and may make life increasingly difficult for others. It is not surprising that growing numbers should decide to play it safe, as they see it, in choosing what and where to study. Although most graduate jobs continue to be open to students of any discipline, some arts subjects may now seem more of a gamble, and there may be pressure at home to go for a science or business subject if you have the right qualifications.

Your choices must be realistic, however. The course must not only be within your capabilities, but will have to maintain your interest for at least three years – possibly much longer than that if it is then going to determine your field of employment. Ideally, higher education should broaden your options in later life, not narrow them. Most of today's graduates will almost certainly work in several different fields during their careers. In any case, no one can be sure which skills will be required in four or more years' time, when today's applicants enter the graduate labour market.

Some subjects and universities will be more marketable than others, but which ones? This *Guide* may give some pointers – medicine is unlikely to go into decline, for example – but times do change. Computer science, for instance, went through years of falling numbers after the dotcom bubble burst, before recovering strongly in recent years. Applications for the group of subjects that includes architecture and building are only now returning to the totals reached before the recession.

Why applicants have reached some of the conclusions they have remains a mystery. Languages, for example, have been hardest hit in terms of applications and enrolments. Yet business leaders are constantly stressing the need for linguists. In this case, decisions made on entry to the sixth-form may be the biggest factor behind falling applications – the numbers taking languages at A level have been dropping for a number of years, perhaps because they are seen as more difficult than other arts subjects.

There will be a number of different factors influencing your choice of university and course, ranging from the limitations imposed by your qualifications to favoured geographical locations. You may want to stay within reach of home – or to get as far away as possible. You may have heard good things about a particular course from friends, or a teacher. This *Guide* – and the tables it contains – offers a reality check to supplement such opinions, and the opportunity to narrow down your options.

Is higher education for you?

Before you start, there is one important question to ask yourself: what do you want out of higher education? The answer will make it easier to choose where (and if) to be a student. With three in ten school-leavers going on to university, it is easy to drift that way without much thought, opting for the subject in which you expect the best A-level grades, and looking for a university with a reasonable reputation and a good social life. Your career will look after itself – you hope.

With graduate debt soaring, however, and job prospects varying widely between subjects, now is the time to look at your own motivation. Fewer young people than predicted have opted out of higher education since higher fees were introduced, but apprenticeships and big firms' training schemes are now offering attractive alternatives. Many of those who do choose higher education appear to be rethinking their choice of course to give themselves the best possible chance of a satisfying and lucrative career.

Love of a subject is an excellent reason for taking a degree, and one that allows you to focus almost exclusively on the search for a course that corresponds with your passions. If, however, higher education is a means to an end, you need to think about career ambitions and look carefully at employment rates for any courses you might consider. These are examined in more detail in chapter 3.

Many graduates look back on their student days as the best years of their lives, and

Key reasons for going to university

To improve job opportunities	71%
To improve knowledge in an area of interest	56%
To improve salary prospects	53%
To specialise in a certain subject/area	51%
Obtain an additional qualification	49%
Essential for my chosen profession	45%
To become more independent	43%
Meet new people	39%
It's the obvious next step – just what you do	36%
To experience a different way of life	33%
To have a good social life	21%
My parents expected me to	21%
I didn't want to get a job straight away	24%
Can live at home and still go to university	12%

Sodexo University Lifestyle Survey 2016

there is nothing wrong with wanting to have a good time. Remember, though, that you will be paying for it later (literally) and there will be more studying than partying. If you have not enjoyed sixth-form or college courses, you may be better off in a job and possibly becoming one of the hundreds of thousands each year who return to education later in life.

Setting your priorities

Even in the world of £9,000-plus fees, there are good reasons to believe that the right degree will still be a good investment. Research by London Economics for the MillionPlus group of universities suggested that, on average, a degree would add £115,000 to lifetime earnings. A more recent Labour Force Survey showed working-age graduates earning 50 per cent more on average than non-graduates – a bigger premium than graduates enjoy in most countries. The majority of graduate jobs are not subject-specific; employers value the transferable skills that higher education confers. Rightly or wrongly, however, most employers are influenced by which university a graduate attended, so the choice of institution remains as important as ever.

Those who want to add value to their degree in the jobs market will find that growing numbers of universities are offering employment-related schemes that are considered in more detail in chapter 3. In many cases, this will involve work experience or extra activities organised by the careers service. A growing number of universities now run certificated employability programmes, while others, such as Liverpool John Moores, have built such skills into degree courses. Such programmes are also highlighted in chapter 3 and in the university profiles in chapter 14

Narrowing down the field

Once you have decided that higher education is for you, the good news is that, as long as you start early enough, finding the right university can be relatively straightforward. Media attention focuses on the scramble for places on a relatively small proportion of courses where competition is intense, but there are plenty of places at good universities for candidates with the basic qualifications – it's just a matter of finding the one that suits you best. For older applicants, relevant work experience and demonstrable interest in a subject may be enough to win a place.

If anything, the problem is that of too much choice, although universities have reduced the number of degree combinations in anticipation of tougher financial conditions. Students prepared to move away from home will still have more than 100 universities and numerous specialist colleges to consider, most with hundreds – even thousands – of course combinations on offer. Institutions come in all shapes and sizes, so there is work to do at the outset narrowing down your options.

Deciding what you want to study may reduce the field considerably – there are only eight institutions offering veterinary medicine for example, although the total is around 100 in subjects such as law and English. By the time you have factored in personal preferences about the type or location of your ideal university, the list of possibilities may already be reduced to manageable proportions.

After that, you can take a closer look at what the courses contain and what life is really like for students. Prospectuses and university websites will give you an accurate account of course combinations, and important facts like the accommodation available to new students, but it is their job to sell the university. To get a true picture, you need more – preferably a visit not just to the university, but to the department where you would be studying. If that is

The UCAS tariff

The UCAS tariff allocates points to a wide range of qualifications so that the worth of different qualifications can be compared. The system was first introduced in 2001. Since then more qualifications have been added and the comparative values between different qualifications have sometimes been questioned. As a result a major overhaul of the system has been introduced for applicants from 2017 onwards. In the new system the points allocated to every qualification has been lowered and the relative value of some qualifications has been altered – for example AS levels are now worth 40 per cent of an A level rather than 50 per cent, while the value of BTECs has been increased. The new UCAS tariff includes the International Baccalaureate, where the tariff is built up from the component parts of the diploma.

Full details are given on the UCAS website (**www.ucas.com**), which also includes a tariff calculator.

The chart below shows the changes for A level, AS level, Scottish Highers and Scottish Advanced Highers.

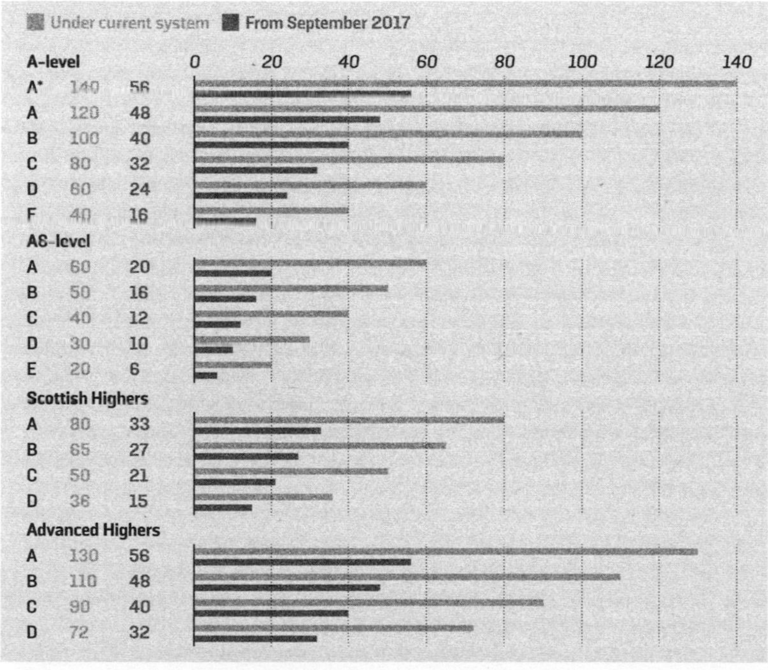

	Under current system	From September 2017
A-level		
A*	140	56
A	120	48
B	100	40
C	80	32
D	60	24
F	40	16
AS-level		
A	60	20
B	50	16
C	40	12
D	30	10
E	20	6
Scottish Highers		
A	80	33
B	65	27
C	50	21
D	36	15
Advanced Highers		
A	130	56
B	110	48
C	90	40
D	72	32

not possible, there are plenty of other sources of objective information, such as the National Student Survey (which is available online, with a range of additional data about the main courses at each institution, at **www.unistats.com**).

Some students' unions publish alternative prospectuses, giving a "warts and all" view of the university, and those that do not provide this service may be able to arrange a brief discussion with a current student, either by phone or email. Your school or college may put you in contact with someone who went to a university that you are considering. Guides and collections of statistics may give you valuable information about a course or a university, but there is no substitute for personal experience.

What to study?

Most people seeking a place in higher education start by choosing a subject and a course, rather than a university. If you take a degree, you are going to spend at least three years immersed in your subject. It has to be one you will enjoy and can master – not to mention one that you are qualified to study. Many economics degrees require maths A level, for example, while most medical schools demand chemistry or biology. The UCAS website (**www.ucas.com**) contains course profiles, including entrance requirements, which is a good starting point, while universities' own sites contain more detailed information. In chapter 5, we describe 67 subject areas and provide league tables for each of them.

Your school subjects and the UCAS tariff

The official yardstick by which your results will be judged is the UCAS tariff, which gives a score for each grade of most UK qualifications considered relevant for university entrance, as well as for the International Baccalaureate (IB). The tariff has changed this year. You can compare the previous points system with the new one on page 31, but most applicants will not be affected – two-thirds of offers are made in grades, rather than tariff points, in any case. This allows universities to stipulate the grades that they require in particular subjects, if they wish, and to determine which vocational qualifications are relevant to different degrees. In certain universities, some departments, but not others, will use the tariff to set offers. Course profiles on the UCAS website and/or universities' own sites should show whether offers are framed in terms of grades or tariff points. It is important to find out which, especially if you are relying on points from qualifications other than A level or Scottish Highers, more of which are included in the new tariff.

Entry qualifications listed in the *Guide* relate not to the offers made by universities, but to the actual grades achieved by successful candidates who are under 21 on entry. For ease of comparison, a tariff score is included even where universities make their offers in grades. These scores use the old UCAS tariff as the data predate the introduction of the new tariff.

"Soft" subjects

There is a related issue for many of the most selective universities about the subjects studied in the sixth-form or at college. Not only have growing numbers of students been applying with vocational (usually BTEC) qualifications, but the variety of A-level courses now available includes many subjects that top universities usually will not consider on a par with traditional academic subjects. For many years a minority of universities have refused to accept General Studies as a full A level for entrance purposes (although even some leading universities do). The growth of supposedly "soft" subjects, such as media studies and photography, has prompted a few universities to produce lists of subjects that will only be accepted alongside at least two traditional academic subjects.

The Russell Group of 24 leading universities publishes an extremely useful report, called *Informed Choices*, on the post-16 qualifications preferred by its members for a wide range of degrees. Although it names media studies, art and design, photography and business studies among the vocational subjects that would normally be given this label, it does not subscribe to the notion of a single list of "soft" subjects. The report suggests you choose at most a single vocational course and primarily select from a list of "facilitating subjects", which are required for many degrees and welcomed generally at Russell Group universities. The list comprises: maths and further maths, English, physics, biology, chemistry, geography, languages (classical and modern) and history. In addition their guide indicates the "essential" and "useful" A-level subjects for 60 different subject areas studied at Russell Group universities.

For most courses at most universities, there are no such restrictions, as long as your main subjects or qualifications are relevant to the degree you hope to take. Nevertheless, when choosing A levels it would be wise to bear the Russell Group lists in mind if you are likely to apply to one or more of the leading universities. At the very least, it is an indication of the subjects that admissions tutors may take less seriously than the rest. Although only the London School of Economics identifies "non-preferred" subjects publicly (see below), others may adopt less formal weightings.

Vocational qualifications

The Education Department downgraded many vocational qualifications in school league tables from 2014. This has added to the confusion surrounding the value placed on diplomas and other qualifications by universities. The engineering diploma has won near-universal approval from universities (for admission to engineering courses and possibly some science degrees), but some of the other diplomas are in fields that are not on the curriculum of the

---

"Traditional academic" and "non-preferred" subjects

The London School of Economics expects applicants to offer at least two of the traditional subjects listed below, while any of the non-preferred subjects listed should only be offered with two traditional subjects.

Traditional subjects

» Ancient history
» Biology
» Classical civilisation
» Chemistry
» Computing
» Economics
» English
» Further mathematics
» Geography
» Government and politics
» History
» Modern or classical languages
» Mathematics
» Music
» Philosophy
» Physics
» Psychology
» Religious studies
» Sociology

Non-preferred subjects

» Any Applied A level
» Accounting
» Art and design
» Business studies
» Citizenship studies
» Communication and culture
» Creative writing
» Design and technology
» Drama/theatre studies
» Film studies
» Health and social care
» Home economics
» Information and communication technology
» Law
» Leisure studies
» Media studies
» Music technology
» Physical education/Sports studies
» Travel and tourism

General studies, critical thinking, thinking skills, knowledge and enquiry and project work A levels will only be considered as fourth A-level subjects and will not therefore be accepted as part of a conditional offer.

most selective universities. Regardless of the points awarded under the tariff, it is essential to contact universities direct to ensure that a diploma or another vocational qualification will be an acceptable qualification for your chosen degree.

Admission tests

The growing numbers of applicants with high grades at A level have encouraged the introduction of separate admission tests for some of the most oversubscribed courses. There are national tests in medicine and law that are used by some of the leading universities, while Oxford and Cambridge have their own tests in a growing number of subjects. The details are listed below. In all cases, the tests are used as an extra selection tool, not as a replacement for A level or other general qualifications.

Making a choice

Your A levels or Scottish Highers may have chosen themselves, but the range of subjects across the whole university system is vast. Even subjects that you have studied at school may be quite different at degree level – some academic economists actually prefer their undergraduates not to have taken A-level economics because they approach the subject so differently. Other students are disappointed because they appear to be going over old ground when they continue with a subject that they enjoyed at school. Universities now publish quite detailed syllabuses, and it is a matter of going through the fine print.

The greater difficulty comes in judging your suitability for the many subjects that are not on the school or college curriculum. Philosophy and psychology sound fascinating (and are), but you may have no idea what degrees in either subject entail – for example, the level of statistics that may be required. Forensic science may look exciting on television – more glamorous than plain chemistry – but it opens fewer doors, as the type of work portrayed in

---

Admissions tests

Some of the most competitive courses now have additional entrance tests. The most significant tests are listed below. Note that registration for many of the tests is before 15 October and you will need to register for them as early as possible. All the tests have their own websites. Institutions requiring specific tests vary from year to year and you must check course website details carefully for test requirements. In addition over 50 universities also administer their own tests for certain courses. Details are given at: **www.ucas.com/ucas/undergraduate/getting-started/entry-requirements/admissions-tests**

Law

Law National Admissions Test (LNAT): for entry to law courses at Bristol, Durham, Glasgow, King's College London, Nottingham, Oxford, SOAS, University College, London. Register from August; tests held from September to January.

Mathematics

Mathematics Admissions Test (MAT): for entry to mathematics at Imperial College, London and mathematics and computer science at Oxford. Test held in early November.

Sixth Term Examination Papers (STEP): for entry to mathematics at Cambridge and Warwick (also encouraged by Bath, Bristol, Imperial College London, King's College London, Loughborough, Nottingham, Southampton and University College London). Register by end April; tests held in June.

Silent Witness or Raising the Dead is very hard to find.

Academic or vocational?

There is frequent and often misleading debate about the differences between academic and vocational higher education. It is usually about the relative value of taking a degree, as opposed to a directly work-related qualification. But it also extends to higher education itself, with jibes about so-called "Mickey Mouse" degrees in areas that were not part of the higher education curriculum when most of the critics were students.

Such attitudes ignore the fact that medicine and law are both vocational subjects, as are architecture, engineering and education. They are not seen as any less academic than geography or sociology, but for some reason social work or nursing, let alone media studies and sports science, are often looked down upon. The test of a degree should be whether it is challenging and a good preparation for working life. Both general academic and vocational degrees can do this.

Nevertheless, it is clear that the prospect of much higher graduate debt is encouraging more students into job-related subjects. This is understandable and, if you are sure of your future career path, possibly also sensible. But much depends on what that career is – and whether you are ready to make such a long-term commitment. Some of the programmes that have attracted public ridicule, such as surf science or golf course management, may narrow graduates' options to a worrying extent, but often boast strong employment records.

As you would expect, many vocational courses are tailored to particular professions. If you choose one of these, make sure that the degree is recognised by the relevant professional body (such as the Engineering Council or one of the institutes) or you may not be able to

---

Medical subjects
BioMedical Admissions Test (BMAT): for entry to medicine at Brighton and Sussex Medical School, Cambridge (also for veterinary medicine), Imperial College London, Keele (international applicants only), Lancaster, Leeds (also for dentistry), Oxford and University College London. Register by 1 October; test held early November.
Graduate Medical School Admissions Test (GAMSAT): for graduate entry to medicine and dentistry at Cardiff, Exeter, Liverpool, Nottingham, Plymouth, St. George's, University of London, Swansea. Register by early August; test held mid-September
Health Professions Admissions Test (HPAT-Ulster): for certain health profession courses at Ulster.Register by start January; test held late January.
UK Clinical Aptitude Test (UKCAT): for entry to medical and dental schools at Aberdeen, Birmingham, Bristol, Cardiff, Dundee, East Anglia, Edinburgh, Exeter, Glasgow, Hull York Medical School, Keele, King's College London, Leicester, Liverpool, Manchester, Newcastle, Nottingham, Plymouth, Queen Mary, University of London, Queen's University Belfast, Sheffield, Southampton, St Andrews, St George's, University of London, Warwick. Register between May and mid-September; tests held between July and early October.

Cambridge University
Pre-interview or at-interview assessments take place for all subjects. Full details given on the Cambridge admissions website. See also STEP and BMAT above.

Oxford University
Pre-interview tests take place in many subjects that candidates are required to register for specifically by early October. Full details given on the Oxford admissions website. Tests held in early November, usually at candidate's educational institution. See also LNAT, MAT and BMAT above.

use the skills that you acquire. Most universities are only too keen to make such recognition clear in their prospectus; if no such guarantee is published, contact the university department running the course and seek assurances.

Even where a course has professional recognition, bear in mind that a further qualification may be required to practise. Both law and medicine, for example, demand additional training to become a fully qualified solicitor, barrister or doctor. Nor is either degree an automatic passport to a job: only about half of all law graduates go into the profession. Both law and medicine also provide a route into the profession for graduates who have taken other subjects. Law conversion courses, though not cheap, are increasingly popular, and there are a growing number of graduate-entry medical degrees, for example at Warwick.

One way to ensure that a degree is job-related is to take a "sandwich" course, which involves up to a year in business or industry. Students often end up working for the organisation which provided the placement, while others gain valuable insights into a field of employment – even if only to discount it. The drawback with such courses is that, like the year abroad that is part of most language degrees, the period away from university inevitably disrupts living arrangements and friendship groups. But most of those who take this route find that the career benefits make this a worthwhile sacrifice.

Employers' organisations calculate that more than half of all graduate jobs are open to applicants from any subject, and recruiters for the most competitive graduate training schemes often prefer traditional academic subjects to apparently relevant vocational degrees. Newspapers, for example, often prefer a history graduate to one with a media studies degree; computing firms are said to take a disproportionate number of classicists. A good degree classification and the right work experience are more important than the subject for most non-technical jobs. But it is hard to achieve a good result on a course that you do not enjoy, so scour prospectuses, and email or phone university departments to ensure that you know what you are letting yourself in for. Their reaction to your approach will also give you an idea of how responsive they are to their students.

Studying more than one subject

You may find that more than one subject appeals, in which case you could consider Joint Honours – degrees that combine two subjects – or even Combined Honours, which will

The ten most popular subject areas for applications, 2016		The ten most popular subject areas for acceptances, 2015	
1 Subjects allied to medicine	401,910	1 Business and admin. studies	66,510
2 Business and admin. studies	347,550	2 Creative arts and design	55,425
3 Biological sciences	281,300	3 Subjects allied to medicine	53,540
4 Creative arts and design	273,870	4 Biological sciences	52,250
5 Social studies	247,980	5 Social studies	46,575
6 Engineering	170,450	6 Engineering	30,850
7 Law	133,870	7 Computer sciences	25,940
8 Computer sciences	129,140	8 Law	24,300
9 Physical sciences	107,830	9 Physical sciences	20,945
10 Education	92,840	10 Education	20,425

UCAS, applications by 30 June 2016

UCAS, end of 2014 cycle

Subject areas covered in this Guide

The list below gives each of the 67 subject areas that are covered in detail later in the book (in chapter 12). For each subject area in that chapter, there is specific advice, a summary of employment prospects and a league table of universities that offered courses in 2014–15, ranked on the basis of an overall score calculated from research quality, entry standards, teaching quality, student experience and graduate employment prospects.

Accounting and Finance
Aeronautical and Manufacturing
   Engineering
Agriculture and Forestry
American Studies
Anatomy and Physiology
Animal Science
Anthropology
Archaeology and Forensic Science
Architecture
Art and Design
Biological Sciences
Building
Business Studies
Celtic Studies
Chemical Engineering
Chemistry
Civil Engineering
Classics and Ancient History
Communication and Media Studies
Computer Science
Creative Writing
Criminology
Dentistry
Drama, Dance and Cinematics
East and South Asian Studies
Economics
Education
Electrical and Electronic Engineering
English
Food Science
French
General Engineering
Geography and Environmental Sciences
Geology

German
History
History of Art, Architecture and Design
Hospitality, Leisure, Recreation and
Tourism
Iberian Languages
Italian
Land and Property Management
Law
Librarianship and Information Management
Linguistics
Materials Technology
Mathematics
Mechanical Engineering
Medicine
Middle Eastern and African Studies
Music
Nursing
Other Subjects Allied to Medicine
Pharmacology and Pharmacy
Philosophy
Physics and Astronomy
Physiotherapy
Politics
Psychology
Radiography
Russian
Social Policy
Social Work
Sociology
Sports Science
Theology and Religious Studies
Town and Country Planning and
Landscape
Veterinary Medicine

cover several related subjects. Such courses obviously allow you to extend the scope of your studies, but they should be approached with caution. Even if the number of credits suggests a similar workload to Single Honours, covering more than one subject inevitably involves extra reading and often more essays or project work.

The numbers taking such degrees is falling, but there are advantages to them. Many students choose a "dual" to take their studies in a particular direction, perhaps by combining history with politics, or statistics with maths. Others want to add a vocational element to make themselves more employable – business studies with languages or engineering, for example, or media studies with English. Some simply want to add a completely unrelated interest to their main subject, such as environmental science and music, or archaeology and event management – both combinations that are available at UK universities.

Number of first degree students by subject area, 2013/14 and percentage of total

Business and admin. studies	203,385	13.3%
Biological sciences	167,185	11.0%
Subjects allied to medicine	156,575	10.3%
Social studies	147,090	9.7%
Creative arts and design	138,095	9.1%
Engineering and technology	108,255	7.1%
Languages	84,520	5.5%
Computer science	71,865	4.7%
Physical sciences	71,545	4.7%
History and philosophy	65,550	4.3%
Law	65,240	4.3%
Education	58,380	3.8%
Medicine and dentistry	45,120	3.0%
Mass communications	37,355	2.5%
Mathematical sciences	35,515	2.3%
Architecture, building and planning	29,430	1.9%
Combined subjects	24,755	1.6%
Agriculture and related subjects	9,300	0.6%
Veterinary science	5,070	0.3%
Total for all subjects	**1,524,225**	**100.0%**

HESA 2016

At most universities it is not necessary to take a degree in more than one subject in order to broaden your studies. The spread of modular programmes ensures that you can take courses in related subjects without changing the basic structure of your degree. You may not be able to take an event management module in a single-honours archaeology degree, but it should be possible to study some history or a language. The number and scope of the combinations offered at many of the larger universities is extraordinary. Indeed, it has been criticised by academics who believe that "mix-and-match" degrees can leave a graduate without a rounded view of a subject. But for those who seek breadth and variety, close scrutiny of university prospectuses is a vital part of the selection process.

What type of course?

Once you have a subject, you must decide on the level and type of course. Most readers of this *Guide* will be looking for full-time degree courses, but higher education is much broader than that. You may not be able to afford the time or the money needed for a full-time commitment of three or four years at this point in your life.

Part-time courses

Tens of thousands of people each year opt for a part-time course – usually while holding down a job – to continue learning and to improve their career prospects. The numbers studying this way have dropped considerably, but loans are available for students whose courses occupy between a quarter and three-quarters of the time expected on a full-time course. Repayments are on the same conditions as those for full-time courses, except that repayments will begin after three years of study even if the course has not been completed by then. The downside is that many universities have increased their fees in the knowledge that part-time students will be able to take out student loans to cover fees and employers are now less inclined to fund their employees on such courses. At Birkbeck, University of London, for example, a compromise has been found with full-time courses taught in the evening. For courses classified as part-time, students pay fees in proportion to the number of credits they take.

Part-time study can be exhausting unless your employer gives you time off, but if you have the stamina for a course that will usually take twice as long as the full-time equivalent, this route should still make a degree more affordable. Part-time students tend to be highly committed to their subject, and many claim that the quality of the social life associated with their course makes up for the quantity of leisure time enjoyed by full-timers.

Distance learning

If you are confident that you can manage without regular face-to-face contact with teachers and fellow students, distance learning is an option. Courses are delivered mainly or entirely online or through correspondence, although some programmes offer a certain amount of local tuition. The process might sound daunting and impersonal, but students of the Open University (OU), all of whom are educated in this way, are among the most satisfied in the country, according to the results of the annual National Student Survey. Attending lectures or oversized seminars at a conventional university can be less personal than regular contact with your tutor at a distance.

Of course, not all universities are as good at communicating with their distance-learning students as the OU, or offer such high-quality course materials, but this mode of study does give students ultimate flexibility to determine when and where they study. Distance learning is becoming increasingly popular for the delivery of professional courses, which are often needed to supplement degrees. The OU now takes students of all ages, including a growing number of school-leavers, not just mature students.

In addition, there is now the option of Massive Open Online Courses (MOOCs) provided by many of the leading UK and American universities, usually free of charge. As yet, such courses are the equivalent of a module in a degree course, rather than the entire qualification. Some are assessed formally but none is likely to be seen by employers as the equal of a conventional degree, no matter how prestigious the university offering the course. That may change – some commentators see in MOOCs the beginning of the end of the traditional, residential university – but their main value at the moment is as a means of dipping a toe in the water of higher education. For those who are uncertain about committing to a degree, or who simply want to learn more about a subject without needing a high-status qualification, they are ideal.

A growing number of UK universities are offering MOOCs through the Futurelearn platform, run by the Open University (**www.futurelearn.com**). But the beauty of MOOCs is that they can come from all over the world. Perhaps the best-known providers are Coursera (**www.coursera.org**), which originated at Stanford University, in California, and now involves a large number of American and international universities including Edinburgh, and edX (**www.edx.org**), which numbers Harvard among its members. MOOCs are also being used increasingly by sixth-formers to extend their subject knowledge and demonstrate their enthusiasm and capability to admissions tutors.

Foundation degrees

Even if you are set on a full-time course, you might not want to commit yourself for three or more years. Two-year vocational Foundation degrees have become a popular route into higher education in recent years. Many other students take longer-established two-year courses, such as Higher National Diplomas or other diplomas tailored to the needs of industry or parts of the health service. Those who do well on such courses usually have the option of converting their qualification into a full degree with further study, although many are satisfied without immediately staying on for the further two or more years that completing a BA or BSc will require.

Other short courses

A number of universities are experimenting with two-year degrees, squeezing more work into an extended academic year. The so-called "third semester" makes use of the summer vacation for extra teaching, so that mature students, in particular, can reduce the length of their career break. Several universities are offering accelerated degrees as part of a pilot project initiated under the last government. But only at the University of Buckingham, the UK's longest-established private university, is this the dominant pattern for degree courses. Other private institutions – notably BPP University – are following suit.

Other short courses, usually lasting a year, are designed for students who do not have the necessary qualifications to start a degree in their chosen subject. Foundation courses in art and design have been common for many years, and are the chosen preparation for a degree at leading departments, even for many students whose A levels would win them a degree place elsewhere. Access courses perform the same function in a wider range of subjects for students without A levels, or for those whose grades are either too low or in the wrong subjects to gain admission to a particular course. Entry requirements are modest, but students have to reach the same standard as regular entrants to progress to a degree.

Yet more choice

No single guide can allow for personal preferences in choosing a course. You may want one of the many degrees that incorporate a year at a partner university abroad, or to try a six-month exchange on the Continent through the European Union's Erasmus Programme (or whatever scheme might replace it after Brexit). Either might prove a valuable experience

---

Subjects with the highest ratio of applications to acceptances, 2015

1	Medicine	9.9
2	Dentistry	9.0
3	Nursing	8.4
4	Anatomy, physiology and pathology	8.1
5	Medical technology	7.9
6	Veterinary medicine	7.2
7	Economics	6.4
=8	Management studies	6.2
=8	Pharmacology, toxicology and pharmacy	6.2
=8	Mechanical engineering	6.2

UCAS 2016 (for subjects with over 1,000 acceptances)

Universities with the highest ratio of applications to acceptances, 2015

1	Buckingham	14.2
2	St George's, University of London	13.0
3	London School of Economics	10.7
4	Edinburgh	10.2
=5	London South Bank	10.1
=5	City, University of London	10.1
7	St Andrews	10.0
8	Brunel London	9.8
9	Surrey	9.4
10	Queen Mary, University of London	9.2

UCAS 2016

and add to your employability. Or you might prefer a January or February start to the traditional autumn start – there are plenty of opportunities for this, mainly at post-1992 universities.

In some subjects – particularly engineering and the sciences – the leading degrees may be Masters courses, taking four years rather than three (in England). In Scotland, most degree courses take four years and some at the older universities will confer a Masters qualification. Those who come with A levels may apply to go straight into the second year. Relatively few students take this option, but it is easy to imagine more doing so in future at universities that charge students from other parts of the UK the full £9,250 for all years of the course.

Where to study

Once you have decided what to study, there are still several factors that might influence your choice of university or college. Obviously, you need to have a reasonable chance of getting in, you may want reassurance about the university's reputation, and its location will probably also be important to you. On top of that, most applicants have views about the type of institution they are looking for – big or small, old or new, urban or rural, specialist or comprehensive. Campus universities tend to produce the highest levels of student satisfaction, but big city universities continue to attract sixth-formers in the largest numbers. You may surprise yourself by choosing somewhere that does not conform to your initial criteria, but working through your preferences is another way of narrowing down your options.

Entry standards

Unless you are a mature student or have taken a gap year, your passport to your chosen university will probably be a conditional offer based on your predicted grades, previous exam performance, personal statement, and school or college reference. A growing number of universities have followed Birmingham's lead in making unconditional offers to candidates in selected subjects who have a strong academic record and are predicted high grades. But at most institutions, only those who already have their grades receive unconditional offers.

Supply and demand dictate whether you will receive an offer. Beyond the national picture, your chances will be affected both by the university and the subject you choose. A few universities (but not many) at the top of the league tables are heavily oversubscribed

Most popular universities by applications, 2015		Most satisfied with students' union 2016	
1 Manchester	63,980	1 Sheffield	96%
2 Edinburgh	59,255	2 Leeds	92%
3 Manchester Metropolitan	56,765	3 Loughborough	90%
4 Leeds	51,855	4 Dundee	88%
5 Nottingham	49,230	5 Cardiff	87%
6 Birmingham	49,080	=6 Nottingham Trent	85%
7 Bristol	43,465	=6 Harper Adams	85%
8 Liverpool	43,100	=8 Teesside	84%
9 King's College London	43,010	=8 Keele	84%
10 University College London	40,355	=8 Buckinghamshire New	84%
UCAS 2015		National Student Survey 2016	

in every subject; others will have areas in which they excel, but may make relatively modest demands for entry to other courses. Even in many of the leading universities, the number of applicants for each place in languages or engineering is still not high. Conversely, three As at A level will not guarantee a place on one of the top English or law degrees, but there are enough courses to ensure that three Cs will put you in with a chance somewhere.

University prospectuses and the UCAS website will give you the "standard offer" for each course, but in some cases this is pitched deliberately low in order to leave admissions staff extra flexibility. The standard A-level offer for medicine, for example, may not demand A*s, but nearly all successful applicants will have one or more.

As already noted, the average entry scores in our tables give the actual points obtained by successful applicants – many of which are far above the offer made by the university, but which give an indication of the pecking order at entry. The subject tables (in chapter 12) are, naturally, a better guide than the main table (in chapter 1), where average entry scores are influenced by the range of subjects available at each university.

Location

The most obvious starting point is the country you study in. Most degrees in Scotland take four years, rather than the UK norm of three. It goes without saying that four years cost more than three, especially given the loss of the year's salary you might have been earning after graduation. A later chapter will go into the details of the system, but suffice to say that students from Scotland pay no fees, while those from the rest of the UK do. Nevertheless, Edinburgh and St Andrews remain particularly popular with English students, despite charging them £9,250 a year for the full four years of a degree starting in 2017. The number of English students going to Scottish universities has increased every year since the fees went up, despite the fact that there would be no savings, perhaps because the institutions tried harder to attract them. Fees – or the lack of them – are by no means the only influence on cross-border mobility: the number of Scots going to English universities has risen sharply in the last two years, in spite of the cost, probably because the number of places is capped in Scotland, but not any longer in England.

Non-academic factors considered when choosing a university

Location-related

Close to transport links	35%
Able to live away from parental home but close enough for support	30%
Quality of accommodation	27%
Low cost of living	23%
Cost of accommodation	22%
Able to live at parental home	17%
Opportunities for part-time jobs	12%

University-related

Good impression from open days	46%
Campus university	36%
Attractive environment	33%
Active social life / good social facilities	28%
IT / Resource / study facilities	28%
Good links to business or other organisations	27%
Clubs and societies	27%
City centre university	24%
Careers advice / support	17%
Good sporting facilities	15%
Accommodation is located on campus	14%
Good catering and retail facilities	8%

Sodexo University Lifestyle Survey 2016

Close to home

Far from crossing national boundaries, however, growing numbers of students choose to study near home, whether or not they continue to live with their family. This is understandable for Scots, who will save themselves tens of thousands of pounds by studying at their own fees-free universities. But there is also a gradual increase in the numbers choosing to study close to home either to cut living costs or for personal reasons, such as family circumstances, a girlfriend or boyfriend, continuing employment or religion. Some simply want to stick with what they know.

The trend for full-time students who do go away to study, is to choose a university within about two hours' travelling time. The assumption is that this is far enough to discourage parents from making unannounced visits, but close enough to allow for occasional trips home to get the washing done, have a decent meal and see friends. The leading universities recruit from all over the world, but most still have a regional core.

University or college?

This *Guide* is primarily concerned with universities, the destination of choice for the vast majority of higher education students. But there are other options – and not just for those searching for lower fees. A number of specialist higher education colleges offer a similar, or sometimes superior, quality of course in their particular fields. The subject tables in chapter 12 chart the successes of various colleges in art, agriculture, music and teacher training in particular. Some colleges of higher education are not so different from the newer universities and may acquire that status themselves in future years, as ten did in 2012–13 and one more in the following year.

Further education colleges

The second group of colleges offering degrees are further education (FE) colleges. These are often large institutions with a wide range of courses, from A levels to vocational subjects at different levels, up to degrees in some cases. Although their numbers of higher education students have been falling in recent years, the new fee structure presents them with a fresh opportunity because they tend not to bear all the costs of a university campus. For that reason, too, they may not offer a broad student experience of the type that universities pride themselves on, but the best colleges respond well to the local labour market and offer small teaching groups and effective personal support.

FE colleges are a local resource and tend to attract mature students who cannot or do not want to travel to university. Many of their higher education students apply nowhere else. But, as competition for university places has increased, they also have become more of an option for school-leavers to continue their studies, as they always have done in Scotland. Ministers hope that they will now also become more attractive by virtue of price.

Their predominantly local, mature student populations do FE colleges no favours in statistical comparisons with universities. But it should be noted that the proportion of college graduates unemployed six months after graduation is invariably higher than at universities, as are average graduate salaries.

Both further and higher education colleges are audited by the Quality Assurance Agency and appear in the National Student Survey, where their results usually show wide variation. Some demonstrate higher levels of satisfaction among their students than most universities, while others are at the bottom of the scale

Private universities and colleges

The final group of colleges that present an alternative to university was insignificant in terms of size until recently, but may also prosper under the current fee regime. This is the private sector, seen mainly in business and law, but also in some other specialist fields. By far the longest established – and the only one to meet the criteria for inclusion in our main table – is the University of Buckingham. The best-known "newcomer" currently is BPP University, which became a full university in 2013 and offers degrees, as well as shorter courses, in both law and business subjects. Like Buckingham, BPP offers two-year degrees with short vacations to maximise teaching time – a model that other private providers are likely to follow. Fees are £13,500 a year for a two-year degree in 2017 and £9,000 a year for the three-year equivalent.

At the other end of the cost spectrum, the New College of the Humanities graduated its first students in 2015. Offering economics, English, history, law and philosophy, the college charged almost £18,000 a year in 2015–16 for guaranteed small-group teaching and some big-name visiting lecturers, but has reduced this to £12,000 for 2017. Many students are offered bursaries for University of London external degree courses and 22 Combined Honours degrees validated by Southampton Solent.

Two other private institutions have been awarded university status in the last four years. Regent's University, attractively positioned in London's Regent's Park, caters particularly for the international market with courses in business, arts and social science subjects priced at £16,400 a year for courses starting in autumn 2017. However, about half of the students at the not-for-profit university, which offers British and American degrees, are from the UK or other parts of Europe. The University of Law, as its name suggests, is more specialised. It has been operating as a college for more than 100 years and claims to be the world's leading professional law school. Law degrees, as well as professional courses, are available in London and Manchester, with fees totalling £18,000 in the current academic year for a full-time course for a UK student, whether taken over two or three years.

There are also growing numbers of specialist colleges offering degrees, especially in the business sector. GSM London (formerly the Greenwich School of Management), with more than 3,500 students on two London campuses, is probably the largest in terms of full-time students, but there are others that have forged partnerships with universities or are going it alone. The London Institute of Banking and Finance, for example, also dates back more than 100 years and now has university college status for its courses in finance and banking. Some others that rely on international students have been hit by tougher visa regulations, but the

The top universities for quality of teaching, feedback and support in the 2017 *Times and Sunday Times* table		The top universities for overall student experience in the 2017 *Times and Sunday Times* table	
1 Buckingham	90.2%	1 Buckingham	91.5%
2 Liverpool Hope	89.9%	2 St Andrews	91%
3 St Andrews	88.4%	3 Keele	90.4%
4 Coventry	87.6%	=4 Coventry	89.8%
5 Keele	87.2%	=4 Harper Adams	89.8%
6 Bishop Grosseteste	86.3%	6 Liverpool Hope	89.6%
7 Dundee	85.9%	7 Dundee	88.8%
=8 Harper Adams	85.1%	8 Queen's, Belfast	88.7%
=8 Lincoln	85.1%	9 Lincoln	88.5%
=10 Aberystwyth	85%	=10 Exeter	87.9%
=10 Edge Hill	85%	=10 Loughborough	87.9%

government is keen to encourage the development of a private sector to compete with the established universities.

City universities

The most popular universities, in terms of total applications, are nearly all in big cities with other major centres of population within a two-hour travelling window. For those looking for the best nightclubs, top sporting events, high-quality shopping or a varied cultural life – in other words, most young people, and especially those who live in cities already – city universities are a magnet. The big universities also, by definition, offer the widest range of subjects, although that does not mean that they necessarily have the particular course that is right for you. Nor does it mean that you will actually use the array of nightlife and shopping that looks so alluring in the prospectus, either because you cannot afford to, because student life is focused on the university, or even because you are too busy working.

Campus universities

City universities are the right choice for many young people, but it is worth bearing in mind that the National Student Survey shows that the highest satisfaction levels tend to be at smaller universities, often those with their own self-contained campuses. It seems that students identify more closely with institutions where there is a close-knit community and the social life is based around the students' union rather than the local nightclubs. Few UK universities are in genuinely rural locations, but some – particularly among the more recently promoted – are in relatively small towns. Several longer-established institutions in Scotland and Wales also share this type of setting, where the university dominates the town.

Importance of Open Days

The only way to be certain if this, or any other type of university, is for you is to visit. Schools often restrict the number of Open Days that sixth-formers can attend in term-time, but some universities offer a weekend alternative. Confirmed university Open Days for 2017 (as at the end of November 2016) are listed at the back of this book, and a full calendar of events is regularly updated at **www.opendays.com** and on universities' own websites. Bear in mind, if you only attend one or two, that the event has to be badly mismanaged for a university not to seem an exciting place to someone who spends his or her days at school, or even college. Try to get a flavour of several institutions before you make your choice.

How many universities to pick?

When that time comes, of course, you will not be making one choice but five; four if you are applying for medicine, dentistry or veterinary science. (Full details of the application process are given in chapter 6.) Tens of thousands of students each year eventually go to a university that did not start out as their first choice, either because they did not get the right offer or because they changed their mind along the way. UCAS rules are such that applicants do not list universities in order of preference anyway – indeed, universities are not allowed to know where else you have applied. So do not pin all your hopes on one course; take just as much care choosing the other universities on your list.

The value of an "insurance" choice

Until recently, nearly all applicants included at least one "insurance" choice on that list – a university or college where entry grades were significantly lower than at their preferred institutions. This practice has been in decline, presumably because candidates expecting high grades think they can pick up a lower offer either in Clearing or through UCAS Extra, the service that allows applicants rejected by their original choices to apply to courses that still have vacancies after the first round of offers. However, it is easy to miscalculate and leave yourself without a place that you want. You may not like the look of the options in Clearing, leaving yourself with an unwelcome and potentially expensive year off at a time when jobs are thin on the ground.

The lifting of recruitment restrictions in 2015 increased competition between universities and has seen even more of the leading institutions taking part in Clearing. For those with good grades, this makes it less of a risk to apply only to highly selective universities. However, if you are at all uncertain about your grades, including an insurance choice remains a sensible course of action – especially since entry requirements have risen in recent years in response to increased demand for places. Even if you are sure that you will match the standard offers of your chosen universities, there is no guarantee that they will make you an offer. Particularly for degrees demanding three As or more at A level, there may simply be too many highly qualified applicants to offer places to all of them. The main proviso for insurance choices, as with all others, is that you must be prepared to take up that place. If not, you might as well go for broke with courses with higher standard offers and take your chances in Clearing, or even retake exams if you drop grades. Thousands of applicants each year end up rejecting their only offer when they could have had a second, insurance, choice.

Reputation

The reputation of a university is something intangible, usually built up over a long period and sometimes outlasting reality. Before universities were subject to external assessment and the publication of copious statistics, reputation was rooted in the past. League tables are partly responsible for changing that, although employers are often still influenced by what they remember as the university pecking order when they were students.

The fragmentation of the British university system into groups of institutions is another factor: the Russell Group (**www.russellgroup.ac.uk**) represents 24 research-intensive universities, nearly all with medical schools; the MillionPlus group (**www.millionplus.ac.uk**) contains many of the former polytechnics and newer universities; the University Alliance (**www.unialliance.ac.uk**) provides a home for 19 universities, both old and new, that did not fit into the other categories; while GuildHE (**www.guildhe.ac.uk**) represents specialist colleges and the newest universities. The Cathedrals Group (**www.cathedralsgroup.ac.uk**) is an affiliation of 16 church-based universities and colleges, some of which are also members of other groups. The university profiles in chapter 14 give the affiliation of each university.

Many of today's applicants will barely have heard of a polytechnic, let alone be able to identify which of today's universities had that heritage, but most will know which of two universities in the same city has the higher status. While that should matter far less than the quality of a course, it would be naïve to ignore institutional reputation entirely if that is going to carry weight with a future employer. Some big firms restrict their recruitment efforts to a small group of universities (see chapter 3), and, however short sighted that might be, it is something to bear in mind if a career in the City or a big law firm is your ambition.

Cost

Quite apart from the level of fees, the cost of studying in different parts of the UK inevitably varies. Some cities – notably London – are notoriously expensive for students and non-students alike. But even these comparisons can be complicated by the availability of part-time employment – an important factor for a growing number of students today. The 2010 RBS survey rated London as the cheapest place in the UK to study once earning opportunities were taken into account, although no other surveys have reached this conclusion, and by the 2016 RBS survey it had dropped to 19th place. If you intend to take part-time employment while studying, check that your chosen university has a "job shop", or some other organisation to help you find reasonably paid work.

Accommodation costs listed alongside the university profiles in this *Guide* are probably the nearest proxy for a cost-of-living indicator. Universities also offer financial support through bursaries and scholarships, and you should check university websites for full details. The size of bursaries varies, as do the rules governing eligibility. Scholarships are awarded for academic or other achievements, regardless of family income.

Facilities

A 2015 survey commissioned by university directors of estates found that the quality of campus facilities was an important factor in choosing a university for two thirds of applicants. Only the course and the university's location had a higher priority. Accommodation is the main selling point for those living away from home, but sports facilities, libraries and computing equipment also play an important part. Even campus nightclubs have become part of the facilities race that has followed the introduction of top-up fees.

Many universities guarantee first-year students accommodation in halls of residence or university-owned flats. But it is as well to know what happens after that. Are there enough places for second- or third-year students who want them, and if not, what is the private market like? Rents for student houses vary quite widely across the country and there have been tensions with local residents in some cities. All universities offer specialist accommodation for disabled students – and are better at providing other facilities than most public institutions. Their websites give basic information on what is provided, as well as contact points for more detailed inquiries.

Special-interest clubs and recreational facilities, as well as political activity, tend to be based in the students' union – sometimes knows as the guild of students. In some universities, the union is the focal point of social activity, while in others the attractions of the city seem to overshadow the union to the point where facilities are underused. Students' union websites are included with the information found in the university profiles (chapter 14).

Sources of information

With more than 120 universities to choose from, the Unistats and UCAS websites, as well as guides such as this one, are the obvious places to start your search for the right course. Unistats now includes figures for average salaries at course level, as well as student satisfaction ratings and some information on contact hours, although this does not distinguish between lectures and seminars. The site does not make multiple comparisons easy to carry out, but it does contain a wealth of information for those who persevere. Once you have narrowed down the list of candidates, you will want to go through undergraduate prospectuses. Most are available online, where you can select the relevant sections rather than waiting for an account of every course to arrive in the post. Beware of generalised claims about the standing of the university, the quality of courses, friendly atmosphere and legendary social life. Stick, if you can, to the factual information.

If the material that the universities publish about their own qualities is less than objective,

Checklist

Choosing a subject and a place to study is a major decision. Make sure you can answer these questions:

Choosing a course

» What do I want out of higher education?
» Which subjects do I enjoy studying at school?
» Which subject or subjects do I want to study?
» Do I have the right qualifications?
» What are my career plans and does the subject and course fit these?
» Do I want to study full-time or part-time?
» Do I want to study at a university or a college?

Choosing a university

» What type of university do I wish to go to: campus, city or smaller town?
» How far is the university from home?
» Is it large or small?
» Is it specialist or general?
» Does it offer the right course?
» How much will it cost?
» Have I arranged to visit the university?

---

much of what you will find on the internet is equally unreliable, for different reasons. A simple search on the name of a university will turn up spurious comparisons of everything from the standard of lecturing to the attractiveness of the students. These can be seriously misleading and are usually based on anecdotal evidence, at best. Make sure that any information you may take into account comes from a reputable source and, if it conflicts with your impression, try to cross-check it with this *Guide* and the institution's own material.

Useful websites

The best starting point is the UCAS website (**www.ucas.com**). On the site there is extensive information on courses, universities and the whole process of applying to university. UCAS has an official presence on Facebook (**www.facebook.com/ucasonline**) and Twitter (**@ucas_online**) and now also has a series of video guides (**www.ucas.com/connect/videos**) on the process of applying, UCAS resources and comments from other students.

For statistical information which allows limited comparison between universities (and for full details of the National Student Survey), visit: **www.unistats.com**

On appropriate A-level subject choice, visit: **www.russellgroup.ac.uk/informed-choices**
Narrowing down course choices: **www.ukcoursefinder.com**

For a full calendar of university and college open days: **www.opendays.com**

Students with disabilities:
Disability Rights UK: **www.disabilityrightsuk.org/how-we-can-help**

3 Assessing Graduate Job Prospects

Graduate employment levels have improved in the last two editions of the *Guide* – although there have been more mixed messages since those statistics were collected. Particularly since the vote to leave the European Union, employers have been less positive in their planning for the recruitment of graduates. Nevertheless, across the working population, graduate unemployment was only 3 per cent at the end of 2015, compared with over 6 per cent for non-graduates. The jobless rate for students graduating over the last five years was 4.9 per cent, compared with 8.6 per cent for non-graduates in their 20s. It would be premature to assume that the graduate labour market has returned to normal, however, because salary levels have taken longer to show the same progress, and there is a growing debate about underemployment – the proportion of graduates in jobs that do not require a degree.

Of course, what matters to readers of this book is how the market will look in four or five years' time, when this year's applicants graduate in a post-Brexit world. Although no one knows that, there would have to be seismic changes in the economy for graduates not to be in a much better position than those without a degree. That has been the case for several decades and all the projections suggest that a growing proportion of the jobs created in the coming years will require a degree. This does not mean, however, that every degree will be a passport to a well-paid job and worth the debts that graduates are going to accrue in the era of high fees. Recent salary figures for graduates five and ten years into their careers show startling differences between universities.

Graduate employment and underemployment

Ever since the move to mass higher education, critics have been predicting that the graduate employment market would become saturated and the financial benefits of having a degree would begin to diminish. In overall terms, this has not happened yet: the average graduate earns at least £100,000 more than non-graduates over a working lifetime, and the returns do not seem to be falling. Employment rates for graduates are higher than they have been since 2007 and the "young graduate high-skilled employment rate", which more closely resembles the measure used in our league tables, is also back to pre-recession levels. Certainly, competition for graduate jobs remains stiff – there are now 12 million graduates in the UK, and in Inner London they represent 60 per cent of the working-age population. Today's graduates may take longer than their predecessors to find the right opening and may experiment with internships before committing themselves. The proportion of graduates starting out in "non-professional" jobs dropped in 2015, but it was still well over 20 per cent, while many others felt the skills and knowledge they had acquired at university were not being utilised, regardless of their job title.

Aside from anecdotal reporting of the difficulties young graduates face in the labour market, this is why underemployment has come to the fore. It is an important debate, but one with little precision and where the practice of collecting employment data only six months after graduation can be extremely misleading. This *Guide* uses the definition from Higher Education Statistics Agency (HESA) of a graduate job in order to address this issue (see below), but employers' idea of which jobs require a degree – or at least, the jobs for which they prefer graduates – changes over time. Nurses now require a degree partly because the job has changed and requires skills that were not needed 20 years ago. The same is true of many occupations, while in others it may be possible to do the job without a degree, but having one makes it much easier to be employed in the first place.

Nevertheless, Accenture found that 60 per cent of 2013 and 2014 graduates considered themselves underemployed or working in a job that did not require a degree. Eight out of ten said they had considered the availability of jobs in their intended field before selecting their degree course, but only 55 per cent were working in their chosen field. Almost 60 per cent said they would trade salary for a more fulfilling job.

The graduate labour market

Government reports take a longer-term view of the whole labour market, which continue to support the case for taking a degree if you have the opportunity. The first "experimental statistics" from its Longitudinal Education Outcomes (LEO) data were published at the end of 2016, showing average salaries and employment status three, five and ten years after graduation. More are due in the months following the publication of this *Guide*, which may become part of the basket of measures by which universities' teaching will be judged. The first figures show predictable differences between subjects in employment and salary rates, some of which are shown in the table below. While the institutional comparisons would require more work to be consistent with other measures in the *Guide*, they did illustrate the lasting impact of choices of university. Among law graduates, for example, the top earners at Oxford and Cambridge average more than £75,000 (and the lowest some £35,000) after five

---

Average earnings by degree subject five years after graduation for 2009 graduates

Medicine and dentistry	£46,500	Law	£25,000
Economics	£37,500	Languages	£25,000
Veterinary science	£36,500	History and philosophy	£25,000
Mathematical sciences	£33,000	Social studies (excluding economics)	£24,500
Engineering and technology	£31,500	Education	£24,500
Architecture, building, planning	£29,500	Combined subjects	£24,500
Subjects allied to medicine	£27,500	Biological sciences	£23,500
Computer science	£27,500	Mass communications	£22,500
Physical sciences	£27,000	Agriculture and related subjects	£22,000
Business	£26,500	Creative arts and design	£20,000

Source: Department for Education, "Employment and earnings outcomes of higher education graduates", 2016

years, compared with under £10,000 for low earners at East London.

Overall, however, graduates continued to earn 43 per cent more than non-graduates in 2015. This may be a smaller premium than they enjoyed before the financial crash – it was over 50 per cent in 2006 – but it remains one of the biggest differentials in the western world. Inevitably, national surveys average out the experiences of millions of people and often take no account of the mix of subjects at different universities. The material in this *Guide* – particularly in the subject tables – should help to create a more nuanced picture. A close examination of individual universities' employment rates in your subject – possibly supplemented by the salary figures on the Unistats website (**www.unistats.com**) – will tell you whether national trends apply to your chosen course.

Even without the uncertainty caused by Brexit, there would be swings in employment trends before anyone starting a degree in 2018 graduates. In 2016, the Association of Graduate Recruiters found that the number of vacancies advertised by its members had dropped for the first time in four years, as they put more investment into apprenticeships. The Association, which represents mainly large organisations, blamed the Brexit vote but stressed that thousands of openings were still available for graduates. *The Times* Top 100 employers, surveyed by High Fliers for the 2016 Graduate Market report, had been planning for a 7.5 per cent increase at the beginning of the year.

However, the High Fliers survey covers only the upper end of the market. For the boom years of graduate employment to return, there will have to be stronger recruitment by small- and medium-sized companies. Increasingly, there will also be a greater proportion of self-employed graduates – and not simply because they cannot find the jobs they want. Many universities report growing demand for the services they provide to help those who want to set up their own companies.

Subject choice and career opportunities

For those thinking of embarking on higher education in 2018, the signs are still positive, but in any year some universities and some subjects produce better returns than others. The tables in this edition of the *Guide* show that at the end of 2015, the unemployment rate for those who had graduated six months earlier was 10 per cent, marginally higher than in the previous year, but the proportion going into professional jobs (54 per cent) was higher than it had been for more than a decade.

The tables on the pages that follow give a more detailed picture of the differences between subjects, while the rankings in chapters 1 and 12 include figures for each university and subject area. There are a few striking changes, but mainly among subjects with relatively small and fluctuating numbers of graduates.

This is the fourth year of a new classification developed by HESA to distinguish between "graduate-level" work and jobs that do not normally require a degree. In the employment table, subjects are ranked on "positive destinations", which include professional jobs and further study, whether or not combined with a job. Some similar tables do not make a distinction between different types of job. These tend to give the misleading impression that all universities and subjects offer uniformly rosy employment prospects.

It should also be noted that the definition of a graduate job is a controversial one. The statistics include internships and temporary jobs, for example, which may or may not lead to permanent employment. New universities in particular often claim that the whole concept of a graduate job immediately after graduation fails to reflect the employment reality for their alumni, especially in subjects such as media studies or art. In any case, a degree is about

What graduates are doing six months after graduation by subject studied

	Subject	Professional job	Professional job and studying	Studying	Non-professional job and studying	Non-professional job	Unemployed	Positive destinations
1	Medicine	93%	1%	5%	0%	0%	1%	99%
2	Dentistry	94%	4%	1%	0%	1%	1%	98%
3	Nursing	93%	2%	1%	0%	1%	2%	97%
4	Veterinary medicine	91%	1%	3%	0%	2%	2%	96%
5	Radiography	93%	1%	1%	0%	2%	3%	95%
6	Physiotherapy	91%	1%	1%	0%	3%	3%	94%
7	Pharmacology and pharmacy	75%	9%	8%	1%	4%	3%	93%
8	Building	79%	3%	3%	0%	8%	7%	85%
9	Civil engineering	71%	3%	10%	1%	7%	9%	84%
10	Land and property management	78%	2%	3%	0%	7%	9%	84%
11	Other subjects allied to medicine	62%	3%	14%	2%	11%	8%	81%
12	General engineering	62%	4%	14%	1%	9%	11%	81%
13	Chemical engineering	59%	2%	19%	1%	9%	10%	80%
14	Architecture	65%	5%	10%	0%	9%	11%	80%
15	Town and country planning and landscape	61%	4%	11%	2%	13%	9%	78%
16	Mechanical engineering	64%	2%	11%	1%	10%	13%	77%
17	Economics	55%	6%	14%	1%	12%	11%	77%
18	Physics and astronomy	36%	4%	36%	1%	11%	13%	76%
19	Chemistry	40%	3%	33%	1%	13%	11%	76%
20	Mathematics	46%	6%	23%	1%	13%	11%	76%
21	Electrical and electronic engineering	62%	2%	11%	1%	13%	12%	75%
22	Education	59%	2%	12%	1%	20%	5%	74%
23	Anatomy and physiology	38%	4%	30%	3%	16%	10%	74%
24	Materials technology	49%	1%	21%	2%	17%	9%	74%
25	Computer science	64%	2%	8%	1%	14%	12%	73%
26	German	49%	4%	19%	1%	18%	9%	73%
27	Food science	56%	2%	13%	2%	16%	11%	73%
28	Russian	47%	3%	21%	1%	19%	8%	73%
29	Law	32%	6%	29%	5%	18%	10%	72%
30	Aeronautical and manufacturing engineering	56%	3%	12%	1%	14%	13%	72%
31	Social work	58%	3%	8%	2%	19%	10%	71%
32	Geology	33%	3%	34%	1%	19%	10%	71%
33	Theology and religious studies	34%	4%	29%	4%	20%	9%	71%
34	French	47%	3%	17%	2%	20%	10%	70%
35	Celtic studies	21%	1%	39%	7%	25%	7%	69%
36	Middle Eastern and African studies	46%	1%	18%	3%	18%	13%	69%
37	Iberian languages	49%	3%	15%	1%	21%	11%	68%

Subject	Professional job	Professional job and studying	Studying	Non-professional job and studying	Non-professional job	Unemployed	Positive destinations
38 Librarianship and information management	56%	3%	6%	3%	25%	7%	68%
39 Accounting and finance	47%	10%	8%	2%	23%	10%	67%
40 Politics	41%	4%	20%	2%	21%	12%	67%
41 Biological sciences	31%	3%	30%	2%	22%	12%	66%
42 Business Studies	54%	3%	7%	1%	24%	11%	65%
43 Philosophy	33%	4%	24%	3%	23%	12%	64%
44 Anthropology	36%	2%	22%	3%	22%	14%	64%
45 Geography and environmental sciences	40%	3%	19%	3%	24%	12%	64%
46 History of art, architecture and design	35%	4%	22%	3%	23%	13%	63%
47 Sport science	38%	4%	18%	3%	29%	8%	63%
48 Linguistics	37%	3%	20%	3%	27%	10%	63%
49 Music	41%	4%	15%	2%	28%	10%	63%
50 English	34%	3%	22%	4%	27%	10%	62%
51 Classics and ancient history	31%	2%	25%	3%	25%	13%	62%
52 Italian	45%	2%	13%	1%	23%	15%	62%
53 East and South Asian studies	41%	3%	17%	2%	20%	18%	62%
54 History	31%	3%	23%	4%	28%	11%	61%
55 Archaeology and forensic science	34%	2%	20%	4%	28%	11%	60%
56 Art and design	51%	1%	5%	1%	30%	11%	59%
57 Psychology	32%	4%	18%	5%	32%	10%	58%
58 American studies	35%	3%	16%	4%	30%	13%	58%
59 Communication and media studies	48%	1%	6%	1%	31%	12%	57%
60 Drama, dance and cinematics	43%	2%	8%	2%	36%	10%	54%
61 Agriculture and forestry	38%	6%	8%	2%	30%	17%	54%
62 Hospitality, leisure, recreation and tourism	45%	1%	5%	1%	36%	11%	53%
63 Social policy	33%	2%	15%	3%	34%	14%	52%
64 Sociology	29%	2%	16%	3%	37%	13%	50%
65 Criminology	30%	3%	12%	3%	41%	11%	48%
66 Creative writing	26%	2%	13%	3%	39%	17%	44%
67 Animal science	21%	1%	13%	4%	50%	10%	40%
Total	**51%**	**3%**	**14%**	**2%**	**21%**	**10%**	**70%**

Note: Table is ranked on the total of positive destinations, the sum of the first four columns, which represent activities that require an undergraduate degree.

Source: 2014/15 DHLE return.

What graduates earn six months after graduation by subject studied

	Subject	Professional employment	Non-professional employment
1	Dentistry	£30,432	..
2	Chemical engineering	£28,603	£17,187
3	Medicine	£28,191	..
4	Economics	£28,157	£18,132
5	General engineering	£27,207	£16,585
6	Veterinary medicine	£26,872	..
7	Mechanical engineering	£26,376	£18,478
8	Building	£26,316	£19,824
9	Electrical and electronic engineering	£26,146	£17,253
10	Mathematics	£25,840	£17,108
11	Aeronautical and manufacturing engineering	£25,588	£16,239
12	Civil engineering	£25,555	£19,067
13	Computer science	£25,142	£16,542
14	Physics and astronomy	£25,047	£15,847
15	Geology	£24,818	£15,839
16	Social work	£24,792	£15,384
17	Land and property management	£24,505	..
18	Philosophy	£24,383	£16,103
19	Librarianship and information management	£24,168	£15,448
20	Materials technology	£24,009	£19,106
21	Russian	£23,973	£18,043
22	East and South Asian studies	£23,723	£17,112
23	Politics	£23,591	£19,911
24	Business studies	£23,476	£22,221
25	Accounting and finance	£23,182	£17,810
26	Nursing	£22,840	£18,221
27	Chemistry	£22,817	£15,547
28	Town and country planning and landscape	£22,775	£17,491
29	Radiography	£22,718	..
30	Classics and ancient history	£22,588	£15,534
31	German	£22,416	£17,407
32	Middle Eastern and African studies	£22,412	£17,378
33	Physiotherapy	£22,331	£13,929
34	Anatomy and physiology	£22,292	£15,530
35	Food science	£22,249	£15,500
36	French	£22,171	£16,517
37	Iberian languages	£22,161	£16,507
38	Geography and environmental sciences	£22,004	£18,041
39	Education	£21,932	£15,525
40	Theology and religious studies	£21,870	£15,168
41	Other subjects allied to medicine	£21,783	£16,211
42	Italian	£21,731	£17,840

Subject	Professional employment	Non-professional employment
43 History	£21,628	£16,767
44 Anthropology	£21,206	£16,553
45 Agriculture and forestry	£21,158	£17,903
46 Sociology	£20,762	£15,804
47 Biological sciences	£20,634	£15,763
48 American studies	£20,618	£15,689
49 Social policy	£20,600	£15,951
50 Law	£20,422	£16,919
51 History of art, architecture and design	£20,370	£16,175
52 Linguistics	£20,224	£15,992
53 Hospitality, leisure, recreation and tourism	£20,148	£17,057
54 English	£20,063	£15,796
55 Music	£19,956	£15,580
56 Psychology	£19,935	£15,745
57 Sport science	£19,899	£16,035
58 Architecture	£19,864	£16,149
59 Criminology	£19,847	£16,205
60 Celtic studies	£19,793	£13,661
61 Pharmacology and pharmacy	£19,746	£17,105
62 Drama, dance and cinematics	£19,673	£15,438
63 Art and design	£19,669	£15,790
64 Animal science	£19,373	£16,431
65 Archaeology and forensic science	£19,255	£15,664
66 Communication and media studies	£19,242	£15,631
67 Creative writing	£18,133	£14,868
Average	**£22,992**	**£16,814**

Note: .. indicates a suppressed mean salary based on 7 or fewer graduates
HESA 2014/15 DLHE return

enhancing your whole career and your view of the world, not just your first job out of college.

The tables on this and the previous pages will help you assess whether your course will pay off in career terms, at least to start with. They show both the amount you might expect to earn with a degree in a specific subject, and the odds of being in work. They reflect the experiences six months after graduation of those who competed their degrees in 2014, and the picture may have improved by the time you leave university. But there is no reason to believe that the pattern of success rates for specific subjects and institutions will have changed radically.

The table of employment statistics does reveal some unexpected results. For example, only 65 per cent of business studies graduates are working in graduate jobs or doing further study. Accounting and finance graduates are only 2 percentage points better off. The figures also explode a few popular myths, such as the suggestion that young people avoid engineering because salaries are low: all five branches of engineering are in the top dozen subjects for graduate earnings.

The employment table also shows that graduates in some subjects, especially sciences such as physics, chemistry and geology, are more likely to undertake further study than in others, such as art and design or hospitality. In both physics and Celtic studies, more than 40 per cent of graduates continued to study. Those going into art and design appreciate that it, too, has its own career peculiarities. Periods of freelance or casual work may be an occupational hazard at the start of their career, and perhaps later on as well. Less surprisingly, doctors and dentists are virtually guaranteed a job if they complete a degree, as are nurses. HESA found that only one graduate in 100 in medicine or dentistry was unemployed six months after graduating.

The second table, on pages 54–5, gives average earnings of those who graduated in 2015, six months after leaving college. It contains interesting, and in some cases surprising, information about early career pay levels. Few would have placed social work among the top 20 for graduate pay. However, nursing, which was in this group in the last edition of the *Guide*, has dropped eight places this time and is one of the few subjects to have seen average salaries drop. Those positions underline the differences between starting salaries and long-term prospects in different jobs. Over time the accountants may well end up with big rewards, despite being only one place higher than nursing in our table.

There are reasons for optimism, too, from the occasional surveys by HESA on the occupations and views of graduates three years into their careers. The last one, published in 2015, again painted a more positive picture than the surveys conducted six months after graduation. Of the UK graduates surveyed for that report, 88 per cent were in employment, 6 per cent were studying full-time and 2.6 per cent were unemployed, compared with 8 per cent when the same cohort was surveyed six months after graduation. The median salary of the 2009 graduates had risen from £22,000 to £26,000 over the same three and a half year period. Almost 6 per cent had seen their incomes rise by over £20,000 and most were at least £5,000 better off than in the initial survey.

Enhancing your employability

Universities are well aware of the difficulties in the graduate employment market and have been introducing all manner of schemes to try to give their graduates an advantage in the labour market. Many have incorporated specially designed employability modules into degree courses; some are certificating extra-curricular activities to improve their graduates' CVs; others are stepping up their efforts to provide work experience to complement degrees.

Opinion is divided on the value of such schemes. Some of the biggest employers restrict their recruitment activities to a small number of universities, believing that these institutions attract the brightest minds and that trawling more widely is not cost-effective. In 2015–16, High Fliers reported that the universities most targeted were Manchester, Nottingham, Warwick, Bristol, Cambridge and Oxford. These companies, often big payers from the City of London and including some of the top law firms, are not likely to change their ways at a time when they are more anxious than ever to control costs. Widening the pool of universities from which they set out to recruit is costly, and unnecessary in a buyers' market like the one we see today. As before, they will expect outstanding candidates who went to other universities to come to them, either on graduation or later in their careers.

The best advice for those looking to maximise their employment opportunities (and who isn't?) must be to go for the best university you can. But most graduates do not work in the City and most students do not go to universities at the top of the league tables.

University schemes

If a university offers extra help towards employment, it is worth considering whether its scheme is likely to work for you. Some are too new to show results in the labour market, but they may have been endorsed by big employers or introduced at an institution whose graduates already have a record of success in the jobs market. In time, these extras may turn into mandatory parts of degree study, complete with course credits.

At Liverpool John Moores University, for example, the World of Work (WoW) programme was devised with the help of the CBI, Shell, Sony, and Marks and Spencer. Originally an option, it is now taken by students in all subjects, including postgraduates, and offers classes in CV writing, interview skills, finance, entrepreneurship and negotiation skills, among many other topics. There are guest lectures and demonstrations, and employers carry out mock interviews to assess students' strengths and weaknesses.

Hertfordshire is another institution which has demonstrated a sustained focus on its students' job prospects. Employer groups are consulted on the curriculum and often supply guest lecturers on degree courses. Like some other universities, such as Derby, it offers career development support to graduates throughout their working life. Other universities, such as Exeter, have taken a different tack and are helping students make the most of their voluntary, sporting and extra-curricular activities by certificating them. It believes that the Exeter Award will encourage employers to take more notice such participation. The well-established York Award offers its students a framework to gain recognition for voluntary and leisure activities that are not formally recognised through the degree programme.

The value of work experience

The majority of graduate jobs are open to applicants from any discipline. For these general positions, employers tend to be more impressed by a good degree from what they consider a prestigious university than by an apparently relevant qualification. Here numeracy, literacy and communications – the arts needed to function effectively in any organisation – are of vital importance. Specialist jobs – for example in engineering or design – are a different matter. Employers may be much more knowledgeable about the quality of individual courses, and less influenced by a university's overall position in league tables, when the job relies directly on knowledge and skills acquired as a student. That goes for medicine and architecture as well as computer games design or environmental management.

In either case, however, work experience has become increasingly important. The High Fliers survey showed that employers in *The Times* 100 expected to fill more than 30 per cent of their vacancies with graduates who had already worked for them, whether in holiday jobs, internships or placements. Sandwich degrees, extended programmes that include up to a year at work, have always boosted employment prospects. Graduates often end up working where they undertook their placement. And while a sandwich year will make your course longer, it will not be subject to a full year's fees.

Many conventional degrees now include shorter work placements that should offer some advantages in the labour market. Not all are arranged by the university so, unless you have an opening that you would like to pursue, that is something to establish and weigh in the balance when choosing a course. The majority of big graduate employers offer some provision of this nature, although access to it can be competitive.

If your chosen course does not include a work placement, you may want to consider arranging your own part-time or temporary employment. The majority of supposedly full-time students now take jobs during term time, as well as in vacations, to make ends meet. But such jobs can boost your CV as well as your wallet. Even working in a bar or a shop shows some experience of dealing with the public and coping with the disciplines of the workplace. Inevitably, the more prosperous cities are likely to offer more employment opportunities than rural areas or conurbations that have been hard hit in the recession.

The ultimate work-related degree is one sponsored by an employer or even taken in the workplace. Middlesex University provides tailored programmes for Asda and Halifax Bank, among other organisations, and has many students taking courses run by its Institute of Work Based Learning. Most such courses are for people already employed by the companies concerned, rather than as a route into the company. But they may become an alternative to entering full-time higher education straight from school or college.

Consider part-time degrees

Another option, also favoured by ministers in successive governments, is part-time study. Although enrolments have fallen sharply both leading up to and since the 2012 increases in fees, there are now loans available for most part-time courses. Employers may be willing to share the cost of taking a degree or another relevant qualification, and the chance to earn a wage while studying has obvious attractions. Bear in mind, however, that most part-time courses take twice as long to complete as the full-time equivalent. If your earning power is linked to the qualification, it will take that much longer for you to enjoy the benefits.

Plan early for your career

Whatever type of course you choose, it is sensible to start thinking about your future career early in your time at university. There has been a growing tendency in recent years for students to convince themselves that there would be plenty of time to apply for jobs after graduation, and that they were better off focusing entirely on their degree while at university. In the current employment market, all but the most obviously brilliant graduates need to offer more than just a degree, whether it be work experience, leadership qualities demonstrated through clubs and societies, or commitment to voluntary activities. Many students finish a degree without knowing what they want to do, but a blank CV will not impress a prospective employer.

Half of the leading employers told High Fliers that they are not interested in graduates without previous work experience and that any such applicants would have "little or no chance" for a place on their graduate programmes. He may be overstating the case, but Martin Burchall, High Fliers' Managing Director, claimed that work placements and internships were now "just as important as getting a 2:1 or first-class degree".

Useful websites

Prospects, the UK's official graduate careers website: **www.prospects.ac.uk**

For career advice, internships and student and graduate jobs: **www.milkround.com**

High Fliers: **www.highfliers.co.uk**

4 Going Abroad to Study

British students have been notoriously reluctant to go abroad even for part of their degree, let alone an entire course. Poor linguistic skills and good universities at home have encouraged them to stay in their own country, while students elsewhere in the world are travelling in unprecedented numbers. France has three times as many studying abroad, Germany more than four times as many, according to UNESCO. Nepal, with half the UK's population, has roughly the same number of students overseas. This may be about to change, however, at least for those including a period of study at a foreign university in their UK degree. The Government and universities themselves have been encouraging students to take advantage of overseas opportunities to strengthen their employment prospects – and finally there appears to be a response. The numbers going abroad as part of a UK degree have grown by 50 per cent in recent years, topping 30,000.

There has been speculation since £9,000 fees were introduced that more students would apply to universities on the Continent, where the equivalent charges are low or even non-existent. More sixth-formers – particularly at independent schools – do appear to be considering it, but the predicted surge has yet to materialise. There has been an increase in the numbers going to universities in the USA, where the fees gap has narrowed, at least with state universities, but it is still very much a minority pursuit. There were over 10,000 UK students at US universities last year, but many were postgraduates and/or the children of Britons working on that side of the Atlantic.

Research by the British Council has shown that one student in three is interested in some form of overseas study. And, good though UK universities are by international standards, other studies suggest that they are right to do so. Research by QS, publishers of the World University Rankings, found that 60 per cent of employers worldwide – and 42 per cent of those in the UK – gave extra weight to an international student experience when recruiting graduates. Of course, everything will depend on what and where that experience was. Harvard is going to carry more weight than the University of Lapland, which has tried to attract British students in the past. But leaving the UK to study, even for a short period, can confer advantages in the employment market. Some universities now have international summer schools and many degrees include the opportunity of a semester or a year abroad, either studying or with an employer.

Some of the obstacles that have held British students back are now being removed. The maximum fee for a year abroad while studying at a UK university is £1,385, for example, and many universities are charging less than that. But there is still one important disincentive to taking a full degree overseas: although support from the Student Loans Company continues for a year abroad during a UK degree course, it is not available for degrees from non-UK institutions.

Universities in some countries – notably the Netherlands and the USA – now mount frequent recruitment campaigns in the UK. Numbers of British students have been rising sharply at Dutch universities, where fees in 2016/17 are €1,984 for most courses, but they still account for only about 1,000 of the 2.5-million UK student population. Leading independent schools report serious interest in American universities and attendance at the Fulbright Commission's recruitment fairs continues to rise, but the numbers enrolling remain modest, despite attractive incentives in the form of scholarships, bursaries and campus employment opportunities.

Nevertheless, it would be surprising if high fees at home and an increasingly international graduate labour market did not encourage continuing growth in overseas study. Most students who go abroad are motivated by a desire to study at a "world-class" institution, according to a study for the Department of Business, Innovation and Skills. Often the trigger is failure to win a place at a leading UK university and being unwilling to settle for second best. Other motivations include a desire for adventure and a belief that overseas study might lead to an international career. The question is how to judge a university that may be thousands of miles from home against more familiar names in the UK. This chapter will make some suggestions, including the use of the growing number of global rankings that are available online or in print.

It is possible to have your academic cake and eat it by going on an international exchange or work placement organised by a UK university, or even to attend a British university in another country. Nottingham University has campuses in China and Malaysia; Middlesex can offer Dubai or Mauritius, where students registered in the UK can take part or all of their degree. Other universities, such as Liverpool, also have joint ventures with overseas institutions which offer an international experience (in China, in Liverpool's case) and degrees from both universities.

In most cases, however, an overseas study experience means a foreign university – through a partnership with a UK institution. Until recently, this was usually for a postgraduate degree – and there are still strong arguments for spending your undergraduate years in the UK before going abroad for more advanced study. Older students taking more specialised programmes may get more out of an extended period overseas than those who go at 18 and, since first degrees in the UK are shorter than elsewhere, it may also be the more cost-effective option.

If cost is the main consideration, however, even the generally longer courses at Continental universities can work out cheaper than a degree in the UK. The main obstacle, apart from British students' traditional reluctance to take degrees anywhere else, concerns the language barrier. Although there are now thousands of postgraduate courses taught in English at Continental universities, first-degree programmes are still much thinner on the ground. A few universities, like Maastricht and others in the Netherlands, are offering a wide range of subjects in English. But most European universities teach undergraduates in the host language – and, up to now, that has always deterred UK students.

The obvious alternative lies in American, Australian and Canadian universities, all of which are keen to attract more international students. Here, cost and distance are the main obstacles. Four-year courses add considerably to the cost of affordable-looking fees, while the state of the pound has been another serious disadvantage. Add in the natural reluctance of most 18-year-olds to commit to life on the other side of the world (or even just the Atlantic), and the prospect of a dramatic increase in student emigration lessens considerably.

Where do students go to?
There is remarkably little official monitoring of how many students leave the UK, let alone where they go. But it seems that for all the economic advantages of studying in Continental Europe, the USA remains by far the most popular student destination. Most surveys put Canada, France and Germany, Ireland and Australia as the biggest attractions outside the USA.

A few British students find their way to unexpected locations, like South Korea or Slovakia, but usually for family reasons or to study the language. The figures suggest that British students are more attracted to countries that are familiar or close at hand, and where they can speak English. Many are doubtless planning to stay in their adopted country after they graduate, although visa regulations may make this difficult.

Studying in Europe
More than 10,000 UK students now attend Continental European universities and colleges, according to UNESCO. But international statistics pick up those whose parents emigrated or are working abroad, as well as those who actually leave the UK to take a degree. A minority are undergraduates, if only because the availability of courses taught in English is so much greater at postgraduate level.

The increased interest in Continental universities arises both from the generally low fees they charge and from the growth in the number of courses offered in English. Some countries charge no fees at all, even to international students, and public universities in the European Union are obliged to charge other member countries' students the same as local residents, as well as allowing them to get a job while studying. Of course, when the UK is no longer a member, students will not enjoy these advantages, but fee levels will remain lower than at home across most of Europe.

At present, undergraduates can study at a French university for less than £150 a year but, not surprisingly, nearly all first degrees are taught in French. Only 68 of the 1,249 programmes taught in English and listed on the Campus France website (**www. campusfrance.org/en**) are at the Licence (Bachelors equivalent) level – and 21 of them have some teaching in French. Germany is much the same, despite attracting large numbers of international students. The DAAD website (**www.daad.de/en**) lists 152 undergraduate programmes taught wholly or mainly in English – seven fewer than last year – but many are at private universities like Jacobs University in Bremen, which charges up to €10,000 a semester. There are cheaper alternatives in the public sector, where tuition fees have been abolished, but they remain relatively scarce.

Any potential saving has to be considered with care. In spite of the Bologna process – an intergovernmental agreement which means that degrees across Europe are becoming more similar in content and duration – most Continental courses are longer than their UK equivalents, adding to the cost and to your lost earnings from attending university. And, of course, you will have higher travel costs. It is harder to generalise about the cost of living. It can be lower than the UK in southern Europe, but frighteningly high in Scandinavia.

Obviously, the cost of an international experience and the commitment involved is much reduced if you opt for an exchange scheme or other scheme arranged by a UK university, many of which have partners all over the world. There are opportunities for everything from a summer school of less than a month to a full year abroad, and a number of universities now have targets to increase the numbers taking advantage of such schemes.

The most common offering is the EU's Erasmus scheme, which funds exchanges of between three months and a year, the work counting towards your degree. More than 2 million students throughout Europe have used the scheme, and there are 2,000 universities to choose from in 30 countries. It is uncertain whether UK students will have access to the scheme after Brexit but, for the moment at least, applications are made through universities' international offices, and must be approved by the UK university as well as by the Erasmus administrators. Erasmus students do not pay any extra fees and they are eligible for grants to cover the extra expense of travelling and living in another country. During the 2015–16 academic year, this amounted to €250–€300 a month for studying abroad, and €350–€400 a month for doing a traineeship abroad, depending on the country you choose to go to.

Studying in America

American universities remain the first choice of British students going abroad to take a degree, just as the UK is the first choice for Americans. Regardless of any special relationship, this is not surprising since international rankings consistently show US and UK universities to be the best in the world (as well as teaching in English).

Around half of the British students taking courses in the USA are undergraduates. Already by far the most popular student destination, the attractions of an American degree have multiplied since fees trebled in England. The Fulbright Commission, which promotes American higher education, has seen a 30 per cent increase in the number of Britons taking US university entrance exams. Even before the latest rise in UK fees, the top American universities had seen demand rise sharply, and this is spreading to universities further down the rankings.

The sheer depth of the US university system means that if you are thinking of studying abroad, the USA is almost bound to be on the list of possibilities. Tuition fees at Ivy League institutions are notoriously high – Harvard's are $47,074 in 2016–17 and the university put the full cost of attendance at $63,025 a year plus health insurance of $2,630 – but generous student aid programmes ensure that most pay far less than the "sticker price". Outside

Top ten countries, as destinations for UK students, 2014		Top ten student cities in the world, 2016	
1 United States of America	9,689	1 Paris	France
2 France	2,110	2 Melbourne	Australia
3 Ireland	2,106	3 Tokyo	Japan
4 Australia	1,618	4 Sydney	Australia
5 Germany	1,499	5 London	United Kingdom
6 Canada	1,337	6 Singapore	Singapore
7 Netherlands	888	7 Montreal	Canada
=8 Denmark	709	8 Hong Kong	Hong Kong
=8 United Arab Emirates	630	9 Berlin	Germany
10 Austria	606	10 Seoul	South Korea
UNESCO Institute for Statistics, 2016		QS Best Student Cities in the World, 2016	

the Ivy League, the fee gap for UK students has been narrowing, but fees at many state universities have shot up in the last three years as politicians have tried to balance the books. At Texas A&M University, for example, ranked in the top 200 in the world, international students now pay $30,208 a year for tuition, and the university put undergraduates' total costs at $48,000. Fees are up to $24,000 at the State University of New York, although the university puts the total cost for those living on campus at up to $40,000. Only at much lower-ranked state universities do the costs compare with those in the UK – at South Dakota State University, for example, the yearly cost is put at $19,400 (£15,500 at the time of writing).

The individual systems of state universities and private universities mean that there is a great variation in the financial support given to international students. Fulbright advises students considering a US degree to assess and negotiate a funding package at the same time as pursuing their application. Otherwise, they may end up with a place they cannot afford, losing valuable time in the quest for a more suitable one.

Which countries are best?
Anyone going abroad to study will be in search of a memorable and valuable all-round experience, not just a good course. Most international students are motivated by location – both the country and the city in which a university is based – as well as by the reputation of the institution. QS publishes an annual ranking of student cities, based on quality of life indicators as well as the number of places at world-ranked universities. Paris topped the ranking in 2016, with Melbourne second, Tokyo third and Sydney fourth.

Many Asian countries are looking to recruit more foreign students, both as part of a broader internationalisation agenda and to compensate for falling numbers of potential students at home. Japan is a case in point. The high cost of living may put off many potential students, as may the unfamiliarity of its language, but more support is being offered to attract foreign students and more courses are being taught in English. However, as with any non-English speaking country, the language of instruction is only part of the story. You will need to know enough of the local language to manage the shops and the transport system, and, of course, to make friends and get the most out of being there.

Another option of growing interest is China, although Western students are often put off by the dormitory accommodation that is the norm at most universities. The country has already grown massively in importance. Its university system is growing in quality, with the leading institutions climbing the world rankings and improving their facilities. Familiarity with China is unlikely to be a career disadvantage for anyone in the 21st century. Some see Hong Kong, which has several world-ranked universities and a familiar feel for Britons, as the perfect alternative to mainland Chinese universities.

Will my degree be recognised?
Even in the era of globalisation, you need to bear in mind that not all degrees are equal. At one extreme is the MBA, which has an international system for accrediting courses, and a global admissions standard. But with many professional courses, study abroad is a potential hazard. To work as a doctor, engineer or lawyer in the UK, you need a qualification which the relevant professional body will recognise. It is understandable that to practise law in England, you need to have studied the English legal system. For other subjects, the issues are more to do with the quality and content of courses outside UK control.

There are ways of researching this issue in advance. One is to contact NARIC, the National Recognition Centre for the UK (**www.naric.org.uk**). NARIC exists to examine

Top universities in the world, averaged from their positions in the QS World University Ranking (QS), the Academic Ranking of World Universities (ARWU) and *Times Higher Education* (*THE*) for 2016

Rank	Institution	Country
1	Stanford University	USA
2	Harvard University	USA
3	Massachusetts Institute of Technology	USA
4	University of Cambridge	UK
5	Oxford University	UK
6	California Institute of Technology	USA
7	Princeton University	USA
8	University of Chicago	USA
9	ETH Zurich (Swiss Federal Institute of Technology)	Switzerland
10	Yale University	USA
=11	University College London	UK
=11	Imperial College London	UK
13	University of California, Berkeley	USA
14	Columbia University	USA
15	Cornell University	USA
16	University of Pennsylvania	USA
17	Johns Hopkins University	USA
18	University of California, Los Angeles	USA
=19	Duke University	USA
=19	University of Michigan	USA
21	Northwestern University	USA
22	University of Toronto	Canada
23	University of Edinburgh	UK
24	University of Tokyo	Japan
25	University of California, San Diego	USA
26	University of Washington	USA
=27	King's College London	UK
=27	New York University	USA
=29	University of British Columbia	Canada
=29	University of Melbourne	Australia
31	Tsinghua University	China
32	National University of Singapore	Singapore
33	University of Manchester	UK
34	University of Illinois at Urbana-Champaign	USA
35	McGill University	Canada
36	École Polytechnique Fédérale de Lausanne	Switzerland
37	Peking University	China
38	Australian National University	Australia
=39	Carnegie Mellon University	USA
=39	Ludwig-Maximilian University of Munich	Germany
41	Technical University of Munich	Germany

42	Kyoto University	Japan
43	University of Texas at Austin	USA
44	Heidelberg University	Germany
=45	London School of Economics	UK
=45	University of Queensland	Australia
47	Nanyang Technological University	Singapore
=48	University of North Carolina at Chapel Hill	USA
=48	University of Bristol	UK
50	University of Hong Kong	Hong Kong

Note: The ARWU ranking only gives band positions above 100. For this exercise universities in the band 101–150 were given a position of 101. If they were given a position of 125 then the ranking at the bottom of the table would alter: 45 University of Queensland; =46 University of North Carolina at Chapel Hill; =46 University of Bristol; 48 University of Wisconsin at Madison; =49 Washington University in St Louis; =49 École Normale Supérieure, Paris.

the compatibility and acceptability of qualifications from around the world. The other approach is to ask the UK professional body in question – maybe an engineering institution, the relevant law society or the general teaching, medical or dental councils – about the qualification you propose to study for.

Which are the best universities?

Going abroad to study is a big and expensive decision, and you want to get it right. Whether your ultimate aim is to become an internationally mobile high-flyer, or simply to broaden your experience, you will want to know that the university you are going to is taken seriously around the world.

At the moment there are three main systems for ranking universities on a world scale. One is run by QS (Quacquarelli Symonds), an educational research company based in London (**www.topuniversities.com**). Another is by Shanghai Ranking Consultancy, a company set up by Shanghai Jiao Tong University, in China, and is called the Academic Ranking of World Universities (ARWU) (**www.shanghairanking.com**). These two have been joined by *Times Higher Education* (**www.timeshighereducation.com/world-university-rankings**), a weekly magazine with no connection to *The Times*, which produced its own ranking for the first time in 2010, having previously published the QS version.

There are several more international ranking systems that an online search might throw up, but most are either specialist – like the Webometrics ranking of universities' web activity – or limited in their readership and influence. Some are still developing: the European Commission's U-Multirank (**www.umultirank.org**), for example, is still limited in the subjects it covers, but may become a more widely used source of information in time.

The QS system uses a number of measures including academic opinion, employer opinion, international orientation, research impact and staff/student ratio to create its listing, while the ARWU uses measures such as Nobel Prizes and highly cited papers, which are more related to excellence in scientific research. *Times Higher Education* has added a number of measures to the QS model, including research income and a controversial global survey of teaching quality.

Naturally, the different methodologies produce some contrasting results – the three main rankings each have a different (American) university at the top, for example. The table opposite and above is a composite of the three main rankings, which places Stanford at the top and includes four UK universities in the top 20. In practice, however, if you go to a university that features strongly in any of the tables, you will be at a place that is well-regarded around the world. After all, even the 200th university on any of these rankings is an elite institution in a world with more than 4,000 universities.

These systems tend to favour universities which are good at science and medicine. Places that specialise in the humanities and the social sciences, such as the London School of Economics, can appear in deceptively modest positions. In addition, the rankings tend to look at universities in the round, and contain only limited information on specific subjects. QS published the first 26 global subject rankings in 2011 and has since increased this to 42. One advantage of the QS ranking system is that 10 per cent of a university's possible score comes from a global survey of recruiters. So you can look at this column of the table for an idea about where the major employers like to hire. Note that the author of this *Guide* has a role in developing the QS rankings.

Other options for overseas studies

For the growing numbers who want to study abroad without committing themselves to a complete degree, a number of options are available. A language degree will typically involve a year abroad, and a look at the UCAS website will show many options for studying another subject alongside your language of choice. UK universities offer degrees in information technology, science, business and even journalism with a major language such as Chinese.

Many universities offer a year abroad, either studying or in a work placement, even to those who are not taking a language. At Aston University, for example, 70 per cent of students do a year's work placement and a growing number do so abroad. China and Chile have been among recent destinations. Other universities offer the opportunity to take shorter credit-bearing courses with partner institutions overseas. American universities are again the most popular choice. The best approach is to decide what you want to study and then see if there is a UK university that offers it as a joint degree or with a placement abroad. Make sure that all the universities involved are well-regarded, for example by looking at their rankings on one or other of the websites of global rankings.

Useful websites

Prospects: studying abroad: **www.prospects.ac.uk/postgraduate-study/study-abroad**
Association of Commonwealth Universities: **www.acu.ac.uk**
Campus France: **www.campusfrance.org/en**
College Board (USA): **www.collegeboard.org**
DAAD (for Germany): **www.daad.de/en**
Study in Holland: **www.studyinholland.co.uk**
Education Ireland: **www.educationinireland.com/en**
Erasmus Programme (EU): **www.erasmusplus.org.uk**
Finaid (USA): **www.finaid.org**
Fulbright Commission: **www.fulbright.org.uk**
Study in Australia: **www.studyinaustralia.gov.au**
Study in Canada: **www.studyincanada.com**

5 Understanding Tuition Fees

Barring some unexpected political reverse, undergraduates in September 2017 in England will be hit with the first increase in fees for five years, and those starting courses in 2018 will pay more again. The good news for students, if it can be called that, is that both increases will be no more than the rate of inflation. In future years, some universities may be prevented from increasing fees further – or even required to reduce them. But for the first two years, all the English universities in our table will be able to go above £9,000 – and nearly all plan to charge the maximum £9,250 – at least for Honours degrees, although bursaries and fee waivers will bring the actual cost down for those from low-income families. Only the University of St Mark and St John (at £9,000) and University College Birmingham (£9,076) have set lower maximum fees for 2017–18.

Bursaries, scholarships and fee waivers mean that the average fees charged in England, let alone other parts of the UK, will vary much more widely than media reporting might suggest. But this only matters to those who qualify for one of the awards, usually by virtue of family income or their academic performance; most students will pay the maximum. For the record, the average fee for UK and European Union undergraduates at higher education institutions in England, in 2017–18, after fee waivers are taken into account, will be £9,090. After all forms of financial support, the average will range from £8,648 at UCB and £8,707 at Sunderland to the full £9,250, if inflation allows universities to charge that much, at more than 30 institutions. A few further education colleges will still be offering average fees of less than £6,000 after accounting for financial support.

This *Guide* quotes the higher headline fees, but even these may vary according to whether you are from inside or outside the EU, studying full-time or part-time, and whether you are taking a Foundation degree or an Honours programme. Non-European medical students may pay as much as £49,000 a year for their clinical years, Britons taking part-time Foundation degrees as little as £3,500. But all the attention has been focused on full-time Honours degrees for British and other EU undergraduates because those are the courses for which the maximum fees shot up to £9,000 in 2012.

Fees and loans
Student numbers dropped in the first year of higher fees, but prospective students long since appear to have resigned themselves to the new charges. The numbers starting courses

rose by 3 per cent in 2015 and there was another small increase in 2016. There is little sign that applicants are basing their choices on the marginal differences in fee levels at different universities, and numbers from the poorest socio-economic groups are at record levels – albeit still severely under-represented compared with more affluent groups. Concern remains, however, over the impact on part-time courses and on the numbers prepared to continue to postgraduate study.

Most readers of *The Times and Sunday Times Good University Guide* will be choosing full-time undergraduate or Foundation degree courses. The fees for 2017–18 are listed alongside each university's profile in chapter 14, and access agreements for universities in England, including details of bursaries and scholarships, are on the website of the Office for Fair Access (OFFA). Institutions in Scotland, Wales and Northern Ireland will continue to have lower charges for their own residents, but will charge varying amounts to students from other parts of the UK. Only those living in Scotland and studying at Scottish universities will escape all fees, although there will be reduced fees for those living in Wales and Northern Ireland.

The number of bursaries and scholarships offered to reduce the burden on new students has been falling since OFFA has suggested that such initiatives do little to attract students from low-income households. Most of the evidence pre-dates £9,000 fees so may no longer be correct, but universities have acted on its advice and the Government has switched its National Scholarship Programme from an undergraduate to a postgraduate scheme. It has also turned the grants paid to the poorest students into loans from 2016–17.

Variations among universities

The lowest full-time fee at an English university in 2017–18 will be £3,500 a year, charged for the small number of Foundation degrees in education at York St John University. But even there, Honours degree students will pay £9,250, if that is the maximum allowable. A total of 33 universities are planning to charge £9,250 for every course, and at several others the only exceptions will be during work placements or years abroad, when fees cannot exceed £1,850 for work placements and £1,385 for a year abroad, and are often less.

Many universities will continue to devote a substantial proportion of the income they receive from higher fees to access initiatives, whether in the form of bursaries or outreach activities. In the case of the London School of Economics, half of all of its fee income above £6,000 will be spent in this way. The lowest proportion will be 10 per cent at Wolverhampton. These measures appear to be having some success in attracting students from disadvantaged backgrounds. There have been successive increases in enrolments by students from disadvantaged groups, as the gap between rich and poor has begun to close to some extent.

Even if it is closer to business as usual than many universities dared hope in the run-up to £9,000 fees, that does not mean that financial considerations will be irrelevant to the decision-making process. In the current economic circumstances, students will want to keep their debts to a minimum and are bound to take the cost of living into account. They will also want the best possible career prospects and may choose their subject accordingly.

Alternative options

Some further education colleges will offer substantial savings on the cost of a degree, or Foundation degree, but they tend to have very local appeal, generally in a limited range of vocational subjects. Similarly, the private sector may be expected to compete more vigorously in future, following the success of two-year degrees at the University of Buckingham and

BPP University in particular. Most will continue to undercut the traditional universities, although Regent's University, one of the latest to be awarded that title, will be charging £16,400 in autumn 2017, while the New College of the Humanities, also in London, has surprisingly reduced its charges from £17,992 to £13,560 (including examination fees) in 2017–18.

Impact on subject and university choice

Fee levels have had little impact on students' choices of university, but that is not the case for choices of subject. Predictions that old universities and/or vocational subjects would prosper at the expense of the rest have been shown to be too simplistic. Some, but not all, arts subjects have suffered, while in general science courses have prospered. For many young people, the options have not changed. If you want to be a doctor, a teacher or a social worker, there is no alternative to higher education. And, while there are now more options for studying post A level, it remains to be seen whether they offer the same promotion prospects as a degree.

Most subjects continued to attract increased applications in 2016, although they were down in medicine and dentistry, veterinary science, business and management, classics, modern languages, creative arts, education and combined subject degrees. Some others saw significant increases, but even some of these subjects are yet to return to the level of applications seen before the fees went up.

It is enrolments that matter in the end, however, and here the pattern is slightly different. Although the numbers starting higher education courses rose by 1.3 per cent in 2016, several areas had reached at least a temporary halt in the rising numbers they had seen in the previous two years. Veterinary and physical sciences, technologies, classics, modern languages, creative arts, education and combined degrees were all down, albeit only marginally.

It will take time to be certain whether the new fees regime brings about more fundamental changes in subject choice, starting at A level or the equivalent, if not before that. Sixth formers studying English, history and French cannot suddenly switch to a chemistry degree, but those entering university in 2016 will have made choices after GCSE knowing what a university education would cost. Not all of the trends in undergraduate education are shaped by fee levels: there were signs in schools, well before the fees went up, of a renaissance in the sciences and a decline in languages.

There is little doubt, however, that applicants are looking more carefully at future career prospects when choosing a degree, and they have decided (rightly or wrongly) that some careers are more secure, or more lucrative, than others. Applications for law remain buoyant and medicine is holding its own, despite a long and now much more expensive training. Enrolments in architecture and building are only now matching the levels seen before the construction industry went in to decline in 2008.

With no real pattern yet established, those hoping to start courses in 2018 would be unwise to jump to conclusions about levels of competition in different subjects, or between whole universities. A drop in applications may mean less competition for places, or it may lead universities to close courses and possibly even intensify the race for entry. The only reliable forecast is that competition for places on the most popular courses will remain stiff, just as it has been since before students paid any fees.

Getting the best deal

There will still be a certain amount of variation in student support packages in 2018–19, so it will be possible to shop around, particularly if your family income is low. But remember that the best deal, even in purely financial terms, is one that leads to a rewarding career. By all means compare the full packages offered by individual universities, but consider whether marginal differences in headline fees really matter as much as the quality of the course and the likely advantages it will confer in the employment market. Higher career earnings will soon account for a few hundred pounds in extra fees to be repaid over 30 years. It is all a matter of judgement – Scottish students can save themselves £27,000 by opting to study north of the border. That is a very different matter to the much smaller saving that is available to students in England, particularly if the Scottish university is of comparable quality to the alternatives elsewhere.

Those who are eligible for means-tested bursaries may not be able to afford to ignore the financial assistance they offer. No one has to pay tuition fees while they are a student, but you still have to find thousands of pounds in living costs to take a full-time degree. In some cases, bursaries may make the difference between being able to afford higher education and having to pass up a potentially life-changing opportunity. Some are worth up to £3,000 a year, although most are less generous than this, often because large numbers of students qualify for an award.

Some scholarships are even more valuable, and are awarded for sporting and musical prowess, as well as academic achievement. Most scholarships are not means-tested, but a few are open only to students who are both high performers academically and from low-income families.

How the £9,250 fee system works

What follows is a summary of the position for British students at the end of 2016. While there are substantial differences between the four countries of the UK, there is one important piece of common ground. Up-front payment of fees is not compulsory, as students can take out a fee loan from the Student Loans Company to cover them (see chapter 8). This is repayable in instalments after graduation, when earnings reach £21,000 for English students, a threshold set by the Government.

With undergraduate fees expected to reach £9,250, the most you can borrow to pay fees will be £9,250, with lower sums set for private colleges and part-time study. As this figure increases over the coming years, so the size of the loan to cover fees will also. There are different levels of fees and support for UK students who are not from England. In 2017 at least, students from other EU countries will pay the same rate as home students in the UK nation in which they study. Those from outside the EU are not affected by the changes, and may well have to pay quite a lot more than home and European students. The latest information on individual universities' fees at the time of going to press is listed at the end of this chapter and alongside their profiles in chapter 14.

With changes, large or small, becoming almost an annual occurrence, it is essential to consult the latest information provided on the websites of the relevant Government agencies.

Fees in England

In England, the maximum tuition fee for full-time undergraduates from the UK or anywhere in the European Union will be £9,250 a year in 2017–18, depending on the rate of inflation. Most courses will demand fees of £9,250, or close to it, in order to recoup the money removed from their Government grants and leave room for further investment and student support.

In many public universities, the lowest fees will be for Foundation degrees and Higher National Diplomas. Although some universities have chosen to charge the same for all courses, in many universities and further education colleges, these two-year courses will remain a cost-effective stepping stone to a full degree or a qualification in their own right. Those universities that offer extended work placements or a year abroad, as part of a degree course, will charge much less than the normal fee for the "year out". The maximum fees for a placement year is 20 per cent of the full tuition fee (£1,850) and for a year abroad, 15 per cent (£1,385).

Fees in Scotland

At Scottish universities and colleges, students from Scotland and those from other EU countries outside the UK pay no fees directly. The universities' vice-chancellors and principals have appealed for charges to be introduced at some level to save their institutions from falling behind their English rivals in financial terms, but Alex Salmond, when he was Scotland's First Minister, famously declared that the "rocks will melt with the sun" before this happens.

Students whose home is in Scotland and are who studying at a Scottish university apply to the Student Awards Agency for Scotland (SAAS) to have their fees paid for them. Note, too, that three-year degrees are rare in Scotland, so most students can expect to pay four years of living costs.

Students from England, Wales and Northern Ireland studying in Scotland will pay fees at something like the level that applies in England and will have access to finance at similar levels to those available for study in England. Several Scottish universities are offering a "free" fourth year to bring their total fees into line with English universities, but Edinburgh, Heriot-Watt and St Andrews are charging £9,250 in all four years of their degree courses.

Fees in Wales

Welsh universities have, in previous years, applied a range of fees up to £9,000, but for 2017–18 all have opted for £9,000. Students who live in Wales will be able to apply for a Tuition Fee Loan as well as a Tuition Fee Grant, wherever they study. The grant was intended to pay fees beyond £4,046 a year in 2017–18.

Tuition fees

The figures below show the maximum fees that students can be charged in 2017–18.

Domicile of student	Location of institution			
	England	Scotland	Wales	Northern Ireland
England	£9,250	£9,250[1]	£9,000	£9,000
Scotland	£9,250	No fee	£9,000	£9,000
Wales[2]	£4,296	4,296[1]	£4,046	£4,046
Northern Ireland	£9,250	£9,250[1]	£9,000	£4,030
European Union	£9,250	No fee	£9,000	£4,030
Other international	Variable	Variable	Variable	Variable

1 Note that Honours degrees in Scotland take four years and some universities charge £9250 for each year.
2 Welsh-domiciled students are entitled to a tuition fee grant for any fees above £4,046 in Wales and £4,296 in the rest of the UK
   (when total fee is £9,250).

The system is expected to change in 2018, however, following a review led by Professor Sir Ian Diamond. The fee grant of up to £4,954 will be scrapped and maintenance grants of up to £11,000 for the poorest families introduced instead. Others will receive loans in order to pay full-cost fees. About 70 per cent of students – those whose families earn up to £59,000 – are expected to receive support. The maximum will be £11,000 in London and £8,000 elsewhere. At the time of writing, the introduction of the system in September 2018 was dependant on Treasury approval, the results of a consultation and the capacity of the Student Loans Company to administer it.

Fees in Northern Ireland

The two universities of Northern Ireland are expected to charge local students £4,030 a year for 2017–18. Students can receive a fee loan to postpone paying this until their earnings are above £17,495 a year. For students from elsewhere in the UK, the fee is currently £9,000 a year at Ulster and Queen's, Belfast. The arrangements for 2018–19 are more uncertain than usual because of large cuts in the two universities' budgets.

Useful websites

With changes, large or small, becoming almost an annual occurrence, it is essential to consult the latest information provided by Government agencies. You should check the following websites for the latest information:

England: **www.gov.uk/student-finance**

Wales: **www.studentfinancewales.co.uk**

Scotland: **www.saas.gov.uk**

Northern Ireland: **www.studentfinanceni.co.uk**

University tuition fees for UK/EU and international students

England

The fees given for UK/EU undergraduates are those for **2017–18**. The fees shown are for full degrees and do not include the sometimes lower fees charged for Foundation degrees or for Foundation years (Year 0). The International student (non-EU) fees are for 2017–18, unless indicated otherwise.

	Undergraduate fees UK / EU students 2017–18	Undergraduate fees International students 2017–18
Anglia Ruskin	£9,250	£11,700–£12,200
Arts University Bournemouth	£9,250	£15,000
University of the Arts London	£9,250	£17,230[1]
Aston	£9,250	£14,000–£17,200
Bath	£9,250	£15,200–£19,000
Bath Spa	£9,250	£11,600[1]
Bedfordshire	£9,250	£10,500[1]
Birkbeck	£9,250	£13,000[1]
Birmingham	£9,250	£15,210–£19,710; £19,710–£35,640 (medicine and dentistry)
Birmingham City	£9,250	£12,000; £15,500 (Conservatoire and acting)
University College Birmingham	£9,076	£9,600[1]
Bishop Grosseteste	£9,250	£11,500
Bolton	£9,246	£12,000
Bournemouth	£9,250	£13,500
Bradford	£9,250	£14,250–£16,970
Brighton	£9,250	£12,680–£13,920; £28,000[1] (medicine)
Bristol	£9,250	£15,800–£19,400
		£19,400–£35,400 (dentistry, medicine, veterinary medicine)
Brunel	£9,250	£14,100–£17,200
Buckingham	£12,444; £36,000 (medicine)[2]	£17,160; £36,000 (medicine)[2]
Buckinghamshire New	£9,250	£10,500
Cambridge	£9,250	£16,608–£25,275; £40,200 (medicine)[3]
Canterbury Christ Church	£9,250	£11,000
Central Lancashire	£9,250	£11,950–£17,500; £36,600 (medicine)
Chester	£9,250	£11,800
Chichester	£9,250	£10,620–£12,240[1]
City	£9,250	£14,000–£16,500
Coventry	£9,250	£11,359–£13,476[1]
University for the Creative Arts	£9,250	£12,350
Cumbria	£9,250	£10,500
De Montfort	£9,250	£11,750–£12,250[1]
Derby	£9,250	£11,750–£12,250
Durham	£9,250	£17,400–£22,000
East Anglia	£9,250	£14,800–£18,200; £30,000 (medicine)
East London	£9,250	£11,440
Edge Hill	£9,250	£11,575
Essex	£9,250	£13,350–£15,450
Exeter	£9,250	£16,500–£21,000; £29,500 (medicine)

	Undergraduate fees UK / EU students 2017–18	Undergraduate fees International students 2017–18
Falmouth	£9,250	£15,000
Gloucestershire	£9,250	£11,750[1]
Goldsmiths	£9,250	£13,500–£19,990
Greenwich	£9,250	£11,500
Harper Adams	£9,250	£10,200
Hertfordshire	£9,250	£11,350–£11,850
Huddersfield	£9,250	£13,000–£14,000
Hull	£9,250	£12,800–£15,300; £29,400 (medicine)
Imperial	£9,250	£25,000–£28,000; £38,500 (medicine)
Keele	£9,250	£13,000–£16,000; £27,800 (medicine)
Kent	£9,250	£13,810–£16,480
King's College London	£9,250	£17,050–£22,800; £33,000 (medicine); £39,200 (dentistry)
Kingston	£9,250	£12,000–£14,500
Lancaster	£9,250	£14,500–£17,470; £28,050 (medicine)
Leeds	£9,250	£15,750–£19,750; £29,750 (medicine); £32,750 (dentistry)
Leeds Beckett	£9,250	£10,500
Leeds Trinity	£9,250	£11,250
Leicester	£9,250	£15,290–£18,855; £18,855–£35,170 (medicine)
Lincoln	£9,250	£12,800–£14,500
Liverpool	£9,250	£13,400–£16,800 £30,850 (medicine, dentistry and veterinary medicine)
Liverpool Hope	£9,250	£10,800[1]
Liverpool John Moores	£9,250	£11,630–£12,660
London Metropolitan	£9,250	£11,400
London School of Economics	£9,250	£18,408
London South Bank	£9,250	£11,600[1]
Loughborough	£9,250	£16,000–£19,900
Manchester	£9,250	£17,000–£21,000; £21,000–£38,000 (medicine)
Manchester Metropolitan	£9,250	£12,720–£14,100
Middlesex	£9,250	£11,500–£12,500
Newcastle	£9,250	£13,980–£17,935; £17,935–£33,190 (medicine and dentistry)
Newman	£9,250	£11,100
Northampton	£9,250	£10,900–£11,900[1]
Northumbria	£9,250	£12,500–£14,500
Norwich University of the Arts	£9,250	£13,000[1]
Nottingham	£9,250	£15,570–£20,070; £29,730 (veterinary medicine) £21,120–£35,010 (medicine)
Nottingham Trent	£9,250	£12,900
Oxford	£9,250	£23,105–£30,540; £25,430–£34,956 (medicine)[4]
Oxford Brookes	£9,250	£12,640–£13,730
Plymouth	£9,250	£12,250–£12,500; £17,800–£33,000 (medicine)[1]
Portsmouth	£9,250	£12,600–£14,400
Queen Mary, London	£9,250	£14,500–£19,550; £31,800 (medicine and dentistry)
Reading	£9,250	£15,300–£18,860
Roehampton	£9,250	£12,500[1]

	Undergraduate fees UK / EU students 2017–18	Undergraduate fees International students 2017–18
Royal Agricultural University	£9,250	£10,000
Royal Holloway, London	£9,250	£14,000–£15,600
St George's, London	£9,250	£15,170–£15,970; £31,960 (medicine)
St Mark and St John	£9,000	£10,500–£11,250
St Mary's, Twickenham	£9,250	£11,000[1]
Salford	£9,250	£11,500–£13,300[1]
Sheffield	£9,250	£16,000–£20,470; £20,470–£35,500 (medicine)
Sheffield Hallam	£9,250	£12,250–£12,750
SOAS, London	£9,250	£16,250[1]
Southampton	£9,250	£16,054–£19,725; £19,725–£40,230 (medicine)
Southampton Solent	£9,250	£11,000
Staffordshire	£9,250	£10,900
Suffolk	£9,250	£10,080–£11,580
Sunderland	£9,250	£10,750
Surrey	£9,250	£15,000–£19,500; £30,000 (veterinary medicine)
Sussex	£9,250	£15,000–£18,750; £28,000[1] (medicine)
Teesside	£9,250	£10,750[1]
University College London	£9,250	£17,710–£23,710; £32,670 (medicine)
Warwick	£9,250	£17,460–£22,260; £20,338–£35,520 (medicine)
West London	£9,250	£10,650[1]
West of England	£9,250	£11,750–£12,500
Westminster	£9,250	£12,500
Winchester	£9,250	£11,600
Wolverhampton	£9,250	£11,475
Worcester	£9,250	£11,700
York	£9,250	£16,290–£20,500; £29,400 (medicine)
York St John	£9,250	£10,000–£11,500

1 Fees for 2016–17; fees for 2017–18 not announced when book went to print.
2 Courses starting in January 2018. Note that courses only lasts two years (eight terms), except medicine (4.5 years).
3 Plus Cambridge College fees (£6,000–£8,500). UK and EU students who are eligible for tuition fee support not liable for College fees.
4 Includes Oxford College fees £7,350 (£2,848 for clinical medicine years). UK and EU students who are eligible for tuition fee support not liable for College fees.

Wales

For **2017–18**, universities can to charge up to £9,000, with the Welsh Assembly paying fees above £4,046 (2017–18) for Welsh students.

	Undergraduate fees UK / EU students 2017–18	Undergraduate fees International students 2017–18
Aberystwyth	£9,000	£13,200–£14,750
Bangor	£9,000	£12,500–£15,300
Cardiff	£9,000	£15,080–£18,980; £18,980–£33,540 (medicine and dentistry)
Cardiff Metropolitan	£9,000	£11,500–£12,000
South Wales	£9,000	£11,900
Swansea	£9,000	£12,900–£16,950; £33,320 (medicine)
Trinity St David (UWTSD)	£9,000	£10,400
Wrexham Glyndŵr	£9,000	£11,500

Scotland

In 2017–18 there are no fees for Scottish and EU students, but there are fees for students from elsewhere in the UK.

	Fees for Scottish students and eligible non-UK EU students 2017–18[1]	Fees for students from elsewhere in the UK 2017–18[2]	Undergraduate fees International students 2017–18
Aberdeen	No fee	£9,000	£14,300–£18,000; £39,000 (medicine)
Abertay	No fee	£8,000	£12,500–£13,500
Dundee	No fee	£9,250	£14,950–£17,950
			£21,300–£35,000 (medicine)
			£28,600–£40,000 (dentistry)
Edinburgh	No fee	£9,250	£17,700–£23,200
			£32,100–£49,900 (medicine)
			£30,200 (veterinary medicine)
Edinburgh Napier	No fee	£9,000	£11,950–£13,900
Glasgow	No fee	£9,250	£16,000–£19,500
			£42,000 (medicine); £39,000 (dentistry)
			£26,750 (veterinary medicine)
Glasgow Caledonian	No fee	£9,000	£11,500
Heriot Watt	No fee	£9,250	£13,770–£17,440
Highlands and Islands	No fee	£8,000–£9,000	£10,000–£11,000
Queen Margaret	No fee	£7,000	£11,250–£12,500
Robert Gordon	No fee	£5,000–£6,750	£12,000–£15,300
		£8,820 (pharmacy)	
St Andrews	No fee	£9,250	£20,570; £28,200 (pre-clinical medicine)
Stirling	No fee	£6,750	£11,845–£14,105
Strathclyde	No fee	£9,250	£13,500–£19,100
West of Scotland	No fee	£9,250	£12,300–£13,800

1 For all eligible students, SAAS will pay fees of £1,820 direct to the universities.
2 As Scottish Honours degrees are four years in length, the cost of some degrees in Scotland for students from the rest of the UK will be higher than in England. Some universities have put a maximum cap on charges to maintain equality with English fees. Consult university websites for details.

Northern Ireland

For 2016–17 there are different fees for students resident in Northern Ireland and students coming from other parts of the UK.

	Fees for Northern Irish students and eligible non-UK EU students 2017–18	Fees for students from elsewhere in the UK 2017–18	Undergraduate fees International students 2017–18
Queen's, Belfast	£4,030	£9,000	£15,100–£18,800
			£19,000–£35,900 (medicine)
			£29,140 (dentistry)
Ulster	£4,030	£9,000	£12,890

6 Making Your Application

There will be nothing you can do about your grades once you have taken your exams, but making your application is firmly under your own control – and much more important than many students realise. The art of conveying knowledge of, and enthusiasm for, your chosen subject – preferably with supporting evidence from your school or college – can make all the difference.

Too many people take their eye off the ball when actually applying for a higher education place. Surprising numbers of applicants each year spell their own name wrongly, or enter an inaccurate date of birth, or the wrong course code. And that is to say nothing of the damage that can be done in the personal statement and teachers' references. While UCAS will decode misspelt names, other errors in grammar or spelling present admissions officers with an easy starting point in cutting applications down to a more manageable number.

There is renewed support for a change of system to one in which applications are made after students have their results, but for the moment decisions have to be made well before that point. You will be able to make up to five choices, although you do not have to use all five if you do not want to. Some people make only a single application, perhaps because they do not want to leave home or they have very particular requirements – but you will give yourself the best chance of success if you go for the maximum.

A number of relatively minor changes were made to UCAS application procedures for entry in 2014, but, at the time of writing, no more were planned for 2017 or 2018, apart from the introduction of the new tariff (see page 31). Perhaps the most important recent change allowed candidates to submit a new personal statement if their initial applications are unsuccessful and they use the UCAS Extra process. This and other changes are outlined below.

The application process

Most applications for full-time higher education courses go through UCAS, although there is still a different process for the music conservatoires. The trend is towards the UCAS model even among specialist providers, however: recruitment to nursing and midwifery diploma and degree courses in Scotland switched to the UCAS system in 2010, and the art and design courses that used to recruit using the separate "Route B" scheme have also moved to the main system.

Some universities that have not filled all their places, even during Clearing, will accept direct applications up to and sometimes after the start of the academic year, but UCAS is both the official route and the only way into the most popular courses.

All UCAS applications are made online. The Apply electronic system is accessed via the UCAS website and is straightforward to use. For those who do not have the internet at home and prefer not to use school or college computers, the UCAS website lists libraries all over the UK where you can make your application. Apply is available 24 hours a day, and, when the time comes, information on the progress of your application may arrive at any time.

Registering with Apply

The first step in the process is to register. If you are at a school or college, you will need to obtain a "buzzword" from your tutor or careers adviser – it is used when you log on to register. It links your application to the school or college so that the application can be sent electronically to your referee (usually one of your teachers) for your reference to be attached. If you are no longer at a school or college, you do not need a "buzzword", but you will need details of your referee. More information is given on the UCAS website.

To register, go to the UCAS website and click on "Apply". The system will guide you through the business of providing your personal details and generating a username and password, as well as reminding you of basic points, such as amending your details in case of a change of address. You can register separate term-time and holiday addresses – a useful option for boarders, who could find offers and, particularly, the confirmation of a place, going to their school when they are miles away at home. Remember to keep a note of your username and password in a safe place.

Throughout the process, you will be in sole control of communications with UCAS and your chosen universities. Only if you nominate a representative and give them your unique nine-digit application number (sent automatically by UCAS when your application is submitted), can a parent or anyone else give or receive information on your behalf, perhaps because you are ill or out of the country.

Improved video guides on the application process are available on the UCAS website. Once you are registered, you can start to complete the Apply screens. The sections that follow cover the main screens.

Personal details

This information is taken from your initial registration, and you will be asked for additional information, for example, on ethnic origin and national identity, to monitor equal

---

The main screens to be completed in UCAS Apply

» Personal and contact details and some additional non-educational details for UK applicants.

» Student finance, a section for UK-resident applicants.

» Your course choices.

» Details of your education so far, including examination results and examinations still to be taken.

» Details of any jobs you have done.

» Your personal statement.

» A declaration that you confirm that the information is correct and that you will be bound by the UCAS rules.

» Pay for the application (applications for 2017 cost £24, or £13 to apply to just one course).

» A reference from one of your teachers.

opportunities in the application process. UK students will also be asked to complete a student finance section designed to speed up any loan application you might make.

Choices

In most subjects, you will be able to apply to a maximum of five universities and/or colleges. The exceptions are medicine, dentistry and veterinary science, where the maximum is four, but you can use your fifth choice as a back-up to apply for a different subject.

The other important restriction concerns Oxford or Cambridge, because you can only apply to one or the other; you cannot apply to both Oxford and Cambridge in the same year, nor can you apply for more than one course. All courses at Cambridge and most at Oxford will require you to take a written test, either before or at interview (see pages 34–5). In addition, for Cambridge, you will be asked to complete an online Supplementary Application Questionnaire once the university has received your application from UCAS. The deadline for Oxbridge applications – and for all medicine, dentistry and veterinary science courses – is 15 October 2017. For all other applications the deadline is 15 January 2018 (or 24 March 2018 for some specified art and design courses). The other exceptions to this rule are the small but growing number of courses that start in January or February. If you are considering one of these, contact the university concerned for application deadlines.

Most applicants use all five choices. But if you do choose fewer than five courses, you can still add another to your form up to 30 June, as long as you have not accepted or declined any offers. Nor do you have to choose five different universities if more than one course at the same institution attracts you – perhaps because the institution itself is the real draw and one course has lower entrance requirements than the other. Universities are not allowed to see where else you have applied, or whether you have chosen the same subject elsewhere. But they will be aware of multiple applications within their own institution. Remember that it is more difficult to write a convincing personal statement if it has to cover two subjects.

For each course you select, you will need to put the UCAS code on the form – and you should check carefully that you have the correct code and understand any special requirements that may be detailed on the UCAS description of the course. It does not matter what order you enter in your choices as all your choices are treated equally. You will also need to indicate whether you are applying for a deferred entry (for example, if you are taking a gap year – see page 88–2).

Education

In this section you will need to give details of the schools and colleges you have attended, and the qualifications you have obtained or are preparing for. The UCAS website gives plenty of advice on the ways in which you should enter this information, to ensure that all your relevant qualifications are included with their grades. While UCAS does not need to see qualification certificates, it can double-check results with the examination boards to ensure that no one is tempted to modify their results.

In the Employment section that follows, add details of any paid jobs you have had (unpaid or voluntary work should be mentioned in your personal statement).

Personal statement

As the competition for places on popular courses has become more intense, so the value attached to the personal statement has increased. Admissions officers look for a sign of potential beyond the high grades that growing numbers of applicants offer. Many academics responsible for admissions value success in extracurricular activities such as drama, sport or the Duke of Edinburgh's Award scheme. But your first priority should be to demonstrate an enthusiasm for and understanding of your subject beyond the confines of the exam syllabus.

This is not easy in a relatively short statement that can readily sound trite or pretentious. You should resist any temptation to exaggerate, let alone lie, particularly if there is any chance of an interview. A claim to have been inspired by a book that you have not read will backfire instantly under questioning and, even without an interview, experienced academics are likely to see through grandiose statements that appear at odds with a teacher's reference.

Genuine experiences of after-hours clubs, lectures or visits, work experience or actual reading around the syllabus are much more likely to strike the right note. If you are applying for medicine, for example, any practical work experience or volunteering in medical or caring settings should be included. Take advice from teachers and, if there is still time before you make your application, look for some subject-related activities that will help fill out your statement.

UCAS top ten personal statement tips

1　Express interest in the subject and show real passion.
2　Go for a strong opening line to grab the reader's attention.
3　Relate outside interests to the course.
4　Think beyond university.
5　Get the basics right.
6　Don't try to sound too clever.
7　Take time and make it your best work.
8　Don't leave it until the last minute – remember the 15 January deadline!
9　Get a second opinion.
10　Honesty is the best policy

Admissions officers are also looking for evidence of character that will make you a productive member of their university and, eventually, a successful graduate. Taking responsibility in any area of school or college life suggests this – leading activities outside your place of learning even more so. Evidence of initiative and self-discipline is also valuable, since higher education involves much more independent study than sixth-formers are used to.

Your overall aim in writing your personal statement is to persuade the admissions officer to pick yours out from the piles of applications. That means trying to stand out from an often rather dull and uniform set of statements based around the curriculum and the more predictable sixth-form activities. Everyone is going to say they love reading, for example; narrow your interest down to an area of (real) interest. Don't be afraid to include the unusual, but bear in mind that an academic's sense of humour may not be the same as yours.

Give particular thought to why you want to study your chosen subject – especially if it is not one you have taken at school or college. You need to show that your interests and skills are well suited to the course and, if it is a vocational degree, that you know how you envisage using the qualification. Admissions officers want to feel that you will be committed to their subject for the length of the course, which could be three, four or even five years, and capable of achieving good results. If your five choices cover more than one subject, be careful not to focus too much on one; try to make more general comments on your academic strengths and enthusiasms. And, since the same statement goes to all your chosen departments, avoid expressing any preference for an individual institution.

Your school or college should be the best source of advice, since they see personal statements every year, but there are others. The UCAS website has a useful checklist of themes that you may wish to address, while sites such as **www.studential.com** also provide tips. But do not fall into the trap of cutting and pasting from the model statements included on such sites

– both UCAS and individual universities have software that will spot plagiarism immediately. In one year, no fewer than one in 20 applicants came to grief in this way. Plagiarists of this type are unlikely to be disqualified, but they destroy the credibility of their application.

Try not to cram in more than the limited space will allow – admissions officers will have many statements to go through, and judicious editing may be rewarded. As long as you write clearly – preferably in paragraphs and possibly with sub-headings – it will be up to you what to include. It is a personal statement. But consider the points listed below and make sure that you can answer all the questions raised. Once you have completed your statement show it to others you trust. It is really important to have others read your statement before submitting it – sometimes things that are clear to you may not be to fresh eyes.

The Apply system allows 4,000 characters (including spaces) or 47 lines for your statement. While there is no requirement to fill all the space, it should not look embarrassingly short. Indeed, from 2014, your statement has had to be at least 1,000 characters long. It is hard to believe that many candidates could not rustle up 200 words to support their application, but presumably significant numbers were not doing so. UCAS recommends using a word-processing package to compile the statement before pasting it into the application system. This is because Apply will time-out after 35 minutes of inactivity, so there is a danger of losing valuable material. Working offline also has the advantage of leaving you with a copy and making it easier to show it to others.

References

Hand in hand with your personal statement goes the reference from your school, college or, in the case of mature students, someone who knows you well, but is not a friend or family member. Since 2014, even referees who are not your teachers have been encouraged to predict your grades, although they are allowed to opt out of this process. Whatever the source, the reference has to be independent – you are specifically forbidden to change any part of it if you send off your own application – but that does not mean you should not try to influence what it contains.

Most schools and colleges conduct informal interviews before compiling a reference, but it does no harm to draw up a list of the achievements that you would like to see included, and ensure your referee knows what subject you are applying for. Referees cannot know every detail of a candidate's interests and most welcome an aide memoire.

The UCAS guidelines skirt around the candidate's right to see his or her reference, but it does exist. Schools' practices vary, but most now show the applicant the completed reference.

Key points to consider in writing your personal statement

» What attracts you to this subject (or subjects, in the case of dual or combined honours)?

» Have you undertaken relevant work experience or voluntary activities, either through school or elsewhere?

» Have you taken part in other extra-curricular activities that demonstrate character – perhaps as a prefect, on the sports field or in the arts?

» Have you been involved in other academic pursuits, such as Gifted and Talented programmes, widening participation schemes, or courses in other subjects?

» Which aspects of your current courses have you found particularly stimulating?

» Are you planning a gap year? If so, explain what you intend to do and how it will affect your studies. Some subjects – notably maths – actively discourage a break in studies.

» What other outside interests might you include that show that you are well-rounded?

Timetable for applications for university admission in 2018

At the time of writing UCAS had not confirmed the exact dates for the application schedule after 15 January 2018. Please check the UCAS website for the most recent information.

2017

January onwards	Find out about courses and universities. Check schedule of open days.
February onwards	Attend open days.
early July	Registration starts for UCAS Apply.
mid September	UCAS starts receiving applications.
15 October	Final day for applications to Oxford and Cambridge, and for most courses in medicine, dentistry and veterinary science.

2018

15 January	Final day for all other applications from UK and EU students including all art and design courses except those which have a 24 March deadline (specified in UCAS Course Search).
16 January–end June	New applications continue to be accepted by UCAS, but only considered by universities if the relevant courses have vacancies.
late February	Start of applications through UCAS Extra.
24 March	Final day for applications to art and design courses that specify this date.
end March	Universities should have sent decisions on all applications received by 15 January.
early May	Final time by which applicants have to decide on their choices if all decisions received by end March (exact date for each applicant will be confirmed by UCAS). **If you do not reply to UCAS, they will decline your offers.** UCAS must have received all decisions from universities if you applied by 15 January.
early June	Final time by which applicants have to decide on their choices if all decisions received by early May.
start of July	Any new application received from this time held until Clearing starts. End of applications through UCAS Extra.
5 July	International Baccalaureate results published.
7 August	SQA results published. Scottish Clearing starts.
16 August	A level results published. Full Clearing and Adjustment starts.
end August	Adjustment closes. Last time for you to meet any offer conditions, after which university might not accept you.
late October	End of period for adding Clearing choices and last point at which a university can accept you through Clearing.

Where this is not the case, the candidate can pay UCAS £10 for a copy, although at this stage it is obviously too late to influence the contents. Better, if you can, to see it before it goes off, in case there are factual inaccuracies that can be corrected.

Timing

The general deadline for applications through UCAS is 15 January, but even those received up to 30 June will be considered if the relevant courses still have vacancies. After that, you will be limited to Clearing, or an application for the following year. In theory – and usually in practice – all applications submitted by the January deadline are given equal consideration. But the best advice is to get your application in early: before Christmas, or earlier if possible. Applications are accepted from mid-September onwards, so the autumn half-term is a sensible target date for completing the process. Although no formal offers are made before the deadline, many admissions officers look through applications as they come in and may make a mental note of promising candidates. If your form arrives with the deadline looming, you may appear less organised than those who submitted in good time; and your application may be one of a large batch that receives a more cursory first reading than the early arrivals. Under UCAS rules, last-minute applicants should not be at a disadvantage, but why take the risk?

Next steps

Once your application has been processed by UCAS, you will receive an email confirming that your application has been sent to your university choices and summarising what will happen next. The email will also confirm your Personal ID, which you can use to access "Track", the online system that allows you to follow the progress of your application. Check all the details carefully: you have 14 days to contact UCAS to correct any errors. Universities can make direct contact with you through Track, including arranging interviews.

After that, it is just a matter of waiting for universities to make their decisions, which can take days, weeks or even months, depending on the university and the course. Some obviously see an advantage in being the first to make an offer – it is a memorable moment to be reassured that at least one of your chosen institutions wants you – and may send their response almost immediately. Others take much longer, perhaps because they have so many good applications to consider, or maybe because they are waiting to see which of their applicants withdraw when Oxford and Cambridge make their offers. Universities are asked to make all their decisions by the end of March, and most have done so long before that.

Interviews

Unless you are applying for a course in health or education that brings you into direct contact with the public, the chances are you will not have a selection interview. For prospective medics, vets, dentists or teachers, a face-to-face assessment of your suitability will be crucial to your chances of success. Likewise in the performing arts, the interview may be as important as your exam grades. Oxford and Cambridge still interview applicants in all subjects, and a few of the top universities see a significant proportion. But the expansion of higher education has made it impractical to interview everyone, and many admissions experts are sceptical about interviews.

What has become more common, however, is the "sales" interview, where the university is really selling itself to the candidate. There may still be testing questions, but the admissions staff have already made their minds up and are actually trying to persuade you to accept an offer. Indeed, you will probably be given a clear indication at the end of the interview that an offer is on its way. The technique seems to work, perhaps because you have invested time and nervous energy in a sometimes lengthy trip, as well as acquiring a more detailed impression of both the department and the university.

The difficulty can come in spotting which type of interview is which. The "real" ones require lengthy preparation, revisiting your personal statement and reading beyond the exam syllabus. Impressions count for a lot, so dress smartly and make sure that you are on time. Have a question of your own ready, as well as being prepared to give answers.

While you would not want to appear ignorant at a "sales" interview, lengthy preparation might be a waste of valuable time during a period of revision. Naturally, you should err on the side of caution, but if your predicted grades are well above the standard offer and the subject is not one that normally requires an interview, it is likely that the invitation is a sales pitch. It is still worth going, unless you have changed your mind about the application.

Offers

When your chosen universities respond to your application, there will be one of three answers:

» Unconditional Offer (U): This used to be a possibility only if you applied after satisfying the entrance requirements – usually if you are applying as a mature student, while on a gap year, after resitting exams or, in Scotland, after completing Highers. However, a growing number of universities competing for bright students have begun to make unconditional offers to those who are predicted high grades – just how high will depend on the university. If you are fortunate (and able) enough to receive one, do not assume that grades are no longer important because they may be taken into consideration when you apply for jobs as a graduate.

» Conditional Offer (C): The vast majority of students will still receive conditional offers, where each university offers a place subject to you achieving set grades or points on the UCAS tariff.

» Rejection (R): You do not have the right qualifications, or have lost out to stronger competition.

If you have chosen wisely, you should have more than one offer to choose from, so you will be required to pick your favourite as your firm acceptance – known as UF if it was an unconditional offer and CF if it was conditional. Candidates with conditional offers can also accept a second offer, with lower grades, as an Insurance choice (CI). You must then decline any other offers that you have.

You do not have to make an Insurance choice – indeed, you may decline all your offers if you have changed your mind about your career path or regret your course decisions. But most people prefer the security of a back-up route into higher education if their grades fall short. You must be sure that your firm acceptance is definitely your first choice because you will be allocated a place automatically if you meet the university's conditions. It is no good at this stage deciding that you prefer your Insurance choice because UCAS rules will not allow a switch.

The only way round those rules, unless your results are better than your highest offer (see Adjustment, below), is through direct contact with the universities concerned. Your firm acceptance institution has to be prepared to release you so that your new choice can award you a place in Clearing. Neither is under any obligation to do so but, in practice, it is rare for a university to insist that a student joins against his or her wishes. Admissions staff will do all they can to persuade you that your original choice was the right one – as it may well have been, if your research was thorough – but it will almost certainly be your decision in the end.

UCAS Extra

If things do go wrong and you receive five rejections, that need not be the end of your higher education ambitions. From the end of February until the end of June, you have another chance through UCAS Extra, a listing of courses that still have vacancies after the initial round of offers. Extra is sometimes dismissed (wrongly) as a repository of second-rate courses. In fact, even in the boom years for applications, most Russell Group universities still have courses listed in a wide variety of subjects.

You will be notified if you are eligible for Extra and can then select courses marked as available on the UCAS website. In order to assist students who choose different subjects after a full set of rejections in their original application, you will be able to submit a new personal statement for Extra. Applications are made, one at a time, through UCAS Track. If you do not receive an offer, or you choose to decline one, you can continue applying for other courses until you are successful. About half of those applying through Extra normally find a place. Some 7,500 were successful this way in 2015.

Results Day

Rule Number One on results day is to be at home, or at least in easy communication – you cannot afford to be on some remote beach if there are complications. The day is bound to be stressful, unless you are absolutely confident that you achieved the required grades – more of a possibility in an era of modular courses with marks along the way. But for thousands of students, Track has removed the agony of opening the envelope or scanning a results noticeboard. On the morning of A-level results day, the system informs those who have already won a place on their chosen course. You will not learn your grades until later, but at least your immediate future is clear.

If you get the grades stipulated in your conditional offer, the process should work smoothly and you can begin celebrating. Track will let you know as soon as your place is confirmed and the paperwork will arrive in a day or two. You can phone the university to make quite sure, but it should not be necessary and you will be joining a long queue of people doing the same thing.

If the results are not what you hoped – and particularly if you just miss your grades you need to be on the phone and taking advice from your school or college. In a year when results are better than expected, some universities will stick to the letter of their offers, perhaps refusing to accept your AAC grades when they had demanded ABB. Others will forgive a dropped grade to take a candidate who is regarded as promising, rather than go into Clearing to recruit an unknown quantity. Admissions staff may be persuadable – particularly if there are extenuating personal circumstances, or the dropped grade is in a subject that is not relevant to your chosen course. Try to get a teacher to support your case, and be persistent if there is any prospect of flexibility.

If your results are lower than predicted, one option is to ask for papers to be re-marked, as growing numbers do each year. The school may ask for a whole batch to be re-marked, and you should ensure that your chosen universities know this if it may make the difference to whether or not you satisfy your offer. If your grades improve as a result, the university will review its decision, but if by then it has filled all its places, you may have to wait until next year to start.

If you took Scottish Highers, you will have had your results for more than a week by the time the A-level grades are published. If you missed your grades, there is no need to wait for A levels before you begin approaching universities. Admissions staff at English universities may not wish to commit themselves before they see results from south of the border, but Scottish universities will be filling places immediately and all should be prepared to give you an idea of your prospects.

Adjustment

If your grades are better than those demanded by your first-choice university, there is now an opportunity to "trade up". Introduced in 2009, the Adjustment Period runs from when you receive your results until 31 August, and you can only use it for five 24-hour periods during that period, so there is no time to waste. First, go into the Track system and click on "Register for Adjustment" and then contact your preferred institutions to find another place. If none is available, or you decide not to move, your initial offer will remain open. The number of students switching universities in this way slipped back slightly in 2015, but there were still 1,100 successful candidates. The process has become an established part of the system and, without the previous restrictions on the number of students they could recruit, many leading universities see it as a good source of talented undergraduates. UCAS does not publish a breakdown of which universities take part – some, such as Oxford and Cambridge, simply do not have places available – but it is known that many students successfully go back to institutions that had rejected them at the initial application stage. Even if you are eligible for Adjustment, you may decide to stick with the offer you have, but it is worth at least exploring your options.

Clearing

If you do not have a place on Results Day, there will still be plenty of options through the UCAS Clearing scheme. A record 64,300 people – almost one successful applicant in eight – found a place through this route in 2015 and the numbers rose again in 2016. With recruitment restrictions lifted, universities that used to regard their absence from Clearing as a point of pride are appearing in the vacancy lists. It is likely that this trend will continue, as more universities seek to expand, particularly in arts, social science and business subjects.

Although the most popular courses may still fill up quickly, many remain open up to and beyond the start of the academic year. And, at least at the start of the process, the range of courses with vacancies is much wider than in Extra. Most universities will list some courses, and most subjects will be available somewhere.

Clearing runs from A-level Results Day until the end of September, matching students without places to full-time courses with vacancies. As long as you are not holding any offers and you have not withdrawn your application, you are eligible automatically. You will be sent a Clearing number via Track to quote to universities.

There are now two ways of entering Clearing: the traditional method of ringing universities that still have vacancies, or by using the system introduced in 2015 which allows universities to approach candidates with suitable grades for one of their courses. You will be given the option of signing up for this service in an email from UCAS and issued with a code word to be used by universities contacting you on Results Day or subsequently. You will be approached by a maximum of five universities or colleges. UCAS advises students to approach universities themselves in any case, but the new system does add an extra string to their bow and may take some of the anxiety out of Clearing.

Assuming you are making your own approaches, the first step is to trawl through the lists on the UCAS website, and elsewhere, before ringing the university offering the course that appeals most, and where you have a realistic chance of a place – do not waste time on courses where the standard offer is far above your grades. Universities run Clearing hotlines and have become adept at dealing with a large number of calls in a short period, but you can still spend a long time on the phone at a time when the most desirable places are beginning to disappear. If you can't get through send an email setting out your grades and the course that interests you.

The best advice is to plan ahead and not to wait for Results Day to draw up a list of possible Clearing targets. Many universities publish lists of courses that are likely to be in Clearing on their websites from the start of August. Think again about some of the courses that you considered when making your original application, or others at your chosen universities that had lower entrance requirements. But beware of switching to another subject simply because you have the right grades – you still have to sustain your interest and be capable of succeeding over three or more years. Many of the students who drop out of degrees are those who chose the wrong course in a rush during Clearing.

In short, you should start your search straight away if you do find yourself in Clearing, and act decisively, but do not panic. You can make as many approaches as you like, until you are accepted on the course of your choice. Remember that if you changed your personal statement for applications in Extra, this will be the one that goes to any universities that you approach in Clearing, so it may be difficult to return to the subjects in your original application.

Most of the available vacancies will appear in Clearing lists, but some of the universities towards the top of the league tables may have a limited number of openings that they choose not to advertise – either for reasons of status or because they do not want the administrative burden of fielding large numbers of calls to fill a handful of places. If there is a course that you find particularly attractive – especially if you have good grades and are applying late – it may be worth making a speculative call.

What are the alternatives?

If your results are lower than expected and there is nothing you want in Clearing, there are several things you can do. The first is to resit one or more subjects. The modular nature of some courses means that you will have a clear idea of what you need to do to get better grades. You can go back to school or college, or try a "crammer". Although some colleges have a good success rate with re-takes, you have to be highly focused and realistic about the likely improvements. Some of the most competitive courses, such as medicine, may demand higher grades for a second application, so check before you commit yourself.

Other options are to get a job and study part-time, or to take a break from studying and return later in your career. You may have considered an apprenticeship before applying to university, but the number and variety are growing all the time, so it may be worth another look. The UCAS Progress service provides information on apprenticeship opportunities post-16 and a new search tool has been established for higher and degree apprenticeship vacancies.

The part-time route can be arduous – many young people find a job enough to handle without the extra burden of academic work. But others find it just the combination they need for a fulfilling life. It all depends on your job, your social life and your commitment to the subject you will study. It may be that a relatively short break is all that you need to rekindle your enthusiasm for studying. Many universities now have a majority of mature students, so you need not be out of place if this is your chosen route.

Taking a gap year

The other popular option is to take a gap year. In most years, about 7 per cent of applicants defer their entry until the following year while they travel, or do voluntary or paid work. A whole industry has grown up around tailor-made activities, many of them in Asia, Africa or Latin America. Some have been criticised for doing more for the organisers than the underprivileged communities that they purport to assist, but there are programmes that are useful and character-building, as well as safe. Most of the overseas programmes are not cheap, but raising the money can be part of the experience.

Various organisations can help you find voluntary work. Some examples include vInspired (**https://vinspired.com/**), Lattitude Global Volunteering (**https://lattitude.org. uk/**) and Volunteer Africa (**www.volunteerafrica.org**). Voluntary Service Overseas (**www. vsointernational.org**) works mainly with older volunteers but has an offshoot, run with five other volunteering organisations, International Citizen Service (**www.volunteerics.org**), that places 18–25-year-olds around the world.

The alternative is to stay closer to home and make your contribution through organisations like Volunteering Matters (**http://volunteeringmatters.org.uk**) or to take a job that will make higher education more affordable when the time comes. Work placements can be casual or structured, such as the Year in Industry Scheme (**www.etrust.org.uk**). Sponsorship is also available, mainly to those wishing to study science, engineering or business.

Many admissions staff are happy to facilitate gap years because they think it makes for more mature, rounded students than those who come straight from school. The longer-term benefits may also be an advantage in the graduate employment market. Both university admissions officers and employers look for evidence that candidates have more about them than academic ability. The experience you gain on a gap year can help you develop many of the attributes they are looking for, such as interpersonal, organisational and teamwork skills, leadership, creativity, experience of new cultures or work environments, and enterprise.

There are subjects – maths in particular – that discourage a break because it takes too long to pick up study skills where you left off. From the student's point of view, you should also bear in mind that a gap year postpones the moment at which you embark on a career. This may be important if your course is a long one, such as medicine or architecture.

If you are considering a gap year, it makes sense to apply for a deferred place, rather than waiting for your results before applying. The application form has a section for deferments. That allows you to sort out your immediate future before you start travelling or working, and leaves you the option of changing your mind if circumstances change.

Useful websites

The essential website for making an application is UCAS: **www.ucas.com**

Gap years

To help you consider options and start planning: **http://gapadvice.org/**
For links to volunteering opportunities in the UK: **https://do-it.org/**
For links to many gap year organisations: **www.yearoutgroup.org**

7 Financing Your Studies

Student debt has become an emotive (and politically sensitive) issue, but there is little agreement about the scale of the problem or the best way for an individual to minimise it. There is little chance of avoiding debt altogether but, depending on your subsequent earnings, you might never have to pay most of it back if you have taken out a student loan. Despite that, a recent study described student loans as "one of the most expensive ways of funding a university education" because of the interest charged over the 30-year repayment period. This chapter will examine the options for students – although even some of these are set to change by the time the academic year begins in 2018.

The last significant change was the abolition of grants for students from low-income families in England and their replacement by loans has focused attention once more on the cost of higher education. As with the introduction of £9,000 fees, there is no immediate impact on students because repayments will begin only after graduation when the borrower's salary reaches £21,000, but the prospect of yet more debt may still deter applicants from this already under-represented section of society. That was not the case when the fees went up in 2012, but no one can be sure what will happen this time.

Most new undergraduates, who would not have qualified for grants in any case, will be marginally better off than their predecessors because they will be able to borrow up to £500 more to help with living expenses, although that naturally brings increased debt on graduation.

There are different arrangements in other parts of the UK, which are addressed later in this chapter. But wherever you study, there are two quite different timescales to consider: in the short term the calculations are all about affordability, while the long term is more about value for money. Most commentary on the subject conflates the two, focusing on the total debt that the average student will have at graduation. Although an intimidating figure and one that should not be ignored by those contemplating a degree, it has little to do with whether you can afford three or more years as an undergraduate.

Affordability

While the introduction of £9,000 fees added enormously to graduates' debts, it has made no difference to the amount of money you will need as a student. That calculation is about bridging the gap between a maintenance loan, which in England will now be worth up to

£8,430 (or £11,002 in London) in 2017–18, and the real cost of living. With hall fees topping £5,000 a year at some universities, there will be a gap for most students, but this was so before the fees went up. Through a combination of parental help, part-time employment and institutional bursaries, most students find a way to make ends meet.

How well you can live on these sums will vary from person to person. But analysis by the National Union of Students suggests that it is not possible to get by on student loans alone. Savings, earnings, and help from family and friends have to be added to the pot. The information provided here will help you understand how big your pot needs to be, and what you can expect to be added and taken away from it. But it takes careful budgeting to avoid adding credit card debt to the income-contingent variety offered by the Government and repaid (or not) over 30 years.

Value for money

Only when you are sure you can cope with the costs of student life should you move on to the longer-term question of whether your chosen degree will be worth repaying £40,000 or more in student loans. Even in purely financial terms, there are too many uncertainties to be sure of the answer. You may never earn enough (£21,000 a year) to be required to repay any of it – although no one goes to university with those expectations and very few will be in that position. Or your degree may help you land such a well-paid job that university was cheap at the price. Most graduates will be somewhere in the middle, and the system is too new for any to have experienced the impact of loan repayments of 9 per cent of salary above £21,000 for such an extended period.

Contrary to some alarmist media coverage of graduate employment prospects, most surveys suggest that, on average, a degree is still a worthwhile investment in terms of future salary expectations, even after adding in the amount you might have earned while you were at university. A study by London Economics for the MillionPlus group of universities put the average graduate premium at £115,000 over a working lifetime. But averages can be deceiving: more recent research suggested that almost half of the graduates of post-1992 universities were earning less than young people who took higher apprenticeships.

This *Guide* should help to fill in some of the detail on employment rates on different courses at different universities. Salary data by course is available on the Unistats website, but no one can be certain of salary prospects over an entire career, possibly spanning a number of employment fields. Many satisfying jobs are open only to graduates, while in others the vast majority of new entrants have degrees.

Even before higher fees arrived, graduates and current students still on courses owed more than £40 billion between them in England alone, making them a major component of the public finances. Virtually all of this debt was in the form of income-contingent loans. The money was owed by 3.8 million borrowers, of whom 2.5 million were earning enough to make repayments, making the average debt just over £10,000 per person. Those figures are rising rapidly, and a report by the Sutton Trust in 2016 put the average debt of final-year undergraduates at £44,000.

Planning your finances

This chapter will focus on the costs while at university and the support that is available to get you through your undergraduate years. Like maximum fees, national student support schemes are the responsibility of the devolved UK administrations. There are separate sections for Northern Ireland, Wales and Scotland that follow the advice given for English students below. Where the rates for 2017–18 had not been announced when this book went to press, the figures quoted are for 2016–17.

With changes, large or small, becoming almost an annual occurrence, it is essential to consult the latest information provided by Government agencies. It is worth checking the following websites for the latest information:

» England: **www.gov.uk/student-finance**
» Wales: **www.studentfinancewales.co.uk**
» Scotland: **www.saas.gov.uk**
» Northern Ireland: **www.studentfinanceni.co.uk**

Student loans for English students

More than 80 per cent of students take out a student loan, and it is not difficult to see why. The National Union of Students estimates that undergraduates spend £12,000 a year outside London and £13,500 in the capital. While some other estimates are marginally lower, most students find it impossible to cover all their living costs on savings and earnings alone and would require significant family support to cover the difference if they did not take out a loan.

Most experts, such as Martin Lewis, who writes regularly on student finance, agree that student loans are a good deal compared with other forms of borrowing – although he has accused the Government of breaking its word by holding the repayment threshold at £21,000 when students had been told it would rise with inflation. In particular, he counsels against using family savings to pay fees upfront, especially since the Government's own estimates suggest that most graduates will not repay the whole amount that they borrow.

There are two types of student loan – one to cover the cost of tuition fees and another to help you cover the cost of living.

Tuition fees loan

You can borrow up to the full amount needed to cover the cost of your tuition fees wherever you study in the UK and it is not dependent upon your household income.

Tuition fees loans for part-time students

The most that universities or colleges can charge for part-time courses in 2017–18 is between £4,625 and £6,935 year. They cannot charge more than 75 per cent of the full time course fee. New part-time students will be able to apply for a tuition fee loan that is not dependent on household income or on age, which has led to some courses having a surprising number of pensioner students. Eligibility depends on the "intensity" of the course being at least 25 per cent of a full-time course. This measure works by comparing the course to a full-time equivalent. So if a course takes six years to complete and the full-time equivalent takes three, the intensity will be 50 per cent.

Maintenance loan

The second type of student loan, a maintenance loan, is means-tested. The amount you can borrow depends on a number of factors, including your family income, where you intend to study, and whether you expect to be living at home.

Although you are legally an adult, your student finance options depend heavily on your family income, frequently termed "household income", which in practice means your mother's and father's earning power. If your parents are separated, divorced or widowed, then only the income of the parent with whom you normally live will be assessed. However, if that parent has married again, entered into a civil partnership or has a partner of the opposite sex, then both their incomes will be taken into account.

For 2017 entry, the maximum loan for those living at home is £7,097, but only if the combined household income is £25,000 or less. The size of the loan is then reduced on a sliding scale to £3,124 for incomes over £60,000.

For students living away from home outside London, the maximum loan is £8,430, and for those living away from home in London, £11,002, but again these are rates for a household income of £25,000 or less.

For students outside London, the loan is reduced on a sliding scale to £3,928 for those whose parents earn £65,000 and above, while for students in London the loan reduces to £5,479 for incomes of £70,000 and above.

You can even get up to £9,654 for a year studying abroad as part of a UK course. Final-year students receive less than those in earlier years. Sixty-five per cent of the maintenance loan is available to you regardless of your family circumstances, while the remaining 35 per cent is means-tested. Note, too, that there is extra cash available for future teachers, social workers and healthcare workers, including doctors and dentists.

Those who qualify for benefits and would have received a Special Supplementary Grant will now receive an increased loan of £9,609 (studying away from home), £11,998 (in London) and £8,372 (at home).

Repaying loans

Full-time students will begin accumulating interest during their course and will start repaying in the April after graduation, if they earn over £21,000. They will then pay 9 per cent of their income above £21,000, but repayments will stop during any period in which annual income falls below the threshold. Repayments are normally taken automatically through tax and National Insurance. If the loan has not been paid off after 30 years, no further repayments will be required.

During the repayment period, the amount of interest will vary according to how much you earn. If you earn less than £21,000, interest will be at the rate of inflation as measured

---

Maintenance loan for a first-year English student 2017–18

Household income	Living at home	Living away from home but not in London	Living away from home in London
£25,000 and below	£7,097	£8,430	£11,002
£30,000	£6,499	£7,825	£10,387
£35,000	£5,901	£7,220	£9,771
£40,000	£5,303	£6,615	£9,155
£42,875	£4,959	£6,266	£8,801
£45,000	£4,705	£6,009	£8,539
£50,000	£4,107	£5,404	£7,924
£55,000	£3,509	£4,799	£7,308
£60,000	£3,124	£4,193	£6,692
£65,000	£3,124	£3,928	£6,076
£70,000 and above	£3,124	£3,928	£5,479

Department for Education, July 2016

by the Retail Price Index (1.6 per cent for 2016–17); between £21,000 and £41,000 you will be charged inflation plus up to 3 per cent; and if you earn over £41,000, interest will be at inflation plus the full 3 per cent. The Student Loans Company website (**www.studentloanrepayment.co.uk**) has information to guide prospective students through these arrangements and gives examples of levels of repayment. At the time of writing, anyone earning £25,000 a year would face monthly repayments of £30. If you are on £35,000, the sum rises to £105 a month, a fair bite even from that healthy paycheque. By the time you graduate, the interest rate will probably have changed and the repayment threshold may have risen, if only by inflation. Currently the threshold is fixed at £21,000 until 2021.

Student loans and grants for Northern Ireland students
Maintenance loans in 2016–17 vary from a maximum of £3,750 for students living at home, £4,840 for those studying away from home, all the way to £6,780 for those studying in London (and only 25 per cent of the loan is means-tested). There are also extra sums for people taking courses longer than 30 weeks a year, worth up to £108 a week if you are in London. Tuition fee loans are available for the full amount of tuition fees, regardless of where you study in the UK. For 2016–17, maintenance grants range from £3,475 for students with household incomes of £19,203 or below, to zero if the figure is £41,066 or above. Your maximum loan is reduced by the size of any grant you receive. Loan repayments of 9 per cent of salary start once your income reaches £17,495 and interest is calculated on the retail price index or 1 per cent above base rate, whichever is lowest. In 2016–17, the rate is 1.25 per cent. The loan will be cancelled after 25 years.

As in England, there are also special funds for people with disabilities and other special needs, and for those with children or adult dependants. There are modest special bursaries of up to £2,000 for students studying in the Republic of Ireland, who also have their fees paid by their local Education and Library Board. Decisions are yet to be announced on levels for 2017–18.

Student loans and grants for Welsh students
The Welsh Government has been offering a range of support for students from Wales, regardless of whether or not they remain in the country. But the system is set to change in 2018, with maintenance grants for students from low-income homes increasing substantially in exchange for the scrapping of the universal fee grant.

For 2017–18, the maximum maintenance loan is £5,358 for students living at home, £6,922 for those living away from home and outside London, £9,697 for a year studying abroad, and £8,253 for those living in London (and only 25 per cent of the loan is means-tested). Tuition fee loans are available to cover the first £4,056 of tuition fees in Wales, where the maximum is £9,000, and £4,296 for the rest of the UK when tuition fees are £9,250. The remainder is covered by a non-means-tested grant of up to £4,954. Repayment of loans starts once a graduate's income reaches £21,000. Interest repayments and the length of loan are as for England (see above).

In addition, students in Wales are also able to apply for Welsh Government Learning Grants of up to £5,161. They are scaled according to household income, which in 2016–17 ranges from £18,370 for a full grant to £50,020 for the smallest payment of £50. The loan you can get is reduced by 50p for every £1 of grant you receive up to £2,575. There are also special funds for people with disabilities and other special needs, and for those with children or adult dependants.

If the latest proposals are confirmed and can be implemented in time, there will be grants of up to £11,000 for the poorest Welsh students at institutions in London and up to £8,000 elsewhere from 2018–19. About 70 per cent of students – those with a family income of up to £59,000 – are expected to receive support. There will be loans for the rest.

Student loans and grants for Scottish students

The Scottish Government has a commitment to a minimum income of £7,625 a year for students from poorer backgrounds – not bad in a setting where tuition is also free. In 2016–17, students from a family with an income below £19,000 can get a £1,875 Young Students' Bursary (YSB) as well as a loan of £5,750. This bursary does not have to be repaid. It tapers off to zero for family incomes of £34,000, at which point the maximum loan also falls from £5,750 to £4,750. The loan does not vary in size depending on whether you live at home or where you are studying in the UK. Higher loans but more limited bursaries are available for "independent" students – those who are married, mature or without family support. Note that you must be under 50 when you first apply for a loan. Repayment of the loan starts when your income reaches £17,495 and is set at 9 per cent of your income above the £17,495 threshold. Interest is linked to the Retail Price Index. Repayments will continue until the loan is paid off, with any outstanding amount being cancelled after 35 years. Arrangements for 2017–18 had not been announced at the time of writing.

As elsewhere in the UK, there are also special funds for people with disabilities and other special needs, and for those with children or adult dependants. No tuition fee loans are required by Scottish students studying in Scotland, but such loans are available for Scottish students studying elsewhere in the UK.

A review of the student support system was announced in October 2016, led by Jayne-Anne Gadhia, the CEO of Virgin Money. It will report in autumn 2017.

Living in one country, studying in another

As each of the countries of the UK develops its own distinctive system of student finance, the effects on students leaving home in one UK nation to go and study in another have become knottier. UK students who cross borders to study pay the tuition fees of their chosen university and are eligible for a fee loan, and maybe a partial grant, to cover them. They are also entitled to apply for the scholarships or bursaries on offer from that institution. Any maintenance loan or grant will still come from the awarding body of their home country. If you are in this position, you must check with the authorities in your home country about the funding you are eligible for.

Scottish maintenance bursaries and loans 2016–17[1]

Young student (under 25 at start of course)				Independent student			
	Bursary	Loan	Total		Bursary	Loan	Total
£0–£18,999	£1,875	£5,750	£7,625	£0–£18,999	£875	£6,750	£7,625
£19,000–£23,999	£1,125	£5,570	£6,875	£19,000–£23,999	0	£6,750	£6,750
£24,000–£33,999	£500	£5,750	£6,250	£24,000–£33,999	0	£6,250	£6,250
£34,000 and over	0	£4,750	£4,750	£34,000 and over	0	£4,750	£4,750

Repayments start at a salary above £17,495. Any outstanding amount will be written off after 35 years.
1 At the time of writing the figures for 2017–18 had not been released by the Scottish Government.

While the UK remains in the European Union, EU students from outside the UK must be charged the same tuition fees as those paid by nationals of the country where they are studying, rather than the higher fees paid by students from outside the EU. They can also apply for a fee loan and may be considered for some of the scholarships and bursaries offered by individual institutions. Only students who have been living and studying in the UK for at least three years can apply for a maintenance loan or grant. If you haven't, then you will need to apply for such assistance from the authorities in your own country. Tuition fee rules for non-UK European Union students are the same in Scotland as for Scottish students – that is, they do not have to pay tuition fees. There are also no fees to pay for exchange students coming to the UK, including those on the Socrates Programme.

Applying for support

English students should apply for grants and loans through Student Finance England, Welsh students through Student Finance Wales, Scottish students through the Student Awards Agency for Scotland, and those in Northern Ireland through Student Finance NI or their Education and Library Board. You should make your application as soon as you have received an offer of a place at university. Maintenance loans are usually paid in three instalments a year into your bank or building society account. European Union students from outside the UK will usually be sent an application form for tuition fee loans by the university that has offered them a place.

Funding timetable

It is vital that you sort out your funding arrangements before you start university. Each funding agency has its own arrangements, and it is very important that you find out the exact details from them. The dates below give general indications of key dates.

March/April

» Online and paper application forms become available from funding agencies.
» You must contact the appropriate funding agency to make an application. This will be the funding agency for the region of the UK that you live in, even if you are planning to study elsewhere in the UK.
» Complete application form as soon as possible. At this stage select the university offer that will be your first choice.
» Check details of bursaries and scholarships available from your selected universities.

May/June

» Funding agencies will give you details of the financial support they can offer.
» Last date for making an application to ensure funding is ready for you at the start of term (exact date varies significantly between agencies).

August

» Tell your funding agency if the university or course you have been accepted for is different from that originally given them.

September

» Take letter confirming funding to your university for registration.
» After registration, the first part of funds will be released to you.

University scholarships and bursaries

As well as taking out student loans for both tuition and living costs, you can shop around for university bursaries, scholarships and other sponsorship packages, and seek out supplementary support to which you may be entitled. There may be reductions for a range of other groups, including local students, which vary widely from university to university and which are usually detailed on university websites. The details of the financial support offered by all universities in England are listed in the access agreements published on the website of the Office for Fair Access (**www.offa.org.uk**).

Although English universities have continued to scale back their support for 2017–18, there is still a bewildering variety of bursaries and scholarships on offer at UK universities. Some awards are guaranteed depending on your financial circumstances, while scholarships are available through open competition. In general, bursaries that provide students with the money to make ends meet at university have (rightly) proved more popular than fee waivers giving relief from repayments that may stretch over 30 years. Some universities offer eligible students the choice of accommodation discounts, fee waivers or cash. Most also have hardship funds for those who find themselves in financial difficulties.

Do take note of the application procedures for scholarships and bursaries, as these vary from institution to institution, and even from course to course within individual institutions. There may be a deadline you have to meet to apply for an award. In some cases the university will work out for you whether you are entitled to an award by referring to your funding agency's financial assessment. If your personal circumstances change part-way through a course, your entitlement to a scholarship or bursary may be reviewed.

If you feel you still need more help or advice on scholarships or bursaries, you can usually find it on a university's website or in its prospectus. Some institutions also maintain a helpline. Some questions you will need answered include whether the bursary or scholarship is automatic or conditional and, if the latter, when you will find out whether your application has been successful. For some awards, you won't know whether you have qualified until you get your exam results. Another obvious question is how the scholarship or bursary on offer compares with awards made by another university you might consider applying to. Watch out for institutions that list entitlements that others don't mention, but which you would get anyway.

Students with disabilities

Extra financial help is available to disabled students studying whether full-time or part-time through Disabled Students' Allowances, which are paid in addition to the standard student finance package. They are available for help with education-related conditions such as dyslexia, and for other physical and mental disabilities. They do not depend on income and do not have to be repaid.

The cash is available for extra travel costs, equipment and to pay helpers. For 2017–18 the maximum for a non-medical helper is £21,305 a year, or £15,978 a year for a part-time student. In addition there is a maximum equipment allowance of £5,358 for the duration of the course and £1,790 for general expenses a year, although most students get less than these amounts.

Further sources of income

If you are feeling daunted by the potential costs, you can take some comfort from this section, which outlines just some of the ways you can raise additional funds.

Taking a gap year

Gap years (see chapter 6) have become increasingly popular both for travelling and to earn some money to help pay for higher education. Many students will simply want to travel, but others will be more focused on boosting the bank balance in preparation for life as a student. Work opportunities can be structured or casual. An example of the structured variety is the Year in Industry Scheme (**www.etrust.org.uk**).

Further support

There are various types of support available for students in particular circumstances, other than the main loans, grants and bursaries.

» Undergraduates in financial difficulties can apply for help to their university's student hardship fund. These are allocated by universities to provide support for anything from day-to-day study and living costs to unexpected or exceptional expenses. Many universities have committed to increasing the size of their hardship funds. The university decides which students need help and how much money to award them. These funds are often targeted at older or disadvantaged students, and finalists who are in danger of dropping out. The sums range up to a few thousand pounds, are not repayable and do not count against other income.

» Students with children can apply for a Childcare Grant, worth up to £159.59 a week if you have one child and up to £273.60 a week if you have two or more children under 15, or under 17 with special needs; and a Parents' Learning Allowance, for help with course-related costs, of between £50 and £1,617 a year.

» Any students with a partner, or another adult family member who is financially dependent on them, can apply for an Adult Dependants' Grant of up to £2,834 a year.

If you do not qualify for any of this kind of financial support you may still be able to apply for a Professional and Career Development Loan available from certain banks, in partnership with the National Careers Service. Students on a wide range of vocational courses can borrow from £300 to £10,000 at a fixed rate of interest to fund up to two years of learning, but the loans cannot be used for first full-time degrees.

Part-time work

The need to hold down a part-time job during term time is now a fact of life for almost half of students. Students from a working-class background are more likely to need to earn while they learn.

If you need to earn during term time, it is important to try to ensure that you do not work so many hours that it starts to affect your studies. A survey by the NUS found that 59 per cent of students who worked felt it had an impact on their studies, with 38 per cent missing lectures and over a fifth failing to submit coursework because of their part-time jobs. You may find that new universities are better geared-up to cope with working students than more traditional institutions.

Student employment agencies, which can now be found on many university campuses, can help you get the balance right. These introduce employers with work to students seeking work, sometimes even offering jobs within the university itself. But they also abide by codes of practice that regulate both minimum wages and the maximum number of hours worked in term time (typically 15 hours a week).

Some firms, such as the big supermarkets, offer continuing part-time employment to their school part-time employees when they go to university. Some students make use of their expertise in areas like web design to earn some extra money, but most take on casual work in retail stores, restaurants, bars and call centres.

Most students, including those who don't work during term time, get a job during vacations. A Government survey found that 86 per cent of students in their second year of study or above worked during their summer vacation. Most of this kind of work is casual, but some is formalised in a scheme like STEP (**www.step.org.uk**) or may be part of a sponsorship programme. Many vacation jobs are fairly mundane, but it is possible to find more interesting work. Some students broaden their experience by working abroad, others work as film extras, do tutoring, or do a variety of jobs at big events such as festivals. It is also a good idea to try to use the summer holidays to get some work experience in a field that has some relevance to your career aspirations. Even if you don't get paid, this can significantly enhance your chances of finding employment after graduation.

What you will need to spend money on
Living costs

Certain costs are unavoidable. You have to have a roof over your head, eat enough, clothe yourself, and probably do a certain amount of travelling. But the cost of even these essential items can be cut down significantly through a mixture of shopping around and careful budgeting. If you set aside a certain amount of money a week for food, you will find it goes much further if you keep takeaways and ready-meals to a minimum, and stick to a shopping list when you go to a supermarket. Some catering outlets at your university or in the students' union may well offer good value meals, but probably the most economical way to eat is to cook and share meals with fellow students with whom you may be living in a shared house. Make sure you make full use of student travel cards and other offers and facilities available locally to help you cut the cost of travel. In certain locations, a bicycle is a very worthwhile investment (as is buying a lock for it).

If you can keep your essential costs down, you will have more money for what you would probably prefer to spend your money on – going out and personal items. Most students spend a proportion of their budget on socialising, and this is certainly an important part of the university experience. You can have plenty of fun and keep your leisure costs down by making the most of your student union's facilities and events.

It is easy to let "other costs" get out of hand to the extent that they start to eat into your budget for day-to-day living. Mobile phone bills are a case in point: the latest edition of an annual survey of student life by RBS put average spending at £4.40 a week, but Sodexo found that some students were spending over £20 a week on them. Look at your previous bills, or think carefully about your usage, and then shop around for the best deal to cover what you need. Extras like downloading games or music, or sending pictures, can add significantly to your bill. Most of all, try to avoid getting tied up with an expensive and inflexible contract.

The RBS survey also shows that students spend almost twice as much on groceries (£19.78 a week) as they do on the next-biggest item, which is household bills. Alcohol comes further down the list, at £6.85 a week on average – perhaps a slightly misleading figure since a growing number of students spend nothing on it. An earlier survey by Sodexo suggested that half of all students have altered their eating and socialising habits for lack of money. It is not just leisure that is being cut back: 65 per cent of students claimed to spend nothing on books in a typical week. Perhaps the most striking item in the RBS survey was the £6.47-a-week average spent on computer games, more than twice the spending on football.

Studying costs

An NUS survey estimated that the average student spent about £1,000 a year on costs associated with course work and studying, mainly books and equipment. The amount you spend will be determined largely by the nature of your course and what you study. Additional financial support may be available for certain expenditure, but this is unlikely to cover you fully for spending on books, stationery, equipment, fieldwork or electives. A long reading list could prove very expensive if you tried to buy all of the required books brand new. Find out as soon as possible which books are available either in your university library or local libraries. Another approach is to buy books second-hand from students who no longer need them. Your students' union or your university may run second-hand book sales or offer a service helping students to buy and sell books.

Overdrafts and credit cards

Other costs it is best to avoid are the more expensive forms of debt. Many banks offer free overdraft facilities for students, but if you go over that limit without prior arrangement, you can end up paying way over the odds for your borrowing. Credits cards can be useful if managed properly. The best way to manage a credit card is to set up a direct debit to pay off your balance in full every month, which means you will avoid paying any interest. One of the worst ways is just paying the minimum charge each month, which can cost you a small fortune over a long period. If you are the kind of person who spends impulsively and doesn't keep track of your spending, you are probably better off without a credit card. That way, you can't spend money you don't have.

Insurance

One kind of additional spending that can actually end up saving you money is getting insurance cover for your possessions. Most students arrive at university with laptops and other goodies such as digital cameras, mobile phones and iPods, not to mention bikes, that are tempting to petty thieves. It is estimated that around a third of students fall victim to crime at some point during their time at university. If you shop around, you should be able to get a reasonable amount of cover for these kinds of items without it costing you an arm and a leg. It may also be possible to add this cover cheaply to your parents' domestic contents policy.

Planning your budget

One in four freshers spend their first student loan instalment in under a month, according to Endsleigh Insurance. But university websites, the National Union of Students and many other sites offer guidance on preparing a budget, usually with the basic headings provided for you to complete. First, list all your likely income (bursaries, loans, part-time work, savings, parental support) and then see how this compares with what you will spend. Try to be realistic, and not too optimistic, about both sides of the equation. With care, you will end up either only slightly in the red, or preferably far enough in the black for you to be able to afford things you would really like to spend your money on.

Above all, keep track of your finances so that your university experience isn't ruined by money worries, or finding you can't go to the ball because the cash machine has eaten your card. Spreadsheets make doing this simpler, and it is one skill you can learn at college that you are definitely going to need for the rest of your life.

If all else fails, your campus almost certainly has a student money adviser who is a member of NASMA, the National Association of Student Money Advisers. You can find them via **www.nasma.org.uk.** NASMA reports that some students, especially those with children, are struggling financially. However, the bargains available in student shops can mean that you might not experience the most exorbitant prices on the high street.

More than two-thirds of young people aged 18–24 say they received no financial education at school. This chimes with the experience of NASMA, which finds that many students have low levels of basic financial awareness and planning ability. In addition, advisers have noticed that students are increasingly likely to spend money they cannot afford on TV and online gambling, so make sure to avoid this temptation.

Useful websites

For the basics of fees, loans, grants and other allowances:
www.gov.uk/student-finance
www.gov.uk/browse/education/student-finance

UCAS provides helpful advice: **www.ucas.com/ucas/undergraduate/undergraduate-finance-and-support**

For England, visit Student Finance England: **www.sfengland.slc.co.uk**
Office for Fair Access: **www.offa.org.uk**
For Wales, visit Student Finance Wales: **www.studentfinancewales.co.uk**
For Scotland, visit the Student Awards Agency for Scotland: **www.saas.gov.uk**
For Northern Ireland, visit Student Finance Northern Ireland: **www.studentfinanceni.co.uk**

All UK student loans are administered by the Student Loans Company: **www.slc.co.uk**

For guidance on the tax position of students, visit HM Revenue and Customs:
www.gov.uk/student-jobs-paying-tax

For finding out about availability of scholarships: **www.scholarship-search.org.uk**

8 Finding Somewhere to Live

Students spend almost three times as much on rent as any other area of expenditure, so it is vital to make the right choice of accommodation. It would be a key decision whatever the financial implications because where you live will have an impact on your whole university experience.

Particularly in your first year – and especially if it is your first time away from home – you are likely to be happier and more successful academically in accommodation of reasonable quality, preferably in a setting that helps you meet other students. Fortunately, there is more choice than ever, with a number of private providers supplementing what universities and individual landlords provide.

Of course, whatever you choose has to be affordable, but if your budget will stand it, that may mean a hall of residence or university flat. Three-quarters of applicants hope to live in a hall of residence, but only 60 per cent actually do so, according to research by Unite Students. Indeed, the survey showed halls gaining in popularity among second- and third-year undergraduates, with the proportion opting for shared houses in their second year falling to little more than half.

With tastes apparently changing and the numbers going to university continuing to rise, the student market has become the biggest growth area in the property market. Rents have been rising at more than 3 per cent a year and billions of pounds have been committed to student housing deals in 2016 alone.

Particularly in the big student cities, but increasingly in other university towns as well, student accommodation now comes in all shapes and sizes – and prices. Despite considerable expansion by universities themselves, property consultants JLL estimate that more than a third of residential places for students are now in private hands. Most of the developments are in big complexes, but there are also niche providers such as Student Cribs, which convert properties and rent them to students, providing a rather higher spec than the traditional student landlord.

Of the big providers, Unite Students has more than 46,000 beds in 28 towns and cities, some provided in partnership with universities and others in developments that serve more than one institution. UPP manages over 30,000 residential places in complexes it has built for 14 universities, where rents are negotiated with the university, often in consultation with the students' union.

There is even an award for the best private halls of residence – won for the last three years by the Student Housing Company, which has over 7,000 beds in nine UK cities and has plans for many more. The best university halls in 2016 were judged to be at Edge Hill, with Lancaster and Northumbria runners-up.

For most students, it will not matter whether the owner of their accommodation is the university, a private landlord or larger organisation if the quality and the price are right. But successive reports by the National Union of Students (NUS) have told a story of increasingly unaffordable rents, often poor facilities and rushed decisions by inexperienced students. While those who can afford it – or think they can – are living in luxury, NUS has found others coping with mice, slugs, mould, cold or all of these. So it is worth putting some effort into basic decisions on this subject.

Living at home

Although student loan repayments start only after graduation, many undergraduates are understandably cautious about the debts they run up, so the option of avoiding big accommodation charges is a tempting one for those who are attracted by a local university.

Term-time type of accommodation of full-time and sandwich students

	2014/15
University maintained property	19.4%
Private-sector halls	7.0%
Parental/guardian home	19.3%
Own residence	15.2%
Other rented accommodation	30.8%
Other	3.3%
Not known	3.7%

HESA 2016 (adapted)

The pattern of recent applications shows that the trend towards studying at home is accelerating, albeit only gradually, and there is no reason to think that this will change in the near future. Indeed it may be a permanent shift, given the rising costs of student housing and the willingness of many young people to live with their parents well into their twenties.

The proportion of students living at home was already rising before undergraduate fees went up, according to research by Sodexo. Including mature students, many of whom live at home because of their family circumstances, the proportion is now close to 20 per cent. Among younger students, women are more likely than men to stay at home, and Asian women are particularly likely to take this option. Home study is also four times more common at post-1992 universities than older institutions, again reflecting the larger numbers of mature students at the newer universities and a generally younger and more affluent student population at the older ones.

For those considering studying from home, there are important considerations – the relationship with your parents and the availability of quiet space are the most obvious ones. You will still be entitled to a maintenance loan, although it will be a maximum of £7,097 in England, rather than £8,430 if you were living away from home outside London.

There may be advantages in terms of academic work if the alternative involves shopping, cooking and cleaning as well as the other distractions of a student flat. The downside is that you may miss out on a lot of the student experience, especially the social scene and the opportunity to make new friends.

There is no evidence that students living at home do any worse academically. You can always move out at a later date if you think you are missing out – many initially home-based students do so in their second year.

Living away from home

Most of those who can afford it still see moving away to study as integral to the rite of passage that student life represents. Some have little option if, in spite of the expansion of higher education, the course they want is not available locally. Others are happy to travel to secure their ideal place and widen their experience.

For the lucky majority, the search for accommodation will be over quickly because the university can offer a place in one of its halls of residence or self-catering flats. The choice may come down to the type of accommodation and whether or not to do your own cooking. But for others, there will be an anxious search for a room in a strange city. Most universities will help with this if they cannot offer accommodation of their own.

Going to university will oblige those who take the "away" route to think for the first time about the practicalities of living independently. This can make the decision about where to live – in terms of location and the type of accommodation – doubly difficult. It may even influence your choice of university, since there are big differences across the sector and the country in the cost and standard of accommodation, and in its availability.

How much will it cost?

Rents vary so much across the UK that national averages are almost meaningless. The 2016 NatWest survey found a range from £73.81 a week in Belfast to £135.38 in Oxford. Most of the 25 student cities in the survey averaged more than £100 a week. However accurate such figures may be, they conceal a wide range of actual rents, particularly in London. This was always the case, but has become even more obvious with the rapid growth of a luxury market at the same time as many students are willing to accept sub-standard accommodation to keep costs down.

A series of recent reports suggest that the need for good Wi-Fi has overtaken reasonable rents as students' top priority in choosing accommodation. A big bedroom with a double bed was another top priority for British students, according to a Europe-wide survey for the Uniplaces website. But obviously you have to be able to afford the rent in the first place. The last annual NUS/Unipol survey found a dwindling amount of "affordable" housing, judged against the loans available to students. Most universities with a range of accommodation find that their most expensive rooms fill up first, and that students appear to have higher expectations than they used to. More than half of all the rooms in the NUS survey had en-suite facilities.

It is important to remember that both your living costs and your potential earnings should be factored into your calculations when deciding where to live. While living costs in London are by far the highest, potential part-time earnings are nearly double those in other parts of the country, according to the NatWest index.

Most important factors for student accommodation

1	Location	39%
2	En suite facilities	36%
3	High speed Wifi	26%
4	Study space	18%
5	Overall cleanliness	16%
6	Multi-use outside games space	14%
=7	Security presence	12%
=7	On-site retail shop	12%
=7	24/7 helpdesk	12%
10	Gym	11%
=11	Environmentally friendly	10%
=11	Social space (café/bar)	10%
13	Cleaning service for room	8%
14	Laundrette	7%
15	Vending machines	5%

Sodexo University Lifestyle Survey, 2016

The choices you have

The NUS puts accommodation into 16 categories, ranging from luxurious university halls to a bedsit in a shared house. The choices include:

» University hall of residence, with individual study bedrooms and a full catering service. Many will have en-suite accommodation.
» University halls, flats or houses where you have to provide your own food.
» Private, purpose-built student accommodation.
» Rented houses or flats, shared with fellow students.
» Living at home.
» Living as a lodger in a private house.

This chapter will help you decide where you would like to live and whether you can afford it.

Making your choice

Finance is not the only factor you should consider when deciding where to live. It is worth investing time to find the right place, and to avoid the false economy of choosing somewhere cheap, where you may end up feeling depressed and isolated. Most students who drop out of university do so in the first few months, when homesickness and loneliness can be felt most acutely.

Being warm and well fed is likely to have a positive effect on your studies. Perhaps for these reasons, most undergraduates in their first year plump for living in university halls, which offer a convenient, safe and reliable standard of accommodation, along with a supportive community environment. The sheer number of students – especially first years – in halls also makes this form of accommodation an easy way of meeting people from a wide range of courses and making friends.

If meals are included, this extra adds further peace of mind both for students and their parents. The NUS survey found that the difference in cost between full board and self-catering is less than £40 a week on average, not unreasonable for two hot meals a day. But only 7.6 per cent of places are now catered, compared with 27 per cent in 1994. Most are self-catering, with groups of students sharing a kitchen.

Wherever you choose to live, there are some general points you will need to consider, such as how safe the neighbourhood seems to be, and how long it might take you to travel to and from the university, especially during rush hour. A survey of travel time between term-time accommodation and the university found that most students in London can expect a commute of at least 30 minutes and often over an hour, while students living in Wales are usually much less than 30 minutes away from their university.

In chapter 14, we provide details of what accommodation each university offers, covering the number of places, the costs, and policy towards first-year students.

What universities offer

You might think that opting to live in university accommodation is the most straightforward choice, especially since first-year students are invariably given priority in the allocation of places in halls of residence, and it is possible to arrange university accommodation in advance and at a distance. Searching for private housing can often be a matter of having to be in the right place at the right time. However, you may still need to select from a range of options, because most universities will have a variety of accommodation on offer. You will need to consider which best suits your pocket and your preferred lifestyle.

New student accommodation

At the top end of the market, private firms usually lead the way, at least in the bigger student cities. Companies such as UPP, Unite Students and Liberty Living offer some of the most luxurious student accommodation the UK sector has ever seen, either in partnerships with universities or in their own right. Rooms in these complexes are nearly always en suite and may include facilities such as your own phone line, satellite TV and internet access. Shared kitchens are top-quality and fitted out with all the latest equipment.

This kind of accommodation naturally comes at a higher price, but offers the advantages of flexibility both in living arrangements and through a range of payment options. An earlier NUS survey found little difference between the rents charged by higher education institutions for their own accommodation and those for rooms managed by private companies under contract, but private providers operating outside institutional links charged over £20 a week more.

Halls of residence

Many new or recently refurbished university-owned halls offer a standard of accommodation that is not far short of the privately built residences. This is partly because rooms in these halls can be offered to conference delegates during vacations. Even though these halls are also at the pricier end of the spectrum, you will probably find that they are in great demand, and you may have to get your name down quickly to secure one of the fancier rooms. That said, you can often get a guarantee of some kind of university accommodation if you give a firm acceptance of an offered place by a certain date in the summer. If you have gained your place through Clearing, this option might have gone, although rooms in private halls might still be on offer at this stage.

While a few halls are single-sex, most are mixed, and often house over 500 students. Indeed, in student villages the numbers are now counted in thousands. They are therefore great places for making friends and becoming part of the social scene. One possible downside is that they can also be noisy places where it can be difficult at times to get down to some work. Indeed, 44 per cent of those responding to a Unite Students survey identified noise as the biggest challenge in student accommodation. Peace and quiet was a higher priority than access to public transport or good nightlife. The more successful students learn, before too many essay deadlines and exams start to loom, to get the balance right between all-night partying and escaping to the library for some undisturbed study time. Remember that some libraries, especially new ones, are now open 24 hours a day.

University self-catering accommodation

An alternative to halls, now offered by most universities, are smaller, self-catering properties fitted out with a shared kitchen and other living areas. Students looking for a more independent and flexible lifestyle often prefer this option. But as well as having to feed yourself, you may also have heating and lighting bills to pay. University properties are often on campus or nearby, so travel costs should not be a problem.

Catering in university accommodation

Many universities have responded to an increase in student demand for a more independent lifestyle by providing more flexible catering facilities, ranging from fast food outlets to the more traditional refectories on campus or in student villages. Students in university accommodation may be offered pay-as-you-eat deals as an alternative to full-board packages.

What after the first year?

After your first year of living in university residences you may well wish, and will probably be expected, to move out to other accommodation. The main exceptions are the collegiate universities – particularly Oxford and Cambridge – which may allow you to stay on in college for another year or two, and particularly for your final year. Students from outside the EU are also often guaranteed accommodation. At a growing number of universities, where there is a sufficiently large stock of residential accommodation, it is not uncommon for students to move back in to halls for their final year.

Practical details

Whether or not you have decided to start out in university accommodation, you will probably be expected to sign an agreement to cover your rent. Contract lengths vary. They can be for around 40 weeks, which includes the Christmas and Easter holiday periods, or for just the length of the three university terms. These term-time contracts are common when a university uses its rooms for conferences during vacations, and you will be required to leave your room empty during these weeks. It is therefore advisable to check whether the university has secure storage space for you to leave your belongings. Otherwise you will have to make arrangements to take all your belongings home or to store them privately between terms. International students may be offered special arrangements by which they can stay in halls during the short vacation periods. Organisations like **www.hostuk.org** can arrange for international students to stay in a UK family home at holiday times such as Christmas.

Parental purchases

One option for affluent families is to buy a house or flat and take in student lodgers. This might not be the safe bet it once appeared, but it is still tempting for many parents. Agents Knight Frank have had a student division since 2007, mostly working with new developers to sell specially adapted homes. The Sodexo University Lifestyle Survey for 2014 found that a surprising 7 per cent of students live in houses owned by their own or fellow students' parents. Those who are considering this route tend to do so from their first year of study to maximise the return on the investment.

Being a lodger or staying in a hostel

A small number of students live as a lodger in a family home, an option most frequently taken up by international students. The usual arrangement is for a study bedroom and some meals to be provided, while other facilities such as the washing machine are shared. Students with particular religious affiliations or those from certain countries may wish to consider living in a hostel run by a charity catering for a specific group. Most of these are in London.

Renting from the private sector

Around a third of students live in privately rented flats or houses. Every university city or town is awash with such accommodation, available via agencies or direct from landlords. Indeed, this type of accommodation has grown to the point where so-called "student ghettoes", in which local residents feel outnumbered have become hot political issues in some cities. Into this traditional market in rented flats and houses have come the new private-sector complexes and residences, adding to the options. Some are on university campuses, but others are in city centres and usually open to students of more than one university. Examples can be seen online; some sites are listed at the end of this chapter.

While there are always exceptions, a much more professional attitude and approach to managing rented accommodation has emerged among smaller providers, thanks to a combination of greater regulation and increasing competition. Nevertheless, it is wise to take certain precautions when seeking out private residences.

How to start looking for rented property

Contact your university's accommodation service and ask for its list of approved rented properties. Some have a Student Accommodation Accreditation Scheme, run in collaboration with the local council. To get onto an approved list under such schemes, landlords must show they are adhering to basic standards of safety and security, such as having an up-to-date gas and electric safety certificate. University accommodation officers should also be able to advise you on any hidden charges. For instance, you may be asked to pay a booking or reservation fee to secure a place in a particular property, and fees for references or drawing up a tenancy agreement are sometimes charged. The practice of charging a "joining fee", however, has been outlawed, and other fees are also set to be banned. It would be wise to speak to older students with first-hand experience of renting in the area. Certain companies in the area may be notorious among second and third years and you can try to avoid them. In addition to websites and accommodation services designed for students, you can also use sites such as Gumtree that cater for the population at large.

Making a choice

Once you have made an initial choice of the area you would like to live in and the size of property you are looking for, the next stage is to look at possible places. If you plan to share, it is important that you all have a look at the property. If you will be living by yourself, take a friend with you when you go to view a property, since he or she can help you assess what you see objectively, and avoid any irrational or rushed on-the-spot decisions. Don't let yourself be pushed into signing on the dotted line there and then. Take time to visit and consider a number of options, as well as checking out the local facilities, transport and the general environment at various times of the day and different days of the week.

If you are living in private rented accommodation, it is likely that at least some of your neighbours will not be students. Local people often welcome students, but resentment can build up, particularly in areas of towns and cities that are dominated by student housing. It is important to respect your neighbours' rights, and not to behave in an anti-social manner.

Preparing for sharing

The people you are planning to share a house with may have some habits that you find at least mildly irritating. How well you cope with some of the downsides of sharing will be partly down to the kind of person you are – where you are on the spectrum between laid back and highly strung – but it will help a lot if you are co-habiting with people whose outlook on day-to-day living is not too far out of line with your own. According to the Unite Students report, 31 per cent of female students find sharing more difficult than they had expected, compared with 22 per cent of men.

Some students sign for their second year houses as early as November. While it is good to be ahead of the rush, you may not yet have met your best friends at this stage. If you have not selected your own group of friends, universities and landlords can help by taking personal preferences and lifestyle into account when grouping tenants together.

Potential issues to consider when deciding whether to move into a shared house include whether any of the housemates smoke or own a loud musical instrument. It will also be important to sort out broadband arrangements that will work for everyone in the house, and that you will be able to arrange access to the university system. It is also a good idea to agree a rota for everyone to share in the household cleaning chores from the start. Otherwise it is almost certain that you will live in a state of unhygienic squalor or that one or two individuals will be left to clear up everyone else's mess.

The practical details about renting

It is a good idea to ask whether your house is covered by an accreditation scheme or code of standards. Such codes provide a clear outline of what constitutes good practice as well as the responsibilities of both landlords and tenants. Adhering to schemes like the National Code of Standards for Larger Student Developments compiled by Accreditation Network UK (**www. anuk.org.uk**) may well become a requirement for larger properties, including those managed by universities, now that the Housing Act is in force.

At the very least, make sure that if you are renting from a private landlord, you have his or her telephone number and home address. Some can be remarkably difficult to contact when repairs are needed or deposits are due to be returned.

Multiple occupation

If you are renting a private house it may be subject to the 2004 Housing Act in England and Wales (similar legislation applies in Scotland and Northern Ireland). Licenses are compulsory for all private Houses in Multiple Occupation (HMOs) with three or more storeys and that house five or more unrelated residents. The provisions of the Act also allow local authorities to designate whole areas in which HMOs of all sizes must be licensed. The good news is that these regulations can be applied in sections of university towns and cities where most students live. This means that a house must be licensed, well-managed and must meet various health and safety standards, and its owner subject to various financial regulations. The bad news is that this could lead to a reduction in the number and range of privately rented properties on the market, or an increase in rental prices.

Tenancy agreements

Whatever kind of accommodation you go for, you must be sure to have all the paperwork in order and be clear about what you are signing up to before you move in. If you are taking up residence in a shared house, flat or bedsit, the first document you will have to grapple with is a tenancy agreement or lease offering you an "assured shorthold tenancy". Since this is a binding legal document, you should be prepared to go through every clause with a fine-tooth comb. Remember that it is much more difficult to make changes or overcome problems arising from unfair agreements once you are a tenant than before you become one.

You would be well advised to seek help in the likely event of your not fully understanding some of the clauses. Your university accommodation office or students' union is a good place to start – they should know all the ins and outs, and have model tenancy agreements to refer to. A Citizens Advice Bureau or Law Advice Centre should also be able to offer you free advice. In particular, watch out for clauses that may make you jointly responsible for the actions of others with whom you are sharing the property. If you name a parent as a guarantor to cover any costs not paid by you, they may also be liable for charges levied on all tenants for damage that was not your fault. A rent review clause could allow your landlord to increase the rent at will, whereas without such a clause, they are restricted to one rent rise a year. Make sure you keep a copy of all documents, and get a receipt (and keep it somewhere safe) for anything you have had to pay for that is the landlord's responsibility.

Contracts with private landlords tend to be longer than for university accommodation. They will frequently commit you to paying rent for 52 weeks of the year. Leaving aside the cost, there are probably more advantages than disadvantages to this kind of arrangement. It means you don't have to move out during vacation periods, which you will have to in most university halls. You can store your belongings in your room when you go away (but don't leave anything really valuable behind if you can help it). You may be able to negotiate a rent discount for those periods when you are not staying in the property. The other advantage, particularly important for cash-strapped students, is that you have a base from which to find work and hold down a job during the vacations. Term dates are also not as dictatorial as they might be in halls; if you rent your own house then you can come back when you wish.

Deposits

On top of the agreed rent, you will need to provide a deposit or bond to cover any breakages or damage. This will probably set you back the equivalent of another month's rent. The deposit should be returned, less any deductions, at the end of the contract. However, be warned that disputes over the return of deposits are common, with the question of what constitutes reasonable wear and tear often the subject of disagreements between landlord and tenant. To protect students from unscrupulous landlords who withheld deposits without good reason, the 2004 Housing Act introduced a National Tenancy Deposit Scheme under which deposits are held by an independent body. This is designed to ensure that deposits are fairly returned, and that any disputes are resolved swiftly and cheaply.

Inventories and other paperwork

You should get an inventory and schedule of condition of everything in the property. This is another document that you should check very carefully – and make sure that everything listed is as described. Write on the document anything that is different. The NUS even suggests taking photographs of rooms and equipment when you first move in (setting the correct date on your camera), to provide you with additional proof should any dispute arise when your contract ends and you want to get your deposit back. If you are not offered an inventory, then make one of your own. You should have someone else witness and sign this, send it to your landlord, and keep your own copy. Keeping in contact with your landlord throughout the year and developing a good relationship with him or her will also do you no harm, and may be to your advantage in the long run.

Security in rented accommodation

Students in private housing are twice as likely to be burgled as those in university halls. When looking at accommodation, use this NUS security checklist:

» Check that the front and back doors are fitted with five-lever mortise locks in addition to standard catch locks.
» Make sure the door to your room has a lock, and always lock up when you leave it, especially for long periods such as during vacations.
» Check the locks and catches on accessible windows, especially those at ground-floor level.
» Before you move in, try to talk to neighbours about how safe the area is and whether there have been many instances of burglary.
» Ask your landlord to ensure that all previous tenants and holders of keys no longer have copies.
» If you find a property that you like but have some security concerns, discuss these with the letting agency or landlord.

You should ask your landlord for a recent gas safety certificate issued by a qualified CORGI engineer, a fire safety certificate covering the furnishings, and a record of current gas and electricity meter readings. Take your own readings of meters when you move in to make sure these match up with what you have been given, or make your own records if the landlord doesn't supply this information. This also applies to water meters if you are expected to pay water rates (although this isn't usually the case).

Finally, students are not liable for Council Tax. If you are sharing a house only with other full-time students, then you will not have to pay it. However, you may be liable to pay a proportion of the Council Tax bill if you are sharing with anyone who is not a full-time student. You may need to get a Council Tax exemption certificate from your university as evidence that you do not need to pay Council Tax.

Safety and security

Once you have arrived and settled in, remember to take care of your own safety and the security of your possessions. You are particularly vulnerable as a fresher, when you are still getting used to your new-found independence. This may help explain why so many students are burgled or robbed in the first six weeks of the academic year. Take care with valuable portable items such as mobile phones, tablet computers and laptops, all of which are tempting for criminals. Ensure you don't have them obviously on display when you are out and about and that you have insurance cover. If your mobile phone is stolen, call your network or 08701 123123 to immobilise it. Students' unions, universities and the police will provide plenty of practical guidance when you arrive. Following their advice will reduce the chance of you becoming a victim of crime, and help you to enjoy living in the new surroundings of your chosen university town.

Useful websites

For advice on a range of housing issues, visit: **www.nus.org.uk/en/advice/housing-advice**

The Shelter website has separate sections covering different housing regulations in England, Wales, Scotland and Northern Ireland: **www.shelter.org.uk**

As examples of providers of private hall accommodation, visit:
www.upp-ltd.com
www.unitestudents.com
www.libertyliving.co.uk
https://student-cribs.com
http://thestudenthousingcompany.com

A number of sites will help you find accommodation and/or potential housemates, including:
www.accommodationforstudents.com
https://sturents.com
www.studentpad.co.uk
www.let4students.com
http://student.spareroom.co.uk
http://uk.easyroommate.com

For guidance on national codes for private accommodation:
The ANUK/Unipol National Codes are owned by a consortium consisting of three organisations, the Accreditation Network UK (ANUK), the NUS and Unipol Student Homes: **http://nationalcode.org**
See also **www.anuk.org.uk** and **www.unipol.org.uk**

For advice on tenancy agreements:
Find and contact your nearest Citizen's Advice Bureau: **www.citizensadvice.org.uk**
Find and contact your nearest law centre: **www.lawcentres.org.uk**

University websites have much advice and information on student accommodation and also provide guidance on student safety.

9 Enjoying University Sport

Olympic years always provide a reminder of how far university sport has come at competitive level, and 2016 was no exception. At the Rio Games, over half Team GB's medals were won by university students or alumni. Loughborough was quick to let the world know that five of the gold medal-winning ladies hockey team (and the coach) were its graduates. Such successes are the result of considerable investment in sports scholarships, training programmes and campus facilities, which are a boon to ordinary students as well as elite performers.

Most people will never again have as much opportunity to exercise and play different sports as they do in their undergraduate years. Even those whose timetable dictates long hours in the laboratory will find plenty of activity in the evenings and at weekends. Especially at the big universities – but also at many of the smaller ones – sporting provision is now both diverse and high quality. And it is not going to waste: two-thirds of students take part in sport of some sort while at university and participation levels are still rising. More than half of all students use the facilities at least once a week.

The quality of those facilities will not be the clinching factor in most students' choice of university – and nor should it be – but nearly a third of applicants say it played some part in their decision-making. Universities are well aware of this and have invested on an unprecedented scale to expand and upgrade their provision. Some of the biggest multi-sports developments of recent years have been on university campuses, where facilities nationally are said to be worth an astonishing £20 billion. As a result, half of all universities were chosen as training bases for Great Britain squads in the run-up to the 2012 Olympic Games and 30 hosted other nations' teams. Nor has the process ended yet: Nottingham opened a £40-million sports complex in autumn 2016 and other universities are building on a smaller scale.

The impact on elite student sport has been obvious for some time. If the students and alumni of UK universities and colleges had been a team at the London Games, they would have finished fifth in the medals table. They repeated their successes in 2014 at the Commonwealth Games and European Championships, and returned from the 2015 World Student Games in South Korea with a record medal haul. The UK's 60-strong team came from 30 different universities. Loughborough was the most successful university in Rio, and would have been 17th in the overall medal table, but it was not the only one – St Mary's,

Twickenham, would have been 25th in the table. The British Universities and Colleges Sport (BUCS) 2015 Sportsman of the Year, Mohamed Elshorbagy of the University of the West of England, was the current world number one in men's squash, while Aimee Wilmott of the University of East London, the 2015 Sportswoman of the Year, won three medals at the 2014 Commonwealth Games. Their 2016 Sportsman of the Year, Max Litchfield of Sheffield Hallam, came fourth in the 400m individual medley final at Rio, while the Sportswoman of the Year, Poppy Leitch of Exeter, played rugby for England in the 2016 Women's Six Nations competition.

Naturally, most students will never aspire to such heights, but may still welcome the chance to use top-grade facilities. Research for BUCS suggests that at least 1.7 million students take part in regular physical activity, from gym sessions to competitive individual or team sports. There are good reasons, beyond fitness, for doing so, according to the BUCS research. In 2013, graduates who had played and/or volunteered in sport were found to be earning between £4,624 and £5,616 more than those who had not, and were 25 per cent less likely to have been unemployed. Nine out of ten employers thought that participation in university sport helped to develop valuable skills in potential employees.

Sporting opportunities

Some specialist facilities may be reserved at times for elite performers, but all universities are conscious of the need for wider access. Surveys show that two-thirds of sessions at university sports facilities are taken by students, roughly a quarter by the local community and the rest by staff. Many institutions still encourage departments not to schedule lectures and seminars on Wednesday afternoons, to give students free time for sport. There are student-run clubs for all the major sports and – particularly at the larger universities – a host of minor ones. In addition, there are high-quality gyms, with staff on hand to devise personalised training regimes and to run popular activities such as Zumba and Pilates. The cost varies widely between universities, and membership fees can represent a large amount to lay out at the start of the year, but most provide good value if you are going to be a regular user.

Sport for all

For most universities, it is in the area of "sport for all" that most attention has been focused. Beginners are welcomed and coaching provided in a range of sports, from Ultimate Frisbee to tai-chi, that would be difficult to match outside the higher education system. Check on university websites to see whether your usual sport is available, but do not be surprised if you come across a new favourite when you have the opportunity to try out something different as a student. Many universities have programmes designed to encourage students to take up a new sport, with expert coaching provided.

All universities are conscious of the need to provide for a spread of ability. Sports scholarships for elite performers are now commonplace, but there will be plenty of opportunities, too, for beginners. University teams demand a hefty commitment in terms of training and practice sessions – often several times a week – and in many sports standards are high. University teams often compete in local and national leagues.

For those who do not aspire to such heights, or whose interests are primarily social, there are thriving internal, or intramural, leagues. These provide opportunities for groups from halls of residence or faculties, or even a group of friends, to form a team and participate on a regular basis. A recent BUCS survey found 41,000 participants in the intramural programmes of 41 institutions. The largest programme was at the University of Brighton, where more than

6,000 students were playing sports ranging from football, rugby and badminton to softball, orienteering and fencing. Nor is university sport a male preserve – student teams were among the pioneers in mixed sport and are still strong in areas such as women's cricket, football and rugby.

Some universities have cut back sports budgets, but representative sport continues to grow. There are plans for a home nations competition at international level and in London, 33 institutions take part in the London Universities Sport League. This now involves more than 460 teams – male, female and mixed – competing at a variety of levels in 14 different sports, not all of which are in the main national competitions.

First-year sport

Halls of residence and university-owned flats will often have their own sports teams. At some universities, these are part of the intramural network of leagues, while others have separate arrangements for first years. In such cases, a Sports Captain, elected the year previously as part of the Junior Common Room, takes responsibility for organising trials and picking the teams, as well as arranging fixtures for the year. Hall sport is a great way of meeting like-minded people from your accommodation and over the course of the years, friendly rivalries often develop with other halls or flats. Generally there will be teams for football (both 5- and 11-a-side), hockey, netball, cricket, tennis, squash, badminton and even golf. If your lodgings are smaller then don't worry, they are often twinned with similar flats to enable as many first-year students as possible to get involved in freshers' sport.

Other opportunities

You may even end up wanting to coach, umpire or referee – and this is another area in which higher education has much to offer. Many university clubs and sports unions provide subsidised courses for students to gain qualifications that may be of use to the individual in later life, as well as benefiting university teams in the short term. Or you might want to try your hand at some sports administration, with an eye to your career.

In most universities there is a sports (or athletic) union, with autonomy from the main students' union, which organises matches and looks after the wider interests of those who play. There are plenty of opportunities for those seeking an apprenticeship in the art of running a club, or larger organisation. Southampton Solent University, for example, deploy students on volunteer coaching placements in more than 70 local schools. These placements increase a university's community engagement as well as enhancing student employability with minimal investment.

Universities that excel

A few universities are known particularly for sport. Exeter and Loughborough men's teams have played national Premier League hockey, for example, while Bath, Loughborough and Northumbria have teams in the Netball Super League. The University of London women's volleyball team has won the English Volleyball Championships, and "Team Bath" have tasted success in the FA Cup.

Several of this elite group had a head start as former physical education colleges. Loughborough is probably the best-known of them, but Leeds Beckett and Brunel are others with a similar pedigree. Other universities with different traditions, such as Bath and East Anglia, also have a variety of outstanding facilities, while the likes of Stirling and Cardiff Metropolitan have the same in a narrower range of sports.

As in so much else, Oxford and Cambridge are in a category of their own. The Boat Race and the Varsity Match (in rugby union) are the only UK university sporting events with a big popular following – although there are varsity matches in several university cities that have become big occasions for students – and there is a good standard of competition in other sports. But you should not assume that success in school sport will be a passport to an Oxbridge place, for the days of special consideration for sporty undergraduates are long since over.

Representative sport

Competitive standards have been rising in university sport, as have the numbers taking part in it. More than 6,000 students were expected to compete in ten sports at the February 2017 BUCS Nationals in Sheffield. BUCS runs competitions in almost 50 sports, and ranks participating institutions based on the points earned in the competitive programme. A table showing the final 2015–16 and 2014–15 rankings is shown overleaf. Over 4,700 teams compete in BUCS leagues, making the organisation the largest provider of league sport across Europe. More than a third of those teams are female and many others mixed. There is also international competition in a number of sports, and the World Student Games have become one of the biggest occasions in the international sporting calendar.

BUCS is the national organisation for higher education sport in the UK, providing a comprehensive, multi-sport competition structure and managing the development of services and facilities for participative, grass-roots sport and healthy campuses, through to high-performance elite athletes. Its mission is to raise the profile of student sport and drive the university sport agenda by influencing government and key stakeholders in the sector.

University sports facilities

Even the smallest university should provide reasonable indoor and outdoor sports facilities – a sports hall, modern gym equipment and outdoor pitches (usually including an all-weather surface and floodlights). Many will also have a swimming pool and extras such as climbing walls, but some smaller universities make arrangements for students to use local sports centres and clubs when it is not feasible to provide for minority sports. The same goes for the really expensive sports, like golf, which is usually the subject of an arrangement with one or more local clubs that give students a discount. Specialist facilities, like boat houses and climbing huts, obviously depend on location, but the most landlocked university is likely to have a sailing club that organises regular activities away from campus, and a skiing club that runs at least annual trips to the mountains.

Many of the larger universities have spent millions of pounds improving their sports facilities, sometimes in partnership with local authorities or national sporting bodies. University campuses are ideal locations for national coaching centres, and many have been established in recent years. Although elite coaching generally takes place in closed sessions, students may occasionally find themselves rubbing shoulders with star players.

It is estimated that close to £500 million has been spent on new or upgraded sports facilities at UK universities over the past decade, and planned investment will add at least £170 million to this figure. Universities now boast a significant proportion of the UK's 50-metre pools, for example the latest of which, at the University of Surrey, has some of the most advanced facilities in the country. Innovative schemes include Leeds Beckett's development of the Headingley cricket and rugby league grounds, providing teaching space for students during the week as well as improved facilities for players and spectators.

British Universities and Colleges Sports (BUCS) league table positions

University	2015–16	2014–15	University	2015–16	2014–15
Loughborough	1	1	Sussex	43	58
Durham	2	2	Hertfordshire	44	45
Edinburgh	3	3	Lancaster	45	48
Nottingham	4	4	Leicester	46	47
Exeter	5	6	Coventry	47	40
Birmingham	6	5	East London	48	63
Bath	7	7	Gloucestershire	49	39
Northumbria	8	8	South Wales (Pontiprydd)	50	54
Newcastle	9	11	Kent	51	62
Oxford	10	9	Brighton (Brighton)	52	43
Cardiff	11	16	Brighton (Eastbourne)	52	43
Leeds Beckett	12	10	Plymouth	53	44
Bristol	13	15	Dundee	54	55
Leeds	14	14	East Anglia	55	50
Cardiff Metropolitan	15	13	Royal Holloway	56	52
Cambridge	16	12	Chichester	57	57
Stirling	17	26	Queen Mary, University of London	58	64
Manchester	18	17	St Mary's, Twickenham	59	56
Nottingham Trent	19	21	Heriot-Watt	60	60
Warwick	20	20	Worcester	61	59
Sheffield	21	20	LSE	62	63
Southampton	22	23	Central Lancashire	63	53
Sheffield Hallam	23	18	Derby	64	61
Imperial College	24	19	Anglia Ruskin	65	77
Liverpool	25	30	Bangor	66	67
Glasgow	26	27	Lincoln	67	70
University College London	27	24	Robert Gordon	68	78
Surrey	28	31	Liverpool John Moores	69	66
St Andrews	29	25	Aberystwyth	70	65
Bournemouth	30	28	Southampton Solent	71	74
Oxford Brookes	31	33	Chester (Chester)	72	79
Essex	32	37	Canterbury Christ Church	73	73
Swansea	33	29	Keele	73	72
Strathclyde	34	42	St Mark and St John (Marjon)	75	71
West of England (UWE)	35	32	West of England, Hartpury	76	68
Brunel	36	38	University of London	77	
King's College London	37	41	Middlesex	78	76
Manchester Metropolitan (MMU)	38	34	Hull	79	69
MMU (Cheshire)	38	34	Kingston	80	84
Reading	39	51	Northampton	81	81
York	40	36	Bedfordshire	82	75
Portsmouth	41	46	Edinburgh Napier	83	86
Aberdeen	42	35	De Montfort	84	87

University	2015–16	2014–15	University	2015–16	2014–15
Edge Hill	85	92	Queen Margaret	115	131
York St John	86	83	Leeds Trinity	116	122
City	87	90	Birmingham City	117	107
Salford	88	82	Royal Agricultural University	118	111
Bradford	89	93	Bath Spa	119	110
Glasgow Caledonian	90	89	Cumbria (Ambleside)	121	133
Roehampton	91	98	Cumbria (Carlisle)	121	133
Sunderland	92	85	Cumbria (Lancaster)	121	133
Abertay	93	95	Cumbria (Penrith)	121	133
Buckinghamshire New	94	80	Cumbria (Preston)	121	133
Huddersfield	95	100	Chester (Warrington)	124	144
London South Bank	96	94	Wrexham Glyndŵr	125	119
Aston	97	88	Newman	126	135
Wolverhampton	98	96	Trinity Saint David (Swansea)	127	128
Wolverhampton (Walsall)	98	96	University College Birmingham	128	126
Staffordshire	99	91	University of the Arts London	130	115
Winchester	100	97	Ulster	131	114
Teesside	101	101	London Metropolitan	131	127
Queen's, Belfast	102	109	West London	135	135
Harper Adams	103	106	Bishop Grosseteste	135	140
FXU (Falmouth and Exeter			Goldsmiths	138	136
Students' Union)	104	108	Suffolk	141	142
Liverpool Hope	105	112	SOAS	142	138
St George's, University of London	107	103	Bolton	143	125
Trinity Saint David (Carmarthen)	108	120	Creative Arts	144	145
West of Scotland	109	104	Trinity Saint David (Lampeter)	144	-
Highlands and Islands	110	113	South Wales (Newport)		105
Greenwich	111	121	Arts University Bournemouth	-	-
Westminster	112	99	Buckingham	-	-

Beyond scrutinising the prospectus for the extent of university facilities, there are two important questions to ask: how much do they cost and where are they? Neither is easy to track down on the average university website.

How much?

University prospectuses tend to major on the quality of the sports facilities without being as forthcoming about the prices. Students who are used to free facilities at school often get a nasty surprise when they find that they are expected to pay to join the Athletic Union and then pay again to use the gym or play football. Because most university sport is subsidised, the charges are reasonable compared to commercial facilities, but the best deal may require a considerable outlay at the start. Some campus gyms and swimming pools now charge more than £300 a year, for example, which is still considerably cheaper than paying per visit if you intend to use the facilities regularly (and provides an incentive to carry on doing so). Some universities are offering sports facility membership as part of the £9,250 fee, but most offer a variety of on- and off-peak membership packages – some for the entire length of your course.

Outdoor sports are usually charged by the hour, although clubs will also charge a membership fee. You may be required to pay up to £60 for membership of the Athletic Union (although not all universities require this). Fees for intramural sport are seldom substantial; teams will usually pay a fee for the season, while courts for racket sports tend to be marginally cheaper per session than in other clubs.

How far away?

The other common complaint by students is that the playing fields are too far from the campus – understandable in the case of city-centre universities, but still aggravating if you have to arrange your own transport. This is where campus universities have a clear advantage. For the rest, there has to be some trade-off between the quality of outdoor facilities and the distance you have to travel to use them. But universities are beginning to realise that long journeys depress usage of important (and expensive) facilities, and some have tried to find suitable land closer to lectures and halls of residence. Indoor sports centres should all be within easy reach.

Sport as a degree subject

Sports science and other courses associated with sport had seen consistent increases in applications until the imposition of higher fees, and their popularity has returned, with over 15,000 students starting courses in 2015, making it one of the ten most studied degree subjects. A separate ranking for the subject is on page 262. If you are hoping to be rewarded with an academic qualification for three or four years on the sports field, you will be disappointed because there is serious science involved. However, sport is a growing employment field and one that demands qualifications like any other.

Other degrees in the sports area are more closely focused on management, with careers in the leisure industry in mind – golf course management, for example, has proved popular with students despite being a target of those who see anything beyond the traditional academic portfolio as "dumbing down". The question is not whether the courses are up to standard, but whether a less specialised one will offer more career flexibility if a decline in popularity for the particular sport limits future opportunities.

Sports scholarships

The number and range of sports scholarships have expanded just as rapidly as courses in the subject, but the two are usually not connected. Sports scholarships are for elite performers, regardless of what they are studying – indeed, they exist at universities with barely any degrees in the field. Imported from the USA, scholarships now exist in an array of sports. At Birmingham University, for example, there are specialist golf awards (as there are at ten other universities) and a scholarship for triathletes, as well as others open to any sport.

The value of scholarships varies considerably – sometimes according to individual prowess. The Royal and Ancient scholarships for golfers, for example, range from £500 for promising handicap golfers to £10,000 for full internationals, and are available at eleven universities. All of them demand that you meet the normal entrance requirements for your course and maintain the necessary academic standards, as well as progressing in your sport. In practice, most departments will be flexible about attendance and deadlines, as long as you make your requests well in advance.

Many sports scholarships offer benefits in kind, in the form of coaching, equipment or access to facilities. The Government-funded Talented Athlete Scholarship Scheme (TASS), which is restricted to students at English universities who have achieved national recognition at under-18 level and are eligible to represent England in one of 30 different sports, is one such example. Winning Students is a similar scheme in Scotland. Around 100 current or former TASS athletes took part in the Rio Olympics, winning 37 medals including 18 gold. The scholarships are worth £3,500 a year and can be put towards costs such as competition and training costs, equipment or mentoring. Further details are available at **www.tass.gov.uk**.

Leading performers in many sports still look first to US universities – often unfamiliar ones – for sports scholarships. In some sports, such as American football or basketball, this is the main route into professional sport, while in others it may provide bigger awards – and in some cases better coaching – than are available in the UK. Half of the UK's six-strong tennis team at the World Student Games were from US universities. The gold medal winners in the men's doubles, Darren Walsh and Joe Salisbury, were from the Southern Methodist University in Texas and the University of Memphis respectively – not household names on this side of the Atlantic. For the most promising athletes, US scholarships can cover the full cost of university; for others they may be worth only a few thousand dollars, but may make the difference in gaining admission. Further details are available at **www.fulbright.org.uk/study-in-the-usa/undergraduate-study/funding/sports-scholarships**.

Part-time work

University sports centres are an excellent source of term-time (and out-of-term) employment. You may also be trained in first aid, fire safety, customer care and risk assessment – all useful skills for future employment. The experience will help you secure employment in commercial or local authority facilities – and even for jobs such as stewarding at football grounds and music venues. Most universities also have a sabbatical post in the Athletic Union or similar body, a paid position with responsibility for organising university sport and representing the sporting community within the university.

Useful websites

The BUCS website provides a wide range of information on competitive university sports: **www.bucs.org.uk**

University sports websites are given in the university profiles (chapter 14).

10 How Parents Can Help

Parents are more involved in the higher education process than they have ever been. Many take an active role in selecting courses, may have their say subsequently on the student experience – and, of course, contribute large sums towards their children's time at university. Under such circumstances, there is a thin line between helping and meddling. But it is a balance that every parent wants to get right – and naturally the same applies to step-parents and guardians.

Nearly half of all parents in the UK think university is now poor value for money, according to a survey by HSBC. But a larger proportion also believe that higher education is essential to their children's career prospects and are willing to help them through it. Indeed, nine out of ten expect to make a financial contribution to their children's time at university – and to spend up to eight years paying off the debts they incur in the process.

The introduction of £9,000 fees was meant to make the student responsible for his or her higher education – including paying for it – but parents' involvement has, if anything, increased under the new system. That is because most parents are paying towards students' living costs, not their tuition. Maintenance loans may be larger than they were, but few students will get by only on them alone. For undergraduates outside London, they range from £8,430 for students with a family income below £25,000 to £3,928 with a family income above £65,000 for 2017–18. Those parents who can are often anxious to spare their children yet more debt on top of the cost of tuition. Surprising numbers of students from affluent families are not taking out loans at all, and are relying instead on support from parents or sometimes grandparents. Up to half the students at some leading universities are doing without Government maintenance loans, although throughout England, well over 80 per cent are taking them up.

Operating the "bank of mum and dad" may be the most indispensable role played by parents, but there are plenty of others, from chauffeur on open days to cookery coach in their first experience of living away from home. The scale of parental involvement naturally depends on individual relationships, but the right advice and encouragement before, during and after the selection process can be invaluable. Many parents have been to university themselves and will be more adept than a teenager at reading between the lines of a self-congratulatory prospectus or website. But it is important to remember who is going to be the student and not to allow your own (inevitably dated) preconceptions to muddy the waters.

Those who are not graduates are just as capable of doing the necessary research to offer a second opinion on universities and courses.

Laying the ground

The first thing any parent can do to smooth the path to university is to be encouraging about the value of higher education. Ideally, this should have started long before the application process, but it is especially important at this point. Now that student debt and variable graduate employment prospects have become frequent media topics, it is only natural for sixth-formers and others to have second thoughts about higher education.

The lure of a regular wage packet will be tempting, should one be available, and there are plenty of young people who are not suited to full-time higher education. More big companies are choosing to employ promising 18-year-olds, rather than rely entirely on graduate recruitment, and there has been a rapid development of apprenticeships. Even after the years of enormous university expansion, most people still do not go to university. Nevertheless, those who are capable of going generally do not regret the decision. Many people look back on their student days as the best period of their life, as well as the one that shaped their personality and their career. Time as a student should still pay off for the individual in terms of lifetime earnings, as well as personal development. A little reassurance at this stage may make all the difference.

There are important decisions to be made before the sixth form even begins because the choice of A levels or vocational qualifications – and even GCSEs – can close off avenues at degree level. A core of traditional academic subjects will help to keep options open, but there are specific requirements for some degrees that can easily be overlooked until it is too late. Maths A level will be needed for many economics courses, for example, as well as for most sciences.

Making the choice

Any parent wants to help a son or daughter through the difficult business of choosing where and what to study. How big a role you play will depend on a number of factors, not the least of which is the extent to which your advice is wanted. If the quality of advice available at school or college is good, parental involvement may be marginal. But often that is not the case, and you may have to call on other resources, including your own research. Avoid second-hand opinions gleaned through the media or dinner party gossip. You may think that some subjects are a sure-fire route to lucrative employment, while others are shunned by employers, but are you right? And do you really know the strengths and weaknesses of more than 100 universities? Above all, do not try to rewind your own career decisions through your children. The fact that you enjoyed – or hated – a subject or a university does not mean that they will. You may have always regretted missing out on the chance to go to Oxbridge or to become a brain surgeon, but they have their own lives to lead. Students who switch courses or drop out frequently complain that they were pressured into their original choice by their parents. The tables in chapters 1 and 3 offer a reality check, but even they cannot take account of the differences within institutions. The subject tables in chapter 12 show that the best graduate employment rates are often not at the obvious universities.

Parents are encouraged by many schools and colleges to play an active role in the process of choosing a course. At the most basic (but vital) level, this means keeping an eye on deadlines, but it is also about acting as a sounding board and trying to guide your child towards the right university and course. Check that choices are being made for sensible reasons, not on the basis of questionable gossip or trivial criteria. But beyond that, you should stay in the background unless there is a very good reason to play a more substantive role. Make a point of looking for important aspects of university life that the applicant might miss. Security, for example, usually does not feature near the top of a teenager's list of priorities; likewise other practical issues, such as the proximity of student accommodation to lectures, the library and the students' union.

Many universities now publish guides specifically for parents and put on programmes for them at Open Days. The latter may be a way of separating prospective applicants from their more demanding "minders", but the programmes themselves can be interesting and informative. Do not worry that you will be an embarrassment by attending Open Days – thousands of parents do so, and you may add a critical edge to the proceedings. Like prospectuses, Open Days are part of the sales process, and it is easy for a sixth-former to be carried away by the excitement surrounding a lively university. You are much more likely to spot the defects – even if they are ignored in the final decision. The programme for Open Days in 2017 is given at the back of the book. As Open Days at popular institutions are often on the same day, assistance in planning Open Day visits is important.

Most of today's sixth-formers and college students seem happy to have their parents' help and advice – even if they do not take it in the end. Research by the Knowledge Partnership consultancy found that more than half of the parents of first-year undergraduates felt they had exerted some influence on their children's choices of university and course, although only about 7 per cent characterised this as "a lot".

UCAS also publishes its own guide for parents, offering useful tips and outlining the deadlines that applicants will have to meet. The school should be on top of the timing and offering the necessary advice, but there is no harm in providing a little back-up, especially on parts of the process that take time and thought, such as writing the personal statement. There is little a parent can do as the offers and/or rejections come rolling in, other than to be supportive. If the worst happens and there are five rejections, you may have to start the advice process all over again for a new round of applications through UCAS Extra. If so, a cool head is even more necessary, but the same principles apply.

Results day

Then, before you know it, results day is upon you. Make sure you are at home, rather than in some isolated holiday retreat. Your son or daughter needs to have access to instant advice at school or college, and to be able to contact universities straight away if Clearing or Adjustment is required. And your moral support will be much more effective face to face, rather than down a telephone line. Whatever happens, try not to transmit the anxiety that you will inevitably be feeling to your son or daughter, especially if the results are not what was wanted. It is easy to make rash decisions about re-sitting exams or rejecting an insurance offer in the heat of the moment. Try to slow the process down and encourage clear and realistic thinking. Make sure you know in advance what might be required, such as where to access Clearing lists, and if Clearing or Adjustment is being used, you will need to be on hand to offer advice and help with visits to possible universities. For most applicants, Clearing or Adjustment is all but over in a week, so the agony should be short-lived.

Before they go

Little more than a month after the tension of results day, everything should be ready for the start of term. Unless your son or daughter chooses to stay at home to study – as one in five now does, according to NatWest – there will be forms to fill in to secure university accommodation, as well as student loans to sort out and registration to complete. You can perform useful services, like supplying recipe books if the first year is to be spent in self-catering accommodation, but now is the time for independence to become reality. Make sure that important details like insurance are not forgotten, but otherwise stand clear.

Then it is just a matter of agreeing a budget, assuming you are in a position to make a financial contribution. How large that contribution is will depend on family circumstances and your attitude to independent living. Some parents want to ensure that their children leave university debt-free; others could never afford to do that. The important thing is that students and parents know where they stand.

Student finance and parental involvement

After a mortgage, a university degree can be the most significant debt families have to repay, according to HSBC. The debt usually combines student loans for tuition fees and maintenance, and is repayable only when a graduate is paid £21,000 a year and can never amount to more than 9 per cent of his or her salary above that threshold. The immediate priority, however, is budgeting for the cost of living, which the National Union of Students puts at £12,000 a year outside London and at least £13,500 in the capital. Other estimates are slightly lower – Manchester University puts average costs for its students at £9,400 for a 40-week year – but the final bill is still substantial.

Hundreds of thousands of undergraduates – particularly mature students – pay their own way through university. Many undergraduates of all ages supplement their income with term-time and vacation jobs. But every survey shows that families play an important (and growing) role where students move straight from school to higher education. More than half of all students consider the family contribution crucial to their ability to afford university. This may rise with the withdrawal of grants for students from the poorest families in 2016, although there will actually be more cash available through the replacement loan system.

Costs are likely to be higher if the choice is an overseas university, although most American institutions have generous scholarships and employment opportunities. Even so, HSBC found that most parents were prepared to pay more for the experience, although they would prefer that their children stayed closer to home.

A frank discussion on what the family can afford is essential before the student leaves home. It is all too easy for a young person who has never had to budget for themselves to get into financial difficulties in the social whirl that is the first term of a degree course. In the worst cases, this can lead to excessive term-time employment to keep up with spiralling debts and pressures that contribute towards a student dropping out.

After they've left

Any new student is going to be nervous if he or she is leaving home for the first time and having to settle into a strange environment. But in most cases it is not going to last long because everyone is in the same boat and freshers' weeks hardly leave time for homesickness. In any case, they will not want to let their apprehension show. The people who are most likely to be emotional are the parents – especially if they are left with an empty nest for the first time. It can take a while to get used to an orderly, quiet house after all those years of mayhem.

Resist any temptation to decorate their bedroom and turn it into an office – it is more common than you might think, and psychologists say it can do lasting damage to family relationships. Keep in touch by phone, text or email, but try not to pry. You're not going to be told everything anyway – which is probably just as well. They will be back soon enough and, just as you were getting used to having the place to yourself, a weekend visit or the Christmas vacation will remind you of how things used to be. If things are not going smoothly at university, this may be the time for more reassurance – more students drop out at Christmas of their first year than at any other time.

"Helicopter parents"

Growing numbers of parents now want to play their part in ensuring that their children get value for money at university, but there is a fine line between constructive involvement and unwelcome interference. Universities report that anxious mothers and fathers are more inclined than ever to question what their children are getting for their now substantial fees. There have been stories of parents challenging not just the amount and quality of tuition, but even the marking of essays and exams. The phenomenon, first reported in the USA, has given rise to the phrase "helicopter parents" – so called because they hover over their children's education when they should be letting go. No one wants to think of themselves in that category, but it is not surprising – or reprehensible – that parents are taking more of an interest.

One of the reasons that some overstep the mark is that they are shocked that the amount of teaching and size of seminar groups are not what they recall from their own "free" higher education. The new fees are meant to herald improvements in the student experience, including more contact hours, but these have been marginal in most universities so far. It may be that fewer and larger seminars are here to stay in the arts and social sciences, where almost all state support for teaching has been withdrawn, and more learning opportunities will be provided online.

An associated reason for greater parental involvement is that family relationships have changed. Many teenage applicants are glad to accept a lift to an open day to get a second opinion on a university and their prospective course. They are also more likely than previous generations of students to come home at the weekend – or to live there in the first place – and to air any grievances. By all means, give advice, but leave direct contact with university administrators and academics to the student. Universities will cite the Data Protection Act, in any case, to say they can only deal with students, not parents. What they really mean is that students are adults and should look after themselves.

Useful websites

Many universities have sections on their websites for parents of prospective students. UCAS has a Parents section and a guide on its website: **www.ucas.com/ucas/undergraduate/getting-started/ucas-undergraduate-parents-and-guardians**

To find out more about Open Days, visit: **www.opendays.com**

11 Coming to the UK to Study

The vote to leave the European Union and Government proposals for an even tougher visa regime for international students and their families have added to the impression in many parts of the world that the UK no longer welcomes students from other countries. Nothing could be further from the truth where universities are concerned, which value the cultural contribution of international students, as well as the fee income they bring. It remains to be seen what obstacles will be put in their way as they recruit overseas, however. There have been suggestions that the new Teaching Excellence Framework could be used to determine whether individual universities should be allowed to admit international students at all and who should be allowed to remain in the country after graduation. At the very least, such talk is likely to reduce the number of applications from abroad, especially in the Indian subcontinent, where existing visa policy was sufficiently controversial to top Prime Minister Modi's agenda at his first meeting with Theresa May.

In some ways, however, the Brexit vote and its aftermath may provide additional opportunities for international students. The fall in the value of the pound has made a UK degree better value for money – the country has been regarded as an expensive study destination, even though its degrees and postgraduate programmes are short by international standards – and there may be less competition for places on popular courses. UK universities have been a magnet for international students for many years – only the huge higher education system in the USA attracts more. Global surveys have shown that UK universities are seen as offering high quality in a relatively safe environment, with the added advantage of allowing students to learn and immerse themselves in English. The UK's 11 per cent share of the world's young people who choose to study outside their own country is important to its universities and welcomed by British students.

The number of new undergraduates coming from other EU countries and farther afield rose again in 2016, but at a slower rate than previously, with nearly all the increase coming from other EU countries.

The future prospects for EU students are far from certain as a result of the UK's decision to leave the union. Those starting their studies in 2017 have been guaranteed that fee levels will remain the same as for UK students for the duration of their course, but, with the UK expected to leave the EU during the 2018–19 academic year, there is, as yet, no indication of what position that year's new EU students will face. At present, EU students pay no fees in Scotland and are eligible for student loans in the rest of the UK. It must be assumed that numbers will decline if these benefits are withdrawn.

More than 4 million people now travel abroad to study, and universities in many parts of the world compete aggressively to attract them. The students concerned may see other countries' universities as better than their own, or they may want to master another language and/or experience another culture, but most also see international study as a boost to their career prospects. Surveys in a number of countries have shown that employers – particularly those engaged in global markets – favour applicants with an international education.

While international students have continued to favour UK universities, the numbers of undergraduates coming from individual countries have varied considerably over recent years. The source of most stability has been China, which sends by far the largest numbers (almost 18 per cent of all those coming to the UK), but there has been fluctuation elsewhere, often due to economic or political factors. Most significant has been the decline in Indian students and the increase in students from Hong Kong, Malaysia and Singapore. Universities in the UK continue to be extremely proactive in the recruitment of international students, participating in international fairs and sometimes opening their own offices in target countries. That will not change unless individual universities are prevented from taking foreign students.

The top countries for sending international students to the UK

EU countries (top 20)		%	Non-EU countries (top 20)		%
Cyprus (European Union)	7,052	9.6	China	35,596	25.7
France	6,759	9.2	Hong Kong	13,796	10.0
Germany	5,730	7.8	Malaysia	12,168	8.8
Romania	5,412	7.3	Nigeria	6,381	4.6
Bulgaria	5,304	7.2	Singapore	5,794	4.2
Ireland	5,077	6.9	India	5,693	4.1
Italy	4,885	6.6	United States of America	4,910	3.5
Greece	4,599	6.2	Norway	4,084	2.9
Lithuania	3,880	5.3	Canada	2,836	2.0
Spain	3,843	5.2	Saudi Arabia	2,727	2.0
Poland	3,666	5.0	South Korea	2,652	1.9
Sweden	2,269	3.1	Pakistan	2,502	1.8
Belgium	1,863	2.5	Russia	2,380	1.7
Portugal	1,459	2.0	Vietnam	2,016	1.5
Finland	1,454	2.0	United Arab Emirates	1,964	1.4
Netherlands	1,353	1.8	Switzerland	1,874	1.4
Latvia	1,294	1.8	Qatar	1,626	1.2
Hungary	1,212	1.6	Kuwait	1,570	1.1
Slovakia	1,044	1.4	Thailand	1,539	1.1
Austria	1,013	1.4	Brunei	1,346	1.0
All EU students	73,829		All non-EU students	138,545	

Note First degree non-UK students. Figures from 2014–15.

Why study in the UK?

Aside from the strong reputation of UK degree courses and the opportunity to be taught and surrounded by English, research shows that most graduates are handsomely rewarded when they return home. A report from the Department for Business, Innovation and Skills (BIS) showed that UK graduates earn much higher salaries than those who studied in their own country. The starting salaries of UK graduates in China and India were more than twice as high as those for graduates educated at home, while even those returning to the USA enjoyed a salary premium of more than 10 per cent.

Some premium is to be expected – you are likely to be bright and highly motivated if you are prepared to uproot yourself to take a degree. And, unless they have government scholarships, most students have to be from a relatively wealthy background to afford the fees and other expenses of international study. A higher salary will probably be a necessity to compensate for the cost of the course. But the scale of increase demonstrated in the report suggests that a UK degree remains a good investment. Three years after graduation, 95 per cent of the international graduates surveyed were in work or further study. More than 90 per cent had been satisfied with their learning experience and almost as many would recommend their university to others.

A popular choice

Nearly all UK universities are cosmopolitan places that welcome international students in large numbers. Recent surveys by i-graduate, the student polling organisation which also produced the BIS report, put the country close behind the USA among the world's most attractive study destinations. Students from outside the EU now make up around 19 per cent of all students at UK universities and colleges. More full-time postgraduates – the fastest-growing group – come from outside the UK than within it. In many UK universities you can expect to have fellow students from over 100 countries.

More than 90 per cent of international students declare themselves satisfied with their experience of UK universities in i-graduate surveys, although they are less enthusiastic in the National Student Survey and more likely than UK students to make official complaints. Nevertheless, satisfaction increased by 8 percentage points in four years, according to i-graduate, reflecting greater efforts to keep ahead of the global competition. International students are particularly complimentary about students' unions, multiculturalism, teaching standards and places of worship. Their main concerns tend to be financial, with the UK considered the second-most expensive study location in the world (after the USA) before the collapse of the pound, partly because of a lack of employment opportunities. In one survey, only 56 per cent were satisfied with the ability to earn money while studying, and statements from ministers in the UK Government suggest that controls on this, and particularly on the opportunity to work after completing a degree, are likely to become tougher still.

One way round this in a growing number of countries is to take a UK degree through a local institution, distance learning or a full branch campus of a UK university. Indeed, there are now more international students taking UK first degrees in their own country than there are in Britain – around 480,000 of them outside the EU. The numbers grew by 70 per cent in a decade and are likely to rise further if UK Government policies obstruct universities' efforts to increase the number of students coming to Britain.

Where to study in the UK

The vast majority of the UK's universities and other higher education institutions are in

England. Of the 133 universities profiled in this *Guide*, 108 are in England, 15 in Scotland, 8 in Wales and 2 in Northern Ireland. Fee limits in higher education for UK and EU students are determined separately in each administrative area, which in some cases has brought benefits for EU students. All undergraduates from other EU countries are currently charged the same fees as those from the part of the UK where their chosen university is located, so EU students currently pay no tuition fees in Scotland, for example. With the UK expected to leave the EU in March 2019, it is unclear whether this arrangement will operate for students starting in 2018–19 or what system might replace it.

Within the UK, the cost of living varies by geographical area. Although London is the most expensive, accommodation costs in particular can also be high in many other major cities. You should certainly find out as much as you can about what living in Britain will be like. Further advice and information is available through the British Council at its offices worldwide, at more than 60 university exhibitions that it holds around the world every year, or at its Education UK website (**www.educationuk.org**). Another useful website for international students is provided by the UK Council for International Student Affairs (UKCISA) at **www.ukcisa.org.uk**.

Universities in all parts of the UK have a worldwide reputation for high-quality teaching and research, as evidenced in global rankings such as those shown on pages 64–5. They maintain this standing by investing heavily in the best academic staff, buildings and equipment, and by taking part in rigorous quality assurance monitoring. Although this system

The universities most favoured by EU and non-EU students

Institution (top 20)	EU students	Institution (top 20)	Non-EU students
Glasgow	2,307	Manchester	5,124
Edinburgh	2,022	Liverpool	4,499
Aberdeen	1,997	University College London	4,023
University College London	1,703	University of the Arts, London	3,954
King's College London	1,657	Coventry	3,871
University of the Arts, London	1,618	Edinburgh	3,431
Coventry	1,451	Sheffield	3,228
Westminster	1,446	Nottingham	3,156
Manchester	1,426	Imperial College	2,614
Essex	1,317	Warwick	2,501
Middlesex	1,268	Portsmouth	2,228
Kent	1,191	St Andrews	2,138
Warwick	1,132	Southampton	2,056
Imperial College	1,115	Newcastle-upon-Tyne	2,023
Portsmouth	1,055	Exeter	2,015
Edinburgh Napier	1,027	King's College London	2,001
Queen Mary, University of London	1,001	City, University of London	1,995
Cambridge	999	Sunderland	1,985
Lancaster	991	Leeds	1,974
London Metropolitan	991	Sussex	1,954

Note: First degree non-UK students. Figures for 2013–14.

is set to change, at present the main regulatory bodies include the Quality Assurance Agency for Higher Education (QAA), higher education funding councils for each country of the UK, and the Office for Standards in Education, all of which publish reports on their websites. Professional bodies also play an important role, and there is an Independent Adjudicator for Higher Education who handles student complaints that have not been resolved by universities' own internal procedures.

Although many people from outside the UK associate British universities with Oxford and Cambridge, in reality most higher education institutions are nothing like this. Some universities do still maintain a traditional culture, but most are modern institutions that place at least as much emphasis on teaching as on research and offer many vocational programmes, often with close links with business, industry and the professions. The table opposite shows the universities that are most popular with international students at undergraduate level. Although some of those at the top of the lists are among the most famous names in higher education, others achieved university status only in the last 20 years.

What subjects to study?
One of the reasons for such diversity is that strongly vocational courses are favoured by international students. The table below shows the most popular subjects studied by international students. Many of these in professional areas such as architecture or medicine

The most popular subjects for international students

Subject	EU students	Non-EU students	Total students	% of all international students
Business studies	10,570	26,018	36,588	17.2
Accounting and finance	2,422	14,493	16,915	8.0
Law	3,676	9,984	13,660	6.4
Economics	2,660	7,257	9,917	4.7
Art and design	3,588	6,224	9,812	4.6
Computer science	4,485	4,697	9,182	4.3
Mechanical engineering	1,749	5,363	7,111	3.3
Politics	3,445	3,416	6,861	3.2
Electrical and electronic engineering	1,362	5,169	6,531	3.1
Biological sciences	3,189	3,195	6,384	3.0
Psychology	3,075	2,751	5,826	2.7
Mathematics	1,394	4,225	5,619	2.6
Communication and media studies	2,605	2,782	5,387	2.5
Civil engineering	1,030	3,405	4,435	2.1
Medicine	977	3,391	4,368	2.1
Architecture	1,745	2,589	4,334	2.0
Drama, dance and cinematics	2,293	1,761	4,055	1.9
Hospitality, leisure, recreation and tourism	1,828	2,192	4,020	1.9
Pharmacology and pharmacy	632	2,416	3,048	1.4
Chemical engineering	632	2,513	3,048	1.4

Note: First degree non-UK students. Figures for 2014–15.

take one or two years longer to complete than most other degree courses. Traditional first degrees are mostly awarded at Bachelor level (BA, BEng, BSc, etc.) and last three to four years. There are also some "enhanced" first degrees (MEng, MChem, etc.) that take four years to complete. The relatively new Foundation degree programmes are almost all vocational and take two years to complete as a full-time course, with an option to study for a further year to gain a full degree. Remember, though, that you need to consider the details of any university course that you wish to study and to look at the ranking of that university in our main league table in chapter 1 and in the subject tables in chapter 12.

English language proficiency

The universities maintain high standards partly by setting demanding entry requirements, including proficiency in English. For international students, this usually includes a score of at least 5.5 in the International English Language Testing System (IELTS), which assesses English language ability through listening, speaking, reading and writing tests.

Under visa regulations introduced in 2011, universities are able to vouch for a student's ability in English. This proficiency will need to be equivalent to an "upper intermediate" level (level B2) of the CEFR (Common European Framework of Reference for Languages) for studying at an undergraduate level (roughly equivalent to an overall score of 5.5 in IELTS).

There are many private and publicly funded colleges throughout the UK that run courses designed to bring the English language skills of prospective higher education students up to the required standard. However, not all of these are Government approved. Some private organisations such as INTO (**www.intohigher.com**) have joined with universities to create centres running programmes preparing international students for degree-level study. The British Council also runs English language courses at its centres around the world.

Tougher student visa regulations were introduced in 2012 and have since been refined. Although under the current system, universities' international students should not be denied entry to the UK, as long as they are found to have followed immigration rules, some lower-level preparatory courses taken by international students have been affected. It is, therefore, doubly important to consult the official UK government list of approved institutions (web address given at the end of this chapter) before lodging an application.

How to apply

You should read the information below in conjunction with that provided in chapter 6, which deals with the application process in some detail.

Some international students apply directly to a UK university for a place on a course, and others make their applications via an agent in their home country. But most applying for a full-time first degree course do so through the Universities and Colleges Admissions Service (UCAS). If you take this route, you will need to fill in an online UCAS application form at home, at school or perhaps at your nearest British Council office. There is lots of advice on the UCAS website about the process of finding a course and the details of the application system (**www.ucas.com/ucas/undergraduate/getting-started/ucas-undergraduate-international-and-eu-students**).

Whichever way you apply, the deadlines for getting your application in are the same. For those applying from within an EU country, application forms for most courses starting in 2018 must be received at UCAS by 15 January 2018. Note that applications for Oxford and Cambridge and for all courses in medicine, dentistry and veterinary science have to be received at UCAS by 15 October 2017, while some art and design courses have a later deadline of 24 March 2018.

If you are applying from a non-EU country to study in 2018, you can submit your application to UCAS at any time between 1 September 2017 and 30 June 2018. Most people will apply well before the 30 June deadline to make sure that places are still available and to allow plenty of time for immigration regulations, and to make arrangements for travel and accommodation.

Entry and employment regulations

Visa regulations have been the subject of continuing controversy in the UK and many new rules and regulations have been introduced, often hotly contested by universities. The Government was criticised for increasing visa fees, doubling the cost of visa extensions, and ending the right to appeal against a refusal of a visa.

It also introduced a points system for entry – known as Tier 4 – which came into effect in 2009. Under this scheme, prospective students can check whether they are eligible for entry against published criteria, and so assess their points score. Universities are also required to provide a Confirmation of Acceptance for Studies (CAS) to their international student entrants, who must have secured an unconditional offer, and the institutions must appear as a "Tier 4 Sponsor" on the Home Office's Register of Sponsors. Prospective students have to demonstrate that, as well as the necessary qualifications, they have English language proficiency and enough money for the first year of their specified course. This includes the full fees for the first year and, as at July 2016, living costs of £1,265 a month, up to a maximum of nine months, if studying in London (£1,015 a month in the rest of the UK). Under the new visa requirements, details of financial support are checked in more detail than before.

All students wishing to enter the UK to study are required to obtain entry clearance before arrival. The only exceptions are British nationals living overseas, British overseas territories citizens, British Protected persons, British subjects, and non-visa national short-term students who may enter under a new Student Visitor route. Visa fees have been increased again (to £328 for a Tier 4 visa, plus £150 a year healthcare surcharge). As part of the application process, biometric data will be requested and this will be used to issue you with a Biometric Residence Permit (BRP) once you have arrived in the UK. You will need a BRP to open a bank account, rent accommodation, establish your eligibility for benefits and services or to work part-time, for example. The details of the regulations are continually reviewed by the Home Office. You can find more about all the latest rules and regulations for entry and visa requirements at **www.gov.uk/tier-4-general-visa**.

The rules and regulations governing permission to work vary according to your country of origin and the level of course you undertake. If you are from a European Economic Area (EEA) country (the EU plus Iceland, Liechtenstein and Norway) or Switzerland, you do not need permission to work in the UK, although you will need to be ready to show an employer your passport or identity card to prove you are a national of an EEA country. However, the regulations that will apply after the UK leaves the EU are unknown at the time of writing and you will need to check for the latest information before making an application.

Students from outside the EEA who are here as Tier 4 students are allowed to work part-time for up to 20 hours a week during term time and full-time during vacations. These arrangements apply to students on degree courses; stricter limits were introduced in 2010 for lower-level courses. If you wish to stay on after you have graduated, you can apply for permission under Tier 2 of the new points-based immigration system, but you will need a sponsor and the work must be considered "graduate level", commanding a salary of at least £20,800. The reforms abolished the Tier 1 two-year post-study period for graduates who do not have such a sponsor. They will be required to apply for a new visa from scratch. Full details are on the Home Office study visas website.

A new Tier 1 Graduate Entrepreneur Scheme enables up to 1,900 graduates to remain in the UK if they have "genuine and credible business ideas and entrepreneurial skills". Successful applicants, who will be selected by their university, will be allowed to stay in the UK for 12 months, with the possibility of a further 12-month extension.

Bringing your family

Since 2010, international students on courses of six months or less have been forbidden to bring a partner or children into the UK, and the latest reforms extend this prohibition to all undergraduates except those who are government sponsored. Postgraduates studying for 12 months or longer will still be able to bring dependants to the UK, and most universities can help to arrange facilities and accommodation for families as well as for single students. The family members you are allowed to bring with you are your husband or wife, civil partner (a same-sex relationship that has been formally registered in the UK or your home country) or long-term partner and dependent children. You can find out more about getting entry clearance for your family at **www.ukcisa.org.uk**.

Support from British universities

Support for international students is more comprehensive than in many countries, and begins long before you arrive in the UK. Many universities have advisers in other countries. Some will arrange to put you in touch with current students or graduates who can give you a first-hand account of what life is like at a particular university. Pre-departure receptions for students and their families, as well as meet-and-greet arrangements for newly arrived students, are common. You can also expect an orientation and induction programme in your first week, and many universities now have "buddying" systems where current students are assigned to new arrivals to help them find their way around, adjust to their new surroundings and make new friends. Each university also has a students' union that organises social, cultural and sporting events and clubs, including many specifically for international students. Both the university and the students' union are likely to have full-time staff whose job it is to look after the welfare of students from overseas.

International students also benefit from free medical and subsidised dental and optical care and treatment under the UK National Health Service (non-EU students will have had to pay a healthcare surcharge of £150 a year when paying for their visa to benefit from this), plus access to a professional counselling service and a university careers service.

At university, you will naturally encounter people from a wide range of cultures and walks of life. Getting involved in student societies, sport, voluntary work, and any of the wide range of social activities on offer will help you gain first-hand experience of British culture, and, if you need it, will help improve your command of the English language.

Useful websites

The British Council, with its dedicated Education UK site designed for those wishing to find out more about studying in the UK:
www.educationuk.org

The UK Council for International Student Affairs (UKCISA) provides a wide range of information on all aspects of studying in the UK:
www.ukcisa.org.uk

UCAS, for full details of undergraduate courses available and an explanation of the application process:
www.ucas.com/ucas/undergraduate/getting-started/ucas-undergraduate-international-and-eu-students

For the latest information on entry and visa requirements:
www.gov.uk/tier-4-general-visa

Register of sponsors for Tier 4 educational establishments:
www.gov.uk/government/publications/register-of-licensed-sponsors-students

For a general guide to Britain, available in many languages:
www.visitbritain.com

12 Subject by Subject Guide

The rankings of whole institutions capture all the headlines when university guides appear, but recent surveys suggest that subject tables are becoming increasingly influential. Knowing where a university stands in the pecking order of higher education is a vital piece of information for any prospective student, but the quality of the course is what matters most – particularly in the short term. Your chosen course, rather than the character of the whole university, will determine what you get out of taking a degree and may have a big bearing on your employment prospects. As the 2014 Research Excellence Framework confirmed, the most modest institution may have a centre of specialist excellence, and even famous universities have mediocre departments. This chapter offers some pointers to the leading universities in a wide range of subjects. With a number of universities reviewing the courses they will offer in the future, it is possible that not all institutions listed in a particular subject area will be running courses in 2017 or 2018.

The subject tables in this *Guide* include scores from the National Student Survey (NSS). These distil the views of final-year undergraduates on various aspects of their course, and this year the results presented in two columns. The teaching quality indicator reflects the average scores of the teaching, assessment and feedback, and academic support sections of the survey. The student experience indicator is drawn from the average of the organisation and management, learning resources, and personal development sections and the overall satisfaction question. The three other measures used are research quality, students' entry qualifications and graduate employment prospects. None of the measures is weighted. A full explanation of the measures is given on the next page.

Many subjects, such as dentistry or sociology, have their own table, but others are grouped together in broader categories, such as "Other Subjects Allied to Medicine". For the first time Criminology appears in a separate subject table, while the Anthropology table has been renamed 'Anthropology and Forensic Science' to reflect the mix of courses included in this category. Scores are not published where the number of students is too small for the outcome to be statistically reliable. In the NSS, a 50 per cent response rate is required from a minimum of 10 students. Cambridge is again the most successful university. It tops 31 of the 67 tables. Oxford and St Andrews have the next highest number of top places with five each, followed by Birmingham and Glasgow with three, Imperial, Lancaster, Leeds and Newcastle with two, while 12 others also gain top spots.

Research quality

This is a measure of the quality of the research undertaken in the subject area. The information was sourced from the 2014 Research Excellence Framework (REF), a peer-review exercise used to evaluate the quality of research in UK higher education institutions, undertaken by the UK Higher Education Funding Bodies. The approach mirrors that in the main table, with the REF results weighted and then multiplied by the percentage of eligible staff entered for assessment.

For each subject, a research quality profile was given to those university departments that took part, showing how much of their research was in various quality categories. These categories were: 4* world-leading; 3* internationally excellent; 2* internationally recognised; 1* nationally recognised; and unclassified. The funding bodies decided to direct more funds to the very best research by applying weightings. The English, Scottish and Welsh funding councils have slightly different weightings. Those adopted by HEFCE (the funding council for England) for funding in 2012–13 are used in the tables: 4* is weighted by a factor of 3 and 3* is weighted by a factor of 1. Outputs of 2* and 1* carry zero weight. This results in a maximum score of 3. In the interests of consistency, the above weightings continue to be applied this year.

The scores in the table are presented as a percentage of the maximum score. To achieve the maximum score all staff would need to be at 4* world-leading level.

Universities could choose which staff to include in the REF, so, to factor in the depth of the research quality, each quality profile score has been multiplied by the number of staff returned in the REF as a proportion of all eligible staff.

Entry standards

This is the average old UCAS tariff score for new students under the age of 21, based on A and AS Levels and Scottish Highers and Advanced Highers and other equivalent qualifications (including the International Baccalaureate), taken from HESA data for 2014–15. Each student's examination grades were converted to a numerical score using the old UCAS tariff and added up to give a total score. HESA then calculated an average score for each university. See page 31 for an explanation of how the old UCAS tariff compares with the new UCAS tariff being used from 2017 onwards.

Teaching quality and student experience

This year we have split the student satisfaction measure into two components which give the students' views of the quality of their courses. These measures are taken from the National Student Survey (NSS) results published in 2015 and 2016. A single year's figures are used when that is all that is available, but an average of the two years' results is used in all other cases. The NSS covers six aspects of a course, with an additional question gauging overall satisfaction. Students answer on a scale from 1 (bottom) to 5 (top) and the scores in the table are calculated from the percentage of positive responses (4 and 5) in each section. The teaching quality indicator reflects the average scores of the teaching, assessment and feedback, and academic support sections. The student experience indicator is drawn from the average scores of the organisation and management, learning resources, and personal development sections and the additional question on overall satisfaction. Teaching quality is favoured over student experience and accounts for 67 per cent of the overall student satisfaction score, with student experience making up the remaining 33 per cent.

Graduate prospects

This is the percentage of graduates undertaking further study or in a professional job ("positive destinations"), in the annual survey by HESA six months after graduation. Two years of data (2014 and 2015 graduates) are aggregated to make the data more reliable. A low score on this measure does not necessarily indicate unemployment – some graduates may have taken jobs that are not categorised as professional work. The averages for each subject are given close by the relevant subject table in this chapter and in two tables in chapter 3 (see pages 52–5).

The Education table uses a fifth measure: Ofsted, a measure of the quality of teaching based on the outcomes of Ofsted inspections of teacher training courses.

Note that in the tables that follow, when a figure is followed by *, it refers solely to data from 2013–14 because no data for 2014–15 are available.

The subjects listed below are covered in the tables in this chapter:

Accounting and Finance
Aeronautical and
  Manufacturing
  Engineering
Agriculture and Forestry
American Studies
Anatomy and Physiology
Animal Science
Anthropology and Forensic
  Science
Archaeology
Architecture
Art and Design
Biological Sciences
Building
Business Studies
Celtic Studies
Chemical Engineering
Chemistry
Civil Engineering
Classics and Ancient
  History
Communication and Media
  Studies
Computer Science
Creative Writing
Criminology
Dentistry
Drama, Dance and
  Cinematics

East and South Asian
  Studies
Economics
Education
Electrical and Electronic
  Engineering
English
Food Science
French
General Engineering
Geography and
  Environmental Sciences
Geology
German
History
History of Art, Architecture
  and Design
Hospitality, Leisure,
  Recreation and Tourism
Iberian Languages
Italian
Land and Property
  Management
Law
Librarianship and
  Information Management
Linguistics
Materials Technology
Mathematics
Mechanical Engineering

Medicine
Middle Eastern and African
  Studies
Music
Nursing
Other Subjects Allied to
  Medicine (see page 237
  for subjects included in
  this category)
Pharmacology and
  Pharmacy
Philosophy
Physics and Astronomy
Physiotherapy
Politics
Psychology
Radiography
Russian and East European
  Languages
Social Policy
Social Work
Sociology
Sports Science
Theology and Religious
  Studies
Town and Country Planning
  and Landscape
Veterinary Medicine

Accounting and Finance

The numbers starting degrees in accounting rose by almost 10 per cent in 2015 after four years of decline. Nearly 7,000 places represented a record entry after an increase in applications of almost 11 per cent, and there was further progress in 2016. Finance degrees were already faring better than the larger accounting group in terms of both applications and acceptances, attracting more than 2,000 students for the first time in 2015.

Employment rates in both areas come a surprisingly long way down the table of subjects, however – only just inside the top 40 of 67 subjects. Those who do find graduate jobs are relatively well paid, however. At an average of more than £23,000 in 2015, they were just in the top 25.

Leeds remains at the top of the table, having moved up from tenth place two years ago. Buckingham and Ulster recorded the best scores in the sections of the National Student Survey (NSS) devoted to teaching, feedback and academic support, while students at London South Bank and second-placed Lancaster were the most satisfied with other aspects of their course. The London School of Economics was far ahead of the rest on research and entry standards, but still did not make the top ten overall because of low scores in the NSS.

The table again shows wide variation in graduates' employment prospects. Loughborough saw nearly 95 per cent of graduates go straight into professional jobs or further study, but at 14 of the 99 universities offering accounting and/or finance the proportion was below 50 per cent. Approaching one student in five takes a further qualification after completing a degree, but only 8 per cent do so full-time.

Some of the leading universities demand maths A level and all welcome it, but with nearly 100 universities qualifying for the table, there is considerable variation in entry standards. Almost 150 institutions offer accounting, either alone or in combination, in 2017.

Accounting and Finance	Research quality %	Entry standards	Teaching quality %	Student experience %	Graduate prospects %	Overall score
1 Leeds	39.3	467	88.7	92.9	86.9	100.0
2 Lancaster	42.6	401	90.1	94.9	86.5	99.1
3 Strathclyde	44.3	514	82.4	88.8	76.8	98.5
=4 Loughborough	32.6	421	84.8	92.7	94.7	97.8
=4 Queen's, Belfast	32.7	409	87.9	94.2	90.9	97.8
6 Warwick	40.4	494	76.0	84.9	86.1	96.7
7 Bath	41.8	497	76.9	83.8	80.8	96.3
8 Ulster	40.4	318	92.0	93.3	80.8	95.7
9 Exeter	24.4	460	84.3	88.6	86.4	95.6
10 Glasgow	22.1	495	81.5	91.9	83.2	95.5
11 Nottingham	32.6	389	83.4	91.4	84.3	94.7
12 London School of Economics	52.3	521	65.3	74.2	80.1	94.6
13 Queen Mary, London	31.3	421	86.8	87.5	75.8	94.4
=14 Reading	29.3	385	86.3	89.0	83.5	94.3
=14 Stirling	25.2	402	84.9	88.6	87.3	94.3
=16 Bristol	32.1	439	75.8	83.5	83.5	93.0
=16 Newcastle	20.7	408	82.0	89.8	86.1	93.0

Accounting and Finance cont	Research quality %	Entry standards	Teaching quality %	Student experience %	Graduate prospects %	Overall score
18 East Anglia	28.1	406	84.9	90.9	73.0	92.9
19 Swansea	22.0	334	89.3	90.0	85.7	92.8
20 Leicester	24.3	379	84.9	91.8	79.2	92.6
=21 Cardiff	32.0	411	78.7	85.2	76.5	92.0
=21 Durham	23.1	414	76.9	82.0	90.8	92.0
23 Sheffield	26.8	381	80.0	86.8	83.6	91.9
24 Birmingham	29.1	394	77.1	83.6	85.0	91.8
25 Aston	19.7	384	87.1	89.1	76.2	91.7
26 Kent	24.8	368	80.1	85.5	83.6	91.1
27 City	27.8	419	75.9	84.0	77.8	90.9
=28 Heriot-Watt	18.8	389	77.4	86.4	86.7	90.7
=28 Manchester	33.3	449	74.7	85.8	64.8	90.7
=28 Sussex	23.7	351	77.6	84.5	90.3	90.7
31 Surrey	15.8	402	88.9	90.2	66.7	90.6
32 Southampton	24.0	393	77.7	85.8	79.5	90.5
33 Liverpool	20.1	388	86.3	89.9	67.2	90.4
=34 Aberdeen	24.9	430	68.8	80.1	84.6	89.6
=34 Bangor	23.4	303	86.9	92.0	72.1	89.6
36 Robert Gordon	2.6	446	79.3	84.5	83.2	89.3
37 Buckingham		273	92.2	93.6	88.9	89.0
38 Lincoln	4.8	325	88.3	93.1	76.3	88.3
=39 Edinburgh	25.8	472	67.6	75.6	71.8	88.1
=39 Liverpool John Moores		323	91.6	93.7	75.0	88.1
=41 De Montfort	10.7	274	84.9	86.7	82.3	87.1
=41 Essex	25.1	300	80.8	85.8	69.3	87.1
=43 Brunel	23.0	317	75.8	83.3	74.2	86.4
=43 Keele	10.2	317	84.4	90.9	68.2	86.4
=43 York St John	0.8		78.6	84.4	83.3*	86.4
46 Dundee	12.1	371	71.3	79.4	84.3	86.2
47 Aberystwyth	14.5	270	86.2	84.5	71.7	85.9
=48 Coventry	1.6	305	88.6	90.6	69.4	85.8
=48 Plymouth	13.1	301	88.7	89.0	59.5	85.8
50 Huddersfield	4.1	333	81.1	85.5	76.1	85.7
51 Portsmouth	9.5	313	81.7	86.1	71.6	85.5
52 Nottingham Trent	4.6	304	84.4	84.0	75.5	85.4
53 West of England	5.5	292	84.5	88.9	72.1	85.3
54 Hull	10.2	336	78.9	82.6	69.2	84.8
55 South Wales	0.2	332	80.7	81.5	78.4	84.7
56 Chester	0.5	265	88.7	88.8	71.9	84.6
57 Northumbria	4.0	348	80.9	84.4	66.7	84.4
58 Bradford	11.8	326	79.5	85.8	60.0	83.8
=59 Glasgow Caledonian	1.8	377	78.2	87.4	60.3	83.6
=59 London South Bank	2.1	232	88.8	96.1	63.3	83.6

=61 Edge Hill		312	85.1	87.4	63.0	83.5
=61 Salford	5.9	296	86.1	91.0	55.6	83.5
63 Oxford Brookes	5.1	308	81.2	91.8	59.7	83.3
64 Middlesex	10.5	293	80.5	81.8	64.6	83.1
65 West of Scotland	2.9	328	82.5	86.4	58.8	83.0
66 Edinburgh Napier	2.3	321	82.9	84.1	61.3	82.9
=67 Hertfordshire	0.9	284	81.0	87.3	68.5	82.7
=67 Gloucestershire		286	82.7	86.8	66.7	82.7
=67 Manchester Metropolitan	4.7	324	80.4	85.4	59.9	82.7
70 Leeds Beckett	0.8	247	88.3	91.3	58.3	82.2
71 Greenwich	3.3	354	79.8	79.8	57.1	82.1
72 Westminster	2.4	348	79.1	87.7	53.3	82.0
73 Bolton		235	83.6	92.5	64.7	81.8
74 Wrexham Glyndŵr		264*	88.5	88.5	53.3	81.5
75 Bournemouth	8.8	313	70.2	82.3	64.9	81.0
76 Central Lancashire	4.4	335	79.2	83.4	49.8	80.9
77 Sunderland	0.4	282	83.9	89.8	50.0	80.6
78 Sheffield Hallam	0.6	285	76.5	82.0	66.1	80.5
=79 Staffordshire	2.6	235	91.2	91.6	41.7	80.3
=79 Worcester	0.9	297	71.7	76.1	74.4	80.3
81 Teesside	2.0	232	81.5	84.1	60.9	79.8
82 Kingston	9.2	291	77.4	86.8	45.5	79.7
83 West London		246	83.7	88.8	49.4	79.2
84 Birmingham City	1.3	265	80.1	82.7	47.9	78.1
85 Brighton	6.5	276	67.0	72.4	67.2	77.9
86 Derby	0.9	259	78.4	82.8	49.6	77.7
87 Cardiff Metropolitan		282	71.9	77.8	58.8	77.5
88 Chichester		225	79.0	80.1	54.7	77.3
89 East London	0.8	232	83.1	79.3	45.3	76.9
90 Winchester		256	79.3	82.0	42.5	76.5
91 Southampton Solent		231	76.5	85.3	48.1	76.4
92 London Metropolitan	0.6	227	75.8	86.1	45.2	75.9
93 Canterbury Christ Church		253	78.9	80.2	39.8	75.6
94 Roehampton	4.5	243	70.9	77.3		75.2
=95 Anglia Ruskin	3.4	217	72.5	76.5	51.6	74.9
=95 Buckinghamshire New	1.8	238	77.8	78.7	39.3	74.9
97 Liverpool Hope		279	70.6	64.6	54.1	74.6
98 Northampton	1.0	243	72.2	75.6	42.0	73.6
99 Bedfordshire	3.1	201	61.0	66.1	42.3	68.8

Employed in professional job:	47%	Employed in non-professional job and studying:	2%
Employed in professional job and studying:	10%	Employed in non-professional job:	23%
Studying:	8%	Unemployed:	10%
Average starting professional salary:	£23,182	Average starting non-professional salary:	£17,810

Aeronautical and Manufacturing Engineering

Most of the courses in this ranking focus on aeronautical or manufacturing engineering, but the category includes some with a mechanical title. To add to the confusion, manufacturing degrees often go under the rubric of production engineering.

Degree apprenticeships at leading firms like Rolls-Royce provide an attractive alternative to a conventional degree in this area, but both applications and enrolments for traditional higher education courses in aeronautical engineering have risen in each of the last four years. The numbers starting degrees passed 3,000 in 2015. The smaller field of production and manufacturing engineering has also seen small increases.

The subjects are just outside the top ten of the 67 subject groups for starting salaries, despite an average increase of more than £600 in the latest survey of professional jobs. However, aeronautical and manufacturing engineering are only just in the top 30 for the proportion of graduates going straight into professional jobs or further study, and only six subjects have a higher unemployment rate.

Cambridge has extended its lead at the top of the table, registering by far the best scores for research, entry standards and graduate prospects. Bristol is now the nearest challenger, although Coventry registered the highest levels of satisfaction with teaching quality and Queen's, Belfast was top for the broader student experience.

Many universities demand maths and physics at A level, and give extra credit for further maths, computing and/or design technology. Entry grades are high at the leading universities, with Cambridge averaging almost 630 points and Imperial College within a whisker of 600. Only two universities average less than 250 points. Coventry is the only post-1992 university in this year's top 20, but the University of the West of England is just one place off it. About one student in seven secured a place through Clearing in 2015.

Almost 60 per cent of the 2015 graduates went straight into high-level work, and there was less variation between institutions than in many subjects. Although Cambridge saw almost 95 per cent of its graduates go straight into graduate jobs or further study and Manchester Metropolitan less than 40 per cent, good scores were distributed throughout the table.

Aeronautical and Manufacturing Engineering	Research quality %	Entry standards	Teaching quality %	Student experience %	Graduate prospects %	Overall score
1 Cambridge	67.0	629	74.7	87.2	94.6	100.0
2 Bristol	52.3	530	80.1	87.5	82.7	94.3
3 Imperial College	59.6	599	63.0	75.5	89.3	93.2
=4 Bath	37.4	523	76.2	87.8	87.9	92.3
=4 Leeds	40.9	433	87.4	91.4	82.6	92.3
=6 Loughborough	41.8	429	75.8	88.3	89.6	90.7
=6 Surrey	30.8	470	82.4	89.0	83.9	90.7
8 Southampton	52.3	470	65.2	79.5	93.3	90.6
9 Sheffield	36.0	421	72.7	80.4	90.3	88.2
10 Nottingham	40.8	400	77.7	87.1	79.2	88.1
11 Queen's, Belfast	36.7	387	88.2	94.8	66.7	88.0
12 Glasgow	47.2	480	69.2	79.4	74.1	87.2
13 Manchester	35.1	460	70.6	75.7	81.2	86.3

14 Swansea	45.5	354	70.0	74.2	85.7	85.5
15 Liverpool	32.1	405	74.9	85.3	73.7	85.1
16 Strathclyde	37.2	468	66.7	80.1	72.0	84.7
17 Coventry	10.3	314	90.4	91.8	77.1	84.5
18 Queen Mary, London	46.7	373	64.8	75.4	74.7	83.1
=19 Aston	20.6	371	69.3	77.8	83.3	82.3
=19 Ulster		301	76.8	89.2	91.3	82.3
21 West of England	10.6	341	74.7	79.4	84.4	81.7
22 Brunel	23.7	394	68.8	77.8	72.4	81.1
23 Teesside	5.8	342*	75.4	85.3		80.0
24 City	20.2	356	80.3	84.5	56.0	79.8
25 Hertfordshire	16.5	306	71.8	78.0	78.5	79.7
26 West of Scotland	9.0	299*	87.9	88.3	53.3	78.4
27 South Wales		307	78.9	78.6	68.3	77.1
28 Sussex		293	72.4	80.7	75.0	76.9
29 Portsmouth	9.1	290	75.1	82.4	61.4	76.2
30 Sheffield Hallam		288	73.8	77.9	72.0	76.1
=31 Buckinghamshire New		249	83.4	77.1	66.7	76.0
=31 Salford	4.4	325	67.6	76.9	70.9	76.0
33 Plymouth	15.7	250	75.3	80.0	59.3	75.4
34 Staffordshire	5.7	218	72.6	66.3	72.1	73.3
35 Manchester Metropolitan	16.3	323*	75.1	80.4	37.5	73.2
36 Kingston	2.9	295	67.6	75.5	57.9	72.3
37 Brighton	7.4	369	51.7	67.2	60.7	70.9

Employed in professional job:	56%	Employed in non-professional job and studying:	1%
Employed in professional job and studying:	3%	Employed in non-professional job:	14%
Studying:	12%	Unemployed:	13%
Average starting professional salary:	£25,588	Average starting non-professional salary:	£16,239

Agriculture and Forestry

Lincoln has leapt from only five places off the bottom of the table for agriculture and forestry last year to top in this edition. Triumphant in the measures derived from the National Student Survey, it benefits from not having enough students to compile an average entry score. In such cases, the scoring system generates a figure from the university's performance on the other measures. Nottingham, only a fraction of a point behind in second place, might have held onto the leadership if Lincoln had more undergraduates studying agriculture – it was tenth on this measure in the 2014 *Guide*, the last time its entry grades could be published.

With only 2,500 undergraduates studying the two subjects across the UK, this table tends to be volatile. Newcastle, the leader two years ago, is now seventh, while Reading has dropped from first to third in the latest edition. Two of the 16 institutions in the table are specialist universities: the Royal Agricultural University and Harper Adams, which has this year's best employment record. Newcastle is the only other university to register positive destinations for more than 80 per cent of graduates, while the rate is below a third at three institutions.

Agriculture and Forestry cont

Both applications and enrolments reached record levels again in 2015, when there was an increase in applications of almost 10 per cent. But with fewer than four applicants to the place (and less than that in forestry and arboriculture), entry standards remain low. Only Nottingham averages more than 400 points at A level, although only two universities average less than 300 points.

Satisfaction rates are high, with only one university dropping below 70 per cent for teaching quality and no institution falling below this figure for student experience. Nottingham Trent again registered the best teaching score and would have finished higher than 12th if it had entered the Research Excellence Framework in this subject. Overall, the subjects are in the bottom 10 for employment, but they do rather better in the salary table, taking 45th place out of 67 subject groupings. The unemployment rate of 17 per cent was one of the three highest, but those who found graduate jobs were paid an average of £21,158.

Agriculture and Forestry	Research quality %	Entry standards	Teaching quality %	Student experience %	Graduate prospects %	Overall score
1 Lincoln	31.1		93.0	93.8	77.3	100.0
2 Nottingham	36.4	403	86.5	86.6	72.0	99.3
3 Reading	50.7	370	82.8	88.3	76.5	99.1
4 Bangor	29.7	362	90.0	88.5	65.8	95.8
5 Glasgow	42.3	362	84.5	79.6		94.9
6 Queen's, Belfast	56.3	351	69.5	81.0	74.6	94.7
7 Newcastle	28.4	360	78.0	85.1	81.1	94.5
8 Aberystwyth	38.2	319	90.8	92.3	58.3	93.9
9 Harper Adams	5.7	346	83.1	89.3	81.6	92.1
10 Oxford Brookes		362	93.3	80.2	57.1	90.3
11 Kent		363	81.6	89.8	59.4	89.4
12 Nottingham Trent		331	93.7	89.8	51.7	88.8
13 Plymouth	17.4		82.9	84.3	30.8	84.5
14 Royal Agricultural University	2.1	294	72.7	83.7	57.8	82.4
15 Greenwich	19.5	303			31.3	81.5
16 Cumbria		272	78.0	70.0	27.0	76.2

Employed in professional job:	38%	Employed in non-professional job and studying:	2%
Employed in professional job and studying:	6%	Employed in non-professional job:	30%
Studying:	8%	Unemployed:	17%
Average starting professional salary:	£21,158	Average starting non-professional salary:	£17,903

American Studies

American Studies is back in the bottom ten for graduate prospects after a brief escape last year, but it is only just in the bottom 20 for starting salaries in professional jobs, after a £1,200 rise in the latest average. The volume of applications increased in 2015, but still remains well below the levels enjoyed before fees reached £9,000. The same was true of acceptances, which are not yet back to 500 nationally.

The small numbers inevitably make for some volatility. Birmingham, which has the highest entry standards, has taken over the leadership from Sussex, which has dropped to fourth. Hull again has the most satisfied students where teaching quality is concerned, and Dundee maintains its lead on the other sections of the National Student Survey. Warwick, which topped the ranking for almost a decade, has rejoined the top 10. It achieved the best results in the Research Excellence Framework, but satisfaction levels for course administration, learning resources and personal development are the lowest in the table.

Student satisfaction is generally high: only one university drops below 75 per cent on each of the two measures. By contrast, only Sussex reaches this level for graduate prospects and entry scores remain modest. Birmingham is the only university to average more than 400 points, while five of the 20 universities with enough students to compile reliable scores average less than 300 points.

Fifty universities and colleges expect to offer American studies in some form in 2017. Some focus on Latin America, whereas most concentrate on the culture and politics of the USA and Canada. A growing number of courses offer the opportunity of a year at an American or Canadian university as part of a four-year degree. The leading universities are likely to expect English or history at A level or the equivalent.

American Studies	Research quality %	Entry standards	Teaching quality %	Student experience %	Graduate prospects %	Overall score
1 Birmingham	48.8	401	84.5	88.4	69.0	100.0
2 Nottingham	39.9	370	89.3	90.9	72.3	99.3
3 Manchester	49.1	395	82.4	87.0	66.6	98.7
4 Sussex	45.6	363	76.9	85.4	80.8	97.9
5 Leicester	34.3	381	85.8	89.7	67.4	96.9
6 Portsmouth	32.2	200	93.1	92.5	63.8	94.0
7 Hull	26.1	314	94.0	93.8	59.0	93.9
8 Goldsmiths, London	34.9	375	90.2	79.6	51.6	93.8
=9 East Anglia	33.1	397	81.0	87.5	54.7	93.6
=9 Warwick	51.7		79.6	73.9	67.5	93.6
11 Liverpool	33.4		86.2	90.8	55.6	92.9
12 Keele	29.8	316	86.5	87.7	59.5	92.2
13 Dundee	30.4		87.2	95.2	48.5*	91.7
14 Kent	47.3	310	72.7	79.8	60.0	90.8
15 Swansea	18.5	301	86.5	89.2	64.5	90.7
16 Essex		313	90.6	92.4	50.0	86.8
17 York St John		279	82.5	87.8	55.6	83.9
18 Canterbury Christ Church	16.3	258	88.1	85.9	35.3	83.5
19 Winchester		245	93.1	91.9	41.9	83.3
20 Derby	13.5	255	77.8	91.6	38.5	81.8

Employed in professional job:	35%	Employed in non-professional job and studying:	4%
Employed in professional job and studying:	3%	Employed in non-professional job:	30%
Studying:	16%	Unemployed:	13%
Average starting professional salary:	£20,618	Average starting non-professional salary:	£15,689

Anatomy and Physiology

This table covers a broad range of courses, including the biomedical science degrees that have been growing in popularity over recent years. Very few actually have the title of anatomy or physiology, but they include degrees in cell biology, neurosciences and pathology. The numbers starting courses slipped a little for the second successive year in 2015 despite increased applications, which reached 35,000 for the first time. At well over eight applications to the place, it is one of the most competitive areas.

In some cases, the courses are used as a fall-back for candidates whose real target was medical school, so average entry qualifications at some of the leading universities are extremely high – more than 630 points in Cambridge's case. Partly because of the range of courses included in the category, entry grades also vary widely, however, with three universities averaging less than 300 points. Entry requirements often include at least two science subjects – usually biology and chemistry – although some new universities will accept just one science.

St Andrews tops the table for the first time, having moved up from third place. Cambridge, last year's leader, still has by far the highest entry standards, but the top scores on the other measures are spread around the table. Dundee, in equal tenth place, shared the best results in the Research Excellence Framework (REF) with fourth-placed University College London, while the best graduate prospects are at Northampton, which is only 26th overall, partly because it did not enter the REF in this category. Student satisfaction is generally high, with third-placed Newcastle leading the way on both of the measures derived from the National Student Survey.

Employment levels are good – a third of the 41 universities in the table recorded positive destinations for more than 80 per cent of graduates. But the subjects have slipped out of the top 20 in the employment table and are not in the top 30 for starting salaries. Only 42 per cent of graduates go straight into professional jobs, but that is partly because 37 per cent go on to further study.

Anatomy and Physiology	Research quality %	Entry standards	Teaching quality %	Student experience %	Graduate prospects %	Overall score
1 St Andrews	37.6	580	97.2	95.8		100.0
2 Cambridge	52.5	636	86.6	86.9	87.5	98.1
3 Newcastle	47.8	474	97.4	96.4	76.5	93.6
4 University College London	55.4	499	80.4	89.4	82.8	92.5
5 Oxford	50.9	596	79.2	76.4	78.2	92.0
6 Sussex	46.8	387	82.9	92.2	87.1	90.0
7 Leeds	40.9	429	85.9	93.2	79.8	89.4
8 Aberdeen	34.7	428	89.3	96.1	77.2	88.9
9 Bristol	49.7	446	82.1	84.1	74.9	88.3
=10 Dundee	55.4		82.2	86.4	75.5	87.6
=10 Queen's, Belfast	33.3	416	84.9	93.3	79.1	87.6
12 Glasgow	33.4	502	78.0	84.7	76.8	87.2
13 Huddersfield	7.8	363	87.1	89.8	98.1	87.0
14 Loughborough	52.1	402	79.3	88.8	72.1	86.7

15 King's College London	38.0	463	75.6	85.6	74.8	85.9
16 Salford	12.7	319	93.2	94.0	86.9	85.6
17 Liverpool	31.7	416	89.5	92.9	65.2	85.2
18 Manchester	38.3	451	76.9	87.0	68.1	84.5
19 Brighton	4.8	313*	91.6	92.8	88.9	84.3
20 Manchester Metropolitan	12.0	350	85.4	89.5	86.4	84.2
21 Queen Margaret, Edinburgh		318	88.4	89.1	94.4	84.0
22 Glasgow Caledonian	8.1	331	83.0	86.9	91.2	83.4
23 Leicester	36.5	411	79.8	86.4	66.4	83.3
24 Nottingham	26.5	415	83.5	85.5	66.7	82.8
25 St George's, London	20.0	358	70.9	71.0	96.0	82.7
26 Northampton		267	83.7	87.4	98.4	82.3
27 Keele	16.5	349	93.1	94.0	61.2	81.2
=28 Central Lancashire	8.3	356	84.8	88.1	72.2	80.4
=28 Sheffield Hallam	10.4	334*	94.1	94.9	61.8	80.4
30 Portsmouth	8.1	344	87.7	88.3	69.6	80.0
31 Coventry	4.5	286	90.6	94.6	71.7	79.6
32 Reading	26.6	367	72.8	82.8	68.3	79.3
33 Plymouth		340	81.5	83.2	76.0	78.4
34 Bangor		320	75.2	79.5	83.3	77.8
35 Edinburgh	52.8		69.8	82.3	60.7	77.7
36 Ulster		321	75.7	87.3	76.3	77.1
37 Oxford Brookes	21.3	323	76.5	79.3	65.2	77.0
38 East London		338	78.4	82.3	72.8	76.9
39 Cardiff Metropolitan		341	63.3	51.1	96.2	75.9
40 Derby	1.6	265	83.5	83.5		75.5
41 Westminster	21.2	302	69.3	80.1	62.8	74.5

Employed in professional job:	38%	Employed in non-professional job and studying:	3%
Employed in professional job and studying:	4%	Employed in non-professional job:	16%
Studying:	30%	Unemployed:	10%
Average starting professional salary:	£22,292	Average starting non-professional salary:	£15,530

Animal Science

A record 11,685 students applied for animal science courses in 2015 – twice as many as in 2007. Acceptances were up as well, to 2,860, in spite of the subject finishing rock bottom of the employment table with 60 per cent of graduates either unemployed or in non-professional jobs. The animal science table was first published only two years ago and was a reflection of growing interest in the group of subjects under this heading. Extracted from the agriculture category, degree courses range from animal behaviour to equine science and veterinary nursing.

Again there are big changes in the table, with Glasgow leaping to the top from eighth place last year, when it suffered from a poor year for graduate employment. Surrey, last year's leader, still has the highest entry standards and the best graduate prospects, but is handicapped because it did not enter the Research Excellence Framework in this category. Many of the other employment scores are worryingly low, albeit better than in the last

Animal Science cont

edition of the *Guide*. Three universities are below 20 per cent for positive destinations, one of them below 5 per cent. The subject has also slipped into the bottom five for salaries in graduate jobs, despite a £1,000 increase, which took the average to £19,373.

For all its problems in the employment market, animal science does not do badly in terms of student satisfaction. Five universities, led by Nottingham Trent, have ratings of at least 90 per cent in the three teaching sections of the National Student Survey, and the same is true in relation to the broader student experience, where third-placed Reading satisfied 97 per cent of final-year undergraduates. Reading also achieved the best results in the Research Excellence Framework, but only 12 of the 18 universities in the table entered.

Animal Science	Research quality %	Entry standards	Teaching quality %	Student experience %	Graduate prospects %	Overall score
1 Glasgow	42.3	471	79.1	82.4	70.6	100.0
2 Surrey		477	85.0	92.2	83.3*	96.2
3 Reading	50.7	369	93.5	97.0	30.0	96.0
4 Nottingham	36.4	386	79.0	87.8	68.6	94.9
5 Liverpool	32.9	438	69.9	87.5	53.7	92.9
6 Aberystwyth	38.2	320	89.2	89.8	40.3	90.6
7 Lincoln		381	93.0	93.8	60.8	90.2
8 Royal Veterinary College		394	87.4	88.8	58.2	88.7
9 Middlesex		361	94.5	86.6	60.0	88.5
=10 Harper Adams	5.7	363	85.9	90.0	31.1	84.5
=10 Nottingham Trent	4.1	304	95.6	92.3	38.8	84.5
12 Anglia Ruskin	24.6	295	77.9	81.8	37.9	82.9
13 Greenwich	19.5	324			31.5	82.5
14 Oxford Brookes	21.3		93.3	80.2	3.6	82.4
15 Bristol	33.2	366	66.7	67.4	11.1	80.4
16 Plymouth		342	82.9	84.3	22.2	79.7
17 Chester	7.9	345	69.4	74.2	15.9	76.4
18 Canterbury Christ Church		256	76.8	75.4	25.7	73.4

Employed in professional job:	21%	Employed in non-professional job and studying:	4%
Employed in professional job and studying:	1%	Employed in non-professional job:	50%
Studying:	13%	Unemployed:	10%
Average starting professional salary:	£19,373	Average starting non-professional salary:	£16,431

Anthropology

The unexpected rise of anthropology since the introduction of £9,000 fees continued in 2015, with further growth in applications and acceptances. Although still small, at 1,600, the numbers starting courses had doubled in four years and, with six applications to the place, there is scope for continued expansion. Instead of prompting a decline, as its own association predicted, higher charges have coincided with an extraordinary increase in the demand for places. Some attribute the subject's rise in popularity to television series, but there has been no firm explanation. Much of the growth has come in joint Honours degrees, pairing the subject with everything from accountancy to linguistics or law. The number of universities in the table has jumped from 20 to 30 in two years, and 48 have courses advertised for 2017 on the UCAS website.

There are no subject-specific requirements for most degree courses, although some Russell Group universities favour candidates with biology or another science at AS level. The subject has tended to be the preserve of old universities, but there are ten post-1992 institutions in the latest table. Cambridge maintains its accustomed leadership, but University College London and Oxford – tied together in second place – are only a fraction of a point behind. The most satisfied students are at East London, only eight places off the bottom in 22nd place, which boasts unusually high scores in both of the measures derived from the National Student Survey.

Employment prospects will be the main concern of those considering a degree in anthropology. Although it has moved out of the bottom 20 for the proportion of graduates going into "professional" jobs or further study after a marked improvement in the latest survey, seven of the 30 universities reported positive destinations for fewer than half of their graduates. Only two universities, Birmingham and Sussex, reached over 80 per cent on this measure. The picture is similar in salary terms. Anthropology is only just outside the bottom 20 of the 67 subject groups for those who do secure graduate-level jobs, although average salaries rose by more than £1,000 in 2015.

Anthropology	Research quality %	Entry standards	Teaching quality %	Student experience %	Graduate prospects %	Overall score
1 Cambridge	40.4	550	83.0	81.6	76.2	100.0
=2 Oxford	38.8	522	85.7	82.7	74.8	99.4
=2 University College London	49.3	480	83.4	89.5	69.7	99.4
4 St Andrews	25.0	507	94.0	95.4	70.0	99.0
5 London School of Economics	41.3	478	81.4	88.8	73.2	97.8
=6 Queen's, Belfast	49.0	334	92.4	92.1	60.8	95.8
=6 Sussex	34.4	391	82.4	87.1	84.1	95.8
8 Birmingham	50.9	330	80.0	71.3	87.6	95.4
9 Manchester	36.7	400	85.2	88.3	70.4	94.9
10 Edinburgh	42.2	480	74.2	85.4	61.1	93.5
11 Durham	29.1	484	73.4	77.8	74.6	92.6
12 SOAS London	31.1	432	87.1	87.3	53.1	92.0
13 Kent	20.5	354	87.2	89.3	68.6	90.7
14 Bristol	11.2	389	86.4	87.2	71.8	90.1
15 Aberdeen	31.8	402	86.0	88.8	45.5	89.7
=16 Bournemouth	19.9	319	89.4	89.9	63.8	89.2
=16 East Anglia	38.6		84.2	76.7	54.5*	89.2
18 Goldsmiths, London	34.5	341	84.0	83.1	54.8	88.9
19 Liverpool John Moores	15.1	332	91.3	94.2	58.1	88.6
20 Brunel	29.3	331	89.9	94.3	41.0	87.9
21 Roehampton	27.7	258	88.2	88.3	59.8	87.6

Anthropology cont	Research quality %	Entry standards	Teaching quality %	Student experience %	Graduate prospects %	Overall score
22 East London	13.7	252	96.9	97.9	51.4	86.6
23 Leeds		411	83.3	85.1	63.8	86.1
24 Stirling		395*	89.0	91.8	51.4	85.6
25 Chester	6.4		83.1	76.6	64.6*	85.3
26 Oxford Brookes	17.3	331	86.4	86.4	46.9	84.8
27 Sheffield Hallam		307*	82.4	81.4	46.4	79.0
28 South Wales		318*	70.5	77.3	36.4	73.9
29 Southampton Solent		253*	72.3	78.9	42.6	73.7
30 Birmingham City	3.8	314*	72.1	62.3	32.3	72.5

Employed in professional job:	36%	Employed in non-professional job and studying:	3%
Employed in professional job and studying:	2%	Employed in non-professional job:	22%
Studying:	22%	Unemployed:	14%
Average starting professional salary:	£21,206	Average starting non-professional salary:	£16,553

Archaeology and Forensic Science

Archaeology and forensic science are in the bottom three for starting salaries in professional jobs, but 43 per cent of graduates do not find this level of employment in any case. Some are not looking for career advancement – degrees in archaeology attract retired people as well as younger students – while others are well aware that archaeologists are not highly paid. Nevertheless, the subjects were among the few to suffer a decline in salary levels since the last survey. With only 455 starting degrees in 2015 – slightly more than in the previous year – some fluctuation is inevitable. Applications have yet to regain the levels seen before £9,000 fees arrived, but the 2015 total of 2,200 was a slight improvement on 2014.

The top six in the table are identical to last year, but Durham has closed the gap on Cambridge to a fraction of a point. Cambridge has the highest entry standards, while Dundee achieved the best results in the Research Excellence Framework. De Montfort, in 21st place overall, is the only university to see more than 85 per cent of its graduates go straight into professional jobs or start postgraduate courses. Manchester and Coventry tied for the highest levels of satisfaction with the quality of teaching, while Derby, in 32nd place overall, had the best scores in the other sections of the National Student Survey.

There are no specific subject requirements for a degree in archaeology, although geography, history and science subjects are all considered relevant. The growing number of universities offering archaeology or forensic science has had the effect of spreading out entry scores, which now range from less than 250 points to 550. Only eight of the 56 universities in the ranking averaged more than 400 points in 2015. More than a quarter of all archaeologists and forensic scientists stay on for a postgraduate qualification, either full or part-time, but almost one in three starts work in a "non-professional" job.

Archaeology and Forensic Science	Research quality %	Entry standards	Teaching quality %	Student experience %	Graduate prospects %	Overall score
1 Cambridge	47.2	550	83.0	81.6	76.6	100.0
2 Durham	41.2	461	88.5	91.5	82.9	99.8
3 Oxford	42.9	538	86.2	80.6	72.7	98.9
4 Dundee	55.4	447	87.4	86.0	68.4	98.2
5 University College London	51.4	432	91.0	94.2	60.8	97.6
6 Glasgow	16.4	470	92.8	88.7	81.0	96.4
7 York	35.1	375	92.8	91.8	68.4	94.6
8 Newcastle	25.8	391	91.2	87.3	76.1	94.0
9 Manchester	24.7	358	94.5	94.0	72.9	93.8
10 Leicester	37.2	376	87.7	89.8	70.1	93.7
11 Liverpool	33.5	377	89.3	87.7	68.4	93.0
12 Exeter	33.6	425	80.8	77.0	78.5	92.9
13 Reading	44.7	340	92.0	92.1	57.0	92.8
14 Birmingham	40.3	393	78.7	70.5	82.0	92.3
15 Southampton	43.5	357	82.4	89.3	66.4	92.1
16 Sheffield	31.6	364	85.5	88.4	65.7	90.9
17 Middlesex	21.1		89.2	85.9	63.3	89.9
18 Nottingham	23.7	390	85.6	81.2	66.7	89.8
19 Swansea	39.4	301	82.0	79.2	75.0	89.7
20 Kent	33.1	346	82.5	85.6	61.5	88.8
21 De Montfort		294	91.7	90.1	85.7	88.7
22 Plymouth	25.8		91.3	89.5	46.2*	87.6
23 Edinburgh	20.9	458	75.1	78.6	60.0	87.5
24 Bradford	23.0	207	83.9	80.7	73.9	86.5
25 Robert Gordon	8.8	351	78.5	88.1	73.7	86.4
26 Keele		364	87.6	88.1	64.4	86.1
27 Queen's, Belfast	36.9	336	85.9	85.8	38.9	86.0
28 Hull	31.7	330	77.3	81.9	56.7	85.4
29 Coventry		312	94.5	92.6	52.2	84.5
=30 Bournemouth	19.9	304	83.0	83.3	57.5	84.4
=30 Liverpool John Moores		352	88.4	89.7	55.2	84.4
32 Derby		290	90.7	94.5	56.9	83.9
33 Teesside		330	84.9	91.8	58.2	83.6
34 Staffordshire		317	89.3	90.1	54.3	83.4
35 Winchester	7.5	255	86.5	87.1	63.0	83.0
36 West of Scotland		329	81.5	92.0	58.9	82.9
37 West of England		343	85.4	84.5	53.9	82.6
38 Huddersfield		353	74.8	75.3	73.1	82.4
39 Aberdeen	29.4		77.9	66.6	57.9	82.1
=40 Cardiff	31.1	310	73.0	78.8	49.6	82.0
=40 Nottingham Trent	4.1	293	81.8	82.9	62.9	82.0
42 Greenwich		304	83.5	92.2	54.9	81.9
43 Lincoln		330	75.1	88.5	62.3	81.5

Archaeology and Forensic Science cont	Research quality %	Entry standards	Teaching quality %	Student experience %	Graduate prospects %	Overall score
44 West London		307	80.4	87.3	59.3	81.4
=45 Chester	15.4	292	85.5	71.8	50.0	81.3
=45 Worcester	8.1	279	76.8	82.3	65.2	81.3
47 Anglia Ruskin	24.6	238	78.8	84.1	53.0	81.2
48 Central Lancashire	9.8	343	76.7	81.4	48.9	80.7
49 Glasgow Caledonian	4.7	391	73.9	76.8	50.0	80.4
50 Kingston	6.9		80.7	77.8	52.4	80.1
51 Birmingham City		309	69.1	76.8	64.4	78.2
52 South Wales		311	80.1	83.8	42.6	78.1
53 Canterbury Christ Church	16.3	241	77.2	74.0	47.2	77.4
54 London South Bank		236	86.3	86.2	33.3	75.9
55 Cumbria	1.5	231	83.1	83.8	27.3	73.9
56 Manchester Metropolitan		332	75.5	75.8	21.7	73.1

Employed in professional job:	34%	Employed in non-professional job and studying:	4%
Employed in professional job and studying:	2%	Employed in non-professional job:	28%
Studying:	20%	Unemployed:	11%
Average starting professional salary:	£19,255	Average starting non-professional salary:	£15,664

Architecture

Three years into their careers, architects are among the least likely of all graduates to say that they wished they had taken a different degree or chosen a different profession. It is not a matter of money, at that stage at least – architecture is not in the top 50 subjects for starting salaries, although earning potential is much greater later for successful architects. The workload on degree courses is above average (16 hours a week, compared to 14 for all subjects) but initial employment prospects are good: architecture is in the top 15 of the 67 subject groups for the proportion of graduates finding high-level work or continuing to study. Seven out of ten graduates went straight into a professional role in 2015.

Applications were up in 2015, but the subject is yet to recover the popularity it had established before £9,000 fees were introduced. The length of courses may be one reason that architecture is yet to share fully in the recovery taking place in other subjects. Qualification usually takes seven years, in which the first degree is but a step on the way. That is a considerable financial commitment, especially when course materials can add another £1,000 to the burden. Nevertheless, there were still close to six applications per place in 2015 and satisfaction rates are higher after graduation than during the course itself.

Bath has taken the lead from Cambridge, surprisingly posting higher entry standards, while Sheffield has moved up to third place. The University of the West of England boasts the highest levels of satisfaction in both of the indicators derived from the National Student Survey, while Strathclyde was the most successful in terms of graduate prospects. The table contains one name that may be unfamiliar: Manchester School of Architecture is a joint enterprise between Manchester and Manchester Metropolitan universities.

Architecture

	Research quality %	Entry standards	Teaching quality %	Student experience %	Graduate prospects %	Overall score
1 Bath	52.9	576	92.3	91.3	94.5	100.0
2 Cambridge	49.0	535	82.8	83.7	96.0	96.0
3 Sheffield	36.6	462	94.6	95.9	88.6	93.6
4 University College London	54.1	515	75.9	72.7	90.9	92.6
5 Cardiff	40.7	489	83.9	80.6	88.7	91.5
6 Newcastle	43.7	495	78.1	81.9	88.6	91.2
7 Edinburgh	35.1	499	73.3	82.6	89.2	89.3
8 Nottingham	14.8	448	90.1	91.2	91.0	88.9
9 Liverpool	43.5	438	75.2	76.3	86.8	88.0
10 Strathclyde	23.0	477	74.1	70.9	96.7	87.4
11 Kent	33.3	405	74.5	83.1	89.0	86.5
12 West of England	10.6	340	95.9	96.8	88.8	86.3
13 Dundee	8.7	404	83.9	87.3	94.4	86.0
14 Queen's, Belfast	35.2	352	87.0	88.9	78.9	85.8
15 Oxford Brookes	17.6	429	84.0	83.3	81.8	84.7
16 Manchester School of Architecture	12.6	457	75.6	80.7	86.2	84.0
17 Cardiff Metropolitan		277	95.4	94.1	95.2	83.9
=18 Brighton	13.1	328	91.3	89.5	84.6	83.7
=18 Lincoln	3.2	370	91.5	92.4	84.8	83.7
20 Northumbria	5.9	398	85.7	85.2	86.4	83.5
21 Edinburgh Napier	5.7	396	76.2	86.2	92.9	83.4
22 Robert Gordon	8.3	400	74.3	79.9	90.5	82.3
23 Nottingham Trent	3.4	296	94.3	93.0	82.7	81.7
24 Coventry	10.3	317	87.1	85.9	82.2	81.2
25 Arts University, Bournemouth	2.4	307	86.1	86.5	87.5	80.8
=26 De Montfort	35.9	290	66.0	71.6	87.5	80.5
=26 Huddersfield		324	86.3	89.8	84.0	80.5
28 University for the Creative Arts	3.4	316	85.2	88.1	84.1	80.4
29 Plymouth	13.2	308	80.4	81.5	82.9	79.9
30 Liverpool John Moores	4.9	342	86.4	87.0	77.0	79.8
31 Westminster	10.7	361	86.6	87.4	69.9	79.7
32 Portsmouth		325	82.6	89.1	81.5	79.2
33 Birmingham City	9.6	304	85.7	87.9	75.3	79.1
34 Ulster	28.6	294	67.5	75.5	82.7	79.0
35 Central Lancashire	3.0	325	77.6	78.6	84.4	78.3
36 Salford	19.6	316	89.1	91.3	59.2	78.2
37 London Metropolitan	7.2	313	83.3	82.0	76.3	78.1
38 Sheffield Hallam	13.4	312	76.4	82.8	76.5	78.0
39 London South Bank	19.6	255	87.4	90.3	67.1	77.9
=40 University of the Arts London		335	79.3	78.9	78.8	77.1
=40 Leeds Beckett	5.6	274	79.6	84.8	79.4	77.1
42 Derby	6.7	270	79.1	83.3	79.0	76.8

Architecture cont	Research quality %	Entry standards	Teaching quality %	Student experience %	Graduate prospects %	Overall score
43 Greenwich	2.0	352	76.6	77.0	76.0	76.6
44 Anglia Ruskin	5.2	235	83.6	82.7	78.8	76.2
45 Northampton		254	87.4	82.3	73.7	75.4
46 East London	8.1	298	90.8	90.3	54.8	74.9
47 Kingston	10.1	319	68.9	76.0	72.7	74.7
48 Southampton Solent		262	86.9	85.0	67.2	74.3
49 Middlesex	13.3	249	82.4	80.9	64.7	74.2
50 Bedfordshire		254	88.1	83.0	54.5	71.0
51 Bolton	2.5		60.3	70.6	75.0	69.6
52 Glasgow Caledonian	9.1		46.9	55.7	59.3	59.0

Employed in professional job:	65%	Employed in non-professional job and studying:	0%
Employed in professional job and studying:	5%	Employed in non-professional job:	9%
Studying:	10%	Unemployed:	11%
Average starting professional salary:	£19,864	Average starting non-professional salary:	£16,149

Art and Design

The numbers starting courses in both fine art and design were at near-record levels in 2015, almost reaching the levels seen before £9,000 fees were introduced. Always one of the most popular choices for students, there were more than 19,000 enrolments in design degrees, with demand still strong in 2016. The same was true in fine art, with more than 25,000 applications and close to 5,000 acceptances. Only nursing attracts more applications than art and design, taken together, despite the fact that the subjects always feature in the lower reaches of the tables for employment and earnings. They remain just outside the bottom ten for the numbers going into graduate-level jobs or further study, but in the bottom five for starting salaries. However, artists and designers have always accepted that they are likely to have a period of lowly paid self-employment early in their career while they find a way to pursue their vocation.

Most courses in art and design are at post-1992 institutions – including several specialist arts universities – but older foundations fill the top 13 places. Newcastle tops the table for the first time, moving up from fourth place with good scores across the board. Oxford, last year's leader, has much the highest entry standards, but Winchester, which is just inside the top 40 largely because it did not enter the Research Excellence Framework, has the best graduate prospects. Only 15 of the 82 universities average 400 points or more, but most artists would argue that entry grades are of less significance than in other subjects. Selection in art and design rests primarily on the quality of candidates' portfolios, and many undergraduates enter through a one-year Art Foundation course.

Aberystwyth has the highest levels of student satisfaction with teaching, feedback and academic support – up almost 15 percentage points on last year – and has jumped 40 places in the table as a result of its overall performance in the National Student Survey. Worcester just pipped it to the best score for student satisfaction with the broader student experience, despite finishing only just inside the top 40 in the table.

Art and Design

		Research quality %	Entry standards	Teaching quality %	Student experience %	Graduate prospects %	Overall score
1	Newcastle	37.3	497	92.5	91.8	70.6	100.0
2	University College London	44.7	454	89.8	91.8	71.4	99.2
3	Oxford	39.7	577	72.3	80.3	68.0	95.8
4	Leeds	33.6	444	87.7	87.1	66.3	95.3
5	Loughborough	35.3	473	80.6	81.9	73.2	95.2
6	Kent	44.3	400	81.6	83.8	73.8	94.8
7	Lancaster	48.0	416	82.3	83.9	60.1	93.6
8	Glasgow	37.2	505*	70.1	77.3	75.0	93.5
=9	Brunel	32.8	369	80.6	80.8	84.0	93.4
=9	Reading	38.9	372	84.2	83.8	71.3	93.4
11	Heriot-Watt	31.1	388	84.6	86.4	70.8	93.2
12	Dundee	39.9	369	87.2	87.1	62.5	93.1
13	Aberystwyth	21.6	360	94.8	91.9	58.4	92.2
14	West of England	15.0	361	92.2	91.5	63.9	91.6
=15	Falmouth	3.0	344	87.8	87.9	83.6	91.4
=15	Manchester Metropolitan	9.7	439	86.9	84.1	66.2	91.4
=15	Southampton	35.4	384	85.5	82.1	59.8	91.4
18	Lincoln	7.1	347	93.0	91.7	67.8	91.1
19	Kingston	10.1	413	86.0	84.9	68.9	91.0
20	Northumbria	13.3	412	85.2	87.3	63.5	90.6
21	Bangor		310	89.1	83.8	87.5	90.4
22	Ulster	57.2	314	79.3	80.6	59.0	90.3
=23	Essex	46.9	250	91.2	91.5	51.9	90.2
=23	Goldsmiths, London	25.9	445	82.3	83.3	53.2	90.2
25	Coventry	18.1	359	84.8	85.3	67.5	89.9
26	Westminster	22.5	400	85.5	84.5	55.1	89.7
27	Edinburgh	27.9	475	75.8	75.2	56.9	89.4
28	Nottingham Trent	4.7	363	82.0	84.2	76.7	89.1
29	Hull	11.2		88.2	89.2	55.6	88.7
30	Portsmouth		362	92.6	90.2	57.8	88.5
31	Middlesex	13.3	342	84.6	84.8	65.9	88.4
32	Robert Gordon	11.5	376	87.1	82.8	58.4	88.2
33	De Montfort	10.2	331	82.3	83.2	73.2	88.1
34	Bath Spa	9.6	363	86.6	83.4	59.6	87.7
35	London Metropolitan	4.7	316	89.5	87.7	61.8	87.4
36	Bournemouth	15.0	310	79.7	77.8	74.1	86.9
37	Huddersfield	4.8	349	83.4	81.5	65.8	86.7
=38	Winchester		278	78.9	80.3	88.2	86.5
=38	Worcester	11.1	294	91.8	92.7	49.0	86.5
40	Teesside	2.9	311	90.4	90.5	54.9	86.4
41	Gloucestershire		344	89.8	90.5	49.8	85.9
42	Norwich University of the Arts	5.6	398	78.3	78.1	61.3	85.8
43	Arts University, Bournemouth	2.4	317	81.7	81.5	67.8	85.3

Art and Design cont

	Research quality %	Entry standards	Teaching quality %	Student experience %	Graduate prospects %	Overall score
=44 Anglia Ruskin	8.5	323	85.7	85.8	52.2	85.2
=44 Cardiff Metropolitan	7.9	286	84.9	83.4	62.4	85.2
=44 Edinburgh Napier		390	77.7	78.5	64.1	85.2
=47 Abertay		375	80.3	77.2	61.3	84.7
=47 Birmingham City	9.6	356	83.6	81.5	48.7	84.7
=47 Hertfordshire	5.8	311	78.3	76.4	71.4	84.7
50 Brighton	13.1	341	81.3	75.9	56.0	84.6
=51 London South Bank	12.8	259	85.5	86.9	55.0	84.4
=51 Sheffield Hallam	15.5	309	80.5	82.6	54.7	84.4
=51 Sunderland	9.8	314	82.6	82.7	55.2	84.4
54 Liverpool Hope		350	86.9	78.9	52.2	84.3
=55 Chichester		295	85.6	87.3	56.4	84.1
=55 University for the Creative Arts	3.4	328	83.4	82.4	54.8	84.1
57 Staffordshire	2.3	315	85.4	88.6	49.8	84.0
=58 Derby	5.1	350	80.8	80.9	53.5	83.9
=58 Greenwich	3.5	382	78.8	74.5	56.9	83.9
=58 Wrexham Glyndŵr	7.8	279	85.3	84.9	54.5	83.9
61 University of the Arts London	8.0	334	77.9	74.8	62.3	83.8
62 Canterbury Christ Church	7.3	302	84.2	82.4	51.3	83.4
63 Liverpool John Moores	7.2	370	79.0	80.1	48.1	83.3
64 Chester	6.2	328	82.7	80.4	49.7	83.1
=65 Oxford Brookes	10.4	347	82.4	77.3	44.4	82.9
=65 Suffolk		313	89.3	84.7	42.9	82.9
67 Salford	8.0	343	82.3	79.7	44.3	82.7
68 Central Lancashire	3.9	307	80.0	79.2	56.6	82.6
69 Cumbria	6.1	343	77.8	79.5	50.0	82.3
=70 Buckinghamshire New	6.1	254	83.7	80.0	56.5	82.2
=70 South Wales	3.3	309	78.1	79.2	57.3	82.2
72 York St John		314	81.4	75.5	56.6	82.1
73 Leeds Beckett	1.2	292	84.2	83.4	47.6	81.8
=74 East London	9.8	286	85.3	83.1	40.0	81.7
=74 Northampton	2.9	305	82.7	81.2	47.1	81.7
76 Plymouth	14.7	317	78.3	81.0	40.8	81.4
=77 Bolton		313	82.0	80.8	46.8	81.3
=77 Glasgow Caledonian	1.8	416	68.3	79.9	47.8	81.3
79 Highlands and Islands		290	76.8	81.4	56.8	81.1
80 Southampton Solent	1.6	282	80.2	81.5	47.3	80.2
81 West London	4.5	295	73.0	69.5	55.1	79.0
82 Bedfordshire		215	84.6	87.5	30.8	77.0

Employed in professional job:	51%	Employed in non-professional job and studying:	1%
Employed in professional job and studying:	1%	Employed in non-professional job:	30%
Studying:	5%	Unemployed:	11%
Average starting professional salary:	£19,669	Average starting non-professional salary:	£15,796

Biological Sciences

Another increase in enrolments in 2016 confirmed the biological sciences as the most popular choice for those seeking a classic science degree. Record numbers had started courses in biology itself in 2015, as a 10 per cent increase in places took the total beyond 7,000 for the first time – almost 1,000 more than in 2013. Applications have been rising in parallel and there are more than five to every place. The demand for places on more specialist courses, in botany, zoology, genetics and microbiology, remains strong but has not matched the growth in general biology degrees. Graduates are less enthusiastic, however: three years after graduation one in three biologists wish they had chosen a different subject – one of the biggest proportions in the arts or sciences.

Cambridge and Oxford (in that order) make it 12 years in a row at the head of the table. But there is plenty of movement in the rest of the table, notably at Edinburgh, which followed last year's rise of 13 places with a similar decline in this edition. King's College London enjoyed the biggest rise: up 17 places to ninth in the table. Cambridge's Natural Sciences degree boasts some of the highest entry grades in any subject, averaging 636 points. Nationally, microbiology provides the stiffest competition, with more than six applications to the place, but the leading universities' requirements can be tough across the whole area. Many will demand two sciences at A level, or the equivalent – usually biology and chemistry – for any of the biological sciences.

The most satisfied students are to be found at Lincoln, which is outside the top 50 overall, having chosen not to enter the 2014 Research Excellence Framework in this category. Satisfaction with the broader student experience there was over 95 per cent, while the result for teaching, feedback and academic support was 24 percentage points higher than at fourth-placed Imperial College. Employment rates and graduate salaries are surprisingly modest, with the biological sciences outside the top 40 for both. More than a third of graduates stay on for a postgraduate qualification, either full- or part-time, but the 12 per cent unemployment rate is above average for all subjects.

Biological Sciences	Research quality %	Entry standards	Teaching quality %	Student experience %	Graduate prospects %	Overall score
1 Cambridge	52.5	636	86.6	86.9	87.4	100.0
2 Oxford	50.9	573	81.0	85.1	83.9	96.1
3 University College London	55.4	509	77.5	85.3	82.3	94.0
4 Imperial College	61.6	541	69.1	81.0	83.3	93.7
5 Sheffield	57.4	445	82.8	91.8	76.1	93.3
6 St Andrews	37.6	501	87.8	91.6	71.8	92.1
=7 Surrey	37.5	422	88.2	90.0	82.0	91.9
=7 Sussex	46.8	389	81.7	87.8	87.9	91.9
9 King's College London	38.0	490	81.8	87.8	78.4	91.5

	Research quality %	Entry standards	Teaching quality %	Student experience %	Graduate prospects %	Overall score
Biological Sciences cont						
10 Warwick	37.1	435	90.1	89.8	75.8	91.3
11 York	41.9	477	83.2	89.6	73.3	91.2
12 Durham	32.9	547	75.5	84.0	80.1	90.9
13 Manchester	38.3	460	82.9	87.9	77.0	90.7
14 Exeter	39.7	457	84.3	90.2	72.0	90.4
15 Dundee	55.4	446	85.1	87.7	62.1	90.2
16 Birmingham	38.1	418	82.5	85.4	80.8	89.9
17 Edinburgh	62.9	503	73.0	83.1	61.8	89.8
18 Leeds	40.9	429	79.0	87.8	78.2	89.7
19 Lancaster	46.5	411	78.5	85.6	78.0	89.6
20 Strathclyde	52.2	450	77.6	85.3	68.7	89.4
21 Bristol	46.8	465	75.7	84.6	70.8	89.0
22 Queen's, Belfast	47.3	375	83.5	91.1	69.0	88.7
23 Bath	31.5	457	77.5	83.6	79.0	88.5
24 Glasgow	33.4	499	79.3	83.4	69.5	88.3
=25 Aberdeen	34.7	431	84.2	88.6	68.6	88.1
=25 Kent	39.1	352	85.2	90.2	73.8	88.1
27 East Anglia	38.8	411	81.7	89.0	69.7	88.0
28 Swansea	38.6	331	83.5	88.4	77.5	87.6
29 Southampton	34.2	398	80.9	90.8	71.0	87.3
30 Aston	39.1	372	79.4	87.1	72.6	86.8
31 Leicester	36.5	390	79.4	86.8	71.3	86.7
32 Nottingham	26.5	418	81.7	85.7	72.8	86.6
33 Liverpool	33.9	405	82.7	84.8	67.0	86.2
34 Newcastle	28.4	404	80.5	84.0	71.8	85.8
35 Brunel	18.2	345	87.8	93.3	70.6	85.2
36 Stirling	49.0	396	78.7	83.6	56.2	85.0
37 Nottingham Trent	24.1	313	88.6	90.5	69.8	84.9
38 Royal Holloway	25.7	391	83.3	84.8	66.9	84.8
39 Cardiff	33.3	397	73.5	84.0	65.7	83.8
40 Heriot-Watt	26.3	380	72.7	75.3	78.7	83.6
41 Keele	16.5	360	84.8	87.9	67.1	83.4
42 Oxford Brookes	21.3	323	81.9	88.6	70.1	83.3
43 St George's, London	20.0	409	70.3	75.4	78.9	83.1
=44 Queen Mary, London	26.1	421	66.9	75.6	74.7	82.8
=44 Reading	26.6	360	80.5	87.1	61.2	82.8
46 Portsmouth	24.3	317	81.4	84.3	69.7	82.7
47 Aberystwyth	38.2	298	82.6	86.0	56.0	82.0
48 Central Lancashire	8.3	347	82.0	81.1	74.0	81.9
49 Bath Spa		310	89.8	88.5	70.9	81.6
50 Bangor	31.5	374	77.9	83.6	54.6	81.5
=51 Bradford	9.5	301	78.3	86.2	77.2	81.4
=51 Glasgow Caledonian	8.1	395	78.5	81.1	68.6	81.4

53 Lincoln		334	93.6	95.1	57.1	81.2
54 Edinburgh Napier	8.9	376	80.4	81.4	65.7	80.8
55 West of Scotland	29.0	333	85.4	90.0	45.9	80.7
=56 Hull	31.7	336	74.4	82.2	59.3	80.6
=56 Sheffield Hallam	10.4	299	80.3	86.9	70.3	80.6
=58 Edge Hill	6.2	309	85.8	91.7	62.3	80.4
=58 Essex	17.8	313	81.0	85.6	62.1	80.4
=58 Huddersfield	7.8	310	78.5	83.7	73.5	80.4
61 Plymouth	17.4	341	85.1	83.3	55.9	80.3
62 Northumbria	14.0	345	74.6	83.4	67.7	80.2
=63 Abertay	4.3	343	80.2	83.1	68.1	80.0
=63 Liverpool Hope		271	89.2	86.2	70.3	80.0
=65 Robert Gordon	4.9	395	71.4	70.6	75.0	79.4
=65 Teesside		296	84.6	88.4	66.7	79.4
67 West of England	8.2	307	86.8	88.3	56.1	79.2
68 Ulster		289	82.8	92.3	64.5	79.0
69 Hertfordshire	10.9	277	73.0	78.2	77.1	78.8
70 Worcester	10.9	276	83.9	82.9	62.7	78.7
71 Manchester Metropolitan	12.0	346	78.8	81.3	56.6	78.4
72 Coventry	4.5	256	85.6	86.4	61.1	77.8
73 Bedfordshire	25.1	236	80.5	84.2	54.0	77.5
74 Sunderland	7.5	236	78.5	82.0	69.2	77.3
75 Cardiff Metropolitan		272	69.7	74.0	82.3	77.0
76 Gloucestershire	14.5	286	89.4	90.6	37.7	76.7
=77 Kingston	2.6	272	78.8	84.7	61.3	76.5
=77 Queen Margaret, Edinburgh		316	80.7	85.8	54.5	76.5
=77 Staffordshire		267	85.3	88.3	55.1	76.5
80 South Wales		327	70.7	81.6	59.6	76.4
81 Derby	1.6	302	86.0	89.3	46.7	76.3
=82 Leeds Beckett	3.5	272	72.7	80.0	68.3	76.2
=82 Liverpool John Moores	15.1	344	79.0	82.3	42.5	76.2
=82 Salford	12.7	323	79.4	83.6	46.1	76.2
85 Greenwich	7.4	305	70.4	85.8	58.9	76.1
86 Bolton		218	80.8	82.0	67.4	75.9
87 Brighton	4.8	288	73.0	81.8	60.5	75.5
88 Middlesex	10.0	271	62.4	85.1	66.7	75.4
89 Canterbury Christ Church	11.9	237	79.0	79.0	57.2	75.3
90 Bournemouth	4.7	299	81.1	81.8	49.0	75.1
91 Westminster	21.2	299	60.9	77.3	57.8	74.7
92 Roehampton	20.6	256	73.2	77.5	45.3	73.4
93 Anglia Ruskin	2.2	217	82.7	84.7	46.4	72.8
94 Chester	12.0	292	66.5	76.8	47.9	72.3
95 Northampton		267	75.6	74.8	47.9	71.4
96 London Metropolitan		258	68.0	76.7	54.8	71.3
97 London South Bank	35.0	226	39.0	64.9	51.9	67.6
98 Suffolk		353	51.4	63.2	46.2	67.1
99 East London		273	68.7	72.1	28.0	66.0

Biological Sciences cont

Employed in professional job:	31%	Employed in non-professional job and studying:	2%
Employed in professional job and studying:	3%	Employed in non-professional job:	22%
Studying:	30%	Unemployed:	12%
Average starting professional salary:	£20,634	Average starting non-professional salary:	£15,763

Building

Building is among the top eight subjects both for employment prospects and starting salaries in professional jobs, averaging £26,300 in 2015 after a rise of more than 10 per cent on the previous year. Nearly 80 per cent of those finishing degrees went straight into graduate-level jobs. Only recently has this encouraging message begun to filter through to sixth-forms and colleges, however. The numbers of applications and enrolments for building grew in 2015, but they are still at least 30 per cent lower than they were when the recession began in 2008. Applicants and careers advisers can be forgiven for not realising the scale of the improvement in the labour market: only four years ago, building was 40th in the employment table. But, with only four applications to the place and entry qualifications among the lowest in the *Guide*, the subject is surely a good bet once more.

The top two in the table remain unchanged, with University College London recording the highest entry grades on its project management for construction degree. Second-placed Loughborough achieved the best grades in the Research Excellence Framework, while fourth-placed Reading has the best graduate prospects. Derby managed unusually high levels of satisfaction for teaching, feedback and academic support – almost 98 per cent – while Edinburgh Napier was the star performer on the broader student experience. Only two universities slipped below 70 per cent satisfaction overall.

Courses in this category include surveying and building services engineering, as well as construction. The table is dominated by post-1992 universities, although older foundations take the top five places. No fewer than 88 institutions are offering courses in this area in 2017. Many are colleges, the majority of which focus on Foundation degrees and Higher National Diplomas.

Building	Research quality %	Entry standards	Teaching quality %	Student experience %	Graduate prospects %	Overall score
1 University College London	54.1	407	79.2	89.6	92.6	100.0
2 Loughborough	58.3	374	70.6	85.0	96.2	97.7
3 Heriot-Watt	38.1	395	78.2	85.7	96.6	97.3
4 Reading	40.0	356	80.7	87.3	97.9	96.8
5 Ulster	28.6	311	83.3	89.5	85.6	91.1
=6 Edinburgh Napier	5.7	327	91.2	93.3	86.2	90.5
=6 Nottingham	14.8	404	88.2	90.3	68.8	90.5
8 Oxford Brookes	17.6	297	80.5	90.0	95.2	90.4
9 West of England	10.6	323	78.8	85.2	95.0	89.5
10 Aston	20.6	344	72.5	84.3	89.5	89.4
11 Robert Gordon	8.3	366	74.3	76.1	94.3	89.0

12 East London	8.1		90.2	91.8	78.6	88.9
13 Liverpool John Moores	4.9	337	85.5	90.4	84.0	88.8
14 Glasgow Caledonian	9.1	359	73.6	80.2	89.0	87.9
15 Derby		315	97.7	91.7	75.0	87.7
16 Sheffield Hallam	13.4	289	83.6	90.3	84.3	87.6
17 Nottingham Trent	3.4	277	82.4	85.4	92.9	86.7
18 Portsmouth		289	78.4	82.2	96.4	86.3
19 Northumbria	5.9	353	72.6	77.2	85.9	86.0
20 Salford	19.6	310	74.4	76.1	82.3	85.6
21 Westminster	10.7	290	76.6	81.2	87.3	85.5
22 Anglia Ruskin	5.2	287	77.1	82.6	88.1	84.9
23 Brighton		275	78.4	79.0	94.3	84.8
24 Coventry	10.3	277	71.8	78.3	88.1	83.7
25 Leeds Beckett	5.6	271	72.5	78.8	88.2	82.9
26 Central Lancashire	3.0	299	76.9	81.3	76.9	82.5
27 Plymouth	13.2	254	74.4	80.7	76.9	81.5
28 Birmingham City	2.7	291	76.4	79.0	75.6	81.4
29 Southampton Solent		210*	88.5	89.0	68.8	79.5
30 Greenwich	2.0	292	66.0	68.3	77.5	78.5
31 Kingston		258	60.1	65.4	89.5	77.8
32 London South Bank	19.6	200	66.7	74.7	69.0	76.1
33 Bolton	2.5	229*	79.5	83.1	50.0	74.1

Employed in professional job:	79%	Employed in non-professional job and studying:		0%
Employed in professional job and studying:	3%	Employed in non-professional job:		8%
Studying:	3%	Unemployed:		7%
Average starting professional salary:	£26,316	Average starting non-professional salary:		£19,824

Business Studies

The various branches of business and management are the largest recruiters of undergraduates in the UK, with almost 60,000 students starting courses in 2016. That represented a 4 per cent increase on the previous year and nearly 10,000 more than when £9,000 fees were introduced. Management is the more competitive field, attracting nearly six applications for every place, one more than for business studies. The subjects are the mainstay of many new universities, but some of the most famous business schools are absent from this ranking because they do not offer undergraduate courses. Manchester Business School provides Manchester's undergraduate courses.

St Andrews is top of the table for the first time, moving up from third place last year partly because it has the best graduate prospects – an impressive 97 per cent of graduates found professional jobs or continued studying in 2015. Oxford remains second and has the highest entry scores, while Bath, last year's leader, has dropped to third. The highest levels of student satisfaction are to be found rather lower in the table. Harper Adams, which is only just inside the top 30 overall, secured the best scores in the National Student Survey (NSS) for teaching, feedback and academic support, while Bristol did best on the broader student experience. Student satisfaction is much higher throughout the table in relation to the

Business Studies cont

student experience than in the teaching sections of the NSS. Only two universities reached 90 per cent satisfaction on teaching, compared with ten for the student experience.

More than half of the institutions in one of our biggest tables are post-1992 universities, but only five appear in the top 50. Employment scores are extremely variable, ranging from 97 per cent at St Andrews to less than 40 per cent at East London. Overall, business and management have moved up the employment table this year, but still do not make the top 40. The subjects do much better in the earnings table, however. The average starting salary of almost £23,500 is just outside the top 20 this year, and the average of £22,221 in non-professional jobs is by some distance the highest in any subject. In spite of this, however, three years after graduation almost a third of respondents say they would have chosen a different subject.

	Business Studies	Research quality %	Entry standards	Teaching quality %	Student experience %	Graduate prospects %	Overall score
1	St Andrews	43.8	556	85.1	90.8	97.2	100.0
2	Oxford	32.0	581	77.1*	87.3*	91.4	95.7
3	Bath	41.8	487	80.5	88.9	90.0	95.5
4	University College London	43.9	499	78.2	84.8	89.8	95.0
5	Lancaster	42.6	417	84.2	90.6	89.4	94.9
=6	Loughborough	32.6	420	82.3	91.0	92.0	93.6
=6	Warwick	40.4	521	73.8	86.1	86.1	93.6
8	Strathclyde	44.3	492	81.0	90.7	71.1	93.5
9	King's College London	38.2	506	75.3	81.8	88.4	93.0
10	Leeds	39.3	440	79.6	87.0	83.3	92.5
11	Durham	23.1	441	81.6	86.4	90.1	91.7
12	London School of Economics	52.3	523	63.2	74.0	89.5	91.6
=13	Bristol	32.1	429	77.2	93.7	81.0	91.3
=13	Exeter	24.4	487	79.4	87.6	80.8	91.3
15	Nottingham	32.6	389	79.4	88.4	80.9	90.1
16	Sussex	23.7	373	81.0	87.4	89.0	89.9
17	Kent	24.8	377	81.1	88.8	84.8	89.8
18	York	24.0	385	83.9	88.2	78.0	89.4
19	Queen's, Belfast	32.7	369	80.5	89.3	75.3	89.1
=20	Aston	19.7	385	82.7	89.5	79.9	89.0
=20	Sheffield	26.8	388	79.4	88.7	79.0	89.0
22	Aberdeen	24.9	454	79.7	89.1	67.5	88.8
=23	Birmingham	29.1	410	73.1	82.6	87.0	88.7
=23	Manchester	33.3	419	74.3	85.1	77.3	88.7
=23	Reading	29.3	402	75.7	84.2	82.5	88.7
=26	City	27.8	417	76.1	83.7	76.4	88.0
=26	Leicester	24.3	391	83.8	86.7	68.5	88.0
28	Harper Adams		312	91.3	92.8	86.4	87.9
29	Surrey	15.8	414	79.1	88.6	76.5	87.7
30	Cardiff	32.0	403	73.3	83.9	72.1	86.9

31	Heriot-Watt	18.8	393	80.8	85.9	71.1	86.8
32	Keele	10.2	343	86.3	90.0	74.3	86.7
33	Liverpool	20.1	393	78.8	86.1	70.3	86.4
34	Newcastle	20.7	411	70.5	79.2	84.9	86.2
35	Ulster	40.4	300	82.8	90.2	55.3	86.1
=36	Dundee	12.1	412	79.7	84.8	70.5	85.8
=36	East Anglia	28.1	413	75.2	80.3	66.8	85.8
38	Coventry	1.6	314	86.4	89.3	76.9	85.1
39	Southampton	24.0	387	70.0	78.9	79.1	85.0
40	Robert Gordon	2.6	423	79.5	85.7	70.3	84.9
=41	Royal Holloway	27.0	418	75.4	82.2	58.2	84.8
=41	Stirling	25.2	385	73.7	82.9	67.3	84.8
43	Swansea	22.0	328	75.9	82.3	76.1	84.7
44	SOAS London	25.0	373	76.8	85.9	60.8	84.6
45	De Montfort	10.7	288	80.4	88.4	78.5	84.4
46	Buckingham		284	84.9	89.5	79.4	84.2
=47	Glasgow	22.1	426	66.4	78.3	74.0	84.0
=47	Portsmouth	9.5	332	78.0	85.3	76.1	84.0
49	Edinburgh	25.8	477	64.5	76.6	66.0	83.9
50	Bangor	23.4	323	82.2	83.0	58.7	83.7
=51	Lincoln	4.8	324	79.0	85.8	77.5	83.6
=51	Nottingham Trent	4.6	314	80.5	84.5	77.7	83.6
=53	Abertay		374	79.9	87.1	69.5	83.4
=53	Essex	25.1	296	79.3	84.1	62.8	83.4
=53	Falmouth		289	79.9	84.1	86.5	83.4
56	Huddersfield	4.1	331	82.5	87.6	67.1	83.2
57	Oxford Brookes	5.1	332	80.1	86.3	70.4	83.1
58	Queen Mary, London	23.5	411	70.2	76.7	63.3	82.9
=59	Bournemouth	8.8	321	78.6	84.7	69.6	82.7
=59	Hull	10.2	342	75.4	83.6	71.1	82.7
61	Aberystwyth	14.5	300	80.4	82.2	66.7	82.6
62	Northumbria	4.0	353	75.0	83.5	74.0	82.5
63	West of England	5.5	307	78.9	86.9	70.4	82.4
64	Plymouth	13.1	275	80.5	86.6	65.2	82.2
65	Central Lancashire	4.4	323	80.0	84.3	65.6	81.8
66	Liverpool John Moores		336	81.5	86.0	62.4	81.6
=67	Edge Hill		298	85.4	90.2	56.2	81.3
=67	Hertfordshire	0.9	300	79.9	88.1	66.3	81.3
=69	Liverpool Hope		293	85.3	89.3	57.6	81.2
=69	Sunderland	0.4	284	82.3	87.6	65.3	81.2
71	Manchester Metropolitan	4.7	335	73.9	82.8	68.7	81.0
72	Bradford	11.8	334	71.7	80.2	63.1	80.2
73	Brunel	23.0	353	68.0	79.2	55.8	80.1
=74	Anglia Ruskin	3.4	227	85.3	86.5	60.3	80.0
=74	Bath Spa		296	80.7	82.1	63.1	80.0
=74	Leeds Trinity		263	81.3	86.2	63.8	80.0
77	Newman		305	80.7	86.2	57.4	79.9

Business Studies cont		Research quality %	Entry standards	Teaching quality %	Student experience %	Graduate prospects %	Overall score
=78	Derby	0.9	268	81.1	84.3	61.9	79.7
=78	Edinburgh Napier	2.3	350	74.1	83.0	59.5	79.7
80	Sheffield Hallam	0.6	304	73.0	82.0	69.9	79.5
81	Glasgow Caledonian	1.8	405	70.2	82.2	56.0	79.4
=82	Gloucestershire		302	75.9	79.0	67.5	79.3
=82	Worcester	0.9	306	73.4	81.5	68.5	79.3
84	York St John	0.8	282	78.6	84.4	60.4	79.2
=85	Brighton	6.5	282	74.8	82.5	61.5	79.0
=85	Cumbria	5.6	244	90.5	86.3	40.9	79.0
87	West of Scotland	2.9	334	74.7	79.4	58.1	78.8
88	Southampton Solent		262	78.3	82.8	61.9	78.5
=89	Chester	0.5	282	72.2	78.5	71.1	78.4
=89	London South Bank	2.1	231	82.0	90.5	51.4	78.4
91	Royal Agricultural University		279	71.7	78.3	72.7	78.3
92	Birmingham City	1.3	288	79.7	82.6	52.5	78.2
93	Salford	5.9	296	76.7	85.1	47.1	77.9
94	Chichester		262	74.6	80.6	65.4	77.8
95	Bolton		291	75.5	79.1	58.6	77.5
96	St Mary's, Twickenham		260	80.0	83.9	50.0	77.2
97	Staffordshire	2.6	241	80.0	79.9	52.2	76.9
=98	University of the Arts London		345	73.3	73.4	53.6	76.8
=98	Teesside	2.0	260	80.2	79.6	49.0	76.8
=100	Middlesex	10.5	280	71.9	80.7	49.6	76.7
=100	Roehampton	4.5	253	70.9	77.2	64.4	76.7
=102	Greenwich	3.3	333	70.8	76.5	51.6	76.5
=102	Northampton	1.0	266	72.7	80.7	57.9	76.5
104	Winchester		281	67.4	74.6	69.2	76.4
105	Cardiff Metropolitan		298	68.6	75.1	63.7	76.3
106	Westminster	2.4	337	67.9	79.8	51.2	76.2
=107	Kingston	9.2	282	69.5	80.7	50.6	76.1
=107	Leeds Beckett	0.8	269	66.9	78.5	66.2	76.1
=109	Canterbury Christ Church		250	74.9	80.9	53.1	75.8
=109	West London		262	74.7	78.7	53.5	75.8
111	South Wales	0.2	332	68.0	75.8	53.0	75.5
112	Wrexham Glyndŵr		256	72.7	74.1	58.5	75.3
113	Queen Margaret, Edinburgh		297	76.0	78.1	42.3	75.2
114	Buckinghamshire New	1.8	265	73.4	77.1	49.6	75.0
115	East London	0.8	261	75.0	79.8	39.5	74.0
116	Suffolk		286	68.7	74.0	47.5	73.4
117	Bedfordshire	3.1	191	72.4	78.5	46.2	72.8
118	London Metropolitan	0.6	237	66.5	74.3	48.6	71.9

Employed in professional job:	54%	Employed in non-professional job and studying:	1%
Employed in professional job and studying:	3%	Employed in non-professional job:	24%
Studying:	7%	Unemployed:	11%
Average starting professional salary:	£23,476	Average starting non-professional salary:	£22,221

Celtic Studies

Only 175 students started full-time Celtic studies degrees in 2015, making it one of the smallest categories in the *Guide*. But that represented a 30 per cent increase on the previous year and took the subject above its levels of demand seen before the switch to higher fees, while the wider languages group was still struggling to attract students. The number of universities in our table remains at ten this year, although the total offering degree courses in 2017, either in Celtic studies or one of the Celtic languages, is down from 17 to 13.

The ranking is split between four universities from Wales, which naturally major in Welsh, and the remaining six, which focus on Irish or Gaelic studies. Ironically, it is the only one from England that tops the table for the fifth year in a row. Cambridge's average entry grades are almost 100 points ahead of its nearest rival and it posted the best scores in the 2014 Research Excellence Framework (REF). Aberystwyth, which is up to a share of third place in the latest table, has the highest satisfaction levels for teaching, feedback and academic support – more than 10 percentage points better than last year. Second-placed Queen's, Belfast did best on the other sections of the National Student Survey.

Swansea's rare 100 per cent rate for graduate prospects is the exception in terms of employment, although Aberystwyth also comes close to the 90 per cent mark. Although only 7 per cent of graduates nationally were unemployed at the time of the latest survey, Celtic studies has dropped out of the top half of the employment table. The small numbers make for extremely volatile results from year to year, especially for graduate prospects. However, for the second year in a row, Celtic studies had the largest proportion of graduates of any subject continuing their studies. The story is not as positive where graduate salaries are concerned: the average in graduate-level jobs was in the bottom ten of the 67 subject groupings and the figure for non-professional jobs was the lowest for any subject, at only £13,661.

Celtic Studies	Research quality %	Entry standards	Teaching quality %	Student experience %	Graduate prospects %	Overall score
1 Cambridge	54.0	538	92.6	89.8	65.6	100.0
2 Queen's, Belfast	53.6	363	90.4	93.8	58.7	93.0
=3 Aberystwyth	23.7	386	97.5	92.3	89.2	92.9
=3 Bangor	39.6	443	84.2	85.7	76.3	92.9
5 Glasgow	41.1		89.5	87.3	64.6	91.0
6 Cardiff	32.5	399	90.5	92.3	69.1	90.9
7 Swansea	19.4	328	87.7	88.9	100.0	89.2
8 Ulster	35.7	311	93.0	93.3	47.0	86.1
9 Liverpool	38.9		84.2	85.1	45*	84.2
10 Highlands and Islands			67.0	69.5	84.6	82.2

Celtic Studies cont

Employed in professional job:	21%
Employed in professional job and studying:	1%
Studying:	39%
Average starting professional salary:	£19,793

Employed in non-professional job and studying:	7%
Employed in non-professional job:	25%
Unemployed:	7%
Average starting non-professional salary:	£13,661

Chemical Engineering

Chemical engineering now has more than twice as many applicants and enrolments as it did at the start of the decade. Engineering degrees in general have been growing in popularity, but the chemical, process and energy courses have seen the biggest rises of all. There was a 16 per cent increase in applications in 2015, overtaking both civil and general engineering courses for the first time. High graduate salaries may have something to do with it: although the average salary in graduate-level jobs dropped slightly in 2015, the figure of £28,603 was bettered only by dentistry. The subject remains in the top fifteen for employment this year.

Cambridge tops the table for the 15th year in a row, with the highest entry standards, the best employment record and the top research score. Both Cambridge and second-placed Imperial were ranked by QS among the top six universities in the world for chemical engineering in 2016. By far the most satisfied students where teaching quality is concerned are those at West of Scotland, which was the highest-placed of five post-1992 universities in the table. Nottingham produced the best scores in the remaining sections of the National Student Survey.

Forty universities, one more than last year, plan to offer chemical engineering in 2017. They include specialist options such as petroleum engineering at London South Bank and chemistry with green nanotechnology at Wrexham Glyndŵr. Degree courses normally demand chemistry and maths A levels or their equivalent and often physics as well. Four out of five chemical engineers come with A levels or equivalent qualifications, and average entry grades are the highest for any engineering subject – more than half of the 27 universities in the table average at least 400 points at entry. This helps produce engineering's largest proportion of Firsts and 2:1s. Most courses offer industrial placements in the final year and lead to Chartered Engineer status.

Chemical Engineering	Research quality %	Entry standards	Teaching quality %	Student experience %	Graduate prospects %	Overall score
1 Cambridge	62.0	662	84.0	92.9	95.1	100.0
2 Imperial College	59.6	596	83.3	89.6	90.2	96.2
3 Birmingham	47.0	466	82.4	89.0	94.1	91.9
4 Bath	37.4	522	82.0	89.6	84.9	89.5
5 Manchester	48.4	506	72.5	85.5	82.8	88.0
6 Loughborough	41.8	432	77.6	88.8	85.0	86.9
7 Newcastle	30.2	436	80.9	89.3	86.2	86.3
=8 Heriot-Watt	47.8	428	65.8	80.8	88.0	85.6
=8 Nottingham	40.8	435	81.4	93.4	75.6	85.6
10 Surrey	30.8	440	80.1	90.3	80.0	84.8

11 Sheffield	36.8	401	72.5	88.2	85.9	84.7
=12 Edinburgh	50.3	500	55.3	67.3	85.5	83.9
=12 Strathclyde	37.2	513	62.6	81.1	81.4	83.9
14 University College London	44.6	491	68.5	80.1	75.3	83.8
15 Leeds	30.7	451	66.6	79.8	86.1	83.2
16 Swansea	45.5	352	70.6	74.7	83.3	82.3
=17 Lancaster	41.6	379	72.6	84.3		82.2
=17 West of Scotland	9.0	379	94.4	91.8	77.8	82.2
19 Queen's, Belfast	36.7	413	73.1	79.3	78.0	82.1
20 Hull	16.5	326	86.2	89.3		80.9
21 Bradford	7.7	318	86.3	91.5	79.6	79.5
22 Aberdeen	28.4	464	62.6	64.4	74.1	77.7
23 Huddersfield	10.2	305	80.1	82.2		76.5
24 Aston	20.6	351	69.3	77.8	71.2	75.5
25 Portsmouth	9.1	339	71.0	79.5	65.9	72.6
26 London South Bank	19.6	266	68.7	77.7	68.4	72.3
27 Teesside	5.8	318	77.3	85.9	57.5	71.2

Employed in professional job:	59%	Employed in non-professional job and studying:	1%
Employed in professional job and studying:	2%	Employed in non-professional job:	9%
Studying:	19%	Unemployed:	10%
Average starting professional salary:	£28,603	Average starting non-professional salary:	£17,187

Chemistry

For many, chemistry is the classic science, a stepping stone to numerous careers and research opportunities. Some courses require maths as well as chemistry, and most successful candidates for the leading universities take more than one science at A level. The skills acquired on degree courses are much in demand: chemistry is firmly established in the top 20 in the employment table, with more than a third of all graduates going on to further study. Starting salaries for graduates in professional jobs are also in the top 30, although four places lower in the earnings table than in the last edition of the *Guide*. Applications and enrolments both rose in 2015, as they had the previous year, with record numbers starting undergraduate courses. In 2017, 106 universities and colleges – 11 more than in the current academic year – plan to offer the subject.

Cambridge remains at the head of the table with the highest entry standards and the best research grades – 97 per cent of the work submitted for the Research Excellence Framework was considered world-leading or internationally excellent. Second-placed Oxford was the only university to see more than nine out of ten graduates go straight into professional jobs or embark on postgraduate study. Both Oxford and Cambridge are among the top six universities in the world for chemistry, according to QS. Keele, which shared 20th place overall, has the most satisfied students for its teaching quality, while Loughborough, one place lower, has the highest score for the broader student experience.

Chemistry is mainly old university territory, with no post-1992 institutions in the top 30, although Nottingham Trent remains only one place outside it. There are now 14 modern universities in the table as a whole, however, with Central Lancashire and Sheffield Hallam

Chemistry cont

also in the top 40. The contrast between the top and bottom of the table in terms of entry grades is starker than ever. While Cambridge entrants average 636 points and those at four other universities top 500 points, eight universities in the latest table average less than 300 points on the old UCAS tariff. Nearly nine out of ten undergraduates have A levels or their equivalent.

Chemistry	Research quality %	Entry standards	Teaching quality %	Student experience %	Graduate prospects %	Overall score
1 Cambridge	70.3	636	86.6	86.9	87.5	100.0
2 Oxford	63.1	594	79.6	85.0	91.1	97.3
3 Durham	49.1	563	88.0	92.8	83.0	95.8
4 York	44.6	486	91.3	94.7	86.4	95.3
5 St Andrews	50.3	513	80.9	88.3	83.9	93.0
6 Warwick	50.8	438	87.1	90.2	82.4	92.6
7 Liverpool	55.6	401	84.5	91.2	83.4	92.2
8 Imperial College	54.6	536	73.4	83.3	85.0	92.1
9 Manchester	46.0	461	85.1	89.8	77.9	91.1
10 Sussex	25.8	390	90.9	89.1	89.5	90.9
=11 Nottingham	48.5	435	81.0	85.5	82.9	90.6
=11 Southampton	50.7	414	82.9	88.0	81.2	90.6
13 Heriot-Watt	34.2	407	90.2	87.6	83.2	90.5
14 Bath	43.0	435	86.0	87.7	79.4	90.4
15 University College London	56.0	498	73.3	77.4	82.0	90.0
16 Surrey	30.8	430	85.4	90.2	83.3	89.9
17 Birmingham	37.3	448	81.7	84.5	84.1	89.8
=18 Bristol	56.6	486	79.2	85.4	71.7	89.7
=18 Sheffield	38.9	416	83.3	90.9	81.0	89.7
=20 Glasgow	41.1	458	77.8	80.9	85.7	89.6
=20 Keele	41.1	342	93.7	92.2	76.4	89.6
22 Loughborough	23.9	354	93.0	96.1	82.0	89.4
=23 Edinburgh	48.4	485	72.1	75.8	85.8	89.3
=23 Leicester	32.8	392	91.5	93.6	76.1	89.3
25 Lancaster	37.5	404	86.4	86.1		89.2
26 Queen's, Belfast	34.7	394	76.1	86.8	89.5	88.6
=27 East Anglia	39.2	438	79.8	85.5	76.0	87.7
=27 Leeds	35.9	439	79.1	87.0	77.5	87.7
29 Cardiff	30.9	374	77.4	85.7	88.0	87.5
30 Newcastle	28.5	413	81.4	87.8	75.1	86.2
31 Nottingham Trent	24.1	292	86.1	90.7	82.1	86.0
32 Aston	20.6	381	90.6	82.2	75.0	85.8
33 Strathclyde	40.1	452	65.2	68.5	84.2	84.9
34 Bangor	19.1	327	84.6	88.5	77.9	84.6
35 Sheffield Hallam		296	90.7	95.4	81.2	84.5
36 Hull	24.2	332	79.6	89.0	77.3	84.2

37 Central Lancashire	11.7	288	85.0	85.9	82.6	83.8
38 Aberdeen	31.6	422	84.0	83.9	61.2	83.7
39 Kent	27.5	330	85.4	87.8	68.7	83.6
40 Queen Mary, London	37.0	378	72.3	77.1	75.8	83.5
41 Liverpool John Moores	6.0	338	84.5	84.5	79.7	83.2
42 South Wales		285	81.5	90.6	86.2	82.9
43 Plymouth	25.3	296	80.7	86.4	72.9	82.5
44 Northumbria	14.0	340	88.6	90.2	64.2	82.2
45 Reading	27.3	325	78.6	82.4	71.1	82.0
46 Greenwich	7.4	305	85.1	85.9	72.5	81.3
47 Bradford	9.5	269	83.9	86.9	74.3	81.0
48 Brighton	4.8	320	80.5	87.5	73.0	80.6
49 Huddersfield	11.0	309	76.9	75.7	76.8	79.8
50 Manchester Metropolitan	16.3	327	78.6	80.3	67.6	79.7
51 West of Scotland	29.0	302	80.0	86.5	52.6	78.2
52 Kingston	2.6	246	70.2	71.8	71.1	74.3
53 London Metropolitan		233*	81.7	87.8	52.0	73.6

Employed in professional job:	40%	Employed in non-professional job and studying:	1%
Employed in professional job and studying:	3%	Employed in non-professional job:	13%
Studying:	33%	Unemployed:	11%
Average starting professional salary:	£22,817	Average starting non-professional salary:	£15,547

Civil Engineering

Civil engineering managed its first increase in enrolments in five years in 2015, as the subject began to share in the popularity of other branches of engineering. Applications were up by almost 5 per cent, reversing a decline that set in before the introduction of £9,000 fees and may have had more to do with applicants' concerns about the state of the construction industry. Any such concerns are not borne out by the latest employment figures: civil engineering is in the top ten subjects for graduate jobs and only just outside it for starting salaries. Even the 7 per cent of graduates who start out in "non-professional" jobs earn more than in most other subjects, averaging more than £19,000 in 2015. This is reflected in this table, where 22 of the 52 universities saw at least nine out of ten leavers go straight into graduate-level jobs or on to postgraduate study.

Imperial College London has taken over from Cambridge at the top of the table, mainly because student satisfaction has risen at Imperial while it declined at Cambridge. Both are rated among the top five universities in the world by QS. Undergraduates at West London, near the bottom of the table, were the most satisfied both with their teaching, feedback and academic support, and with the overall student experience. Only two universities failed to satisfy at least three-quarters of final-year undergraduates, taking all sections of the survey into account.

Some of the top degrees in civil engineering are four-year courses leading to an MEng; others are sandwich courses incorporating a period at work. The leading departments will expect physics and maths A levels or their equivalent. Fewer than half of all civil engineering undergraduates are admitted with A levels, however, reflecting the popularity of BTEC.

Civil Engineering cont

Almost half of the universities in the table are post-1992 institutions, but none reaches the top 20 this year. There is considerable variation in entry scores: the top four all average more than 500 points, but 14 universities average less than 300 points on the old UCAS tariff.

Civil Engineering	Research quality %	Entry standards	Teaching quality %	Student experience %	Graduate prospects %	Overall score
1 Imperial College	61.5	559	92.4	95.8	97.7	100.0
2 Cambridge	67.0	629	74.7	87.2	94.6	97.1
3 Glasgow	47.2	531	79.8	90.3	98.1	94.8
4 Bath	52.9	526	82.3	85.9	94.3	94.3
5 Leeds	32.0	416	91.0	94.3	89.8	90.9
=6 Dundee	46.2	399	84.4	85.8	91.6	90.5
=6 Southampton	52.3	469	73.6	83.6	91.9	90.5
8 Sheffield	43.1	427	78.7	88.7	92.6	90.2
9 Edinburgh	50.3	496	73.9	85.4	87.8	90.1
=10 Loughborough	26.9	394	83.1	91.9	96.2	89.7
=10 Newcastle	40.9	401	82.0	88.6	91.7	89.7
12 Cardiff	35.0	411	80.8	89.2	93.4	89.6
13 Queen's, Belfast	31.3	353	84.6	91.9	95.8	89.5
14 Bristol	52.3	509	72.3	79.5	84.5	88.8
15 Exeter	36.4	446	71.8	85.7	94.4	88.7
16 Nottingham	40.8	448	75.9	83.7	89.9	88.6
17 Heriot-Watt	47.8	412	79.8	87.3	83.9	88.3
18 Aberdeen	28.4	470	75.1	82.4	92.6	88.0
19 Swansea	45.5	347	76.0	81.1	92.7	87.4
20 Strathclyde	35.7	465	71.6	78.9	87.2	86.4
21 Birmingham	21.9	437	72.6	79.5	94.7	86.3
22 Abertay	16.3	322	92.6	94.3	83.1	85.6
23 Coventry	10.3	319	87.2	92.8	90.0	85.4
24 Surrey	30.8	407	81.0	86.8	79.7	85.3
25 Manchester	36.4	453	65.7	69.6	92.1	85.2
26 Northumbria	30.7	354	80.1	76.8	88.9	85.1
27 Liverpool	32.1	358	75.5	86.6	83.6	84.2
28 Brunel	23.7	353	77.4	84.8	85.7	83.8
29 West of Scotland	9.0	314	90.0	92.0	82.3	83.6
30 University College London	23.1	496	58.4	70.7	90.9	83.1
31 City	20.2	376	82.7	86.1	76.9	82.8
32 Ulster		278	78.2	90.3	95.5	82.7
33 Salford	19.6	321	83.7	87.3	79.2	82.5
34 Glasgow Caledonian	9.1	381	75.3	83.3	86.5	82.4
35 Nottingham Trent		266	84.4	86.3	91.4	82.1
36 South Wales		344	80.9	82.5	88.7	82.0
37 Derby	6.7	226	81.3	82.1	95.2	81.9
38 Bradford	17.8	292	72.2	79.2	89.8	81.2

39 Liverpool John Moores		352	73.2	77.9	92.1	81.1
40 Leeds Beckett	5.6	286	78.3	88.3	85.7	80.8
41 Anglia Ruskin	5.2	255	83.7	85.9	85.0	80.6
42 Edinburgh Napier	7.7	316	79.6	87.6	80.4	80.5
43 Portsmouth	9.1	288	77.7	84.8	84.6	80.4
44 West of England	10.6	275	80.1	82.3	82.4	79.9
45 London South Bank	19.6	263	78.3	84.5	78.7	79.7
46 Plymouth	15.7	271	75.3	80.0	83.6	79.6
47 Brighton	5.1	277	75.9	84.0	84.8	79.3
48 Greenwich	5.5	332	82.1	86.2	72.7	79.0
49 East London	2.3	290	85.7	89.4	73.5	78.9
50 West London		224*	99.2	98.3	58.8	77.0
51 Teesside	5.8	320*	70.4	82.2	75.7	76.8
52 Kingston	2.9	266	63.2	70.4	65.0	69.9

Employed in professional job:	71%	Employed in non-professional job and studying:	1%
Employed in professional job and studying:	3%	Employed in non-professional job:	7%
Studying:	10%	Unemployed:	9%
Average starting professional salary:	£25,555	Average starting non-professional salary:	£19,067

Classics and Ancient History

Applications and enrolments for classics both rose in 2015, as modern languages continued to struggle. Indeed, the numbers starting degrees passed 1,000 for the first time and applications were at their highest point since 2007. Ancient history was already sharing in the increases enjoyed by other history departments. Independent schools dominate provision of Latin and Greek at A level, producing some of the highest average grades of any subjects. However, most universities offering classics teach the subject from scratch, as well as to more practised students.

Cambridge has topped the table with Oxford in second place for the last 11 years, but the gap between the two has narrowed this year. Cambridge has the highest scores in the table for research and entry grades, while St Andrews, which has moved up to third place, has the most satisfied students in all aspects of the National Student Survey. St Andrews is also the only university to see nine out of ten graduates go straight into professional employment or onto postgraduate courses, leaving it only a fraction of a point behind Oxford overall.

Satisfaction rates are high throughout the table, but graduate prospects are generally disappointing. Although starting salaries in graduate-level employment are in the top 30, the proportion going into such jobs or on to further study is now outside the top 50. About a third of graduates opt for postgraduate courses, but the unemployment rate of 13 per cent was well above average in 2015.

More than 30 universities plan to offer classics courses in 2017. They are mainly older institutions – Roehampton is the only post-1992 university in our ranking. Several universities teach the subjects as part of a modular degree scheme, but not as a degree in its own right, while most providers now broaden their offering with degrees in classical studies or classical civilisation that range beyond language.

Classics and Ancient History

	Research quality %	Entry standards	Teaching quality %	Student experience %	Graduate prospects %	Overall score
1 Cambridge	65.0	572	89.7	89.4	81.7	100.0
2 Oxford	58.3	556	84.3	86.3	83.9	97.3
3 St Andrews	43.2	478	95.4	94.2	90.3	97.1
4 Durham	54.3	557	91.6	88.2	72.1	96.2
5 Exeter	45.0	469	88.2	87.4	73.3	91.7
6 Warwick	45.0	427	93.7	88.4	71.5	91.6
7 Nottingham	52.0	399	86.4	86.7	69.3	89.9
8 University College London	42.7	470	80.0	79.2	80.4	89.8
9 Newcastle	44.7	392	82.8	85.9	76.1	88.8
10 Birmingham	40.3	398	86.2	83.2	76.3	88.7
11 Glasgow	32.7	434	92.9	90.8	57.7	87.0
12 King's College London	43.6	431	78.3	79.3	66.2	86.0
=13 Edinburgh	34.9	471	79.6	81.0	56.9	84.2
=13 Liverpool	28.9	375	86.2	86.8	64.2	84.2
=13 Royal Holloway	20.4	411	91.1	87.5	61.6	84.2
16 Reading	45.2	360	87.9	86.6	47.5	84.0
17 Bristol	42.2	472	73.3	64.9	65.0	83.8
18 Manchester	31.0	369	81.9	82.3	62.5	82.6
19 Kent	33.1	321	82.7	82.2	60.0	81.5
20 Leeds	29.1	402	74.4	77.5	63.2	81.0
21 Swansea	25.0	294	82.5	81.4	69.2	80.9
22 Roehampton		256	90.6	80.8	49.5	73.5

Employed in professional job:	31%	Employed in non-professional job and studying:	3%
Employed in professional job and studying:	2%	Employed in non-professional job:	25%
Studying:	25%	Unemployed:	13%
Average starting professional salary:	£22,588	Average starting non-professional salary:	£15,534

Communication and Media Studies

Courses in communication and media studies continue to confound the sceptics who believed that a combination of £9,000 fees and poor employment prospects would bring about the decline in recruitment long predicted in the media itself. Both journalism and media studies registered increased applications and enrolments for the third year in a row in 2015, and the communications group as a whole saw further growth in 2016.

Communication and media studies used to be the preserve of the new universities, but older institutions have been moving in and now occupy the top 26 places. Newcastle heads the table for the first time without having the top score on any individual measure. Exeter has an unusually high 99 per cent satisfaction rate for teaching, feedback and academic support, but only just makes the top 20 because it did not enter the 2014 Research Excellence Framework in this category. Queen's, Belfast had the best scores in the sections of the National Student Survey devoted to the broader student experience, while Strathclyde again has the highest entry standards.

The division of jobs into professional and non-graduate fields of employment hits communication and media studies harder than most other subjects. Academics in the field argue that it is normal for students completing media courses to take "entry level" work that is not classified as a graduate job. The subjects remain in the bottom ten for graduate prospects, while starting salaries for those who do find graduate-level work are in the bottom two, despite a £1,000 increase on last year's average. For the second year in a row, Kent is well ahead of the field with 93 per cent of graduates going straight into professional jobs or staying on for a postgraduate course. Of the remaining 90 institutions, only Sheffield, Lancaster, Sussex and Newcastle managed positive destinations for 80 per cent graduates and the rate was below 40 per cent at seven universities. Entry scores remain modest: although no institution averages less than 230 points, 40 of the 91 universities averaged below 300 points in 2015.

Communication and Media Studies	Research quality %	Entry standards	Teaching quality %	Student experience %	Graduate prospects %	Overall score
1 Newcastle	37.8	431	90.9	91.3	86.7	100.0
2 Loughborough	62.3	393	82.9	87.9	77.9	98.1
3 Sheffield	37.9	403	89.3	91.0	83.6	97.8
4 Lancaster	51.4	391	85.3	81.8	81.8	97.0
5 Leeds	54.5	411	76.0	85.6	70.5	94.4
6 Cardiff	55.4	375	85.5	88.8	63.9	94.2
=7 Leicester	46.1	385	86.1	89.2	66.2	93.8
=7 Warwick	61.7	427	84.1	82.1	51.7	93.8
9 King's College London	55.8	431	81.3	77.1	57.0	93.0
10 Kent		339	94.7	94.1	93.3	92.8
11 East Anglia	43.8	417	81.0	83.6	62.4	92.3
=12 Queen Mary, London	35.1	419	88.1	88.0	56.6	92.0
=12 Sussex	43.6	353	74.9	81.8	82.6	92.0
14 Stirling	36.0	409	86.4	87.2	56.7	91.3
15 Goldsmiths, London	60.0	392	78.0	77.6	56.1	91.1
16 Queen's, Belfast	38.3	347*	91.2	96.6	49.8	89.7
17 City	30.1	409	77.1	79.1	67.6	89.6
18 Southampton	42.7	370	84.0	86.1	50.0	88.6
19 Keele	25.0	347	82.6	84.0	68.9	88.2
20 Exeter		429	99.1	88.0	47.7*	87.9
21 Strathclyde	39.4	442	78.1	81.8	40.0	87.4
22 Surrey	30.2	399	68.0	74.8	68.4	86.8
23 Liverpool	27.5	363	81.9	85.0	56.5	86.7
24 Royal Holloway	38.1	383	76.8	74.1	52.4	86.0
25 Swansea	18.5	304	88.8	90.7	59.6	85.6
26 Salford	36.9	369	77.0	77.2	51.1	85.3
27 Glasgow Caledonian	15.2	404	72.3	75.9	62.9	84.8
=28 De Montfort	31.2	273	80.4	82.5	66.2	84.7

Communication and Media Studies cont	Research quality %	Entry standards	Teaching quality %	Student experience %	Graduate prospects %	Overall score
=28 Robert Gordon	7.5	371	75.7	74.2	72.5	84.7
30 Liverpool Hope		269	94.2	93.3	68.5	84.6
=31 Coventry	18.1	292	87.0	87.3	61.0	84.5
=31 Leeds Beckett	11.0	286	87.7	91.5	64.3	84.5
=31 Oxford Brookes	25.3	333	83.0	86.8	51.4	84.5
=34 Lincoln	4.0	348	80.4	83.5	68.3	84.4
=34 Northumbria	22.2	354	81.5	83.8	51.8	84.4
=34 Westminster	28.3	351	74.1	80.2	58.3	84.4
37 Liverpool John Moores	6.2	332	86.9	89.9	58.4	84.3
38 Bangor	24.7	319	88.2	89.7	45.8	84.2
39 Nottingham Trent	10.0	291	82.9	86.5	69.6	84.0
40 Bournemouth	15.1	347	74.3	79.7	65.0	83.6
41 Brunel	23.0	322	80.0	77.1	59.3	83.5
42 Roehampton	26.4	248	84.8	87.8	60.4	83.4
43 Falmouth		289	80.7	80.9	75.3	82.4
44 Portsmouth	12.8	301	83.6	83.0	57.9	82.2
45 Sunderland	13.0	303	80.0	82.1	60.5	82.0
46 Edinburgh Napier	9.5	377	77.0	75.2	53.2	81.8
=47 Ulster	34.0	293	78.6	83.0	45.1	81.4
=47 West of England	18.6	286	84.0	86.1	50.4	81.4
49 Kingston	15.7	299	81.4	84.3	49.7	80.6
50 Birmingham City	6.0	336	73.5	74.8	62.4	80.5
51 Anglia Ruskin	26.4	244	87.9	90.3	41.1	80.3
52 Huddersfield		301	78.9	79.4	64.3	80.2
53 Southampton Solent	0.8	274	82.8	86.5	56.8	79.3
54 Manchester Metropolitan	29.0	328	67.6	66.1	51.8	79.1
=55 University for the Creative Arts	3.4	267	84.6	84.4	52.7	78.7
=55 Queen Margaret, Edinburgh	14.0	343	76.3	77.9	41.5	78.7
=55 West of Scotland	11.3	320	75.6	72.7	51.9	78.7
58 Aberystwyth	9.2	297	82.9	86.7	42.0	78.6
=59 Brighton	16.2	278	78.2	81.7	48.5	78.5
=59 Middlesex	11.0	288	73.2	74.9	59.3	78.5
=61 St Mark and St John		344	88.9	90.4	27.7	78.2
=61 Winchester	15.8	295	71.6	73.9	55.1	78.2
=63 Staffordshire	6.7	260	79.3	81.7	55.1	77.9
=63 York St John	4.4	281	83.5	77.6	50.0	77.9
65 Bath Spa	13.9	306	71.8	70.7	54.3	77.8
66 Derby	13.5	278	79.6	79.9	45.4	77.6
=67 Cumbria		253	97.1	92.7	33.3	77.4
=67 Sheffield Hallam	14.4	293	72.1	78.4	49.3	77.4
69 Leeds Trinity	3.9	270	76.5	75.4	58.9	77.3
70 Bradford		282	70.0	74.2	66.4	77.2
71 Central Lancashire	7.9	317	66.3	74.1	55.9	76.9

72 Canterbury Christ Church	7.3	245	81.1	79.0	51.6	76.7
73 London South Bank	12.8	234	87.2	82.3	40.4	76.6
74 East London	13.9	236	86.3	81.3	39.1	76.2
75 Hull	11.2	342	72.3	69.2	39.7	76.0
76 Chester	4.3	271	76.5	79.1	47.6	75.6
77 Edge Hill	10.2	301	74.5	75.2	39.9	75.4
78 Buckinghamshire New		256	78.6	77.9	50.7	75.2
79 University of the Arts London		268	69.2	68.2	61.3	74.7
80 Gloucestershire	9.3	295	69.0	67.6	47.6	74.4
81 Worcester	8.2	257	75.0	74.6	45.7	74.3
82 Chichester		287	75.9	80.3	40.6	74.2
=83 St Mary's, Twickenham	9.1	284	68.7	72.0	45.8	74.0
=83 Wrexham Glyndŵr	7.8	251	71.3	71.9	51.3	74.0
85 Bedfordshire	8.2	229	80.8	80.5	39.0	73.8
=86 Teesside	2.9	239	78.9	75.6	44.6	73.5
=86 West London	4.5	280	65.5	70.7	52.2	73.5
88 London Metropolitan	5.9	243	68.8	65.2	56.6	73.1
89 Northampton		257	79.8	80.7	35.7	72.9
90 Greenwich	3.5	318	62.2	68.1	44.8	72.5
91 South Wales		310	66.0	66.5	40.0	71.3

Employed in professional job:	48%	Employed in non-professional job and studying:	1%
Employed in professional job and studying:	1%	Employed in non-professional job:	31%
Studying:	6%	Unemployed:	12%
Average starting professional salary:	£19,242	Average starting non-professional salary:	£15,631

Computer Science

Computer science is the ultimate example of students reacting to their perception of the jobs market when they choose courses. After the dot.com bubble burst, applications declined for a decade but, with the exception of a single year when £9,000 fees were introduced, they have risen strongly throughout this decade. There was another 5 per cent increase in the numbers starting degrees in 2016, making growth of more than 40 per cent in four years. The latest survey showed around two-thirds of graduates going straight into professional roles and the subject was 13th in the salary league, averaging more than £25,000 in graduate-level jobs.

Cambridge has taken over the leadership of the table that it lost to Oxford last year. Both are rated in the top six in the world for computer science by QS, but Cambridge has more satisfied students and the highest entry standards in the table. The most satisfied students of all, at least in relation to teaching, feedback and academic support, are at Liverpool Hope. Fourth-placed St Andrews is again the top university for the broader student experience, while Imperial College, in third place, produced the best grades in the Research Excellence Framework.

Although computer science has a good employment record overall, the table shows the advantage of winning a place at one of the leading universities. Nineteen of the top 22 universities registered positive destinations for at least 90 per cent of graduates, whereas only one of the bottom 50 reached 80 per cent. Lancaster had the best record in 2015, with 98 per cent of graduates going straight into professional employment or continuing their studies.

Computer Science cont

Entry standards also vary more widely than in most subjects, with average scores on the old UCAS tariff ranging from more than 500 points at the top five universities to less than 250 points at six of the lower-ranked institutions.

Some of the leading universities demand maths at A level, or the equivalent, while others want computing or computer science. The most competitive area is the small field of artificial intelligence, where there were only 85 places in 2015, while the strongest growth has been in computer games courses.

Computer Science	Research quality %	Entry standards	Teaching quality %	Student experience %	Graduate prospects %	Overall score
1 Cambridge	57.1	645	87.1	83.6	92.9	100.0
2 Oxford	60.6	584	82.7	82.3	94.5	97.8
3 Imperial College	64.1	544	78.0	86.2	92.3	96.2
4 St Andrews	33.4	512	92.5	96.8	92.7	96.0
5 Durham	38.8	522	85.3	91.5	95.2	95.2
6 Warwick	54.8	488	82.0	89.0	90.8	94.4
7 University College London	62.7	515	72.7	84.8	94.7	94.3
8 Sheffield	51.1	388	89.8	90.9	93.6	93.5
9 Leeds	41.6	424	92.9	93.2	86.9	93.1
10 Manchester	50.7	461	78.5	88.6	92.3	92.6
11 Southampton	48.2	462	78.0	88.1	93.3	92.3
12 Swansea	47.5	360	86.0	87.3	97.4	91.7
13 Bristol	49.2	503	70.2	76.8	97.0	91.1
14 Birmingham	46.4	451	77.7	81.8	92.7	90.8
15 York	46.9	440	79.1	79.3	93.1	90.6
=16 Glasgow	50.3	459	78.7	85.8	83.6	90.5
=16 Loughborough	18.7	394	91.3	94.4	94.2	90.5
18 Lancaster	44.8	411	75.6	84.2	98.0	90.3
19 Surrey	25.3	426	84.6	86.8	95.5	90.1
20 Exeter	40.7	444	78.8	82.9		89.2
21 Dundee	29.4	366	85.6	91.5	92.0	89.0
22 Bath	33.3	448	77.2	79.0	93.6	88.8
23 Nottingham	45.4	386	80.2	86.9	84.5	88.5
=24 Heriot-Watt	39.5	405	80.4	84.3	86.4	88.4
=24 King's College London	47.6	421	75.5	81.5	86.3	88.4
26 Newcastle	49.7	408	74.7	81.3	86.3	88.1
27 Liverpool	40.5	389	80.1	85.7	85.6	88.0
28 Royal Holloway	35.1	372	81.7	85.2	88.7	87.7
29 Edinburgh	54.3	482	64.7	77.9	82.1	87.4
30 Aston	21.7	364	81.9	83.5	94.0	86.6
31 Kent	37.8	360	72.2	83.5	91.8	86.0
32 Aberystwyth	38.4	295	80.8	84.6	89.9	85.9
33 East Anglia	35.9	370	74.7	81.5	88.7	85.8

34 Cardiff	25.0	405	72.6	80.7	90.7	85.2
35 Queen's, Belfast	29.5	372	76.2	79.8	88.2	85.0
36 Stirling	14.0	370	76.4	80.0	94.9	84.4
37 Bangor	17.6	333	83.6	84.6	85.4	84.2
=38 Keele	10.8	330	87.5	90.8	80.6	84.0
=38 Leicester	30.2	394	68.2	77.6	89.4	84.0
40 Strathclyde	21.1	460	63.6	78.8	89.4	83.8
41 Essex	34.3	318	74.0	81.8	83.3	83.0
42 Lincoln	13.6	350	79.5	84.9	82.6	82.8
43 Liverpool Hope	8.8	298	93.0	91.9	72.5	82.7
=44 Aberdeen	37.4	377	69.1	73.4	81.5	82.6
=44 Abertay	3.4	366	87.1	87.8	74.9	82.6
46 Hull	22.2	349	72.0	77.3	88.7	82.4
47 Queen Mary, London	37.4	359	67.4	73.1	84.7	82.3
48 Reading	16.3	367	73.8	72.6	89.9	82.2
=49 Brunel	25.2	348	75.7	79.4	78.5	82.0
=49 Huddersfield	7.4	360	83.6	85.2	75.8	82.0
51 Sussex	21.6	369	67.2	76.9	89.3	81.9
52 De Montfort	13.4	288	81.2	82.2	84.1	81.3
53 City	19.2	386	75.0	78.0	74.2	81.2
54 West of England	5.9	332	77.4	83.0	84.6	81.0
55 Coventry	3.3	318	84.5	84.6	78.2	80.9
56 Edinburgh Napier	5.2	324	82.9	85.3	74.7	80.4
57 Robert Gordon	4.3	349	80.3	81.8	74.8	80.0
=58 Bournemouth	8.5	321	78.5	78.8	79.5	79.8
=58 Plymouth	21.8	328	73.1	73.3	79.4	79.8
60 Portsmouth	7.2	328	82.7	85.4	68.2	79.6
61 Edge Hill	0.3	322	83.1	86.2	71.0	70.1
=62 Derby	5.0	301	80.1	80.1	74.3	78.4
=62 Hertfordshire	7.8	286	77.3	82.3	77.0	78.4
=62 Salford	15.3	360	79.4	80.8	58.2	78.4
65 Nottingham Trent	5.2	289	77.3	77.3	80.8	78.3
=66 Central Lancashire		341	77.2	82.3	70.2	77.8
=66 Ulster	16.6	300	74.3	81.2	69.8	77.8
68 Chester	1.3	287	83.3	77.0	73.6	77.7
69 Liverpool John Moores	3.2	348	76.8	79.6	67.5	77.5
=70 Birmingham City	4.9	308	79.0	82.5	66.9	77.3
=70 Staffordshire	0.4	298	81.7	81.1	69.3	77.3
72 South Wales	3.6	329	79.4	76.1	67.4	77.1
=73 Leeds Beckett	0.2	274	84.2	83.0	67.3	77.0
=73 Sheffield Hallam		295	77.2	80.8	74.1	77.0
75 Goldsmiths, London	29.2	325	63.2	63.5	76.7	76.7
76 Manchester Metropolitan	5.6	339	72.7	76.5	69.3	76.6
=77 Brighton	6.4	301	71.6	74.6	76.9	76.5
=77 Oxford Brookes	13.0	327	65.5	70.8	78.5	76.5
79 Middlesex	14.2	280	76.9	80.0	63.6	76.3
=80 Northampton		292	75.7	74.3	75.3	76.0

Computer Science cont	Research quality %	Entry standards	Teaching quality %	Student experience %	Graduate prospects %	Overall score
=80 Sunderland	1.8	285	77.7	76.5	71.2	76.0
82 Northumbria	4.0	352	70.0	70.4	70.2	75.6
=83 Gloucestershire		307	78.6	75.1	65.2	75.4
=83 Teesside	3.4	322	79.6	79.7	56.2	75.4
=83 West London	1.2	277	87.7	90.0	48.2	75.4
=86 Glasgow Caledonian	4.0	336	71.0	76.7	65.4	75.2
=86 Worcester		280	76.5	74.6	71.4	75.2
88 West of Scotland	3.2	323	75.2	76.3	61.9	75.0
89 Greenwich	7.3	346	70.1	74.4	60.4	74.5
90 East London	2.3	246	82.9	86.0	53.6	74.1
91 Buckinghamshire New		216	82.9	79.8	61.6	73.6
92 London Metropolitan	0.7	229	81.0	85.0	57.0	73.5
93 Bradford		300	67.5	75.8	68.2	73.3
=94 Anglia Ruskin		225	81.7	78.8	59.9	73.2
=94 Southampton Solent		260	75.8	73.8	65.1	73.2
96 Cardiff Metropolitan		291	67.0	70.2	72.3	73.0
=97 Bolton		281	72.6	71.7	63.8	72.6
=97 Westminster	2.9	285	71.0	77.6	59.2	72.6
=97 Wrexham Glyndŵr	3.9	257	79.4	79.0	51.6	72.6
100 London South Bank	19.6	227	69.9	78.8	55.1	72.2
101 Kingston	5.3	262	67.4	71.5	62.5	71.3
102 Bedfordshire	9.1	203	71.2	75.3	59.2	70.8
103 Suffolk		255	74.7	72.9	50.0	70.0
104 Canterbury Christ Church		276	49.4	58.4	69.4	66.8

Employed in professional job:	64%	Employed in non-professional job and studying:	1%
Employed in professional job and studying:	2%	Employed in non-professional job:	14%
Studying:	8%	Unemployed:	12%
Average starting professional salary:	£25,142	Average starting non-professional salary:	£16,542

Creative Writing

Creative writing – or imaginative writing, as it is known by UCAS – has been a significant, but little-noticed area of growth in higher education over recent years. More than 90 universities and colleges plan to offer undergraduate courses in the subject starting in 2017. Many are part of a joint honours programme or are still too small to qualify for our table, which is now in its third year. Creative writing is paired with subjects as diverse as ceramics, business and biology, but more normally with English. The numbers starting courses dropped slightly in 2015, but there were still 3,300 applications. Some 830 students took up places.

Warwick remains top of the table, with the highest entry grades and the best performance in the 2014 Research Excellence Framework. Bolton, in a share of 24th place, posted the best scores for teaching, feedback and academic support in the National

Student Survey. Students at Westminster were again the most satisfied with other elements of the student experience.

Employment is, perhaps not surprisingly, the Achilles heel of creative writing when compared with other subjects. It is just one place off the bottom of the employment table, with only 28 per cent of graduates starting out in professional jobs and an unemployment rate of 17 per cent. Average salaries for those who did find a professional job in 2015 were the lowest in any subject, at little more than £18,000. Half of the universities with enough graduates to compile an employment score saw less than 50 per cent of their graduates go into professional employment or further study.

With only four applications to the place, entry standards are generally low – only six of the 49 universities averaged more than 400 points on the old UCAS tariff. The table is largely composed of post-1992 universities, although the top ten are all older foundations.

Creative Writing	Research quality %	Entry standards	Teaching quality %	Student experience %	Graduate prospects %	Overall score
1 Warwick	59.8	482	89.8	89.3	75*	100.0
2 Newcastle	54.3	458	91.3	84.3		97.7
3 Birmingham	37.0	449	90.6	86.2	76.1	95.4
4 Queen's, Belfast	53.1	393	84.5	87.2	70.3	93.6
5 Surrey	39.1	371	90.1	86.9	72.3	92.4
6 Lancaster	47.0	416	76.4	84.9	69.3	91.2
7 Nottingham	56.6	386	84.0	82.9	53.7	90.7
8 Bangor	46.3	373	90.6	87.6	47.4	89.9
9 East Anglia	36.2	464	81.0	85.8	52.5	89.8
10 Royal Holloway	49.9	422	77.1	77.1	60.0	89.6
11 Birmingham City	30.9	305	90.9	88.5	62.9	87.8
12 Reading	36.3		82.4	78.1	66.7	87.5
13 Coventry	18.1	322	90.1	85.6	70.0	87.1
14 Brunel	30.9	359	85.0	83.0	58.7	87.0
15 Hull	22.7	352	84.1	83.4	67.1	86.7
16 Westminster	28.9	293	89.5	94.7	54.8	86.3
17 Bath Spa	23.5	316	89.3	88.2	53.0	85.2
18 Aberystwyth	31.2	283	86.4	87.7	55.7	84.8
19 De Montfort	24.1	298	81.4	83.3	68.4	84.5
20 West of England	35.4		85.0	78.6	48.1	84.0
21 Liverpool John Moores	17.9	348	88.9	90.1	40.0	83.6
22 Portsmouth	17.1	302	80.8	81.1	67.4	83.1
23 Manchester Metropolitan	29.0	329	81.6	73.7	51.3	82.5
=24 Bedfordshire	45.8	229	91.3	90.2	24.0	81.7
=24 Bolton	14.4	264	91.7	82.3	51.7	81.7
26 Plymouth	30.5	276	80.7	83.9	48.7	81.5
27 Northampton	15.3	283	85.9	75.3	55.6	80.8
28 Central Lancashire	9.9	351	74.2	76.4	54.4	79.5
29 Derby	13.5	306	85.8	82.9	34.6	79.0
30 Chester	10.7	308	87.1	79.8	35.8	78.7

Creative Writing cont

	Research quality %	Entry standards	Teaching quality %	Student experience %	Graduate prospects %	Overall score
31 Gloucestershire	9.3	274	81.3	80.6	48.7	78.1
=32 Canterbury Christ Church	8.0	267	87.0	81.4	41.7	78.0
=32 Middlesex	11.0	255*	87.5	84.9	37.9	78.0
=32 Winchester		299	86.1	84.7	41.0	78.0
35 St Mary's, Twickenham	14.6	267	80.8	79.9	45.7	77.9
36 Bournemouth	15.1	339	71.2	73.9	43.6	77.1
=37 London South Bank	12.8	232	83.9	82.8	41.3	76.9
=37 Roehampton	20.8	269	80.1	77.0	36.6	76.9
39 Chichester	16.3	274	86.4	80.0	25.8	76.7
=40 Kingston	15.7	303	74.2	72.7	43.6	76.5
=40 South Wales	12.8	311	75.7	69.8	44.7	76.5
42 Greenwich	14.4	348	68.1	69.8	41.4	75.7
43 York St John	9.7	277	78.0	77.4		75.6
44 Salford	7.8	267	80.6	74.3	33.7	74.3
45 Sheffield Hallam	14.6	306	72.0	75.6	26.5	73.6
46 Edge Hill	12.1	312	73.2	70.0	29.5	73.5
47 Worcester	8.2	248	84.9	76.0	22.2	73.2
48 Southampton Solent		240	73.9	73.4	50.0	73.0
49 Staffordshire		228*	76.0	71.4	33.8	70.3

Employed in professional job:	26%	Employed in non-professional job and studying:	3%
Employed in professional job and studying:	2%	Employed in non-professional job:	39%
Studying:	13%	Unemployed:	17%
Average starting professional salary:	£18,133	Average starting non-professional salary:	£14,868

Criminology

Criminology is the latest discipline to be added to our separate subject tables. The data previously appeared in the sociology and law tables, but the growth in demand for degrees in criminology justifies a ranking of its own. More than 130 universities and colleges now offer the subject, albeit sometimes only as part of a broader social science degree. About half that number had enough students to qualify for the inaugural table, which is based on some 3,700 students aged 21 or less. The graduate prospects data refers to just one year, 2015.

York, one of the pioneers in criminology degrees, tops that first table although it does not lead on any of the individual measures. Gloucestershire is the only university to reach 90 per cent satisfaction for teaching, feedback and academic support and 95 per cent for the broader student experience, but it is restricted to a share of 25th place because it did not enter the Research Excellence Framework (REF) in this category. Second-placed Kent had the top scores in the REF, while Durham has the highest entry standards and is one of only two universities to average more than 400 points on entry. Sociology or psychology A level will be welcomed by some departments, but there are no specific entry requirements for criminology degrees apart, possibly, from a GCSE in maths since the course is likely to involve statistics.

Durham is also the only university to have registered positive destinations for three-quarters of its 2015 graduates. The figure was below 40 per cent at eight of the 53 universities in the table. Criminology has started out in the bottom three for graduate prospects, largely because more than 40 per cent of graduates begin their careers in lower-level employment. It is a little higher in the earnings table, but still in the bottom ten. Many criminology graduates eventually find employment in the police force, prison service, the Home Office, charities or law practices.

Criminology	Research quality %	Entry standards	Teaching quality %	Student experience %	Graduate prospects %	Overall score
1 York	47.5	386	84.3	85.4	66.7	100.0
2 Kent	59.0	330	81.6	87.2	74.0	99.9
3 Leeds	40.1	404	82.7	84.3		98.8
4 Manchester	27.2	386	83.4	84.7	68.7	97.5
5 Stirling	33.8	392	87.6	90.7	48.4	97.4
6 Durham	28.7	416	74.4	79.0	78.9	97.2
7 Essex	44.3	318	80.5	91.1	68.3	97.1
8 Southampton	52.8	370	76.9	80.8	55.2	95.7
=9 Nottingham	43.5	356	77.7	82.6		94.1
=9 Swansea	20.4	329	83.1	86.1	65.8	94.1
11 Cardiff	30.8	387	78.0	83.7	51.3	93.8
12 Liverpool Hope	8.6	292	88.8	86.8	70.6	93.6
13 Portsmouth	12.1	330	85.9	87.0	62.6	93.5
14 Leicester	26.3	389	82.7	83.6	44.0	93.4
15 Edinburgh Napier		375	84.0	88.5	56.3	92.5
16 Lincoln	5.8	333	85.2	88.6	59.2	92.4
17 Sussex	27.9	341	79.3	83.1		92.0
18 Hull	14.3	335	76.1	87.5	61.7	91.4
19 Edge Hill	12.1	315	84.8	85.3		91.2
20 Northumbria	12.7	354	80.4	84.6	50.0	90.8
=21 Plymouth	16.0	303	82.5	86.0		90.3
=21 Wrexham Glyndŵr		318	84.3	85.3	58.8	90.3
23 City	19.2	354	77.3	79.3		90.1
24 Derby	2.4	304	89.7	84.5	49.5	90.0
=25 Gloucestershire		310	93.5	95.3	30.9	89.7
=25 West of England	10.9	329	82.5	84.3	47.1	89.7
27 Nottingham Trent	5.1	277	84.6	85.2	59.9	89.6
28 Sheffield Hallam	14.4	297	83.1	83.4	50.3	89.4
29 Manchester Metropolitan	6.9	328	83.7	85.4	42.2	88.9
30 Middlesex	14.9	298	77.4	79.2	59.4	88.8
31 Central Lancashire	11.8	336	78.4	83.9	44.1	88.5
32 Bradford	10.6	328	79.6	87.2	41.2	88.4
33 Teesside	15.0	272	81.6	82.9	52.0	88.3
=34 Bangor		319	86.5	84.6	37.3	87.6
=34 De Montfort	11.2	280	76.4	82.0	58.0	87.6

Criminology cont

		Research quality %	Entry standards	Teaching quality %	Student experience %	Graduate prospects %	Overall score
36	Brighton	12.4	296	81.5	83.0	40.0	87.1
37	Aberystwyth	14.3	281	76.9	77.8	53.4	86.8
38	Greenwich	2.1	329	79.4	78.3	45.5	86.7
39	Anglia Ruskin	5.4	233	89.3	85.6	41.0	86.4
40	London South Bank	20.1	225	75.7	81.3	55.2	85.9
41	East London	10.6	262	80.5	82.9		85.8
=42	Birmingham City	3.8	313	78.4	76.2	45.1	85.7
=42	Westminster		276	83.4	86.7	39.1	85.7
44	London Metropolitan	8.8	261	77.3	78.5	51.6	85.3
45	Chester	0.3	278	83.1	76.6	41.6	84.7
46	Winchester	4.4	267	80.9	79.8	41.1	84.6
47	Northampton		245	79.5	82.9	44.2	83.7
48	Canterbury Christ Church	3.2	233	84.6	85.9	31.6	83.5
49	South Wales	15.4	317	70.2	75.4	32.0	83.0
50	Roehampton		263	74.8	75.7	48.4	82.8
51	Suffolk		281	76.6	82.3	33.3	82.7
52	Kingston		259	75.2	76.6	36.8	81.1
53	Southampton Solent		256	72.3	78.9	36.4	80.5

Employed in professional job:	30%	Employed in non-professional job and studying:	3%
Employed in professional job and studying:	3%	Employed in non-professional job:	41%
Studying:	12%	Unemployed:	11%
Average starting professional salary:	£19,847	Average starting non-professional salary:	£16,205

Dentistry

For the fourth year in a row, dentistry is the only subject whose graduates were paid more than £30,000 in "professional" jobs six months after leaving university. There is no figure for less skilled work because virtually everyone who completes a degree goes on to become a dentist, so the subject is also in the top two in the employment table. None of the 15 undergraduate dental schools saw less than 97 per cent of graduates going into professional jobs or further study. This measure is not used to determine positions so as not to exaggerate the impact of tiny numbers delaying their entry into the profession. Even so, in 2015, for the fourth year in a row, applications declined, this time by more than 10 per cent.

Most degrees last five years, although several universities offer a six-year option for those without the necessary scientific qualifications. The number of places has been increased in recent years to tackle shortages, but there are still nine applications to the place – more than in any subject except medicine. Entry standards are correspondingly high: none of the schools averages less than 460 points and five have an average of more than 500 on the old UCAS tariff. Most demand chemistry and biology, and some also demand maths or physics.

Scores in the subject are so close that the ranking changes frequently. Cardiff jumped eight places – more than half the ranking – to take the lead last year, but it is back down to ninth in the latest edition. Glasgow, the previous leader, is back at the top, with the highest entry standards and a good performance in the National Student Survey. Second-placed Queen's, Belfast has the best scores for teaching quality and overall student experience – an unusually high satisfaction rating of around 99 per cent for both measures. Sixth-placed Manchester produced the best results in the Research Excellence Framework, as it did in the 2008 assessments.

Dentistry	Research quality %	Entry standards	Teaching quality %	Student experience %	Graduate prospects %	Overall score
1 Glasgow	29.3	555	91.4	96.2	99.2	100.0
2 Queen's, Belfast	50.7	475	98.8	99.1	97.6	97.4
3 Newcastle	43.6	503	90.3	93.9	97.5	96.3
4 Queen Mary, London	48.3	505	87.6	88.8	100.0	95.9
5 Dundee	22.1	509	96.2	96.0	100.0	94.9
6 Manchester	57.1	510	74.2	79.3	99.2	93.2
7 Bristol	47.1	493	80.9	84.8	99.0	92.1
8 King's College London	40.9	495	81.6	86.4	99.2	91.7
9 Cardiff	36.8	493	82.5	87.1	99.3	91.1
10 Liverpool	31.7	465	92.3	92.8	100.0	90.3
=11 Birmingham	19.2	489	86.1	83.4	99.2	87.7
=11 Leeds	31.7	497	74.3	82.0	99.3	87.7
13 Sheffield	28.5	463	84.4	89.0	99.2	87.0
14 Plymouth	9.5	464	89.7	87.9	100.0	84.8
15 Central Lancashire	8.3		86.3	86.7	100.0	84.5

Employed in professional job:	94%	Employed in non-professional job and studying:	0%
Employed in professional job and studying:	4%	Employed in non-professional job:	1%
Studying:	1%	Unemployed:	1%
Average starting professional salary:	£30,432	Average starting non-professional salary:	..

Drama, Dance and Cinematics

Drama has become one of the most popular subjects in UK higher education, with cinematics and photography not far behind. As a group, the three main subjects in this table attracted more than 95,000 applications between them in 2015, the third successive improvement, although still nowhere near the numbers seen before fees reached £9,000 a year. The numbers actually starting degrees has now surpassed pre-2012 levels in drama and photography, however, and is close to doing so in dance.

There are now more than six applications to the place in drama, although the ratio is nearer 5:1 in dance and in cinematics and photography. The subjects' popularity has never been reflected in high entry grades. Although 18 of the 95 universities and colleges in the table average more than 400 points at entry, none reaches 500 and 18 universities have averages of less than 300 points. East Anglia has the highest entry standards, but Lancaster has jumped from tenth place to take over the leadership of the table. Lancaster has the most satisfied undergraduates in all aspects of the National Student Survey and by far the best graduate prospects.

Three other institutions, including the specialist Royal Conservatoire of Scotland saw more than 80 per cent of graduates go straight into professional employment or continue

Drama, Dance and Cinematics cont

their studies. The subjects are in the bottom ten for employment and, in spite of a £2,700 increase in average starting salaries in graduate-level jobs, they are still in the bottom six in the earnings table. Although the unemployment level of 10 per cent is no higher than average for the 67 subject groups, approaching 40 per cent of graduates start out in low-level jobs. As in other performing arts, freelancing and periods of temporary employment are common for new graduates.

The majority of institutions offering drama, dance or cinematics are post-1992 universities, but none of them feature in this year's top 20. Standards of performance will be influential in the selection process for dance and drama, as will a portfolio of work for photography, but drama courses at leading universities are likely to require English literature A level.

Drama, Dance and Cinematics	Research quality %	Entry standards	Teaching quality %	Student experience %	Graduate prospects %	Overall score
1 Lancaster	48.0	391	97.1	96.1	86.9	100.0
2 Warwick	61.7	456	87.3	87.1	64.5	97.0
3 Exeter	46.3	466	90.9	95.6	62.9	96.8
4 Sussex	45.6	381	90.6	93.3	80.8	96.3
5 Queen Mary, London	68.4	434	87.8	89.5	57.0	95.7
6 Glasgow	53.9	456	81.1	85.9	66.7	95.0
7 Birmingham	36.9	417	81.7	86.3	80.7	94.0
8 Essex	37.7	393	90.9	91.1	71.3	93.6
9 Sheffield	60.0	403	85.6	87.9	61.4	93.5
10 Manchester	58.6	443	82.3	81.0	58.8	93.1
11 Edinburgh Napier	37.9	417	86.1	82.2	72.2	92.9
12 East Anglia	43.8	488	78.8	86.8	53.3	91.9
13 Leeds	28.0	410	87.2	89.6	67.7	91.3
14 Central School of Speech and Drama	47.7	363	88.4	86.1	64.3*	91.0
15 Bristol	48.7	483	72.7	72.3	59.8	90.8
16 Surrey	27.2	402	87.8	84.5	68.3	90.6
17 Bangor	24.7		96.3	92.9	56.6*	90.4
18 Kent	44.3	363	85.7	85.3	64.3	89.9
19 Loughborough	32.4	424	85.7	83.3	54.9	88.9
20 Edinburgh	48.0	433	74.1	74.8	57.9	88.6
21 Robert Gordon	11.5		86.8	82.9	69.6	88.0
22 Coventry	18.1	340	90.5	87.7	70.2	87.9
23 York	26.0	432	79.1	84.3	58.3	87.8
24 Nottingham	45.8	360	86.7	87.7	51.3	87.7
=25 Middlesex	16.1	330	90.0	89.8	71.1	87.5
=25 Royal Holloway	50.6	410	74.7	76.5	54.1	87.5
27 Huddersfield	28.0	323	90.1	86.3	64.5	87.0
28 Royal Conservatoire of Scotland	11.3	321	83.0	83.6	81.3	86.3
29 Roehampton	46.6	312	83.5	83.9	52.5	84.9
30 Chichester	9.7	334	93.7	95.1	53.8	84.6

=31	Queen's, Belfast	38.3	368	82.8	86.5	41.0	84.0
=31	Reading	34.8	360	80.1	74.2	54.4	84.0
33	Nottingham Trent		362	89.3	87.7	58.9	83.8
34	Oxford Brookes	27.8	330	88.3	87.3	47.5	83.5
35	De Montfort	14.5	317	82.1	83.4	66.6	83.4
36	Birmingham City	11.6	345	86.2	85.7	55.1	83.0
=37	East London	11.2	339	88.2	86.0	53.5	82.8
=37	Falmouth	6.2	319	78.9	79.5	74.3	82.8
39	Hull	11.2	338	89.9	92.8	47.6	82.6
40	Aberdeen	29.3	408	85.1	85.4	28.1	82.3
41	West of Scotland		389	83.2	79.6	55.6	82.2
42	Manchester Metropolitan	7.5	370	86.8	85.8	47.4	82.1
43	Lincoln	6.5	349	83.6	83.4	56.8	82.0
44	Brunel	32.6	344	79.2	79.0	46.9	81.8
45	Liverpool John Moores		357	87.6	88.4	50.9	81.6
46	Northumbria	13.3	366	85.5	83.2	44.4	81.5
=47	Aberystwyth	30.3	299	82.8	86.9	47.2	81.1
=47	Liverpool Hope	3.0	319	84.9	85.1	58.8	81.1
=47	Portsmouth		346	83.4	84.0	57.3	81.1
=50	Central Lancashire	3.9	323	85.5	81.5	57.8	80.9
=50	Hertfordshire	5.3	332	75.6	77.0	67.5	80.9
52	Arts University, Bournemouth	2.4	333	77.8	79.6	65.0	80.7
53	Norwich University of the Arts		336	82.5	81.5	58.3	80.4
54	Sunderland	4.2	274	87.5	86.8	59.8	80.2
55	Ulster	40.0	276	82.5	82.3	43.7	80.1
56	Derby	5.1	333	81.6	74.8	58.0	80.0
57	West of England		329	85.1	81.4	55.0	79.9
58	Queen Margaret, Edinburgh	14.0	417	75.6	75.6	37.8	79.5
=59	Bath Spa	10.7	338	75.8	74.4	55.1	79.1
=59	St Mary's, Twickenham		331	87.8	80.5	48.3	79.1
=61	Goldsmiths, London	28.3	356	68.9	62.0	52.0	78.8
=61	Newman	0.6	313	91.5	83.9	39.1	78.8
63	Teesside	2.9	300	90.2	89.1	43.8	78.6
64	University for the Creative Arts	3.4	319	86.5	85.4	44.0	78.4
65	Greenwich	3.5	368	76.4	80.0	45.6	78.2
=66	Bolton		320	93.7	82.5	38.6	78.1
=66	Winchester	11.2	313	85.1	80.4	42.7	78.1
68	Chester	4.3	307	81.8	75.8	53.4	77.9
69	University of the Arts London		342	77.9	75.2	51.7	77.6
70	Kingston	15.7	312	77.6	76.0	46.2	77.3
71	Gloucestershire		351	78.8	79.3	44.0	77.1
72	Bournemouth	15.1	388	58.9	65.2	53.6	77.0
73	London South Bank		275	86.4	84.1	49.5	76.9
74	Westminster		310	79.7	79.3	50.5	76.8
75	Plymouth	20.2	312	75.1	77.2	40.8	76.4
76	Northampton		322	78.9	75.8	47.9	76.2
77	Staffordshire		283	85.7	83.6	45.0	76.1

Drama, Dance and Cinematics cont

	Research quality %	Entry standards	Teaching quality %	Student experience %	Graduate prospects %	Overall score
=78 Cardiff Metropolitan		291	82.4	86.6	44.4	76.0
=78 Edge Hill	3.8	340	76.7	73.1	44.1	76.0
=78 South Wales	6.4	332	78.0	77.1	41.1	76.0
81 London Metropolitan		241	88.2	86.8	47.8	75.8
82 Salford	7.2	328	78.4	70.5	43.0	75.7
83 Bedfordshire	5.6	269	82.6	85.6	42.6	75.3
=84 Brighton	13.1	318	70.0	67.0	49.0	75.2
=84 York St John	10.5	296	76.6	75.9	44.1	75.2
86 Leeds Beckett	1.7	307	83.7	83.3	35.4	75.0
87 Canterbury Christ Church	15.2	272	81.8	78.7	37.8	74.8
88 Bishop Grosseteste		288	80.6	76.9	45.5	74.7
89 Sheffield Hallam		289	79.5	79.5	43.4	74.3
90 West London	2.3	318	70.9	68.2	49.3	74.1
91 Buckinghamshire New		278	82.0	80.3	41.4	74.0
92 Anglia Ruskin	16.9	256	78.2	79.1	33.2	72.7
93 Southampton Solent		298	72.7	73.6	43.0	72.6
94 Worcester	3.5	263	86.9	82.8	28.2	72.4
95 Cumbria		296	74.0	74.9	39.8	72.2
96 Suffolk		332	67.7	65.4	38.9	71.3
97 Wrexham Glyndŵr		227	42.5	48.8	55.5	62.8

Employed in professional job:	43%	Employed in non-professional job and studying:		2%
Employed in professional job and studying:	2%	Employed in non-professional job:		36%
Studying:	8%	Unemployed:		10%
Average starting professional salary:	£19,673	Average starting non-professional salary:		£15,438

East and South Asian Studies

The apparent surge in interest in China, including the promotion of Mandarin in some sixth forms, has barely impacted on higher education, but the numbers starting courses in East and South Asian studies as a whole have at least passed 500 for the first time. Japanese is the main draw, attracting a record number of students in 2015 – some 40 per cent more than Chinese. The subjects have suffered the same recruitment problems that have afflicted all modern language programmes since higher fees arrived in 2012. Most undergraduates learn their chosen language from scratch, although universities expect to see evidence of language-learning potential in other modern language qualifications.

Degrees in these subjects are afforded extra protection by the Government because of their small size and their economic and cultural importance, but the low numbers can make for exaggerated swings in the ranking. This year's table is relatively stable, with Cambridge retaining the lead and again registering the highest entry grades. Oxford Brookes, only two places off the bottom of the table, is nine percentage points ahead of its nearest challenger for the proportion of students satisfied with teaching, feedback and academic support.

Second-placed Durham produced the best scores in the remaining sections of the National Student Survey.

Forty universities are offering Chinese studies and 24 Japanese in 2017. Others include modules in modern languages or area studies degrees, while the School of Oriental and African Studies (SOAS London) offers a range of languages, including Burmese, Indonesian, Thai, Tibetan and Vietnamese. South Asian studies is available at only four universities. The small numbers make for exaggerated swings, especially in the employment table. As a group, East and South Asian studies have escaped the bottom ten this year, but still have the highest unemployment rate in our table, at 18 per cent. Those who secured professional employment in 2015 did much better, however. The subjects are just outside the top 20 in the earnings table, more than 30 places higher than in the last edition of the *Guide*.

East and South Asian Studies	Research quality %	Entry standards	Teaching quality %	Student experience %	Graduate prospects %	Overall score
1 Cambridge	45.0	592	75.2	76.7	75.3	100.0
2 Durham	34.6	536	81.6	84.4		98.3
3 Manchester	48.9	407	82.5	79.9	66.2	96.2
4 Oxford	36.2	545	73.5	73.3	75.0	96.0
5 SOAS London	26.3	449	80.4	80.7	63.6	91.9
6 Leeds	30.6	420	77.7	79.8	64.8	91.5
7 Nottingham	27.3	396	72.8	77.3	75.5	90.8
8 Edinburgh	30.1	506	75.6	79.8	49.2	90.2
9 Sheffield	16.7	391	80.8	80.0	59.3	87.6
10 Oxford Brookes		380	91.6	80.8	47.7	84.3
11 Westminster	11.3		63.6	79.2	46.2	78.5
12 Central Lancashire		305	79.8	63.8	46.6	76.9

Employed in professional job:	41%	Employed in non-professional job and studying:	2%
Employed in professional job and studying:	3%	Employed in non-professional job:	20%
Studying:	17%	Unemployed:	18%
Average starting professional salary:	£23,723	Average starting non-professional salary:	£17,112

Economics

Economics has moved into the top four for graduate starting salaries, reflecting the value that employers place on a subject that they see combining the skills of the sciences and the arts. Although it is lower for overall employment rates, the subject is still in the top 20. Its reputation as a highly marketable degree has helped economics to withstand the impact of higher fees. More than 8,000 students started undergraduate courses in 2014, a record number, like the 52,000 applications. Competition for places is correspondingly stiff, with Oxford and Cambridge entrants averaging more than 600 points on the old UCAS tariff and another five universities averaging more than 500. The range of entry scores has been widening: eight have averages of less than 250 points. Many of those considering a degree in economics underestimate the mathematical skills required. Most of the leading universities demand maths at A level or its equivalent as part of offers that are consistently high.

Economics cont

Oxford has retained the top position it won last year, but its lead has narrowed with Cambridge moving back up to second place with the highest entry grades and the best graduate prospects. The London School of Economics took the laurels in the Research Excellence Framework, but Oxford's lead over Cambridge on this measure was enough to keep it on top overall. The most satisfied students for teaching, feedback and academic support in the National Student Survey are at Buckingham and Central Lancashire, which is also top for the general student experience, but only just inside the top 50 in the table because of low scores for research and entry standards.

More than 60 per cent of economists go straight into jobs categorised as professional, while 21 per cent continue studying, either full- or part-time. The leading universities invariably produce some of the highest graduate salaries of the year. While the average for 2015 in "professional" jobs was £28,157, graduates of Oxford's degree in economics and management earned an average of £38,000.

Economics	Research quality %	Entry standards	Teaching quality %	Student experience %	Graduate prospects %	Overall score
1 Oxford	58.0	600	77.1	86.6	88.4	100.0
2 Cambridge	45.0	635	76.7	82.0	93.9	99.3
=3 University College London	70.2	545	69.8	77.6	89.5	97.8
=3 Warwick	49.6	548	77.2	87.5	87.8	97.8
5 Nottingham	31.7	470	85.6	94.4	87.6	96.6
6 St Andrews	23.6	558	82.5	84.7	89.5	95.7
7 London School of Economics	70.7	569	64.7	71.7	85.6	95.6
=8 Bath	41.8	489	75.5	80.3	93.5	95.2
=8 Loughborough	32.6	411	80.8	93.3	93.3	95.2
10 Bristol	43.6	488	77.6	85.2	83.0	94.6
11 Surrey	33.0	427	86.8	92.3	80.7	94.5
12 Leeds	39.3	449	78.5	87.2	86.0	94.2
=13 Exeter	26.9	496	80.7	86.5	86.1	94.0
=13 Heriot-Watt	18.8	369	88.5	94.2	91.5	94.0
15 Durham	23.1	538	73.8	82.5	92.3	93.4
=16 East Anglia	25.7	397	87.1	91.6	78.4	92.4
=16 Stirling	25.2	365	88.6	79.9	89.5	92.4
=18 Birmingham	26.6	415	80.4	83.8	85.8	91.7
=18 Queen Mary, London	31.3	435	83.1	84.9	76.5	91.7
20 Glasgow	26.4	441	74.2	84.1	89.2	91.5
=21 Newcastle	20.7	432	81.2	89.8	80.9	91.4
=21 Strathclyde	44.3	477	84.9	89.0	55.8	91.4
23 Queen's, Belfast	32.7	377	80.3	90.1	79.2	91.3
24 Lancaster	42.6	395	72.5	82.8	81.2	90.6
25 York	22.6	422	77.3	83.5	84.7	90.4
26 Kent	14.6	377	79.6	84.4	89.8	89.9
27 Sussex	25.1	365	71.6	84.5	90.2	89.4
=28 Cardiff	32.0	395	75.1	80.8	80.3	89.3

=28 Reading	29.3	352	79.2	86.2	77.9	89.3
=30 Royal Holloway	31.3	369	81.9	85.7	70.7	89.1
=30 SOAS London	22.9	404	80.6	82.0	77.4	89.1
32 Essex	43.6	293	79.7	87.6	71.8	89.0
33 Aston	19.7	351	79.3	81.8	84.4	88.6
=34 Edinburgh	30.2	479	67.9	78.0	77.4	88.3
=34 Keele	10.2	339	87.3	86.6	78.0	88.3
=34 Liverpool	20.1	389	77.8	85.1	77.8	88.3
37 De Montfort	10.7	255	90.2	92.3	77.8	88.0
38 Hull	10.2	359	80.6	90.0	78.8	87.9
39 Coventry	1.6	294	90.0	93.2	77.9	87.7
40 Buckingham		312	91.7	91.1	75.9	87.6
=41 Manchester	26.8	431	68.8	79.7	76.9	87.2
=41 West of England	5.5	288	91.2	94.3	70.6	87.2
=43 Aberdeen	16.0	379	72.7	83.1	83.0	87.1
=43 Sheffield	16.6	409	69.1	79.0	86.4	87.1
=43 Southampton	23.4	407	70.6	81.3	78.5	87.1
46 Leicester	21.4	370	75.7	81.8	75.0	86.6
47 Ulster		312	86.6	90.9	75.8	86.4
48 City	15.1	369	74.8	80.4	79.8	86.3
49 Central Lancashire	4.4	289	91.7	95.4	64.5	86.1
50 Nottingham Trent		295	87.7	89.1	74.1	85.7
51 Swansea	22.0	307	73.6	78.4	81.4	85.6
52 Manchester Metropolitan	4.7	328	82.3	87.1	73.4	85.4
53 Salford	5.9	282	81.5	90.3		85.2
54 Brunel	9.9	331	79.8	84.8	72.6	85.1
55 Huddersfield	4.1	299	82.2	86.8		85.0
56 Portsmouth	9.5	303	78.1	83.3	70.7	84.7
57 Plymouth	13.1	258	83.1	86.6	68.3	84.2
58 Bradford	12.7	245	76.5	81.8	78.3	83.6
59 Hertfordshire	0.9	268	84.5	87.6	69.7	83.5
■60 Dundee	12.1	381	76.5	82.2	60.8	83.2
=60 Goldsmiths, London	16.8	344	73.5	77.5		83.2
62 Sheffield Hallam		285	81.8	88.3	66.7	82.6
63 Aberystwyth	14.5	234	77.4	83.6	66.9	81.9
64 Bangor	23.4	317	71.3	76.4	63.6	81.8
=65 Middlesex	10.5	229	73.6	78.8	75.0	81.2
=65 Oxford Brookes	5.1	328	75.2	82.3	63.2	81.2
67 Greenwich	3.3	337	77.9	81.3	56.5	80.4
68 London Metropolitan		183	89.9	89.2	55.3	80.3
69 Cardiff Metropolitan		225	76.3	89.1	65.4	80.0
70 Anglia Ruskin	3.4	237	84.8	89.1	51.4	79.9
71 East London	0.8	252*	79.4	80.1	59.1	78.9
72 Leeds Beckett	0.8	252	72.6	84.3	60.8	78.3
73 Kingston	9.2	236	74.9	77.6	58.4	78.2
74 Northampton		233	72.4	80.8	50.7	75.3
75 Birmingham City	1.3	252	68.9	77.9	51.2	74.8

Economics cont

Employed in professional job:	55%	Employed in non-professional job and studying:	1%
Employed in professional job and studying:	6%	Employed in non-professional job:	12%
Studying:	14%	Unemployed:	11%
Average starting professional salary:	£28,157	Average starting non-professional salary:	£18,132

Education

Morale is often said to be low in the teaching profession, but the official survey of graduates three years into their careers shows that those who studied education are among the least likely to wish they had taken a different subject. Only those who took medicine or dentistry are more satisfied. Applications for teacher training courses recovered in 2015, after a three-year decline as the Government promoted other routes into the profession. By contrast, courses classified as Academic Studies in Education, which had been recruiting more strongly, saw the demand for places falter. Entry to the BEd courses that train teachers at undergraduate level is still competitive, with nearly six applications to the place, but the chances of winning a place on the other education courses – which include early years qualifications, as well as those for youth work and outdoor education – is more than twice as good. The BEd remains the most common route into primary teaching, accounting for most of the 9,000 students starting courses in 2015, whereas alternatives such as the Postgraduate Certificate in Education, Teach First and the Government's Schools Direct programme have limited the demand for undergraduate training at secondary level.

Education	Research quality %	Ofsted	Entry standards	Teaching quality %	Student experience %	Graduate prospects %	Overall score
1 Cambridge	36.6	4.0	544	82.8	83.3	87.9	100.0
2 Durham	38.9	4.0	429	88.4	89.1	88.0	98.3
3 Birmingham	40.9	4.0	378	91.5	91.4	85.7	97.5
4 Glasgow	32.5	..	430	81.3	86.9	96.2	96.6
5 Stirling	29.2	..	438	80.1	83.3	96.0	95.7
6 Dundee	11.7	..	399	89.2	87.6	97.2	95.2
7 West of Scotland	7.5	..	384	92.5	91.1	92.0	94.6
8 Reading	25.8	3.5	368	90.2	88.6	87.0	93.1
=9 Edinburgh	23.1	..	432	71.3	80.7	97.2	92.2
=9 Southampton	41.1	3.0	411	91.8	91.3	62.5	92.2
11 Strathclyde	19.8	..	450	74.5	84.4	85.2	92.0
12 Manchester	46.0	4.0	373	80.4	79.1	62.5	91.6
13 Royal Conservatoire of Scotland	..	..	438	76.9	80.7	97.4	91.2
14 West of England	5.3	3.8	366	89.0	89.0	82.7	91.0
15 Northumbria	..	4.0	338	82.1	90.3	90.0	89.8
16 Brunel	20.4	4.0	338	81.2	86.2	71.2	89.4
17 Brighton	1.6	4.0	334	82.9	82.6	88.6	89.0
=18 Edge Hill	1.4	4.0	335	84.7	86.6	81.2	88.9

=18 Sheffield	32.9	3.0	382	88.6	88.1	59.0	88.9
=20 St Mary's, Twickenham	1.8	4.0	286	84.5	90.0	90.2	88.8
=20 York	43.3	3.0	385	78.0	78.7	73.6	88.8
22 East Anglia	27.2	3.0	396	83.3	87.9	66.7	88.5
23 Chichester	..	4.0	305	84.6	86.4	85.1	88.2
24 Coventry	18.1	..	..	82.0	83.5	77.3	88.1
=25 Bangor	39.6	..	316	79.4	81.3	75.6	87.9
=25 Cardiff	35.3	..	383	78.2	85.2	58.8	87.9
=27 Winchester	2.2	3.5	334	85.7	89.8	81.6	87.7
=27 Worcester	2.5	4.0	312	84.8	87.2	75.3	87.7
29 Canterbury Christ Church	2.8	4.0	335	76.7	78.5	90.3	87.6
30 Huddersfield	5.9	3.5	313	86.7	89.5	80.3	87.5
31 Birmingham City	1.8	4.0	316	82.7	79.6	82.7	87.3
32 Keele	25.0	3.5	352	78.2	82.3	66.5	86.9
33 Liverpool Hope	7.3	3.0	315	93.0	94.4	72.3	86.8
34 York St John	1.5	3.3	334	86.2	88.5	79.8	86.7
35 Gloucestershire	..	3.7	327	84.2	88.6	73.2	86.6
36 Leeds	31.6	3.0	393	79.2	80.4	57.8	86.2
=37 Aberdeen	7.6	..	412	65.9	69.1	95.7	86.0
=37 University College London	40.2	3.5	279	75.6	84.8	65.6	86.0
39 Warwick	43.6	3.7	379*	67.6	72.4	51.8	85.8
=40 Chester	1.4	3.8	316	82.3	81.6	74.2	85.7
=40 Derby	1.1	3.4	320	88.3	90.4	65.3	85.7
42 Oxford Brookes	3.3	3.5	344	79.6	84.0	74.6	85.5
43 Bath Spa	3.2	3.4	327	79.6	84.9	74.8	84.7
44 Hertfordshire	..	3.0	309	82.2	89.0	83.0	84.2
45 Liverpool John Moores	3.0	3.5	344	75.3	82.3	72.0	84.1
=46 Aberystwyth	..	..	313	85.2	84.9	66.4	83.7
=46 Middlesex	14.9	3.0	311	76.0	81.8	80.3	83.7
=46 Plymouth	9.4	3.5	300	76.4	79.6	74.9	83.7
=49 Leeds Beckett	2.3	3.0	290	86.7	88.3	73.8	83.6
=49 Nottingham Trent	2.6	3.3	302	84.6	87.2	65.2	83.6
=51 De Montfort	11.2	..	312	78.5	81.7	69.4	83.2
=51 Sheffield Hallam	2.0	3.3	307	79.4	84.3	72.9	83.2
=53 Manchester Metropolitan	5.8	2.7	345	80.0	79.9	78.4	83.0
=53 South Wales	..	..	332	82.7	83.1	62.5	83.0
55 Bolton	3.1	..	305	88.7	80.0	60.0	82.9
56 Bishop Grosseteste	1.4	3.1	288	85.6	86.2	69.7	82.8
=57 Bedfordshire	3.1	3.0	265	86.7	86.9	71.2	82.4
=57 Northampton	1.8	3.0	298	83.4	86.6	69.0	82.4
59 Leeds Trinity	..	3.0	300	79.5	80.3	82.2	82.3
60 Portsmouth	..	3.5	323	77.3	81.1	61.7	82.1
=61 Cumbria	0.4	3.0	303	79.7	79.3	78.8	82.0
=61 Greenwich	0.8	3.3	327	78.6	81.3	62.6	82.0
63 Wrexham Glyndŵr	..	..	230	91.7	92.3	58.9	81.7
=64 Roehampton	20.2	3.0	294	72.0	74.8	72.8	81.3
=64 Sunderland	3.8	2.7	347	72.7	70.3	87.3	81.3

	Research quality %	Ofsted	Entry standards	Teaching quality %	Student experience %	Graduate prospects %	Overall score
66 Hull	5.0	3.0	333	69.2	75.3	76.4	80.7
=67 Cardiff Metropolitan	..	..	325	78.9	84.7	50.8	80.0
=67 Central Lancashire	..	..	312	79.6	80.9	56.5	80.0
=67 Newman	2.2	3.0	310	74.3	76.1	70.6	80.0
=70 Kingston	..	3.0	278	79.2	81.6	66.4	79.8
=70 Staffordshire	7.6	4.0	264	79.8	85.3	27.3	79.8
72 Ulster	27.5	..	285	76.2	82.1	44.2	79.4
73 Goldsmiths, London	17.4	3.0	323	75.4	80.1	39.7	79.3
74 Teesside	15.0	..	282	79.8	83.8	41.3	78.6
75 St Mark and St John	..	2.0	275	82.6	84.6	78.4	78.5
76 East London	2.8	3.0	271	79.2	81.1	41.1	76.9
77 London Metropolitan	3.3	2.3	257	84.7	85.2	50.5	76.6
78 Anglia Ruskin	0.8	3.0	287	71.8	68.7	55.0	76.0

Employed in professional job:	59%	Employed in non-professional job and studying:	1%
Employed in professional job and studying:	2%	Employed in non-professional job:	20%
Studying:	12%	Unemployed:	5%
Average starting professional salary:	£21,932	Average starting non-professional salary:	£15,525

Education is the only ranking that contains inspection scores – because teacher training assessments are carried out by Ofsted at English universities. Fourteen universities tie for the best of these scores, only one of them – Staffordshire – in the bottom half of the table overall. Cambridge has regained the lead it lost last year, thanks partly to its usual high entry standards. The Cambridge course is an example of those that do not offer Qualified Teacher Status, but combines the academic study of education with other subjects. Liverpool Hope posted the best scores on both of the student satisfaction measures derived from the National Student Survey.

Employment scores at different universities reflect to some extent the variations in demand for new staff between primary and secondary schools, as well as between different parts of the UK – the top seven are all Scottish. Universities that specialise in primary training are at an advantage at the moment in terms of employment. Some of the best-known education departments are absent from the table because they offer only postgraduate courses. University College London's Institute of Education, which is ranked top in the world in this field by QS, and Oxford, which achieved the top grades in the 2014 Research Excellence Framework, are two examples.

Electrical and Electronic Engineering

The demand for places in electrical and electronic engineering took longer to recover from the introduction of £9,000 fees than was the case in other branches of the discipline, but it has got there now. The numbers starting courses are still marginally lower than in 2010, the last year unaffected by higher charges, but applications are running at record levels. Some natural applicants have been diverted into courses such as computer games design and, at around five applications to the place, selection is less competitive than in most other branches of engineering. Nevertheless, only mechanical courses attract more students. The subject is just outside the top 20 for employment prospects and in the top ten for salaries in graduate-level jobs.

Cambridge maintains its lead in electrical and electronic engineering this year, with the best research grades and a lead of almost 60 points over second-placed Imperial College on entry standards. The scores are close together for much of the top 20: Surrey, for example, dropped from second place to equal 13th last year, but is back up to sixth in the latest edition. Sunderland achieved a rare 100 per cent employment score among its 2015 graduates, but did not enter the Research Excellence Framework in this category and fails to make the top 50 overall. Northumbria is the only post-1992 institution in the top 30, although East London, only nine places off the bottom of the table, has much the highest levels of student satisfaction.

Most of the top courses demand maths and physics at A level or the equivalent, but the table displays a big divide in entry standards. Cambridge and Imperial College average more than 550 points on the old UCAS tariff, but there are 13 universities with averages of less than 300 points. There are also considerable variations in employment rates and the gap in earnings between those in professional jobs and lower-level employment is among the widest of any subject, at almost £9,000. Three-quarters of graduates go straight into professional jobs or continue their studies, but the 12 per cent unemployment rate is above the average for all subjects.

Electrical and Electronic Engineering	Research quality %	Entry standards	Teaching quality %	Student experience %	Graduate prospects %	Overall score
1 Cambridge	67.0	629	74.7	87.2	94.6	100.0
2 Imperial College	65.0	570	83.5	89.0	87.0	97.5
3 Southampton	53.3	497	82.1	85.0	93.5	93.9
4 University College London	59.0	488	75.6	85.9	88.8	92.3
5 Bristol	52.3	459	78.3	86.8	91.5	91.4
6 Surrey	36.3	445	88.2	93.3	88.6	89.9
7 Queen's, Belfast	47.3	415	81.4	81.6	93.3	89.5
8 Leeds	41.8	423	89.8	93.4	84.4	89.3
9 Glasgow	47.2	516	70.0	81.6	85.7	89.2
10 Manchester	37.0	447	81.6	88.6	90.3	88.9
11 Edinburgh	50.3	512	73.7	81.0	80.2	88.8
12 Bath	28.6	453	81.0	87.8	93.9	88.4
13 Strathclyde	41.7	476	76.9	87.9	81.1	87.5
=14 Nottingham	40.8	394	82.2	86.8	87.5	86.9
=14 Sheffield	42.6	383	78.5	82.3	92.1	86.9
16 Birmingham	32.1	406	83.9	82.3	90.7	86.5
=17 Dundee	34.1		79.0	84.1	90*	86.3
=17 Lancaster	41.6	391	77.3	85.8	88.9	86.3
19 Heriot-Watt	47.8	420	64.9	76.7	92.7	86.2

Electrical and Electronic Engineering cont

		Research quality %	Entry standards	Teaching quality %	Student experience %	Graduate prospects %	Overall score
20	Exeter	36.4	458	66.6	73.6	92.0	85.5
21	Cardiff	30.2	424	77.8	81.8	88.6	85.2
22	Newcastle	39.4	370	79.5	91.2	81.0	84.2
23	Loughborough	23.8	381	80.1	87.3	89.7	83.8
24	Brunel	26.4	354	90.4	95.2	80.8	83.7
25	Swansea	45.5	338	72.6	81.4	86.2	83.2
=26	Aberdeen	28.4	412	64.2	73.3	95.5	82.9
=26	Northumbria	30.7	350	89.5	89.6	78.0	82.9
28	York	21.4	369	88.5	86.9	81.6	82.4
29	Liverpool	30.4	387	81.8	86.9	74.1	81.6
30	Bangor	31.9	301	91.4	91.2	75.8	81.3
31	Kent	27.3	322	78.6	86.3	86.9	81.2
32	West of England	10.6	295	90.1	88.0	89.1	80.2
33	Hull	16.5	330	89.3	89.7	78.6	79.9
34	Reading	16.3	330	78.6	80.0	89.5	79.7
=35	Aston	25.8	367	67.3	64.3	90.5	79.4
=35	Bedfordshire	9.1		83.5	90.3	76.9	79.4
37	Essex	34.3	342	74.4	80.6		79.3
38	Ulster	22.8	312	81.5	90.8	76.7	78.6
39	Wrexham Glyndŵr	20.1		82.6	85.8	70*	77.9
40	Hertfordshire	16.5	295	87.3	86.8	76.9	77.7
41	Sheffield Hallam	17.8	278	84.4	87.5	79.2	77.4
42	Portsmouth	7.2	347	75.7	82.3	84.4	77.3
43	Manchester Metropolitan	16.3	334	76.0	82.9	78.9	77.1
=44	City	20.2	379	73.3	79.9	72.4	77.0
=44	Coventry	10.3	292	86.7	91.7	77.6	77.0
46	Glasgow Caledonian	4.7	393	76.3	84.2	76.7	76.9
47	Sussex	24.0	404	63.4	72.0	75.0	76.7
48	Robert Gordon	8.8	387	64.1	74.3	84.4	76.2
=49	Huddersfield	10.2	337	83.2	84.0	72.3	76.0
=49	Queen Mary, London	41.9	335	63.8	72.8	69.5	76.0
51	Derby	6.7	291	83.1	85.9	80.4	75.9
=52	De Montfort	12.5	261	77.0	81.5	79.6	74.1
=52	Plymouth	13.3	332	72.8	74.4	74.3	74.1
54	Sunderland		246	69.6	63.1	100.0	73.4
=55	Anglia Ruskin	9.1	269	88.6	87.3	65.9	73.1
=55	Southampton Solent		239*	87.1	82.6	79.2	73.1
57	Liverpool John Moores	8.7	375	66.2	70.0	71.9	72.7
58	London South Bank	19.6	285	76.0	77.3	63.2	71.6
59	Brighton	7.4		65.5	66.2	78.3	71.5
60	Birmingham City		335	81.6	82.8	60.8	71.0
61	Central Lancashire	11.7	321	69.0	70.1	63.2	69.6
62	East London	2.3	260*	98.9	96.7	45.5	69.4

63 Salford	4.4	345	71.4	69.9	60.3	69.0
=64 Greenwich	7.5	324	62.0	63.3	67.2	68.2
=64 South Wales		314	61.6	67.3	72.7	68.2
66 Teesside	5.8	319	73.2	76.8	53.6	67.6
67 Bradford		295	72.7	79.4	58.3	67.1
68 Westminster	2.9	285	59.5	70.8	63.8	65.4
69 Staffordshire	5.7		47.1	52.0	63.0	58.8
70 Bolton		338	34.4	45.4	58.3	58.7

Employed in professional job:	62%	Employed in non-professional job and studying:	1%
Employed in professional job and studying:	2%	Employed in non-professional job:	13%
Studying:	11%	Unemployed:	12%
Average starting professional salary:	£26,146	Average starting non-professional salary:	£17,253

English

Degrees in English are a perennial favourite of university applicants, despite the fact that they seldom feature among the top 50 subjects for employment prospects or starting salaries in professional jobs. There were small increases in both applications and enrolments in 2015, when English remained among the top dozen choices for a degree. The demand for places remains well short of the level reached before the introduction of £9,000 fees, but the table remains one of the largest in the *Guide* and entry standards are high at the leading institutions. Five of the top seven average more than 500 points on the old UCAS tariff.

St Andrews has deposed Durham at the top of the table this year without registering the top score in any of the individual measures. Durham is only a fraction of a point behind after posting the highest entry scores – an achievement in a table that contains both Oxford and Cambridge, neither of which is in the top three overall. Queen Mary, London, in equal 17th place, produced the best results in the Research Excellence Framework, with University College London its nearest challenger.

Less predictable names dominated the 2015 National Student Survey: Southampton Solent, in 72nd place overall, satisfied 97 per cent of final-year undergraduates on teaching, feedback and academic support, while Surrey, in tenth place, had the best scores on the questions relating to the student experience. Only De Montfort, of the modern universities, made the top 30.

Almost three English graduates in ten continue their studies, while more than a third went into graduate-level jobs in 2015. Unemployment was no higher than average for all subjects, but approaching a third of all graduates started out in lower-level jobs. Employment rates have improved in the last two editions of the *Guide*, but only Sussex, Cambridge, Nottingham, Durham and Birmingham saw eight out of ten graduates go straight into graduate-level work or further study. English has produced consistently good levels of student satisfaction, however. In the 2016 survey, every one of the 105 universities in the table satisfied at least three-quarters of the final-year undergraduates.

Employed in professional job:	34%	Employed in non-professional job and studying:	4%
Employed in professional job and studying:	3%	Employed in non-professional job:	27%
Studying:	22%	Unemployed:	10%
Average starting professional salary:	£20,063	Average starting non-professional salary:	£15,796

English

	Research quality %	Entry standards	Teaching quality %	Student experience %	Graduate prospects %	Overall score
1 St Andrews	60.4	521	93.0	90.5	79.8	100.0
2 Durham	57.9	560	87.9	86.8	82.6	99.2
3 University College London	61.7	513	88.5	84.9	77.0	97.7
4 Oxford	50.7	542	87.8	86.3	76.9	97.1
5 Exeter	46.2	487	90.9	90.8	75.8	96.7
6 Nottingham	56.6	429	87.3	87.3	80.6	95.8
7 Cambridge	50.0	536	80.6	83.8	80.6	95.3
8 Birmingham	37.0	419	90.5	88.2	80.6	94.4
9 York	61.5	463	81.6	85.5	72.9	94.3
10 Surrey	39.1	390	94.1	95.6	67.2	94.0
=11 Lancaster	47.0	433	84.1	88.3	78.4	93.9
=11 Sussex	45.6	377	86.1	87.9	84.8	93.9
=11 Warwick	59.8	480	82.0	81.3	72.2	93.9
14 King's College London	47.6	468	83.2	82.5	76.9	93.5
15 Newcastle	54.3	447	85.0	87.0	67.2	93.4
16 Kent	47.3	362	88.3	87.2	74.7	92.8
=17 Loughborough	32.4	408	88.6	88.0	77.4	92.7
=17 Queen Mary, London	64.0	409	83.7	84.1	65.5	92.7
19 Leeds	38.6	451	83.0	86.2	74.4	92.2
20 Glasgow	52.0	441	85.3	86.6	60.8	92.1
21 Bangor	46.3	347	92.7	89.2	61.6*	91.8
22 Leicester	45.4	388	85.4	89.0	68.3	91.7
23 Stirling	29.8	376	90.8	89.0	72.3	91.6
24 Manchester	49.1	421	81.7	82.3	70.9	91.3
25 Sheffield	42.2	420	83.0	87.8	67.7	91.2
26 Royal Holloway	49.9	410	84.5	85.8	60.2	90.8
27 Strathclyde	39.4	445	87.4	89.8	53.2	90.7
28 Southampton	38.4	402	85.1	86.5	65.5	90.4
=29 De Montfort	24.1	281	94.7	94.6	69.3	90.3
=29 Queen's, Belfast	53.1	384	84.9	90.5	53.0	90.3
=31 Bedfordshire	45.8	247	91.1	92.9	64.3	90.1
=31 Bristol	30.0	497	81.0	77.2	71.6	90.1
=31 Dundee	32.8	399	88.6	89.5	59.4	90.1
34 Edinburgh	43.6	485	77.0	81.5	64.6	89.9
=35 Aberdeen	46.3	429	84.0	85.8	54.0	89.8
=35 Swansea	43.6	297	82.9	84.8	78.8	89.8
37 Edinburgh Napier	37.9	373	92.3	86.3	52.1	89.5
38 Aberystwyth	31.2	290	91.6	91.3	64.8	89.4
39 East Anglia	36.2	451	81.4	84.6	59.0	89.1
40 Liverpool	47.8	394	82.2	82.7	58.6	89.0
41 Reading	36.3	374	83.8	87.2	60.4	88.6
42 Keele	29.8	342	87.2	90.7	58.4	88.2
43 Huddersfield	29.9	318	87.4	81.3	69.5	88.1

44 Cardiff	35.1	389	83.9	84.1	57.6	87.9
45 Bolton	14.4	208*	97.1	93.3	65.9	87.6
46 Buckingham		290	93.8	91.3	71.2	87.4
47 West of England	35.4	315	88.1	87.8	53.2	87.3
=48 Derby	13.5	351	91.5	93.7	52.5	87.2
=48 Lincoln	16.2	334	87.7	87.4	65.1	87.2
=50 Aston	23.4	331	83.8	85.1	67.6	87.0
=50 Birmingham City	30.9	286	90.8	88.4	53.4	87.0
=50 Oxford Brookes	27.8	329	86.2	86.3	59.5	87.0
=50 Teesside	15.6	278	93.3	90.8	60.0	87.0
54 Coventry	18.1	302	85.2	83.7	73.3	86.7
55 Northumbria	27.2	355	85.5	83.4	55.2	86.3
56 Brunel	30.9	313	87.0	89.3	47.6	85.9
57 Manchester Metropolitan	29.0	316	87.6	85.1	51.2	85.8
=58 Essex	37.7	315	79.2	83.3	59.7	85.7
=58 Portsmouth	17.1	296	85.8	85.9	64.7	85.7
60 Plymouth	30.5	296	89.1	83.6	48.7	85.4
61 Nottingham Trent	30.0	260	85.7	84.7	58.9	85.3
62 Liverpool Hope	26.9	281	82.7	81.1	65.9	85.2
63 Goldsmiths, London	34.9	353	78.6	75.1	59.9	84.9
64 Hull	22.7	338	82.2	85.1	54.7	84.8
65 Falmouth		290	89.6	84.3	66.7	84.7
66 Cumbria		243	96.5	92.8	52.9	84.6
67 Roehampton	20.8	276	84.9	82.9	61.1	84.5
=68 Gloucestershire	9.3	300	92.8	90.7	44.0	84.3
=68 Liverpool John Moores	17.9	334	85.7	89.8	45.4	84.3
70 Bishop Grosseteste	6.7	293	87.7	82.5	61.7	84.1
71 Ulster	35.1	276	88.5	89.3	34.0	84.0
72 Southampton Solent		254	97.2	88.4	48.6	83.8
73 Bath Spa	23.5	318	84.4	84.1	47.1	83.7
74 Newman	9.6	275	88.1	88.3	52.2	83.5
75 Edge Hill	12.1	321	80.8	83.1	60.2	83.4
=76 Chester	10.7	307	87.3	82.4	50.9	83.1
=76 Greenwich	14.4	332	87.1	81.8	45.6	83.1
78 Bournemouth	15.1	335	80.4	79.5	57.1	83.0
79 Westminster	28.9	287	80.2	82.8	50.7	82.9
80 Middlesex	11.0	228*	80.3	79.8	74.1	82.7
=81 Kingston	15.7	286	83.3	87.1	48.6	82.5
=81 Northampton	15.3	241	87.5	84.0	51.4	82.5
=83 Anglia Ruskin	16.3	245	88.3	86.0	46.1	82.4
=83 South Wales	12.8	317	90.0	88.3	32.2	82.4
=85 Hertfordshire	7.8	288	83.2	81.2	58.2	82.3
=85 Suffolk		276	89.8	89.8	46.3	82.3
87 Central Lancashire	9.9	341	80.0	82.6	52.4	82.2
=88 Chichester	16.3	248	88.0	88.8	41.4	82.1
=88 Leeds Trinity	6.2	256	84.1	87.9	55.0	82.1
90 Winchester		299	84.4	85.1	54.0	81.9

English cont	Research quality %	Entry standards	Teaching quality %	Student experience %	Graduate prospects %	Overall score
=91 Staffordshire		220	87.2	88.5	57.3	81.8
=91 York St John	9.7	287	83.2	83.0	52.3	81.8
93 Sunderland	15.3	275	77.5	78.8	62.0	81.6
=94 Leeds Beckett	11.0	288	83.7	81.3	48.1	81.3
=94 Sheffield Hallam	14.6	298	79.7	82.0	50.0	81.3
96 Salford	7.8	278	87.3	82.4	44.3	81.2
97 Brighton	16.2	288	74.5	75.8	61.2	80.7
98 London South Bank	12.8	218	87.7	91.2	34.1	80.3
99 Canterbury Christ Church	8.0	256	79.9	84.2	50.9	80.1
100 East London	13.7	262	89.4	83.9	28.8	80.0
101 Worcester	8.2	291	79.7	78.3	46.8	79.4
102 St Mary's, Twickenham	14.6	273	73.3	79.8	52.6	79.2
103 Cardiff Metropolitan		278	81.8	76.4	49.2	78.9
104 London Metropolitan		234	82.1	83.8	39.8	77.6
105 St Mark and St John		241*	79.4	72.5	33.7	74.7

Food Science

The courses classified by UCAS as Food and Beverage Studies may be beginning to reap the benefits of television's obsession with cookery. Although only 770 students started courses in 2015, that represented a 33 per cent increase on the previous year. Applications have grown for seven of the last eight years, and are now twice what they were at the start of the decade. Employment levels have been rising, too – food science is well inside the top 30 for positive destinations in the latest table, with 58 per cent of graduates finding "professional" jobs within six months of completing a course. The subject does less well in the earnings table, but the national average of £22,250 in graduate-level employment is well up on last year and only just in the bottom half of the 67 subjects.

Degrees range from professional cookery to food manufacturing and nutrition. Almost a third of entrants to food science courses arrive with alternative qualifications to A levels, usually BTECs. Entry standards have been rising – none of the universities in this year's ranking averages less than 250 points – but there were still little more than three applications per place in 2015.

Surrey has retained the lead in food science that it won last year, although it does not lead on any of the individual measures. Leeds, which has moved up from third place with the highest entry standards, could not be closer to top place. Hertfordshire, in 13th place, has the best graduate prospects – a creditable 97 per cent registering positive destinations – while Queen's, Belfast produced the best results in the 2014 Research Excellence Framework (REF). Edge Hill has the most satisfied students for teaching, feedback and academic support in the National Student Survey, while Greenwich, closely followed by Edge Hill, performs best on the overall student experience. Edge Hill would have finished higher than 15th place if it had entered the REF in this category. Most of the institutions offering food science are post-1992 universities, but only Lincoln and Coventry feature in the top ten.

Food Science

Food Science	Research quality %	Entry standards	Teaching quality %	Student experience %	Graduate prospects %	Overall score
1 Surrey	37.5	434	84.5	84.4	94.4	100.0
2 Leeds	36.8	444	88.0	89.5	84.4	99.9
3 King's College London	46.8	440	77.7	82.5	81.8	97.7
=4 Queen's, Belfast	56.3	381	69.5	92.8	85.3	96.2
=4 Reading	50.7	385	78.4	83.9	83.3	96.2
6 Nottingham	36.4	377	83.3	85.5	87.8	95.9
7 Newcastle	28.4	407	78.7	90.4	86.1	95.4
8 Lincoln	31.1		89.6	93.7	70.0	93.6
9 Ulster	42.5	319	86.7	90.9	75.4	93.1
10 Coventry		363	86.7	88.2	96.4	92.6
11 Glasgow Caledonian	8.1		87.6	94.7	80.0	92.5
12 Plymouth	17.4	359	89.7	93.0	72.3	91.8
13 Hertfordshire	14.8	326	79.9	81.2	97.0	90.7
14 Robert Gordon	4.9	433	76.2	80.2	77.4	90.0
15 Edge Hill		339	94.8	97.4	70.8	89.8
16 Greenwich	19.5		83.6	98.0	65.2	89.4
17 Harper Adams	5.7	296	85.0	84.5	93.5	88.9
18 Manchester Metropolitan	12.0	344	86.5	89.4	70.0	88.8
19 Liverpool Hope		321	94.2	91.0	74.2	88.6
20 Leeds Beckett		330	86.5	92.1	77.3	88.0
21 Huddersfield		310	90.2	93.3	73.2	87.3
22 Northumbria	14.0	346	79.7	83.0		87.0
23 Kingston	2.6		90.9	93.6	57.6	86.6
24 Chester	12.0	322	72.6	77.9	85.2	86.0
25 Sheffield Hallam		304	86.0	89.2	73.3	85.6
26 Liverpool John Moores	6.0	346	80.7	82.7	66.7	85.4
27 Bournemouth	4.7	334	79.5	88.3	65.6	84.8
28 London Metropolitan		302	80.8	87.1	75.7	84.6
29 Roehampton	20.6	258	86.5	89.3	60.0	84.2
30 Central Lancashire	8.3	360	83.4	83.0	50.0	84.1
31 Queen Margaret, Edinburgh		384	77.6	78.0	54.0	82.8
32 Oxford Brookes	3.0	317	76.9	77.1	66.1	82.0
33 Worcester		278	92.9	92.9	46.2	81.6
34 Cardiff Metropolitan		292	73.7	77.6	66.0	79.8
35 Bath Spa		307	77.7	84.6	51.5	79.6
36 St Mary's, Twickenham		273	77.7	82.5	56.0	78.5
37 Royal Agricultural University	2.1		65.4	70.6	73.3	78.3
38 Westminster		288	71.3	84.8	56.6	78.2
39 Suffolk		305	71.0	79.6	52.6	77.6
40 Leeds Trinity		254	70.4	67.1	61.1	75.1

Food Science cont

Employed in professional job:	56%	Employed in non-professional job and studying:	2%
Employed in professional job and studying:	2%	Employed in non-professional job:	16%
Studying:	13%	Unemployed:	11%
Average starting professional salary:	£22,249	Average starting non-professional salary:	£15,500

French

Languages have suffered a well-publicised decline in recent years – enrolments were dropping before the introduction of £9,000 fees and the process has accelerated since. Applications were down for the sixth year in a row in 2015, and the numbers actually starting courses dropped again in 2016. Some universities are now closing their language departments, but 76 of them (two more than last year) are offering full-time undergraduate courses in or including French for 2017. Only 430 students started degrees in French in 2015 – 90 fewer than in the previous year – but another 2,700 opted for broader modern language courses. French remains the most popular language at degree level, but a continuing decline at A level suggests more tough times ahead.

Nevertheless, entry standards remain relatively high. In spite of the falling numbers, there were almost six applications to the place in 2015 and many of the candidates came from high-achieving independent schools. Just under half of the 50 universities in the table averaged more than 400 points on the old UCAS tariff and only seven were below 300. Perhaps not surprisingly, nine out of ten undergraduates enter with A levels or their equivalents, although many universities will teach the language from scratch, especially as part of joint degrees.

Cambridge remains well clear at the top of the table, with the best research grades and the highest entry standards, but the top performers on the other measures are spread through the table. Coventry had the best scores in all aspects of the National Student Survey (NSS), for example, but remains outside the top 30, partly because it did not enter the Research Excellence Framework in this category. Aberystwyth, in equal 18th place despite also doing well in the NSS, has the best of a mixed set of employment scores. Only ten universities saw eight out of ten graduates go straight into "professional" jobs or continue their studies, and the rate was below 50 per cent at three institutions. French is outside the top 30 subjects for employment and earnings, although an increase of more than £1,500 took average starting salaries beyond £22,000 in 2015.

French	Research quality %	Entry standards	Teaching quality %	Student experience %	Graduate prospects %	Overall score
1 Cambridge	54.0	570	88.0	87.7	87.6	100.0
2 Lancaster	47.0	436*	85.7	85.4	87.2	94.4
=3 Oxford	41.3	558	82.8	88.3	75.3	94.3
=3 Warwick	45.2	460	89.9	88.2	76.8	94.3
5 Durham	34.6	554	81.8	85.0	86.0	94.1
6 St Andrews	26.4	510	90.7	90.8	81.2	93.5
=7 Birmingham	33.7	426	91.0	91.6	82.7	93.1
=7 Newcastle	36.3	423	90.2	92.7	81.0	93.1

9	Surrey	39.1		92.2	95.7	67.2	92.8
10	King's College London	42.1	448	83.0	81.8	86.3	92.7
11	York	37.3	443	88.3	95.4	71.1	92.0
=12	Queen's, Belfast	53.6	395	83.7	87.4	71.9	91.7
=12	Southampton	42.7	435	81.5	90.1	78.6	91.7
14	Exeter	35.1	460	85.8	91.1	72.0	91.1
15	Manchester	48.9	418	81.5	82.5	72.1	90.4
16	Nottingham	39.4	406	79.2	87.3	79.5	89.7
17	Sheffield	41.2	413	81.2	83.8	75.7	89.6
=18	Aberystwyth	16.6	335	94.1	91.7	89.0	89.5
=18	Strathclyde	42.0	460	89.6	90.7	50.0	89.5
20	Glasgow	26.3	498	87.8	88.0	64.0	89.3
21	Heriot-Watt	26.3	425	88.7	89.2	72.6	89.2
=22	Bath	27.4	441	81.7	82.3	82.1	89.0
=22	Kent	41.9	354	83.1	84.7	77.0	89.0
=22	Royal Holloway	48.3	368	86.4	85.5	63.1	89.0
25	University College London	43.7	483	75.8	77.4	70.0	88.9
26	Bristol	36.0	439	79.7	81.6	74.4	88.6
27	Leeds	30.6	419	83.4	88.4	72.5	88.4
28	Cardiff	32.5	362	84.7	88.0	75.6	88.1
29	Liverpool	33.4	366	87.4	85.8	66.7	87.3
30	Aston	23.4	338	88.4	95.0	67.3	86.2
31	Edinburgh	30.3	496	71.2	80.4	67.9	85.8
32	Queen Mary, London	35.1	377	78.9	73.6	73.4	85.5
=33	Reading	41.7	356	83.5	84.8	52.5	85.0
=33	Swansea	22.8	297	87.6	90.8	71.4	85.0
35	Hull	22.7	349	83.3	89.7	67.9	84.6
36	Coventry		281	95.2	97.7	78.9	84.5
37	Aberdeen	29.3	490	73.2	78.4	58.5	84.1
38	Central Lancashire	15.2		86.7	85.7	62.4	83.7
39	Leicester	16.9	387	81.1	88.8	64.1	83.3
40	Stirling	29.8	389	72.3	70.0	74.0	83.2
=41	Bangor	39.6	322	85.4	81.3	45.4	82.6
=41	Sussex		392*	75.1	83.6	88.9	82.6
43	Manchester Metropolitan	29.0	310	77.7	79.3	54.9	80.0
44	Portsmouth	32.2	279	79.3	82.6	46.2	79.0
45	Chester	17.3	282	82.2	76.1	60.2	78.8
46	Oxford Brookes		315*	90.0	85.6	54.4	78.6
47	Nottingham Trent	7.6	280	80.8	82.0	66.5	78.4
48	Edinburgh Napier		361	80.1	85.5	53.1	77.2
49	Ulster	22.4	292	75.8	75.0	44.7	75.7
50	Westminster	2.0	291	78.3	85.3	51.5	75.0

Employed in professional job:	47%	Employed in non-professional job and studying:	2%
Employed in professional job and studying:	3%	Employed in non-professional job:	20%
Studying:	17%	Unemployed:	10%
Average starting professional salary:	£22,171	Average starting non-professional salary:	£16,517

General Engineering

Applications for general engineering courses rose by almost 10 per cent in 2015, following an even bigger increase in the previous year. The numbers starting undergraduate courses also grew significantly for the fourth year in a row. Although they do not yet attract as many applications as the established specialist branches of engineering, the general courses attract students who are looking for maximum career flexibility. Another reason for its success may be that general engineering has become a fixture in the top five of the graduate salaries table. Although the subject was one of the few to see a drop in average starting salaries in professional jobs at the end of 2015, the figure was still above £27,200 a year. The subject is just outside the top ten in the overall employment table, with two-thirds of graduates going straight into "professional" roles.

Cambridge remains at the top of the table with an extended lead. Oxford, which had the best results in the 2014 Research Excellence Framework, is now the nearest challenger, having overtaken Imperial College London. The best scores in the sections of the National Student Survey relating to teaching, feedback and academic support came at Coventry, while Bristol was the top performer on the broader student experience. Exeter's graduates were most successful in the employment market, with more than 95 per cent going straight into high-level work or starting postgraduate courses. Coventry, in 13th place, has taken over from Lincoln as the leading modern university in the subject.

The growth in applications has brought rising entry grades, but five universities still average less than 300 points on the old UCAS tariff. Most of the leading universities will require both maths and physics at A level, with further maths, design technology and/or computing welcome additions. Nearly one student in five goes on to a postgraduate course, either full or part-time.

General Engineering	Research quality %	Entry standards	Teaching quality %	Student experience %	Graduate prospects %	Overall score
1 Cambridge	67.0	629	74.7	87.2	94.6	100.0
2 Oxford	68.7	604	74.8	82.3	90.6	98.1
3 Imperial College	60.1	543	76.6	81.5	94.7	96.7
4 Nottingham	40.8	494*	89.4	91.7	89.1	95.2
5 Durham	39.4	568	78.7	82.8	93.1	94.7
6 Bristol		569	90.3	98.6	91.9	93.1
7 Glasgow	47.2	507	79.8	90.3	82.1	92.5
8 Warwick	47.2	450	72.6	81.5	87.1	89.9
9 Heriot-Watt	47.8	458	73.9	84.8		89.7
10 Exeter	36.4	449	62.7	76.2	95.7	87.9
11 Sheffield	51.4	422	76.5	88.6	72.5	87.7
12 Liverpool	32.1	445*	75.5	86.6	78.6	86.7
13 Coventry	10.3	245	95.5	94.9	88.2	86.3
14 Lincoln	12.4	324	85.1	85.7	90.3	85.9
15 Bournemouth	8.5	301	92.2	86.2	87.5	85.6
16 West of England	10.6	317	90.7	95.1	81.9	85.5
17 City	20.2	346	75.8	81.3	88.2	84.5

18 Aberdeen	28.4	518	66.1	70.7			84.4
19 Ulster		304	85.6	94.1	86.3		83.7
20 Leicester	34.4	365	70.4	81.4	77.2		83.1
21 Cardiff	30.2	421	58.6	67.8	89.7		83.0
22 Swansea	45.5	340	72.8	77.4	70.0		82.3
23 Aston	20.6	306	73.6	91.3			81.2
=24 London South Bank	19.6	240	75.6	74.9	83.7		80.0
=24 Queen Mary, London	46.7		67.3	76.5	70.3*		80.0
=24 West of Scotland	9.0		90.3	96.0	56.5		80.0
27 Glasgow Caledonian	4.7	369	76.1	85.3	74.4		79.9
28 Derby	6.7	276	81.3	82.1			79.1
29 Edinburgh Napier		339	73.4	80.9	77.0		78.2
30 Central Lancashire	7.1	334	76.9	80.9	68.5		77.6
31 Greenwich	5.5		76.3	85.3	66.7		77.1
32 Bradford	7.7	316	79.7	85.3	62.8		76.9
33 Sheffield Hallam		296	68.7	72.8	80.8		76.2
34 De Montfort	12.5		75.6	78.3	64.3*		75.9
35 Northampton		253	70.2	80.9	74.4		74.7
36 Liverpool John Moores	14.2	337	64.6	58.1	64.6		72.6

Employed in professional job:	62%	Employed in non-professional job and studying:	1%
Employed in professional job and studying:	4%	Employed in non-professional job:	9%
Studying:	14%	Unemployed:	11%
Average starting professional salary:	£27,207	Average starting non-professional salary:	£16,585

Geography and Environmental Sciences

Geography and environmental sciences continue to benefit from strong interest in green issues among young people. The numbers starting degrees in human or physical geography, as well as in what UCAS describes as the "science of terrestrial and aquatic environments", were all up in 2015. Human and social geography had already enjoyed two years of growth, while physical courses and environmental science had been broadly steady, regardless of fee levels, throughout the decade. The subjects' attractions do not seem to be related to immediate career prospects since geography and environmental science are not in the top 40 in the employment table. They fare only a little better in the comparison of earnings, where an average starting salary of £22,000 in professional jobs places them 38th out of 67 subject groups.

Cambridge is back at the top of the table after an absence of two years, registering the highest entry grades, while Durham has moved up to second. Geography is one of the subjects where student satisfaction bears little relation to positions in the table. None of the six universities scoring more than 90 per cent on teaching quality in the National Student Survey is in the top ten overall. Coventry, in 30th place, just pips Liverpool Hope, in 41st, to the best score on this indicator and is also the top performer on other aspects of the student experience. UCL registered the best of a variable set of scores for graduate prospects. Winchester was the only other institution to see nine out of ten graduates go straight into professional jobs or continue their studies, and the proportion was below 40 per cent at three universities.

Geography and Environmental Sciences cont

Physical geography courses may give preference to candidates with a science or maths A level in addition to geography, while for environmental science, most of the leading universities will ask for two from biology, chemistry, maths, physics and geography at A level or the equivalent. Average entry scores range from over 500 points at the top four universities to less than 300 at almost a third of the institutions in the table. Satisfaction ratings are generally good in both branches of geography and in environmental science.

Geography and Environmental Sciences	Research quality %	Entry standards	Teaching quality %	Student experience %	Graduate prospects %	Overall score
1 Cambridge	57.3	561	81.6	84.5	87.2	100.0
2 Durham	55.0	526	86.9	91.3	79.7	99.5
3 Oxford	41.1	538	85.7	89.8	87.2	98.7
4 St Andrews	44.2	524	85.6	85.7	80.5	97.0
5 Exeter	43.7	444	88.1	94.0	76.8	95.7
6 Bristol	61.3	488	75.6	87.3	76.4	95.6
7 Lancaster	46.5	423	82.3	89.6	84.3	94.9
8 Leeds	42.3	425	83.4	90.5	81.5	94.2
=9 Newcastle	43.1	407	87.3	89.0	77.8	93.9
=9 University College London	52.3	482	70.9	74.0	90.8	93.9
11 Manchester	36.6	430	89.8	93.0	72.6	93.8
12 Royal Holloway	45.8	384	91.4	90.7	71.2	93.7
13 East Anglia	47.4	420	84.2	90.6	70.1	93.0
14 Loughborough	24.3	376	86.1	91.9	88.0	92.3
15 Southampton	45.8	401	82.8	88.5	71.3	91.9
16 Winchester	7.5		84.0	89.5	90.6	91.5
17 Nottingham	39.6	410	82.2	88.5	72.0	91.3
=18 Birmingham	42.0	393	83.1	82.2	75.8	91.2
=18 Sussex	35.8	375	84.9	91.5	74.7	91.2
20 London School of Economics	46.9	517	67.9	72.0	79.2	91.1
21 Edinburgh	38.2	469	78.3	83.5	69.9	90.8
=22 Aberystwyth	38.6	307	88.9	90.6	75.8	90.7
=22 Glasgow	42.4	446	75.6	84.2	72.9	90.7
24 King's College London	40.0	426	76.3	79.9	78.6	90.4
=25 Cardiff	36.8	387	84.0	88.5	66.5	89.7
=25 York	23.9	383	87.9	90.4	71.1	89.7
27 Aberdeen	38.2	426	77.4	87.3	67.0	89.4
28 Liverpool	26.3	369	83.9	86.6	74.4	88.8
29 Sheffield	31.1	419	78.1	85.8	70.0	88.6
=30 Coventry	2.0	311	94.3	94.3	78.6	87.9
=30 Keele	16.4	343	90.5	92.9	67.8	87.9
32 Queen's, Belfast	36.9	337	82.9	91.2	62.6	87.7
33 Swansea	39.4	333	81.8	87.9	63.5	87.4
34 Dundee	28.3	357	85.5	91.9	59.5	87.2
35 Reading	35.0	348	80.0	85.8	64.6	86.7

=36 Queen Mary, London	45.1	373	72.1	79.3	66.0	86.4
=36 Stirling	30.3	404	74.6	80.8	68.8	86.4
38 Hull	31.7	327	84.5	87.7	59.6	86.1
39 Oxford Brookes	17.3	322	84.0	90.6	69.3	85.9
40 Bangor	31.5	309	84.1	85.5	62.2	85.6
41 Liverpool Hope	1.6	298	94.1	87.7	70.6	85.2
42 Leicester	29.7	368	75.9	80.0	66.1	85.1
43 Portsmouth	14.9	311	88.0	88.6	61.5	84.5
=44 Northumbria	15.4	337	83.6	84.3	61.1	83.7
=44 West of England	6.4	316	88.1	89.8	61.6	83.7
46 Plymouth	25.8	301	80.0	85.7	56.4	82.7
47 Edge Hill	6.2	289	86.9	92.7	57.6	82.3
48 Gloucestershire	14.5	286	90.8	91.5	43.1	81.6
=49 Salford	16.7	254	80.4	80.5	67.9	81.5
=49 Worcester	8.1	268	88.9	86.9	56.2	81.5
51 Bradford	23.6		71.6*	73.8*	70.8	81.3
52 Nottingham Trent	4.1	257	90.9	88.4	55.8	81.2
53 Manchester Metropolitan	14.9	304	85.1	80.1	50.1	80.6
54 Staffordshire		214	92.3	90.9	58.2	80.5
55 Liverpool John Moores		331	88.2	90.3	44.2	80.3
56 Chester	6.4	293	87.4	82.9	51.2	80.2
57 Brighton	5.1	267	82.9	85.9	55.6	79.3
=58 Central Lancashire	9.8	270	87.9	88.3	41.1	79.1
=58 Leeds Beckett	5.6	261	85.4	94.3	45.3	79.1
60 Northampton	7.7	258	87.6	89.5	42.9	78.8
61 Highlands and Islands		320			50.0	78.7
=62 Hertfordshire		283	73.3	79.2	69.7	78.5
=62 Kingston	6.9	247	80.8	78.1	60.7	78.5
64 Sheffield Hallam		296	79.1	83.6	56.3	78.4
65 Greenwich	7.4	328	75.6	85.0	47.8	78.2
66 Derby	3.6	271	76.0	78.5	63.9	78.1
67 St Mary's, Twickenham		249	80.0	77.3	64.3	77.9
68 Canterbury Christ Church		244	83.7	87.7	51.6	77.7
69 Ulster		270	84.6	93.7	39.9	77.4
70 Strathclyde	31.9		68.8	81.6	48.3	77.1
71 South Wales		295	72.5	77.3	61.5	76.9
72 Bournemouth	19.9	269	65.7	70.7	61.7	76.6
73 Bath Spa		288	74.4	82.8	43.2	74.7
=74 Cumbria	1.5	303	69.2	63.8	32.2	69.8
=74 Southampton Solent		210	72.2	75.9	35.7	69.8

Employed in professional job:	40%	Employed in non-professional job and studying:	3%
Employed in professional job and studying:	3%	Employed in non-professional job:	24%
Studying:	19%	Unemployed:	12%
Average starting professional salary:	£22,004	Average starting non-professional salary:	£18,041

Geology

The surge in interest in geology since the introduction of £9,000 fees came to at least a temporary halt in 2015. Applications and enrolments were both down marginally, although the numbers starting courses were still close to record levels after a series of increases in the first half of the decade. There are still more than five applications to the place and entry standards are high. Cambridge recorded its normal high entry grades (636 points in 2015) and another seven of the 31 universities in the table topped 450 points. Some of the leading universities expect candidates to have two scientific or mathematical subjects at A level, or the equivalent.

High graduate salaries and the prospect of an international career no doubt contribute to the subject's growing popularity. Geology is in the top 15 in the salary table after an increase in average earnings of almost £1,800 in 2015. The subject is lower in the overall employment ranking, but still in the top half of the table. More of those graduating in 2015 opted for a postgraduate course than went straight into professional jobs. Only 10 per cent were unemployed at the time of the last survey, but the 20 per cent starting out in lower-level employment cost the subject its place in the top 30.

Imperial College has maintained its lead over Cambridge at the top of the table, with the best research grades and exceptional scores in the National Student Survey for the fourth year in a row. Over 99 per cent of final-year undergraduates were satisfied both with teaching quality and the broader student experience. Cambridge still has by far the highest entry standards, while fourth-placed St Andrews again has much the best employment record. Third-placed Oxford was the only other university to see more than 90 per cent of graduates gain a professional job or go on to further study. No post-1992 university reaches the top 20, but Plymouth is only two places outside it.

Geology	Research quality %	Entry standards	Teaching quality %	Student experience %	Graduate prospects %	Overall score
1 Imperial College	59.6	526	99.9	99.6	89.6	100.0
2 Cambridge	58.0	636	86.6	86.9	87.5	97.9
3 Oxford	52.1	592	82.6	94.1	90.2	96.6
4 St Andrews	44.2	490	90.3	93.2	95.0	95.5
5 Durham	42.2	491	85.5	92.8	82.5	91.3
6 Bristol	55.8	423	84.5	89.0	77.6	89.9
7 Exeter	45.7	433	74.3	83.8	86.7	88.2
8 Edinburgh	38.2	481	84.0	90.2	75.6	88.1
9 Liverpool	30.3	393	91.4	91.2	81.8	87.9
=10 Glasgow	38.5	470	82.9	87.7	75.4	87.4
=10 Leeds	41.9	430	79.0	83.8	82.4	87.4
12 Royal Holloway	43.4	387	80.8	81.0	80.4	86.2
13 Southampton	58.3	396	74.1	84.6	71.1	85.5
14 University College London	47.9	460	75.6	79.3	71.4	85.3
15 Leicester	37.2	397	87.5	91.7	68.8	85.2
16 Aberystwyth	34.9	288	87.1	91.1	78.1	84.3
17 East Anglia	47.4	393	75.5	85.9	70.7	84.1

	Research quality %	Entry standards	Teaching quality %	Student experience %	Graduate prospects %	Overall score
18 Birmingham	38.6	380	83.1	85.1	71.4	84.0
19 Manchester	44.5	395	68.6	75.4	72.2	81.6
20 Bangor	31.5	310	80.2	92.3	70.6	81.3
21 Aberdeen	38.2	426	67.1	77.2	65.1	79.5
22 Plymouth	25.3	305	85.3	88.2	61.5	78.6
23 Cardiff	21.3	367	75.4	86.7	62.7	77.6
24 Keele	12.2	328	88.6	91.2	58.1	77.3
25 Derby	3.6	278	90.8	93.8	63.1	76.7
26 Portsmouth	19.8	293	78.7	79.7	65.9	76.3
27 Brighton	5.1	283	76.7	80.8	72.2	75.1
28 Edge Hill		292	86.4	88.8	57.4	73.8
29 Hull	31.7	296	69.1	66.8		73.5
30 South Wales		250	81.4	85.3	65.2	73.2
31 Kingston	6.9	226	63.7	66.6	66.7	68.6

Employed in professional job:	33%	Employed in non-professional job and studying:	1%
Employed in professional job and studying:	3%	Employed in non-professional job:	19%
Studying:	34%	Unemployed:	10%
Average starting professional salary:	£24,818	Average starting non-professional salary:	£15,839

German

The number of students starting degrees in German dropped below 200 for the first time in living memory in 2015, although many others are learning the language through broader modern languages degrees. German has suffered more than other European languages from the decline in the numbers taking courses in the sixth-form, or even earlier. The introduction of £9,000 fees undoubtedly contributed to falling numbers, but there has been a worldwide decline in the language that has been worrying the German government, as well as academic linguists. Courses in the language will be available at 59 universities – two more than last year – in 2017, but only about half are offering single Honours in the language.

Cambridge makes it 11 years in a row at the top of the table for German and has a big lead in the new *Guide*, with the highest entry standards and the best score from the Research Excellence Framework (REF). The small numbers of students make for big swings elsewhere in the table, however. Last year, Bristol moved up 13 places to second, whereas it is back in tenth place in the latest edition, with Lancaster jumping 15 places to take its place.

German	Research quality %	Entry standards	Teaching quality %	Student experience %	Graduate prospects %	Overall score
1 Cambridge	54.0	570	88.0	87.7	87.6	100.0
2 Lancaster	47.0	437	93.3	92.3	81.8	95.6
3 Warwick	45.2	454	92.0	90.1	82.3	95.2
4 Newcastle	36.3	436	94.0	95.6	83.0	94.1
5 Durham	34.6	554	81.8	85.0	86.1	93.6
6 St Andrews	26.4	491	88.4	95.2	88.8	93.3

German cont

		Research quality %	Entry standards	Teaching quality %	Student experience %	Graduate prospects %	Overall score
7	Oxford	41.3	534	82.8	84.9	77.4	92.8
=8	Birmingham	33.7	368	95.1	88.9	81.5	91.0
=8	Glasgow	26.3	536	90.0	86.6	74.7	91.0
10	Bristol	36.0	421	83.9	83.8	81.9	89.9
=11	Exeter	35.1	460	85.8	91.1	71.7	89.7
=11	King's College London	42.1	444	93.8	91.9	57.7	89.7
13	York	37.3	448	82.3	89.1		89.5
14	Manchester	48.9	405	78.5	78.5	76.8	89.2
15	Sheffield	41.2	424	85.0	87.7	69.8	89.1
16	Leeds	30.6	444	81.7	87.1	80.6	88.9
17	Nottingham	39.4	400	84.1	78.4	78.0	88.7
18	Southampton	42.7	462	82.3	91.5	62.8	88.6
19	Liverpool	33.4	397*	90.0	88.8	70*	88.1
20	University College London	43.7	508	77.3	77.3	64.7	87.9
21	Aston	23.4	372	90.9	87.0	80.7	87.7
22	Queen Mary, London	35.1	373	76.4	62.9	95.4	87.5
23	Heriot-Watt	26.3	425	84.7	86.8	74.5	86.9
24	Royal Holloway	48.3		83.5	84.3	59.7	85.8
=25	Bangor	39.6	324	83.0	85.7	70.4	85.6
=25	Edinburgh	30.3	481	81.6	84.2	62.1	85.6
27	Cardiff	32.5	355	81.8	79.1	75.5	85.1
28	Reading	41.7	347	80.4	78.8	67.7	84.8
29	Aberystwyth	16.6		81.7	91.0	74.7	84.4
30	Bath	27.4	410	70.3	73.6	85.0	84.3
31	Kent	41.9	318	81.8	75.6	66.7	83.9
32	Portsmouth	32.2	289	82.0	85.9	70.5	83.0
33	Hull	22.7	335	92.7	95.2	57.7	82.9
34	East Anglia		410	94.9	95.0	64.6	82.2
35	Central Lancashire	15.2		86.7	85.7	61.6*	80.9
36	Swansea	22.8	274	83.2	83.8	60.7	78.7
37	Aberdeen	29.3		74.0	79.8	61.8	78.6
38	Chester	17.3	294	75.4	81.1	71.8	78.3
39	Nottingham Trent	7.6	267	85.1	89.8	66.1	77.5
40	Manchester Metropolitan	29.0	302*	79.4	67.8	56.4	77.3

Employed in professional job:	49%	Employed in non-professional job and studying:	1%
Employed in professional job and studying:	4%	Employed in non-professional job:	18%
Studying:	19%	Unemployed:	9%
Average starting professional salary:	£22,416	Average starting non-professional salary:	£17,407

Birmingham had the highest levels of satisfaction in the teaching quality sections of the National Student Survey (NSS), while fourth-placed St Andrews followed by Hull, which is in the bottom ten, did best in the other sections of the survey. Most universities scored well in the NSS; only two failed to satisfy at least 75 per cent of final-year undergraduates. Portsmouth remains the highest-placed of just five post-1992 universities in the ranking.

Most universities in the table offer German from scratch as well as catering for those who took the subject at A level. Employment prospects are better than in other modern languages, although the small numbers mean that the differences can be slight. German is in the top 30 for the proportion of graduates going into professional jobs or onto postgraduate courses. Queen Mary, University of London has by far the best graduate prospects and was the only university to record 90 per cent positive destinations in 2015. The language is only just outside the top 30 in the earnings table, after the second successive increase of more than £1,200 in average starting salaries in graduate-level jobs.

History

History has enjoyed four years of growth in both applications and enrolments, and now has far more of both than there were before the arrival of £9,000 fees. Yet the subject is in the bottom 15 for employment, with almost as many graduates starting out in low-level jobs as in those categorised as professional occupations. History has also fallen in the earnings table and is now outside the top 40 subjects, although surveys have suggested that historians often rise to the top later in their careers.

Durham and Cambridge had taken it in turns to lead the history table for the last seven years. Cambridge remains in first place with the highest entry standards and the top score from the 2014 Research Excellence Framework (REF). Most of the leading scores for satisfaction with teaching quality are to be found outside the top 30, however. Suffolk has the best of all, an impressive 97 per cent satisfaction rate, despite finishing in equal 73rd place, partly because it did not enter the REF in history. Lincoln, in 32nd place, has the best scores in the remaining sections of the National Student Survey. Satisfaction levels are high throughout the ranking: only three universities failed to satisfy at least 70 per cent of final-year undergraduates.

The older institutions continue to dominate the table: only Lincoln, Huddersfield, Northumbria and De Montfort of the modern universities appear in the top 40. Average entry scores are high at the leading universities since, with half of the top ten averaging more than 500 points on the old UCAS tariff – the equivalent of more than four As at A level. Perhaps more surprisingly, six universities average less than 250 points. Employment scores are disappointing at many of the 94 universities in the table, although slightly better than last year. More than 30 institutions saw fewer than half of those graduating in 2015 go into professional jobs or start postgraduate courses by the end of the year, and the figure was below 40 per cent at nine of them.

History	Research quality %	Entry standards	Teaching quality %	Student experience %	Graduate prospects %	Overall score
1 Cambridge	56.3	569	89.4	91.1	81.3	100.0
=2 Durham	41.4	561	87.2	89.3	83.3	97.0
=2 Oxford	56.1	558	80.2	87.2	81.9	97.0
4 St Andrews	46.7	520	90.6	90.9	73.3	96.3

History cont

		Research quality %	Entry standards	Teaching quality %	Student experience %	Graduate prospects %	Overall score
5	Exeter	45.6	480	89.1	89.9	77.5	95.2
6	Warwick	51.7	470	86.2	81.4	80.2	94.6
7	University College London	51.9	504	79.0	81.3	78.2	93.4
=8	Birmingham	48.8	418	83.9	85.3	83.3	93.1
=8	King's College London	45.3	474	82.0	83.5	81.8	93.1
=8	York	43.3	468	88.7	89.4	69.2	93.1
11	Leeds	43.6	448	87.7	88.3	73.3	92.9
12	Lancaster	37.0	438	88.9	88.8	78.9	92.8
13	Sheffield	53.7	424	84.6	86.1	69.3	92.2
=14	East Anglia	47.4	411	89.6	91.0	60.0	91.3
=14	Sussex	41.3	374	83.6	88.2	85.1	91.3
16	Glasgow	47.7	440	86.0	87.7	62.4	91.1
17	Southampton	50.6	396	86.3	87.7	65.3	91.0
18	London School of Economics	46.8	501	71.3	74.8	82.1	90.4
19	Nottingham	36.9	416	83.8	84.5	77.1	90.1
20	Kent	41.3	364	85.4	86.7	74.7	89.8
=21	Bristol	40.6	488	76.8	79.9	71.9	89.5
=21	Loughborough	22.5	374	86.7	91.9	84.4	89.5
23	Queen Mary, London	43.7	379	87.5	83.3	66.4	89.4
=24	Manchester	39.8	407	85.0	85.8	66.3	89.1
=24	Royal Holloway	40.6	389	87.7	85.0	64.4	89.1
26	Liverpool	38.9	394	85.6	85.1	61.2	87.9
=27	Edinburgh	46.9	472	73.2	79.4	63.2	87.8
=27	Queen's, Belfast	46.3	360	84.4	86.7	59.2	87.8
29	Newcastle	29.0	436	82.9	83.2	68.6	87.7
30	Strathclyde	42.0	448	84.5	87.3	42.1	86.9
31	Keele	32.8	344	87.6	88.2	62.6	86.8
=32	Leicester	34.3	371	84.2	87.7	60.3	86.5
=32	Lincoln	25.9	311	96.0	94.6	55.4	86.5
34	Reading	35.4	374	85.7	84.8	58.4	86.4
35	Aberdeen	36.1	427	78.8	82.8	60.0	86.2
36	SOAS London	20.8	381	83.8	86.8	71.2	86.0
=37	Dundee	30.4	399	84.0	83.7	59.2	85.9
=37	Essex	34.8	306	85.5	89.8	63.7	85.9
39	Huddersfield	22.3	310	91.7	82.2	69.7	85.6
=40	De Montfort	23.4	259	92.0	90.9	69.4	85.5
=40	Hull	26.1	336	88.2	89.3	60.5	85.5
=40	Northumbria	30.7	342	88.4	88.1	55.6	85.5
43	Teesside	27.9	272	92.9	92.0	53.5	84.5
44	Cardiff	31.4	398	80.7	82.9	53.0	84.1
45	Aberystwyth	19.5	314	90.1	90.4	58.0	84.0
46	Coventry	5.6	289	91.2	92.0	72.7	83.9
47	Swansea	25.0	303	84.2	85.5	65.7	83.8

=48 Liverpool Hope	15.7	278	89.5	82.8	72.4	83.7
=48 Stirling	28.5	384	77.8	79.8	62.1	83.7
50 Bangor	24.3	314	92.2	88.1	48.4*	83.6
51 Goldsmiths, London	34.5	317	83.6	79.9	57.1	83.5
52 Brunel	32.4	306	90.1	89.3	42.9	83.4
=53 Hertfordshire	46.7	305	78.7	78.6	53.9	83.3
=53 Portsmouth	32.2	284	85.4	84.3	57.3	83.3
55 Edge Hill	23.6	293	89.0	88.0	54.5	83.1
56 Oxford Brookes	35.0	336	84.0	81.9	47.4	82.9
=57 Roehampton	21.4	271	86.3	84.0	60.4	81.9
=57 West of England	28.9	304	84.5	82.3	51.0	81.9
59 Liverpool John Moores	15.9	317	90.6	87.2	47.5	81.7
=60 Newman	12.0	280	93.0	88.6	52.2	81.6
=60 Plymouth	22.6	277	91.3	89.5	43.5	81.6
=62 Bishop Grosseteste	7.0	260	89.2	87.0	66.4*	81.3
=62 Manchester Metropolitan	18.0	325	88.7	82.3	48.4	81.3
64 Winchester	19.1	287	88.7	88.9	46.0	80.9
65 Derby	13.5	272	95.1	93.5	39.0	80.7
66 Northampton	21.5	276	86.3	85.2	46.5	80.1
67 Chester	9.1	302	89.8	83.5	46.7	79.5
68 Nottingham Trent	17.5	269	84.4	81.2	54.0	79.4
69 Canterbury Christ Church	16.3	273	90.6	84.5	40.9	79.3
70 Chichester	15.8	242	91.3	89.5	41.0	79.2
71 Bath Spa	8.3	319	85.2	84.3	48.4	79.0
72 Leeds Beckett	11.0	264	91.1	90.4	40.0	78.9
=73 Sheffield Hallam	38.3	277	76.9	79.9	40.1	78.8
=73 Suffolk		315	97.3	87.9	33.7	78.8
=75 Greenwich	8.6	313	89.5	77.3	45.1	78.6
=75 South Wales	15.8	310	86.3	84.8	37.0	78.6
77 St Mary's, Twickenham	11.0	238	85.6	85.0	53.8	78.3
78 Salford		286	87.5	85.6	51.9	78.1
=79 Central Lancashire	12.0	281	85.3	79.7	46.6	77.8
=79 Sunderland	7.7	282	83.6	86.3	48.2	77.8
=79 Worcester	19.5	258	84.0	78.0	46.4	77.8
82 Wrexham Glyndŵr		282*	94.5	87.4	36.1	77.5
83 Highlands and Islands		281	83.3	78.7	30.4	77.0
84 York St John		278	85.4	83.0	50.8	76.9
85 Brighton	13.1	309	71.6	65.4	66.2	76.6
=86 Anglia Ruskin	15.3	232	89.6	86.2	31.1	76.5
=86 Westminster	11.8	277	81.4	80.3	44.7	76.5
88 Kingston		243	80.7	77.8	49.9	74.0
89 Ulster	24.0	282	75.0	76.0	28.1	73.9
90 Staffordshire		202	89.3	84.8	35.7	73.8
91 East London	13.9	214	77.4	72.8	45.6	73.4
92 Bradford	12.7		69.0	71.2	55.8	73.0
93 Gloucestershire	11.2	310	64.4	59.4	45.2	70.6
94 Leeds Trinity	10.3	257	69.9	59.9	29.2	68.1

Employed in professional job:	31%	Employed in non-professional job and studying:	4%
Employed in professional job and studying:	3%	Employed in non-professional job:	28%
Studying:	23%	Unemployed:	11%
Average starting professional salary:	£21,628	Average starting non-professional salary:	£16,767

History of Art, Architecture and Design

History of Art may be about to lose its A level, but it is alive and well in universities. Forty-seven are offering the subject at degree level in 2017, compared with 44 last year, and student numbers are recovering after a decline that coincided with the introduction of £9,000 fees. Entry standards are high: only two universities in the table average less than 300 points and four have averages of more than 500 points on the old UCAS tariff. Cambridge, whose entrants had the highest of those grades, remains the leader after a big rise up the table last year. The Courtauld Institute, an independent college of the University of London based in Somerset House and previously the only specialist institution to top any of our league tables, is back up to second. It had the best results in the Research Excellence Framework, when 95 per cent of its submission was rated as world-leading or internationally excellent.

Employment levels are much improved in the latest edition of the table, particularly at the leading institutions. The relatively small numbers taking degrees in the history of art, architecture or design make for considerable volatility in the statistics, but the subjects are now well inside the top 50. Whereas two of the top ten universities managed positive destinations for 75 per cent of graduates in 2014, five of the top ten did by the end of 2015, and Birmingham topped 90 per cent. Nationally, although the unemployment rate remained higher than average, at 13 per cent, the numbers starting out in low-level employment was down from a third to just over a quarter. Average starting salaries in professional jobs remain outside the top 50, however.

Satisfaction levels are high throughout the table. Indeed, the best scores in the section of the National Student Survey dealing with teaching, feedback and academic support came at Plymouth, only two places off the bottom of the table overall. The best ratings for the broader student experience were at fourth-placed St Andrews and East Anglia, which finished 13th overall.

History of Art, Architecture and Design	Research quality %	Entry standards	Teaching quality %	Student experience %	Graduate prospects %	Overall score
1 Cambridge	49.0	545	87.9	89.0	82.9	100.0
2 Courtauld Institute	66.0	470	84.6	82.5	80.6	98.3
3 Exeter	35.1	515	88.5	88.8		96.9
4 St Andrews	42.1	461	90.4	91.0	74.2	96.6
5 Essex	46.9		85.9	89.9	74.4	95.8
=6 Birmingham	43.7	412	83.8	84.7	91.4	95.1
=6 Oxford	39.7	514	80.4	87.0	79.2	95.1
8 Leicester	42.0		84.7	87.8	75.6	94.5
9 Warwick	53.0	444	86.2	81.3	67.1	94.4

10 York	53.2	405	89.1	90.0	59.0	94.3
11 University College London	44.7	534	79.2	81.8	69.2	94.1
12 Manchester	54.0	379	85.7	86.3	64.1	92.9
13 East Anglia	36.9	419	89.6	91.0	59.6	92.7
14 Glasgow	37.2	412	86.9	88.0	68.2	92.6
15 Sussex	25.2	392	83.6	88.2	82.9	91.3
16 Kent	44.3	316	85.5	87.1	69.6	90.7
17 Leeds	30.0	394	88.0	88.4	61.8	90.6
=18 Bristol	28.3	467	78.3	80.9	67.4	89.5
=18 Nottingham	30.9	372	84.0	84.3	69.6	89.5
=18 SOAS London	40.9	402	83.8	86.0	50.0	89.5
21 Aberystwyth	21.6		90.1	90.4	46.7*	88.9
22 Goldsmiths, London	25.9	392	83.7	79.9	59.8	87.5
23 Edinburgh	27.9	460	74.0	79.3	60.4	87.0
24 Oxford Brookes	35.0	295	84.0	81.9	52.5	85.6
25 Manchester Metropolitan	9.7	411	88.7	82.3	39.3	84.8
26 Liverpool John Moores	7.2	359	90.6	87.2	40.9	84.4
27 Aberdeen	36.1		78.4	82.5	41.2	83.6
28 Plymouth	14.7	302	91.3	89.5	32.5	83.4
29 Brighton	13.1	271	72.8	66.0	39.4	75.2

Employed in professional job:	35%	Employed in non-professional job and studying:	3%
Employed in professional job and studying:	4%	Employed in non-professional job:	23%
Studying:	22%	Unemployed:	13%
Average starting professional salary:	£20,370	Average starting non-professional salary:	£16,175

Hospitality, Leisure, Recreation and Tourism

This group of subjects covers a variety of courses directed towards management in the leisure and tourism industries, mainly delivered at modern universities. Taken together with sports studies, it remains in the top 20 for applications, although the numbers dropped a little in 2015. Because so many graduates begin their careers in low-level jobs, the subjects are never far from the foot of the employment table. Although they have escaped the bottom four in the latest edition, they are still well inside the bottom ten. The subjects do better in the earnings table, but are still outside the top 50.

The numbers starting courses dropped for the first time in three years in 2015 and are not yet back at the level seen in 2010, the last year unaffected by the move to £9,000 fees. Entry standards are modest – only second-placed Exeter and Surrey, in fourth place, average more than 400 points on the old UCAS tariff. Birmingham has retained the top position it won for the first time last year, boasting by far the best results in the Research Excellence Framework, when 90 per cent of its submission was considered world-leading or internationally excellent, as well as the best graduate prospects. It was one of only three universities to see three-quarters of graduates go straight into professional employment or onto a postgraduate course, while at two universities the proportion was below a quarter.

Only ten of the 62 institutions in the table are pre-1992 universities, but they include the top four. Lincoln, the highest-placed modern university, in fifth place, had the most

Hospitality, Leisure, Recreation and Tourism cont

satisfied students with all aspects of their course. Satisfaction rates are invariably high: only four universities failed to achieve at least 70 per cent approval in the National Student Survey. A total of 117 universities and colleges are offering courses in one or more of the hospitality, leisure, recreation and tourism subjects in 2017.

Hospitality, Leisure, Recreation and Tourism	Research quality %	Entry standards	Teaching quality %	Student experience %	Graduate prospects %	Overall score
1 Birmingham	63.7	379	80.0	84.0	81.6	100.0
2 Exeter	24.4	487	79.4	87.6	80.8	99.0
3 Strathclyde	44.3		93.4	90.8	68.4	97.7
4 Surrey	33.6	411	83.6	89.8	57.5	93.6
5 Lincoln	11.4	330	97.7	97.3	68.2	90.9
6 Arts University, Bournemouth		335	94.7	93.8	72.7	88.9
=7 Coventry	1.6	334	88.0	93.7	72.6	87.6
=7 Liverpool John Moores	45.3	339	78.1	78.6	47.9	87.6
9 Oxford Brookes	5.1	350	85.0	92.5	64.4	86.9
=10 De Montfort		336	83.6	88.6	72.9	86.0
=10 Manchester		366	75.0	77.8	81.0	86.0
12 Glasgow Caledonian	15.2	390	78.7	82.3	47.5	85.5
=13 Gloucestershire	6.0	315	78.5	86.3	71.4	84.3
=13 Ulster	31.0	298	88.3	92.4	35.3	84.3
15 Hertfordshire	0.9	325	88.8	88.7	57.3	84.0
16 South Wales	10.8	334	80.3	84.2	56.8	83.8
17 Manchester Metropolitan	4.7	344	79.3	83.2	61.4	83.7
=18 Edinburgh	26.1	335	64.7	73.7	65.2	83.5
=18 Greenwich	3.3	361	77.4	79.8	60.7	83.5
20 Sunderland	2.4	293	95.1	94.1	50.7	83.3
21 Leeds Beckett	12.6	291	81.4	87.4	61.8	83.2
=22 Brighton	10.9	301	82.8	88.3	53.7	82.5
=22 Sheffield Hallam	8.5	310	81.8	85.4	56.3	82.5
=24 Central Lancashire	5.1	317	83.5	85.5	52.0	81.9
=24 Huddersfield		306	79.2	83.2	67.6	81.9
=26 Bolton		342	77.7	82.8	58.3	81.8
=26 Winchester		276	91.5	93.2	55.1	81.8
=28 Falmouth		273	80.7	87.3	70.5	81.3
=28 Plymouth	13.1	290	82.7	85.3	50.0	81.3
30 Chester	6.6	317	80.1	79.8	54.4	81.2
31 Edinburgh Napier	2.3	352	81.0	83.3	42.8	80.9
32 Cardiff Metropolitan	7.7	305	73.9	81.5	60.3	80.6
33 Robert Gordon	2.6	335	74.5	79.5	55.4	80.4
34 Queen Margaret, Edinburgh		321	85.3	85.7	43.3	80.0
=35 Bournemouth	9.0	299	75.3	79.6	56.3	79.9
=35 London South Bank	35.0	238	79.9	81.3	42.4	79.9
37 Liverpool Hope	10.9	334	78.0	68.3	42.9	79.2

=38 Derby	0.9	307	82.0	78.2	50.3	79.1
=38 Southampton Solent	0.6	289	78.1	84.8	56.6	79.1
=38 West of Scotland	9.1	331	75.4	78.5	42.3	79.1
41 Westminster	10.7	323	78.7	83.0	34.9	78.9
42 Staffordshire	19.1	274	76.1	78.7	43.5	78.1
=43 University of the Arts London		341	73.3	73.4	47.6	78.0
=43 Salford	5.9	336	67.2	84.7	43.9	78.0
45 Middlesex	10.5	317	74.0	79.6	38.6	77.7
46 Aberystwyth	14.5	322	81.2	87.9	17.4*	77.5
47 West of England		316	74.5	77.9	46.7	77.2
48 Hull	10.2		76.8	83.3	36.4	76.5
49 Chichester		250	72.8	89.1	58.3	76.4
50 Northampton		290	78.4	80.2	42.3	76.1
51 Portsmouth	8.1	267	73.3	77.6	48.8	76.0
52 London Metropolitan		284	75.8	76.7	48.1	75.8
53 Cumbria	3.2	247	87.7	80.4	37.5	75.5
54 Canterbury Christ Church	19.0	271	65.1	73.0	46.2	75.4
55 West London		288	75.1	82.4	40.6	75.2
56 Suffolk		346	67.5	73.9	36.0	75.0
57 Bedfordshire	6.7	219	79.3	84.2	39.3	73.5
58 St Mary's, Twickenham	4.8	262	78.0	85.4	28.2	73.4
59 Highlands and Islands		276	62.9	62.1	60.6	73.1
60 Anglia Ruskin	3.4	259	80.4	86.8	20.8	72.4
61 Buckinghamshire New	0.9	256	73.4	73.8	39.7	72.1
62 East London	0.8	281	59.8	57.0	45.6	69.7

Employed in professional job:	45%	Employed in non-professional job and studying:	1%
Employed in professional job and studying:	1%	Employed in non-professional job:	36%
Studying:	5%	Unemployed:	11%
Average starting professional salary:	£20,148	Average starting non-professional salary:	£17,057

Iberian Languages

Spanish gained on French as the most popular language at degree level in 2015, following a small rise in the numbers starting courses, but there were still only 325 entrants in total. Those statistics do not capture students who learn the language as part of a broader modern languages programme, but even the rise in applications in 2015 did not take numbers close to the levels seen before £9,000 fees were introduced. The table also includes Portuguese, but not a single student embarked on a single Honours degree in the language since 2012. Nevertheless, Portuguese will still be available – either alone or as part of a modern languages degree – at 26 universities in 2017. It can even be combined with Czech at Bristol.

Cambridge has widened an already clear lead at the top of the table, with Durham regaining the second place it lost last year to Oxford. Cambridge has the highest entry grades, the top results in the 2014 Research Excellence Framework and the best graduate prospects. Coventry, in 33rd place, just pipped Surrey to the top score for student satisfaction with teaching, feedback and academic support, but there was no stopping Surrey in the

Iberian Languages cont

sections of the National Student Survey devoted to the broader student experience, where it recorded a rare 100 per cent rating.

The languages have arrested their decline in the employment table, but remain in the bottom half of the 67 subject groups. The relatively small numbers of students can cause volatility in the statistics. In 2014, for example, there was a £500 decline in average starting salaries in professional jobs, whereas the latest average shows a rise of £2,000. This also applies to the number of universities in the table – last year there had been a rise of six; this time a decline of one. Ten of the 51 institutions are post-1992 universities, but none features in this year's top 30. Roehampton, at 31st, comes closest to doing so.

Iberian Languages	Research quality %	Entry standards	Teaching quality %	Student experience %	Graduate prospects %	Overall score
1 Cambridge	54.0	570	88.0	87.7	87.6	100.0
2 Durham	34.6	554	81.8	85.0	86.1	93.8
3 Warwick	45.2	446	91.0	88.8		93.4
4 Oxford	41.3	554	80.7	84.8	77.4	93.2
5 Newcastle	36.3	426	89.5	89.7	86.1	92.3
6 Birmingham	33.7	389	91.2	91.4	83.9	90.8
7 St Andrews	26.4	475	90.9	92.2	77.4	90.6
=8 Queen's, Belfast	53.6	371	87.9	89.3	68.3	90.2
=8 Surrey	39.1	455	97.7	100.0	54.5	90.2
10 King's College London	42.1	430	85.0	88.8	72.3	89.8
11 Exeter	35.1	460	85.8	91.1	71.6	89.6
12 University College London	43.7	456	72.2	79.4	82.3	89.4
13 East Anglia	33.1	410	93.3	95.0	68.5	89.0
=14 Lancaster	47.0	404	75.7	79.9	80.9	88.9
=14 Southampton	42.7	432	80.7	87.7	71.5	88.9
16 Nottingham	39.4	418	77.0	83.1	82.4	88.8
17 York	37.3	425	82.1	91.4		88.7
=18 Bath	27.4	423	82.6	87.1	83.6	88.3
=18 Royal Holloway	48.3	373	83.9	84.8	70.1	88.3
20 Bristol	36.0	429	81.6	84.9	76.1	88.2
21 Manchester	48.9	400	84.7	87.5	62.3	88.1
22 Aberdeen	29.3	476	76.5	84.8	78.6	87.8
23 Kent	41.9	351	80.3	84.1	80.9	87.7
24 Strathclyde	42.0	459	86.6	89.8	55.0	87.6
25 Leeds	30.6	416	81.3	87.3	73.2	86.4
26 Sheffield	41.2	410	80.0	84.1	65.4	86.2
27 Liverpool	33.4	361	87.3	92.3	67.5	85.9
28 Heriot-Watt	26.3	425	80.8	88.4	72.3	85.6
29 Glasgow	26.3	460	85.5	86.4	58.0	84.5
30 Edinburgh	30.3	490	70.2	76.2	69.5	84.4
31 Roehampton	21.8		91.7	84.3	65*	84.2
32 Aberystwyth	16.6	284	93.0	95.5	79.9	84.1

33 Coventry	18.1	303	97.8	97.1	69.4	84.0
34 Aston	23.4	343	85.6	88.0	73.5	83.7
35 Swansea	22.8	309	87.9	88.1	68.2	82.0
36 Queen Mary, London	35.1	365	71.4	75.0	68.4	81.5
=37 Leicester	16.9	372*	85.9	92.8	61.1	81.4
=37 Northumbria		341	91.8	95.4	75.6	81.4
39 Portsmouth	32.2	289	71.7	87.8	72.8	81.0
40 Manchester Metropolitan	29.0	318	84.5	87.9	57.3	80.6
=41 Cardiff	32.5	338	76.2	77.6	60.4	79.7
=41 Stirling	29.8	373	67.2	74.0	68.2	79.7
43 Sussex		366	85.1	85.3	72.9	79.2
44 Hull	22.7	348	72.5	77.1	68.7	79.0
45 Nottingham Trent	7.6	290	89.8	90.6	65.7	78.5
46 Bangor	39.6	291	89.1	91.5	33.0	78.3
47 Chester	17.3	287	79.9	76.3	67.3	77.1
48 Central Lancashire	15.2	291*	80.7	84.6	61.4	76.7
49 Westminster	2.0	297	77.4	82.8	53.5	71.8
50 Ulster	22.4	271	72.5	78.1	33.7	69.7
51 Leeds Beckett		261*	60.5	60.2	75.8	68.9

Employed in professional job:	49%	Employed in non-professional job and studying:	1%
Employed in professional job and studying:	3%	Employed in non-professional job:	21%
Studying:	15%	Unemployed:	11%
Average starting professional salary:	£22,161	Average starting non-professional salary:	£16,507

Italian

Only 25 students started degrees in Italian in 2015, the same low total as in 2013 and less than a third of the numbers seen six years earlier. Even allowing for the much larger numbers of students who included Italian in broader language degrees or as one or more modules in another subject, demand is worryingly low. Forty universities offered the language in 2016, compared with only 28 in 2017. Most students have no previous knowledge of Italian, although they are likely to have taken another language at A level.

As in Iberian languages, the small numbers make for exaggerated swings in the graduate employment statistics. Average starting salaries in professional jobs dropped by over £700 in 2014, for example, but were up by almost £2,000 in the following survey. Italian has fallen ten places in the employment table, to 52nd out of the 67 subject groups. Cambridge has the best employment score, as well as the highest entry standards and research grades, leaving it well clear of the field.

St Andrews has jumped nine places to second, despite having one of the lowest research scores in the table. Its results in the National Student Survey, which included the best scores for course organisation, learning resources and personal development, were mainly responsible, although satisfaction levels were high throughout the table. Nottingham Trent, only one place off the bottom, was the star performer on the sections relating to teaching quality.

Italian cont

Entry standards remain surprisingly high, given the small numbers of applicants. The top four of the 23 universities in the ranking all average at least 550 points at entry and only two drop below 300 points. There is a high response rate and scores have generally been good in the National Student Survey. No university failed to satisfy at least seven out of ten final-year undergraduates taking Italian.

Italian	Research quality %	Entry standards	Teaching quality %	Student experience %	Graduate prospects %	Overall score
1 Cambridge	54.0	570	88.0	87.7	87.6	100.0
2 St Andrews	26.4	552*	93.1	93.8		96.1
3 Durham	34.6	554	81.8	85.0	86.1	94.2
4 Oxford	41.3	550	80.0	87.0	76.2	93.5
5 Warwick	45.2	426	90.3	91.6	65.9	92.6
6 Exeter	35.1	460	85.8	91.1	72.0	91.5
7 Manchester	48.9	392	88.2	86.6	61.7	90.7
8 Leeds	30.6	420	90.5	92.7	68.4	90.4
9 Birmingham	33.7	428	86.9	85.5	73.7	90.3
10 Bath	27.4	408	85.1	83.6	84.3	89.8
11 Bristol	36.0	439	83.9	81.0	74.0	89.7
12 University College London	43.7	432	73.9	80.9	75.4	89.0
13 Royal Holloway	48.3	388*	83.2	81.6	53.2	87.3
14 Kent	41.9	338	83.5	86.2		87.0
15 Hull	22.7		81.9	91.7	67.0	86.7
16 Glasgow	26.3	462*	77.5	86.3		86.4
17 Manchester Metropolitan	29.0	302*	92.8	90.3	56.8	85.7
18 Reading	41.7	349	91.0	90.5	37.5	85.5
19 Portsmouth	32.2	289	82.0	85.9	71.1	85.4
20 Central Lancashire	15.2		86.7	85.7	60.0*	84.0
21 Edinburgh	30.3	491	73.4	74.9	55.9	83.8
22 Nottingham Trent	7.6	283	94.0	92.5	66.2	83.5
23 Cardiff	32.5	344	74.7	77.0	65.2	83.0

Employed in professional job:	45%	Employed in non-professional job and studying:		1%
Employed in professional job and studying:	2%	Employed in non-professional job:		23%
Studying:	13%	Unemployed:		15%
Average starting professional salary:	£21,731	Average starting non-professional salary:		£17,840

Land and Property Management

The property market has definitely recovered if our labour market statistics for graduates in land and property management are anything to go by. The subject is in the top ten of our 67 groupings for employment, with eight out of ten graduates going straight into professional jobs in 2015. Three years of substantial salary increases had taken the average in those jobs to £24,500 and there were too few graduates in lower-level employment to calculate a reliable figure. In the main, the subject table reflects those high employment rates: 96 per cent of graduates at sixth-placed Sheffield Hallam found high-level work or continued to study.

The table is still less than half the size it was in 2006, with no representation from Scotland or Wales, but here, too, there are signs of recovery. One more university – Oxford Brookes – has joined the table, and 26 universities and colleges are offering courses in this area in 2017. They include degrees in woodland ecology and conservation, property management and valuation, and even a Foundation degree in sports turf, as well as the real estate degrees that are the largest recruiters. Cambridge has a predictably big lead, with the best research score and entry grades that are 200 points ahead of the nearest challenger.

The subjects have acquired a reputation for recruiting disproportionate numbers from independent schools, but property firms have donated more than £500,000 to support a "Pathways to Property" scheme to try to widen participation. Those who take the courses appear to enjoy the experience: only one university in the table recorded less than 70 per cent satisfaction in the teaching or student experience sections in the National Student Survey. Oxford Brookes, the leading post-1992 institution in fourth place, had the highest levels of satisfaction with teaching quality and tied with third-placed Ulster for the best scores for course organisation, learning resources and personal development.

Land and Property Management	Research quality %	Entry standards	Teaching quality %	Student experience %	Graduate prospects %	Overall score
1 Cambridge	49.0	600	78.8	83.7	95.9	100.0
2 Reading	40.0	393	74.2	83.1	95.1	93.8
3 Ulster	28.6	288	80.5	89.3	94.1	93.1
4 Oxford Brookes	17.6	327	82.8	89.3	89.2	92.7
5 Nottingham Trent	3.4	297	80.4	83.2	92.2	89.0
6 Sheffield Hallam	13.4	270	72.3	82.0	96.1	87.7
7 Birmingham City	2.7	260*	80.4	83.2	70.6	86.5
8 Greenwich	2.0	308*	71.5	78.9	68.8	84.1
9 Westminster	10.7	285	67.3	79.3	72.9	84.0
10 Plymouth	13.2		79.7	86.3	16.7*	83.4

Employed in professional job:	78%	Employed in non-professional job and studying:		0%
Employed in professional job and studying:	2%	Employed in non-professional job:		7%
Studying:	3%	Unemployed:		9%
Average starting professional salary:	£24,505	Average starting non-professional salary:		..

Law

The numbers starting law degrees have risen for seven years in a row, reaching almost 24,000 in 2016. It remains one of the most popular subjects, with more than 100,000 applications, unaffected by the move to higher fees. Entry standards reflect this: only in medicine do so many universities make such testing demands. Ten of the 100 universities in the table average

Law cont

at least 500 points and almost a third have average entry scores of over 400 points. However, so many universities now offer law that it was still possible to find one (Bolton) where the average was below 200 points in 2015.

Cambridge has held on to the top place it regained from Oxford three years ago, extending its lead in the new *Guide*. Oxford has the highest entry grades, but Cambridge again had the greatest proportion of graduates – 94 per cent – going straight into professional jobs or continuing their studies. Although most of the scores for graduate prospects are good, the proportion enjoying "positive destinations" was below half at four universities. Law is only just in the top 30 in the employment table and is 50th out of the 67 subjects for early career earnings. Only about half of all graduates go on to practise law, and training contracts for those who do keep the average in graduate-level jobs to £20,400.

The London School of Economics achieved the best results in the 2014 Research Excellence Framework (REF) but once again, the most satisfied students are not at one of the leading universities in the table. For the second year in a row, Abertay has that distinction, producing the top scores in both of the indicators derived from the National Student Survey. It remains the only post-1992 university in the top 20, despite recording one of the lowest scores in the REF.

Aspiring solicitors in England go on to take the Legal Practice Course, while those aiming to be barristers take the Bar Vocational Course, so it is no surprise that 40 per cent of all law graduates are engaged in postgraduate study six months after completing a degree. Note that in Scotland, most law courses are based on the distinctive Scottish legal system, which also has different professional qualifications.

Law	Research quality %	Entry standards	Teaching quality %	Student experience %	Graduate prospects %	Overall score
1 Cambridge	58.7	574	88.9	91.6	94.2	100.0
2 Oxford	51.8	598	83.3	86.3	85.5	96.2
3 London School of Economics	64.5	571	76.8	76.3	84.3	94.1
4 Durham	32.8	564	83.3	87.4	83.0	92.9
=5 Nottingham	45.2	488	84.7	92.0	76.1	92.5
=5 University College London	57.7	560	73.5	80.3	82.0	92.5
7 Leeds	40.1	446	86.3	91.6	81.4	92.3
8 Bristol	50.5	495	74.6	86.1	81.9	91.3
9 Queen's, Belfast	40.3	415	81.6	90.9	84.6	91.1
10 Dundee	16.3	451	88.1	93.9	85.4	90.9
11 King's College London	39.2	580	72.1	81.3	83.3	90.7
=12 East Anglia	26.5	414	92.2	94.6	75.1	90.5
=12 York	30.3	465	80.4	91.2	83.6	90.5
14 Kent	43.9	394	79.9	87.8	85.1	90.4
15 Aberdeen	20.9	469	81.0	89.6	89.2	90.3
16 Edinburgh	40.8	526	72.8	82.2	84.2	90.2
17 Warwick	41.9	500	74.3	82.3	84.1	90.1
18 Glasgow	33.8	534	71.6	82.5	87.0	89.8
19 Abertay	1.2	350	92.9	95.5	91.3	89.2

20 Newcastle	25.4	446	82.6	91.2	78.5	89.1
21 Queen Mary, London	23.7	495	81.6	85.5	79.3	89.0
=22 Lancaster	38.9	426	75.8	83.8	81.4	88.3
=22 Strathclyde	29.4	505	77.0	90.4	71.9	88.3
24 Birmingham	33.6	423	76.9	79.4	86.4	88.1
25 Sheffield	31.9	403	80.1	85.0	79.4	87.7
26 Heriot-Watt	18.8	410*	78.6	83.9	89.4	87.6
27 Sussex	23.3	374	81.3	87.3	84.2	87.5
28 Exeter	21.4	491	76.3	82.8	80.8	87.4
29 Keele	30.5	334	77.3	88.1	86.1	87.1
30 Leicester	26.4	395	77.4	84.0	83.4	86.9
31 SOAS London	26.7	412	72.3	82.2	86.8	86.5
32 Reading	31.2	387	74.7	80.1	85.0	86.4
33 Ulster	48.5	304	85.9	89.9	60.2	86.3
34 Aston	19.7	384	83.4	88.8	73.7	86.1
35 Portsmouth	32.2	350	77.7	88.0	75.9	85.9
36 Swansea	20.4	309	82.8	87.1	82.6	85.8
37 Robert Gordon	3.9	388	83.8	84.8	83.8	85.6
38 Bangor	12.0	373	88.7	91.2	68.0	85.4
39 Manchester	27.2	433	69.8	80.4	81.6	85.3
40 Southampton	18.2	424	77.1	83.0	77.2	85.2
=41 Buckingham		298	87.4	91.3	83.1	84.8
=41 Cardiff	27.2	399	74.7	83.3	74.4	84.8
43 Lincoln	5.0	338	85.4	90.3	76.5	84.5
44 Essex	31.6	304	76.0	83.4	78.5	84.4
45 Liverpool	19.6	377	75.2	81.6	79.4	84.1
46 Coventry	5.6	296	86.4	88.6	78.5	84.0
47 Surrey	8.5	410	82.2	85.8	69.8	83.9
=48 Edge Hill	12.1	301	92.6	94.1	59.0	83.6
=48 Stirling	19.4	387	77.8	82.2	71.5	83.6
50 City	9.1	350	77.1	83.1	81.3	83.3
51 London South Bank	20.1	226	91.3	94.2	60.9	83.1
52 Manchester Metropolitan	14.9	326	79.5	84.8	74.1	83.0
=53 Edinburgh Napier		342	84.4	88.0	73.4	82.9
=53 Nottingham Trent	2.3	295	85.4	87.0	76.7	82.9
55 Glasgow Caledonian	1.8	410	78.8	88.8	69.8	82.8
56 De Montfort	5.2	265	83.2	84.3	82.1	82.7
=57 Huddersfield		319	80.9	82.3	82.1	82.4
=57 Oxford Brookes	5.1	337	81.1	86.7	72.7	82.4
59 Salford	5.9	296	87.9	88.9	65.2	82.1
=60 Bradford	11.8	329	80.0	86.8	68.3	82.0
=60 Northumbria	2.5	348	81.2	85.5	72.0	82.0
=62 Aberystwyth	14.3	308	79.5	83.5	70.5	81.7
=62 Gloucestershire		309	89.6	86.9	64.7	81.7
64 Brunel	20.3	367	71.7	82.6	68.5	81.5
65 Buckinghamshire New		279	86.4	86.6	70.4	81.3
=66 Teesside	15.0	278	92.2	94.0	46.2	81.2

Law cont

		Research quality %	Entry standards	Teaching quality %	Student experience %	Graduate prospects %	Overall score
=66	West of England	3.5	310	77.7	87.4	74.0	81.2
68	Greenwich	2.1	346	80.7	83.2	69.8	81.1
=69	Hull	12.6	339	71.8	85.3	71.9	81.0
=69	St Mary's, Twickenham		240	83.0	86.5	77.9	81.0
=71	Derby	2.4	328	75.0	78.3	80.1	80.7
=71	South Wales		324	86.5	86.5	61.6	80.7
73	Plymouth	16.0	306	83.3	85.8	54.9	80.3
74	Central Lancashire	5.3	293	79.5	85.5	68.2	80.2
75	Sheffield Hallam		293	85.2	86.2	63.0	80.0
76	Sunderland	0.7	264	88.5	88.1	59.4	79.8
=77	Cumbria		274	85.3	90.9	59.8	79.7
=77	Liverpool John Moores	2.7	336	79.0	84.2	64.0	79.7
79	Southampton Solent		249	89.1	92.4	56.1	79.6
80	Chester		293	82.2	81.2	68.0	79.5
81	Brighton	6.5	270	77.0	82.1	70.1	79.2
82	Kingston		306	74.8	83.9	71.4	79.1
83	Middlesex	21.4	247	75.7	80.8	64.4	79.0
84	Hertfordshire		278	73.3	82.2	76.3	78.8
85	Leeds Beckett		264	82.9	85.9	62.1	78.7
86	Westminster	7.5	310	68.0	79.6	71.7	78.1
87	Bedfordshire	3.6	209	85.4	84.5	59.6	77.9
=88	Bournemouth	8.8	326	69.4	81.9	63.2	77.7
=88	Staffordshire		278	81.6	83.2	58.5	77.7
90	Liverpool Hope		301	88.3	83.8	46.2*	77.5
91	Birmingham City	2.8	276	77.5	77.0	63.8	77.1
92	West London		276	77.2	83.4	59.3	76.8
93	Northampton		256	76.9	82.5	60.1	76.4
=94	Anglia Ruskin	5.2	242	75.4	84.0	55.1	75.7
=94	Canterbury Christ Church	3.2	277	82.5	80.6	45.8	75.7
96	East London	8.6	243	76.7	82.2	49.3	75.2
97	Bolton		189	74.4	80.9	63.6	74.8
98	West of Scotland		295	73.5	72.6	56.3	74.4
99	London Metropolitan	0.3	220	74.5	81.8	54.8	74.1
100	Winchester		281	64.3	66.9	58.4	71.7

Employed in professional job:	32%	Employed in non-professional job and studying:	5%
Employed in professional job and studying:	6%	Employed in non-professional job:	18%
Studying:	29%	Unemployed:	10%
Average starting professional salary:	£20,422	Average starting non-professional salary:	£16,919

Librarianship and Information Management

Only five universities are left in the table for librarianship and information management – half the number of a decade ago – and none of them has a degree with librarianship in the title. Librarianship is now more normally studied at Masters level; indeed, some postgraduate training is required to enter the profession after completing a first degree. Most of the courses in this category focus on broader information services, but only 145 students started undergraduate courses in 2015 – five fewer than in the previous year.

As in other subjects with small enrolments, there can be huge swings in some of the statistics. Librarianship and information management is back in the top 20 in the graduate earnings table, for example, after jumping 22 places as a result of a £4,000 increase in average salaries in professional jobs. At the same time, however, the subjects have dropped seven places in the employment table. Unemployment is still low, at 7 per cent, but there has not been the growth in positive destinations seen in other subjects in the top 40. Only Loughborough saw more than three-quarters of its graduates find professional employment or enrol on postgraduate courses.

Loughborough remains top of the table, with by far the highest employment rate and the best of the entry scores at the three universities attracting enough students to meet our threshold for publication. It was the only university to average more than 350 points on the old UCAS tariff. Leeds, in second place, produced the best score in the Research Excellence Framework and has the highest satisfaction levels in both of the measures derived from the National Student Survey. Only a low score for graduate prospects prevented it from mounting more of a challenge to Loughborough.

Librarianship and Information Management	Research quality %	Entry standards	Teaching quality %	Student experience %	Graduate prospects %	Overall score
1 Loughborough	45.1	393	86.1	92.2	89.4	100.0
2 Leeds	54.5		86.6	93.6	52.4	93.2
3 Northumbria	21.0	346	75.3	79.2	72.3	86.8
4 Manchester Metropolitan	4.7	336	69.0	76.8	58.0	80.2
5 Aberystwyth	9.2		61.7	65.4	40.9	74.5

Employed in professional job:	56%	Employed in non-professional job and studying:	3%
Employed in professional job and studying:	3%	Employed in non-professional job:	25%
Studying:	6%	Unemployed:	7%
Average starting professional salary:	£24,168	Average starting non-professional salary:	£15,448

Linguistics

Fewer than 600 students started degrees in linguistics in 2015, but the number of universities offering the subject at degree level is still going up – 68 in 2017, two more than in the current academic year – albeit sometimes as the language component of a degree in English. There are also three more universities in the latest table than in the last edition of the *Guide*. In its pure form, linguistics examines how language works, and can lead to

Linguistics cont

work in speech therapy or the growing field of teaching English as a foreign language. The subject has fared much better than might have been expected since the introduction of £9,000 fees. Both applications and enrolments are well ahead of the levels seen at the start of the decade.

Almost three-quarters of the students are female. There are about five applications for each place and entry standards are comparatively high. Only four of the 32 universities in the table average less than 300 points, while the norm at top-placed Oxford and at Cambridge, which has dropped to fourth, is more than 550 points. Cambridge's decline is due to a dramatic fall in student satisfaction, down more than 15 percentage points in a year. The best scores in all aspects of the National Student Survey are at Bangor, in equal 14th place, while the best graduate prospects are at sixth-placed Newcastle.

Linguistics is just inside the top 50 in the employment table, as it was last year. Three graduates in ten start off in low-level jobs and only Newcastle, Cambridge and University College London saw eight out of ten of those completing a linguistics degree go straight into professional work or onto a postgraduate course. The subject is outside the top 50 for graduate earnings, although higher than in the last edition of the *Guide* after a £1,250 increase in average salaries in professional employment.

Linguistics	Research quality %	Entry standards	Teaching quality %	Student experience %	Graduate prospects %	Overall score
1 Oxford	41.3	551	82.4	86.1	76.2	100.0
2 University College London	43.7	492	82.5	85.9	81.2	99.8
3 Aberdeen	46.3		92.4	93.2	65.0	98.1
4 Cambridge	54.0	599	64.8	61.3	81.4	98.0
5 Lancaster	47.0	425	88.9	87.1	72.1	97.6
6 Newcastle	36.3	420	81.8	83.8	85.5	97.0
7 Warwick	45.2	499	81.8	80.8		96.6
8 Edinburgh	57.7	489	77.1	81.7	62.0	95.6
9 York	37.3	421	91.5	94.0	60.9	94.5
10 Leeds	30.6	412	87.6	87.0	71.7	94.0
11 Sheffield	42.2	431	77.5	86.8	70.6	93.9
12 King's College London	42.1	413	80.7	82.2	69.6	93.4
13 Queen's, Belfast	53.1		84.8	89.3	57.2	93.1
=14 Bangor	39.6	328	97.1	95.3	54.5	91.9
=14 Manchester	48.9	395	77.1	78.3	66.7	91.9
16 Queen Mary, London	50.3	374	74.4	75.3	65.6	90.3
17 Glasgow	26.3		85.3	86.6	60.0	89.3
18 Cardiff	35.1		83.9	84.1	57.9	89.1
19 Kent	41.9	335	69.5	77.9	74.7	89.0
20 Manchester Metropolitan	29.0	315	91.0	82.9	49.3	85.6
21 SOAS London	26.0	394	72.4	65.5	66.7	85.5
22 Central Lancashire	15.2	350	81.4	83.8	62.2	85.3
23 West of England	9.5	336	92.9	94.7	50.7	85.0
24 York St John	9.7	287	85.8	90.3	60.8	83.9

25 Ulster	22.4	304	88.6	89.9	40.5	82.2
26 Salford	4.8		88.1	83.8	48.1	81.7
27 Nottingham Trent	10.0	264	84.1	85.7		81.3
28 Essex	36.0	309	73.7	75.8	47.2	81.2
29 Westminster	2.0	286	87.0	83.3	54.1	80.4
30 Greenwich	8.2		69.3	71.7	65.2	80.0
31 Brighton	16.2	316	71.1	69.7	55.0	78.7
32 Hertfordshire		280	80.0	73.3	49.2	75.9

Employed in professional job:	37%	Employed in non-professional job and studying:	3%
Employed in professional job and studying:	3%	Employed in non-professional job:	27%
Studying:	20%	Unemployed:	10%
Average starting professional salary:	£20,224	Average starting non-professional salary:	£15,992

Materials Technology

Courses in this table cover four distinct areas: materials science, mining engineering, textiles technology and printing, and marine technology. The various subjects are highly specialised and attract relatively small numbers – less than 500 started courses in 2015 – but recruitment has begun to pick up after a dip when £9,000 fees were introduced. More than 300 students started courses in materials technology itself in 2015, a small increase to follow much larger ones in the previous two years. Although there are only 14 universities in the table, 52 institutions are offering courses in this area in 2017 – four more than in the current academic year. The leading universities demand chemistry and sometimes also physics, maths or design technology at A level or its equivalent.

Materials Technology	Research Quality %	Entry Standards	Teaching Quality %	Student experience %	Graduate prospects %	Overall score
1 Cambridge	78.3	636	86.6	86.9	87.5	100.0
2 Oxford	70.8	587	74.8	82.3	81.5	93.5
=3 Birmingham	49.3	421	80.5	86.4	90.7	92.1
=3 Imperial College	62.3	528	74.4	82.7	84.8	92.1
=5 Exeter	36.4	383	84.2	87.1	88.0	91.2
=5 Swansea	45.5	307	84.1	90.6	88.6	91.2
7 Loughborough	41.8	381	83.1	84.8	87.0	90.9
8 Sheffield	41.0	428	78.0	85.3	86.1	90.0
9 Queen Mary, London	40.0	374	81.2	87.7	70.8	88.4
10 Manchester	36.4	418	76.3	82.9	77.7	87.6
11 Sheffield Hallam	17.8	299	79.0	81.6	57.7	82.1
12 Huddersfield	10.2	344	81.9	74.2	55.0	81.8
13 De Montfort	12.5	318	77.1	73.5	68.9	81.7
14 Buckinghamshire New		300	84.9	79.6	44.4	80.4

Materials Technology cont

Cambridge enjoys a big lead in the table, with much the highest scores for entry standards and research: only 3 per cent of the university's submission to the Research Excellence Framework was considered less than world-leading or internationally excellent. Cambridge students are also the most satisfied with the teaching, feedback and academic support they receive, while Swansea again posted the best scores in the remaining sections of the National Student Survey. Oxford has overtaken Imperial College to take second place in the table, but the best graduate prospects are at Birmingham, which now shares third place with Imperial.

Materials technology is in the top 20 subject groups for salaries in graduate-level jobs, with an average that topped £24,000 in 2015. The subjects have moved up nine places in the table based on graduate destinations and are now in the top 25. Almost a quarter of graduates continue their studies, either full or part-time, and half are in professional jobs six months after graduation.

Employed in professional job:	49%	Employed in non-professional job and studying:	2%
Employed in professional job and studying:	1%	Employed in non-professional job:	17%
Studying:	21%	Unemployed:	9%
Average starting professional salary:	£24,009	Average starting non-professional salary:	£19,106

Mathematics

Maths is often cited as one of the subjects most likely to lead to a lucrative career, and our earnings table seems to bear this out. The subject is in the top ten for average salaries in professional jobs six months after graduation – approaching £26,000 at the end of 2015. It is lower in the table based on the proportion of graduates going straight into professional jobs or becoming postgraduate students, but still in the top 20.

Three graduates in ten continue their studies after graduation, while more than half find high-level employment. Employment scores in the table reflect this, with more than half of the 71 universities, including all the top 20, recording positive destinations for at least 75 per cent of their graduates.

There was a brief decline in applications and enrolments when £9,000 fees were introduced, but maths remains one of the most popular subjects among those considering higher education. The numbers starting are now at record levels – close to 7,000 in 2016, almost 1,000 more than in 2012. With rising numbers taking A level and universities in England receiving funding for new teaching facilities in maths, engineering and the sciences, further increases must be likely in future years. Entry standards are already high: the top six in this year's table all average more than 550 points. The scores are boosted by the fact that most successful candidates for the leading universities have taken two A levels in the subject, as well as two or three others. But the table also covers a wide spread of entry scores: 14 universities (compared with 11 last year) average less than 300 points.

Oxford and Cambridge shared the lead last year, but Cambridge has now pulled ahead with the highest entry grades and the one of the two employment scores of more than 90 per cent. Sussex had the best graduate prospects of all, while Oxford produced the best results in the Research Excellence Framework. Salford, only eight places off the bottom of the table, was the star performer for both the teaching quality and the broader student experience in the National Student Survey.

Mathematics

	Research quality %	Entry standards	Teaching quality %	Student experience %	Graduate prospects %	Overall score
1 Cambridge	60.7	632	87.9	85.9	92.0	100.0
2 Oxford	67.5	611	82.8	83.1	87.7	98.1
3 Imperial College	59.7	580	80.0	84.6	86.9	95.9
=4 Durham	44.0	588	84.1	90.3	86.3	95.5
=4 St Andrews	44.2	569	85.2	87.2	88.8	95.5
6 Warwick	55.8	555	80.3	84.1	82.7	94.0
7 Dundee	48.2	393	90.6	93.3	82.8	93.3
8 University College London	42.0	529	81.0	83.8	87.3	92.8
9 Lancaster	45.8	434	85.3	89.3	85.6	92.7
10 Bath	35.7	512	85.9	80.9	88.0	92.5
11 Bristol	57.3	504	78.5	80.2	82.4	92.2
12 Nottingham	44.8	472	80.6	87.1	82.7	91.4
=13 Leeds	42.0	456	81.0	86.3	84.4	91.1
=13 Surrey	31.5	441	88.5	89.5	82.4	91.1
15 Edinburgh	43.7	510	80.5	84.6	78.0	90.7
=16 Exeter	37.9	464	81.7	87.6	82.5	90.6
=16 Newcastle	32.0	424	87.6	90.8	81.6	90.6
18 Loughborough	31.0	419	85.9	89.3	85.2	90.5
19 Heriot-Watt	42.3	419	86.3	86.7	78.5	90.4
20 Glasgow	41.4	501	81.5	83.4	76.7	90.0
=21 Birmingham	34.1	449	82.1	84.3	82.5	89.5
=21 Southampton	41.9	433	80.2	82.9	82.3	89.5
23 Manchester	44.3	484	78.6	83.3	75.2	89.1
24 Sussex	28.5	362	79.0	84.8	94.4	88.8
25 Sheffield	34.0	415	82.1	89.1	74.7	87.8
26 Keele	19.5	346	92.6	91.0	77.6	87.7
27 York	27.0	426	84.1	83.8	77.8	87.6
28 Leicester	25.0	381	83.3	90.8	79.8	87.5
29 East Anglia	33.7	385	83.5	89.2	73.3	87.2
30 Essex	34.3	308	84.3	87.6	80.0	87.1
31 King's College London	37.1	481	71.7	73.9	82.2	86.9
32 Swansea	20.7	321	83.2	83.8	86.7	86.3
33 Queen's, Belfast	25.0	430	77.5	78.4	82.4	86.2
34 Stirling	14.0	379	89.6	85.5	76.6	86.1
35 Liverpool Hope	8.8	283	86.7	93.3	86.8	86.0
36 Royal Holloway	35.5	384	85.0	81.3	68.4	85.8
37 Strathclyde	34.6	454	76.1	83.9	68.7	85.5
38 London School of Economics	28.7	543	65.6	71.3	82.5	85.4
39 Coventry	9.4	301	91.7	93.5	75.2	85.2
40 Reading	35.3	361	78.7	84.0	72.7	85.1
=41 Aberdeen	32.0	393	79.6	86.5	68.4	85.0
=41 Cardiff	31.6	411	74.4	78.8	77.3	85.0
43 South Wales	10.1	333	94.9	88.6	70.2	84.9

Mathematics cont

	Research quality %	Entry standards	Teaching quality %	Student experience %	Graduate prospects %	Overall score
44 West of England	10.6	322	90.4	82.8	78.3	84.7
45 Aberystwyth	19.4	299	90.3	88.6	70.0	84.4
46 Liverpool	29.8	389	74.3	78.4	74.2	83.6
47 Brighton	6.4	284	87.2	89.8	77.8	83.5
48 City	30.2	356	85.4	87.6	57.9	83.3
49 Kent	28.2	326	77.5	79.9	74.2	83.0
50 Chester	7.1	282	85.3	81.9	81.5	82.9
=51 Aston	21.7	342	79.8	81.2	72.4	82.8
=51 Nottingham Trent	18.4	277	87.9	88.6	67.7	82.8
53 Northumbria	16.7	335	81.8	82.9	71.7	82.6
54 Hertfordshire	20.2	270	81.8	79.5	77.2	82.4
=55 Plymouth	9.3	329	84.1	86.5	69.4	82.0
=55 Sheffield Hallam		286	82.0	89.4	80.0	82.0
57 Greenwich	5.1	328	87.5	92.0	64.7	81.9
58 Central Lancashire	19.8	313	89.1	88.6	57.1	81.8
59 Brunel	25.8	329	75.7	79.8	70.9	81.7
60 Liverpool John Moores	3.2	342	81.3	83.6	74.1	81.4
=61 Bolton		280*	92.2	90.7	64.2	81.0
=61 Manchester Metropolitan	5.6	327	88.2	85.3	63.5	81.0
63 Salford	4.4	288	95.5	93.9	53.3	80.7
64 Queen Mary, London	30.3	387	70.8	73.8	65.7	80.5
65 Portsmouth	11.2	288	78.7	81.5	69.7	79.7
66 Derby	5.0	277	74.2	81.4	77.2	79.2
67 Staffordshire		205*	90.0	91.2	64.3	79.1
68 Hull	24.2	339	71.3	70.3		77.9
69 London Metropolitan	13.5	217	87.6	89.8	48.5	77.2
70 Oxford Brookes	13.9	319	76.4	78.8	51.8	76.1
71 Kingston		244	73.1	77.3	60.4	73.7

Employed in professional job:	46%	Employed in non-professional job and studying:	1%
Employed in professional job and studying:	6%	Employed in non-professional job:	13%
Studying:	23%	Unemployed:	11%
Average starting professional salary:	£25,840	Average starting non-professional salary:	£17,108

Mechanical Engineering

Mechanical engineering is by far the biggest branch of engineering, attracting twice as many applicants as any of the other subjects. Indeed, it is only just outside the top ten for all degree choices. The introduction of higher fees has only increased the subject's popularity: the 7 per cent rise in applications in 2015 was the seventh in succession. Enrolments have not quite kept pace, but the 8 per cent rise in 2015 was the third increase in succession, and numbers were up throughout engineering in 2016. It is not hard to see why. During the economic downturn, mechanical engineering was among the top ten subjects for early career prospects and for starting salaries in graduate-level employment. It is now seventh in the earnings table, with average salaries of more than £26,000 in professional jobs. The subject is a little lower this year (16th) in the employment table, but two-thirds of graduates go straight into such jobs.

Cambridge remains top in mechanical engineering, extending its lead over Imperial College London. The two universities are both ranked in the top five in the world for the subject by QS. Cambridge has by far the highest entry standards and the best research grades. But Lancaster, in sixth place, again has the best graduate prospects, over 95 per cent of graduates finding professional work or beginning a postgraduate course within six months of graduating. Student satisfaction with the quality of teaching is relatively low, compared with other subjects, however. Only Sunderland, in 26th place, had a rating of more than 90 per cent on this measure, and ten universities were below 70 per cent. Scores were better in the sections of the National Student Survey dealing with the broader student experience, with Sunderland again the highest scorer.

No fewer than 127 universities and colleges are offering mechanical engineering in 2017. Most of the leading universities demand maths – preferably with a strong component of mechanics – and another science subject (usually physics) at A level or its equivalent. With more than six applications to the place, entry standards are high at the leading universities, five of which averaged more than 500 points in 2015. Only one institution averaged less than 250 points.

Mechanical Engineering	Research quality %	Entry standards	Teaching quality %	Student experience %	Graduate prospects %	Overall score
1 Cambridge	67.0	629	80.8	94.0	94.6	100.0
2 Imperial College	59.6	596	75.0	84.7	85.4	93.8
3 Leeds	40.9	461	84.3	88.5	90.6	91.3
4 Bath	37.4	534	77.0	86.5	90.5	91.0
5 Bristol	52.3	514	74.2	88.6	82.2	90.2
6 Lancaster	41.6	388	79.7	90.8	95.8	90.0
7 Loughborough	41.8	433	78.0	85.2	91.5	89.3
8 Surrey	30.8	446	80.3	91.7	89.3	88.8
9 Southampton	52.3	443	72.6	84.7	86.4	88.6
10 Sheffield	36.0	444	79.9	88.6	86.4	88.3
11 Nottingham	40.8	429	78.6	86.2	86.6	88.1
12 Glasgow	47.2	488	71.8	82.0	83.3	87.9
13 Heriot-Watt	47.8	431	81.3	88.2	78.2	87.8
14 Manchester	35.1	463	75.4	84.6	87.5	87.6
15 Strathclyde	37.2	512	69.6	83.4	84.5	87.2
=16 Birmingham	37.7	433	74.9	79.0	88.3	86.6
=16 Edinburgh	50.3	487	63.5	76.5	85.6	86.6
18 Swansea	45.5	356	78.8	85.3	85.5	86.5
=19 Brunel	23.7	394	85.9	90.1	83.0	85.9
=19 Cardiff	30.2	419	74.4	87.7	87.1	85.9
=21 Queen's, Belfast	36.7	381	76.4	84.7	87.1	85.8

Mechanical Engineering cont	Research quality %	Entry standards	Teaching quality %	Student experience %	Graduate prospects %	Overall score
=21 University College London	44.6	489	59.6	74.9	89.2	85.8
=23 Coventry	10.3	338	88.4	90.3	93.5	85.7
=23 Exeter	36.4	447	64.5	80.4	91.2	85.7
25 Newcastle	30.2	425	74.4	84.7	86.3	85.5
26 Sunderland	8.8	253	93.1	94.4	91.4	84.1
=27 Aberdeen	28.4	439	70.4	73.9	87.0	83.8
=27 Aston	20.6	383	75.7	85.5	87.7	83.8
29 Liverpool	32.1	385	71.7	80.7	84.1	83.2
30 Sussex	24.0	338	76.7	85.3	83.9	82.4
31 Teesside	5.8	317	86.2	91.3	84.3	82.0
32 Northumbria	30.7	348	75.2	81.5	79.1	81.6
33 Dundee	34.1	408	70.7	81.4	72.4	81.2
34 Plymouth	15.7	310	75.2	77.8	91.0	81.1
35 Robert Gordon	8.8	445	64.6	79.7	87.5	81.0
=36 Liverpool John Moores	4.7	349	84.2	87.3	78.9	80.6
=36 Queen Mary, London	46.7	381	63.1	73.0	76.2	80.6
38 Oxford Brookes	13.9	351	81.3	82.4	77.2	80.3
39 Ulster		310	84.2	90.0	82.4	80.0
40 Harper Adams		308	81.7	87.9	82.6	79.3
41 Huddersfield	10.2	318	73.5	82.6	84.4	79.2
42 Hull	16.5	315	72.4	86.5	79.1	78.9
43 Portsmouth	9.1	308	82.6	85.7	75.5	78.8
44 Salford	4.4	281	83.0	90.6	75.6	78.1
45 Derby	6.7	284	77.5	76.2	84.2	77.9
46 Bradford	7.7	292	79.6	80.6	78.5	77.7
47 Greenwich	29.5	321	76.4	82.3	64.6	77.6
48 Manchester Metropolitan	16.3	335	74.0	79.2	73.3	77.5
49 De Montfort	12.5	268	73.9	77.3	83.3	77.4
50 West of England	10.6	319	74.0	80.7	76.5	77.3
51 Hertfordshire	16.5	296	73.4	78.5	76.3	77.0
52 Central Lancashire	7.1	300	84.8	87.5	66.7	76.8
53 City	20.2	331	78.0	81.8	63.2	76.6
54 Glasgow Caledonian	4.7	358	72.7	82.1	71.9	76.3
55 Sheffield Hallam		284	71.0	79.0	81.1	75.3
56 London South Bank	19.6	294	72.3	81.1	60.0	73.6
57 West of Scotland	9.0	379	74.6	78.8	55.3	73.4
58 Staffordshire	5.7	264	77.4	77.3	67.5	73.3
59 Anglia Ruskin	9.1	244	78.5	81.8	64.3	73.2
60 South Wales		356	64.5	68.6	71.4	72.4
61 Birmingham City		288	61.8	65.1	72.2	69.9
62 Kingston	2.9	283	62.5	68.0	62.6	68.3
63 Brighton	7.4	319	47.7	62.0	65.8	67.1

Employed in professional job:	64%	Employed in non-professional job and studying:	1%
Employed in professional job and studying:	2%	Employed in non-professional job:	10%
Studying:	11%	Unemployed:	13%
Average starting professional salary:	£26,376	Average starting non-professional salary:	£18,478

Medicine

Even after a 12 per cent decline in the demand for places in medicine, there were almost ten applications for every place in 2015 – easily the highest ratio in any subject and all the more remarkable since candidates can only apply to four medical schools. Entry standards are correspondingly fearsome: only three of the 33 schools, compared with six last year, averaged less than 500 points, all of them were within 15 points of this mark. In spite of this, medicine is in the top six subjects for the volume of applications. Nearly all schools demand chemistry and most biology. Physics or maths is required by some, either as an alternative or addition to biology. Universities will want to see evidence of commitment to the subject through work experience or voluntary work. Almost all schools interview candidates, and several use one of the two specialist aptitude tests (*see* chapter 2).

The subject carries unique prestige and is back on top of the employment table this year. Employment scores for individual schools are no longer used in the ranking (although they are still shown for guidance) to avoid small differences distorting positions in a subject where virtually all graduates become junior doctors or researchers. Fifteen schools reported full employment in 2015, and only two dropped below 99 per cent. The average starting salary of £28,191 for junior doctors was £500 lower than in 2014, but still in the top three.

The top two in the table have been the same for the last six years, with Oxford widening its lead over Cambridge in the latest edition. Queen Mary, University of London has moved up to third place but the two London giants, Imperial and University College London, have both lost ground. Oxford has by far the most satisfied students – it is one of only two schools with a rating of more than 90 per cent for teaching quality, the other being Brighton and Sussex Medical School, overall in 29th place. Cambridge has the highest entry standards. There was little to separate the leading universities in the Research Excellence Framework, but Lancaster came out on top.

Undergraduates have to be prepared to work long hours, particularly towards the end of the course, which will usually be five years long. Many students are now opting for the postgraduate route into the medical profession instead, although this is even longer. Levels of satisfaction on the undergraduate courses are generally high, but at six schools the approval rate dropped below 70 per cent on the three sections of the National Student Survey covering teaching, feedback and academic support.

Employed in professional job:	93%	Employed in non-professional job and studying:	0%
Employed in professional job and studying:	1%	Employed in non-professional job:	0%
Studying:	5%	Unemployed:	1%
Average starting professional salary:	£28,191	Average starting non-professional salary:	..

Medicine

Medicine	Research quality %	Entry standards	Teaching quality %	Student experience %	Graduate prospects %	Overall score
1 Oxford	48.9	612	93.2	97.5	99.6	100.0
2 Cambridge	52.0	632	71.4	79.8	98.5	94.8
3 Queen Mary, London	40.2	573	85.6	91.8	99.8	91.6
=4 Keele	50.0	528	89.6	92.4	100.0	91.4
=4 Imperial College	54.6	566	74.7	85.6	100.0	91.4
=4 Newcastle	44.8	558	84.5	92.6	99.8	91.4
7 University College London	53.3	578	69.9	82.2	99.4	90.4
8 Glasgow	42.3	571	81.9	85.7	99.3	90.2
9 Swansea	44.7		80.9	89.2	100.0	89.8
10 Lancaster	55.2	492	88.2	91.3		89.1
11 Exeter	41.6	542	83.7	92.5	100.0	88.9
12 Edinburgh	49.8	588	66.2	76.9	99.7	88.6
=13 Bristol	47.5	534	74.8	82.7	99.8	86.2
=13 Dundee	25.1	568	83.4	90.2	99.6	86.2
15 East Anglia	31.8	534	85.7	93.3	100.0	86.1
16 Leeds	32.1	540	80.1	92.0	99.1	85.2
17 Birmingham	31.5	552	77.6	88.8	99.9	85.0
18 Aberdeen	20.2	568	81.9	92.6	99.7	84.9
19 St Andrews	19.8	548	87.9	94.8	98.8	84.8
=20 Queen's, Belfast	34.6	505	84.2	92.7	100.0	83.9
=20 Southampton	35.6	531	77.5	87.0	100.0	83.9
22 Cardiff	34.5	514	81.0	91.6	99.8	83.7
=23 Hull-York Medical School	36.2	518	78.6	84.8	99.6	83.0
=23 Plymouth	23.1	533	83.7	92.5	100.0	83.0
25 Sheffield	36.5	488	86.2	89.3	100.0	82.8
26 Manchester	34.6	524	71.7	81.8	99.9	80.9
27 Nottingham	36.8	505	72.8	82.3	100.0	80.2
28 King's College London	48.3	507	59.0	71.8	99.5	78.7
29 Brighton and Sussex Medical School	8.6	500	91.0	92.5	100.0	77.9
30 Leicester	33.3	519	63.6	79.3	100.0	77.8
31 St George's, London	22.4	502	73.5	79.8	100.0	75.7
32 Liverpool	31.7	486	62.7	75.3	100.0	73.7
33 Warwick	26.2		63.4	70.6	100.0	71.8

Middle Eastern and African Studies

St Andrews is the new leader in Middle Eastern and African studies, having dropped out of the table for the last two years because it did not have enough students in these subjects for a reliable score to be compiled. It was not for the lack of options: St Andrews is offering 85 combinations of Arabic, Persian and Middle Eastern studies in 2017. There still were too few entrants to compile a score for entry standards in 2015, but the university's normal high levels of student satisfaction have taken it to top place. St Andrews had the best scores in the teaching sections of the National Student Survey and was second only to seventh-placed Leeds for the broader student experience.

This is one of the smallest categories in the *Guide* in terms of student numbers at degree level. Only 90 students started courses in Middle Eastern studies in 2014, and the total for African studies was a mere 10. Although Arabic shared in a small increase in enrolments for non-European languages, fewer than 100 students started degrees in the entire group. The subjects enjoy some official protection because they are classed as "vulnerable" and of national importance. It is just as well, because applications remain well down on the norm before the introduction of £9,000 fees.

Nevertheless, there is one more university in the ranking than last year, albeit none from Wales or Northern Ireland. Second-placed Birmingham, last year's leader, has much the best scores both for research and graduate prospects. Again, the small numbers make for big swings even in the national statistics. The unemployment rate is five percentage points lower and the average starting salary in professional jobs is £3,000 higher than in the last edition of the *Guide*. As a result the subjects have moved up 18 places in the earnings table and are just outside the top 30. Applicants for courses in Arabic or African languages are not expected to have previous knowledge of the language, although they would normally be expected to demonstrate an aptitude for learning other languages.

Middle Eastern and African Studies	Research quality %	Entry standards	Teaching quality %	Student experience %	Graduate prospects %	Overall score
1 St Andrews	46.7		87.0	89.5	85.3	100.0
2 Birmingham	50.9	346	87.2	82.6	91.1	96.7
3 Durham	34.6	531	81.6	84.4	83.3	94.5
4 Cambridge	45.0	592	75.2	76.7	67.9	91.9
5 Exeter	36.0	454	75.1	84.1	82.4	91.2
6 Oxford	36.2	591	60.0	66.2	84.4	90.4
7 Leeds	30.6	409	84.6	90.8	75.9	89.5
8 Edinburgh	30.1	475	87.9	72.0	81.8	87.5
9 SOAS London	26.3	416	79.4	83.7	67.6	84.5
10 Manchester	48.9	354	67.8	63.1	66.7	83.5
11 Westminster	11.3	281	72.2	77.0	63.3	74.2

Employed in professional job:	46%	Employed in non-professional job and studying:	3%
Employed in professional job and studying:	1%	Employed in non-professional job:	18%
Studying:	18%	Unemployed:	13%
Average starting professional salary:	£22,412	Average starting non-professional salary:	£17,378

Music

Universities responded to the third successive rise in applications for degrees in music by increasing the number of places by 10 per cent in 2015. The subject seems to be well and truly over the impact of £9,000 fees, with both applications and enrolments running at record

Music cont

levels. One effect has been that the number of applications per place has dropped from more than five to a little over four. Entry grades are relatively low at most universities – 16 average less than 300 UCAS points – although music grades and the quality of auditions carry more weight in selecting students. Nine out of ten degree applicants come with A levels and most university departments expect music to be among them, although they may accept a distinction or merit in Grade 8 music exams. The character of courses varies considerably, from the practical and vocational programmes in conservatoires to the more theoretical degrees in some of the older universities, and everything from creative sound design and new media to sonic arts elsewhere. Almost 200 universities, colleges and other providers are offering undergraduate courses in 2017.

Durham has leapfrogged both Oxford and Manchester to take the lead in the new table. It has the highest entry grades and good scores on the other measures. The most satisfied students are at the University of St Mark and St John, in 47th place, which produced the top scores on both of the measures derived from the National Student Survey, but was hampered in the overall table by the university's decision not enter the Research Excellence Framework.

The Royal College of Music again has the best employment score, with an impressive 98.7 per cent of graduates going straight into professional work or postgraduate study. The four specialist institutions do far better than most university departments on this measure. Music invariably finishes ahead of the other performing arts in the employment table, although it is only just in the top 50. The 10 per cent unemployment rate is no worse than the average for all subjects, but 30 per cent of leavers were in non-graduate occupations six months after graduation. Music has improved considerably this year in the earnings table, with average salaries in professional jobs close to £20,000, but is still only 55th out of 67 subjects.

Music	Research quality %	Entry standards	Teaching quality %	Student experience %	Graduate prospects %	Overall score
1 Durham	64.9	564	82.0	81.2	88.1	100.0
2 Oxford	66.3	509	82.4	86.7	88.3	98.9
3 Manchester	56.3	556	85.3	87.9	77.3	98.0
4 Bristol	48.0	491	90.5	88.7	76.8	95.6
5 Birmingham	50.7	470	84.5	86.3	85.3	95.1
6 Royal Holloway	55.0	468	85.5	83.7	76.0	93.9
7 Nottingham	55.4	391	91.9	91.8	74.1	93.2
8 Leeds	44.2	470	88.2	88.8	71.2	92.7
=9 Cambridge	48.0	545	67.9	68.3	87.0	92.1
=9 Cardiff	47.0	440	86.3	90.4	72.6	92.1
=9 Southampton	70.7	404	81.4	82.8	72.0	92.1
12 York	37.1	384	92.6	90.5	80.8	91.5
13 SOAS London	60.0	345	88.3	84.0	77.3	91.0
14 King's College London	43.5	472	76.6	74.0	84.3	90.9
15 Surrey	27.2	462	89.0	84.6	76.4	90.7
=16 Edinburgh	48.0	479	79.3	77.7	70.2	90.2
=16 Sheffield	60.0	394	83.5	85.3	67.8	90.2

18 Newcastle	40.8	409	88.0	90.0	69.6	89.8
19 Glasgow	46.0	474	80.5	78.8	61.6	88.6
20 Bangor	24.7	357	96.4	93.0	69.1	87.7
21 Royal Academy of Music	23.9	328	83.5	84.5	94.4	87.3
22 Huddersfield	28.0	350	88.8	89.0	74.8	86.9
23 Royal College of Music	10.9	316	83.7	84.8	98.7	85.9
24 Queen's, Belfast	38.3	397	79.4	78.9	67.3	85.5
=25 Royal Northern College of Music	12.3	359	84.6	81.7	85.1	85.0
=25 Sussex	30.2	366	81.0	69.4	80.8	85.0
27 Kent	44.3	345	82.0	78.6	66.7	84.9
28 Keele	41.7	311	80.1	80.3	76.6	84.8
29 City	34.0	349	79.8	78.8	75.7	84.7
30 Middlesex	16.1	305	90.7	90.3	76.8	84.4
31 Aberdeen	32.0	443	71.8	76.9	66.9	84.3
32 Birmingham City	11.6	333	88.9	81.9	80.8	84.2
=33 Goldsmiths, London	51.1	374	70.8	69.8	70.0	84.0
=33 Ulster	40.0	334	90.7	89.2	50.4	84.0
35 Edinburgh Napier		424	89.1	89.4	64.3	83.8
36 Greenwich		408	89.4	93.6	61.9	83.3
37 Bath Spa	10.7	338	88.7	89.0	68.2	82.7
38 Hull	11.2	389	87.4	88.1	57.6	82.4
39 Royal Conservatoire of Scotland	11.3	385	69.7	71.6	89.5	82.2
40 Coventry	18.1	331	90.0	88.3	59.4	82.1
41 Brunel	32.6	350	94.8	91.0	34.8	81.9
42 Liverpool	31.4	386	78.6	77.3	47.7	80.2
=43 Bournemouth	15.0	308	85.2	83.9	60.0	79.4
=43 Falmouth	6.2	320	84.8	84.0	65.1	79.4
=43 West London	2.3	342	86.9	86.5	59.6	79.4
46 Chester	4.3	324	84.1	80.4	65.9	78.9
47 St Mark and St John		288	96.5	94.1	52.0	78.8
48 Westminster	22.5	304	74.1	76.9	65.2	78.0
49 Edge Hill	3.8	338	82.5	78.5		77.9
=50 Essex		253	92.4	91.7	59.7	77.7
=50 Sunderland	4.2	275	90.9	83.6	58.6	77.7
52 Liverpool Hope	15.5	322	79.2	71.5	60.9	77.5
53 Salford	7.2	317	91.2	87.3	43.2	77.3
54 De Montfort	14.5	283*	90.8	82.1	45.8*	76.9
55 Gloucestershire		294	95.3	91.7	42.9	76.8
56 Leeds Beckett	1.7	307	84.8	78.9		76.7
57 Hertfordshire	5.3	312	76.9	73.8	67.2	76.5
58 West of Scotland	11.3	373	74.6	74.7	50.7	76.2
59 Bolton		287	86.9	81.8	55.6	75.8
60 Derby		294	85.0	84.9	51.7	75.3
61 York St John	10.5	287	75.9	81.2	56.8	75.0
62 Cumbria		313	79.5	80.9	54.5	74.9
63 Winchester	11.2	329*	88.9	89.1	25.0	74.7
64 Oxford Brookes	30.2	337	66.0	66.8	48.9	74.5

Music cont

	Research quality %	Entry standards	Teaching quality %	Student experience %	Graduate prospects %	Overall score
65 Plymouth	20.2	303	77.3	75.0	42.5	74.1
66 Kingston		314	75.0	79.8	55.5	74.0
67 Manchester Metropolitan	7.5	326	78.1	77.0	43.1	73.6
68 Central Lancashire	3.9	299	73.3	72.8	58.3	73.3
69 Canterbury Christ Church	15.2	274	78.3	75.8	44.5	73.0
70 Southampton Solent		284	82.5	87.8	41.8	72.9
=71 Chichester	9.7	330	70.9	71.7	44.7	72.1
=71 Northampton		302	83.2	82.2	35.9	72.1
73 Buckinghamshire New		278	77.5	80.3	48.9	72.0
=74 Brighton	13.1	238	76.0	64.0	56.6	71.7
=74 South Wales	6.4	317	65.1	60.1	61.5	71.7
76 London South Bank	12.8	268	74.1	65.0	47.6	70.8
77 Anglia Ruskin	16.9	256	65.5	68.3	46.6	69.2
78 University of the Arts London		241	69.6	63.7	54.2	68.0
79 East London	11.2	306	54.8	54.7	54.0	67.7

Employed in professional job:	41%	Employed in non-professional job and studying:		2%
Employed in professional job and studying:	4%	Employed in non-professional job:		28%
Studying:	15%	Unemployed:		10%
Average starting professional salary:	£19,956	Average starting non-professional salary:		£15,580

Nursing

Nursing continues to attract more than twice as many applications as any other subject, although the numbers dropped by 5,000 in 2015. There has been phenomenal growth since the move towards an all-graduate profession, with the number of applications passing 100,000 for the first time in 2008 and now in excess of 230,000. There was another small increase in enrolments in 2015, but there were still almost nine applications to every place. Even so, entry requirements are low. Although for the first time no universities averaged less than 250 points, still only four have averages of more than 400 points. Almost two-thirds of the students arrive without A levels, many of them upgrading other health-related qualifications. A quarter of those who join pre-registration programmes drop out, but the rate is nearer 10 per cent thereafter.

Glasgow remains at the top of the table, despite not leading on any of the individual measures. Edinburgh, which has the highest entry standards, has moved up to second, while Bangor has jumped 10 places to third with greatly increased entry grades and one of the five 100 per cent employment scores. The others are at Brunel, Manchester Metropolitan, Essex and De Montfort. Only the bottom two in the table score less than 90 per cent for graduate prospects, and the subject remains in the top three for employment. The same is not true of the earnings table, however, where nursing has dropped from 18th to 26th this year, with average salaries in professional jobs lower at the end of 2015 than at the time of the previous survey.

Portsmouth's remarkable record for student satisfaction, exceeding 96 per cent on both of our measures derived from the National Student Survey, has taken the university up to fourth place this year – the highest any post-1992 university has finished for eight years. Southampton, in ninth place, produced much the best results of all in the Research Excellence Framework, when 94 per cent of its work was rated as world-leading or internationally excellent.

Nursing	Research quality %	Entry standards	Teaching quality %	Student experience %	Graduate prospects %	Overall score
1 Glasgow	42.3	454	94.2	93.3	98.2	100.0
2 Edinburgh	53.4	458	84.9	89.5	97.5	99.3
3 Bangor	34.7	422	83.8	78.7	100.0	97.0
4 Portsmouth	24.3		97.8	96.3	97.2	96.5
=5 Brunel	18.2		90.3	92.7	100.0	96.3
=5 Leeds	31.7	406	82.0	84.3	99.7	96.3
7 Surrey	37.5	393	79.1	82.3	99.0	95.5
8 Keele	20.9	353	91.0	94.7	99.5	95.4
9 Southampton	65.7	382	66.7	75.2	98.9	95.3
=10 Liverpool	35.3	356	92.3	89.1	96.8	95.1
=10 Manchester Metropolitan	12.0	366	91.3	90.8	100.0	95.1
12 Birmingham	37.0	387	79.3	85.8	98.0	95.0
13 Manchester	57.1	386	72.7	74.8	97.9	94.9
14 East Anglia	24.9	399	80.1	82.8	98.4	94.5
15 Nottingham	31.4	379	78.7	74.6	99.4	94.2
16 Bradford	9.5	355	89.0	92.3	99.1	94.0
=17 Northumbria	14.0	371	85.1	83.2	99.1	93.7
=17 York	40.2	370	75.3	82.2	97.5	93.7
19 Queen Margaret, Edinburgh	1.5	362	92.2	95.9	97.8	93.5
=20 King's College London	34.6	380	71.3	77.8	98.6	93.4
=20 South Wales	2.2	381	87.5	86.9	98.6	93.4
22 Cardiff	36.8	376	75.2	74.5	97.8	93.3
=23 Huddersfield	13.2	351	86.7	87.3	98.6	93.2
=23 Queen's, Belfast	34.7	341	87.0	90.1	95.2	93.2
25 West London	2.5	342	91.7	91.3	98.5	93.0
26 Swansea	14.5	379	83.2	84.1	97.2	92.9
=27 City	19.2	332	86.2	84.6	98.4	92.7
=27 Coventry	4.5	344	88.9	91.3	98.3	92.7
=29 Chester	12.0	323	87.3	85.3	99.4	92.6
=29 Worcester	2.6	357	87.3	89.5	98.2	92.6
31 Teesside	2.4	335	90.1	91.3	98.3	92.4
=32 Birmingham City	1.5	352	85.4	86.3	99.0	92.3
=32 Central Lancashire	8.3	362	83.7	84.8	97.9	92.3
34 Dundee	22.1	280	87.0	89.9	98.5	91.9
35 Bournemouth	4.7	354	81.3	81.8	98.9	91.8
36 Essex		308	87.7	86.1	100.0	91.6

Nursing cont

	Research quality %	Entry standards	Teaching quality %	Student experience %	Graduate prospects %	Overall score
37 Lincoln	22.6	338	72.1	80.4	99.0	91.5
=38 Edge Hill	2.0	346	91.6	91.4	95.1	91.4
=38 Ulster	27.7	331	76.6	85.9	96.6	91.4
=40 De Montfort	13.0	329	76.5	76.3	100.0	91.2
=40 Leeds Beckett	3.5	361	80.2	84.2	97.4	91.2
=42 Anglia Ruskin	3.1	302	87.0	88.3	98.8	91.1
=42 Oxford Brookes	3.0	339	86.6	82.5	97.3	91.1
=44 Liverpool John Moores	6.0	356	78.5	82.9	97.3	90.9
=44 West of England	8.2	340	75.6	78.0	99.4	90.9
46 Hull	16.7	367	80.1	83.4	94.3	90.8
=47 Glasgow Caledonian	8.1	329	80.2	81.1	97.9	90.6
=47 Stirling	34.1	281	78.9	81.4	97.1	90.6
=49 Derby		312	82.8	82.8	99.3	90.5
=49 Middlesex	10.0	297	86.5	86.5	97.3	90.5
51 Sheffield Hallam	3.7	349	75.1	74.5	99.0	90.4
=52 Bedfordshire	25.1	295	76.5	76.1	98.2	90.2
=52 Greenwich	2.2	312	81.3	83.3	98.6	90.2
54 Salford	3.8	362	75.1	79.9	96.8	90.0
=55 Cumbria	0.7	320	80.2	78.8	98.4	89.8
=55 Hertfordshire	4.0	315	78.1	80.0	98.6	89.8
=55 Northampton	1.6	304	81.3	87.2	97.9	89.8
=55 Plymouth	9.5	318	83.3	80.2	96.1	89.8
=55 West of Scotland	29.0	271	83.9	85.7	95.2	89.8
60 London South Bank	13.7	321	70.9	76.8	98.3	89.5
=61 Canterbury Christ Church	2.2	308	80.7	82.5	96.8	89.1
=61 Suffolk		332	71.4	70.8	99.5	89.1
63 Brighton	4.8	337	71.9	68.3	98.1	88.8
64 Edinburgh Napier	5.3	291	78.8	80.9	97.0	88.5
65 Kingston/St George's, London	2.6	299	71.1	78.7	98.3	88.1
66 Robert Gordon	4.9	312	71.3	71.8	97.0	87.7
67 Buckinghamshire New	1.0	290	86.5	90.6	92.4	87.5
68 Staffordshire		323	73.3	73.7	95.0	87.0
69 Abertay		290	82.2	84.8	93.0	86.8
70 Bolton		284	89.1	87.8	87.1	84.7
71 Highlands and Islands			77.9	71.3	84.6	80.1

Employed in professional job:	93%	Employed in non-professional job and studying:	0%
Employed in professional job and studying:	2%	Employed in non-professional job:	1%
Studying:	1%	Unemployed:	2%
Average starting professional salary:	£22,840	Average starting non-professional salary:	£18,221

Other Subjects Allied to Medicine

This table was shorn of two of the most popular subjects in the group when physiotherapy and radiography were given rankings of their own. But taken together, the remaining subjects still recruit more students than the totals for most other tables. Those subjects include audiology, complementary therapies, counselling, health services management, health sciences, nutrition, occupational therapy, optometry, ophthalmology, orthoptics, osteopathy, podiatry and speech therapy. Only ophthalmology managed increased enrolments when £9,000 fees arrived, but the numbers starting courses in the group as a whole rose slightly in 2015, despite a drop in the number of applications.

Most of the institutions in the table are post-1992 universities, but Kingston, in ninth place, is the only one in the top ten. Strathclyde has taken over from Aston in top position, leaping up from 17th place with much-improved scores across the board. Cambridge, not surprisingly, has much the highest entry grades, but did not enter the Research Excellence Framework (REF) in the relevant category. Southampton, which shares fourth place with Cambridge, was the star performer in the REF. The most satisfied students are to be found at universities much lower down the table – Edge Hill, in 65th place, just pips Worcester, in 32nd, on both of the measures derived from the National Student Survey.

The choice of specialism naturally affects graduate employment rates, which range from better than 90 per cent positive destinations at 20 universities to less than 60 per cent at five others. Surrey (for the second year in a row) and Kingston both reached 100 per cent. Overall, the subjects are just outside the top 10 for employment prospects, after a rise of six places. Almost two-thirds of graduates go straight into professional jobs. Average salaries in professional jobs have not kept pace with those in other areas, however, and the subjects have dropped out of the top 40 – the second successive year in which they have fallen down the earnings table.

Other Subjects Allied to Medicine	Research quality %	Entry standards	Teaching quality %	Student experience %	Graduate prospect %	Overall score
1 Strathclyde	52.2	483	87.4	89.7	82.5	100.0
2 Aston	39.1	409	91.8	95.1	96.7	99.8
3 University College London	48.4	490	78.8	89.6	88.7	99.2
=4 Cambridge		636	86.6	86.9	87.5	98.8
=4 Southampton	65.7	393	82.4	77.9	96.1	98.8
6 Surrey	37.5	417	87.6	86.3	100.0	98.6
7 Cardiff	36.8	409	87.6	87.9	98.2	98.1
8 Newcastle	47.8	463	86.1	92.0	76.3	97.4
9 Kingston	2.6		91.4	94.7	100.0	97.2
10 Manchester	57.1	430	75.7	78.7	92.8	97.0
=11 Dundee	31.3	498	81.9	85.4	85.9	96.6
=11 Lancaster	55.2	433	80.6	87.8	80.7	96.6
=13 City	19.2	376	93.6	92.3	95.5	95.6
=13 Kent	42.3	369*	85.7*	90.7*	89.7	95.6
=13 Reading	42.3	462	78.9	85.8	82.6	95.6
16 Swansea	44.7	374	83.2	84.3	92.3	95.3

		Research quality %	Entry standards	Teaching quality %	Student experience %	Graduate prospects %	Overall score
17	King's College London	34.6	450	77.7	82.5		94.2
18	Robert Gordon	4.9	370	93.5	96.3	95.7	93.8
19	Warwick	25.3	442	89.3	88.9	75.8	93.6
20	Liverpool	35.3	362	82.0	86.8	90.5	93.3
21	East Anglia	24.9	418	78.3	88.4	87.0	92.6
22	Glasgow Caledonian	8.1	435	83.5	87.1	90.8	92.5
23	Sunderland	7.5		86.3	81.2	94.2	92.1
24	Brunel	18.2	385	84.1	87.0	83.0	90.7
25	Hull	16.7		79.8	83.6	89.7	90.5
26	Northumbria	14.0	390	84.2	90.7	81.5	90.4
27	Leeds	31.7	381	65.5	77.3	97.6	90.3
28	Bournemouth	4.7	340	87.9	86.3	93.5	89.9
29	Sheffield	38.3	408	72.2	82.3	75.6	89.8
30	Glyndŵr	3.6		93.1	92.9	73.1	89.5
31	Ulster	27.7	352	85.2	89.0	73.0	89.3
=32	Oxford Brookes	3.0	364	84.8	80.4	93.6	89.2
=32	Worcester	2.6	301	94.2	97.1		89.2
34	Manchester Metropolitan	12.0	408	83.6	86.1	76.6	89.1
35	West of Scotland	29.0	374	80.9	93.3	67.7	88.8
36	Brighton	4.8	316	83.8	84.7	97.4	88.7
37	Northampton	1.6	322	89.7	88.6	89.3	88.6
38	Cumbria	0.7	407	81.6	79.6	86.7	88.3
39	Plymouth	9.5	335	79.9	83.7	92.2	88.1
40	Coventry	4.5	315	89.2	93.8	82.8	88.0
41	Lincoln	22.6	319	87.4	93.7	70.9	87.9
42	Birmingham	31.5	409	70.4	78.5	73.7	87.7
43	Greenwich	2.2	353	85.7	93.5	79.5	87.6
44	Birmingham City	1.5	365	84.8	89.4	80.8	87.5
45	Queen Margaret, Edinburgh	6.7	400	87.5	91.8	64.9	87.3
46	Teesside	2.4	340	87.3	90.9	78.9	87.1
47	Anglia Ruskin	3.1	271	87.4	86.8	93.3	87.0
48	Exeter		480	67.9	69.5	85.7	86.6
49	Cardiff Metropolitan	3.6	346	83.9	80.2	84.1	86.5
50	Salford	3.8	385	82.6	84.5	75.0	86.4
51	Liverpool John Moores	6.0	341	87.6	89.9	72.6	86.3
52	Bedfordshire	25.1	255	76.5	76.1	94.4	86.2
=53	Canterbury Christ Church	2.2	287	81.1	81.5	95.5	86.0
=53	Huddersfield	13.2	309	87.1	85.2	75.3	86.0
55	London South Bank	13.7	350	73.8	73.3	87.8	85.9
56	Edinburgh Napier	5.3		78.8	80.9	82.4*	85.8
57	Derby		348	85.0	82.8	79.3	85.6
58	Essex		296	86.9	93.1	80.2	85.5
59	Sheffield Hallam	3.7	329	82.5	85.2	79.0	85.2

60 Portsmouth	24.3		81.8	82.5	65.0*	84.6
61 Bradford	9.5	357	68.3	76.7	86.3	84.5
62 South Wales	2.2	331	75.8	76.5	86.8	84.1
63 Hertfordshire	4.0	311	75.6	77.7	88.1	84.0
64 Nottingham	31.4		79.4	82.8	61.6	83.8
=65 Edge Hill	2.0		94.8	97.4	50.0	83.7
=65 West of England	8.2	344	75.4	83.9	73.6	83.7
=67 Middlesex	10.0	312	75.5	83.1	77.5	83.4
=67 Westminster	21.2	307	75.9	78.4	72.9	83.4
69 Abertay		356	81.2	81.9	70.3	83.2
70 Leeds Beckett	3.5	298	00.0	03.0	73.1	82.1
71 Chester	12.0	314	71.3	81.8	69.8	81.2
72 De Montfort	13.0	295	65.7	73.3	81.7	80.8
73 York St John	1.9	336	63.8	70.5	84.0	80.5
74 London Metropolitan	5.2		80.4	86.8	56.5	79.7
75 St Mark and St John		313	69.4	73.8	74.2	79.0
=76 Newman		319	79.0	82.7	54.4	78.3
=76 St Mary's, Twickenham		347	55.3	67.9	82.9	78.3
78 East London	7.6	276	75.7	83.0	52.8	76.8
79 Central Lancashire	8.3	343	69.9	77.0	47.8	76.5

Employed in professional job:	62%	Employed in non-professional job and studying:		2%
Employed in professional job and studying:	3%	Employed in non-professional job:		11%
Studying:	14%	Unemployed:		8%
Average starting professional salary:	£21,783	Average starting non-professional salary:		£16,211

Pharmacology and Pharmacy

The Coalition Government decided not to reduce the number of places in pharmacy after a funding council inquiry, but was anxious for applicants to know that a degree in the subject was no guarantee of employment as a pharmacist. The message seems to be getting through because applications were down by 5 per cent in 2015, the fourth decline in succession. Not that the employment table suggests cause for concern in the graduate labour market: the subjects were seventh out of 67 groups, with 84 per cent of graduates going straight into professional jobs and only 3 per cent unemployed. The earnings table is a different matter, however. Partly because of the training structure for pharmacists, the subjects are seldom in the top 40. In the latest edition, they have dropped into the bottom seven.

Pharmacology was not part of the inquiry, which focused on the growth in the numbers taking the MPharm course, the only direct route to professional registration as a pharmacist. The qualification is now offered at 30 institutions, while another 18 are running a BSc in the subject or as part of a broader degree. There was a second successive 5 per cent decline in enrolments across both subjects in 2015, but that still left almost six applications for every place. Departments in England are evenly split between those specialising in pharmacy and pharmacology. Only four cover both. While the MPharm degree takes four years, pharmacology is available either as a three-year BSc or as an extended course. Most degrees require chemistry and another science or maths at A level or the equivalent.

Pharmacology and Pharmacy cont

Cambridge remains top of the table, where the university's normal high entry standards make the difference: they are 100 points ahead of the rest. Third-placed Ulster has a rare 100 per cent employment rate, with more than half of the 44 universities in the table registering over 90 per cent. Students give the subjects high satisfaction ratings. Bristol, which does not always achieve high satisfaction ratings in other tables, has the best ratings throughout the National Student Survey in this one. Queen's, Belfast, which remains second overall, produced the best results in the 2014 Research Excellence Framework.

Pharmacology and Pharmacy	Research quality %	Entry standards	Teaching quality %	Student experience %	Graduate prospects %	Overall score
1 Cambridge	52.5	636	86.6	86.9	87.5	100.0
2 Queen's, Belfast	60.0	419	90.5	95.8	98.6	97.7
3 Ulster	42.5	394	92.1	92.4	100.0	94.9
4 University College London	51.3	458	80.1	90.3	97.0	94.8
=5 Bristol	47.0	440	93.2	99.1	76.5	94.6
=5 Strathclyde	52.2	532	74.9	82.1	94.5	94.6
7 Cardiff	36.8	436	85.3	92.3	97.3	93.7
8 Manchester	57.1	448	78.9	84.5	93.8	93.6
9 Newcastle	47.8	457*	90.9	89.6	75.6	93.4
10 Aston	39.1	378	87.3	92.9	99.5	93.0
=11 Bath	56.2	441	76.4	80.9	97.5	92.9
=11 Nottingham	51.2	453	75.2	83.7	98.6	92.9
13 Keele	20.9	385	93.1	97.8	99.3	92.8
=14 Dundee	55.4	497*	74.3	76.8	91.3	92.7
=14 Leeds	40.9	453	84.9	91.3	84.6	92.7
=14 Reading	34.2	382	88.3	93.3	99.3	92.7
17 Aberdeen	34.7	442	88.7	94.9	81.0	92.4
=18 East Anglia	38.1	421	82.7	86.3	98.6	92.2
=18 Glasgow	33.4	504	79.9	84.6	90.0	92.2
20 Robert Gordon	4.9	477	87.9	92.0	99.4	91.9
21 Kent	42.3	352	85.7*	90.7*	98.6	91.8
22 Liverpool	31.7	400	90.7	94.5	80.9	91.1
23 King's College London	46.8	415	70.7	82.1	94.6	89.5
24 Portsmouth	24.3	347	85.5	88.7	92.6	88.3
25 Huddersfield	13.2	366	80.0	89.3	97.9	87.2
26 Birmingham	19.2	413	78.7	83.7		86.6
=27 Bradford	9.5	352	78.5	86.3	94.4	85.2
=27 Edinburgh	49.8		79.5	89.8	59.2*	85.2
29 Brighton	4.8	365	76.9	85.6	96.9	84.9
30 Liverpool John Moores	6.0	377	77.1	79.3	96.6	84.6
31 De Montfort	13.0	324	77.2	85.0	96.0	84.5
=32 Greenwich	2.7	334	80.8	89.2	88.3	83.8
=32 Lincoln	22.6	345	77.6	85.1		83.8
=34 Coventry	4.5	290	89.1	93.7	76.9	83.3

	Research	Entry				Overall
=34 Hull	16.7		72.8	86.0	82.9	83.3
=34 Queen Margaret, Edinburgh	1.5	317	90.4	89.6	75.0	83.3
37 Hertfordshire	10.9	317	75.6	76.0	93.0	82.0
38 Sunderland	7.5	353	64.3	77.6	98.6	81.4
39 Leicester		411	76.4	84.1	64.2	80.8
40 Kingston	2.6	280	81.4	84.6	82.2	80.7
41 Central Lancashire	8.3	339	60.8	75.3	98.4	80.1
42 Glasgow Caledonian	8.1	375	74.4	91.2	52.9	79.7
43 Westminster	21.2	303	67.9	85.0	54.5	77.1
=44 East London	7.6	308	82.9	83.5	26.0	74.4
=44 London Metropolitan	5.2	240	76.5	82.4	53.1	74.4

Employed in professional job:	75%	Employed in non-professional job and studying:		1%
Employed in professional job and studying:	9%	Employed in non-professional job:		4%
Studying:	8%	Unemployed:		3%
Average starting professional salary:	£19,746	Average starting non-professional salary:		£17,105

Philosophy

The numbers starting degrees in philosophy rose by 8 per cent in 2015, after a similar increase in applications, but the demand for places has still to match the levels seen before £9,000 fees were introduced. Nevertheless, 79 universities — six more than in 2016 – are offering courses starting in 2017. Philosophy is no longer among the most selective subjects in the arts and social sciences, although five universities average more than 500 points at entry and 20 topped 400 points. Relatively few philosophy undergraduates studied the subject at A level – indeed, Bristol used to warn applicants that even an A in the subject was "not necessarily evidence of aptitude for philosophy at university". Degrees can require more mathematical skills than many candidates expect, especially when there is an emphasis on logic in the syllabus.

St Andrews has moved up from third place to take the lead in philosophy this year, partly due to its traditional strength in the National Student Survey (NSS). Students at Gloucestershire, in 19th place, were the most satisfied with teaching, feedback and academic support, but St Andrews has the best score for the broader student experience. Philosophers are generally satisfied with their courses: only four universities had an approval rating below 75 per cent in either the teaching or student experience sections of the NSS. Oxford, which produced the best grades in the 2014 Research Excellence Framework, is only a fraction of a point behind overall. Cambridge has higher entry grades but has dropped from first to third in the new table.

Graduate prospects have been improving gradually. Nine universities, compared with five in the last table and only one in the previous year, saw 80 per cent of philosophers go straight into professional jobs or onto postgraduate courses in 2015, and the number where the rate dropped below half was down from 12 to nine. The best performance was again at Birmingham, where there were positive destinations for 87 per cent of the graduates. There is even better news in the comparison of average salaries in professional-level jobs, which are up by £3,000 since the last *Guide*, taking the subject into the top 20 on this measure.

Philosophy	Research quality %	Entry standards	Teaching quality %	Student experience %	Graduate prospects %	Overall score
1 St Andrews	52.7	512	90.1	96.0	77.4	100.0
2 Oxford	61.3	593	79.3	85.3	83.0	99.8
3 Cambridge	51.6	622	84.9	85.3	75.5	99.4
4 London School of Economics	48.6	542	81.5	80.8	82.9	96.8
5 Birmingham	52.8	420	86.0	83.3	87.1	96.6
6 Lancaster	53.0	412	84.3	88.3	81.5	95.8
7 Exeter	41.0	489	83.0	88.8	80.0	95.5
8 King's College London	53.9	460	82.0	75.5	81.3	94.8
9 Warwick	47.7	487	79.3	81.5	80.9	94.5
10 Durham	30.1	528	79.5	81.1	79.7	92.9
11 Newcastle	54.3	405	80.7	87.3	66.7	92.5
=12 Bristol	40.9	486	80.2	83.1	70.4	92.4
=12 Leeds	39.5	409	85.2	86.4	72.0	92.4
=14 Sussex	34.2	378	81.8	86.9	84.1	92.0
=14 University College London	55.6	495	66.9	77.2	80.1	92.0
16 Nottingham	28.2	411	87.9	87.6	73.4	91.9
17 Southampton	31.7	386	89.1	89.6	69.9	91.8
18 Sheffield	48.3	415	80.4	80.7	70.7	91.6
19 Gloucestershire	6.9	360	98.6	89.4		91.1
20 Manchester	31.9	401	84.7	89.2	69.6	91.0
21 Aberdeen	39.1	409	91.2	87.5	50.3	90.7
22 York	30.7	425	83.1	83.5	72.0	90.6
23 Edinburgh	49.7	461	74.0	79.3	62.1	89.7
24 Essex	44.0	303	81.9	88.8	67.9	89.3
25 Hertfordshire	32.9	290	85.7	88.9	72.4	89.2
26 Queen's, Belfast	40.3	354	85.9	87.3	56.6	89.1
27 Keele	23.7	327	87.9	91.8	63.2	88.3
28 Kent	31.0	333	83.2	83.6	65.8	87.6
29 Cardiff	36.3	361	84.7	82.3	54.2	87.4
30 East Anglia	28.6	383	83.2	82.8	57.9	87.1
31 Royal Holloway	30.5	392	82.9	83.1	54.0	86.9
32 Reading	28.6	332	84.2	81.8	61.5	86.6
33 Liverpool	28.4	364	79.8	80.9	64.0	86.5
34 Stirling	22.7	370	83.8	84.2	56.1	86.1
35 West of England	18.6	303	92.1	93.5	44.7	85.5
36 Dundee	27.7	368	81.7	79.8	52.6	85.0
37 Glasgow	18.9	389	82.5	85.2	49.1	84.7
38 Central Lancashire	8.3	261	97.5	91.2	42.4	83.8
39 Liverpool Hope		285	92.8	87.3	55.0	83.5
40 Oxford Brookes	8.4	317	88.6	89.1	44.6	82.9
=41 Greenwich		308	89.9	88.6	44.9	81.9
=41 Heythrop College		295	86.0	87.3	54.4	81.9
43 Anglia Ruskin		235	92.8	95.3	37.9	80.7

44 Brighton	13.1	281	84.0	72.4	52.0	80.5
=45 Hull	10.5	300	77.3	74.6	59.5	80.3
=45 Manchester Metropolitan	12.5	315	80.0	77.9	48.2	80.3
47 Nottingham Trent	10.0	265	84.0	75.9		79.9
48 Roehampton		260	81.8	86.0	52.5	79.5
49 Bath Spa		304	84.3	75.7	43.6	78.4
50 St Mary's, Twickenham	7.0	245	75.9	76.1	36.5	74.8

Employed in professional job:	33%	Employed in non-professional job and studying:	3%
Employed in professional job and studying:	4%	Employed in non-professional job:	23%
Studying:	24%	Unemployed:	12%
Average starting professional salary:	£24,383	Average starting non-professional salary:	£16,103

Physics and Astronomy

The long decline in the numbers taking physics in the sixth-form and at university was being reversed before higher fees arrived. The numbers starting physics degrees have increased for eight years in a row and went up again in 2015 to almost 5,000. The "Brian Cox effect" has been credited with the recent boom in popularity, in recognition of the engaging Manchester University professor's many television appearances. Applications finally dipped a little in 2015, but there were still approaching six for every place. Astronomy and astrophysics degrees are even more selective and are being offered by over 30 universities in 2017. Entry scores are correspondingly high. Ten universities average more than 500 points at entry, three of which are between 19th and 21st in the table. Cambridge, which leads the table and is in the top four universities in the world according to QS, has the highest entry standards and also produced the best grades in the 2014 Research Excellence Framework. St Andrews' prodigious strength in the National Student Survey keeps it in second place, the university topping the overall student satisfaction measure but just losing out to Keele, in equal 33rd place, for satisfaction with teaching quality.

Sussex was the only university in 2015 where more than 90 per cent of those completing courses were in professional jobs or continuing their studies six months after graduation. Physics and astronomy have dropped out of the top 10 for starting salaries in this edition of the *Guide*, but the average in professional jobs was still more than £25,000. The subjects are also in the top 20 in the overall comparison of graduate prospects, with more than 40 per cent taking postgraduate courses, either full- or part-time.

Most universities demand physics and maths at A level for both physics and astronomy, as well as good grades overall. Only seven of the 47 universities in the table are post-1992 institutions: Northumbria is the highest-placed, just outside the top 30. Just one undergraduate in five is female and a similarly small proportion arrives without A levels or their equivalent. About 5 per cent transfer to other courses or drop out, usually at the end of the first year, but well over half of those who remain get Firsts or 2:1s.

Employed in professional job:	36%	Employed in non-professional job and studying:	1%
Employed in professional job and studying:	4%	Employed in non-professional job:	11%
Studying:	36%	Unemployed:	13%
Average starting professional salary:	£25,047	Average starting non-professional salary:	£15,847

Physics and Astronomy

	Research quality %	Entry standards	Teaching quality %	Student experience %	Graduate prospects %	Overall score
1 Cambridge	55.7	636	86.6	86.9	87.5	100.0
2 St Andrews	51.0	541	93.6	93.7	81.5	98.2
3 Oxford	52.1	624	79.5	82.4	87.4	97.0
4 Durham	46.2	603	81.4	87.1	87.8	96.6
5 Warwick	46.1	525	86.9	86.5	82.4	94.9
6 Birmingham	33.8	535	89.6	90.3	86.7	94.8
7 Manchester	44.9	571	77.7	85.4	85.3	94.1
=8 Bath	40.0	493	87.9	87.4	81.5	93.3
=8 Lancaster	37.6	487	86.8	86.9	86.3	93.3
10 Exeter	42.4	492	82.7	89.0	82.4	92.9
11 Southampton	44.1	430	88.1	91.6	79.2	92.7
12 Strathclyde	45.3	418	91.0	91.4	74.8	92.4
13 Nottingham	48.3	453	83.4	90.2	76.3	92.3
14 Bristol	43.7	472	79.8	86.6	83.2	92.0
15 Queen's, Belfast	44.4	411	85.9	89.1	81.0	91.9
16 Leeds	41.8	451	83.3	89.8	79.1	91.5
17 Surrey	39.6	451	84.4	87.6	80.6	91.4
18 Glasgow	42.0	481	77.2	86.1	83.3	91.3
19 Edinburgh	48.7	523	74.3	77.5	79.0	90.9
20 Imperial College	49.6	604	61.9	67.5	88.1	90.7
21 University College London	45.1	515	69.4	80.2	85.6	90.6
22 Leicester	40.8	395	86.2	91.2	76.8	90.5
23 York	35.8	418	80.6	89.2	82.5	89.7
=24 King's College London	35.8	478	79.3	78.4	81.2	89.2
=24 Sheffield	36.8	434	83.5	87.0	75.0	89.2
26 Sussex	24.7	390	81.2	88.9	92.2	89.1
27 Liverpool	31.5	403	82.9	87.5	83.0	89.0
28 Loughborough	19.0	399	85.3	87.8	87.7	88.1
=29 Cardiff	34.9	400	82.0	92.3	72.2	87.9
=29 Dundee	34.1	432	89.8	92.1	60.9	87.9
31 Aberdeen	32.0	411	87.1	88.3	68.8	87.6
32 Northumbria	30.7	337	88.9	88.9		87.4
=33 Keele	31.8	354	94.2	94.3	60.5	86.9
=33 Hull	24.2	337	85.2	91.0	81.4	86.9
=33 Royal Holloway	31.5	420	82.1	87.4	70.9	86.9
=36 Heriot-Watt	44.1	427	72.5	82.2	69.4	86.3
=36 Swansea	33.0	332	84.0	88.1	73.8	86.3
38 Hertfordshire	20.2	314	93.1	92.4	72.9	85.9
39 Kent	30.7	343	75.7	85.1	79.8	85.1
40 Portsmouth	21.8	244	89.4	91.4	72.7	83.7
41 Queen Mary, London	27.6	374	78.8	81.6	69.1	83.4
=42 Aberystwyth	12.4	283	86.1	92.2	77.9	83.3
=42 Nottingham Trent	20.1	295	91.2	89.5	65.8	83.3

44 Central Lancashire	19.8	325	74.2	77.4	81.8	81.9
45 West of Scotland	19.1	347	85.8	90.3	57.1	81.6
46 Salford	4.4	346	85.3	91.9	47.2	77.1
47 South Wales		334	78.1	72.1	40.0	70.7

Physiotherapy

Nine out of ten physiotherapy graduates go straight into professional jobs – enough to take the subject into the top six in the employment table this year, a rise of 18 places. Applications are well above the level before £9,000 fees arrived and the numbers starting courses rose again in 2015. As a result, over 50 universities and colleges are offering undergraduate courses in physiotherapy, or a related subject such as osteopathy or chiropractic, starting in 2017. Most of the leading courses demand biology A level or equivalent, but some may also want another science or maths. The Chartered Society of Physiotherapy accredits all degrees in the subject in the UK.

The ranking is in its fourth year, the subject having appeared previously as part of the table for "other subjects allied to medicine". Southampton remains top of the table, having produced the best results in the Research Excellence Framework. The highest entry standards were at Glasgow Caledonian, while two universities – Liverpool and Queen Margaret, Edinburgh – saw every graduate find professional work or continue studying within six months of finishing in 2015. Worcester, only ten places off the bottom of the table, has the highest levels of satisfaction with teaching, feedback and academic support, while Robert Gordon, in sixth place, did best in the sections of the National Student Survey relating to other elements of the student experience.

Entry standards have been rising and vary less than in most subjects. Although only four universities average more than 450 points, more than half are over 400 and only three universities average less than 350. Two-thirds of the universities in the table are post-1992 institutions, but only three feature in the top ten. Satisfaction levels are high, with 15 universities topping 90 per cent overall. Employment scores are equally impressive: only the bottom three universities in the table saw fewer than nine out ten leavers find professional jobs or start postgraduate courses within six months of qualifying. The average starting salary of £22,331 in professional roles places physiotherapy just above half way in the earnings table.

Physiotherapy	Research quality %	Entry standards	Teaching quality %	Student experience %	Graduate prospects %	Overall score
1 Southampton	65.7	447	81.3	87.9	96.9	100.0
=2 Birmingham	63.7	432	78.8	83.8	98.8	99.6
=2 East Anglia	24.9	476	90.0	95.3	97.2	99.6
4 Liverpool	35.3	395	89.5	92.9	100.0	98.6
5 Keele	20.9	426	93.1	94.0	98.7	98.5
6 Robert Gordon	4.9	457	95.2	98.3	95.7	97.6
7 Bradford	9.5	436	95.5	92.5	97.2	97.5
8 Cardiff	36.8	415	91.5	95.6	94.4	97.3

Physiotherapy cont	Research quality %	Entry standards	Teaching quality %	Student experience %	Graduate prospects %	Overall score
9 Coventry	4.5	434	90.6	94.6	98.7	97.2
10 Queen Margaret, Edinburgh	1.5	429	88.4	89.1	100.0	96.7
11 Sheffield Hallam	3.7	393	94.1	94.9	98.6	96.1
12 Glasgow Caledonian	8.1	485	83.0	86.9	94.3	95.8
13 Salford	3.8	390	93.2	94.0	98.0	95.6
14 Northumbria	14.0	409	91.1	88.8	95.7	95.4
15 Nottingham	40.6	410	83.5	85.5	93.6	95.3
=16 Brunel	18.2	398	95.1	96.9	92.7	95.0
=16 King's College London	34.6	401	75.6	85.6	96.8	95.0
18 Brighton	4.8	381	91.6	92.8	97.7	94.9
19 Bournemouth	4.7	413	85.2	88.9	97.1	94.6
20 Oxford Brookes	3.0	455	76.5	79.3	97.4	94.4
21 Huddersfield	13.2	379	87.1	89.8	96.6	94.2
22 York St John	1.9	397	90.1	92.3	95.2	93.9
23 Manchester Metropolitan	12.0	422	85.4	89.5	92.7	93.6
24 Hertfordshire	4.0	398	88.5	89.3	94.2	93.2
25 Worcester	2.6	335	97.0	95.1		92.7
26 West of England	8.2	378	78.9	84.4	96.4	92.2
27 Plymouth	9.5	393	81.5	83.2	93.6	91.9
28 Kingston/St George's, London	2.6	411*	70.9	71.0	97.7	91.6
29 Cumbria	0.7	403	78.6	72.6	95.6	91.3
30 Teesside	2.4	356	80.2	85.8	95.8	91.0
31 East London	7.6	326	78.4	82.3	98.2	90.9
32 Ulster	27.7	385	75.7	87.3	88.7	90.3
33 Central Lancashire	8.3	357	84.8	88.1	89.7	89.5
34 Leeds Beckett	3.5	345	91.8	91.8	88.2	89.1

Employed in professional job:	91%	Employed in non-professional job and studying:		0%
Employed in professional job and studying:	1%	Employed in non-professional job:		3%
Studying:	1%	Unemployed:		3%
Average starting professional salary:	£22,331	Average starting non-professional salary:		£13,929

Politics

Applications and enrolments for degrees in politics were both up by more than 12 per cent in 2015 – one of the biggest increases for any subject – continuing a rising trend that has lasted for most of the decade. The numbers starting courses topped 7,000 for the first time, over 1,000 more than before the introduction of £9,000 fees. Even after the provision of more places, there were nearly six applications for every place. Consequently, 113 universities and colleges are offering courses at undergraduate level in 2017.

Oxford remains top of the table and is rated by QS in the top two in the world for politics. It has the highest entry grades in the UK, while Essex, in seventh place, was well ahead of the field in the Research Excellence Framework, with 87 per cent of its work considered world-leading or internationally excellent. Final-year undergraduates at Huddersfield, in 35th place, were the most satisfied with the teaching, feedback and academic support they had received, while Coventry, in equal 26th place, did best in other sections of the National Student Survey (NSS). Politics students are generally satisfied with their courses: only three universities dropped below 70 per cent on either of the measures derived from the NSS.

Employment scores are less impressive, however. Politics is only just in the top 40 of the employment table, with just over a quarter of all politics graduates going on to take postgraduate courses, but almost as many starting their careers in low-level employment. University College London, in fourth place, had the best employment record in 2015, but only 11 other universities registered more than 80 per cent positive destinations and ten were below 50 per cent. Nationally, unemployment is above average at 12 per cent, but still lower than it was two years previously. Politics does much better in the comparison of early-career salaries in professional jobs, however. The subject has moved closer to the top 20 after a £1,600 increase in average salaries since the previous survey.

Politics	Research quality %	Entry standards	Teaching quality %	Student experience %	Graduate prospects %	Overall score
1 Oxford	61.1	595	75.2	85.1	86.9	100.0
2 St Andrews	38.4	559	89.3	89.1	85.5	99.3
3 Warwick	52.7	501	87.1	89.7	83.0	99.2
4 University College London	57.0	561	76.8	79.9	88.1	98.5
=5 Cambridge	38.2	550	83.0	81.6	79.2	95.5
=5 Lancaster	53.0	420	81.1	85.9	84.1	95.5
7 Essex	69.6	305	81.1	88.7	77.6	94.5
8 Sheffield	48.3	445	81.8	86.1	77.5	94.4
9 Exeter	29.8	466	83.6	87.2	84.5	93.9
=10 Durham	27.0	534	77.6	82.6	87.1	93.5
=10 London School of Economics	54.6	535	71.1	71.3	79.8	93.5
12 York	36.9	422	84.5	88.4	77.0	93.0
13 Bristol	30.4	446	86.7	86.9	75.6	92.7
14 Sussex	33.6	373	83.9	90.7	80.9	92.1
15 Leeds	25.1	424	84.0	87.8	79.6	91.5
16 Birmingham	31.1	390	81.0	84.3	83.4	91.0
17 SOAS London	30.5	425	81.0	84.0	77.3	90.7
=18 Kent	27.8	339	85.4	88.7	81.8	90.
=18 King's College London	29.0	487	75.2	79.8	80.7	90.6
=18 Nottingham	30.8	411	78.6	84.7	81.4	90.6
21 Loughborough	22.5	363	85.9	90.8	79.8	90.4
22 East Anglia	35.5	393	85.4	86.3	64.1	89.8
23 Glasgow	30.5	460	75.5	84.3	73.7	89.6
=24 Edinburgh	44.5	487	69.1	80.5	65.6	89.0
=24 Southampton	37.0	372	81.1	86.9	66.8	89.0
=26 Aberystwyth	40.2	306	83.6	85.9	68.8	88.7
=26 Coventry	5.6	295	96.4	97.4	75.0	88.7

Politics cont

	Research quality %	Entry standards	Teaching quality %	Student experience %	Graduate prospects %	Overall score
28 Queen Mary, London	28.1	410	79.0	80.3	74.9	88.6
29 Manchester	28.4	422	78.5	83.3	71.2	88.5
30 Newcastle	22.0	407	82.9	86.9	68.6	88.2
31 Aston	38.6	319	79.7	83.6	70.2	87.7
32 Queen's, Belfast	35.0	368	77.9	87.3	65.6	87.6
33 Bath	27.4	474	68.8	76.8	76.5	87.4
34 West of England	13.8	299	95.7	96.8	60.2	87.3
35 Huddersfield	9.5	300	97.6	93.7	63.2	87.2
36 Portsmouth	32.2	296	85.1	86.3	66.0	87.1
37 Royal Holloway	30.5	403	76.8	77.8	69.4	87.0
38 Surrey	12.5	410	84.7	83.8	68.8	86.9
=39 Aberdeen	18.4	420	76.5	84.8	72.3	86.8
=39 Dundee	10.8	385	90.2	86.1	63.4	86.8
=39 Reading	37.0	361	73.6	80.5	71.2	86.8
=42 Cardiff	30.4	390	76.9	82.0	66.5	86.7
=42 Keele	24.0	328	85.3	89.7	63.6	86.7
=42 Strathclyde	41.6	459	79.9	86.0	40.0	86.7
45 City	24.6	339	81.3	85.2	68.9	86.4
=46 Brunel	32.4	302	82.3	80.7	65.7	85.8
=46 Stirling	33.8	386	76.2	75.8	64.4	85.8
=48 De Montfort	10.7	251	86.7	86.0	77.6	85.1
=48 Hull	10.8	334	85.8	87.0	66.4	85.1
50 Liverpool	12.0	373	83.0	84.1	64.1	84.8
=51 Greenwich	8.6	297	90.3	92.8	60.6	84.6
=51 Leicester	20.0	369	80.5	81.9	61.7	84.6
=51 Northumbria	12.7	352	87.6	84.0	59.3	84.6
=54 Derby	13.5	288	90.5	78.6		84.2
=54 Oxford Brookes	17.8	323	85.2	83.9	59.6	84.2
56 Lincoln	7.7	298	87.2	86.3	62.9	83.4
57 Swansea	18.5	293	76.8	81.1	68.8	82.7
58 Liverpool Hope	7.0	279	92.3	88.2	53.4	82.6
59 Sheffield Hallam		280	96.0	91.3	49.6	82.2
60 Middlesex	14.9	206	86.4	85.8	63.6	82.1
61 East London	13.7	166*	91.1	92.8	56.4	81.7
62 Manchester Metropolitan	18.0	336	78.5	77.6	56.4	81.5
63 Plymouth	25.8	288	76.7	76.8	57.0	81.1
64 Canterbury Christ Church	3.2	250	91.6	87.3	52.6	80.9
65 Leeds Beckett		273	90.3	87.7	52.4	80.7
66 Nottingham Trent		269	85.5	86.3	59.9	80.5
67 Bradford	12.7	285	76.1	72.7	69.1	80.4
68 Westminster	14.3	276	84.0	86.4	46.2	80.1
69 Salford	4.8	269	86.0	89.9	49.2	80.0
70 Goldsmiths, London	16.8	301	75.0	73.3	61.3	79.9

71 Bournemouth	15.1	291	76.2	74.8		78.6
72 Brighton	13.1	236	79.0	87.1	50.0	78.5
73 Winchester		271	87.3	84.2	46.8	78.4
74 Ulster	20.9	277	80.4	82.3	34.8	77.8
75 Chester		267	87.6	79.5	43.1	77.2
=76 London Metropolitan	1.2	221	77.9	82.4	53.7	76.1
=76 Northampton		261*	87.3	90.6	30.4	76.1
78 Central Lancashire	12.0	296	77.2	58.6	44.7	74.8
79 Kingston		242	75.6	74.3	49.7	74.1

Employed in professional job:	41%	Employed in non-professional job and studying:	2%
Employed in professional job and studying:	4%	Employed in non-professional job:	21%
Studying:	20%	Unemployed:	12%
Average starting professional salary:	£23,591	Average starting non-professional salary:	£19,911

Psychology

Psychology was one of only three subjects to attract more than 100,000 applications in 2015, remaining more popular than law. It has the biggest table in the *Guide*, with two more universities joining this year, reflecting another 4 per cent rise in enrolments. For the first time, over 20,000 students started undergraduate courses. Psychology's popularity endures in spite of poor performances in the graduate employment market: it is only just outside the bottom ten for the proportion of graduates gaining professional jobs or continuing studying, and occupies a similar position for average starting salaries in professional-level jobs. More than a third of graduates begin their careers in low-level jobs.

Most undergraduate programmes are accredited by the British Psychological Society, which ensures that key topics are covered, but the clinical and biological content of courses still varies considerably. Some universities require maths and/or biology A levels among three high-grade passes, but others are much less demanding. The contrast is obvious in the ranking, with 31 universities averaging more than 400 points at entry but 13 falling below 270 points. Cambridge again has the highest entry grades in the table, but has lost the overall lead to Oxford. Kent has the best graduate prospects and was one of only four universities where more than 80 per cent of 2015 graduates found professional employment or continued studying. The proportion was below half at no fewer than 31 universities and below 40 per cent at two of them.

Fourth-placed Loughborough achieved the highest scores in the Research Excellence Framework (REF). Buckingham has the highest satisfaction ratings in both of our indicators derived from the National Student Survey but is handicapped in the table because, as a private university, it was not eligible for the REF. Satisfaction levels are high at most universities in the table, as they have been in previous years.

Employed in professional job:	32%	Employed in non-professional job and studying:	5%
Employed in professional job and studying:	4%	Employed in non-professional job:	32%
Studying:	18%	Unemployed:	10%
Average starting professional salary:	£19,935	Average starting non-professional salary:	£15,745

Psychology

		Research quality %	Entry standards	Teaching quality %	Student experience %	Graduate prospects %	Overall score
1	Oxford	58.6	553	93.7	96.3	75.8	100.0
2	Cambridge	57.5	596	86.9	86.3	78.9	98.7
3	Bath	56.2	514	91.2	92.8	77.8	98.0
4	Loughborough	62.3	403	86.8	89.0	80.6	94.9
5	University College London	57.0	517	78.4	86.1	78.7	94.7
6	St Andrews	45.4	528	79.3	87.3	78.5	93.9
7	Durham	37.1	507	82.9	86.7	79.4	93.3
8	York	46.7	448	86.5	93.8	67.5	92.5
=9	Birmingham	55.8	421	74.9	82.2	83.9	91.7
=9	Kent	38.8	406	81.0	88.5	84.7	91.7
11	Newcastle	50.0	442	82.7	89.3	68.4	91.4
12	Exeter	43.3	487	77.2	84.6	75.1	91.2
13	Cardiff	55.7	452	79.6	90.2	63.5	90.9
14	Sussex	42.3	405	77.2	86.1	83.9	90.7
15	Glasgow	52.9	458	71.9	85.8	75.1	90.6
16	Bristol	49.4	460	77.6	86.2	63.3	89.4
17	Swansea	44.7	350	81.2	83.9	78.9	89.2
18	Southampton	47.8	411	77.4	85.2	70.1	88.9
19	Aberdeen	38.7	428	81.7	84.9	66.6	88.6
=20	Leicester	29.6	370	87.2	88.9	68.4	88.1
=20	Nottingham	36.4	443	75.1	84.6	71.3	88.1
=22	Royal Holloway	37.8	446	79.7	86.2	62.3	88.0
=22	Warwick	43.1	449	78.0	81.5	64.0	88.0
=24	East Anglia	33.2	418	85.9	90.5	58.2	87.9
=24	Lancaster	38.5	412	77.3	84.0	71.2	87.9
=24	Surrey	22.0	446	79.1	86.3	73.0	87.9
27	Leeds	33.0	445	73.7	86.8	71.1	87.7
28	Dundee	22.7	413	89.8	91.0	58.6	87.5
29	Edinburgh	52.8	488	69.6	78.1	62.2	87.4
30	Bangor	32.0	332	85.7	91.6	67.6*	87.3
31	Queen's, Belfast	40.2	380	81.7	89.0	60.9	87.1
32	Strathclyde	23.5	451	87.8	89.8	49.0	86.3
=33	Lincoln	7.9	351	90.5	93.2	66.9	86.2
=33	Manchester	44.9	419	76.6	78.8	61.4	86.2
35	Essex	41.0	321	83.4	88.0	61.8	86.0
36	Aston	39.1	369	79.1	80.6	65.4	85.8
37	Buckingham		249	94.7	96.7	75.4	85.5
38	Abertay	15.1	374	86.7	87.3	61.9	85.1
39	De Montfort	11.2	279	88.2	94.5	69.4	84.8
40	Stirling	40.1	373	80.8	81.4	55.2	84.6
41	Sheffield	38.8	419	70.0	78.2	64.1	84.5
42	Northumbria	18.7	367	86.3	89.9	54.2	84.2
43	Goldsmiths, London	40.4	336	79.5	84.4	56.5	84.0

44	Reading	42.3	399	72.9	83.7	53.9	83.9
45	Portsmouth	21.0	350	84.9	85.1	58.2	83.8
46	Edinburgh Napier	5.3	394	85.1	89.9	57.2	83.6
47	Heriot-Watt	26.9	350	78.5	80.7	62.2	83.2
48	Keele	17.7	341	80.6	86.7	61.3	83.0
49	City	23.5	369	79.1	84.6	56.2	82.8
50	Nottingham Trent	19.3	297	85.9	88.3	55.7	82.4
51	Liverpool Hope	5.5	307	83.9	87.3	63.8	81.9
=52	Hull	26.8	337	76.2	82.3	58.4	81.8
=52	West of England	8.2	330	88.6	90.8	49.5	81.8
54	Brunel	26.6	335	80.7	84.8	50.1	81.6
55	West of Scotland	9.4	334	91.3	90.8	43.5	81.5
=56	Aberystwyth		286	87.2	89.8	61.5	81.4
=56	Edge Hill	18.8	312	87.9	88.2	45.9	81.4
=58	Huddersfield	9.5	329	81.0	82.8	61.3	81.3
=58	Manchester Metropolitan	12.0	331	84.3	85.8	53.2	81.3
60	Salford	3.8	349	82.9	83.6	57.4	81.0
=61	Coventry	7.8	311	73.7	84.0	70.7	80.9
=61	Greenwich	6.7	336	85.3	85.0	53.1	80.9
=63	Glasgow Caledonian	8.1	407	79.4	87.8	44.8	80.5
=63	Liverpool	34.6	373	69.8	80.1	50.6	80.5
=65	Gloucestershire		324	85.4	90.0	51.8	80.3
=65	Plymouth	33.8	320	75.6	83.8	47.5	80.3
67	Chichester	10.3	269	87.3	90.8	49.1	80.1
=68	Roehampton	26.4	274	72.8	79.3	64.1	80.0
=68	Staffordshire	8.2	283	85.5	88.3	52.5	80.0
70	Oxford Brookes	18.1	356	73.7	79.7	55.3	79.9
71	Bolton	3.6	296	84.7	84.0	56.2	79.8
72	Teesside	15.0	298	78.9	83.4	55.3	79.7
73	Bradford	9.5	296	76.0	79.3	65.7	79.6
74	Leeds Trinity		297	83.3	80.8	59.0	79.2
75	York St John	11.0	293	80.1	78.8	57.8	79.1
76	Ulster	23.2	297	82.6	89.2	37.9	79.0
77	Cumbria		228	90.0	87.8	54.0	78.9
=78	Brighton	12.4	308	81.0	83.7	47.9	78.8
=78	Chester	7.9	327	85.2	79.5	46.1	78.8
=78	Queen Mary, London	26.1	389	64.2	70.1	58.0	78.8
=78	Worcester	7.1	290	82.8	86.8	49.4	78.8
=82	Bournemouth	13.0	307	81.7	84.1	46.3	78.7
=82	Central Lancashire	12.2	314	76.4	83.5	52.6	78.7
84	Sunderland	7.5	265	78.9	79.5	62.1	78.6
=85	Bedfordshire	25.1	225	78.9	83.1	53.5	78.5
=85	West London	7.6	277	82.9	81.9	53.2	78.5
87	Sheffield Hallam		311	83.1	88.3	47.3	78.4
=88	Middlesex	7.6	317	67.9	78.3	66.1	78.1
=88	Suffolk		281	86.2	86.4	47.5	78.1
=90	Bath Spa		315	79.4	79.7	55.8	78.0

Psychology cont		Research quality %	Entry standards	Teaching quality %	Student experience %	Graduate prospects %	Overall score
=90	Derby	8.4	293	83.1	82.5	46.5	78.0
=90	Liverpool John Moores	7.8	345	76.3	84.0	46.8	78.0
93	Buckinghamshire New		236	85.0	85.0	55.3	77.9
94	Winchester	6.5	300	75.2	82.4	55.6	77.8
95	St Mary's, Twickenham		289	79.4	88.7	47.1	77.0
96	Anglia Ruskin	12.6	263	82.6	84.9	40.6	76.8
=97	Hertfordshire	6.0	278	73.6	78.7	56.8	76.6
=97	Highlands and Islands		290	78.3	73.7	57.1	76.6
99	East London	8.3	281	77.4	82.8	46.3	76.4
100	Newman	0.8	263	83.2	82.0	45.8	76.2
101	Leeds Beckett	6.5	302	75.2	76.8	48.4	75.8
=102	Canterbury Christ Church	2.2	292	74.7	81.3	48.9	75.7
=102	Northampton	0.4	286	77.2	83.6	46.7	75.7
104	Birmingham City		293	75.9	75.8	52.3	75.6
105	Westminster	9.3	310	69.7	81.0	45.7	75.2
106	Kingston	6.5	263	73.7	78.8	49.9	75.0
107	Southampton Solent		256	77.1	81.5	47.3	74.7
108	London South Bank	8.6	264	71.1	77.3	50.5	74.6
109	Queen Margaret, Edinburgh	8.6	339	68.8	75.7	42.5	74.4
=110	London Metropolitan		239	78.4	83.8	42.0	73.9
=110	South Wales	0.9	324	76.0	78.7	35.9	73.9
112	Wrexham Glyndŵr	3.6	228	76.9	80.5	41.9	73.2
113	Cardiff Metropolitan		297	61.3	68.8	49.2	71.0

Radiography

Radiography remained among the top five subjects for employment in 2015. Indeed, only dentistry had a higher proportion of graduates going straight into professional jobs than the 93 per cent of radiographers. The subject has fallen seven places in the earnings table, however, although it is still inside the top 30. Courses are divided into diagnostic and therapeutic specialisms. Diagnostic courses usually involve two years of studying anatomy, physiology and physics followed by further training in sociology, management and ethics, and the practice and science of imaging. The therapeutic branch covers much of the same scientific content in the first year, but follows this with training in oncology, psycho-social studies and other modules. Degrees require at least one science subject, usually biology, among three A levels or the equivalent. A total of 26 universities are offering the subject in 2017, one more than in the current academic year.

The table is in its fourth year, radiography having been listed previously among "other subjects allied to medicine" in the *Guide*. Bangor, which now has the highest entry qualifications, remains top of the table. It is one of five institutions, compared with three last year, to record 100 per cent employment among its radiographers in 2015. Salford, Teesside, Derby and the University of the West of England were the others. Exeter, which remains only a fraction of a point behind Bangor in second place, was the clear leader in the Research Excellence Framework. City, in tenth place, had the most satisfied students in the teaching sections of the National Student Survey, while fourth-placed Robert Gordon again did best on the student experience.

Employment scores reflect the subject's elevated position in the employment table: all but three universities saw more than nine out of ten graduates go straight into professional jobs or further study. Entry grades are not high, but they have been rising: six universities, compared with three in 2014, averaged more than 400 points in the latest survey, and the remaining scores were tightly bunched.

Radiography	Research quality %	Entry standards	Teaching quality %	Student experience %	Graduate prospects %	Overall score
1 Bangor	34.7	447	89.1	87.9	100.0	100.0
2 Exeter	42.4	418	92.3	92.7	97.3	99.4
3 Leeds	31.7	413	91.6	94.8	98.4	98.7
4 Robert Gordon	4.9	440	90.1	95.9	95.5	95.5
5 Salford	3.8	431	82.5	80.7	100.0	94.8
6 Cardiff	36.8	369	72.9	80.3	98.6	94.1
7 West of England	8.2	323	90.8	92.5	100.0	93.5
=8 Bradford	9.5	373	82.2	90.9	98.1	93.3
=8 Liverpool	35.3	341	76.3	83.5	97.0	93.3
10 City	19.2	332	97.4	94.9	93.3	93.2
11 Teesside	2.4	332	92.5	89.0	100.0	93.1
12 Portsmouth	24.3	370	81.8	82.5	95.5	92.9
13 Sheffield Hallam	3.7	343	88.9	91.9	98.4	92.7
14 Derby		357	82.9	88.8	100.0	92.5
=15 Birmingham City	1.5	337	89.6	90.8	97.5	91.9
=15 Cumbria	0.7	344	87.4	84.7	99.0	91.9
17 Ulster	27.7	371	84.8	91.3	88.7	91.5
18 Hertfordshire	4.0	345	79.6	87.4	97.1	90.7
=19 Canterbury Christ Church	2.2	302	92.1	89.8	96.4	90.5
=19 Glasgow Caledonian	8.1	420	71.0	71.8	94.8	90.5
21 Suffolk		354	81.7	85.9	95.9	90.3
22 Queen Margaret, Edinburgh	1.5	371	82.5	91.1	89.5	88.8
23 London South Bank	13.7	335	83.4	86.6	88.7	88.2
24 Kingston/St George's, London	2.6	318	67.4	76.1	98.6	87.7

Employed in professional job:	93%	Employed in non-professional job and studying:	0%
Employed in professional job and studying:	1%	Employed in non-professional job:	2%
Studying:	1%	Unemployed:	3%
Average starting professional salary:	£22,718	Average starting non-professional salary:	..

Russian and Eastern European Languages

Only 50 students started degrees in Russian in 2015 – half the number at the start of the decade – although others studied the language as part of a broader modern languages programme. There had been signs of recovery as three more universities joined the table for Russian and Eastern European languages last year, but only 270 students applied for places in 2015, a drop of 17 per cent on the previous year. Only 20 universities are offering Russian in 2017.

As in other subjects, the small numbers inevitably make for exaggerated swings in the statistics. Having dropped more than 20 places in last year's employment table, Russian has regained almost all that ground in the latest table and is inside the top 30. The unemployment rate has practically halved and seven out of ten graduates went straight into professional employment or continued their studies in 2015. Average starting salaries in professional jobs were on the verge of the top 20.

The top three in the table are unchanged, as they were last year, with Cambridge extending its lead over Oxford. Cambridge has the highest entry standards and the best research score, as well as the best graduate prospects. St Andrews has the most satisfied students, topping both of our measures derived from the National Student Survey. Portsmouth is the sole representative of the post-1992 universities and there are no institutions from Wales or Northern Ireland.

Most undergraduates learn the language from scratch. Despite the small numbers, entry standards remain high throughout the table: the top three all average well over 500 points and only three universities are below 400 points on the old UCAS tariff. Satisfaction levels are also high. Nearly every university in the table satisfied at least three-quarters of its final-year undergraduates.

Russian and Eastern European Languages	Research quality %	Entry standards	Teaching quality %	Student experience %	Graduate prospects %	Overall score
1 Cambridge	54.0	570	88.0	87.7	87.6	100.0
2 Oxford	41.3	546	79.9	81.3	85.1	93.3
3 Durham	34.6	554	79.0	83.8	86.1	92.0
4 St Andrews	26.4	467	93.7	94.3	77.3	90.2
5 Bristol	36.0	426	89.3	89.9	74.4	89.6
6 Birmingham	33.7	428	84.3	83.0	85.6	89.5
7 Exeter	35.1	460	85.8	91.1	72.1	89.2
8 Sheffield	41.2		88.7	91.8	62.2	89.1
9 Leeds	30.6	401	84.4	86.0	80.6	87.3
10 University College London	43.7	488	71.7	73.7	71.0	87.1
11 Manchester	48.9	403	81.6	80.5	57.1	86.3
12 Edinburgh	30.3	494	73.7	82.3		85.3
13 Glasgow	26.3	490*	87.4	86.2	59.6	85.1
14 Bath	27.4	376	79.2	79.7	78.6	83.7
15 Nottingham	39.4	377	77.1	77.4	63.4	83.1
16 Portsmouth	32.2	289	82.0	85.9	71.1	82.4
17 Queen Mary, London	35.1	407*	74.8	70.9		81.6

Employed in professional job:	47%	Employed in non-professional job and studying:	1%
Employed in professional job and studying:	3%	Employed in non-professional job:	19%
Studying:	21%	Unemployed:	8%
Average starting professional salary:	£23,973	Average starting non-professional salary:	£18,043

Social Policy

Social policy has recovered from the drop in applications it experienced in 2014, but is still well short of the demand for places it enjoyed in the year before £9,000 fees were introduced. Although the numbers starting courses rose by 9 per cent in 2015, there were little more than three applications for every place. Yet there are still 38 universities in the table – four more than last year – and 94 universities and colleges have courses in this area starting in 2017. Nor are entry standards especially low: while only three universities average more than 400 points on the old UCAS tariff, just one dropped below 240 points, and this was a figure from 2014 because there were not enough entrants to compile a more recent average.

The London School of Economics (LSE) has lost the lead in social policy for only the second time in the more than 15 years that the table has been published, as a result of some of the lowest student satisfaction scores in the ranking. Leeds has taken over at the top, although it does not lead on any of the individual measures. Edinburgh, which is down to ninth with similar scores to the LSE in the National Student Survey, has the highest entry standards, while fourth-placed Nottingham remains a long way ahead of the rest for the proportion of graduates going straight into professional jobs or joining postgraduate courses. Liverpool Hope did best on the teaching sections of the NSS, while Sheffield Hallam was the top performer for course organisation, learning resources and personal development. Overall, Bolton, at equal 13th, was the top performing post-1992 university.

Nationally, the subject remains in the bottom five for employment, with more than a third of graduates starting out in low-level jobs. This is reflected in the table for social policy, where less than half of the graduates at nine of the 38 universities found professional work or continued studying. The picture is more positive in the comparison of starting salaries in graduate-level jobs, although the average of £20,600 in 2015 was only just in the top 50 subjects.

Social Policy	Research quality %	Entry standards	Teaching quality %	Student experience %	Graduate prospects %	Overall score
1 Leeds	47.6	404	87.1	87.0	68.4	100.0
2 London School of Economics	74.9	469	64.5	65.3	66.8	99.1
3 Glasgow	41.8	392	80.1	85.6	77.9	98.9
4 Nottingham	43.5	374	72.6	72.9	88.0	97.3
5 Kent	59.0	371	76.9	83.6	66.7	97.1
6 York	47.5	357	79.8	84.0	71.7	96.5
=7 Bristol	47.9	374	84.0	84.4	59.7	95.8
=7 Southampton	52.8	390	77.3	80.3		95.8
9 Edinburgh	53.4	473	63.6	66.8	65.2	95.7
10 Loughborough	40.6	363	87.1	87.7	58.5	95.0

Social Policy cont	Research quality %	Entry standards	Teaching quality %	Student experience %	Graduate prospects %	Overall score
11 Bath	43.4	386	80.5	77.8	60.0	94.2
12 Bangor	39.6		82.2	74.3	69.3	93.9
=13 Bolton	1.0		92.2	88.4	67.6	93.6
=13 Stirling	33.8	352	90.3	94.4	51.7*	93.6
15 Sheffield	26.8	375*	79.6	83.3	67.6	93.2
=16 Aston	38.6	328	74.7	83.3	67.8	91.8
=16 Sheffield Hallam		362	96.2	97.1	57.5	91.8
18 Birmingham	40.1	373	62.0	72.9	73.0	91.2
19 Liverpool Hope	8.6	292	96.4	88.3	66.7	90.8
=20 Keele	25.0	335	81.8	82.8	61.3	90.2
=20 Swansea	22.7	277	84.4	89.6	68.8	90.2
22 Salford	27.7	281	90.7	91.2	51.6	89.0
23 Queen's, Belfast	26.2	338*	76.2	87.5	56.1	88.8
24 West of Scotland	9.4		94.4	85.4	43.5	87.3
25 Central Lancashire	11.8	345	82.7	91.5	40.8	85.6
26 Cardiff	30.8	349	77.6	76.0	38.9	85.2
27 Ulster	39.2	278	84.4	93.7	29.4	84.8
28 Middlesex	14.9	302	76.4	74.8	58.3	84.3
29 Lincoln	5.8	300*	75.5	82.3	56.5	83.2
30 Bedfordshire	16.3	240	75.3	80.8	58.0	82.1
31 Northampton		307	78.3	84.3	47.7	81.7
32 Brighton	12.4	271	78.3	82.3	44.6	80.9
33 Chester	0.3	267	83.1	76.6		80.5
34 Canterbury Christ Church	3.2	277	72.5	77.7	52.9	79.8
35 Plymouth	16.0	212*	83.0	85.8	36.7	78.5
36 London Metropolitan	8.8	269	69.1	85.0	38.8	77.4
37 Anglia Ruskin	5.4	250	75.1	84.3	33.3	76.0
38 Birmingham City	3.8	271	62.2	66.8	50.0	75.3

Employed in professional job:	33%	Employed in non-professional job and studying:		3%
Employed in professional job and studying:	2%	Employed in non-professional job:		34%
Studying:	15%	Unemployed:		14%
Average starting professional salary:	£20,600	Average starting non-professional salary:		£15,951

Social Work

Record numbers of students are taking social work degrees, in spite of the fact that applications have dropped from 80,000 to 60,000 in five years. A combination of falling demand and increasing provision has seen the number of applications per place drop from more than seven in 2010 to only 4.3 in 2015. Although five of the top ten universities, compared with two last year, average more than 400 points at entry on the old UCAS tariff, a quarter of the 80 universities in the table have averages below 300 points.

The social work table is particularly volatile, with none of the top ten occupying the same position as last year. Lancaster has taken over the leadership from Glasgow, which has dropped seven places only a year after moving up ten. Strathclyde, in sixth place, has the highest entry standards, while Middlesex, just outside the top 20, has a rare 100 per cent employment rate – an impressive achievement when four universities in the table did not reach 50 per cent on this measure. Bedfordshire, the top post-1992 university, in 13th place, had the most satisfied students in relation to teaching, feedback and academic support, while Liverpool Hope produced the best scores in the National Student Survey for the broader student experience.

A new attempt has been launched to attract graduates of other subjects into social work through the Frontline programme, modelled on Teach First. For the moment, however, social work degrees remain the main route into the profession. Just over 60 per cent of graduates go straight into social work or find other professional employment, leaving the subject on the verge of the top 30. Starting salaries in graduate-level jobs, which averaged almost £24,800 in 2015, are just outside the top 15 of the 67 subject groupings.

Social Work	Research quality %	Entry standards	Teaching quality %	Student experience %	Graduate prospects %	Overall score
1 Lancaster	51.4	386	84.0	87.0	95.6	100.0
2 Bath	43.4	410	87.4	91.9	84.1	99.0
3 Birmingham	40.1	388	85.2	90.9	90.4	98.0
4 Kent	59.0	362	78.6	87.0	88.7	97.5
5 East Anglia	45.8	409*	89.3	90.8	71.8	97.2
6 Strathclyde	31.9	463	89.8	95.2	62.5	96.6
7 Edinburgh	53.4	443	61.6	67.3	92.6	96.2
8 Glasgow	41.8		82.9	84.8	91.7	96.0
=9 Leeds	47.6	413	79.1	86.5	75.4	95.8
=9 Nottingham	43.5	389	74.2	82.0	92.6	95.8
11 Dundee	31.1	319	92.7	90.2	94.9	95.1
12 Sussex	27.9	378	70.0	80.8	95.3	94.0
13 Bedfordshire	16.3		95.3	93.4	81.0	93.9
14 Manchester	57.1		76.7	82.5	83.3	93.7
15 Stirling	33.8	373*	84.3	86.0	81.0	93.6
16 Robert Gordon	18.0	366	85.2	88.5	89.6	92.8
17 York	47.5	344*	77.9	77.1	83.8	92.5
18 Queen's, Belfast	39.3	352	72.5	83.4	89.7	92.3
=19 Keele	25.0	325	84.4	74.8	96.4	91.4
=19 Swansea	22.7		77.6	80.8	94.1	91.4
21 Portsmouth	12.1	354	83.5	90.5	89.4	91.0
22 Middlesex	14.9	301*	84.4	82.8	100.0	90.0
23 Glasgow Caledonian	8.1	366	83.1	88.6	85.3	89.9
24 Ulster	39.2	303	81.7	89.5	76.4	89.5
25 Lincoln	5.8	338	85.1	84.1	90.4	89.0
26 Huddersfield	9.5	353	83.1	87.8	82.9	88.9
27 Suffolk		340	83.5	87.7	93.6	88.8

Social Work cont

	Research quality %	Entry standards	Teaching quality %	Student experience %	Graduate prospects %	Overall score
28 Liverpool Hope	8.6	310	93.0	95.8	80.0	88.7
29 West of England	10.9	385	65.7	73.9	96.6	88.5
30 West of Scotland	9.4	310	87.9	85.7	85.4	87.8
31 De Montfort	11.2	341	78.4	81.8	86.9	87.7
32 Hull	14.3	338	75.3	76.0	87.2	86.8
33 Coventry	5.6	338	85.8	89.2	75.2	86.6
=34 Kingston/St George's, London		319	80.9	86.2	90.1	86.3
=34 Plymouth	16.0	289	91.0	91.7	71.8	86.3
=34 Staffordshire		317	87.6	84.9	84.2	86.3
37 Oxford Brookes		345	78.6	79.0	88.6	86.2
38 Salford	27.7	369	67.0	68.4	74.2	85.6
39 Central Lancashire	11.8	340	82.8	86.1	66.7	85.1
40 Anglia Ruskin	5.4	285	83.5	83.7	86.7	84.9
41 Greenwich	2.2		78.4	83.4	80.8	84.8
42 Leeds Beckett	6.4	309	90.2	85.7	70.4	84.7
43 Cardiff Metropolitan		344	80.2	86.4	75.4	84.6
44 Northumbria	12.7	357	81.6	80.4	62.0	84.4
45 Bournemouth	4.7	353	71.1	72.8	83.8	84.2
46 Bolton	1.0		81.5	76.3	78.6	83.7
47 Manchester Metropolitan	6.9	347	78.5	78.8	67.4	83.2
=48 Gloucestershire		318	76.5	80.8	81.4	83.0
=48 Goldsmiths, London	13.5		70.6	76.8	80.4	83.0
50 South Wales	15.4	282	84.5	86.5	66.7	82.9
51 Brighton	12.4	268*	89.3	87.0	67.5	82.8
=52 Sunderland	1.9	324	86.1	86.3	61.3	82.2
=52 Winchester		287	82.7	82.2	78.4	82.2
54 Derby		309	87.9	83.8	64.2	81.8
=55 Bradford	10.6	314	77.8	84.8	63.4	81.7
=55 London South Bank	20.1	330	66.2	72.0	70.3	81.7
57 Sheffield Hallam		310	69.6	75.3	84.5	81.2
58 Liverpool John Moores	5.8	335	74.2	80.3	64.5	81.1
59 East London	10.6	279*	79.7	83.3	68.6	81.0
=60 Birmingham City	3.8	325	70.2	74.7	75.2	80.9
=60 Essex		299	80.5	88.8	67.2	80.9
=60 Nottingham Trent	5.1	297	82.1	82.6	65.4	80.9
=60 Teesside	15.0	331	59.6	57.9	84.5	80.9
64 Hertfordshire	4.0	320	63.9	67.9	82.9	80.2
=65 Brunel	28.5	377	42.2	40.6	83.3	80.0
=65 Wrexham Glyndŵr		238*	84.8	83.8	77.9	80.0
67 Edge Hill	5.7	320	74.8	80.4	61.7	79.8
68 Southampton Solent		278	65.5	68.8	91.3	79.3
69 Bangor		348	85.2	79.1	44.7	79.0
70 Chichester		297	81.7	83.1	59.6	78.9

=71 Chester	0.3	289	75.2	76.7	68.4	78.3
=71 West London		257*	78.4	71.6	76.9	78.3
73 Northampton		280	73.3	74.7	72.5	77.9
74 Buckinghamshire New		254	76.9	80.1	70.4	77.4
75 Canterbury Christ Church	2.2	298	78.4	82.4	49.8	76.7
76 Newman	2.2	295	81.1	77.9	47.7	76.1
77 Worcester		197*	93.0	90.3	53.6	75.3
78 Cumbria		257	79.0	77.4	52.3	74.1
79 London Metropolitan	8.8	255	63.1	72.3	50.0	71.2
80 St Mark and St John		205	79.3	89.2	40.9	70.3

Employed in professional job:	58%	Employed in non-professional job and studying:	2%
Employed in professional job and studying:	3%	Employed in non-professional job:	19%
Studying:	8%	Unemployed:	10%
Average starting professional salary:	£24,792	Average starting non-professional salary:	£15,384

Sociology

Sociology is enjoying a spectacular renaissance after seeing demand drop when £9,000 fees were introduced. The numbers starting degrees in 2015 increased by 24 per cent – the largest rise in any major subject – as universities responded to two years of double-digit growth in applications. Another seven universities and colleges are offering the subject in 2017, bringing the total to 136. Labour market signals are not responsible in this case: sociology is in the bottom four for the proportion of graduates finding professional work or continuing their studies. More than half of those graduating in 2015 were in low-level jobs or unemployed at the end of the year. Those who did find professional work did rather better, but their average salary of £20,762 was still close to the bottom 20.

Cambridge remains at the top of the table, with the highest entry standards and the best graduate prospects, although even it did not see 80 per cent of sociologists go straight into professional jobs or begin postgraduate courses. The best performance in the Research Excellence Framework (REF) was at Kent, which shares seventh place overall, followed by Southampton and Lancaster. The REF sociology panel was no respecter of reputations, for Cambridge only just made the top 20 for research. The most satisfied students were at Gloucestershire, which produced the best scores in both the measures derived from the National Student Survey, while the London School of Economics has the lowest rate of student satisfaction in the table.

Courses starting in 2017 will include subjects such as urban studies, women's studies and some communication studies, as well as sociology itself, and a large number of institutions teach the subject as part of a combined studies or modular programme. Entry standards are moderate: more than 40 per cent of the 97 universities in the table average less than 300 points on the old UCAS tariff.

Employed in professional job:	29%	Employed in non-professional job and studying:	3%
Employed in professional job and studying:	2%	Employed in non-professional job:	37%
Studying:	16%	Unemployed:	13%
Average starting professional salary:	£20,762	Average starting non-professional salary:	£15,804

Sociology	Research quality %	Entry standards	Teaching quality %	Student experience %	Graduate prospects %	Overall score
1 Cambridge	39.2	550	83.0	81.6	79.2	100.0
2 Exeter	41.0	432	85.6	88.7	74.4	97.5
3 Bath	43.4	392	84.6	88.4	72.4	96.0
4 Bristol	46.7	400	87.0	84.9	67.4	95.9
5 Loughborough	40.6	366	86.4	90.5	69.7	95.1
6 Birmingham	31.1	368	86.9	83.6	78.4	94.5
=7 Edinburgh	48.8	482	75.8	77.7	61.8	94.0
=7 Kent	59.0	322	79.3	86.3	70.5	94.0
9 York	45.1	377	84.3	85.4	63.2	93.7
10 Leeds	47.6	404	82.7	84.3	58.4	93.6
11 Manchester	50.4	374	82.7	83.3	61.1	93.3
=12 Durham	28.7	452	77.0	82.3	72.4	93.1
=12 Glasgow	41.8	452	77.2	82.5	61.0	93.1
14 Keele	25.0	326	89.7	89.3	72.0	92.9
15 Warwick	31.7	408	85.1	86.2	60.2	92.8
16 Stirling	33.8	385	86.4	89.7	56.0	92.5
17 Sheffield	26.8	365	86.5	87.6	65.4	92.2
18 Nottingham	43.5	366	77.7	82.6	66.3	91.7
19 King's College London	42.2	447	75.6	79.6		91.5
20 Surrey	30.2	422	80.1	82.3	61.1	91.4
21 Southampton	52.8	387	76.9	80.8	55.4	91.3
22 Aberdeen	31.0	444	78.3	82.0	58.1	91.2
23 Bangor	39.6	335	86.5	84.6	56.8	91.1
24 Sussex	29.7	362	76.5	79.5	78.2	91.0
25 Essex	44.3	309	80.5	91.1	59.4	90.8
26 Newcastle	30.3	375	85.8	83.5	55.8	90.7
27 Queen's, Belfast	26.2	338	87.9	89.8	56.5	90.5
28 Aston	38.6	323	86.6	87.0	50.5	90.0
29 Portsmouth	32.2	294	85.9	87.0	54.3	88.7
30 London School of Economics	45.2	473	62.6	71.3	58.3	88.5
31 Leicester	18.4	349	82.7	83.6	60.1	88.3
32 Lancaster	51.4	362	77.9	77.4	43.8	88.2
33 Strathclyde	31.9		83.9	89.6	45.0	88.0
34 Cardiff	30.8	369	78.0	83.7	49.8	87.7
=35 Goldsmiths, London	33.4	334	83.0	80.8	48.4	87.6
=35 West of Scotland	9.4	325	90.1	87.2	53.2	87.6
37 Coventry	5.6	295	88.0	89.9	62.1	87.5
=38 East Anglia	45.8		83.3	86.3	38.8	87.4
=38 Liverpool	24.5	363	80.0	82.3	52.4	87.4
40 Lincoln		309	84.4	87.8	67.8	87.0
41 Plymouth	16.0	289	90.3	88.9	48.5	86.9
=42 Gloucestershire	14.5	284	93.5	95.3	38.1	86.5
=42 Huddersfield	9.5	275	81.5	90.8	65.9	86.5

44 Edinburgh Napier	5.3	365	84.0	88.5	49.5	86.4
=45 Bath Spa	13.9	290	92.4	90.8	41.8	86.3
=45 Salford	27.7	310	86.4	89.2	37.6	86.3
47 Brunel	26.0	310	85.0	85.2	44.0	86.2
48 Glasgow Caledonian	12.7	411	80.8	81.6	42.4	85.8
49 Royal Holloway		347	77.9	80.7	67.8	85.5
=50 Bradford	10.6	297	79.6	87.2	59.6	85.3
=50 Oxford Brookes	17.8	323	79.5	78.0	57.0	85.3
52 Nottingham Trent		272	89.8	89.2	54.8	85.2
53 Anglia Ruskin	26.4	247	89.3	85.6	39.9	84.9
54 Robert Gordon	4.9	304	70.1	81.8	64.4	84.8
55 Manchester Metropolitan	14.9	311	83.7	85.4	44.0	84.6
=56 Derby	13.5	263	89.7	84.5	44.8	84.4
=56 Northumbria	12.7	340	80.4	84.6	45.1	84.4
58 City	19.2	345	77.3	79.3	47.3	84.2
59 Abertay	5.0	323	80.5	77.0	59.2	84.1
60 Bournemouth	4.7	269	92.9	86.4	41.4	84.0
61 West of England	10.9	299	82.5	84.3	46.3	83.6
62 Hull	14.3	307	76.3	87.8	48.1	83.5
63 Winchester	4.4	285	80.9	79.8	58.2	83.3
=64 Brighton	12.4	275	83.4	84.5	45.4	83.2
=64 De Montfort	11.2	299	76.4	82.0	55.3	83.2
=66 Middlesex	14.9	276	77.8	81.0	53.9	83.0
=66 Queen Margaret, Edinburgh		327	82.6	87.3	43.2	83.0
=68 Edge Hill	5.7	275	84.8	85.3	46.6	82.9
=68 Highlands and Islands		248	83.4	72.3	69.2	82.9
70 Liverpool Hope	8.6	300	88.8	86.8	30.4	82.7
71 Liverpool John Moores	5.8	321	82.6	86.7	37.2	82.5
72 Teesside	15.0	261	81.6	82.9	41.7	81.8
73 Central Lancashire	11.8	268	78.4	83.9	46.3	81.7
=74 Sunderland	1.9	274	85.1	85.6	40.5	81.5
=74 Westminster		274	83.4	86.7	43.5	81.5
76 Staffordshire		229	90.1	86.3	40.4	81.2
=77 Bedfordshire	16.3	212	80.7	82.1	47.0	81.0
=77 Sheffield Hallam		286	83.4	84.0	40.3	81.0
79 Ulster		264	83.2	87.3	40.9	80.8
=80 Chester	6.4	294	83.1	76.6	37.8	80.5
=80 Worcester		264	80.5	80.0	49.3	80.5
82 Roehampton	24.9	248	72.9	73.9	48.4	80.4
=83 Canterbury Christ Church		247	84.6	85.9	38.0	80.0
=83 East London	13.7	246	78.8	81.4	39.9	80.0
=85 Birmingham City	3.8	280	79.1	77.7	43.7	79.9
=85 Newman	2.2	269	81.1	77.9		79.9
87 London South Bank	20.1	202	75.7	81.3	46.4	79.7
88 Northampton		243	84.1	87.0	35.3	79.5
89 London Metropolitan		294	77.3	78.5	41.8	79.2
90 Greenwich		305	79.4	78.3	35.0	78.9

Sociology cont	Research quality %	Entry standards	Teaching quality %	Student experience %	Graduate prospects %	Overall score
91 St Mary's, Twickenham		256	75.4	76.0	50.0	78.6
92 Suffolk		320	73.4	79.6	37.4	78.5
93 Kingston		275	75.2	76.6	40.2	77.6
=94 Buckinghamshire New		256	77.0	75.0	42.1	77.5
=94 Leeds Beckett	6.4	263	72.7	73.4	43.2	77.5
96 South Wales		306	69.9	73.8	34.7	75.9
97 Cumbria		254	80.9	85.3	16.7	75.8

Sports Science

Sports science has been one of the big growth areas of UK higher education over the past decade: more than 160 universities and colleges – four more than in the current academic year – plan to offer the subject in 2017. Although there was a substantial drop in applications with the introduction of higher fees, both applications and enrolments have recovered strongly. The numbers starting courses are now 50 per cent higher than in 2012, having topped 15,000 for the first time in 2015, leaving sports science among the ten most popular subjects at degree level. Sport and exercise science covers more than 40 specialisms, from sports therapy to equestrian sport studies and marine sport technology. Many courses contain more science and less physical activity than candidates may expect. Essex, for example, requires maths or one of the sciences at A level. Many universities now offer sports scholarships for elite performers, but most are not tied to a particular course and, officially at least, do not mean that the normal entry requirements are waived.

All the universities at the top of the table have excellent sports facilities and successful teams, but it is their performance in research and sports degree courses that counts here. Birmingham is back at the top of the table this year, with the top research score. Exeter, last year's leader, has dropped to second, while Loughborough, the most famous name in university sport, is now down to sixth in the table. Glasgow, in fourth place, has the highest entry standards, as the only university to average more than 500 points on the old UCAS tariff, while Swansea, in eighth position, has the best graduate prospects. The most satisfied students are to be found further down the table. Like last year, Kingston, which is only just in the top 60, has the top scores in the National Student Survey for teaching, feedback and academic support, while Liverpool Hope, just outside the top 30, does best on the broader student experience.

Sports science is almost in the bottom ten for starting salaries in professional jobs, but it remains in the top 50 subjects for graduate prospects. Only 8 per cent of 2015 graduates were unemployed at the end of the year, a rate bettered by just 11 subjects.

Employed in professional job:	38%	Employed in non-professional job and studying:	3%
Employed in professional job and studying:	4%	Employed in non-professional job:	29%
Studying:	18%	Unemployed:	8%
Average starting professional salary:	£19,899	Average starting non-professional salary:	£16,035

Sports Science

	Research quality %	Entry standards	Teaching quality %	Student experience %	Graduate prospects %	Overall score
1 Birmingham	63.7	402	87.0	86.8	84.9	100.0
2 Exeter	50.8	431	88.5	92.4	78.9	99.4
3 Bath	54.0	442	87.0	84.4	76.5	98.3
4 Glasgow	42.3	535	79.0	85.3	73.1	97.8
5 Durham	28.7	426	87.8	90.5	81.6	96.8
6 Loughborough	52.1	422	78.2	85.5	80.2	96.3
7 Leeds	50.5	392	83.5	92.6	69.3	95.0
8 Swansea	38.8	331	83.8	84.2	88.1	94.3
=9 Aberdeen	34.7	433	84.6	87.0	66.7	93.6
=9 Surrey	33.6	403	84.1	88.7		93.6
11 Edinburgh	26.1	438	71.7	77.8	87.5	93.0
12 Portsmouth	8.1	372	93.6	94.3	73.9	92.8
13 Huddersfield		336	91.7	94.2	82.1	91.9
14 Stirling	33.6	378	83.6	89.5	65.6	91.5
15 Robert Gordon	4.9	385	90.4	92.3	68.6	90.9
=16 Coventry	4.5	309	92.0	92.8	78.5	90.7
=16 Salford	3.8	386	89.2	91.9	69.7	90.7
18 Brunel	46.4	380	81.2	82.6	60.5	90.6
19 Lincoln	11.4	375	87.5	91.7	64.3	89.7
=20 Bangor	30.6	376	80.8	82.0	64.9*	89.4
=20 East Anglia	27.2	419	82.3	84.6	56.4	89.4
=22 Bolton		302	91.5	90.0	76.8	89.1
=22 Middlesex	10.0	332	82.3	83.9	80.0	89.1
=22 Nottingham	31.4	366	78.9	85.3		89.1
=25 Brighton	10.9	356	86.9	87.1	67.0	88.8
=25 Liverpool John Moores	45.3	371	76.6	80.7	60.2	88.8
27 Ulster	31.0	347	81.6	87.3	61.5	88.6
28 Chester	6.6	322	91.9	88.6	67.1	88.5
29 Kent	21.0	366	73.7	81.7	75.2	88.4
30 Hull	14.2	379	84.2	86.4	61.1	88.1
31 Liverpool Hope	10.9	312	92.2	96.2	58.4	87.9
32 Nottingham Trent	7.3	339	86.8	87.3	65.5	87.5
33 Chichester	15.2	317	86.2	90.0	62.3	87.3
34 Staffordshire	19.1	303	88.7	90.2	59.3	87.2
35 Cardiff Metropolitan	7.7	355	80.1	86.2	68.4	87.1
36 London South Bank	35.0	216	84.1	89.3	69.6	87.0
37 Bournemouth	9.0	321	81.7	87.4	68.6	86.7
38 Gloucestershire	6.0	368	84.0	86.2	59.8	86.5
=39 Hertfordshire	0.9	314	83.4	83.2	73.6	86.3
=39 Northumbria	4.4	384	80.9	84.2	61.8	86.3
=39 West of Scotland	9.1	347	84.2	88.0	59.3	86.3
42 Central Lancashire	5.1	336	87.9	86.7	59.7	86.2
43 Sheffield Hallam	8.5	331	86.8	89.7	57.6	86.1

Sports Science cont

	Research quality %	Entry standards	Teaching quality %	Student experience %	Graduate prospects %	Overall score
44 Anglia Ruskin		284	92.7	93.5	60.5	86.0
=45 Essex	25.8	346	76.5	86.3	57.1	85.9
=45 Worcester	4.9	333	79.0	84.2	70.3	85.9
47 St Mary's, Twickenham	4.8	310	79.7	84.8	71.4	85.6
=48 Aberystwyth	23.5	311	82.3	87.7	55.2	85.5
=48 Leeds Beckett	12.6	338	76.0	84.1	66.4	85.5
=48 Manchester Metropolitan	12.0	326	83.9	87.3	57.8	85.5
51 Bradford	9.5	365	76.7	82.6		85.3
52 Newman	2.8	315	83.4	87.6	63.7	85.2
53 Southampton Solent	0.6	317	86.9	88.0	59.5	85.0
=54 Bedfordshire	6.7	276	83.8	87.1	66.9	84.9
=54 Derby	1.7	314	88.9	87.6	57.3	84.9
=54 Oxford Brookes	3.0	328	81.6	88.3	61.5	84.9
=54 St Mark and St John		311	85.9	88.3	61.5	84.9
58 Kingston	2.6	280	95.2	89.4	54.2	84.8
=59 Edge Hill	7.7	360	83.7	83.5	51.6	84.4
=59 Winchester		280	85.9	85.8	66.0	84.4
61 Abertay	8.9	306	78.9	81.3	66.4	84.3
=62 Edinburgh Napier	5.3	346	80.0	85.6	57.0	84.2
=62 South Wales	10.8	311	84.7	85.9	54.9	84.2
64 Bishop Grosseteste		269*	82.9	80.2	73.3	84.1
=65 Canterbury Christ Church	19.0	293	82.5	84.8	55.2	84.0
=65 Roehampton	20.6	282	76.9	77.1	67.4	84.0
67 London Metropolitan		258	88.0	88.7	60.1	83.3
68 East London	7.6	294	78.9	82.9	59.7	82.6
69 Teesside	2.4	313	80.3	81.9	58.0	82.5
70 Leeds Trinity	0.8	313	79.8	81.6	58.7	82.3
71 Sunderland	2.4	300	81.3	86.0	53.3	81.9
72 Suffolk		278	87.9	90.1	46.5	81.4
73 Greenwich	7.4	343	67.3	78.8	58.3	80.9
74 Wrexham Glyndŵr	3.6	247	82.9	79.3	56.1	80.2
=75 Northampton		283	82.8	83.6	48.0	80.0
=75 York St John	5.5	302	69.1	71.4	64.6	80.0
77 Cumbria	3.2	263	73.8	75.3	58.7	78.7
78 Buckinghamshire New	0.9	251	70.3	76.1	54.5	76.6

Theology and Religious Studies

Cambridge has held onto first place in theology and religious studies, the first time in seven years that any university has done so. Cambridge, which has the highest entry standards and the best graduate prospects, had been exchanging the lead with Durham on an annual basis. There is still less than a single point between them, with Durham achieving the best results in the Research Excellence Framework, as it did in the previous assessments, in 2008. Competition is particularly keen in Scotland, which has five of the top 14 universities, led by St Andrews, in third place. St Andrews has the highest levels of satisfaction with teaching, feedback and academic support – an impressive rating of nearly 99 per cent – while Liverpool Hope, in equal 17th place, does best in the remaining sections of the National Student Survey (NSS). Theology and religious studies produce high levels of satisfaction in general, with only three universities dropping below 75 per cent satisfaction on either of our NSS measures.

By no means all graduates go into the church, but the vocation has helped to maintain relatively healthy employment records up to now. The two subjects have moved up three places to 33rd for graduate prospects and are still in the top 40 in the earnings table. More than a third of those completing courses take postgraduate degrees, either full- or part-time.

Over 1,000 students began degrees in theology or religious studies in 2015 – slightly fewer than in the previous year and still well short of the totals before higher fees were introduced. Applications have dropped by almost a quarter in that time and there are now little more than four to the place. Nevertheless, 58 universities and colleges – three more than in 2016 – plan to offer courses in the subjects in 2017.

Theology and Religious Studies	Research quality %	Entry standards	Teaching quality %	Student experience %	Graduate prospects %	Overall score
1 Cambridge	44.6	534	89.2	91.8	88.9	100.0
2 Durham	56.6	486	88.7	89.2	85.2	99.3
3 St Andrews	28.9	487	98.9	92.9	82.7	97.9
4 Lancaster	53.0	454	83.9	85.2	79.7	95.4
5 Exeter	38.9	454	89.1	89.3	80.3	95.3
6 Oxford	46.7	532	75.8	84.8	82.3	95.1
7 Nottingham	43.9	388	96.8	95.3	70.3	95.0
8 Birmingham	36.2	394	86.4	85.1	78.3	91.9
=9 Bristol	36.0	440	86.5	85.7	71.0	91.8
=9 Glasgow	21.4	464*	89.9	91.0	70.2	91.8
11 Leeds	44.4	398	84.3	82.5	72.3	91.2
12 Stirling	29.8	407	84.1	79.2	83.0	90.9
13 Aberdeen	39.9	418*	78.8	81.8	77.4	90.7
=14 Edinburgh	43.2	422	74.0	79.3	74.1	89.3
=14 King's College London	37.1	402	79.6	81.3	73.3	89.3
16 Kent	44.1	311	86.5	84.8	66.3	88.7
=17 Liverpool Hope	17.7	295	94.7	97.5	65.2	88.1
=17 Sheffield	25.3	379	85.4	85.8	68.1	88.1
19 SOAS London	34.1	380	79.6	84.5	67.8	87.8

Theology and Religious Studies cont	Research quality %	Entry standards	Teaching quality %	Student experience %	Graduate prospects %	Overall score
20 Manchester	37.2	367	82.9	83.5	60.0	87.1
21 Chester	11.1	290	89.6	86.6	73.2	85.9
=22 Oxford Brookes		311*	89.5	87.8	73.6	85.1
=22 Queen's, Belfast		355	88.8	90.7	66.0	85.1
=22 Winchester	18.0	289	88.4	87.7	64.3	85.1
=25 Heythrop College	14.0	269	86.5	83.8	74.4	84.9
=25 Roehampton	24.3	309	83.2	78.3	69.1	84.9
27 Cardiff	33.5	348	75.9	77.8	60.8	83.9
28 Newman	3.5	272	90.5	84.9	64.9	82.9
29 Chichester		259	90.2	89.1	64.5	82.5
30 Cumbria		256*	83.1	83.8	77.5	82.4
31 Leeds Trinity	9.9	247	91.6	81.1	60.0	82.0
32 Gloucestershire	6.9	343	83.9	84.3	52.0	81.3
33 Canterbury Christ Church	16.3	252	87.9	78.5	57.0	81.2
34 South Wales		288	89.9	90.4	50.7	80.9
35 York St John	4.8	290	84.3	82.1	50.9	79.2
36 Bath Spa	8.3	331	85.0	78.3	37.3	77.9
37 St Mary's, Twickenham	9.4	270	73.6	74.8	60.8	77.8
38 Hull	14.3		70.8	79.3	42.0*	73.0

Employed in professional job:	34%	Employed in non-professional job and studying:	4%
Employed in professional job and studying:	4%	Employed in non-professional job:	20%
Studying:	29%	Unemployed:	9%
Average starting professional salary:	£21,870	Average starting non-professional salary:	£15,168

Town and Country Planning and Landscape

Almost two-thirds of graduates in the planning and landscape groups go straight into professional jobs, placing the subjects in the top 15 in the employment table. But before a 17 per cent rise in enrolments in 2015, the numbers starting courses had fallen for six years in a row. The demand for places began to decline after the 2008 recession, but there were signs of a recovery before the introduction of £9,000 fees. Numbers have held up better in landscape and garden design than in the planning courses, but still only 235 students started landscape courses in 2015, compared with over 600 in planning.

Cambridge, which has much the highest entry standards and the best graduate prospects, continues to have a big lead at the top of the table. There are big changes elsewhere in the table, however, with Cardiff dropping from second to ninth and Loughborough from third to twelfth. University College London is up to second, but it is Queen's, Belfast's rare 100 per cent satisfaction rate for teaching quality that is the outstanding feature of the table. Fourth-placed Queen's also came close to 99 per cent satisfaction for the broader student experience.

About 40 universities and colleges are offering courses in landscape or garden design in 2017, some of them as an element of a broader degree in geography or architecture. Over 70 are expecting to run courses in various areas of planning, including disaster management and emergency planning, rural enterprise and land management, and coastal safety management. Starting salaries and employment prospects vary by course as well as by university. Five universities – Cambridge, Birmingham, Sheffield, Loughborough and Dundee – saw more than nine out of ten graduates go straight into professional jobs or continue studying in 2015, compared with less than half at bottom-placed Westminster.

Town and Country Planning and Landscape	Research quality %	Entry standards	Teaching quality %	Student experience %	Graduate prospects %	Overall score
1 Cambridge	49.0	600	78.8	83.7	95.9	100.0
2 University College London	54.1	499	81.0	90.0	85.0	96.2
3 Heriot-Watt	38.1	422	90.5	90.9	83.9	93.4
4 Queen's, Belfast	35.2	312	100.0	98.7	84.8	92.6
5 Birmingham	42.0	387	79.3	81.9	94.6	92.1
6 Sheffield	36.6	377	85.0	86.3	91.9	92.0
7 Newcastle	43.7	365	86.6	87.3	86.0	91.7
8 Gloucestershire	20.6	344	96.8	95.0	86.4	90.8
9 Cardiff	36.8	393	83.4	87.9	84.9	90.7
10 Reading	40.0	393*	80.7	87.3		90.2
11 Aberdeen	40.6		77.5	85.4	84.0	88.4
12 Loughborough	58.3	371	59.7	64.6	95.2	88.2
13 Edinburgh	35.1	447	75.5	66.2	83.3	87.8
14 Dundee	8.7		80.8	84.8	92.3	87.6
15 West of England	10.6	313	91.6	94.5	87.0	87.4
16 Manchester	36.5	352	77.1	81.5	84.2	87.3
17 Liverpool	26.3		81.6	88.1	80.0	86.6
18 Oxford Brookes	17.6	281	83.9	85.4	85.1	84.4
19 Birmingham City	2.7	264	94.0	91.7	84.0	84.2
20 Glasgow Caledonian	9.1	413	83.3	88.7	67.5	83.3
21 Northumbria	5.9		77.1	79.8	82.4*	81.8
22 Nottingham Trent	3.4	298*	87.9	88.8	75.0	81.7
=23 Manchester Metropolitan	9.7	334*	81.8	79.8	70.0	80.3
=23 Ulster	28.6	286	76.7	83.8	67.3	80.3
25 Leeds Beckett	5.6	247	85.4	87.3	74.3	79.6
26 Sheffield Hallam	13.4	268	74.2	73.7	80.0	78.9
27 Greenwich	2.0		81.5	73.7	63.2	74.8
28 Westminster	10.7	298	73.6	79.6	48.7	72.6

Employed in professional job:	61%	Employed in non-professional job and studying:	2%
Employed in professional job and studying:	4%	Employed in non-professional job:	13%
Studying:	11%	Unemployed:	9%
Average starting professional salary:	£22,775	Average starting non-professional salary:	£17,491

Veterinary Medicine

Only medicine itself has higher entry standards than veterinary medicine, where successful candidates had an average of more than 500 points in 2015 and, even after a 7 per cent drop in applications, there were more than seven of them to every place. An eighth veterinary school opened in 2013 at the University of Surrey, but it will be several years before there are enough data to include it in this table. Nottingham was the last newcomer, opening in 2006, and it had already enjoyed three years at the top of the table, before dropping to fourth last year and remaining there this year. Nottingham still has the most satisfied students, but Edinburgh, which achieved the best results in the Research Excellence Framework, as it did in the 2008 assessments, has taken over the leadership this year from Cambridge. Glasgow has moved up to second, with Cambridge dropping to third after a fall in student satisfaction.

Veterinary medicine is another of the rankings in which employment scores have been removed from the calculations that determine universities' positions. The scores are still shown in the table, but the review group of academic planners consulted on the *Guide* agreed that employment rates in the subject were so tightly bunched that small differences could distort the overall ranking. Veterinary medicine remains in the top four in the employment table, but is still only sixth for earnings in professional jobs.

The number of places in veterinary medicine is centrally controlled. Most courses demand high grades in chemistry and biology, with some accepting physics or maths as one alternative subject. Cambridge and the Royal Veterinary College also set applicants a specialist aptitude test that is used by a number of medical schools. Few candidates win places without evidence of practical commitment to the subject through work experience, either in veterinary practices or laboratories. The norm for veterinary science degrees is five years, but the Cambridge course takes six years and both Bristol and Nottingham offer a "pre-veterinary" year. Both Edinburgh and the Royal Veterinary College run four-year courses for graduates. There are no degrees in the subject in Wales or Northern Ireland, or in the post-1992 universities, although a number of them and several colleges offer veterinary nursing.

Veterinary Medicine	Research quality %	Entry standards	Teaching quality %	Student experience %	Graduate prospects %	Overall score
1 Edinburgh	46.8	555	78.6	83.7	96.9	100.0
2 Glasgow	42.3	546	82.0	86.2	95.3	98.8
3 Cambridge	43.1	573	72.3	75.3	100.0	95.6
4 Nottingham	36.4	469	88.0	91.8	97.8	94.4
5 Royal Veterinary College	40.8	498	80.0	85.6	97.5	94.3
6 Bristol	33.2	508	79.8	84.3	92.6	91.0
7 Liverpool	32.9	473	83.2	87.3	98.3	90.3

Employed in professional job:	91%	Employed in non-professional job and studying:	0%
Employed in professional job and studying:	1%	Employed in non-professional job:	2%
Studying:	3%	Unemployed:	2%
Average starting professional salary:	£26,872	Average starting non-professional salary:	..

13 Applying to Oxbridge

Oxbridge (as Oxford and Cambridge are called collectively) not only dominates UK higher education; the two universities are recognised as among the best in the world, regularly featuring among the top five in global rankings. But that is not why they merit a separate chapter in this *Guide*.

The two ancient universities have different admissions arrangements to the rest of the higher education system. Although part of the UCAS network, they have different deadlines from other universities, you can only apply to one or the other, and selection is in the hands of the colleges rather than the university centrally. Most candidates apply to a specific college, although you can make an open application if you are happy to go anywhere.

There have been reforms to the admissions system at both universities in recent years, in order to make the process more user-friendly to those who do not have school or family experience to draw upon. Most significantly, in 2017, Cambridge is reintroducing 'pre-interview written assessments' in most subjects, with tests on the day of interview in the rest. Both universities have also changed the way applicants are matched to colleges. Candidates are now distributed around colleges more efficiently, regardless of the choices they make initially.

There is little to choose between the two universities in terms of entrance requirements, and a formidable number of successful applicants have the maximum possible grades. However, that does not mean that the talented student should be shy about applying: both have fewer applicants per place than many less prestigious universities, and admissions tutors are always looking to extend the range of schools and colleges from which they recruit. For those with a realistic chance of success, there is little to lose except the possibility of one wasted space out of five on the UCAS application.

Overall, there are about five applicants to every place at Cambridge and six at Oxford, but there are big differences between subjects and colleges. As the tables in this chapter show, competition is particularly fierce in subjects such as medicine and law, but those qualified to read earth sciences or modern languages have a much better chance of success. The pattern is similar to that in other universities, although the high degree of selection (and self-selection) that precedes an Oxbridge application means that even in the less popular subjects the field of candidates is certain to be strong.

The two universities' power to intimidate prospective applicants is based partly on myth. Both have done their best to live down the *Brideshead Revisited* image, but many sixth-formers still fear that they would be out of their depth there, academically and socially. In fact, the state sector produces about 60 per cent of entrants to Oxford and Cambridge, and the dropout rate is lower than at almost any other university. The "champagne set" is still present and its activities are well publicised, but most students are hard-working high achievers with the same concerns as their counterparts on other campuses.

State school applicants

Both universities and their student organisations have put a great deal of effort into trying to encourage applications from state schools, and many colleges have launched their own campaigns. Such has been the determination to convince state school pupils that they will get a fair crack of the whip that a new concern has grown up of possible bias against independent school pupils. In reality, however, the dispersed nature of Oxbridge admissions rules out any conspiracy. Some colleges set relatively low standard offers to encourage applicants from the state sector, who may reveal their potential at interview. Some admissions tutors may give the edge to well-qualified candidates from comprehensive schools over those from highly academic independent schools because they consider theirs the greater achievement in the circumstances. Others stick with tried and trusted sources of good students. The independent sector still enjoys a degree of success out of proportion to its share of the school population.

Choosing the right college

Simply in terms of winning a place at Oxford or Cambridge, choosing the right college is not quite as important as it used to be. Both universities have got better at assessing candidates' strengths and finding a suitable college for those who either make an open application or are not taken by their first-choice college.

Cambridge: The Tompkins Table 2016

College	2016	2015	College	2016	2015
Trinity	1	1	Sidney Sussex	16	17
Pembroke	2	5	St Catharine's	17	13
Christ's	3	14	Clare	18	15
Emmanuel	4	4	Gonville and Caius	19	19
St John's	5	10	Wolfson	20	26
Queens'	6	7	Newnham	21	21
Jesus	7	11	Robinson	22	16
Peterhouse	8	6	Fitzwilliam	23	20
Magdalene	9	2	Homerton	24	27
Corpus Christi	10	22	Murray Edwards	25	23
Churchill	11	3	Lucy Cavendish	26	29
Downing	12	9	Girton	27	24
Trinity Hall	13	8	St Edmund's	28	28
King's	14	18	Hughes Hall	29	25
Selwyn	15	12			

At Oxford, subject tutors from around the university put candidates into bands at the start of the selection process, using the results of admissions tests as well as exam results and references. Applicants are spread around the colleges for interview and may not be seen by their preferred college if the tutors think their chances of a place are better elsewhere. Over a quarter of successful candidates are offered places by a college other than the one they applied to.

Cambridge relies on the "pool", which gives the most promising candidates a second chance if they were not offered a place at the college to which they applied. Those placed in the pool are invited back for a second round of interviews early in the new year. The system lowers the stakes for those who apply to the most selective colleges – typically around 20 per cent of offers come via the pool. Cambridge still interviews more than 80 per cent of applicants, whereas the system at Oxford has resulted in more immediate rejections in some subjects. Overall around 60 per cent of applicants are interviewed, but there is great variation by subject.

However, most Oxbridge applicants still apply direct to a particular college, not only to maximise their chances of getting in, but because that is where they will be living and socialising, as well as learning. Most colleges may look the same to the uninitiated, but there are important differences. Famously sporty colleges, for example, can be trying for those in search of peace and quiet.

Thorough research is needed to find the right place. Even within colleges, different admissions tutors may have different approaches, so personal contact is essential. The tables in this chapter give an idea of the relative academic strengths of the colleges, as well as the varying levels of competition for a place in different subjects. But only individual research will suggest where you will feel most at home. For example, women may favour one of the few remaining single-sex colleges (Murray Edwards, Newnham and Lucy Cavendish at Cambridge). Men have no such option.

Oxford: The Norrington Table 2016

College	2016	2015	College	2016	2015
Merton	1	27	Somerville	16	28
Oriel	2	12	Keble	17	9
Magdalen	3	1	New	18	2
University	4	20	Lincoln	19	5
Trinity	5	19	Hertford	20	14
Wadham	6	3	St Edmund Hall	21	29
Brasenose	7	24	St Hugh's	22	21
Balliol	8	4	Lady Margaret Hall	23	26
Worcester	9	11	Christ Church	24	15
St Catherine's	10	6	Exeter	25	22
Harris Manchester	11	16	St Anne's	26	8
St John's	12	7	St Hilda's	27	17
Pembroke	13	30	St Peter's	28	23
Jesus	14	13	Mansfield	29	18
Corpus Christi	15	10	Queen's	30	25

Oxford applications and acceptances by course

Arts	Applications		Acceptances		Acceptances to Applications %	
	2015	2014	2015	2014	2015	2014
Ancient and modern history	77	73	18	18	23.4	24.7
Archaeology and anthropology	93	72	27	24	29.0	33.3
Classical archaeology and ancient history	79	84	20	24	25.3	28.6
Classics	291	291	111	106	38.1	36.4
Classics and English	42	37	11	12	26.2	32.4
Classics and modern languages	24	30	6	9	40.0	30
Computer science and philosophy	45	50	5	8	11.1	16
Economics and management	1,127	1,149	87	86	7.7	7.5
English	1,044	1,100	227	231	21.7	21
English and modern Languages	128	115	24	18	18.8	15.7
European and Middle Eastern languages	41	37	17	3	41.5	8.1
Fine art	255	193	28	27	11.0	14
Geography	321	322	82	76	25.5	23.6
History	1,004	1,001	237	234	23.6	23.4
History and economics	114	84	13	16	11.4	19
History and English	72	85	9	9	12.5	10.6
History and modern languages	87	106	18	23	20.7	21.7
History and politics	317	288	41	33	12.9	11.5
History of art	137	122	14	13	10.2	10.7
Law	1,298	1,262	195	185	15.0	14.7
Law with law studies in Europe	279	287	31	34	11.1	11.8
Mathematics and philosophy	100	83	14	15	14.0	18.1
Modern languages	491	515	173	172	35.2	33.4
Modern languages and linguistics	70	61	23	27	32.9	44.3
Music	195	208	72	66	36.9	31.7
Oriental studies	163	148	40	45	24.5	30.4
Philosophy and modern languages	60	66	17	15	28.3	22.7
Philosophy and theology	103	121	23	25	22.3	20.7
Physics and philosophy	104	135	16	16	15.4	11.9
Philosophy, politics and economics (PPE)	1,691	1,651	239	240	14.1	14.5
Theology	117	120	35	40	30.0	33.3
Theology and oriental studies	3	4	2	1	66.6	25
Total Arts	**9,972**	**9,778**	**1,875**	**1,851**	**18.6**	**18.9**

The findings in the Tompkins Table (see page 270) are not officially endorsed by Cambridge University, while Oxford University now produces the Norrington Table (see page 271). Sanctioned or not, both tables give an indication of where the academic powerhouses lie – information which can be as useful to those trying to avoid them as to those seeking the ultimate challenge. Although there can be a great deal of movement

Oxford applications and acceptances by course cont

Sciences	Applications		Acceptances		Acceptances to Applications %	
	2015	2014	2015	2014	2015	2014
Biochemistry	511	424	98	102	19.2	24
Biological sciences	541	424	114	103	21.1	24.3
Biomedical sciences	266	229	31	36	11.7	15.7
Chemistry	750	684	189	187	25.2	27.3
Computer science	335	238	30	22	9.0	9.2
Earth sciences (Geology)	110	111	31	26	28.2	23.4
Engineering sciences	1,029	922	154	159	15.0	17.2
Engineering, economics and management	-	-	-	-	-	-
Experimental psychology	257	238	51	46	19.8	19.3
Human science	254	178	27	25	10.6	14
Materials science (including MEM)	145	118	32	33	22.1	28
Mathematics	1,145	1,015	176	178	15.4	17.5
Mathematics and computer science	199	153	29	28	10.1	18.3
Mathematics and statistics	229	143	16	13	7.0	9
Medicine	1,375	1,433	146	152	10.7	10.6
Physics	1,064	1,113	184	176	17.3	15.8
Psychology and philosophy (PPL)	195	161	33	24	16.9	14.9
Total Sciences	**8,405**	**7,584**	**1,341**	**1,310**	**16.0**	**17.3**
Total Arts and Sciences	**18,377**	**17,362**	**3,216**	**3,161**	**17.5**	**18.2**

Note: the dates refer to the year in which the acceptances were made.

year by year, both tables tend to be dominated by the rich, old foundations. Both tables are compiled from the degree results of final-year undergraduates. A first is worth five points; a 2:1, four; a 2:2, three; a third, one point. The total is divided by the number of candidates to produce each college's average.

In both universities, teaching for most students is based in the colleges. In practice, however, in the sciences this arrangement holds good only for the first year. One-to-one tutorials, which are Oxbridge's traditional strength for undergraduates, are by no means universal. Teaching groups remain much smaller than in most universities, and the tutor remains an inspiration for many students.

The applications procedure

Both universities have set a UCAS deadline of 15 October 2017 (at 6pm) for entry in 2018 or deferred entry in 2019. For Cambridge, you may then take admissions tests at the beginning of November at your school or college, or other authorised centre, while some subjects will continue to administer tests when you attend for interview. The Cambridge website lists the subjects setting the pre-interview assessments, which may include reading comprehension, problem-solving test, or thinking skills assessment, in addition to a paper on the subject itself. At Oxford, a number of subjects (but not all) also require applicants to take a written test,

Cambridge applications and acceptances by course

	Applications		Acceptances		Acceptances to Applications %	
Arts, Humanities and Social Sciences	**2015**	**2014**	**2015**	**2014**	**2015**	**2014**
Anglo-Saxon, Norse and Celtic	59	58	20	25	33.9	43.1
Architecture	384	403	49	43	12.8	10.7
Asian and Middle Eastern studies	121	114	43	49	35.5	43
Classics	136	155	74	74	54.4	47.7
Classics (4 years)	45	40	15	13	33.3	32.5
Economics	1,136	1,105	160	152	14.1	13.8
Education	80	113	31	35	38.8	31.0
English	714	767	197	193	27.6	25.2
Geography	345	314	108	101	31.3	32.2
History	625	607	197	198	31.5	32.6
History of art	101	87	23	26	22.8	29.9
Human, social and political sciences	1,012	898	208	186	20.6	20.7
Land economy	246	206	50	53	20.3	25.7
Law	1,015	1,047	208	204	20.5	19.5
Linguistics	88	100	27	30	30.7	30.0
Modern and medieval languages	387	383	173	169	44.7	44.1
Music	151	151	63	66	41.7	43.7
Philosophy	203	235	46	42	22.7	17.9
Theology and religious studies	87	89	41	43	47.1	48.3
Total Arts, Humanities and Social Sciences	**6,935**	**6,872**	**1,733**	**1,702**	**25.0**	**24.8**
Sciences	2,015	2014	2015	2014	2015	2014
Computer science	642	583	91	101	14	17.3
Engineering	2,089	2,161	312	326	14.9	15.1
Mathematics	1,308	1,336	247	236	18.9	17.7
Medical sciences	1,300	1,861	265	287	20.4	15.4
Natural sciences	3,036	3,170	652	660	21.5	20.8
Psychological and behavioural sciences	392	422	61	66	16	15.6
Veterinary medicine	251	347	64	70	26	20.2
Total Science and Technology	**9,018**	**9,880**	**1,692**	**1,746**	**18.1**	**17.7**
Total	**15,953**	**16,752**	**3,425**	**3,448**	**21.5**	**20.6**

Note: the dates refer to the year in which the acceptances were made.

Mathematics includes mathematics and mathematics with physics. Medical sciences includes medicine but does not include the graduate course in medicine.

The Tripos courses in chemical engineering, management studies and manufacturing engineering can be taken only after Part 1 in another subject.

Applications and acceptances for these courses are recorded under the first year subjects taken by the applicants involved.

either before or at the time of interview. In addition, once Cambridge receives your UCAS form, you will be asked to complete an online Supplementary Application Questionnaire (SAQ) by 22 October in most cases. For international applications to Cambridge you must also submit a Cambridge Online Preliminary Application (COPA), by 20 September or 15 October, depending on where interviews are held; check the Cambridge website for full details.

You may apply to either Oxford or Cambridge (but not both) in the same admissions year, unless you are seeking an Organ award at both universities. Interviews take place in December for those short-listed (for international applicants, Cambridge holds some interviews overseas while Oxford holds some interviews over the internet, though medicine interviewees must come to Oxford, as must EU interviewees). Applicants will receive either a conditional offer or a rejection early in the new year.

For more information about the application process and preparation for interviews, visit **www.undergraduate.study.cam.ac.uk** and **www.ox.ac.uk/admissions/undergraduate**.

Oxford College Profiles

Balliol

Oxford OX1 3BJ	01865 277777	www.balliol.ox.ac.uk
Undergraduates: 373	Postgraduates: 279	undergrad.admissions@balliol.ox.ac.uk

Famous as the alma mater of many prominent post-war politicians, Balliol has maintained a strong presence in university life and is usually well represented in the Union and most other societies. Academic standards are formidably high and it usually falls in the top ten of the Norrington Table. The college has an impressive medieval library, which allows students 24 hour access to over 70,000 books and periodicals. Balliol began admitting overseas students in the 19th century and recently students voted unanimously to establish a scholarship for a student with refugee status. The college has cultivated an attractively cosmopolitan atmosphere with a thriving music and drama scene. "Bruce's Brunch", organised by the Welfare Officer, bring a steady stream of interesting speakers to Balliol. Undergraduates are offered guaranteed accommodation in college for their first and final years. Graduate students are usually lodged in the Graduate Centre at Holywell Manor, ten minutes' walk from the main site. Hall food is good quality and the JCR has its own cafeteria.

Brasenose

Oxford OX1 4AJ	01865 277510 (admissions)	www.bnc.ox.ac.uk
Undergraduates: 367	Postgraduates: 203	admissions@bnc.ox.ac.uk

Nestled beside the stunning Radcliffe Camera, Brasenose has an advantageous city-centre position. The college was one of the first to admit women in the 1970s, and now has a near-even split. BNC, as the college is often known, has a strong rugby reputation, having won the rugby cuppers 14 times over the years. Named after the door knocker on the 13th-century Brasenose Hall, the college has a pleasant, intimate ambience conducive to study and made an impressive leap in the Norrington Table in 2016, from 24th to 7th place. Law, PPE, medicine and modern history are traditional strengths, and the main library is open 24 hours and there is also a separate law library. Owing to the college's central location, there is little need for a bike to get around, although Brasenose does offer a free bike rental scheme for those who may need to travel further away. The annexe at Frewin Court, five minutes from the main site, means nearly all undergraduates can live in, and postgraduates are offered accommodation at the St Cross Hollybush Row sites.

Christ Church

Oxford OX1 1DP   01865 276181 (admissions)   www.chch.ox.ac.uk

Undergraduates: 428   Postgraduates: 164   admissions@chch.ox.ac.uk

The college, founded by Cardinal Wolsey in 1525, boasts the largest quad in Oxford, complete with an ornamental pond full of Japanese koi carp, donated by the Empress of Japan. Around half of offers tend to be made to state school pupils, which leaves Christ Church with among the highest proportion of private school students. Christ Church has its own art gallery, hosting a collection of Old Master paintings and drawings. The magnificent 18th-century library is one of the best in Oxford and is supplemented by a separate law library. The river is close by for the aspiring oarsman and the college has two excellent squash courts inside St Aldates Quad. Students also enjoy free membership of the gym at Iffley Road. Accommodation, provided for all three years, is rated by college undergraduates as excellent and includes flats off Iffley Road as well as a number of beautifully panelled shared sets (double rooms) in college. A three-course dinner (served daily in the "Hogwarts" hall) costs less than £3, providing exceptional value. The chapel is also the cathedral of the Diocese of Oxford – England's smallest medieval cathedral. The constant stream of tourists is mildly disruptive to collegiate life, although college porters regularly check for student cards before allowing entry into the grounds.

Corpus Christi

Oxford OX1 4JF   01865 276693 (admissions)   www.ccc.ox.ac.uk

Undergraduates: 249   Postgraduates: 94   admissions.office@ccc.ox.ac.uk

Corpus, one of Oxford's smallest colleges, is naturally overshadowed by its Goliath-like neighbour, Christ Church, but makes the most of its intimate, friendly atmosphere and exquisite beauty. Although the college has only around 350 students including postgraduates, it has an admirable 24-hour library. Academic expectations are high and English, classics, PPE and medicine are especially well-established. Corpus can offer accommodation to all its undergraduates, one of its many attractions to those seeking a smaller community in Oxford. First years recently moved into the newly refurbished Jackson and Hugh Oldham Buildings, and rooms in the off-site Lampl building are modern and en suite. The college is also one of the most generous with bursaries, giving travel, book and vacation grants at an almost unparalleled level across the university. Scholars are particularly well rewarded. The MBI Al-Jaber Auditorium is a large, modern and pleasant space built into a bastion of the medieval city wall and is used for music and drama, as well as for parties, art exhibitions and film screenings. Corpus's drama club, the Owlets, is highly regarded in Oxford.

Exeter

Oxford OX1 3DP   01865 279648 (academic secretary)   www.exeter.ox.ac.uk

Undergraduates: 316   Postgraduates: 186   admissions@exeter.ox.ac.uk

Nestled between the High Street and Broad Street, Exeter is located in the heart of town. The college boasts one of the most spectacular views of the city from its Fellows' Garden, overlooking Radcliffe Square and All Souls' College. Most undergraduates are guaranteed three years of college accommodation, although many second-year students currently live out. Graduate students are housed off-site on the Exeter House campus. The Cohen Quad, located on Walton Street, opened in 2016 and provides a further 90 en-suite bedrooms. Exeter students are known to be lively and outspoken, having recently staged a successful campaign to abolish an £840 catering charge on food in hall. The college also boasts a number of societies. The John Ford Society exists to fund dramatic ventures; the Fortescue Society to talk about the law; the PPE Society to bring in high-profile speakers. The annual Turl Street Arts Festival, in partnership with neighbours Lincoln and Jesus, brings a week of live music, theatre and poetry in February.

Harris Manchester

Oxford OX1 3TD   01865 271009 (admissions tutor)   www.hmc.ox.ac.uk
Undergraduates: 82   Postgraduates: 134   enquiries@hmc.ox.ac.uk

As the university's only college for mature students (21 or older), Harris Manchester can appear out of step with the rest of the university. Students are proud, however, of its closely knit, college community. Founded in Manchester in 1786 to provide education for non-Anglican students, Harris Manchester finally settled in Oxford in 1889 after spells in both York and London. A full university college since 1996, its central location with fine buildings and grounds in Holywell Street is very convenient for the Bodleian, the university's main library, although the college also has an excellent library. All meals are provided – indeed the college encourages its members to dine regularly in hall. Its food is among the finest in Oxford and Harris Manchester is one of the only colleges to serve academics on the high table and students the same food. Most members live in, and the Siew-Sngiem Clock Tower provides five hotel-worthy rooms. The college has renovated the majority of its accommodation on the college site and a new student building will open in July 2017, providing a further eight en-suite student rooms, a lecture hall, new music practice rooms and a student gymnasium.

Hertford

Oxford OX1 3BW   01865 279404 (admissions)   www.hertford.ox.ac.uk
Undergraduates: 394   Postgraduates: 204   admissions@hertford.ox.ac.uk

Though tracing its roots to the 13th century, Hertford is determinedly modern. The college was one of the first colleges to admit women and is popular with state school applicants, thanks to its strong commitment to access. Hertford offers a £1,000 bursary to students from low income families and was the first college to become a living wage employer, further cementing its progressive reputation. The Principal, Will Hutton, a former editor-in-chief of *The Observer*, has helped foster a dynamic atmosphere. His popular panel discussions draw in large audiences and touch on a range of topical issues. Past events include a discussion on the Leveson inquiry with Hugh Grant. The college can lodge undergraduates for the entire course of their study. All first years live in the main college site. Second and third years live in Abingdon House and Warnock House annex near the Thames at Folly Bridge. Those who achieve a first in their preliminary examinations are given preference in the housing ballot. The quality of food in hall is average, while the food at Warnock House has a much better reputation.

Jesus

Oxford OX1 3DW   01865 279721 (admissions)   www.jesus.ox.ac.uk
Undergraduates: 330   Postgraduates: 185   admissions.officer@jesus.ox.ac.uk

Alma mater to T.E. Lawrence and Harold Wilson, Jesus consistently ranks highly for student satisfaction. Founded at the request of a Welsh churchman in 1571, the college continues to maintain strong links with the country. Welsh students form 15 per cent of the student body and chalk drawings of Welsh dragons sit proudly at the entrances to staircases in Second Quad, earning Jesus a reputation for being "the Welsh college". Sporting success has tailed off in recent years, but the college has squash courts and extensive playing fields with hockey, cricket, football and rugby pitches, hard grass tennis courts, netball courts and a sports pavilion. Students can use the university's gym free of charge. The college also has a symphony orchestra shared with St Peter's. Accommodation is almost universally excellent and relatively inexpensive. Self-catering flats in north and east Oxford have enabled every graduate to live in throughout his or her Oxford career. The Ship Street Centre contains 33 en-suite rooms for first-year students and a lecture theatre. The college offers a number of generous bursaries and grants, including one for books as well as a vacation grant, enabling students to study in Oxford outside of term time.

Keble

Oxford OX1 3PG   01865 272711 (admissions)   www.keble.ox.ac.uk
Undergraduates: 416   Postgraduates: 227   college.office@keble.ox.ac.uk

Keble is one of Oxford's most distinct colleges, built of brick in unmistakably extravagant Victorian Gothic style. With around 450 undergraduates, it is one of the biggest colleges in Oxford, and with guaranteed college accommodation for most undergraduates for three years, its vibrant community spirit provides Keble students with a coveted social life. Graduates are currently housed in the Acland site on Banbury Road, a two-minute walk from the main college. Thanks to a £25-million grant, the largest donation in Keble's history, the new H B Allen Centre will house 230 graduate students – more than double the current number – from October 2018. The site will also boast a 120-seat lecture theatre and an exhibition space. The college's sporting record remains exemplary, with rugby and rowing traditional strengths. The college also has thriving music and drama societies, which make use of the modern O'Reilly Theatre and hosts a successful Arts Week every Hilary term. The college hall, where students wishing to dine must wear gowns six nights a week, is one of the most impressive in the university. The annual Keble Ball is one of the best value black tie events in Oxford.

Lady Margaret Hall

Oxford OX2 6QA   01865 274310 (admissions)   www.lmh.ox.ac.uk
Undergraduates: 395   Postgraduates: 213   admissions@lmh.ox.ac.uk

Lady Margaret Hall, Oxford's first college for women, has been co-educational since 1978 and now enjoys an equal gender balance. For many students, LMH's comparative isolation – the college is three-quarters of a mile north of the city centre – is a real advantage, providing welcome refuge from tourists. For others it means a long journey to central facilities. The college's beautiful gardens back onto the Cherwell River, allowing LMH to have its own punt house and tennis courts. The college has a 24-hour library, with particularly strong collections in the arts and humanities and individual study booths prized among finalists seeking solitary working conditions. Accommodation is guaranteed for first-, second- and third-year students since the opening of the Pipe Partridge Building, which also houses a new JCR, dining hall and lecture theatre. The new Clore Graduate centre and Donald Fothergill building will provide just over 40 en-suite study bedrooms for graduate students. Sporting successes include victory in athletics cuppers and blades on the river for the women's firsts.

Lincoln

Oxford OX1 3DR   01865 279836 (admissions)   www.lincoln.ox.ac.uk
Undergraduates: 297   Postgraduates: 316   admissions@lincoln.ox.ac.uk

Lincoln's 15th-century buildings and beautiful library – a converted Queen Anne church – combine to produce a delightful environment in which to spend three years. The college's relaxed atmosphere is justly celebrated and city-centre accommodation is provided by the college for all undergraduates throughout their careers. Graduate students are housed a few minutes' walk away in Bear Lane, at the EPA Science Centre close to the university science area and at a new site on Little Clarendon Street. Lincoln has one of the largest number of scholarships available for graduate students and rewards undergraduates who perform well in examinations. However, the college plummeted 15 places in the Norrington Table in 2016 to 19th place. The recently refurbished Garden Building is a stylish addition to the college, providing much needed space for music practice, dining and teaching. The Oakeshott room is a popular venue and has hosted many shows in the Turl Street Arts Festival. The college JCR is highly proactive. Among several recent initiatives, is the JCR Art Scheme, in which the JCR purchases artworks for their collection, loaning the pieces to students to hang in their rooms.

Magdalen

Oxford OX1 4AU   01865 276063 (admissions)   www.magd.ox.ac.uk
Undergraduates: 393   Postgraduates: 176   admissions@magd.ox.ac.uk

Perhaps the most beautiful Oxbridge college, Magdalen is known around the world for its tower, its deer park and its May morning celebrations. In recent years, the college has worked hard to shake off its public school image, with a large intake from overseas and one of the highest proportion of state school pupils. Undergraduates are studious and ferociously competitive. The college consistently performs strongly in the Norrington Table, though it slipped from the top spot to third place in 2016, and has won University Challenge a record four times over the years. The Longwall library opened in 2016 after a £10.5 million refurbishment, providing three times the number of reader spaces. First-year students are accommodated in the Waynflete Building and all undergraduates can be housed in college for the full length of their course. Rents are not cheap compared to other colleges but the college has agreed to freeze rents for next year. Over 25 per cent of students receive some type of financial support during their studies, ranging from travel grants to funding for creative projects. The college has had a lot sporting of success on the river in recent years and offers students free punting during in the summer.

Mansfield

Oxford OX1 3TF   01865 270920 (admissions)   www.mansfield.ox.ac.uk
Undergraduates: 220   Postgraduates: 130   admissions@mansfield.ox.ac.uk

Formally becoming an Oxford College in 1995, Mansfield's attractive site is fairly central, close to the English faculty and social science library. Its proximity to University Parks facilitates collegiate sporting enthusiasm, most notably for croquet and quidditch. Taking just over 70 undergraduate students per year, the community is close-knit and the atmosphere relaxed. Mansfield has a strong representation of state school students and over 10 per cent of its students are BME. First- and third-year students live in college accommodation; either on site or in an annex in east Oxford, while second years generally find their own accommodation. First-year postgraduates are also housed by the College in off-site accommodation. The College boasts four libraries, which are open 24 hours and the JCR and Crypt Café, are popular for socialising and casual study. From October 2017, the new Love Lane building will provide additional accommodation as well as a home for Oxford's Institute of Human Rights.

Merton

Oxford OX1 4JD	01865 276299 (admissions)	www.merton.ox.ac.uk
Undergraduates: 291	Postgraduates: 253	admissions@admin.merton.ox.ac.uk

Founded in 1264 by Walter de Merton, Bishop of Rochester and Chancellor of England, Merton is one of Oxford's oldest and most prestigious colleges. It has an enduring reputation for academic excellence reflected in its position usually at or near the top of the Norrington Table. After a surprise fall to 27th place in 2015, it regained its place at the top of 2016's table. Accommodation is some of the cheapest in the university, of good standard and offered for all three years. Merton's food is well-priced and among the best in the university; formal hall is served six times a week. The college provides generous support to students, having awarded over £120,000 to students last academic year. Merton's many diversions include the Merton Floats, its dramatic society, the Bodley Club for literary speakers, and an excellent Christmas Ball every three years. Following the establishment of its choral foundation, both its choir and the organ have an ever-growing reputation. The college recently established a scheme inviting local school girls to form a choir at the college, enabling them to participate in Merton's musical tradition.

New College

Oxford OX1 3BN	01865 279512 (admissions)	www.new.ox.ac.uk
Undergraduates: 429	Postgraduates: 256	admissions@new.ox.ac.uk

New College is actually rather old (founded in 1379 by William of Wykeham), large and much more relaxed than most expect behind its daunting facade. It is a bustling place, as proud of its excellent music and its bar as of its academic prestige. Musical students flourish here thanks to the choir, orchestra and chamber groups. There is a band room and a new music building on Mansfield Road is currently under construction. Traditionally poor at attracting state school students, the college has been making particular efforts to change this. It recently established a new bursary for students from the lowest income backgrounds, amounting to £4,500 a year. All first-, second- and fourth-year students can live in college and almost all of the third years can, at a squeeze. The college is currently putting forward proposals for much needed off-site accommodation built around a new quad. New College gardens are a memorable sight, especially the other-worldly mound in the heart of the college. The grounds provide the perfect setting for the Commemoration Ball, held every three years – a highlight of Oxford's social calendar. The college also host an annual boat party in London, which is popular with students from across the university. Students also benefit from summer access to the college chalet (shared with Balliol and University) near Mont Blanc.

Oriel

Oxford OX1 4EW	01865 276522 (admissions)	www.oriel.ox.ac.uk
Undergraduates: 325	Postgraduates: 172	admissions@oriel.ox.ac.uk

Oriel is a friendly, centrally located college. Unlike its neighbour Christ Church, which is inundated with tourists, the college successfully keeps a low profile. Behind this, however, are some impressive achievements. The college is traditionally described as having "a strong crew spirit", reflecting its traditions on the river; the Oriel men's crew retained their position as Head of the River in 2016, for the third year in a row. Academically, the college celebrated its best ever performance in 2016, coming second in the Norrington Table, with just under half of its finalists achieving Firsts. Oriel's sports facilities include a boathouse, impressive sports ground, squash courts and multiple gyms. Meal and rent costs are some of the lowest in Oxford. Accommodation is variable, but is available for the duration of an undergraduate course and extensive (mainly graduate) accommodation is provided one mile away off the popular Cowley Road. Several flats have recently been completed at a former industrial site on Rectory Road, providing some limited facilities for couples. The annual Summer Garden Party is a highlight of Trinity term.

Pembroke

Oxford OX1 1DW   01865 276412 (admissions)   www.pmb.ox.ac.uk

Undergraduates: 365   Postgraduates: 227   admissions@pmb.ox.ac.uk

Tucked away off St Aldate's, Pembroke is a welcoming and inclusive community with an improving state school intake. The college is historically impoverished but the JCR is among the wealthiest, thanks to the savvy purchase of a Francis Bacon painting for £150 in 1953, which it sold in 1997 for £400,000. The college is among the weakest academically, languishing at the bottom of the Norrington Table for two years in a row, before rising to 13th place in 2016. History is a traditionally strong subject, with several students winning university-wide prizes over the years. Pembroke is able to accommodate all undergraduates after a new quad was opened in April 2013, and the Sir Geoffrey Arthur Building on the river, ten minutes' walk away, offers excellent facilities; in addition to 100 student rooms there is a concert room, computer room and a multi-gym. The JCR successfully secured a rent decrease last year, but college food is among the most expensive in Oxford and students must pre-pay for a minimum of six dinners a week. Rowing is strong, with Pembroke men and women traditionally performing well on the river and several going on to represent the university crews.

Queen's

Oxford OX1 4AW   01865 279161   www.queens.ox.ac.uk

Undergraduates: 342   Postgraduates: 138   admissions@queens.ox.ac.uk

With its beautiful neo-Classical dome and bell-tower, Queen's is one of the most striking sights of the High Street. Despite this, it is one of Oxford's least dynamic colleges. Its academic record is average and the college sank five places to last place in 2016. All students are offered accommodation. Unlike most other colleges, Queen's houses first years away from the main site, in modernist annexes in east Oxford. The college has converted a large number of these rooms into en-suite facilities. Finalists are housed in the main college site, closer to the college and university libraries. Postgraduates are accommodated in St Aldate's House, a modern building close to the town centre. Queen's can be insular, but has a strong college enthusiasm for sport. The two refurbished squash courts are said to be the best in Oxford and the college is one of the few to have its own gym. Queen's also provides a generous grant for those participating in university level sport, alongside its book and travel grants. The beer cellar is one of the most popular in the university and the JCR facilities are also better than average.

St Anne's

Oxford OX2 6HS   01865 274840 (admissions)   www.st-annes.ox.ac.uk

Undergraduates: 423   Postgraduates: 322   enquiries@st-annes.ox.ac.uk

Architecturally uninspiring, St Anne's makes up in community spirit what it lacks in awesome grandeur. The dining hall, with its sky-light and absence of portraits, is underwhelming but the food is some of the best in Oxford. The new library and academic centre, on Woodstock Road, is an impressive sight and with 2,000 books added to its shelves every year, library facilities are among the best across the colleges. The college coffee shop, STACS, is quaint and a hit with students wanting to take a break from their studies. The college has recently had a strong presence in the university journalism scene, and its rugby team tends to do well in the inter-college league. Accommodation is guaranteed to undergraduates for three years, and the college also operates an equalisation scheme, giving grants to students wishing to live out. Graduates are housed in an 82-room hall of residence in Summertown, a five-minute cycle ride away. St Anne's students benefit from exclusive access to a number of internships organised by the college.

St Catherine's

Oxford OX1 3UJ   01865 271703 (admissions)   www.stcatz.ox.ac.uk

Undergraduates: 476   Postgraduates: 387   admissions@stcatz.ox.ac.uk

St Catherine's strikes an immediate chord with those seeking to avoid the grandiosity of some other colleges. Arne Jacobsen's modernist design for "Catz", one of Oxford's youngest and largest undergraduate colleges, has attracted much attention as the most striking contrast to the lofty spires of Magdalen and New College. The student body describes itself as "Oxford without the stereotypes". Close to the law, English and social science faculties, the university science area and the pleasantly rural Holywell Great Meadow, St Catherine's is a lot closer to the city centre than it feels. The Wolfson library is open until midnight. Rooms are small but tend to be warmer than in other, more venerable, colleges, and are now available on site for first-, second- and third-year students. There is an excellent theatre, as well as an on-site punt house, gym and squash courts. Like many of the larger colleges, sporting success is high – the women's football team topped the league this year. Six portraits of female college members have been commissioned and are due to be hung in the Library's (currently all male) collection. The college hosts the Cameron Mackintosh Chair of Contemporary Theatre, whose incumbents have included Meera Syal, Kevin Spacey, Arthur Miller and Sir Ian McKellen.

St Edmund Hall

Oxford OX1 4AR   01865 279011 (admissions)   www.seh.ox.ac.uk

Undergraduates: 404   Postgraduates: 291   admissions@seh.ox.ac.uk

St Edmund Hall – "Teddy Hall" – has one of Oxford's smallest college sites but one of its most populous. The college offers students the chance to live in its medieval quads right in the heart of the city. Despite a near equal male/female ratio, the college still has an enduring image as a home for "hearties". The sporting culture is vigorous, with both the men and women's teams securing victory in this year's rugby cuppers. Teddy Hall has a generous sporting fund for students who play sport at university level as well as four annual prizes for journalism. The college has created posts for a disabilities officer and black and minority ethnic officer. Academically, Teddy Hall tends to yo-yo between the middle and the bottom of the Norrington Table. College accommodation is reasonable and can be offered for three years, either on the main site or in three annexes. To add to this, the college recently bought a house adjacent to the existing Norham Gardens site.

St Hilda's

Oxford OX4 1DY   01865 286620 (admissions)   www.st-hildas.ox.ac.uk
Undergraduates: 411   Postgraduates: 163   college.office@st-hildas.ox.ac.uk

October 2008 marked a milestone for St Hilda's and the university as a whole, as the college welcomed its first mixed-sex intake. Although the college, founded in 1893, lasted more than 100 years as an all-female institution, the governing body voted in 2006 to admit men. There are now equal numbers of males and females. The college prides itself on its commitment to fostering an inclusive and laid-back atmosphere, introducing the post of "Class Liberation Officer" to support working-class students. The college has long languished at the lower end of the Norrington Table, lying at 27th in 2016. Like the other originally female colleges, St Hilda's boasts an impressive library, which is particularly well stocked for English. The college has beautiful riverside gardens, allowing students to go punting from the college site, and is close to the lively social scene in multi-ethnic east Oxford. Accommodation is guaranteed to first years and finalists, and the common room and student-run bar have been renovated and enlarged. Many of the rooms offer some of the best river views in Oxford, with the city's spires as a backdrop. St Hilda's commitment to music is particularly strong.

St Hugh's

Oxford OX2 6LE   01865 274910 (admissions)   www.st-hughs.ox.ac.uk
Undergraduates: 432   Postgraduates: 333   admissions@st-hughs.ox.ac.uk

St Hugh's is well liked for its pleasantly bohemian atmosphere and splendid grounds. It was criticised by students in 1986 when it began admitting men. There is now an equal male/female ratio and it has a large student body. The alma mater of Theresa May, St Hugh's is a bicycle ride from the city centre. It is an ideal college for those seeking a place to live and study away from the madding crowd, and its gardens provide the perfect backdrop for the college's springtime outdoor cinema, launched in 2016. Despite having one of the biggest and best college libraries, academic pressure remains comparatively low. St Hugh's guarantees on-site accommodation to undergraduates for the duration of their degree, although the standard of rooms is variable. The quality of food is high and meals are subsidised. The college also boasts a café, and kitchen facilities are among the best in Oxford. The Dickson Poon Building provides an additional place to work and socialise. Sport, particularly football, is taken quite seriously. As the college enjoys extensive grounds compared to most colleges, there is space for a croquet lawn and tennis courts.

St John's

Oxford OX1 3JP   01865 277317 (admissions)   www.sjc.ox.ac.uk
Undergraduates: 385   Postgraduates: 221   admissions@sjc.ox.ac.uk

St John's is one of Oxford's powerhouses, excelling in almost every field and boasting arguably the most beautiful gardens in the university. Founded in 1555 by a London merchant, it is Oxford's wealthiest college, and makes the most of its resources by providing guaranteed college accommodation at a subsidised rate for all its undergraduates in addition to generous annual book grants and prizes. Academic standards are high, with English, chemistry and history among the traditional strengths. All students benefit from the impressive library and work has begun on a new study centre and library extension, allowing for double the number of reader seats. Although St John's fell to 12th place in the Norrington Table in 2016, the college is usually challenging for the top spot and reached the final of University Challenge in 2016. St John's has a strong sporting tradition with a particular strength in women's rowing. As befits such an all-round strong college, entry is fiercely competitive.

St Peter's

Oxford OX1 2DL   01865 278863 (admissions)   www.spc.ox.ac.uk
Undergraduates: 340   Postgraduates: 188   admissions@spc.ox.ac.uk

Opened as St Peter's Hall in 1929, St Peter's has been an Oxford college since 1961. Its medieval, Georgian and 19th-century buildings are in the city centre and close to most of Oxford's main facilities. Though still young, St Peter's is well-represented in university life and has pockets of academic excellence, despite being towards the bottom of the Norrington Table. History tutoring is particularly good and the college Master, Mark Damazer, former Controller of Radio 4, regularly invites high-profile speakers to the college, including Mark Carney and the Archbishop of Canterbury. Accommodation is offered to students in their first and third years, varying from traditional rooms in college to new purpose-built rooms a few minutes' walk away. The college's facilities are impressive, including a recently upgraded JCR and a popular student bar, one of the few that are entirely student run. Linton Quad and the chapel have also undergone recent refurbishment. The college has a proud sporting heritage, being particularly strong at rugby and rowing. Thanks to a partnership with Laura Ashley, a generous bursary scheme will be available for the next five years.

Somerville

Oxford OX2 6HD   01865 270619 (admissions)   www.some.ox.ac.uk
Undergraduates: 385   Postgraduates: 171   secretariat@some.ox.ac.uk

Named after the astronomer Mary Somerville (1780–1872), one of the most celebrated scientific writers of her day, Somerville was one of the first two colleges at Oxford founded to admit women. Members of the college celebrated the news that the pioneering academic would become the first woman, other than a royal, to grace a British bank note. Since 1994, Somerville has admitted men and women equally, while retaining its pioneering and inclusive ethos. Alma mater to Margaret Thatcher, Indira Gandhi and Nobel prizewinner Dorothy Hodgkin, Somerville is one of the most international and diverse colleges. The highly popular principal, Dr Alice Prochaska, who was well liked for her proactive but informal approach, will step down at the end of the 2016/17 academic year. During her time, college accommodation has expanded and rooms in college are now provided for three years to most undergraduates and all first-year postgraduates. There are kitchens in all buildings and subsidised food in hall. The library, one of the most beautiful and largest college libraries, is 24-hour. Students dominate university journalism and Somerville recently had their first President of the Oxford Union.

Trinity

Oxford OX1 3BH   01865 279860 (admissions)   www.trinity.ox.ac.uk
Undergraduates: 286   Postgraduates: 136   admissions@trinity.ox.ac.uk

Architecturally impressive and boasting beautiful lawns (which you can actually walk on), Trinity is one of Oxford's least populous colleges. The college admits some 80 undergraduates each year and is among the strongest academically. It is ideally located, beside the Bodleian,

Blackwell's bookshop and the White Horse pub, a short stroll from the University Parks and the town centre. Whilst members are active in all walks of university life, the college has its own debating and drama societies. The Trinity Players stage at least two productions a year, including one on the college lawns. Facilities are impressive, with a well-equipped college gym and squash courts. The 17th-century chapel opened this spring after a year-long restoration project. Usually, all undergraduates are given a room on the main site in their first and second years, with the majority of third and fourth years living in a purpose-built block a mile and a half north of the main site. Trinity students rate the food highly for both its quality and price. Trinity's Commemoration Ball, held once every three years, has one of the biggest budgets in Oxford and is a popular event.

University

Oxford OX1 4BH   01865 276959 (admissions)   www.univ.ox.ac.uk

Undergraduates: 363   Postgraduates: 199   admissions@univ.ox.ac.uk

"Univ", as it is popularly known, is the first Oxford college to be able to boast a former student in the Oval Office. The former President Clinton was a Rhodes Scholar at University in the late 1960s. The college is probably Oxford's oldest – a claim fought over with Merton – and has made a significant effort to shake off its public school image. After a report revealed it to be one of the worst performing colleges for state-school intake, University took the unprecedented step of reserving up to ten places each year for students from disadvantaged backgrounds. It adds to a generous bursary scheme, and an access programme that is among the best in Oxford. Academic expectations are high and the college prospers in most subjects. Thanks to a newly refurbished accommodation block, first- and third-year undergraduates are guaranteed a college room. University is particularly well represented on the river, with both men and women's crews doing well in recent years. The college also has access to a chalet in the foothills of Mont Blanc, with student parties welcome in the summer.

Wadham

Oxford OX1 3PN   01865 277545 (admissions)   www.wadham.ox.ac.uk

Undergraduates: 451   Postgraduates: 166   admissions@wadh.ox.ac.uk

Wadham is known in about equal measure for its progressive and liberal atmosphere and its leftist politics. The JCR – or student union (SU) as it has rebranded itself – is famously dynamic and politically active, although the breadth of political opinion is greater than its left-wing stereotype suggests. The college is very strong on admitting students from state schools, owing to its successful Student Ambassador Scheme. Its gardens are beautiful and host Shakespearian performances each summer. The college has a good 24-hour library. Wadham is the only college with no formal hall and accommodation is guaranteed in first year and at least one further year. Fourth years and graduates are offered accommodation in Merifield, the college's modern development of shared flats in Summertown. Wadham is planning to develop a new site on Iffley Road, which will enable the College to house all of its students for the duration of their studies. Highlights in the social calendar are Queer Festival, a riotous celebration of LGBTQ culture, and Wadstock, the college's open-air spring music festival. The women's rowing team have been Head of the River for three years and the men's 1st VIII are in the top division. The College also contributes to the local community through a new scheme which delivers food that does not get eaten in hall to a local homeless centre.

Worcester

Oxford OX1 2HB   ·   01865 278391 (admissions)   www.worc.ox.ac.uk
Undergraduates: 428   Postgraduates: 146   admissions@worc.ox.ac.uk

Worcester is to the west of Oxford what Magdalen is to the east: a spacious contrast to the urban rush of the city centre. The college's rather mediocre exterior conceals a delightful environment, including some striking Baroque architecture, extensive gardens and a lake. The college gardeners even post horticultural updates to their own blog and the Buskins dramatic society makes use of the beautiful grounds, with annual summer Shakespeare performances in the gardens. Arts Week is an annual highlight and includes a mix of plays, concerts and recitals. Accommodation, guaranteed for three years, is either within the college grounds or less than 300 metres from it. The college boasts good quality food, with a Michelin-star chef every Wednesday. College chefs have even created an Instagram account to exhibit their fine dishes. Periodic "sustainable halls" feature local produce and the Edible Garden project encourages students to grow their own food in Oxford's only student-run vegetable patch. Like Magdalen and New, it is home to the Commemoration Ball once every three years, a highlight of the Oxford social calendar.

Cambridge College Profiles

Christ's

Cambridge CB2 3BU   01223 334983 (admissions)   www.christs.cam.ac.uk

Undergraduates: 425   Postgraduates: 187   admissions@christs.cam.ac.uk

Enter a gate on St Andrew's Street and you will find yourself in the tranquillity of Christ's College in whose quads have passed many illustrious alumni, including Charles Darwin and John Milton. In front of the college is the bustle of Cambridge's main shopping centre while behind lies Christ's Pieces whose tennis courts and lawns are popular with students in the summer. Students can have rooms close to or in the college itself for all three years of their undergraduate degrees and 40 per cent of rooms are en suite. Thanks to its proximity to the geography and natural sciences faculties, it is strong in these subjects, but also has strengths in the arts helped by its enviable Visual Arts Centre, theatre and annually appointed artist-in-residence. Societies abound from amateur dramatics to one of the universities best attended student film groups. On the sports front, Christ's is particularly strong on the football pitch and also is one of only five Oxbridge colleges to have its own swimming pool. The college has a 60:40 male to female split and came third in the 2016 Tompkins Table with over 30 per cent of degrees achieving a first.

Churchill

Cambridge CB3 0DS   01223 336202 (admissions)   www.chu.cam.ac.uk

Undergraduates: 487   Postgraduates: 246   admissions@chu.cam.ac.uk

It may be a little way out of the centre, but Churchill enjoys all the benefits of the 42 acres of parkland that its location allows. Though the brutalist architecture may not be to everyone's taste, it houses some of the best on-site facilities of any college: a gym, theatre-cum-cinema, music room and recording studio, squash and tennis courts, grass pitches and the largest dining hall in Cambridge allow students a varied experience. A new boathouse was opened in 2016 and a new court housing 68 rooms has just been completed. The college is handily located for the science faculties on the West Cambridge site and it is only a short walk to the University Library and the humanities faculties on the Sidgwick Site. Churchill is one of the least traditional of the colleges: students are allowed to walk on the grass and don't wear academic gowns when dining formally in hall. It is also one of the few not to charge a fixed bill for catering – a move popular with Churchillians. It has a diverse student body, with relatively large numbers of graduates and overseas students and has one of the highest intakes of state school students in Cambridge (typically around 70 per cent). The college performs well academically (11th in the 2016 Tompkins Table), a success sometimes attributed to what students have called its "dangerously comfortable" library.

Clare

Cambridge CB2 1TL   01223 333246 (admissions)   www.clare.cam.ac.uk

Undergraduates: 481   Postgraduates: 215   admissions@clare.cam.ac.uk

Clare, with its central location on the Backs and elegant courts and gardens, is popular with applicants. Amongst the oldest colleges in Cambridge, it has a strong reputation for music and a world-renowned choir. The student bar is in Clare Cellars, which often plays host to DJ and live music nights that draw students from across the university. For accommodation, Old Court offers a traditional experience, while Memorial Court, across the river, is close to the University Library as well as the humanities and science departments. "The Colony", closer to the boathouse, provides diverse accommodation including flats and converted houses. The college has an enthusiastic boat club with the highest participation rate in Cambridge, and very good sports facilities just beyond the university's botanic garden (a ten-minute cycle ride away). In addition to the college choir, it has a thriving musical society as well as regular recitals. Clare is evenly balanced in terms of arts and sciences, and also has a good gender split – almost 50:50 among undergraduates.

Corpus Christi

Cambridge CB2 1RH   01223 338056 (admissions)   www.corpus.cam.ac.uk
Undergraduates: 288   Postgraduates: 190   admissions@corpus.cam.ac.uk

For those who prefer a more familial atmosphere, Corpus is one of Cambridge's smallest colleges with an undergraduate population that hovers at just below 300. Steeped in history, it is the only Oxbridge college to have been founded by the townspeople (in 1352) and is home to the oldest court in either of the universities, and which has been in continuous use since the 14th century. That said, there is plenty that is up-to-date. Accommodation is both in ancient college rooms (walking to the bathroom may involve a quick trip outside) and modern buildings at the college's Leckhampton site just over a mile away where a gym, playing fields and an open-air swimming pool can also be found. Students can be housed for all three years in college accommodation. Rooms are allocated on the basis of exam results, which is not always popular. Many in Cambridge know Corpus for its unusual clock on the corner of Trumpington Street which is only correct every five minutes. Corpus is strong on music with a renowned pipe organ in the chapel. For sports it collaborates with King's and Christ's colleges to form the "CCK" sports teams, which often perform well and are a good way to meet students from other colleges.

Downing

Cambridge CB2 1DQ   01223 334826 (admissions)   www.dow.cam.ac.uk
Undergraduates: 437   Postgraduates: 193   admissions@dow.cam.ac.uk

Downing students are rightly proud of the spacious quadrangle around which the college's neoclassical architecture is set. The college was originally founded for the study of law and natural sciences in 1800 and while it is still popular with scientists, lawyers and geographers thanks to its fall-out-of-bed-and-into-lectures proximity to their faculties, it is now home to an eclectic body of students studying all subjects. Extra-curricular strengths lie on the sports field (Downing is known to be a fearsome opponent on the rugby field) and in the arts thanks to the Howard Theatre, a 120-seat space opened in 2010, and the new Heong Gallery dedicated to modern and contemporary art that opened in 2016 with a small but acclaimed show of Ai Weiwei's works. Unusually for Cambridge all students, both graduate and undergraduate, can be housed on the college's main site, which helps to foster a solid sense of community. Its most recently built accommodation block was unveiled in 2014 and rooms are generally of a high standard.

Emmanuel

Cambridge CB2 3AP   01223 334290 (admissions)   www.emma.cam.ac.uk
Undergraduates: 507   Postgraduates: 166   admissions@emma.cam.ac.uk

"Emma" as Emmanuel is fondly known prides itself on an open, friendly atmosphere that is underpinned by a strong academic ethic. It regularly comes in the top five in the Tompkins

Table (fourth in the 2016 ratings) and after great success winning University Challenge in 2010 the college has once again made it to the TV rounds. Students love it for its central location, busy and cheap bar, well-subsidised accommodation (which includes a free weekly load of washing in the rent) and the spacious grounds. Founded by Puritans in the 1580s it tries to maintain a forward-thinking and egalitarian atmosphere. It has a virtually equal gender split, a female master and two-thirds of the undergraduates hail from the state sector. Societies and sports focus more on inclusion than competition, although both the football team and the boat club do well in inter-college competitions. It's understated yet beautiful Christopher Wren chapel hosts a number of concerts organised by the music society. As one of the better endowed colleges Emmanuel offers a number of bursaries and scholarships and offers accommodation to all undergraduates, some of which has been recently refurbished.

Fitzwilliam

Cambridge CB3 0DG   01223 332030 (admissions)   www.fitz.cam.ac.uk
Undergraduates: 447   Postgraduates: 280   admissions@fitz.cam.ac.uk

Founded in the 19th century to increase access to Cambridge, Fitzwilliam College is proud of its heritage as a college committed to widening participation. It moved to its current location in 1963 and while it doesn't have the archetypal ancient architecture, the college gardens are some of the most beautiful in town. If you climb to the top of its new library, designed by award-winning architect Edward Cullinan, you will be standing at the highest point in the city. The atmosphere in college is one of a tight-knit community and students are accommodated throughout their degrees in one of 400 rooms in college or in houses minutes from the main campus. The friendly feel is also helped by the busy café patronised by both staff and students. At present "Fitz", as its fondly known, is undertaking a major refurbishment programme. Thus far half the freshers' accommodation has been revamped. On the academic front, Fitz is usually in the second half of the Tompkins Table, 23rd place in 2016, and it does well on the sports field thanks to its well-kept pitches, which are only five minutes from college, and a new gym.

Girton

Cambridge CB3 0JG   01223 338972 (admissions)   www.girton.cam.ac.uk
Undergraduates: 481   Postgraduates: 174   admissions@girton.cam.ac.uk

Girton is as far out to the west of Cambridge as Homerton is to the east, but for some the distance out of town is good reason to apply there. Its grounds, which include lawns, orchards, sports pitches and courts, majestic brick buildings and an indoor swimming pool, amount to some 50 acres. Girton students either live on this tranquil campus or in Wolfson Court, a separate three-acre annexe with its own café. The college has just undergone an extensive improvement programme that includes the most significant new building on its site for 75 years – a new wing at Ash Court that contains 50 en-suite bedrooms, student kitchens and a laundry. The swimming pool and gym have also been refurbished. Though it was founded as a women's college in 1869, it was the first college to go co-educational and now has an equal gender balance that is slightly weighted in favour of men. Academically Girton tends towards the bottom of the Tompkins Table, and was 27th in 2016. It is known for the arts and has its own museum and photography dark room. Sports enthusiasts will find the college has a strong boat club, too.

Gonville and Caius

Cambridge CB2 1TA   01223 332440 (admissions)   www.cai.cam.ac.uk
Undergraduates: 571   Postgraduates: 179   admissions@cai.cam.ac.uk

Gonville and Caius (pronounced 'keys') is one of the university's oldest colleges, having been founded as Gonville Hall in 1348, and is a haven of ancient courts and old world traditions. Students wear distinctive blue gowns for formal hall each week night (though often with jeans or sports kit underneath), and pass through symbolic gates in college on matriculation and graduation. Freshers sometimes question the need to pay for a minimum number of dinners in hall every term (it is the only college to do this), but by graduation many appreciate what regular communal eating does for Caius' familial feel. On other fronts, Caius is a forward-looking place. The £13-million Stephen Hawking building offers en-suite accommodation (named in honour of the world-famous physicist who celebrated 52 years as a Fellow of the college in 2016 and is often seen at High Table), as does Harvey Court, which was renovated in 2011. The college holds imaginative events for potential applicants such as its pioneering "Women in Economics" day. New academic prizes for sixth formers are being launched in 2016/17, no doubt with an eye to keeping up an impressive line up of alumni: with J. Michael Kosterlitz sharing the Nobel Prize for Physics in 2016, the college now boasts no fewer than 14 Nobel laureates. The college library used to be the University Library and is set under the arched roof of the Cockerell Building just outside the college.

Homerton

Cambridge CB2 8PH   01223 747252 (admissions)   www.homerton.cam.ac.uk
Undergraduates: 551   Postgraduates: 570   admissions@homerton.cam.ac.uk

Although Homerton is approaching the 250th anniversary of its foundation in the London district of Homerton in 1768, it is both the newest Cambridge college as well as the largest. That is because it only moved to Cambridge in 1894 and formally became a college in 2010. The college had just over 1,100 students – roughly half undergraduates and half postgraduate students – who live on a large, landscaped site in southeast Cambridge. Close to the railway station, it is a 15-minute cycle ride from town. Accommodation is offered to students in all years with largely en-suite study bedrooms of a high standard. The College also has tennis courts, a gym, a squash court and a football pitch (with plans for a new sports facilities close by). There is also an orchard and extensive lawns that can be walked on – Homerton students are quick to talk of the college's friendly and unstuffy atmosphere – though it still holds a feeling of history in its striking neo-Gothic Great Hall, built in 1889, which is used for daily student meals and for candlelit formal dinners. It has a near 50:50 gender split and hosts all courses except veterinary medicine and architecture. It is particularly known for being home to the largest number of students studying education in line with its history as a teaching training college.

Hughes Hall

Cambridge CB1 2EW   01223 334897 (admissions)k   www.hughes.cam.ac.uk
Undergraduates: 111   Postgraduates: 454   admissions@hughes.cam.ac.u

Founded in 1885, Hughes Hall is the oldest graduate college in the university and today welcomes applications for postgraduate courses as well as undergraduates over 21 in all subjects. Two-thirds of the students come from outside the UK with 116 nationalities represented by alumni, and the college has particular flair for sciences, law and business. Hughes lies on the eastern side of the city centre near Mill Road (an area known to be one of Cambridge's more cosmopolitan) and the train station. It is also close to the university cricket ground – one of many reasons that the college boasts a strong record on the sports pitch and on the river. It had eight Blues rowers in 2016, one of whom rowed in the Rio Olympics. Accommodation is provided to all single undergraduates and affiliated students and in 2016, 85 en-suite rooms were built along with a bike store and study rooms in the new Gresham Court building.

Jesus

Cambridge CB5 8BL   01223 339455 (admissions)   www.jesus.cam.ac.uk
Undergraduates: 527   Postgraduates: 294 undergraduate-admissions@jesus.cam.ac.uk
Jesus is the envy of many a Cantabrigian for its spacious grounds near both the river and the centre of town. Its red brick buildings are iconic and many date to the Jesus' founding between 1496 and 1516. Its chapel, once part of a Benedictine nunnery, is believed to be the oldest university building in Cambridge. Not all is old though. The college has just opened a development at West Court with new student common rooms, games room, café and bar and also has on-site football, rugby and cricket pitches as well as squash and tennis courts. As one of the largest colleges it is home to an eclectic student population that is as strong on the sports field as it is in music (the choir has released a number of bestselling albums) and art (a student recently exhibited and sold two works in the Royal Academy Summer Exhibition). The much-loved grounds are often punctuated by modern sculpture exhibitions and students are allowed to roam on most of the grass. The May Ball is very popular. While they might play hard, students still find time to study hard, too, and Jesus regularly performs well in the Tompkins Table coming seventh in the 2016 ratings

King's

Cambridge CB2 1ST   01223 331255 (admissions)   www.kings.cam.ac.uk
Undergraduates: 400 Postgraduates: 161   undergraduate.admissions@kings.cam.ac.uk
Think of a postcard of Cambridge and it is likely that the architecture of King's will come to your mind's eye. The iconic chapel (home to the annual Festival of Nine Lessons and Carols) and elegant facades back onto the river giving King's an enviable location that is ideally located for both arts and science students. Given its appearance and the fact that it was originally founded in 1441 as a college for boys from Eton, King's is proudly the most anti-establishment of the colleges. It hosts an "affair" rather than a May Ball which is highly popular and always has a left-field theme. The college has done away with the Fellows' "High Table" in the dining hall and hangs a hammer and sickle flag in its bar – though its presence there is hotly debated each year. A high state-school intake (just over 80 per cent) is aided by the college actively seeking out those from disadvantaged backgrounds. Accommodation ranges from the archetypically Cambridge (think mullioned windows overlooking the river) to en-suite rooms in newer hostels. It is one of the smaller student bodies and joins up with Corpus and Christ's on the sports field.

Lucy Cavendish

Cambridge CB3 0BU   01223 330280 (admissions)   www.lucy-cav.cam.ac.uk
Undergraduates: 113   Postgraduates: 193   lcc-admissions@lists.cam.ac.uk
Unlike any other Oxbridge college, Lucy Cavendish ("Lucy" to its members) takes only mature female students. This encourages a more staid and studious atmosphere than other colleges, but one that is highly supportive. Founded in 1965 by female academics who

believed that opportunities for women at the university were too restricted, Lucy holds strong to its founding remit and often hosts major conferences, such as 2015's "Where are the Women?" that included contributions from Harriet Harman, Polly Toynbee and Hannah Rothschild. Political journalist and broadcaster Jackie Ashley joined the college as its President in 2015 in time to oversee its 50th anniversary celebrations. Accommodation is provided for all students either in college or in nearby houses, the location of which are near those of St Edmund Hall and Fitzwilliam, making for easy intermingling with these other "hill" colleges. Sport is strong and there is a well-equipped gym, while on the river the Lucy rowing team shared the 2015/16 Michell Cup for best overall performance with Hughes Hall. While Lucy doesn't sit near the top of the Tompkins Table, over 20 per cent of students achieved Firsts or 2:1 degrees in 2016 allowing it climb three places to 26th. The college is better known for its Fiction Prize, which had a record 484 entries this year.

Magdalene

Cambridge CB3 0AG   01223 332135 (admissions)   www.magd.cam.ac.uk
Undergraduates: 375   Postgraduates: 148   admissions@magd.cam.ac.uk

Magdalene rejoices in the longest river frontage of any Cambridge college and is renowned for its ancient and beautiful grounds. It is one of the smaller colleges, but this does mean that students tend to all know each other. Despite a reputation for being more traditional than some – it was the last all-male college to admit women (in 1988) and famously hosts one of the university's few white tie balls every three years – it has a 50:50 gender balance and one of the cheapest formal halls in Cambridge. It also owns its own punts, which are a popular fixture in the summer term. The college's sports pitches are shared with St John's (both colleges have a sporty reputation) and it has its own Eton Fives court on site. Accommodation varies and is found across the college or in 21 houses and hostels nearby. Students are mixed together, which helps inter-year socialising. The college's most famous alumni, Samuel Pepys, is immortalised in its famous Pepys Library that houses a collection of 3,000 of the diarist's books preserved on their original shelves. The Master is the former Archbishop of Canterbury Rowan Williams, who arrived in 2013. Magdalene has fallen from second the Tompkins Table to ninth in 2016, but the college generally performs in the top half of the table.

Murray Edwards

Cambridge CB3 0DF   01223 762229 (admissions)   www.murrayedwards.cam.ac.uk
Undergraduates: 373   Postgraduates: 123   admissions@murrayedwards.cam.ac.uk

One of Cambridge's three colleges for women, Murray Edwards is possibly the most gregarious of them. It is an informal, relaxed college whose students spend as much time mingling with students from other colleges in town as taking advantage of their calm and spacious campus at the top of Castle Hill. It hosts a renowned garden party during May Week, and the Saturday brunch is legendary – voted best in Cambridge last year. Unsurprisingly for an all-female college it does much to promote women in the workplace, most notably running a programme on academic leadership and career development called Gateway that runs once a week during term. The laid-back atmosphere extends to the gardens where students can grow herbs and vegetables as well as, unusually for a Cambridge college, walk on the grass. Sport is strong – during the 2016 season the netball team were the intercollegiate champions and the hockey team were finalists. The college often provides Blues players to the university teams. Murray Edwards is also is home to the second largest collection of women's art in the world, which is displayed around the college, and includes work by Barbara Hepworth and Tracey Emin.

Newnham

Cambridge CB3 9DF   01223 335783 (admissions)   www.newn.cam.ac.uk
Undergraduates: 362   Postgraduates: 211   admissions@newn.cam.ac.uk

Newnham was the first college established for women to attend lectures at Cambridge in 1871 (though it was another 77 years before they were admitted as full members of the university) and it prides itself on academic excellence and creating a supportive atmosphere for women to achieve their potential. Seminars in conjunction with organisations such as Women of the Year are common. Alumnae include Germaine Greer (who is still a fellow at the college), Sylvia Plath, Mary Beard and Emma Thompson. For arts students it is ideally located for the Sidgwick Site and for those who like to socialise, Newnham often joins up with nearby college Selwyn for socials, formals and for its choir (Newnham has no chapel). The grounds of the college are much loved by Newnhamites and stretch to 18 acres that include sports pitches, tennis courts and an on-site arts centre known as "The Old Labs". Extensive work has begun to build 90 en-suite rooms for students as well as a new Porters' Lodge, gym, café and rooms for conferences and supervisions, which are expected to open in September 2018.

Pembroke

Cambridge CB2 1RF   01223 338154 (admissions)   www.pem.cam.ac.uk
Undergraduates: 450   Postgraduates: 190   adm@pem.cam.ac.uk

Given its position at the corner of Pembroke and Trumpington streets, Pembroke is surprisingly large and is home to extensive gardens and a Christopher Wren chapel. Particularly famous for its poets, including Ted Hughes and Edmund Spenser, in 2016 Pembroke marked the 300th anniversary of the birth of the poet Thomas Gray, also an alumnus. Loyal Pembroke students love the college for the cheap rents (though in second year particularly these do somewhat reflect the quality), a lively café and facilities that include an on-site gym and Europe's oldest bowling green. While performing well academically – in 2016 Pembroke regained second position in the Tompkins Table – there is a strong extra-curricular ethos, too. There are dozens of clubs and societies, including the Pembroke College Music Society, the Stokes Scientific Society, Pembroke Politics and the Pembroke Players, who regularly take productions to the Edinburgh Festival and annually take a Shakespeare play to Japan. In sport, the College is currently strong in football, hockey and rowing. In 2015/16 the 1st team were finalists in the inter-college football tournament for the third year running and the 1st XI won hockey "Supercuppers" against Worcester College, Oxford. It is a well-endowed institution, and the Pembroke recently received what is thought to be the largest bequest ever given to a Cambridge college.

Peterhouse

Cambridge CB2 1RD   01223 338223 (admissions)   www.pet.cam.ac.uk
Undergraduates: 254   Postgraduates: 116   admissions@pet.cam.ac.uk

It may be Cambridge's most diminutive college – home to just 254 undergraduates – but Peterhouse's influence belies its size and it boasts five Nobel Prize winners. It is also Cambridge's oldest college and it remains home to some quirky traditions and a famously old-world formal hall. That said it is modern in outlook with a good gender balance and one of the highest state-school intakes. It is also one of the richer colleges and has a roster of travel grants and academic awards available. Accommodation standards are high. Students are housed either on site or not more than five minutes away for all years of their degree. Rooms are allocated on a points-based system that accounts both for academic progress as well as extra-curricular achievements. Though it doesn't have its own sports ground, Peterhouse does have a squash court and a recently built gym. It also has some of Cambridge's wilder outdoor spaces known as "The Deer Park" (without deer). Peterhouse is well located for both the science and arts faculties and is particularly strong in the arts. It has two libraries, the Perne and the Ward, which provide plenty of quiet learning space away from the busier atmospheres of students' faculty libraries.

Queens'

Cambridge CB3 9ET   01223 335540 (admissions)   www.queens.cam.ac.uk
Undergraduates: 519   Postgraduates: 368   admissions@queens.cam.ac.uk

Queens' (the placement of the apostrophe distinguishes it from its Oxford counterpart) is a bustling college that has a central location spanning both sides of the River Cam with Sir Isaac Newton's much-photographed Mathematical Bridge joining the two. It is the third biggest of the colleges in population terms and, especially in the new courts, has a more outgoing feel than some of its calmer counterparts. Drama is popular thanks to the active BATS dramatic society and sport is strong – Queens' won inter-college competitions in both football and squash in 2016 and has sports clubs covering everything from chess to water polo. It is also hosts a well-attended biennial May Ball. An eclectic mix of architecture from the college's founding in 1448 right through to the present day allows for all undergraduates to be housed for the three years of their degree; the accommodation in the Dokett building is currently being upgraded to include en-suite facilities. Queens' is particularly strong in the sciences thanks to a roster of subject bursaries and awards.

Robinson

Cambridge CB3 9AN   01223 339143 (admissions)   www.robinson.cam.ac.uk
Undergraduates: 418   Postgraduates: 165   apply@robinson.cam.ac.uk

Though occasionally ribbed for the austere 1970s redbrick architecture, the college has made a virtue of its appearance: the Red Brick Café is envied by many other colleges' students and Brickhouse, the student drama company makes good use of the outdoor theatre space. The (brick) chapel is renowned for its fantastic acoustic and organ. The college is engaged in a rolling programme of refurbishment that has resulted in very good facilities even if rents are not as well subsidised as some. However, the food served up in the college's canteen is renowned as some of the best in Cambridge. Robinson tends to rest in the second half of the Tompkins Table (it was 22nd in 2016, but has been as high as 3rd). For those who want to focus on academe it is conveniently situated just behind the University Library and minutes away from the arts faculties on the Sidgwick Site and the maths, physics and materials science buildings. For those who like sport, Robinson often fields strong teams, winning the Football Cuppers and with its women's first boat taking blades in both the Lent and May bumps in 2016. The sports grounds are shared with Queens', Selwyn and King's College and are less than a mile from the main college site.

St Catharine's

Cambridge CB2 1RL   01223 338319 (admissions)   www.caths.cam.ac.uk

Undergraduates: 472   Postgraduates: 170   undergraduate.admissions@caths.cam.ac.uk

Despite its unusual open court frontage "Catz", as St Catharine's is fondly known, is one of the least assuming of the colleges strung along Cambridge's King's Parade. It is one of the mid-sized colleges and has not one but two college libraries thanks to the remit for learning instilled by its original benefactor, Robert Woodlark. It came 17th in the Tompkins Table in 2016 and has recently gained a new Master, Sir Mark Welland, who is a renowned professor of nanotechnology. Catz students live on site in first year before moving out to the popular St Chad's complex in second year, where accommodation is split into flats with octagonal bedrooms. Other recent improvements include the McGrath Centre, which houses an auditorium, junior common room and bar, and a refurbished boat house and hockey pitch, with the only collegiate Astroturf pitch in Cambridge. It does well on the river and one alumnus was part of the Olympic gold-medal winning men's coxless four. Film nights and societies are well attended as is the college's drama group, the Shirley Society.

St Edmund's

Cambridge CB3 0BN   01223 336086 (admissions)   www.st-edmunds.cam.ac.uk

Undergraduates: 120   Postgraduates: 309   admissions@st-edmunds.cam.ac.uk

Having just celebrated its 50th year as a graduate college, St Edmund's (called "Eddies" by its members) enjoys a reputation as one of Cambridge's most international colleges with a student body that, though male-heavy, hails from as many as 85 different countries. It is also renowned for providing numerous sportsmen and women to the university's Blues teams. Simon Amor, coach of the 2016 Olympic rugby sevens team, is an Eddies alumnus. Located near Fitzwilliam and Murray Edwards, it is known as one of the most social of the graduate colleges. Accommodation and food is on the expensive side as St Edmund's doesn't enjoy the big endowments of some of the larger colleges, but there are a variety of rooms on offer in the recently built Brian Heap building as well as maisonettes a short walk from college for couples and small families. St Edmund's is unique among Cambridge colleges for having a Catholic chapel and also takes a relaxed approach to traditions. There is no Fellow's High Table in hall, for example.

St John's

Cambridge CB2 1TP   01223 338703 (admissions)   www.joh.cam.ac.uk

Undergraduates: 602   Postgraduates: 219   admissions@joh.cam.ac.uk

St John's and Trinity enjoy a friendly rivalry, which in part sparks from them both being large, rich and architecturally beautiful colleges as well as next door neighbours. St John's is home to Cambridge's famous Bridge of Sighs and a stunning chapel whose tower is the highest building in town. Thanks to a large undergraduate body, St John's is a diverse place, though it is particularly renowned for its prowess on the sports field. The "Red Boys" rugby team has now won the college league two years on the trot and the men's 1st boat came head of the river in the inter-college Bumps. The size of St John's endowments means that it can support a wide range of activities from launching its own record label in aid of the strong music scene in college to two new financial initiatives which aim to help those who would previously have relied on the Government's maintenance grants. Accommodation standards are high and the food in the buttery is considered delicious and well subsidised. St John's also hosts a May Week Ball that has a reputation as one of the most fabulous.

Selwyn

Cambridge CB3 9DQ   01223 335896 (admissions)   www.sel.cam.ac.uk
Undergraduates: 410   Postgraduates: 165   admissions@sel.cam.ac.uk

Selwyn sits on the other side of the River Cam from the city centre and enjoys a roomy location just behind the Sidgwick Site, which makes the lecture commute an easy two-minute walk for arts and humanities students. The only complaint about its location is that it's a ten-minute or so walk to the nearest cash point and supermarket. It was among the first colleges to admit women and has a typically 50:50 balance. Selwyn also has one of the largest contingents of state-maintained undergraduates in the university (a roughly 70:30 ratio). All the students are accommodated for all years of their degrees, thanks to an extensive refurbishment programme. Academically, Selwyn comes in the middle of the Tompkins rankings at 15th, but music is strong and the college choir's recent recording was a Classic FM album of the week. On the sports front, long-standing sports clubs known as the Hermes and Sirens fund grants for various teams, and on the river the men's team recently climbed six places in the inter-college Bumps competition.

Sidney Sussex

Cambridge CB2 3HU   01223 338872 (admissions)   www.sid.cam.ac.uk
Undergraduates: 367   Postgraduate: 151   admissions@sid.cam.ac.uk

Sidney Sussex, which was founded in 1596, is located, happily for students, just opposite the entrance to the city centre's main supermarket. This is not the only plus point of its central situation, however: it is a short cycle ride in one direction to the river, a two-minute walk to the main student theatre, the ADC, and a five-minute walk to the natural science faculties. It is one of the smaller colleges, and celebrated 40 years of women at the college in 2016. Thanks to its size and city centre location, many students are housed off site in one of 11 nearby hostels though there are some atmospheric rooms to be had in the college's main buildings. One of the hostels has been refurbished this year with 22 new student rooms and two large kitchens. The college is a musical one with an award-winning chapel and a newly inaugurated organ. Also in the chapel, more bizarrely, is buried Oliver Cromwell's head (he was among the college's first students). Food is also well reviewed and the college chefs have taken the top prize in the university-wide culinary competitions on numerous occasions. Sports grounds are shared with Christ's, a ten-minute cycle ride away.

Trinity

Cambridge CB2 1TQ   01223 338422 (admissions)   www.trin.cam.ac.uk
Undergraduates: 716   Postgraduates: 246   admissions@trin.cam.ac.uk

The largest of all Oxbridge colleges, Trinity was established in 1546 and occupies extensive grounds that span the River Cam. Like its neighbour St John's, Trinity is incredibly well endowed (it is the wealthiest of all the colleges), which allows it to provide high quality and cheap accommodation as well as lots of bursaries to its undergraduate population which the largest of any college. The Tudor Gothic buildings of New Court have just been renovated to provide 169 student rooms and nearly half the college's accommodation is en suite. Since 1997 Trinity has not come below eighth in the Tompkins Table and regularly tops it, but that's not to say there is not a lot going on in college besides. A two-floor gym and netball, football, rugby and cricket pitches minutes from the main gate mean that sports are easy to enjoy (hockey pitches, badminton, tennis and squash courts are also available) and the college punts are a popular choice on summer afternoons. The chapel is home to an active choir. Though male dominated (about two-thirds), Trinity has recently expanded its access and outreach programmes and it's a diverse place. Some say it is too big and the tourists too many, but others revel in the choice this allows.

Trinity Hall

Cambridge CB2 1TJ   01223 332535 (admissions)   www.trinhall.cam.ac.uk
Undergraduates: 387   Postgraduates: 144   admissions@trinhall.cam.ac.uk

"Tit Hall", as Cambridge's fifth oldest college is known, is tucked behind its more grandiose neighbours, Trinity and Clare, allowing it to enjoy a less tourist-heavy river frontage. That's not to say it's not picturesque and its small size allows its undergraduates to get to know each other quickly. It is also ideally located for strolling into town as well as short cycle rides to the Sidgwick Site for the arts faculties and the University Library. Thanks to its endowments Trinity Hall is one of the richer colleges, which means that accommodation is cheap and facilities are good. A new block with double en-suite rooms called WYNG Gardens opened in autumn 2016 and the 90 rooms at the Wychfield Site (a ten-minute walk from the main college) have recently been refurbished. The college is a sporty one and it fields a strong women's football team as well as a good boat club. The modern Jerwood Library is a much-loved study space for students in part thanks to its river views. Among those who have studied at Trinity Hall are eminent scientists Stephen Hawking and David Thouless as well as the Olympic medal-winning cyclist Emma Pooley.

Wolfson

Cambridge CB3 9BB   01223 335918   www.wolfson.cam.ac.uk
Undergraduates: 169   Postgraduates: 605   ugadministrator@wolfson.cam.ac.uk

Established as University College in 1965, Wolfson took its current name from a generous grant from the Wolfson Foundation just eight years after it was founded. It is first and foremost a college for graduate students but also welcomes 150 or so mature undergraduates each year. All are guaranteed three years of accommodation. The community is varied, with students from over 80 countries and aged from 21 to 60 (the average is 25). It's a forward-thinking place with famously little distinction between fellows and students in rank (there is no High Table in hall, for example) and a President rather than a Master. The 1970s buildings are not the town's most beautiful but the gardens are an oasis of calm, out to the southwest of Cambridge and not far from the path to Granchester. It is also not far from the Sidgwick Site and the University Library though the city centre is about a 20-minute walk. On site the college has one of the university's best gyms as well as a basketball-cum-tennis court and social activities are both regular and popular.

14 University Profiles

This chapter provides profiles of every university that appears in *The Times and Sunday Times* league table. In addition there are profiles for the two major suppliers of part-time degrees, the Open University and Birkbeck College, and also for those institutions which did not release data for use in the table (University College Birmingham, University of Wales Trinity St David and Wolverhampton). However, we do not have separate profiles for specialist colleges, such as the Royal College of Music (**www.rcm.ac.uk**) or institutions that only offer postgraduate degrees, such as Cranfield University (**www.cranfield.ac.uk**). Their omission is no reflection on their quality, simply a function of their particular roles. A number of additional institutions with degree-awarding powers are listed at the end of the book with their contact details.

The federal University of London (**www.london.ac.uk**) is by far Britain's biggest conventional higher education institution, with more than 120,000 students. The majority study at colleges in the capital, but such is the global prestige of the university's degrees that over 54,000 students in 180 different countries take University of London International Programmes. The university, which celebrated its 175th anniversary in 2011, consists of 18 self-governing colleges, the Institute in Paris and the School of Advanced Study, which comprises ten specialist institutes for research and postgraduate education (details at **www.sas.ac.uk**). City University joined the university in 2016. The university does not have its own entry in this chapter, but the following colleges do: Birkbeck College, City, Goldsmiths, King's College London, London School of Economics and Political Science, Queen Mary, Royal Holloway, SOAS and University College London. Contact details for its other constituent colleges are given on page 566.

Guide to the profiles
The profiles contain valuable information about each university. You can find contact details, including postal address, telephone number for admission enquiries, email or web addresses for admissions and prospectus enquiries, web addresses for the university, the students' union and for sports facilities, and any university grouping that the institution is affiliated to (Russell Group, etc.). In addition, each profile provides information under the following headings:

» **The Times and Sunday Times** rankings For the overall ranking, the figure in bold refers to the university's position in 2017 and the figure in brackets to 2016. All the information listed below the heading is taken from the main league table. See chapter 1 for explanations and the sources of the data.

» **Undergraduates** The number of full-time undergraduates is given first followed by part-time undergraduates (in brackets). The figures are for 2014–15, and are the most recent from the Higher Education Statistics Agency (HESA).

» **Postgraduates** The number of full-time postgraduates is given first followed by part-time postgraduates (in brackets). The figures are for 2014–15, and are the most recent from HESA.

» **Mature students** The percentage of undergraduate entrants who were 21 or over at the start of their studies in 2015. The figures are from UCAS.

» **International students** The number of undergraduate overseas students (both EU and non-EU) as a percentage of full-time undergraduates. The figures are for 2014–15, and are from HESA.

» **Applications per place** The number of applicants per place for 2015, from UCAS.

» **From state-school sector** The number of young full-time first-degree entrants from state schools or colleges in 2014–15 as a percentage of total young entrants. The figures are from HESA.

» **From working-class homes** The number of young full-time first-degree entrants in 2014–15 whose parental occupations are skilled, manual, semi-skilled or unskilled (NS-SEC classes 4–7) as a percentage of total young entrants. The figures are from HESA.

» **Accommodation** The information was obtained from university accommodation services, and their help is gratefully acknowledged.

Tuition fees

Details of tuition fees for 2017–18 are given wherever possible. At the time of going to press, a number of universities had not published their international fees for 2017–18. In these cases the fees for 2016–17 are given. Please check university websites to see if they have managed to give updated figures. Fees of 2018–19 will not be published until late summer 2017. While fees in England may increase by inflation if universities meet certain conditions, such increases had not been approved by Parliament when the *Guide* went to press. For Wales, the figures given are for 2017–18, but applicants for places in 2018 need to be aware that the tuition fee grant system for Welsh students is being reviewed for potential reform in 2018.

While EU students have been guaranteed that UK rather than International fees will apply to them if they start in 2017, no such guarantee has yet been given for students planning to start in 2018. It is of the utmost importance that you check university websites for the latest information.

Every university website gives full details of the financial and other support the university provides to its students, from scholarships and bursaries to study support and hardship funds. Some of the support will be delivered automatically but most will not, and you must study the details on the websites, including methods of applying and deadlines, to get the greatest benefit out of your university. In addition, in England the Office for Fair Access (**www.offa. org.uk**) publishes "Access Agreements" for every English university on its website. Each agreement outlines the university's plans for fees, financial support and measures being taken to widen access to that university and to encourage students to complete their courses.

University of Aberdeen

New arrivals at Aberdeen are paired with current undergraduates, often on the same course, under the Students4Students scheme, to help them settle in and get the most from university life. Growing numbers would like to study in the Granite City – applications were up by more than 7 per cent in 2015, when the numbers starting degrees rose for the third year in a row. Established in 1495, Aberdeen is the UK's fifth oldest university. Today's university is a fusion of two ancient institutions which came together in 1860. The original King's College premises are the focal point of an attractive campus, complete with cobbled main street and Georgian buildings, about a mile from the city centre.

Its longevity is celebrated in the university's Sixth Century courses, which are part of a menu of "Enhanced Study" options designed to broaden undergraduate degrees. Students can incorporate a language, business or computing into their degree, or choose from cross-disciplinary programmes with titles such as Global Issues – Global Religions, the Mind Machine, or Northern Light and Landscape. The aim is to give graduates broader knowledge and more intellectual flexibility, and assessors praised the "transformative" effect of curriculum reforms, as well as the quality of online learning resources, personal tutoring and employability initiatives, in Aberdeen's last institutional review.

The university opened its first overseas campus in September 2016, at Changwon in South Korea, making it the only UK university to have a base in that country. The campus is specialising in the offshore-related disciplines that are among Aberdeen's greatest strengths.

The university has been chosen to lead a new MSc programme aimed mainly at people working in the UK oil and gas industry. At its own underwater research facility, Oceanlab, at Newburgh, north of Aberdeen, its engineers lead the world in creating systems capable of operating at depths down to 11,000 metres.

The university's expertise is spread much more widely, however. Three-quarters of the work submitted for the 2014 Research Excellence Framework was rated as world-leading or internationally excellent. The university was placed top in the UK for environmental and soil science and in the top three for psychology and English.

The university will have invested £377 million on capital projects by 2019. The futuristic Sir Duncan Rice Library, named after the Principal who commissioned it, cost £57 million and was chosen as one of the 12 best new buildings in Scotland. A £22-million Aquatic Centre, with 50-

King's College
Aberdeen AB24 3FX

01224 272090/91 (admissions)
sras@abdn.ac.uk
www.abdn.ac.uk
www.ausa.org.uk
Affiliation: none

The Times and Sunday Times **Rankings**
Overall Ranking: **=44** (last year: 45)

Teaching quality:	105	78.1%
Student experience:	=50	84.4%
Research quality:	43	29.9%
Entry standards:	16	443
Student–staff ratio:	=25	13.5
Services & facilities/student:	28	£2,300
Expected completion rate:	=77	84.3%
Good honours:	=33	77.9%
Graduate prospects:	37	78.5%

metre pool and 10-metre diving board, opened in 2014, completing the Aberdeen Sports Village, which offers some of the best facilities at any university in the UK, including a full-size indoor football pitch.

The university established the English-speaking world's first chair in medicine and has produced its share of advances since. Medicine is at Foresterhill, a 20-minute walk away, where the university shares one of Europe's largest health campuses with NHS Grampian, placing researchers, scientists, clinicians and patients together on one site. This has been enhanced by the addition of a new £37-million building for the University of Aberdeen Rowett Institute of Nutrition and Health, a world-leader in food and nutrition research.

Buses link the two sites with the Hillhead residential complex, which has been refurbished recently and new central facilities added to allow students to relax and socialise.

Almost a third of all students come from the north of Scotland, but one in six is from England among a total of 120 nationalities. Although the winters are long, the climate is warmer than the uninitiated might expect and transport links are good.

Students find the city lively and welcoming, if expensive: the JobLink service provides a good selection of part-time employment. Aberdeen has been ranked as the "safest city in the UK" in 2016 by an international consulting firm which surveyed 230 cities across the globe, ranking them on a range of factors, including internal stability, crime levels and the performance of local law enforcement. The region as a whole has been rated as the UK's top environment in which to live and work.

The students' centre in The Hub brings together dining and retail outlets with support services, including the accommodation and careers offices. The Hub includes an International Centre which brings students from around the world together and provides everything from support with language skills to days out, excursions and even camping trips.

The university's ICT network has over 1,500 computers for student use.

All new undergraduates are guaranteed housing – an important benefit in a city with the highest rents in Scotland.

Tuition fees

» Fees for Scottish and EU students 2017–18   No fee
» Fees for Non-Scottish UK (RUK) students 2017–18   £9,000 capped at £27,000 for 4-year courses and £36,000 for 5-year courses; no cap for medicine and dentistry.
» Fees for international students 2017–18   £14,300–£18,000   Medicine   £39,000
» There are particular support schemes for RUK students.
» Check the university's website for the latest information.

Students

Undergraduates:	9,395	(655)
Postgraduates:	2,415	(1,570)
Mature students:	24.2%	
International students:	26.8%	
Applications per place:	7.7	
From state-sector schools:	79.2%	
From working-class homes:	25%	
Satisfaction with students' union	48%	

For detailed information about sports facilities:
www.abdn.ac.uk/sportandexercise

Accommodation

Number of places and costs refer to 2016–17
University-provided places: 3,380 (including private providers)
Percentage catered: 12%
Catered costs: £144 – £169 a week (39 weeks).
Self-catered costs: £99 – £152 a week (39–51 weeks).
First-year students are guaranteed accommodation.
International students: as above.
studentaccomm@abdn.ac.uk
www.abdn.ac.uk/accommodation

Abertay University

Abertay has been going through a period of rapid transition, introducing Scotland's first accelerated degrees as well as new joint degrees and compulsory interdisciplinary courses for all undergraduates. At the same time, a third of the programmes have been cut because they were not considered viable, contributing to a drop in applications in 2015. Despite this, the slimmed-down portfolio produced increased enrolments for the first time in five years.

Among the other changes has been a reduction in the feedback time on assessed work to ten working days, with students submitting work electronically and receiving their feedback and marks the same way. Grading has been simplified and students are guaranteed to have lectures and seminars in the same place at the same time every week. The academic calendar has changed from two semesters to three terms, regularising holidays and making room for feedback and reading weeks.

The university is best known for its courses in computer arts and games design. It introduced the UK's first degree in ethical hacking and cyber security, and remains a leader in the field. American academics surveyed by the *Princeton Review* rated Abertay among the best places in the world to study games design, while Sony chose the university as the site for the largest teaching laboratory in Europe for its PlayStation consoles. The university opened Europe's first research centre dedicated to computer games and digital entertainment, and more recently established a centre for research into systems pathology. It hosts the first Interactive Media Academy in the UK and the national Centre for Excellence in Computer Games Education, and also has the largest number of courses in this area accredited by Skillset, the Government-sponsored training council for the creative industries.

The university has upgraded its own IT facilities to match, investing £3 million in software upgrades and hardware replacement across the campus, including a new Wi-Fi network. Abertay provides almost one computer for every five students – one of the highest ratios of PC to student in Britain – and is promising further improvements.

The seven accelerated degrees include ethical hacking and computer arts, which can be taken in three years, rather than the norm of four north of the border. The final two years consist of 45 weeks rather than the usual 30. Other subjects available in this format – unique so far in Scotland – include business studies, computer game applications development, game design and production management, sports development and coaching, and food and

---

Bell Street
Dundee DD1 1HG

01382 308080
sro@abertay.ac.uk
www.abertay.ac.uk
www.abertaysa.com
Affiliations: MillionPlus;
GuildHE

DUNDEE
Edinburgh
Belfast
London
Cardiff

The Times and Sunday Times **Rankings**

Overall Ranking: **85** (last year: 97)

Teaching quality:	=24	83%
Student experience:	49	84.5%
Research quality:	=90	5.1%
Entry standards:	55	346
Student–staff ratio:	=110	19.3
Services & facilities/student:	97	£1,657
Expected completion rate:	118	77.2%
Good honours:	64	70.9%
Graduate prospects:	83	68.4%

consumer science. The changes were part of a move towards more problem- and work-based approaches to learning, focusing on real-world issues and teamwork, with less time spent in conventional lectures. All courses can be taken on a part-time basis, and new programmes aim to offer students the chance to spend at least 30 per cent of their time in industry.

Based in the centre of Dundee, all the university's teaching and learning buildings are within five minutes' walk of each other. They are modern and functional, such as the innovative White Space facility, the university's flagship creative learning and working environment, where students study alongside industry professionals who are working on real commercial or broadcast projects.

A new graduate school provides dedicated study space for postgraduates, as well as training and professional development opportunities. Abertay has also established a series of specialist research centres in areas as diverse as urban water systems, bioinformatics, earth systems and environmental sciences. The latest are in sustainability assessment, visualisation and enhancement, and food innovation.

The university doubled in size during the 1990s and has grown to around 5,000 students since tuition fees were abolished for Scots. Most are based in Dundee, but Abertay's degrees are also taught as far away as Malaysia.

Entrance requirements have risen consistently over the last five years, even beyond those sought-after computing courses. Law and forensic psychobiology, for example, both demand ABBB in Scottish Highers or BCC at A level. Well-qualified A-level students are eligible for direct entry into second year if they do not opt for an accelerated degree.

The university hosts the Dundee Academy of Sport, launched in partnership with Dundee and Angus College – a venture using sport as a vehicle for learning across the school curriculum and throughout life.

The city has seen considerable investment recently, including the development of its waterfront, centred on the £80-million V&A Dundee design museum, which is due to open in 2018.

The city has a large student population and the cost of living is modest. A 500-bed student village, which opened in 2010, allows all first-years to be guaranteed accommodation.

Tuition fees

» Fees for Scottish and EU students 2017–18   No fee
» Fees for Non-Scottish UK (RUK) students 2017–18   £8,000
» Fees for international students 2017–18   £12,500–£13,500
» There are particular support schemes for RUK students.
» Check the university's website for the latest information on fees, scholarships, bursaries and other forms of student support.

Students

Undergraduates:	3,630	(245)
Postgraduates:	185	(160)
Mature students:	42.4%	
International students:	9.0%	
Applications per place:	5.4	
From state-sector schools:	98.3%	
From working-class homes:	33.8%	
Satisfaction with students' union	64%	

For detailed information about sports facilities:
www.abertay.ac.uk/student-life/sport

Accommodation

Number of places and costs refer to 2017–18
University-provided places: 497
Percentage catered: 0%
Self-catered costs: £59 – £117 a week (38, 42 or 51 weeks).
All new entrants (home and international) given priority for accommodation if conditions are met. Pre-payment discount available (some residential restrictions).
residences@abertay.ac.uk
www.abertay.ac.uk/student-life/accommodation

Aberystwyth University

Both applications and enrolments declined for the third successive year at Aberystwyth in 2015, but the sharpest of turnarounds in student satisfaction in 2016 — up 90 places in both of our measures — should herald better times, reflected in a big rise in our league table this year. Despite the fee concessions offered to Welsh students, who make up nearly a third of Aber's intake, the demand for places has dropped by a third since 2011.

Aberystwyth, a mid-size university set by Cardigan Bay, ranked in the top 50 in the latest research ratings, and employment figures have seen the number of Aber students gaining graduate-level jobs rise to 68.2 per cent, up from 53 per cent two years ago. This has filtered through to improved rankings in our table.

The new vice-chancellor will inherit a strategic plan that stresses the need for improvements in the student experience, which has been the university's Achilles heel in UK rankings. Aber has doubled its planned investment in student accommodation and teaching and research facilities, taking total spending past £100 million.

Fferm Penglais, the new flagship student village has taken its first students, an innovation centre is being developed to serve local businesses and provide opportunities for students, and the School of Management and Business and the Department of Law and Criminology at the Llanbadarn Centre have been fully refurbished. The university is developing more opportunities for work experience through a range of courses with an in-built year in industry. A number of European and international partnerships provide opportunities for undertaking study abroad – for a semester or for an entire year.

Several new degrees involve collaborative teaching across departments. They include data science, which explores the territory where computing and mathematics meet, engineering physics, and adventure tourism management, which takes advantage of the spectacular countryside around Aberystwyth. In addition, there is a new range of four-year Integrated Masters degrees, which reach postgraduate levels of study without the need to source additional funding.

The attractive seaside location remains a draw for applicants: Aberystwyth was officially named a "great town" at the Academy of Urbanism 2015 Awards. Although the oldest of the Welsh universities, Aberystwyth was among the pioneers of the modular degree system, and allowed students flexibility between subjects even before that. Welsh-medium teaching is thriving, with more courses available in the language. Well over 90

Reception
Penglais
Aberystwyth
Ceredigion SY23 3FL

01970 622021 (admissions)
ug-admissions@aber.ac.uk
www.aber.ac.uk
www.abersu.co.uk
Affiliation: none

The Times and Sunday Times Rankings

Overall Ranking: **56** (last year: =79)

Teaching quality:	=10	85%
Student experience:	19	87%
Research quality:	45	28.1%
Entry standards:	104	299
Student–staff ratio:	=108	19.1
Services & facilities/student:	89	£1,694
Expected completion rate:	=46	88.6%
Good honours:	=84	66.9%
Graduate prospects:	84	68.2%

per cent of the undergraduates are state educated – a higher proportion than the mix of subjects would imply – although the proportion from working-class homes is below the university's benchmark. A Student Welcome Centre continues to offer advice on everything from money problems to learning difficulties long after undergraduates have enrolled, helping to produce one of the lowest dropout rates in Wales. The university also has a branch campus in Mauritius, but the project drew criticism when it emerged that only 40 students had enrolled in its first year.

Scores in the 2014 Research Excellence Framework showed improvement on the previous assessments, with international politics, geography and earth science, and the Institute of Biological, Environmental and Rural Sciences (IBERS) doing particularly well. Overall, two-thirds of the research submitted was judged to be world-leading or internationally excellent, with all the submissions in computer science and art judged at this level for their external impact.

IBERS, which serves 1,500 under-graduate and research students and focuses on sustainable land use, climate change, renewable energy, and the security of food and water supplies, has been one of the main growth points. The Institute, which has a link with Bangor University, has 360 staff, making it one of Europe's largest in this field. Aber has the widest range of land-related courses in the UK and is developing an upland agricultural research centre.

The new residences are close to the existing student village and within walking distance of the Penglais and Llanbadarn campuses. They provide self-catering accommodation for 1,000 students, with a central hub that includes social and learning facilities, and there is plenty of out-of-season accommodation to supplement the university's extensive stock.

The original Old College Building is to be redeveloped as an arts centre. There is 24-hour computer network access, and the four university libraries are complemented by the National Library of Wales. Aberystwyth town is compact and travel to other parts of the UK slow, so applicants should be sure that they will be happy spending three years or more in a tight-knit community. The students' guild is the largest entertainment venue in the region. Sports facilities are good and well used, and include a 400-metre running track, 50 acres of playing fields, a 3G pitch, refurbished swimming pool, a climbing wall and specialist outdoor water sports facilities.

Tuition fees

» Fees for UK/EU students 2017–18 £9,000
» Fees for international students 2017–18 £13,200–£14,750
» Welsh Assembly non-means-tested grant to pay fees above £4,046 for Welsh students. Tuition fee grant is under review for 2018.
» Check the university's website for the latest information.

Students

Undergraduates:	6,985	(1,520)
Postgraduates:	790	(545)
Mature students:	15.7%	
International students:	13.1%	
Applications per place:	4.6	
From state-sector schools:	94.7%	
From working-class homes:	33.8%	
Satisfaction with students' union	62%	

For detailed information about sports facilities:
www.aber.ac.uk/en/sportscentre

Accommodation

Number of places and costs refer to 2016–17
University-provided places: 4,000
Percentage catered: 13%
Catered costs: £116.41 (single) a week.
Self-catered costs: £95.41 – £124.88 (single) a week.
Accommodation guaranteed for all new full-time first-year UK/EU students if conditions are met.
International students: guaranteed for fee paying students
accommodation@aber.ac.uk
www.aber.ac.uk/en/accommodation

Anglia Ruskin University

Already *Times Higher Education* magazine's Entrepreneurial University of the Year in 2014, Anglia is one of five institutions shortlisted for the 2016 Duke of York Award for University Entrepreneurship. The university's successes celebrate its work with 2,000 businesses, but also its efforts to instil entrepreneurial values among both students and staff. Many courses are recognised by industry and a large number are professionally accredited. The university has a £7-million business innovation centre in Chelmsford, which includes a Startup Lab for students to test and develop their ideas.

Three-quarters of the full-time undergraduate leavers who find jobs in the UK stay in East Anglia. The university has an innovative scheme placing graduates with the region's small firms – usually the companies that are least likely to take on those emerging from higher education.

A prototype regional university, Anglia Ruskin has campuses in Chelmsford, Cambridge and Peterborough, serving more than 35,000 students, studying at a variety of levels. There are also university centres in Harlow and King's Lynn.

The university has invested £122 million in the last six years, adding facilities such as medical simulation suites, forensic science labs, mock hospital wards and a courtroom, where students can practise their skills in safe but realistic environments. The Cambridge campus has been redeveloped at a cost of £35 million, and two buildings dedicated to Health and Social Care have been added in Chelmsford. There is also a purpose-built music centre and full-size professional theatre on the Chelmsford campus, as well as a sports hall and business centre with a high-tech Bloomberg Financial Markets Lab.

The university plans to spend another £98 million over the next four years, beginning with the development of a new site five minutes' walk from the East Road campus in Cambridge. A new science centre will open there in 2017.

Anglia was the last university to retain a polytechnic title, discarding it only in 2005. It took the name of John Ruskin, who founded the Cambridge School of Art, which evolved into one part of Anglia Ruskin.

The university is planning to grow by another 20 per cent while "driving up" entry qualifications by attracting more applicants. Other targets include exceeding the national average for student retention, achievement, satisfaction and graduate employment, thereby aiming to improve the university's position in league tables. It is a demanding agenda and undergraduate enrolments dipped slightly in 2015.

The university has a history of providing innovative courses: the BOptom (Hons)

Chelmsford Campus:
Bishop Hall Lane
Chelmsford, Essex CM1 1SQ
Cambridge Campus:
East Road
Cambridge CB1 1PT
01245 686868 (enquiries)
answers@anglia.ac.uk
www.anglia.ac.uk
www.angliastudent.com
Affiliation: MillionPlus

The Times and Sunday Times **Rankings**

Overall Ranking: **108** (last year: 108)

Teaching quality:	=19	83.5%
Student experience:	=59	84%
Research quality:	=88	5.4%
Entry standards:	124	257
Student–staff ratio:	=83	17.3
Services & facilities/student:	92	£1,676
Expected completion rate:	=103	80.6%
Good honours:	100	64.8%
Graduate prospects:	=123	56.8%

is the only qualification of its kind in the UK and the hearing aid audiology course was among the first to lead directly to registration. Paramedic science has also been added.

Anglia Ruskin was also the first UK university to sign the Rio+20 Declaration of Higher Education Institutions. Its Global Sustainability Institute, established in 2011, is building an international reputation for its research, and Anglia Ruskin is aiming to make sustainability an important part of every student's experience.

Nearly all the students attended state schools or colleges and almost 40 per cent are from the four poorest socio-economic groups. Each undergraduate has an adviser to help compile a degree package which can look at the chosen subject from different points of view to maximise future job prospects.

The results of the 2014 Research Excellence Framework showed that at least some world-leading research is undertaken in all five faculties. The best results were in music, drama and the performing arts, where 40 per cent of the research was found to have "outstanding" impact, but there were good results, too, in health subjects, media studies, and geography and environmental science.

The social scene naturally varies between the campuses, all of which are within an hour of London by train. The university offers a range of sporting facilities, from swimming and tennis to climbing and studio classes at all of the sites. Chelmsford has an on-campus sports centre with a well-equipped gym, while Cambridge also has a gym, sports centre and swimming pool.

There is limited collaboration with Cambridge University at the Cambridge Centre for Cricketing Excellence, and at the base for Anglia Ruskin's Rowing Club. The university's flourishing programme to encourage sporting participation is particularly successful at elite level in judo. Sports facilities in Cambridge will improve with the planned addition of a new pavilion, and both grass and artificial pitches, including one 3G surface. Anglia Ruskin students have access to Vivacity's clubs in Peterborough, where there are also leisure centres and a lido.

Tuition fees

» Fees for UK/EU students 2017–18 £9,250
Foundation degree £7,500
» Undergraduate courses at associated colleges
£7,750–£9,250
» UK fees are expected to increase by the rate of inflation from 2018–19 onwards.
» Fees for international students 2017–18 £11,700–£12,200
» Check the university's website for the latest information on fees, scholarships, bursaries and other forms of student support.

Students

Undergraduates:	13,090	(3,400)
Postgraduates:	1,650	(1,685)
Mature students:	35.5%	
International students:	10.4%	
Applications per place:	6.6	
From state-sector schools:	97%	
From working-class homes:	38.9%	
Satisfaction with students' union	63%	

For detailed information about sports facilities: www.anglia.ac.uk/sport

Accommodation

Number of places and costs refer to 2016–17
University-provided places: Cambridge: 1,928 (including referral rooms); Chelmsford, 511; Peterborough, 114.
Percentage catered: 0%
Self-catered costs: Cambridge: £91 – £175;
Chelmsford: £115 – £122; Peterborough £98 – £112 a week.
Most first years are accommodated. Restrictions apply.
International students: Most new students housed.
essexaccom@anglia.ac.uk; cambaccom@anglia.ac.uk
www.anglia.ac.uk/student-life/accommodation

Arts University Bournemouth

The Arts University Bournemouth (AUB) opened the first drawing studio to be built at a UK art school for 100 years in 2016. It was designed by AUB alumnus and globally renowned architect Professor Sir Peter Cook, whose first building in the UK this was. The studio, whose curved design produces a softer light for drawing, was described by RIBA judges as "like a squat Buddha, ethereal and likeable". It has already won four prizes. The project is part of a £17-million upgrading of the campus at Wallisdown, on the outskirts of Bournemouth.

The Photography Building, which opened in 2015 with flexible teaching spaces and IT suites, is another highlight. The Gallery showcases work by students and other contemporary artists, hosting talks, events and film nights to support the exhibition programme.

There is also an Enterprise Pavilion (eP) on campus to develop, attract and retain new creative businesses in the South West. The purpose-built library includes the Museum of Design in Plastics, which holds over 12,000 artefacts of predominantly 20th- and 21st-century mass-produced design and popular culture. The items are selected specifically to support the academic courses taught at the university. Laser cutting machinery and a 3-D printer feature among the high-tech equipment available to students.

The university has operated as a specialist institution since 1885 and is now one of only 15 higher education institutions in the UK devoted solely to the study of art, design and media, five of which appear in our table.

There are now around 3,000 students, who are rigorously selected. Fewer than four applicants in ten received offers in 2015 – one of the lowest rates outside Oxford and Cambridge. They take degrees in acting, architecture, dance, event management and film production, as well as art and design subjects. The university describes its courses as having an "highly practical streak" designed to give students an edge in a competitive creative world. Both applications and enrolments have grown every year since university status arrived in 2012.

Only 12 staff were entered for the 2014 Research Excellence Framework, when 43 per cent of their work was rated as world-leading or internationally excellent.

The staff includes many with experience in, and continuing engagement with, the creative industries. Students and staff work together on an innovative programme of professional practice and research, with different disciplines encouraged to work together.

Wallisdown
Poole
Dorset BH12 5HH

01202 533011
hello@aub.ac.uk (enquiries)
www.aub.ac.uk
www.aubsu.co.uk
Affiliation: GuildHE

The Times and Sunday Times Rankings

Overall Ranking: **64** (last year: 81)

Teaching quality:	=62	80.7%
Student experience:	=107	81.2%
Research quality:	116	2.4%
Entry standards:	=69	324
Student–staff ratio:	=43	14.9
Services & facilities/student:	122	£1,214
Expected completion rate:	35	91.5%
Good honours:	=107	62.2%
Graduate prospects:	=52	73.9%

The careers service provides students with subject-specific and generic advice on future employment. Industry liaison groups and visiting tutors keep the university abreast of developments in the creative industries, while alumni return regularly as lecturers.

AUB has a Skillset Media Academy in partnership with Bournemouth University, offering eight accredited courses in areas from animation to make-up for media and performance. The two universities also bid successfully to become a Screen Academy, through which Skillset recognises excellence in film and the broader screen-based media.

The most recent audit of the university by the Quality Assurance Agency resulted in the highest possible grade, commending the academic standards. The MArch programme has recently been validated by the Royal Institute of British Architects, which already validated the BA course, allowing students to qualify entirely through AUB.

More than 30 per cent of the undergraduates are from working-class homes and 96 per cent attended state schools or colleges – both figures close to the national average for AUB's subjects and entry qualifications. The low dropout rate is a point of particular pride – at only 5 per cent, it is half the university's benchmark figure. More than a third of undergraduates receive either scholarships or bursaries. Support for students arriving in 2016 includes bicycle vouchers, support for educational visits and hardship loans.

The university has 550 places in its halls of residence and flats, with priority going to overseas students and those with disabilities or other medical conditions. Most of the places are in the newest development in the centre of Bournemouth, which was completed in 2014. There is plenty of privately rented accommodation in the area. The university keeps a register of approved housing at the **www.aubstudentpad.com** website and runs accommodation days in July and August for current and prospective students to find potential housemates. Bournemouth has a large and cosmopolitan student population and one of the most vibrant club scenes outside London. The capital is less than two hours away by regular train and coach services or via good motorway links.

Tuition fees

» Fees for UK/EU students 2017–18 £9,250
  Year abroad £1,000
» The full-time fee will be held at this level for the duration of the course of study for continuing students.
» Fees for international students 2017–18 £15,000
» Check the university's website for the latest information on fees, scholarships, bursaries and other forms of student support.

Students

Undergraduates:	2,840	(40)
Postgraduates:	65	(10)
Mature students:	9.0%	
International students:	13.6%	
Applications per place:	5.6	
From state-sector schools:	96.3%	
From working-class homes:	30.4%	
Satisfaction with students' union	67%	

For detailed information about sports facilities:
www.aubsu.co.uk/activities/sports

Accommodation

Number of places and costs refer to 2016–17
University-provided places: 550
Percentage catered: 0%
Self-catered costs: £120 (single occupancy double room);
£115 – £135 (single en suite); £125 (double en suite);
£135 – £150 (single studio); £140 – £153 (double studio);
£158 (large double studio) a week
First years with medical conditions/disabilities have priority.
International students have priority.
http://aub.ac.uk/plan-visit-apply/accommodation

University of the Arts London

University of the Arts London (UAL) has been placed among the top five institutions in the world for art and design after another rise in the QS subject rankings, but is yet to reach such heights either in our institutional or subject tables. The main obstacle has been student satisfaction, which is often relatively low both in specialist art institutions and universities in London. Scores for teaching and feedback in the National Student Survey have been rising, but UAL remains near the bottom for the broader student experience.

An ambitious development plan may help in years to come: over the next five years UAL will invest more than £250 million in student facilities. A new campus is planned for London College of Fashion at the Olympic Park, one for London College of Communication is on the way at Elephant and Castle, and there will be significant redevelopment of the Camberwell College of Arts campus. Central Saint Martins has already moved into prize-winning premises in the new King's Cross development.

UAL is the biggest art and design university in Europe and the new developments will allow it to capitalise on the renewed demand for places experienced by the six constituent colleges. Five of the colleges came together as the London Institute in 1989 before becoming a university 15 years later. The five became six when Wimbledon College of Arts joined in 2006, bringing an international reputation in theatre design and the UK's largest school of theatre.

The founding members, which continue to use their own names and enjoy considerable autonomy, were Camberwell College of Arts, Central Saint Martins, Chelsea College of Arts, London College of Fashion and London College of Communication (formerly the London College of Printing). A global reputation attracts 6,600 international students and almost 3,000 from other EU countries among a total of nearly 18,000.

Applications and enrolments dropped slightly in 2015, but there had been big gains in the two previous years. The university also performed well in the 2014 Research Excellence Framework, when 83 per cent of the work submitted was considered world-leading or internationally excellent. All of it reached one of the top two categories for its external impact.

Perhaps more impressively for prospective applicants, more than half of the designers at the 2016 London Fashion Week studied at UAL, and all four nominees for the 2015 Turner Prize studied, taught or carried out research there. Business of

---

272 High Holborn
London WC1V 7EY

0207 514 6000
contact through website
www.arts.ac.uk
www.arts-su.com
Affiliation: none

The Times and Sunday Times Rankings

Overall Ranking: **109** (last year: 99)

Teaching quality:	118	76.4%
Student experience:	127	73.9%
Research quality:	72	8%
Entry standards:	=73	322
Student–staff ratio:	79	17
Services & facilities/student:	90	£1,686
Expected completion rate:	84	83.7%
Good honours:	106	62.7%
Graduate prospects:	=108	61.2%

Fashion has named Central Saint Martins as the best college in the world – and London College of Fashion as eighth best – for undergraduate courses in a ranking based on global impact, learning experience and long-term value.

Big changes were already under way before university status arrived: a £70-million development next door to the Tate Gallery produced prestigious new premises for Chelsea College of Arts, while the £200-million King's Cross development brought Central Saint Martins together on one site for the first time. The Grade II listed former granary was voted the world's best higher education building in 2012. The next two developments will bring together London College of Fashion's 5,600 students and staff for the first time in a new Olympicopolis arts quarter alongside the V&A and a 600-seat theatre for Sadler's Wells, and create a new academic extension and additional student accommodation for Camberwell College of Arts.

All the colleges make good use of visiting lecturers, who keep students abreast of developments in their field. The university also runs weekend classes and summer schools in an attempt to broaden the intake. Around a third of the undergraduates come from the four poorest socio-economic groups, while 95 per cent attended state schools or colleges. Students have access to the largest art and design specialist careers centre in the country, while the pioneering Emerging Artists Programme continues to support graduates early in their careers. The university holds the only recruitment festival tailored to the needs of creative graduates, providing access to hundreds of industry professionals for networking opportunities and advice.

The colleges vary considerably in character and facilities, although a single students' union serves them all. The university's student hub provides a central place for students to work, socialise and share ideas, as well as being the location for student services such as housing and careers. The university has 12 residences spread around the colleges. House-hunting workshops help those who have to rely on the expensive private housing market. The university owns no sports facilities, although it has arranged student discounts with a number of providers.

Tuition fees

» Fees for UK/EU students 2017–18	£9,250
Foundation degree	£9,250
Year abroad	£1,385
Placement year	£1,850

» UK fees are expected to increase by the rate of inflation from 2018–19 onwards.

» Fees for international students 2016–17   £17,230

» Check the university's website for the latest information on fees, scholarships, bursaries and other forms of student support.

Students

Undergraduates:	14,020	(485)
Postgraduates:	2,485	(785)
Mature students:	21.3%	
International students:	42.7%	
Applications per place:	7.8	
From state-sector schools:	94.8%	
From working-class homes:	33.1%	
Satisfaction with students' union	60%	

For detailed information about sports facilities:
www.arts-su.com//arts-active

Accommodation

Number of places and costs refer to 2016–17
University-provided places: 3,333
Percentage catered: 0%
Self-catered costs: £113 – £280 a week.
First-year students are offered accommodation depending on availability and if conditions are met.
Priority for disabled and students under 18, and those from outside London.
International students: guaranteed if conditions met.
www.arts.ac.uk/study-at-ual/accommodation

Aston University

Aston was one of a dozen universities to be awarded prestigious Regius professorships to celebrate the Queen's 90th birthday. Aston's is in pharmacy, one of the university's greatest strengths, but by no means the only area in which the university has shone recently.

Aston has enjoyed one of the biggest increases in applications of any university since the move to £9,000 fees. A recent analysis conducted by *Times Higher Education* magazine of the metrics to be used by the government's new Teaching Excellence Framework, produced even better results for Aston, ranking the university second in the UK for teaching quality. Only Loughborough scored better.

The university also did well in the latest research assessments, doubling the proportion of work in the top two categories to 80 per cent. Life and health sciences led the way, with business and management, politics and engineering also producing good results. New research centres in enterprise, healthy ageing, Europe, and neuroscience and child development proved their worth, and research funding is at record levels.

Aston celebrated its 50th year as a university in 2016 with a newly landscaped campus where the last of the 1970s buildings and facilities have been replaced by modern and spacious student accommodation, open green spaces and the remodelled Chancellor's Lake.

There was another 18 per cent increase in applications in 2015, enabling the university to take 67 per cent more undergraduates than in 2011, a record number. More than a third of them come with ABB or better at A level, attracted by a consistently good graduate employment record, which is the university's main selling point. Seven out of ten students have a work placement, often abroad, and the target is 100 per cent by 2020. Many later secure graduate jobs at the scene of their placement.

Set in the heart of Birmingham, the university has remained resolutely specialist in business, science and technology, languages and social science, concentrating on degrees with professional placements even when they were in decline elsewhere. Aston expects to open its own medical school in 2018, training much-needed doctors for disadvantaged communities. It will also launch new degrees in subjects such as applied physics and neurosciences.

The university has been concentrating on improving the student experience and boosting research performance, with the eventual aim of becoming a top ten university. The MyAston mobile app, used regularly by 80 per cent of students, gives access course materials and other

Aston Triangle
Birmingham B4 7ET

0121 204 4444 (admissions)
ugenquiries@aston.ac.uk
www.aston.ac.uk
www.aston.ac.uk/union
Affiliation: none

The Times and Sunday Times Rankings

Overall Ranking: **33** (last year: 30)

Teaching quality:	=44	81.9%
Student experience:	21	86.8%
Research quality:	48	25.8%
Entry standards:	46	365
Student–staff ratio:	107	19
Services & facilities/student:	37	£2,177
Expected completion rate:	=20	93.7%
Good honours:	9	86.2%
Graduate prospects:	18	82.3%

information remotely and at a time of users' own choosing.

The completion of the Aston Student Village has provided 3,000 en-suite rooms on campus, maintaining the guarantee of accommodation for all first-year students. A £215-million programme of improvements includes an impressive library and the Woodcock Sport Centre, which includes a Grade II listed swimming pool and a new sports hall with indoor courts and team sports facilities. Aston's active students' union is set to be rehoused in purpose-built premises in the middle of the campus. More chemistry and chemical engineering laboratories have been provided and £16.5 million spent on the European Bioenergy Research Institute.

Once a college of advanced technology, Aston remains strong in engineering and the sciences. It was chosen to provide undergraduate programmes in engineering and business for Muscat University, a new venture in Oman. The highly rated business school accounts for almost half of all Aston's students and will relocate to a new centralised position on campus after a £19-million revamp.

New undergraduates are offered 12 online study skills modules before the formal start of their course. Aston has also introduced a free programme of language tuition for all students, covering seven languages including Arabic and Mandarin, as part of its efforts to help boost employability further. More than a quarter of first-year students use the service.

The projected dropout rate has improved considerably in recent years and at less than 6 per cent, is ahead of the national average for Aston's subjects. The intake is diverse, with almost 42 per cent of the undergraduates coming from working-class homes, nine out of ten of whom go on to obtain graduate-level jobs. Six out of ten undergraduates come from outside the West Midlands and around a fifth from outside the UK.

Recent developments have also helped to place Aston among the top dozen universities in the People and Planet Green League of sustainability for the past five years. It was given "Platinum Eco Campus" status for demonstrating a lasting commitment to sustainability.

Tuition fees

- » Fees for UK/EU students 2017–18 £9,250
  Placement year £1,250
  Foundation degree £9,250
- » UK fees are expected to increase by the rate of inflation from 2018–19 onwards.
- » Fees for international students 2017–18 £14,000–£17,200
- » Check the university's website for the latest information on fees, scholarships, bursaries and other forms of student support.

Students

Undergraduates:	8,000	(690)
Postgraduates:	1,340	(1,035)
Mature students:	6.5%	
International students:	16.5%	
Applications per place:	6.5	
From state-sector schools:	92.7%	
From working-class homes:	42.1%	
Satisfaction with students' union	63%	

For detailed information about sports facilities:
www.aston.ac.uk/sport/

Accommodation

Number of places and costs refer to 2016–17
University-provided places: 3,017
Percentage catered: 0%
Self-catered accommodation: £117.60 – £121.10;
£124.60 – £135.45 (en suite).
First years are guaranteed accommodation if they fulfil requirements and apply by the deadline.
International fee-paying students: as above.
accom@aston.ac.uk
www.aston.ac.uk/accommodation

Bangor University

Student satisfaction has been Bangor's trump card for several years. It has had consistently the top scores in Wales in the National Student Survey, until overtaken by Aberystwyth in 2016. It is firmly established in the top 15 in the UK in *Times Higher Education*'s student experience ranking and has now seen its accommodation rated the best in the UK.

A new student village of 600 rooms opened in 2015, close to the city centre, with a range of accommodation from en-suite studio apartments to townhouses. There is also a café, shop, laundrette, student lounges, outdoor recreation and games area, a mini cinema, and performance and music space. Bangor's clubs and societies, which are free to students, have been voted the best in the UK for the last two years.

Bangor is not just about keeping the students happy, however. The university finished among the top 50 universities in the 2014 Research Excellence Framework, with half of the schools rated in the top 20 in the UK, leisure and tourism, languages and psychology leading the way.

Enrolments have been rising steadily and are now close to record levels, but relatively low scores for completion and spending on student facilities have contributed to another fall in our league table.

The small North Wales city's scenic surroundings, from Snowdonia to the sea, are among the attractions to students. Bangor is also among the cheapest places in the UK in which to study, as well as one of the safest. Much of the university estate has been redeveloped or modernised in recent years.

A £40-million Arts and Innovation Centre forms a bridge between the university's upper campus and the nearby science site. In addition to providing a new base for the Students' Union, the new centre houses a bar and café as well as a theatre, studio theatres, cinema, lecture theatres and exhibition spaces.

The main sports centre, Canolfan Brailsford, was refurbished and renamed in 2014. It has a two-storey gym, including 50 cardiovascular machines, a six-platform Olympic lifting area, two sports halls, an aerobics studio, cycling studio, gymnastics hall, climbing wall and squash courts.

Other additions include a £5-million environmental sciences building, a £3.5-million Cancer Research Institute and a Business Management Centre, part-funded by an EU grant, on a waterfront site.

The university has a community focus that dates back to a 19th-century campaign which saw local quarrymen putting part of their weekly wages towards the establishment of a college. The School of Lifelong Learning continues the tradition

---

College Road
Bangor
Gwynedd LL57 2DG

01248 383717 (admissions)
admissions@bangor.ac.uk
www.bangor.ac.uk
www.undebbangor.com
Affiliation: none

The Times and Sunday Times Rankings

Overall Ranking: **61** (last year: 52)

Teaching quality:	12	84.8%
Student experience:	=24	86.4%
Research quality:	47	27.2%
Entry standards:	=57	344
Student–staff ratio:	=76	16.9
Services & facilities/student:	104	£1,528
Expected completion rate:	=91	82.3%
Good honours:	102	64.2%
Graduate prospects:	=92	66.3%

with courses across North Wales, but the university has also built a worldwide reputation in areas such as environmental studies and ocean sciences. The 23 academic schools are all within walking distance of each other, apart from the School of Ocean Sciences, which is two miles away in Menai Bridge. The university is in the top 30 in an international league table for its green credentials.

Bangor is an expanding centre for Welsh-medium teaching. Although a majority of students come from outside Wales, around 20 per cent speak the language and one of the halls of residence is for Welsh-speakers and learners of the language.

Bangor also has a flourishing international exchange programme, which gives students the option of studying overseas for one extra year in a wide variety of destinations. In addition, there is a Peer Guiding scheme, where second- and third-year students mentor new students and arrange social activities for them, which is one of the largest schemes in the UK.

Around 95 per cent of the students come from state schools or colleges, and over a third are from working-class homes. For 2017 entry, the university is offering scholarships and bursaries worth over £3.7 million, which range from merit awards based on pre-entry examinations, to sports scholarships and awards in number of other subjects. The university's Talent Opportunities Programme, which operates in schools across North Wales, targets potential applicants from lower socio-economic families who have little or no history of going on to university.

There is a strong focus on student support, including a pioneering dyslexia service, which offers individual and group support throughout students' courses. The Study Skills Centre helps with the transition to university and provides continuing academic support.

In addition, the Bangor Employability Award (BEA) has been introduced to enhance students' career prospects by accrediting co-curricular and extracurricular activities, such as volunteering and part-time work, that are valued by employers. Social life for most students is concentrated mainly on the students' union.

Tuition fees

- » Fees for UK/EU students 2017–18 £9,000
  Year abroad / Placement year no fee
- » Fees for International students 2017–18 £12,500–£15,500
- » Welsh Assembly non-means-tested grant to pay fees above £4,046 for Welsh students. Tuition fee grant is under review for 2018.
- » Check the university's website for the latest information on fees, scholarships, bursaries and other forms of student support.

Students

Undergraduates:	7,235	(870)
Postgraduates:	1,675	(985)
Mature students:	20.0%	
International students:	14.4%	
Applications per place:	4.8	
From state-sector schools:	94.6%	
From working-class homes:	34.9%	
Satisfaction with students' union	71%	

For detailed information about sports facilities:
www.bangor.ac.uk/brailsford

Accommodation

Number of places and costs refer to 2016–17
University-provided places: around 2,900
Percentage catered: 0%
Self-catered costs: £77 – £100 (standard); £100 – £141 (en-suite, large en suite, premium en suite, premium plus en suite and deluxe en suite) a week (40–42 weeks). Also studios from £144 – £179 a week.
All first-year students are guaranteed places.
International undergraduate students: as above.
halls@bangor.ac.uk; www.bangor.ac.uk/accommodation

University of Bath

Bath has called a halt to expansion on its undergraduate courses after adding 700 places to its intake in three years. With applications rising by almost 50 per cent over the same period, the university was already among the most selective in the UK. There were over eight applicants for every place in 2015.

As it celebrates its 50th anniversary as a university, Bath is the highest-ranked institution in Europe for its age. A perennial high achiever in the National Student Survey, it is never far from the top ten in our league table. With 16,000 students, a third of whom are postgraduates, the university remains relatively small. But it has invested £215 million to improve the campus and cater for the extra students it has taken in recent years.

The modern campus on the edge of Bath cannot live up to the magnificence of the city's architecture, but the 200-acre site has pleasant grounds with a grass amphitheatre and lake, as well as conveniently placed amenities. The university is rated among the top 15 in the world in the GreenMetric environmental ranking. The Quads student accommodation complex added 700 en-suite bedrooms in 75 flats, along with a 350-seater restaurant. The Edge, which opened in 2015, has a theatre, performance studio, rehearsal studios, three galleries and a café for use by the university and the wider community.

It is also home to the School of Management's executive education training suite. Two more academic buildings opened in 2016, one for engineering and design and the other for psychology. The campus features a modern student centre and a dedicated centre for postgraduates, and Bath is also investing £4.5 million in a new learning zone and student services hub in the city centre.

The sports facilities are outstanding and were used as a training base in sports as diverse as athletics, judo, swimming and beach volleyball in the run-up to London 2012 and the Rio 2016 Olympic Games. There is a 50-metre Olympic Legacy swimming pool, indoor running track, multipurpose sports hall, eight indoor tennis courts and indoor facilities for athletics, shooting, fencing and judo. There is even a newly revamped skeleton start area, as used by Lizzy Yarnold, the 2014 Olympic gold medallist, and her predecessor Amy Williams.

Siobhan-Marie O'Connor and Jazz Carlin both won silver medals in the pool at the Rio Games, while other Bath students scored two further silvers and four bronze medals.

The university's Sports Training Village was also chosen to host the Paralympics GB team ahead of the London Olympics

Claverton Down
Bath BA2 7AY

01225 383019 (admissions)
ask-admissions@bath.ac.uk
www.bath.ac.uk
www.bathstudent.com
Affiliation: none

The Times and Sunday Times **Rankings**

Overall Ranking: **12** (last year: 12)

Teaching quality:	49	81.6%
Student experience:	39	85.1%
Research quality:	24	37.3%
Entry standards:	10	481
Student–staff ratio:	=51	15.5
Services & facilities/student:	34	£2,210
Expected completion rate:	5	96.3%
Good honours:	=12	84.5%
Graduate prospects:	7	85.4%

and para athletes continue to train at the university.

Over 1,500 students compete regularly at every level from regional leagues to national tournaments. Bath pioneered sports scholarships more than 20 years ago and there will be a range of them available for 2017. All students are encouraged to use the facilities through the 48 clubs for everything from ultimate frisbee to Latin and ballroom dancing.

Research is thriving: nearly a third of Bath's submission to the 2014 Research Excellence Framework was judged to be world-leading, with 87 per cent in the top two categories. Projects range from developing new drugs to prolong the lives of people with breast cancer and working with Ford to develop fuel-efficient engines to research into child poverty, which won a Queen's Anniversary Prize. The research grants and contracts portfolio is worth £130 million, and there are 25 international multidisciplinary strategic partnerships with top-ranked institutions worldwide.

Bath is a highly internationalised university, with over 20 per cent of its undergraduates coming from outside the UK, representing over 100 nationalities.

Most degree courses have a practical element, and assessors have praised the university for the work placements it offers. Over two-thirds of undergraduates take courses with placements, in the UK or abroad, or a period of overseas study. Graduates enjoy some of the highest rates of employment and starting salaries in the UK. Student entrepreneurship is actively encouraged through a number of initiatives and projects. Recent additions to the portfolio of courses include astrophysics, aerospace, physical health and international development.

A quarter of the undergraduates come from independent schools. Students generally like the city, which is a World Heritage site, and many take advantage of the nightlife of nearby Bristol, which is only a few minutes away by public transport.

The popular students' union has a won an award for being one of the best developed and well managed in the UK. The university's support services include a new virtual learning environment and centralised provision of advisory services.

Tuition fees

- » Fees for UK/EU students 2017–18   £9,250
  Franchised Foundation degree   £7,710
  Year abroad   £1,385
  Placement year   £1,850
- » UK fees are expected to increase by the rate of inflation from 2018–19 onwards.
- » Fees for international students 2017–18   £15,200–£19,000
- » Check the university's website for the latest information on fees, scholarships, bursaries and other forms of student support.

Students

Undergraduates:	11,180	(135)
Postgraduates:	2,130	(2,130)
Mature students:	2.5%	
International students:	21.7%	
Applications per place:	8.2	
From state-sector schools:	74.4%	
From working-class homes:	18.2%	
Satisfaction with students' union	83%	

For detailed information about sports facilities:
www.bathstudent.com/sport

Accommodation

Number of places and costs refer to 2016–17
University-provided places: 4,211
Percentage catered: 25%
Catered cost: £100 – £204 a week.
Self-catered cost: £65 (shared) – £158 (en-suite single).
First years guaranteed accommodation if conditions are met, and applications received by 1 July.
International students: as above. Exchange students are housed on a reciprocal basis.
www.bath.ac.uk/groups/student-accommodation

Bath Spa University

A record number of students started courses at Bath Spa in 2015, when a 17 per cent increase in enrolments was among the largest at any university. Applications had risen by more than 1,000 for the second year in a row, enabling the university to accelerate the gradual growth that had taken place in recent years.

To accommodate the extra students, a student village of 550 study bedrooms has opened on campus and additional housing for 460 students has been built in the city centre, where the Sion Hill Campus is home to the Bath School of Art and Design. A £6-million redevelopment there has produced specialist facilities that are some of the best in the country. They will be further augmented by the conversion of a former factory close to the River Avon, which will become an "academic incubator for the creative industries" and free up space on the university's other campuses.

The university is far from new, although it was awarded the title only in 2005. The history of its predecessor colleges goes back 160 years, and it boasts some famous alumni, including Body Shop founder Anita Roddick and Turner Prize winner Sir Howard Hodgkin. The university's Newton Park headquarters, four miles outside the World Heritage city of Bath, is in grounds landscaped by Capability Brown in the 18th century, with a handsome Georgian manor house owned by the Duchy of Cornwall as its centrepiece.

Newton Park is the base for all students except those taking art and design subjects, and provides a study environment where historic buildings blend sympathetically with modern facilities. A £70-million development completed in 2014 provides impressive new study facilities for students, particularly in the field of digital arts. By contrast, the Creative Writing Centre is housed in the 14th-century gatehouse, a scheduled ancient monument.

There is also a postgraduate centre at Corsham Court, a 16th-century manor house near Chippenham. About a third of Bath Spa's students are postgraduates, including a large cohort training to be teachers who form part of a new Institute for Education.

Bath Spa has forged a series of international partnerships to ensure that its students leave as "global citizens" with insights into the world beyond education. The university focuses on creativity, culture and enterprise, and initiated the Global Academy of Liberal Arts (GALA), which brings together a diverse range of liberal arts providers from around the world. All students have the opportunity to collect a Global Citizenship award by completing a module that covers a range of cross-cutting issues with relevance to all subjects in the

Newton Park
Newton St Loe
Bath BA2 9BN

01225 875875 (enquiries)
enquiries@bathspa.ac.uk
www.bathspa.ac.uk
www.bathspasu.co.uk
Affiliation: MillionPlus

The Times and Sunday Times **Rankings**

Overall Ranking: **75** (last year: 58)

Teaching quality:	=51	81.4%
Student experience:	=99	81.6%
Research quality:	73	7.9%
Entry standards:	=73	322
Student–staff ratio:	=100	18.5
Services & facilities/student:	91	£1,677
Expected completion rate:	=54	87.2%
Good honours:	58	72.8%
Graduate prospects:	=110	61%

arts, humanities and sciences.

The university also offers a pre-entry year for international undergraduates with language tuition, academic instruction and information on UK history and culture, as well as the opportunity to become involved in local community projects. International students now comprise 15 per cent of Bath Spa's intake.

The university is increasingly focused on a liberal arts curriculum, clustering subjects from arts, humanities, social sciences and sciences. Bath Spa is also building a reputation for expertise in the field of creative computing, with several new courses ranging from software development to gaming.

Results in the National Student Survey have been good, especially for teaching quality. Students like the "small and friendly" atmosphere.

Bath Spa also enjoyed its best-ever research assessments in 2014, when more than half of a relatively small submission was rated as world-leading or internationally excellent. The university received an 86 per cent increase in research funding as a result. It had strengthened its research capacity in key areas such as art and design and creative writing through the appointment of high-profile professors, including Fay Weldon and Gavin Turk.

Despite a setting that would seem to be a magnet for applicants from independent schools, 94 per cent of the home intake is state educated, and around a third are from working-class homes. Two-thirds of the students are female, reflecting the arts and social science bias in the curriculum, and a quarter of all students are over 25. The latest projected dropout rate of less than 7 per cent is much better than the national benchmark for the university's courses and entry grades.

The university is also proud of its environmental record and is in the top 30 in the People and Planet Green League. Sports facilities are not extensive, but a new gym in the students' union has improved them, and some of the university's sports teams do well in local competitions.

Tuition fees

» Fees for UK/EU students 2017–18 £9,250
   Franchised Foundation and first degrees £7,500–£9,250
   Year abroad £1,385
   Placement year £1,850
» UK fees are expected to increase by the rate of inflation from 2018–19 onwards.
» Fees for international students 2016–17 £11,600
» Check the university's website for the latest information on fees, scholarships, bursaries and other forms of student support.

Students

Undergraduates:	5,215	(90)
Postgraduates:	1,095	(980)
Mature students:	13.7%	
International students:	7.4%	
Applications per place:	6.3	
From state-sector schools:	94%	
From working-class homes:	33.1%	
Satisfaction with students' union	64%	

For detailed information about sports facilities:
www.bathspasu.co.uk/opps/clubsandsocs/clubs

Accommodation

Number of places and costs refer to 2016–17
University provided places: 2,260
Percentage catered: 0% (catering voucher packages available)
Self-catered: £80 – £238 a week (from 36 weeks)
First years (home/EU/overseas) are housed provided requirements are met. Residential restrictions may apply. Support available for students with accessibility requirements.
www.bathspa.ac.uk/university-life/accommodation

University of Bedfordshire

A decline of almost 8 per cent in the number of students starting degrees in 2015 was among the ten highest at any university – it was the fourth successive year in which enrolments had dropped. But Bedfordshire has been praised for its successes in widening participation, not only in enrolling students from groups that are under-represented in higher education, but also in helping them to achieve good results.

Almost all the undergraduates are state educated and more than half come from the four lowest socio-economic classes. Nearly 40 per cent of undergraduates are 21 or over on entry and nearly one in five students comes from outside the EU, many taking postgraduate courses.

Bedfordshire has also enjoyed recent success in research. The university more than doubled the number of academics it entered for the 2014 Research Excellence Framework, and was rewarded with one of the biggest increases in funding for research at any university. Almost half of the work submitted for assessment was placed in the top two categories, with social work and social policy, health subjects and English producing particularly good results. The university received the Queen's Anniversary Prize in 2013 for applied research on child exploitation, which influenced new safeguarding policy and practice.

Bedfordshire has spent £180 million on its six campuses since the university changed its identity in 2006, when the former Luton University took over De Montfort's campus in Bedford. Another £120 million has been committed for a range of projects over the next few years. The latest major development was the opening of an attractive new campus in Milton Keynes, the fastest-growing city in the UK, in 2013. University Campus Milton Keynes, which is a partnership with the local authority, opened with 100 students and is expected to expand to around 550 by 2018.

However, the bulk of Bedfordshire's students will still be on the university's town-centre site in Luton, where a new £46-million library was completed for the start of the 2016–17 academic year. A new campus centre opened there in 2010, with teaching and exhibition space as well as the students' union, information desks and a careers and employment centre.

A £40-million student halls complex with en-suite facilities, phone and high-speed internet access, a Postgraduate and Continuing Professional Development Centre and a well-equipped media arts centre have followed.

The Bedford Campus, in a leafy setting 20 minutes' walk from the town centre, has a new campus centre comprising a 280-seat auditorium and a students' union, as well as

University Square
Luton
Bedfordshire LU1 3JU

01234 400400
admissions@beds.ac.uk
www.beds.ac.uk
www.bedssu.co.uk
Affiliation: MillionPlus

***The Times and Sunday Times* Rankings**

Overall Ranking: **121** (last year: 110)

Teaching quality:	=72	80.1%
Student experience:	87	82.5%
Research quality:	=77	7%
Entry standards:	128	239
Student–staff ratio:	=86	17.4
Services & facilities/student:	61	£1,969
Expected completion rate:	119	76.3%
Good honours:	128	50.4%
Graduate prospects:	=104	61.7%

an accommodation block for 600 students. The Gateway, a £25-million teaching and learning building, opened in 2015.

The campus is home to the Education and Sport Faculty, with around 2,500 students, making it the UK's largest provider of physical education teacher training, as well as a national centre for other subjects at primary and secondary level. Another 1,000 students take subjects such as performing arts, law and business management.

The Putteridge Bury Campus, a neo-Elizabethan mansion on the outskirts of Luton, doubles as a management centre and conference venue, as well as an academic teaching space. It is also home to the Business School's postgraduate programme.

Nursing and midwifery students in the growing Faculty of Health and Social Sciences are based at the Butterfield Park campus near Luton, or at the Oxford House development in Aylesbury, Buckinghamshire. Placements are available at a wide range of hospitals, including Stoke Mandeville, Wycombe General, Luton and Dunstable, and Bedford.

Vocational courses include a portfolio of two-year Foundation degrees, which range from software development to media production and sport science. Most are taught at partner colleges across the region. The university pioneered electronic assessment, with more than 10,000 students in disciplines from accountancy to biology tested by computer.

Bedfordshire was also awarded a national centre of excellence in personal development planning and employability, aiming to link student learning with life after university. The dropout rate has improved considerably and the latest projection of 12.5 per cent is better than the national average for Bedfordshire's courses and entry qualifications.

Bedfordshire was named among the top 15 universities for its environmental record in the People and Planet League. It was the first university in England to promise not to invest in the fossil fuel industry, following a national student campaign, and is Fairtrade accredited.

Both Luton and Bedford have their share of pubs, clubs and restaurants, and London is 30–40 minutes away by train.

Tuition fees

» Fees for UK/EU students 2017–18	£9,250
Foundation degree	£6,165
Placement year	No fee

» UK fees are expected to increase by the rate of inflation from 2018–19 onwards.

» Fees for international students 2016–17 £10,500

» Check the university's website for the latest information on fees, scholarships, bursaries and other forms of student support.

Students

Undergraduates:	9,235	(2,375)
Postgraduates:	1,495	(2,550)
Mature students:	38.4%	
International students:	11.7%	
Applications per place:	7.5	
From state-sector schools:	97.6%	
From working-class homes:	50.1%	
Satisfaction with students' union	67%	

For detailed information about sports facilities: www.beds.ac.uk/sportbeds

Accommodation

Number of places and costs refer to 2016–17

University-provided places: about 2,312

Percentage catered: 0%

Self-catered costs: £86 – £172 a week.

First years are guaranteed a place, and help is available to find alternative housing in the private sector.

International students: as above.

www.beds.ac.uk/studentlife/accommodation

Bedford and Luton campus: bedfordshire@clvuk.com

Birkbeck, University of London

Birkbeck has transformed itself since higher fees triggered a nationwide collapse in part-time enrolments. Once known exclusively for part-time education, the college is now offering all its undergraduate degrees on a full-time basis, but taught in the evening. By 2018, there will be some 80 three-year undergraduate degrees available, in addition to the four-year part-time programmes that have been Birkbeck's traditional fare.

The new format has been an instant hit with students of all ages, not least because they qualify for student loans and maintenance grants. More than half of the students are now full-time, with applications almost doubling in the two years up to 2015, as more courses were added. Growth in enrolments has been restricted in the last two years, but there is scope for further expansion in 2018–19.

Like the part-timers who still have a portfolio of courses to choose from, students on the new courses appreciate the opportunity to combine daytime work with evening study and believe it will give them a head start in their chosen career when they graduate.

Birkbeck chooses not appear in our league table because the high proportion of part-timers makes it difficult to compare fairly with other universities on some measures. Its academic reputation is not in doubt, however, and it is ranked among the top 250 universities in the world by *Times Higher Education* magazine.

More than 80 per cent of its eligible academics were entered for the 2014 Research Excellence Framework and their results placed the college in the top 30 of all UK institutions. Almost three-quarters of the work submitted was rated world-leading or internationally excellent, with psychology and environmental science in the top six nationally. Archaeology, classics, finance, geology and linguistics were rated top nationally for overall satisfaction in the National Student Survey, when 87 per cent of final-year undergraduates were satisfied with their experience of the college.

Birkbeck is part of the University of London and has its own degree-awarding powers if it chose to exercise that right. For the foreseeable future, it will continue to award University of London degrees.

Founded in 1823 as a mechanics' institute, Birkbeck is based near the University of London's headquarters in Bloomsbury. However, the college expanded beyond central London for the first time in 2013. Since 2005 it had offered courses in Stratford, East London, but it now shares a new five-storey building there with the University of East London. University

---

Malet Street
Bloomsbury
London WC1E 7HX

020 7631 6000 (general enquiries)
contact via website
www.bbk.ac.uk
www.birkbeckunion.org
Affiliation: none

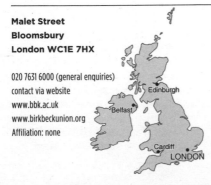

The Times and Sunday Times **Rankings**
The available data do not match the data used to rank the other full-time universities, so Birkbeck could not be included in the league table this year.

Square Stratford is the first shared project of its kind in the capital, and Birkbeck's contribution is courses in law and business as well as a BSc in community development and public policy and a Foundation degree in computing/information technology/web development. A new Foundation degree in management and accounting was introduced at both campuses in January 2017. The Stratford facilities include a 300-seat lecture theatre, learning centre, student support centre and seminar rooms for 3,400 students.

Courses are tailored to the employment market. For example, a BSc in applied accounting and business is run in collaboration with the Institute of Chartered Accountants in England and Wales, allowing trainee accountants to combine work and study to gain their qualifications at a substantially lower cost and much sooner than if they took a degree before completing their professional qualification.

Birkbeck graduates enjoy high average starting salaries – among the best in the sector – partly because many of them are mature students returning to already successful careers. A professional in-house recruitment service, Birkbeck Talent, links employers with Birkbeck students and graduates for both employment opportunities and paid internships.

Birkbeck welcomes applications from people without traditional qualifications and continues to attract non-traditional learners of all ages and backgrounds: over 40 per cent of students are from low socio-economic groups. Applicants who have taken A level or an equivalent qualification recently are made offers based on the UCAS tariff, but others are assessed by the college on the basis of interviews and/or short tests. The My Birkbeck Student Centre acts as a front door to all the college's student support services, from help in choosing courses and submitting applications to information about financial support and study skills.

Almost £20 million has been spent improving the college's buildings. Bloomsbury is easily accessible by public transport and cycle routes. Most Birkbeck students already live in the capital, but full-time students looking for housing have access to the University of London Housing Service. The College also has an agreement with UNITE, which entitles full-time Birkbeck students to apply for places in their halls of residence.

Tuition fees

» Fees for full-time UK/EU students 2017–18	£9,250
Foundation degree	£7,150
» UK fees are expected to increase by the rate of inflation from 2018–19 onwards.	
» Fees for international students 2016–17	£13,000
» Check the university's website for the latest information on fees, scholarships, bursaries and other forms of student support. .	

Students

Undergraduates:	2,340	(7,340)
Postgraduates:	1,030	(3,225)
Mature students:	66.5%	
International students:	11.8%	
Applications per place:	6.3	
From state-sector schools:	90.3%	
From working-class homes:	42.8%	
Satisfaction with students' union	58%	
For detailed information about sports facilities: www.student-central.london/activities		

Accommodation

Number of places and costs refer to 2016–17
The university has 50 places in the intercollegiate halls of residence, and these are normally reserved for full-time international students. The university also has an agreement with UNITE for self-catered places within their halls of residence.

Catered costs: £139.91 (twin) – £247.60 (en-suite single).
Self-catered: £350.66 (studio) – £428.23 (1-bed flat).
Contact: www.bbk.ac.uk/prospective/accommodation
accommodation@bbk.ac.uk

University of Birmingham

Ever an innovator in university admissions, Birmingham has introduced an online Offer Calculator to give prospective students a better idea of whether they are likely to secure a place. Two-thirds of applicants received an offer in 2015, when the demand for places rose by more than 5 per cent. The university's popularity has increased markedly since it started the trend for unconditional offers three years ago. Those who are predicted better than three As at A level are offered a place without needing to achieve set grades. In 2016, the scheme is operating in 55 subjects, from African studies and anthropology, mathematics, modern languages to social work and chemistry, and may be expanded further in 2017.

Another attraction has been Birmingham's focus on employability – the university has invested £5 million in graduate careers services and was our University of the Year for Graduate Employability in 2015. Successful alumni offer mentoring, and the university provides bursaries to support work experience and internships in the UK and overseas.

Birmingham did well in the 2014 Research Excellence Framework, when over 80 per cent of its submission was rated as world-leading or internationally excellent. Its performance took Birmingham into the top 20 for research quality and has helped to maintain its position in our top 20 overall. The university was ranked in the top five for philosophy, history, classics, theology and religion, area studies, chemical engineering, and sport, exercise and rehabilitation studies. Its current research focus includes antibiotic resistance, drone warfare and sustainable energy among a series of "global challenges" identified as priorities. Birmingham, which has a research partnership with the University of Nottingham, has one of the largest clinical trial units in Europe and recently opened the Institute of Translational Medicine. In 2015 Birmingham announced their discovery of one of the world's oldest Koran manuscripts and displayed it to the public in a collaborative exhibition with the Barber Institute and Cadbury Research Library.

Birmingham was the original "redbrick" university. The 230-acre campus in leafy Edgbaston is dominated by a 300-foot clock tower, one of the city's best-known landmarks, and boasts its own train station.

Dentistry is located in the city centre, while part of the School of Education is in Selly Oak, a mile from the Edgbaston campus. Drama is also located there, along with the BBC Drama Village, which is part of a strategic alliance between the university and the corporation. The university is part way through a long-term programme of

Edgbaston
Birmingham B15 2TT

0121 414 3344
admissions@bham.ac.uk
www.birmingham.ac.uk
www.guildofstudents.com
Affiliation: Russell Group

***The Times and Sunday Times* Rankings**

Overall Ranking: **16** (last year: 17)

Teaching quality:	61	80.8%
Student experience:	=50	84.4%
Research quality:	26	37.1%
Entry standards:	22	429
Student–staff ratio:	=31	14
Services & facilities/student:	24	£2,531
Expected completion rate:	=14	94.8%
Good honours:	10	86.1%
Graduate prospects:	=8	85.3%

investment. A new Student Services Hub has seen part of the redbrick Aston Webb Building remodelled to house a number of different services including employability, careers and a 400-seat lecture theatre. A new library building opened in September 2016, and a cultural hub will embrace new and emerging technologies for an enhanced student experience.

The sports facilities are some of the best in the country. A new sports centre boasts Birmingham's first 50-metre swimming pool, a multi sport hall, a range of activity and fitness studios, an extensive gym, six glass-backed squash courts and various other facilities.

The numbers recruited from the poorest social groups have been rising gradually. The Access to Birmingham (A2B) scheme, which encourages students from the West Midlands whose families have little or no experience of higher education to apply to university, is being extended to students in other parts of England. In 2016, students whose household income is less than £36,000 will qualify for the university's Chamberlain awards of between £1,000 and £2,000 a year.

Three-quarters of the undergraduates undertake work experience as part of their course. The university also encourages interdisciplinary study, for example allowing undergraduates to combine technology with subjects ranging from Latin or modern

Greek to the management of floods and other natural disasters.

Most of the halls and university flats are conveniently located in an attractive parkland setting near the main campus. There are more than 5,000 university-owned beds, and accommodation in the private sector is also plentiful.

The campus is less than three miles from the city centre, but the area has plenty of shops, pubs and restaurants. With its own nightclub among the facilities on campus, some students do not even stray that far, but the city is acquiring a growing reputation among the young. Other student facilities on campus are also first-rate, and include a medical practice. There is also an outdoor pursuits centre by Coniston Water in the Lake District. The Active Lifestyles Programme attracts 4,000 students to 150 different courses.

Tuition fees

» Fees for UK/EU students 2017–18   £9,250
   Placement year   £1,850
» UK fees are expected to increase by the rate of inflation from 2018–19 onwards.
» Fees for international students 2017–18   £15,210–£19,710
   Medicine   £20,250–£35,640
   Dentistry   £19,710–£35,640
» Check the university's website for the latest information on fees, scholarships, bursaries and other forms of student support.

Students

Undergraduates:	19,005	(1,095)
Postgraduates:	8,300	(5,760)
Mature students:	6.8%	
International students:	12.7%	
Applications per place:	8.0	
From state-sector schools:	80.3%	
From working-class homes:	22.8%	
Satisfaction with students' union	75%	

For detailed information about sports facilities: www.sport.bham.ac.uk

Accommodation

Number of places and costs refer to 2016–17
University-provided places: 5,184
Percentage catered: 30%
Catered costs: £121 – £188 a week.
Self-catered costs: £85 – £148 a week.
All first years are guaranteed housing (subject to conditions).
International students: as above.
www.birmingham.ac.uk/study/accommodation

Birmingham City University

Birmingham City University (BCU) has thrived since changing its name from the University of Central England in 2007. An overall investment of £260 million will see it concentrate most of its activities on two main sites by the time that new students arrive in 2017.

The university's traditional headquarters, in the northern suburb of Perry Barr, will close completely in 2018, but undergraduate teaching will have moved before then. A new building on the City South Campus, in Edgbaston will enable education to transfer from Perry Barr and will also accommodate the university's new sport and life sciences courses. The campus already has a prize-winning library, IT suites, teaching facilities and recreational space.

At the same time, Birmingham Conservatoire – perhaps BCU's best-known feature – will move into a new home on the growing City Centre Campus, which the university hopes will prove attractive both to students and private sector partners. The campus, close to the eventual HS2 rail terminus, includes the Curzon Building, opened in 2015, which houses all student support services as well as business, law, social science and English. The Parkside Building, opened two years previously, serves the university's highly regarded courses in art

and design and media, and contains what is claimed to be the largest university broadcast centre in the UK and the country's largest "green-screen studio" for special effects sequences. The university also occupies part of the Millennium Point building, helping to create Birmingham's Eastside Learning Quarter.

Meanwhile, the Bournville Campus hosts a new college offering preparatory courses for overseas students to support the university's international ambitions. These include the establishment of the Birmingham Institute of Fashion and Creative Art in Wuhan, China, in partnership with Wuhan Textile University. The Institute is expected to have 3,500 students studying architecture, visual communication and digital media technology by 2022.

Enrolments have risen for three years in a row, some attracted by the prospect of unconditional offers for those who achieve BBC at AS level or a DMM profile in BTEC qualifications and make the university their first choice. In 2015, the university was only just outside the top 20 for the volume of applications.

There are strong links with business and the professions, including pioneering work in green technology, which is attracting support from national and regional partners. There is a strong emphasis on making graduates "job-ready", with support schemes and work placements among a raft of

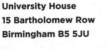

University House
15 Bartholomew Row
Birmingham B5 5JU

0121 331 5595 (enquiries)
www.bcu.ac.uk/courses/choices
www.bcu.ac.uk
www.bcusu.com
Affiliation: none

The Times and Sunday Times Rankings

Overall Ranking: **=93** (last year: 105)

Teaching quality:	=51	81.4%
Student experience:	103	81.5%
Research quality:	=97	4.3%
Entry standards:	84	316
Student–staff ratio:	=108	19.1
Services & facilities/student:	80	£1,788
Expected completion rate:	58	86.5%
Good honours:	95	65.2%
Graduate prospects:	80	69.1%

initiatives designed to help develop skills and knowledge for the workplace. Students have access to learning tools such as Shareville – a virtual learning environment where students can engage with real-life scenarios.

The Faculty of Business, Law and Social Sciences offers a number of three-year professional practice courses, where the first two years of a degree are studied on campus, while the final year is completed and assessed in the workplace.

Several degrees in the Faculty of Computing, Engineering and the Built Environment are available as four-year integrated Master's awards, offering seamless progression from a Bachelor's to a Master's degree. The university has launched a range of scholarships and bursaries to encourage undergraduates to stay on for postgraduate study.

Six out of ten students come from the West Midlands, many from ethnic minorities and nearly 47 per cent from the poorest socio-economic groups. The university is working with schools in the region to encourage more young people to go on to higher education. Many students enter through the network of associated further education colleges, which run foundation and access programmes.

The prize-winning Student Academic Partners scheme has spawned a formal agreement between the university and the students' union to improve the student experience. A new student enquiry service,

"Ask", handles all student queries either in person at helpdesks, over the phone or online.

The university made a relatively small submission to the 2014 national research assessments, but 60 per cent of the work reached the top two categories and almost 90 per cent was judged to have delivered "outstanding" or "very considerable" external impact. Most research is applied, with an accent on employment in the region.

University accommodation is guaranteed for first years whose homes are more than ten miles from their place of study. Another 650 rooms for students on the City Centre Campus are planned for 2016–17. The city's student scene is highly rated and has become a draw for many young applicants.

Tuition fees

» Fees for UK/EU students 2017–18		£9,250
Placement year		no fee
Foundation degree		£6,165

» UK fees are expected to increase by the rate of inflation from 2018–19 onwards.

» Fees for international students 2017–18		£12,000
Conservatoire and acting		£15,500

» Check the university's website for the latest information on fees, scholarships, bursaries and other forms of student support.

Students

Undergraduates:	16,395	(2,810)
Postgraduates:	1,980	(2,150)
Mature students:	24.3%	
International students:	9.0%	
Applications per place:	7.0	
From state-sector schools:	97.6%	
From working-class homes:	46.9%	
Satisfaction with students' union	71%	

For detailed information about sports facilities:
www.bcusu.com/sports

Accommodation

Number of places and costs refer to 2016–17
University-provided places: 2,418
Percentage catered: 0%
Self-catered costs: £90.00 (standard) – £132.50 (extra-large); 2-bed city-centre flats from £128.00 a week (39–43, 51 weeks).
Accommodation guaranteed for first years if conditions are met.
International students are guaranteed accommodation.
www.bcu.ac.uk/student-info/accommodation

University College Birmingham (UCB)

University College Birmingham (UCB) will be one of only two universities in England not to charge the maximum £9,250 fee for UK and EU undergraduates in 2017–18. Its degrees will cost £9,076 and Foundation degrees £7,500. Indeed, it will have the lowest fees of any university after allowing for fee waivers, at £8,648.

UCB is also unique among UK universities in having a third of its students taking further education programmes. It believes that would place it at a disadvantage in league tables such as ours, so it has again instructed the Higher Education Statistics Agency not to release its data. Consequently, UCB does not appear in our main league table or any of the subject tables. Nevertheless, it was above average for overall satisfaction in the 2016 National Student Survey after a rise of 4 percentage points, and it claims the lowest rate of complaints from students through the Office of the Independent Adjudicator. There was a 21 per cent increase in applications in 2015, the second successive year of substantial growth.

UCB chose not to change its name when full university status arrived in 2013, in order to preserve its identity. It was the largest of a dozen colleges to become universities, with more than 5,000 higher education students and nearly 2,500 taking further education courses. The university traces its history back more than 100 years to the foundation of a Municipal Technical School offering cookery and household science courses. It has had degree awarding powers since 2007, although some degrees are still accredited by the University of Birmingham.

The core subjects are hospitality, tourism, business, sport and education. The most recent Ofsted inspection rated the further education provision as outstanding, while 100 per cent of students in the most recent exit survey rated their postgraduate teacher training as good or better. UCB has an international reputation in hospitality and tourism, with about a third of the students coming from outside the UK.

Based in the city centre, UCB is located close to the International Convention Centre, Symphony Hall and the Library of Birmingham, as well as the main shopping areas. The main campus is at Summer Row, with New Street station a five-minute walk away.

UCB is investing £60 million on new teaching facilities in Birmingham's historic Jewellery Quarter – just a short walk from the main campus. The four-storey first phase of the development, which opened in 2014, won an architectural prize. It features dedicated facilities for undergraduate and

---

Summer Row
Birmingham B3 1JB

0121 604 1040 (admissions)
admissions@ucb.ac.uk
www.ucb.ac.uk
www.ucbguild.org.uk
Affiliation: GuildHE

The Times and Sunday Times **Rankings**
University College Birmingham blocked the release of data from the Higher Education Statistics Agency and so we cannot give any ranking information.

postgraduate study, a flexible learning centre, three lecture theatres, teaching rooms, IT facilities and a café. Phase Two will see the development of a new campus, which may allow new subjects to be added. Existing specialist teaching facilities include high-quality training kitchens, commercial training restaurants, a full bakery, and a new £2-million Food Science and Innovation Suite.

The university focuses on giving students an advantage in the highly competitive graduate job market. Many courses include full- or half-year industrial placements, including overseas opportunities in the USA, Hong Kong, Canada and Europe.

As well as arranging placements, the expanded careers and employability team, hired@UCB, provides students with support to develop skills, such as communication, teamwork, problem solving and time management, through work experience, workshops, volunteering, and part time and seasonal work. The Unitemps service finds suitable part-time employment opportunities for students during their studies.

UCB has one of the most socially diverse student bodies in the country – more than half are from a black or minority ethnic background. Student ambassadors promote further and higher education to young people from a range of backgrounds. Almost all the undergraduates are state educated and 53 per cent come from the four poorest socio-economic groups. Retention rates are good for some groups, but the projected dropout rate for all undergraduates remains significantly worse than the national average for UCB's courses and entry qualifications, at nearly 19 per cent.

More than 1,000 students can be accommodated in UCB's halls of residence, and accommodation can be offered to all years and programmes of study. The Maltings halls are a ten minute walk from UCB, and Cambrian Hall is only 150 yards from the main campus. Both offer among the best value in the Midlands. The Spa offers hairdressing salons, beauty therapy suites, a sports therapy clinic, a multi-gym, and a fitness assessment suite. There is also a gym and sports hall at The Maltings site. Two restaurants staffed by the university's students are open to the public, as well as to students and staff.

Tuition fees

» Fees for UK/EU students 2017–18   £9,076
  Placement term or year   no fee
» UK fees are expected to increase by the rate of inflation from 2018–19 onwards.
» Fees for international students 2016–17   £9,600
» Check the university's website for the latest information on fees, scholarships, bursaries and other forms of student support.

Students

Undergraduates:	3,605	(775)
Postgraduates:	355	(120)
Satisfaction with students' union	71%	

For detailed information about sports facilities: www.ucb.ac.uk/facilities/gym-and-sports.aspx

Accommodation

Number of places and costs refer to 2016–17
University-provided places: 1,074
Percentage catered: 0%
Self-catered costs: £86 (shared); £95 (standard); £105 (en suite); £156 (twin) (42 weeks).
Priority is given to disabled students (new and returning) and new full-time students by application date.
International students: guaranteed housing if conditions are met.
Contact: www.ucb.ac.uk/student-life/accommodation

Bishop Grosseteste University

Bishop Grosseteste (BGU) has been expanding its intake in pursuit of a five-year plan to double the number of students it educates. Currently one of the UK's smallest universities, it is aiming for 4,500 students by 2019, and took an additional 100 undergraduates in 2015 as part of this process. It was the fourth year in a row in which enrolments had grown, during which time the proportion of applicants receiving offers has shot up from 50 per cent to 80 per cent. The expansion will include more students from non-traditional backgrounds and more mature students taking work-based courses, as well as increases in the numbers of postgraduates and research students.

At the same time, the university is aiming improve already high levels of student retention, satisfaction and graduate employment. A 2016 review by the Quality Assurance Agency highlighted several areas in which BGU excelled, including employability, rigorous monitoring of standards, student support and a student-centred approach to learning and teaching.

The latest graduate employment data backs this up, ranking BGU third in the UK for outright employment with 97.2 per cent of graduates in work or further study within six months of leaving. Under our analysis, which looks specifically at graduate-level employment, however, BGU ranks 87th, a less impressive performance.

Based on an attractive, leafy campus in uphill Lincoln, not far from the cathedral and castle, Bishop Grosseteste celebrated 150 years of teacher training in 2012. The former university college used to be too small to become a university, but a change of rules allowed it to take the title in 2013.

Named after a theologian and scholar who was bishop of Lincoln in the 13th century, BGU is still proudly associated with the Church of England, although it welcomes students of all faiths and none. It describes itself as a Church university within the Anglican tradition.

The campus has been gearing up for a larger intake. The former college canteen and dining room has been turned into teaching accommodation, and building work has started on more teaching and learning space, which will be ready for the September 2017 intake. A new complex of flats has replaced an older hall of residence, and together with the extensive refurbishment of an existing hall, has brought the number of campus rooms to more than 200.

The university entrance and reception area has been remodelled at a cost of £250,000. Other recent developments have seen the campus theatre equipped with a

Longdales Road
Lincoln LN1 3DY

01522 583658 (admissions)
admissions@bishopg.ac.uk
www.bishopg.ac.uk
www.bgsu.co.uk
Affiliations: GuildHE,
Cathedrals Group

The Times and Sunday Times Rankings

Overall Ranking: **95** (last year: =112)

Teaching quality:	6	86.3%
Student experience:	=26	86.2%
Research quality:	118	2.1%
Entry standards:	=115	287
Student–staff ratio:	127	25.1
Services & facilities/student:	126	£1,031
Expected completion rate:	=40	90%
Good honours:	=77	67.9%
Graduate prospects:	87	67.1%

new digital projection system, surround sound and fully refurbished seating to double as a cinema which can also stage theatrical productions. The Venue is now home to the Lincoln Film Society and is open to staff, students and the public.

The library has been extended and given a new name: the Cornerstone Building. It houses the Student Advice and Learning Development teams, as well as Library Services. A business start-up centre on campus is popular with new businesses and entrepreneurs. BG Futures differs from other incubation centres by emphasising the university's values of equality and diversity.

The strategic plan envisages broadening the range of courses on offer. Business (team entrepreneurship), health and social care, sociology, psychology and counselling, and history and archaeology were introduced in 2015. The portfolio covers a range of arts and social sciences, but teacher training still dominates.

A new report by Ofsted rates the courses for early years, primary and secondary teachers as "Good". The inspectors praised the high quality of training and effective partnerships between the university and schools, adding that "university tutors' involvement in current educational research provides a sharp edge to the training programme." BGU's introduction of courses leading to Early Years Teacher Status has meant that, for the first time, BGU is training teachers of every age group, including adults.

The university is divided into three schools: Teacher Development, Humanities and Social Sciences. A popular psychology degree, which attracted twice the target enrolment when it was introduced in 2013, has been awarded accreditation by the British Psychological Society. Only 11 staff entered the 2014 Research Excellence Framework, but some work was classed as "world-leading" in education, English and history, the three subjects in which the university was assessed.

The Sport and Fitness Centre has a sports hall which can cater for a variety of different sporting activities and fitness classes and a well-appointed fitness suite. Ten acres of sports fields are close by. The city of Lincoln is one of the fastest-growing in the UK, with relatively low living costs. It may not compete with the big cities for youth culture, but it has a growing student population and a range of bars and nightclubs to serve it.

Tuition fees

- » Fees for UK/EU students 2017–18 £9,250
  Foundation degree £6,938
- » UK fees are expected to increase by the rate of inflation from 2018–19 onwards.
- » Fees for international students 2017–18 £11,500
- » Check the university's website for the latest information on fees, scholarships, bursaries and student support.

Students

Undergraduates:	1,730	(10)
Postgraduates:	355	(200)
Mature students:	41.8%	
International students:	0%	
Applications per place:	3.1	
From state-sector schools:	97.7%	
From working-class homes:	44%	
Satisfaction with students' union	68%	

For detailed information about sports facilities:
www.bishopg.ac.uk/student/sportscentre

Accommodation

Places and costs refer to 2016–17
University-provided places: 217 on campus; 76 off campus.
Percentage catered: 0%
Self-catered costs: £101 – £126 a week (33 or 44 weeks).
Priority is given to disabled and new full-time students on a first come, first served basis.
International students: limited accommodation is available.
www.bishopg.ac.uk/student/accommodation

University of Bolton

Having attracted the biggest increase in applications of any university in 2015, Bolton is planning a step change in size by merging with the town's further education college and another in nearby Bury. Both are already partner colleges offering some Bolton courses. Although the 2015 applications did not turn into increased enrolments despite a 27 per cent increase in offers, the university has taken on a new lease of life recently. It is preparing to move its student accommodation, law school and head office into the centre of Bolton, while also investing heavily in its main campus.

A £40-million student village on council-owned land will house 850 students, replacing two existing halls with smaller capacity.

Another collaboration with the council and local NHS produced the Bolton One development, a £31-million health, leisure and research centre on the main campus. It boasts a multi-sports hall, climbing wall and a sports and spinal injuries clinic, as well as a 25-metre competition swimming pool and a therapeutic hydrotherapy pool, fitness suite and community gym.

A new Health Sciences Faculty is teaching biomedical sciences and subjects allied to health and dentistry, and a £10-million facility for science and engineering is on the way. A University Technical College for 14–19 year-olds has opened, and new all-weather sports facilities and a Creative Industries and Technologies Centre to house the industry-leading special effects courses will follow in 2017.

The university traces its roots back 190 years to one of the country's first three mechanics institutes. The student population is one of the most ethnically diverse in the UK, with around a quarter of British students coming from ethnic minority communities. Just under 40 per cent of the undergraduates are 21 or over on entry and more than a quarter study part-time – a significant proportion at a time when part-time numbers have plummeted nationally.

Bolton exceeds all the access measures designed to widen participation in higher education: over half of the undergraduates are from working-class homes and the proportion from areas without a tradition of higher education is among the highest in the UK, at almost 25 per cent. The downside is that, despite successive big improvements, the projected dropout rate remains significantly higher than the national average for Bolton's courses and entry qualifications, at more than 20 per cent.

Perhaps Bolton's most surprising claim to fame is that it is the first university to host a professional motor racing team. Based at the purpose-built Centre for Advanced Performance Engineering (CAPE), which

Deane Road
Bolton BL3 5AB

01204 903394 (admissions)
admissions@bolton.ac.uk
www.bolton.ac.uk
www.boltonsu.com
Affiliation: MillionPlus

The Times and Sunday Times **Rankings**

Overall Ranking: **124** (last year: =123)		
Teaching quality:	=38	82.4%
Student experience:	=99	81.6%
Research quality:	113	2.9%
Entry standards:	=112	290
Student–staff ratio:	60	15.9
Services & facilities/student:	125	£1,136
Expected completion rate:	127	71%
Good honours:	123	55%
Graduate prospects:	115	59.1%

offers degree courses in automotive performance engineering and motorsport technology, the team is run in conjunction with a motorsports company. Students work and learn alongside engineers and mechanics from the team, as well as the university's mechanical engineering lecturers.

General engineering was one of two areas to see a majority of their work rated as world-leading or internationally excellent in the 2014 Research Excellence Framework. The best results were in English and almost a third of the university's submission reached the top two categories. About 1,100 of its students are postgraduates, taking qualifications up to and including PhDs.

The university has partner colleges in several Asian countries and a branch campus in the United Arab Emirates. The Ras al-Khaimah campus opened in 2008, offering a range of undergraduate and postgraduate courses identical to those taught at Bolton. The £1-million development near Dubai is designed to take 700 students. Those at Bolton have the opportunity to study in the UAE for part of their degree course.

Earlier rationalisation of sites has provided additional and enhanced teaching space, facilities to interact with industry and a new students' union. In 2013, the university launched the Bolton Business School, which hosts business, law and accountancy courses, along with the Centre of Islamic Finance.

The building programme at the Deane Campus has included a design studio and three floors of teaching and learning space where students work on actual briefs for companies seeking design solutions. Within the Innovation Factory is a new social learning zone which includes students' union offices, advice centre, bar and social facilities, plus a computer access room.

Bolton has partnered with the owners of ten dental practices in the North of England to offer a state-of-the-art practice on campus and new clinical simulation facilities in Bolton One, where the university has launched a range of dental courses with their input and support. There are new degrees in advanced dental nursing and dental hygiene and therapy, and a Diploma of higher education for clinical dental technicians.

Tuition fees

» Fees for UK/EU students 2017–18 £9,246
Courses at partner colleges £7,500
Placement year £500
Year abroad £1,350
» UK fees are expected to increase by the rate of inflation from 2018–19 onwards.
» Fees for international students 2017–18 £12,000
» Check the university's website for the latest information on fees, scholarships, bursaries and other forms of student support.

Students

Undergraduates:	3,920	(1,370)
Postgraduates:	470	(620)
Mature students:	36.8%	
International students:	6.9%	
Applications per place:	5.8	
From state-sector schools:	99.2%	
From working-class homes:	52.5%	
Satisfaction with students' union	71%	

For detailed information about sports facilities:
www.bolton.ac.uk/Sport/Home.aspx

Accommodation

Number of places and costs refer to 2016–17
University-provided places: 381
Percentage catered: 0%
Self-catered costs: £80 a week (38 weeks).
All first years are generally accommodated.
International students: as above.
accomm@bolton.ac.uk
www.bolton.ac.uk/accommodation

Bournemouth University

Bournemouth will have invested £200 million in new buildings and equipment by the end of 2018, and there is more to come.

A new student centre opened in 2015 and the five-storey Fusion Building opened on the main Talbot campus, in Poole, in 2016. Gateway buildings for the Poole and Bournemouth campuses will be next major projects. They will add to the already impressive media facilities and provide a new home for the Faculty of Health and Medical Sciences by 2019. The university has risen 20 places in our league table this year.

Such is the university's strength in media subjects that 60 animation graduates worked on the Oscar-winning film *Gravity*, another won a BAFTA for special effects on *Star Wars: the Force Awakens* and yet more worked on the 2016 Oscar winner, *Ex Machina*.

Bournemouth was designated as England's only centre for excellence in media practice and hosts the National Centre of Computer Animation. Its state-of-the-art equipment includes a motion capture facility for real-time animation, which is used in teaching and available for use by outside companies.

There have also been successes in other areas. The university's decision to invest £1 million a year on academic appointments and the fusion of teaching and research paid off in the 2014 Research Excellence Framework, when 60 per cent of the university's entry was judged to be world-leading or internationally excellent. It was one of the biggest proportions at any post-1992 university and a considerable improvement on previous results, with Bournemouth finishing top in the UK for tourism research.

The university appointed 150 academics in three years to "foster the development of an academically led culture". Its Fusion Investment Fund is designed to promote "the combination of inspirational teaching, world-class research and the latest thinking in the professions".

All Honours degree students have the opportunity to do work experience as part of their courses. Even in 2013, almost 90 per cent of undergraduates were taking up the offer, the highest proportion in the UK. The policy has improved graduates' employment prospects. The retail management degree, for example, notched up eight successive years of full employment. Both applications and enrolments have been rising, although relatively modest scores in the National Student Survey have held the university back in our league table.

Virtually all students take up the offer of personal development planning, both online and with trained staff, while 1,400 first years also take advantage of peer-assisted

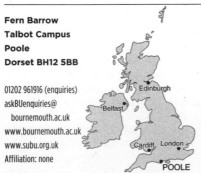

Fern Barrow
Talbot Campus
Poole
Dorset BH12 5BB

01202 961916 (enquiries)
askBUenquiries@
  bournemouth.ac.uk
www.bournemouth.ac.uk
www.subu.org.uk
Affiliation: none

POOLE

The Times and Sunday Times Rankings

Overall Ranking: **62** (last year: =82)

Teaching quality:	=103	78.2%
Student experience:	=92	82.1%
Research quality:	=64	9%
Entry standards:	=73	322
Student–staff ratio:	=83	17.3
Services & facilities/student:	49	£2,112
Expected completion rate:	67	85.5%
Good honours:	=33	77.9%
Graduate prospects:	65	71.6%

learning, receiving advice and mentoring from more experienced undergraduates. Bournemouth has been increasing its use of education technology, for example to enable its part-time students to study from home or the workplace in order to reduce the amount of time they need spend on campus.

In 2015–16, nearly quarter of undergraduates received either a scholarship or a bursary. In addition, the Global Horizons Fund helps students and staff to travel overseas for study, research or work or life experience. For international students, the new Bournemouth International College provides preparatory courses in English and study skills.

The university claims a number of firsts in its portfolio of courses, notably in the areas of tourism, media-related programmes and conservation. Degrees in public relations, retail management, scriptwriting and tax law were all ahead of their time.

Foundation degrees are delivered in four further education colleges in Dorset and Somerset, as well as on the main campus. They support the needs of business in the creative arts, media and tourism. Top-up courses are available for those who wish to turn their qualification into an Honours degree. Bournemouth is also expanding postgraduate opportunities, promising up to 100 doctoral places each year until 2018, many of them fully funded. A total of 33 different professional bodies accredit Bournemouth's degrees.

The subject mix and an increasingly fashionable seaside location, between the World Heritage Jurassic Coast and the New Forest National Park, attract more middle-class students than at most new universities, although nearly 94 per cent attended state schools. The campuses are served by a subsidised bus service and students are discouraged from bringing cars.

The students' union's Old Fire Station bar is among many nightlife options. Sports facilities have been improving following a refurbishment of the gym, with the addition of a new multipurpose large studio. There is a wide range of accommodation: students based in halls of residence in Poole enjoy a millionaire's view of the harbour. The university finished in the top ten in the 2015 People and Planet Green League of environmental performance and has an EcoCampus Gold Award, as well as holding Fairtrade status.

Tuition fees

- » Fees for UK/EU students 2017–18 £9,250
  Foundation degree £6,000
- » The fees will remain the same for students once they have enrolled.
- » Fees for international students 2017–18 £13,500
- » Check the university's website for the latest information on fees, scholarships, bursaries and other forms of student support.

Students

Undergraduates:	12,005	(2,765)
Postgraduates:	1,760	(1,695)
Mature students:	19.3%	
International students:	8.7%	
Applications per place:	5.6	
From state-sector schools:	93.3%	
From working-class homes:	31.4%	
Satisfaction with students' union	78%	

For detailed information about sports facilities:
http://microsites.bournemouth.ac.uk/sportbu

Accommodation

Number of places and costs refer to 2016–17
University-provided places: about 3,200
Percentage catered: 2%
Catered costs: from £173 a week
Self-catered costs: £97 – £141 (single en suite); £139 – £166 (single studio) a week including bus pass.
The university expects to offer all first years a place to live. Residential restrictions apply.
International students: guaranteed if conditions are met.
www1.bournemouth.ac.uk/discover/accommodation

University of Bradford

Bradford is celebrating its 50th anniversary by launching a new scholarship for each year of its existence. Always one of the most diverse of the pre-1992 universities, it draws 58 per cent of its undergraduates from the four poorest socio-economic groups.

Professor Brian Cantor, who made a surprise move from York in 2013 to become vice-chancellor, says the university also has "truly brilliant research and teaching", particularly in engineering, the life sciences, health sciences, business, international studies and political sciences. He is concentrating on those strengths to rebuild self-confidence at Bradford, which had dropped almost 30 places in our league table in ten years and remains stuck in the mid-70s in the table.

The near-stationary overall ranking this year masks its improvement in six of our nine measures, including completion rates and graduate prospects. But these gains were offset by a slump in scores for teaching quality and student experience, measured in the annual National Student Survey, with Bradford now in the bottom 20 for teaching quality nationally.

Bradford is perhaps best known as a pioneer of the green policies that have swept UK universities. In 2016, it was rated as the greenest university in the country and eighth in the world for its sustainable architecture, innovative technologies and other green initiatives.

The university's £120-million modernisation plan is keeping it at the forefront of that movement. The new Bright Building, where the re:centre links the university with local business, was given the highest ever environmental rating at a higher education institution. Built almost entirely from natural and/or recycled products, it took that title from the university's sustainable student village. The Green, with its 1,000 rooms, was the most visible sign of the "ecoversity" programme, which addressed issues of sustainable development in all the university's practices, including the curriculum. Having reduced its carbon footprint by 35 per cent and saved in excess of £7 million, Bradford was named among the top six universities in the world for carbon reduction.

An estates plan that will eventually cost £260 million includes new and upgraded teaching facilities and a major refurbishment of the library, which attracted a Green Gown award for its insulation and natural ventilation. Other recent developments include a £1.5-million engineering laboratory containing equipment that can be used across the engineering disciplines. More than £5 million has been spent on modernising the biomedical science laboratories, the

---

Richmond Road
Bradford
BD7 1DP

0800 073 1225; 0300 456 2666
course-enquiries@bradford.ac.uk
www.bradford.ac.uk
www.bradfordunisu.co.uk
Affiliation: none

The Times and Sunday Times Rankings
Overall Ranking: **76** (last year: 75)

Teaching quality:	116	76.9%
Student experience:	84	83%
Research quality:	=62	9.2%
Entry standards:	=76	321
Student–staff ratio:	=61	16
Services & facilities/student:	57	£2,004
Expected completion rate:	=81	84%
Good honours:	46	75.4%
Graduate prospects:	36	78.8%

forensic enhancement suite, clinical skills and aseptic suites. An Integrated Learning Centre is being developed for the Faculty of Life Sciences that will feature human patient simulators and dedicated facilities for scholarship in pathology and anatomy. The university is also leading a £12-million programme to create a Digital Health Zone for the city to develop new healthcare products and links with practitioners.

Around 15 per cent of the university's students are from overseas, many of them taught in partner institutions in Singapore, Brunei, Malaysia, Pakistan and India. A number of local further education colleges offer Bradford Foundation degrees in areas such as public sector administration, community justice, engineering technology and enterprise in IT. At degree level, too, most courses have a vocational slant, many offering work experience or placements, which regularly place Bradford well up the employment tables. Other distinctive features include the world-renowned peace studies department and a highly rated School of Management, whose distance learning MBA is ranked in the top ten in the world by the *Financial Times*.

A separate online portal is available to applicants and new students to smooth their transition to higher education. Computer-assisted learning is increasing in many subjects, making use of unusually extensive IT provision and a new wireless network.

The university entered less than a quarter of eligible academics for the 2014 assessments of research, but their work produced good results. Almost three-quarters of it was rated in the top two categories, with allied health, management and archaeological science producing particularly good grades. There were also high scores for the impact of Bradford's research in archaeology, politics and management.

The sports facilities have been improved with the addition of a gym, climbing wall, and sports hall. Bradford has recently been awarded £500,000 by the Premier League and the Football Association for a sports hub for students and the local community with a floodlit, 3G football pitch, four tennis courts, refurbished changing pavilion and conditioning suite. Places in halls are reasonably priced and all have internet connections. Bradford has particularly good provision for disabled students, who account for 6 per cent of the university population.

Tuition fees

- » Fees for UK/EU students 2017–18   £9,250
  Placement year   £925
- » UK fees are expected to increase by the rate of inflation from 2018–19 onwards.
- » Fees for international students 2017–18   £14,250–£16,970
- » Check the university's website for the latest information on fees, scholarships, bursaries and other forms of student support.

Students

Undergraduates:	8,025	(795)
Postgraduates:	860	(1,840)
Mature students:	23.4%	
International students:	14.9%	
Applications per place:	7.3	
From state-sector schools:	96.7%	
From working-class homes:	58.3%	
Satisfaction with students' union	78%	

For detailed information about sports facilities:
www.bradford.ac.uk/unique

Accommodation

Number of places and costs refer to 2016–17
University-provided places: 1,026
Percentage catered: 0%
Self-catered costs: £104.30 (standard) – £112.84 (en suite) a week (42 weeks).
All first-year undergraduate students are guaranteed accommodation (terms and conditions apply).
accommodation@bradford.ac.uk
www.bradford.ac.uk/student/accommodation

University of Brighton

Brighton is planning a series of new developments after seeing the volume of applications rise by eight times the national average in 2015. In the event, only 170 additional students started degrees, but that still took the total back to the levels seen before £9,000 fees were introduced. The university's fashionable seaside location is one draw for students, as are the modern campuses, which have seen more than £100 million of investment in the past decade.

Brighton was the first post-1992 university to raise money from the bond markets to fund further campus improvements. In the next phase, an advanced engineering building is under construction on the Moulsecoomb campus, in Brighton itself, where £29 million is being invested in new teaching facilities and social space. Another academic building and 1,300 student bedrooms are also planned there. Meanwhile at nearby Varley Park, £27 million has been spent on new halls of residence and support facilities, with further redevelopment planned.

There are 21,000 students on five campuses. In central Brighton, a development has provided a new home for photography, moving image, and film and screen studies. The School of Education, as well as languages and literature students, moved into a new building on the Falmer Campus, which now also boasts a £7.3-million sports centre. The university's wealth of teaching facilities are designed to build real-life skills, and include a radio station and TV studio, a podiatry hospital, a physiotherapy clinic, a flight simulator, rapid prototyping facilities, industrial textile rooms, and a clinical skills and simulation suite for nursing students.

At Eastbourne there is a modern library and extensive leisure and sports facilities. Sport science laboratories and 354 en-suite residential places have been added, and improvements made to the learning resources centre, lecture theatres and refectory. In addition, a new academic building has opened in Hastings and facilities for the College or Arts and Humanities are being expanded on the Grand Parade campus in Brighton, which also hosts the Design Council's national archive.

Brighton was one of the first post-1992 universities to be awarded a medical school. Run jointly with Sussex University, the school is now training almost 140 doctors a year. Its headquarters, on Brighton's Falmer Campus, has also provided a new base for applied social sciences, such as criminology and applied psychology.

The two universities have been collaborating since Brighton was a polytechnic, and there is a joint research

Mithras House
Lewes Road
Brighton BN2 4AT

01273 600900 (switchboard)
admissions@brighton.ac.uk
www.brighton.ac.uk
www.bsms.ac.uk
www.brightonsu.com
Affiliation: none

The Times and Sunday Times Rankings
Overall Ranking: **104** (last year: 90)

Teaching quality:	107	77.6%
Student experience:	119	79.5%
Research quality:	=73	7.9%
Entry standards:	=92	305
Student–staff ratio:	=86	17.4
Services & facilities/student:	109	£1,426
Expected completion rate:	80	84.1%
Good honours:	=84	66.9%
Graduate prospects:	68	71.3%

building for science policy and management studies.

The university is also engaged in imaginative regional initiatives. Its campus in Hastings, which focuses on digital and broadcast media, runs a number of schemes to draw people from the region into higher education. More than nine out of ten courses include a placement or the option of a sandwich year. The four-year fashion textiles degree, for example, offers work placements in the USA, France and Italy, as well as Britain.

Brighton was in the top quarter of universities for the impact of the research submitted to the 2014 national assessments. Two-thirds of its work was placed in one of the top two categories – a big improvement on 2008, when Brighton was already among the most successful of the post-1992 universities. The university is perhaps best known for its strength in art and design, which was recognised in the award of national teaching centres in design and creativity. But it also has a growing reputation in areas such as sport and hospitality, as well as scoring well in teacher education rankings.

The university has a cosmopolitan atmosphere, with more international students and a more middle-class UK intake than most post-1992 universities. Among the efforts to widen participation are progression partnerships with 22 primary and over 50 secondary schools and colleges in the South East of England, where eligible students are guaranteed offers for many Brighton courses, as well as financial support from the university. Over 2,000 students applied from Compact partnership schools in 2014, the first full year of operation.

The university also holds a Charter Mark for its commitment to care leavers and has a higher-than-average number of disabled students. Students have a personal tutor and there is an award-winning student services department. There are well-established mentoring, entrepreneurship and volunteering schemes for students to develop themselves outside the classroom.

Most students like Brighton's lively social scene, despite the high cost of living for those not in hall. Eastbourne is also popular, and both towns offer plentiful accommodation to supplement the university's growing stock.

Tuition fees

» Fees for UK/EU students 2017–18 £9,250
   Foundation degrees at partner colleges £7,196–£7,710
   Placement year £1,000
» UK fees are expected to increase by the rate of inflation from 2018–19 onwards.
» Fees for international students 2017–18 £12,680–£13,920
   Medicine (2016-17) £28,000
» Check the university's website for the latest information on fees, scholarships, bursaries and student support.

Students

Undergraduates:	14,125	(2,735)
Postgraduates:	1,665	(2,160)
Mature students:	21.4%	
International students:	12.8%	
Applications per place:	7.6	
From state-sector schools:	93.1%	
From working-class homes:	34.2%	
Satisfaction with students' union	59%	

For detailed information about sports facilities:
http://sport.brighton.ac.uk

Accommodation

Number of places and costs refer to 2016–17
University provided places: 2,107 (216 in private sector university-managed houses or flats).
Percentage catered: 55%
Catered costs: £151 – £172 a week.
Self-catered costs: from £108 a week.
First years have priority for housing if conditions are met.
International students: guaranteed accommodation if conditions are met
www.brighton.ac.uk/living-here

University of Bristol

The chances of receiving an offer from Bristol practically doubled in the five years up to 2015, as the university took the opportunity to expand following the lifting of restrictions on the numbers it was allowed to recruit. The undergraduate intake grew by 1,500 places over the same period and offers were made to six out of ten applicants last year, but such is Bristol's popularity that entry standards have been broadly maintained and are still among the highest.

There are now over 16,000 undergraduates, although Bristol remains one of the smaller universities in the Russell Group. The university draws applicants from all types of school, but 40 per cent of entrants in 2014 came from the independent sector, the highest proportion outside Oxbridge and St Andrews.

To broaden the intake, departments may make slightly lower offers to the most promising applicants from the bottom 40 per cent of schools and colleges at A level. Over 2,400 such offers were made in 2014, but the proportion from low-income groups remains less than one in seven. The university has spent more than £18 million since 2006 on recruiting and supporting students from disadvantaged backgrounds. Some 640 local students take the Access to Bristol course while at school or college, for example, and receive a substantial bursary and a year's free tuition if they go on to a Bristol degree and their family income is less than £25,000.

Bristol's place among the leading universities in the UK was confirmed in the 2014 Research Excellence Framework, when the university ranked alongside Oxford in the top four. It entered more than 90 per cent of its eligible staff – a higher proportion than Oxford – and still saw 83 per cent of its research rated as world-leading or internationally excellent. Among the many successes, geography consolidated its position as the leader in its subject, while the entire submissions in clinical medicine, health subjects, economics and sport and exercise sciences were placed in the top categories for their external impact. The results helped to maintain Bristol's position in our top 20, with research outcomes and the proportion of good degrees being the two measures for which Bristol is ranked highest in our league table.

Bristol is just outside the top 40 in the world, according to the QS rankings. International rankings – where the university has enjoyed more recent success than domestic ones – do not take account of the annual National Student Survey in which Bristol has struggled to perform well. Our measures of student satisfaction with teaching quality and the wider

---

Senate House
Tyndall Avenue
Bristol BS8 1TH

0117 394 1649
choosebristol-ug@bristol.ac.uk
www.bristol.ac.uk
www.bristolsu.org.uk
Affiliation: Russell Group

The Times and Sunday Times Rankings

Overall Ranking: **19** (last year: 20)

Teaching quality:	=97	78.8%
Student experience:	=59	84%
Research quality:	6	47.3%
Entry standards:	11	479
Student–staff ratio:	=28	13.8
Services & facilities/student:	55	£2,032
Expected completion rate:	10	95%
Good honours:	6	87.9%
Graduate prospects:	35	79%

student experience have seen significant improvements in scores at the university this year, although it's still the case that just 30 institutions rank lower for student satisfaction with teaching quality.

Since 2010 the university has embarked on the most ambitious construction programme in its history, having spent or committed in excess of £350-million on major projects. A £54-million Life Sciences building was completed in 2014, when new study centres were opened in the university precinct and in the students' union. A new 400-seat lecture theatre has been completed recently and the arts faculty headquarters updated.

There have been academic developments, too. A new innovation programme is being launched so that, for example, a four-year course that combines a core academic subject with extensive training on how to develop and plan a business. Bristol decided to introduce the courses after it found that 30 per cent of its students planned to become entrepreneurs. The programme, which leads to a master's degree, can be taken in anthropology, computer science, electrical and electronic engineering, film and television, geography, history, management, music, physics, psychology and theatre.

An extension to one of the halls at Stoke Bishop has added 320 residential places, helping the university to maintain its guarantee of accommodation for all new undergraduates who accept an offer by the end of July. An impressive sports complex with a well-equipped gym has been developed at the heart of the university precinct, where the careers centre has also been refurbished. The students' union houses one of the city's biggest live music venues as well as a café and swimming pool. A £31-million refurbishment and redesign has provided more space for community activities, student societies and sports clubs.

Bristol possesses a vibrant youth culture and, as one of the country's most prosperous cities, offers job opportunities to students and graduates alike. The university's famous gothic tower dominates the skyline from the junction of two of the main shopping streets. Most students enjoy life there: the dropout rate is among the lowest in Britain, and one student in five stays in the city after graduation. The university won a police-approved Secured Environments award for its crime protection work.

Tuition fees

» Fees for UK/EU students 2017–18 £9,250
» UK fees are expected to increase by the rate of inflation from 2018–19 onwards.
» Fees for international students 2017–18 £15,800–£19,400
  Dentistry, medicine, vet. medicine £19,400–£35,400
» Check the university's website for the latest information on fees, scholarships, bursaries and other forms of student support.

Students

Undergraduates:	15,620	(410)
Postgraduates:	4,265	(1,265)
Mature students:	5.5%	
International students:	14.9%	
Applications per place:	8.4	
From state-sector schools:	60.1%	
From working-class homes:	14.7%	
Satisfaction with students' union	54%	

For detailed information about sports facilities:
www.bris.ac.uk/sport

Accommodation

Number of places and costs refer to 2016–17
University-provided places: about 5,490
Percentage catered: 32.8%
Catered costs: £125.37 (shared room) – £186.34 a week.
Self-catered costs: £81.97 (shared room) – £154.70 a week.
First years are guaranteed one offer of accommodation provided conditions are met.
International students: accommodation is guaranteed provided conditions are met.
www.bristol.ac.uk/accommodation

Brunel University London

Brunel suffered one of the larger falls in our league table last year after a decline in its previously stellar student satisfaction rate. But the university was already taking a number of steps to improve the student experience and graduates' career prospects, helping it to recover some of the lost ground this year.

The new Brunel Educational Excellence Centre provides students with opportunities to enhance their academic skills and encourages innovative teaching, while the Professional Development Centre focuses on employability, bringing together the award-winning placement and careers services, modern foreign languages and the newly established Innovation Hub.

Brunel has always been strong on work placements and also tries to maximise future employment prospects through the inclusion in degree courses of skills modules, such as oral and written communication, business and computer literacy. In 2016, the university also launched its new Brunel+ award, designed to give recognition for non-academic activities that appeal to employers.

The university has been celebrating its 50th anniversary, having invested more than £400 million in recent years on its campus in northwest London. Another £150 million will be spent on new engineering and sports facilities over the next five years.

Brunel is also benefiting from increased research funding after a good performance in the 2014 Research Excellence Framework. Over 60 per cent of a large submission was rated as world-leading or internationally excellent, with sports sciences achieving the best results and ranking in the top five departments in the UK. Brunel did particularly well in the new assessments of the external impact of research. In public health, art and design, politics, and environmental and earth sciences, 100 per cent of the work achieved three or the maximum four stars for impact. There are three autonomous interdisciplinary research institutes to encourage academics from different subjects to work together and produce innovative courses and research projects. The highest-profile example has been the establishment of the first Centre for Comedy Studies Research, launched by Brunel alumni Jo Brand and Lee Mack.

The library and Brunel's already world-class sports facilities have accounted for much of the investment on campus, which retains its original 1960s architecture, but with the addition of striking new buildings and landscaping. There have been many new and refurbished social, teaching and residential facilities, and more green spaces for students to enjoy. The latest major construction project was the £30-million

Kingston Lane
Uxbridge
UB8 3PH

01895 265265 (admissions)
contact via website
www.brunel.ac.uk
http://brunelstudents.com
Affiliation: none

The Times and Sunday Times Rankings

Overall Ranking: **=54** (last year: 60)

Teaching quality:	=100	78.6%
Student experience:	=77	83.2%
Research quality:	49	25.4%
Entry standards:	53	349
Student–staff ratio:	=56	15.7
Services & facilities/student:	59	£1,979
Expected completion rate:	53	87.4%
Good honours:	59	72.2%
Graduate prospects:	=69	71.2%

Eastern Gateway Building, which provided new teaching and research facilities, a large auditorium, a café and an art gallery.

The latest strategic plan commits Brunel to making stronger connections between teaching and research, and further improving the quality of students' experience. There has been significant growth in courses focusing on new technologies such as multimedia design and broadcast media, as well as health and social care. The university is training 40 postgraduates to deliver Robo-Code sessions at secondary schools to encourage more girls to go into engineering and computer programming.

Other innovations include creative writing, professionally accredited journalism, sonic arts, aviation engineering and pilot studies, motorsport engineering and games design. Benjamin Zephaniah took up his first academic position as Chair of Creative Writing, and Will Self has joined as Professor of Contemporary Thought. Brunel's Institute for the Environment won a Queen's Anniversary Prize for pioneering research revealing the link between chemicals in rivers and reproductive health.

Over 40 per cent of the undergraduates are from low-income families – well ahead of the national average for Brunel's courses and entry qualifications. More than half come from the UK's ethnic minorities and there is also a large contingent of international students. The International Pathways and Language Centre was named as Britain's top-performing university centre under the British Council's accreditation framework. A new international strategy promotes study opportunities abroad. Brunel features in the top 25 in *Times Higher Education*'s ranking of the world's leading universities in their 50th year, scoring highly for its international outlook.

A tradition of sporting excellence saw Brunel students and graduates represented at the Rio Olympic and Paralympic Games. The level of facilities is such that Brunel was chosen as a training base for the 2015 Rugby World Cup. The university has won awards for its provision for disabled students, and for its placement and careers service. Campus improvements have transformed student accommodation and there are now more than 4,500 places for first-year, full-time students – enough to guarantee accommodation even for those entering through Clearing.

Tuition fees

- » Fees for UK/EU students 2017–18 £9,250
  Placement year £1,000
- » UK fees are expected to increase by the rate of inflation from 2018–19 onwards.
- » Fees for international students 2017–18 £14,100–£17,200
- » Check the university's website for the latest information on fees, scholarships, bursaries and other forms of student support.

Students

Undergraduates:	9,435	(255)
Postgraduates:	3,030	(995)
Mature students:	11.9%	
International students:	20.6%	
Applications per place:	9.8	
From state-sector schools:	94.3%	
From working-class homes:	43.3%	
Satisfaction with students' union	74%	

For detailed information about sports facilities:
www.brunel.ac.uk/services/sport

Accommodation

Number of places and costs refer to 2016–17
University-provided places: 4,531
Percentage catered: 0%
Self-catered costs: £108.15 (standard) – £137.90 (en suite); £206.15 (studio flat for cohabiting couples) a week.
All new full-time first-year students are eligible for on-campus accommodation.
International students: as above.
www.brunel.ac.uk/life/accommodation
accom-uxb@brunel.ac.uk

University of Buckingham

Buckingham has been celebrating its 40th anniversary by opening its first premises in London and launching a £70-million fundraising campaign for new facilities.

The London Centre will host lectures and other activities, attracting visiting speakers from Parliament and business, as well as acting as recruiting offices. Among others, it will be used by students on the university's new degree in politics, philosophy and economics, which will have distinctive elements such as cross-disciplinary modules on scientific literacy, communication and high-level writing skills.

Buckingham had the best scores once again in the 2016 National Student Survey (NSS) for teaching quality and academic feedback. It also has the highest scores this year for student satisfaction with their overall university experience. Buckingham, therefore, tops three of our nine league table indicators, a number bettered only by Cambridge. It does not finish higher in our rankings – suffering a minor three-place fall this year – as its performance in other measures is less stellar. Barely half the students graduate with a First or 2:1, and as a private institution its absence from the 2014 research ratings also handicaps its overall performance.

For many years Britain's only private university, Buckingham is still the only one in our main league table, now well established in the top 50. Buckingham saw dramatic growth early in this decade before the demand for places levelled off.

The most prestigious recent development saw the opening of the UK's first private not-for-profit medical school in 2015. The "massively oversubscribed" course is 4.5 years long, modelled on Leicester University's MBChB programme, and its costs are in line with the overseas rate at other medical schools. The university has had a postgraduate medical school for seven years, attracting overseas medical graduates, and is now building a teaching and learning centre for undergraduate and postgraduate medical students at Milton Keynes University Hospital.

Sir Anthony Seldon, the political historian who joined as vice-chancellor in 2015, is a campaigner for higher teaching standards in universities. Buckingham had already expanded its library and teaching space before his arrival, as well as boosting spending on student facilities and refurbishing the refectory on the main campus. In addition, £3 million was spent on refurbished buildings for the Medical School, including a new 106-seat lecture theatre and a tablet-style large Anatomage table.

There is a rolling programme of refurbishment of student accommodation

---

Hunter Street
Buckingham MK18 1EG

01280 820313 (admissions)
admissions@buckingham.ac.uk
www.buckingham.ac.uk
www.buckingham.ac.uk/
life/social/su
Affiliation: none

The Times and Sunday Times Rankings

Overall Ranking: **41** (last year: =38)

Teaching quality:	1	90.2%
Student experience:	1	91.5%
Research quality:	n/a	n/a
Entry standards:	79	319
Student–staff ratio:	1	9.6
Services & facilities/student:	56	£2,008
Expected completion rate:	69	85.1%
Good honours:	124	54.7%
Graduate prospects:	67	71.4%

and the first-ever campus bank has been established.

Even before the arrival of £9,000 fees elsewhere, Buckingham claimed to be no more expensive than other universities because its intensive two-year degrees cut maintenance costs and accelerate entry into employment. Total fees for British and EU undergraduates taking the two-year degree from January 2017 will be £24,888 for home and EU students, and £34,320 for those from other countries. There is a range of scholarships for both home and international candidates.

A Conservative-backed experiment of the 1970s, Buckingham has long been an accepted part of the university system, with no party political ties. Its degrees carry full currency in the academic world and teaching standards are high. Small group tutorials are common: the average contains about six students. The Quality Assurance Agency praised the university's culture of responsiveness to students in its last report.

Buckingham has a number of research groups and over 170 research students. It is refurbishing property to accommodate the Humanities Research Institute and plans to enter the REF in future. One high-profile project has involved excavations at Stonehenge, which have led to Buckingham's first Massive Open Online Course (MOOC) about the site.

Students can begin courses in January, July or September, most of which run for two 40-week years. Just over half of the students are from overseas, but the proportion from Britain is growing. They have the option of a three-year degree in the humanities, and other schools are now following suit.

The main campus includes the refectory, bar and fitness centre, with the Radcliffe Centre, which hosts internal and external events, nearby. The law school is within walking distance. The School of Education is based at Whittlebury Hall, near Towcester. A minibus provides transport between the three campuses. Two historic buildings have been refurbished at a cost of almost £2 million, and a new six-acre site has been acquired to make room for future expansion. Buckingham's campus, judged the safest in the country. hosts a university cinema, and the town of Buckingham is pretty. Milton Keynes and Oxford are nearby.

Tuition fees

Note that the degree courses last two years, except medicine (4.5 years).

» Fees for UK/EU students starting Jan. 2017   £12,444
   Medicine   £36,000
» Fees for international students starting Jan. 2017   £17,160
   Medicine   £36,000
» Check the university's website for the latest information on fees, scholarships, bursaries and other forms of student support.

Students

Undergraduates:	1,080	(70)
Postgraduates:	1,040	(55)
Mature students:	28.6%	
International students:	50.5%	
Applications per place:	14.2	
From state-sector schools:	78%	
From working-class homes:	25%	
Satisfaction with students' union	66%	

For detailed information about sports facilities:
www.buckingham.ac.uk/life/thingstodo/sport

Accommodation

Number of places and costs refer to 2016–17
University provided places: 548
Percentage catered: 0%
Self-catered accommodation: £89.32 – £215.77 a week (48 weeks).
All first-year students are guaranteed accommodation if they follow the application process.
International students: same as above.
accommodation@buckingham.ac.uk
www.buckingham.ac.uk/life/accommodation

Buckinghamshire New University

Students at Buckinghamshire New University receive a unique and valuable package of free activities through its "Big Deal" programme, which has been running since before the introduction of £9,000 fees. The programme entitles all students to free entertainment, recreational activities, events and sport. There are now means-tested bursaries of up to £500 a year to cover other academic costs, such as field trips.

Yet satisfaction ratings remain among the lowest in the National Student Survey and continue to hold the university back in our league table. Nevertheless, applications have risen for three years in a row, albeit without parallel increases in enrolments. There are now some 9,000 students, two-thirds of whom are full-time undergraduates, three in ten of them over 21 years old on entry.

Bucks was awarded university status in 2007 and also owns the dedicated conference and events venue, Missenden Abbey. The university specialises in industry-focused degree programmes and professional qualifications across the creative and cultural industries, management and the public sector.

It is a leader in nurse training in north-west London and won the Partnership of the Year at the 2016 Student *Nursing Times* awards. The nursing provision is one of the largest in the London area and has growing links with the Imperial College London Healthcare Trust, including a joint appointment designed to promote innovation. The child nursing courses attract particularly good ratings.

Nursing is based in Uxbridge and there is a new and innovative campus for higher education and professional development in Aylesbury, which hosts programmes taught by the university and Aylesbury College. Employers are helping to shape and develop the curriculum, which will include Foundation degrees, top-up courses and Foundation programmes.

The main campus is in High Wycombe, where a £200-million development programme has seen the prize-winning Gateway Building transform the town-centre campus with improved teaching, social and administrative space. The complex includes a sports hall, gym, treatment rooms and sports laboratory, open to the public as well as to students.

In 2016, the university opened a Human Performance, Exercise and Wellbeing Centre, which is being used by around 270 students following undergraduate programmes from sports therapy to exercise health and fitness management, dance and performance as well as MSc health

---

Queen Alexandra Road
High Wycombe
Buckinghamshire
HP11 2JZ

0330 123 2023 (enquiries)
advice@bucks.ac.uk
www.bucks.ac.uk
www.bucksstudentsunion.org
Affiliations: GuildHE

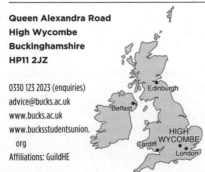

The Times and Sunday Times Rankings

Overall Ranking: **118** (last year: 109)

Teaching quality:	=54	81.2%
Student experience:	=94	81.9%
Research quality:	121	1.5%
Entry standards:	123	260
Student–staff ratio:	92	17.6
Services & facilities/student:	64	£1,947
Expected completion rate:	=108	79.7%
Good honours:	121	55.3%
Graduate prospects:	107	61.4%

rehabilitation and exercise.

The university's travel and aviation students are able to use an Elite S812 flight simulator – a dual pilot simulator to develop and progress such skills as instrument and cross-country flying.

There is also a new social work academy, run in partnership with Buckinghamshire County Council, where the university's academics support the continuing professional development of qualified social workers and managers.

Research is focused on the needs of business, commerce and industry, as well as the public and voluntary sectors. There is a range of research centres and institutes, with focuses including nursing, policing, social work, telehealth, sport and vocational learning. However, Bucks is in the bottom four in our table for research quality, having entered only 24 staff for the 2014 Research Excellence Framework. Almost 40 per cent of their work reached one of the top two categories, with art and design producing much the best results.

The university has continued to do well against the Government's benchmarks for widening participation in higher education: almost all the entrants are from state schools or colleges, and almost half are from working-class homes. The projected dropout rate of little more than 10 per cent for those who entered in 2014 was significantly lower than the national average for its subjects

and entry qualifications.

Sport plays an important part in life at the university, which is involved in a variety of activities with Wycombe Wanderers Football Club, while students in the School of Arts and Creative Industries film matchday footage and produce online magazine programmes for Reading and Watford football clubs. Some Foundation degrees are run at partner colleges including animation and visual effects, protective security management, and sports coaching and performance. Collaboration with two of the world's biggest IT companies is resulting in one of the most advanced student networks in UK higher education.

Two new accommodation blocks in High Wycombe added 108 en-suite rooms to the university's residential stock, doubling the size of the student village and bringing the number of places owned by Bucks to 885. High Wycombe has a range of student pubs and clubs and is within easy reach of London.

Tuition fees

» Fees for UK/EU students 2017–18 £9,250
  Franchised courses at partner colleges £6,165–£9,250
» UK fees are expected to increase by the rate of inflation from 2018–19 onwards.
» Fees for international students 2017–18 £10,500
» Check the university's website for the latest information on fees, scholarships, bursaries and other forms of student support.

Students

Undergraduates:	5,890	(2,080)
Postgraduates:	420	(640)
Mature students:	31.6%	
International students:	7.6%	
Applications per place:	5.6	
From state-sector schools:	96.9%	
From working-class homes:	46.2%	
Satisfaction with students' union	84%	

For detailed information about sports facilities:
www.bucksstudentsunion.org/activities/sports

Accommodation

Number of places and costs refer to 2016–17
University-provided places: 885
Percentage catered: 0%
Self-catered costs: £104.52 (standard) – £174.07 (studio) a week (42 weeks).
First-year students applying before 30 June are guaranteed accommodation.
International students: priority allocation for first years.
accommodation@bucks.ac.uk;
http://bucks.ac.uk/home_eu_students/accommodation

University of Cambridge

Top in almost half of our 67 subject tables and placed among the four best universities in the world in all the main rankings, Cambridge is the clear leader in *The Times and Sunday Times* league table. It is a position the university has occupied for four years in succession, albeit jointly with Oxford in the 2015 *Guide*.

Cambridge has the highest entry standards of any UK university, demanding at least A*AA at A level in arts subjects and A*A*A in the sciences, although candidates may be made a lower offer if their school or personal circumstances are thought to disadvantage them. Cambridge has also introduced pre-interview assessments in more than half of its subjects, with written tests at interview in the rest, to try to pick out the high fliers at an earlier stage.

With around five applicants for each place – fewer if you choose your subject carefully – the competition for places appears less intense than at the popular civic universities, but the difference is that nine out of ten entrants have at least three A grades at A level. That competition shows no sign of easing since the university has barely increased the size of its intake with the relaxation of recruitment restrictions. Until now, four out of five applicants are interviewed – a much higher proportion than at Oxford – but only one in three receives a conditional offer of a place.

Established in 1209, Cambridge possesses some of the most ancient and iconic buildings at any university. But huge sums have been spent modernising the facilities. The first phase of the £1-billion North West Cambridge development opens in 2017, with accommodation for 2,000 postgraduates. The final development will include 100,000 square metres of academic and research space, as well as 1,500 homes for university staff and another 1,500 private houses.

Other recent additions include the £26-million Maxwell Centre, on the West Cambridge site, where research scientists from industry will occupy laboratory and desk space alongside Cambridge research groups. A new £59-million centre for biodiversity and conservation, named after Sir David Attenborough, opened in 2015.

Cambridge produced the best results in the 2014 Research Excellence Framework (REF), helping to keep the university ahead of its main rival. However, both Cambridge and Oxford registered significant declines in the 2016 National Student Survey for satisfaction with teaching quality, for which Cambridge now ranks 32 (Oxford 43) in the UK. Cambridge entered 95 per cent of eligible academics for the REF – no university involved a higher proportion – and 87 per cent of their work was rated as world-leading or internationally excellent.

The Old Schools
Trinity Lane
Cambridge CB2 1TN

01223 333308 (admissions)
admissions@cam.ac.uk
www.cam.ac.uk
www.cusu.co.uk
Affiliation: Russell Group

The Times and Sunday Times Rankings

Overall Ranking: **1** (last year: 1)

Teaching quality:	=27	82.9%
Student experience:	35	85.5%
Research quality:	1	57.3%
Entry standards:	1	600
Student–staff ratio:	4	11
Services & facilities/student:	1	£3,446
Expected completion rate:	1	98.5%
Good honours:	2	91%
Graduate prospects:	3	88.3%

It achieved the UK's best results in aeronautical and electronic engineering, business and management, chemistry, classics and clinical medicine.

More than 60 per cent of undergraduates now come from the state system, but the proportion of working-class undergraduates remains low, at only 10 per cent. Summer schools, student visits and, in some colleges, sympathetic selection procedures are helping to attract more applications from comprehensive schools and further education colleges. There are generous bursaries of up to £3,500 a year, according to parental income.

The application system has been simplified slightly, with candidates no longer required to complete an initial Cambridge form, as well as their UCAS form. However, they are sent the Supplementary Application Questionnaire, after they have submitted their UCAS form, covering the applicant's academic experience in more detail. The tripos system was a forerunner of the currently fashionable modular degree, allowing students to change subjects (within limits) midway through their courses. Students receive a classification for each of the two parts of their degree.

Choosing a college is an additional complication for those not familiar with Cambridge. Brief profiles of all the undergraduate colleges appear in Chapter 13. Making the right choice is crucial, both to maximise the chances of winning a place and to ensure an enjoyable three years if you are successful. Applicants can take pot luck with an open application if they prefer not to opt for a particular college; though the statistics show that this route is equally successful, only a minority takes it. Most teaching is now university-based, especially in the sciences, and a shift of emphasis towards the centre has been taking place more generally.

A £16-million sports centre opened in 2013, featuring a large sports hall and a strength and conditioning wing. Cambridge is not for everyone, however bright. The amount of high-quality work to be crammed into eight-week terms can prove a strain, although the projected dropout rate of 1.4 per cent is the lowest at any university. Most students relish the experience and reap the rewards in their careers.

Tuition fees

» Fees for UK/EU students 2017–18   £9,250
» UK fees are expected to increase by the rate of inflation from 2018–19 onwards.
» Fees for international students 2017–18   £16,608–£25,275
    Medicine   £40,200 (medicine)
    College fees   £6,000–£8,500
» Check the university's website for the latest information on fees, scholarships, bursaries and student support.

Students

Undergraduates:	11,870	(365)
Postgraduates:	6,320	(965)
Mature students:	4.5%	
International students:	20.2%	
Applications per place:	4.8	
From state-sector schools:	61.8%	
From working-class homes:	10.2%	
Satisfaction with students' union	37%	

For detailed information about sports facilities:
www.sport.cam.ac.uk

Accommodation

www.undergraduate.study.cam.ac.uk/why-cambridge/student-life/accommodation

Also see chapter 13 for information about individual colleges. College websites provide accommodation details.

Canterbury Christ Church University

Canterbury Christ Church was short-listed for *Times Higher Education*'s award for the most improved student experience in 2015, after registering particularly good scores for the helpfulness of staff, security and library services. There has been progress, too, in the National Student Survey, but not enough to bring the university back into our top 100.

Applications were down by more than 13 per cent in 2015, although a higher offer rate ensured that enrolments did not drop. There are now 17,000 students, more than half of whom come from Kent, while nearly 1,000 of the rest are from Europe or further afield. The former Church of England college achieved university status in 2005, and is one of the region's largest provider of courses and research for the public services, with teacher training courses that are highly rated by Ofsted, and strong programmes in health and social care, nursing and policing. It also offers a wide range of traditional and professional arts and humanities courses, with a strong focus on employability and excellence in research. The university remains a Church of England foundation and has the Archbishop of Canterbury as its Chancellor.

There are three campuses – Canterbury, Broadstairs and Chatham – and a postgraduate centre in Tunbridge Wells. The purpose-built campus at Broadstairs offers a range of subjects from commercial music to digital media, photography and early childhood studies, while the recently expanded Medway site at Chatham Historic Dockyard specialises in education and health programmes. The majority of the students, however, are at the university's main campus at Canterbury, part of the city's World Heritage Site.

Augustine House, a £35-million library and student services centre, with specialist teaching and IT facilities, was joint winner of the Society of College, National and University Librarians' 2013 award for the best library design. All campuses are interconnected by a high-speed data network, providing access to online teaching and learning materials, the student web portal and email. The student support service – i-zone – can be accessed online or via staff at the i-zone desks.

More student accommodation opened in 2015 in the centre of Canterbury, close to the students' union and other facilities. The university is also developing the former Canterbury Prison site over the next decade, as a major extension to its main campus. A £150-million project is in the pipeline, which will provide contemporary spaces for learning, teaching and research, as well as social facilities. The centrepiece will be

North Holmes Road
Canterbury CT1 1QU

01227 782900 (enquiries)
admissions@canterbury.ac.uk
www.canterbury.ac.uk
https://ccsu.co.uk
Affiliations: Cathedrals
Group; MillionPlus

The Times and Sunday Times Rankings

Overall Ranking: **114** (last year: 107)

Teaching quality:	83	79.8%
Student experience:	111	80.8%
Research quality:	96	4.5%
Entry standards:	=121	276
Student–staff ratio:	=61	16
Services & facilities/student:	117	£1,323
Expected completion rate:	102	80.8%
Good honours:	86	66.8%
Graduate prospects:	=110	61%

an industry-led science, technology and engineering centre, which will provide space for research and development, technology transfer and knowledge exchange to drive innovation. The plans also have an eye to history and would restore the former Pilgrim's Trail from St Martin's Church through the campus to Canterbury Cathedral.

Seven out of ten students are female – partly the result of the subject mix, with its emphasis on health subjects and education. Recent developments have included the introduction of special educational needs and inclusion studies, and a counselling, coaching and mentoring degree, helping to meet the fast-growing demand for careers in both areas

Business degrees have been strengthened with new industry placement years and facilities such as the Bloomberg Trading Room, while computing courses have developed a focus on cybercrime an area of research in which the university is a national leader.

Almost half of Canterbury Christ Church's submission to the 2014 research assessments was placed in the top two categories, resulting in one of the biggest percentage increases in funding at any university. New developments include the opening of a Life Sciences Industry Liaison Lab, which allows students and staff to link up with companies working at the cutting edge of research. The UK Institute for Migration Research is another recent addition, as is the Institute of Medical Sciences, which builds on the university's work in stem cell research and minimally invasive surgery.

The university contributes to Canterbury's cultural life with the Sidney Cooper Gallery, which hosts exhibitions and workshops from visiting artists as well as work by students. It has also renovated St Gregory's Centre for Music, a historic concert venue, and opened separate rehearsal, practice and performance spaces in a building named after Sir Peter Maxwell Davies. Social and sports facilities vary between the campuses, although the students' union is present on all of them. The sports centre in Canterbury includes a large adaptable sports hall and a fitness suite, a sports and exercise studio and performance analysis rooms. The university also has outdoor sports facilities about a mile from the main campus.

Tuition fees

» Fees for UK/EU students 2017–18 £9,250
Placement year £1,850
» UK fees are expected to increase by the rate of inflation from 2018–19 onwards.
» Fees for international students 2017–18 £11,000
» Check the university's website for the latest information on fees, scholarships, bursaries and other forms of student support.

Students

Undergraduates:	10,060	(2,975)
Postgraduates:	995	(1,990)
Mature students:	27.6%	
International students:	5.7%	
Applications per place:	5.0	
From state-sector schools:	97.8%	
From working-class homes:	39.8%	
Satisfaction with students' union	62%	

For detailed information about sports facilities:
www.canterbury.ac.uk/christ-church-sport

Accommodation

Number of places and costs refer to 2016–17
University provided places: 1,933
Percentage catered: 0%. Catering card is available.
Self-catered costs: £94 – £160 a week
Single person accommodation guaranteed for first years, if conditions are met. Limited 1-bed accommodation available for couples.
International students: As above.
Contact: accommodation@canterbury.ac.uk
www.canterbury.ac.uk/study-here/accommodation

Cardiff University

The highest-ranked Welsh university in every edition of *The Times and The Sunday Times* league tables until this year, Cardiff is the only member of the Russell Group of research-led universities in Wales and its sole representative in the top 200 of the world rankings. It is also one of the few universities in the UK to boast two Nobel laureates on its staff.

Both applications and enrolments are running at record levels: the numbers starting degrees at Cardiff in 2015 were more than 20 per cent higher than at the beginning of the decade. The university now has over 30,000 students, including 6,000 from outside the UK.

Cardiff has embarked on a £450-million masterplan that will include a new Innovation Campus and provide much-improved facilities for student services, as well as a new library, on the main Cathays Park site.

There are also plans to open an innovative Centre for Student Life, which will act as a one-stop shop for students seeking advice and be linked to the redesigned students' union, where the facilities have already been upgraded. A new multipurpose venue there provides social, learning and meeting space during the day and then becomes a nightclub.

A third of the students come from Wales, but it is the international dimension that has been Cardiff's main focus recently. Its Global Opportunities Programme provides studying, working and volunteering options across the world to enhance the student experience. The aim is for 17 per cent of undergraduates to undertake at least four weeks study, work or volunteering overseas by 2017.

The university has also launched a Languages for All programme, giving students the chance to learn another language alongside their chosen degree for free. Students are also offered the Cardiff Award to boost their employment prospects by recognising the skills acquired from extracurricular activities, while an enterprise team helps with business start-ups, offering advice and training.

An audit by the Quality Assurance Agency complimented the university on its "powerful academic vision and well-developed and effectively articulated mission to achieve excellence in teaching and research". Student support services, including counselling facilities and the help offered to dyslexics, were among the features singled out for praise.

New degree programmes include Chinese and a revamped range of bioscience degree programmes.

One undergraduate in seven comes from an independent school and little more than

---

Cardiff
CF10 3XQ

029 2087 4455 (enquiries)
enquiry@cardiff.ac.uk
www.cardiff.ac.uk
www.cardiffstudents.com
Affiliation: Russell Group

Edinburgh
Belfast
London
CARDIFF

The Times and Sunday Times **Rankings**

Overall Ranking: **46** (last year: 33)

Teaching quality:	=94	79%
Student experience:	=42	84.8%
Research quality:	34	35%
Entry standards:	34	405
Student–staff ratio:	27	13.7
Services & facilities/student:	66	£1,938
Expected completion rate:	=26	92.6%
Good honours:	42	76%
Graduate prospects:	=52	73.9%

one in five has a working-class background. The 5 per cent projected dropout rate is comfortably the lowest in Wales.

Cardiff would have finished higher in our league table if it had entered more academics for the 2014 Research Excellence Framework: at 62 per cent of eligible staff, the entry was 12 percentage points smaller than that of any other Russell Group university. However, the results were stellar, with 87 per cent of the submission rated as world-leading or internationally excellent. Cardiff was in the top three for the impact of its research, and civil and construction engineering was rated top in the UK. The university attracts more than half of the research funding awarded in Wales.

The university occupies a significant part of Cardiff's civic complex around Cathays Park. The five healthcare schools at the Heath Park Campus share a 53-acre site with the University Hospital of Wales. The £18-million Cochrane Building provides teaching and learning facilities for all healthcare schools based there. The School of Dentistry's Dental Education Clinic offers students some of the UK's most modern training facilities.

Other recent projects have included a £30-million science development and a £13.5-million learning and teaching centre for the Business School, which includes a 60-seat trading room and two large lecture theatres. In 2016, the Queen opened a new £44-million Brain Research Imaging Centre, which contains the most powerful equipment of its kind in Europe and is said to be the equal of any in the world.

Library services have continued to improve. The range of electronic resources has increased and there have been moves to extend self-service provision and improve the environment for the study of rare collections. Students have online access to information about their studies and social life, from reading lists to social events.

The university guarantees a residential place to those making Cardiff their first choice. The main residential site at Talybont boasts a "sports training village", and there is also a newly refurbished city-centre fitness suite and a sports ground. A new student residence with 178 beds opened there in 2014.

Cardiff is a popular student city, relatively inexpensive and with a good range of nightlife and cultural venues.

Tuition fees

» Fees for UK/EU students 2017–18   £9,000
» Welsh Assembly non-means-tested grant to pay fees above £4,046 for Welsh students. Tuition fee grant is under review for 2018.
» Fees for international students 2017–18   £15,080–£18,980
   Medicine and dentistry   £18,980–£33,540
» Check the university's website for the latest information on fees, scholarships, bursaries and other forms of student support.

Students

Undergraduates:	17,960	(3,615)
Postgraduates:	4,425	(4,480)
Mature students:	13.1%	
International students:	14.3%	
Applications per place:	7.0	
From state-sector schools:	84.9%	
From working-class homes:	23.8%	
Satisfaction with students' union	87%	

For detailed information about sports facilities:
www.cardiff.ac.uk/sport

Accommodation

Number of places and costs refer to 2016–17
University-provided places: 5,353
Percentage catered: 6.4%
Catered costs: £112 – £136 a week (39 or 41 weeks).
Self-catered costs: £99 – £123 a week (39 or 41 weeks).
All first-year students are guaranteed accommodation if conditions are met.
Policy for international students: as above.
residences@cardiff.ac.uk
www.cardiff.ac.uk/study/accommodation

Cardiff Metropolitan University

Cardiff Met is going into partnership with a Chinese television company to build a media and communications school for 2,000 students in the Welsh capital. The first joint venture of its kind between a private firm and a Welsh university covers a TV media centre, teaching space and student accommodation. The timing and location of the new school is yet to be determined, but the university hopes that the project will enhance its growing international reputation.

Cardiff Met has an office in China and 1,200 international students, who have voted the university the best in the UK for student support for the past six years. There are also more than 6,500 students studying for Cardiff Met degrees in Bangladesh, Bulgaria, Egypt, Greece, Hong Kong, India, Lebanon, London, Malaysia, Morocco, Singapore, South Korea and Sri Lanka. The international partnerships provide an opportunity for students to spend part of their studies abroad. Cardiff Met has also been awarded the Government's Charter Mark four times, the judges commenting particularly on the level of student satisfaction.

Last year the university celebrated the 150th anniversary of the founding of the Cardiff School of Art, which eventually evolved into Cardiff Met. It adopted its present name in 2011, after a long period as The University of Wales Institute, in order to stress its location in the Principality's capital.

The university had already committed £70 million to improvements on its two campuses. The purpose-built School of Art and Design is now open on the Llandaff Campus and has won an award from the Royal Society of Architects in Wales. A new campus centre, with a shop and catering facilities, was added previously, along with an Information Zone for student services. The Cyncoed Campus had also benefited from a new student centre and there are plans for another 500 new student flats there, as well as a swimming pool and trampolining studio.

Cardiff Met is one of Britain's leading centres for university sport, with team performances that do justice to some excellent facilities. In recent years, the university has had British university champions in sports ranging from archery and gymnastics to squash, weightlifting and judo. More than 300 past or present students are internationals in 30 sports.

The £7-million National Indoor Athletics Centre is the university's pride and joy, but other facilities are also of high quality. As well as participating in a thriving sports club

Llandaff Campus
Western Avenue
Cardiff CF5 2YB

029 2041 6010 (enquiries)
askadmissions@cardiffmet.ac.uk
www.cardiffmet.ac.uk
www.cardiffmetsu.co.uk
Affiliation: University
Alliance

The Times and Sunday Times **Rankings**

Overall Ranking: **89** (last year: 103)

Teaching quality:	=113	77.2%
Student experience:	=105	81.3%
Research quality:	106	3.9%
Entry standards:	=80	318
Student–staff ratio:	94	17.9
Services & facilities/student:	40	£2,162
Expected completion rate:	=91	82.3%
Good honours:	81	67.5%
Graduate prospects:	74	70.4%

scene, around 2,000 students pursue sport and dance related courses.

Cardiff Met entered only 35 academics for the 2014 Research Excellence Framework out of 381 who were eligible – only two universities entered a smaller proportion. But the small submission scored well, with 80 per cent of the work rated in the top two categories. The university has since received a Queen's Anniversary Prize for the use of design and related 3D digital scanning technologies as applied to maxillofacial reconstructive surgery. There is also a new FabLab, accredited by the Massachusetts Institute of Technology, where students and businesses can use the latest digital manufacturing equipment.

Postgraduates and research students make up over a quarter of the student population. All six teacher training courses, including the postgraduate pathways, are rated as excellent by Estyn, the school inspectorate.

Undergraduate applications fell in 2015, but there was only a small drop in the numbers starting degrees. Students from Wales account for two-thirds of the 12,000 full-time students, half of whom are from Cardiff or the Vale of Glamorgan. The two sites in Cardiff are close to the city centre and linked by the Met Rider bus service during term time.

The Cyncoed Campus, housing education and sport, is the main centre of social activity, particularly for first years. As well as the new student centre, the athletics centre is there, together with a multitude of outdoor facilities and also the upgraded Welsh Sports Centre for the Disabled. The IT suite has 250 computers available 24 hours a day.

The Llandaff Campus hosts the School of Management, design, engineering, food science and health courses. The student centre at Llandaff includes a dyslexia support unit among a number of advice and representation services, and a learning centre with more than 300 computers.

There is also a Centre for Entrepreneurship, which offers a wide range of activities and one-to-one support for individuals looking to start a business.

The halls of residence are a mile from the main campus on the Plas Gwyn Residential Campus, where there are enough hall places to accommodate most first years, although the university cannot offer a guarantee.

Tuition fees

» Fees for UK/EU students 2017–18   £9,000
» Welsh Assembly non-means-tested grant to pay fees above £4,046 for Welsh students. Tuition fee grant is under review for 2018.
» Fees for international students 2017–18   £11,500–£12,000
» Check the university's website for the latest information on fees, scholarships, bursaries and other forms of student support.

Students

Undergraduates:	8,365	(555)
Postgraduates:	3,640	(1,105)
Mature students:	24.8%	
International students:	18.0%	
Applications per place:	4.6	
From state-sector schools:	95.2%	
From working-class homes:	38.4%	
Satisfaction with students' union	68%	

For information about sports facilities:
www.cardiffmet.ac.uk/about/sport

Accommodation

Number of places and costs refer to 2016–17
University-provided places: 947
Percentage catered: 34%
Catered cost: £142 – £151 a week during term.
Self-catered costs: £102 – £107 a week.
First-year students have no guarantee; terms and conditions apply.
International students: accommodation is reserved, subject to availability and if conditions are met.
www.cardiffmet.ac.uk/accommodation

University of Central Lancashire (UCLan)

UCLan is in the top ten universities in the UK for the number of undergraduates it educates. With 36,000 students at all levels, it dominates the centre of Preston and, according to independent consultants, brings more than £200 million a year into the local economy. That is also the price tag on the university's masterplan, which is designed to create a unified and sustainable campus that will "integrate seamlessly" with the rest of the city. Recent developments have included the £13-million Sir Tom Finney Sports Centre and a £12.5-million building housing the university's forensic science, chemistry and fire courses. A £30-million Engineering Innovation Centre is due to open in 2018, supplementing facilities such as Europe's largest 3-D lecture theatre, forensic crime scene houses, a moot court room, a motorsports workshop and child observation lab.

Applications reached record levels in 2015, although the numbers actually starting courses were down a little on the previous year.

Always one of the most enterprising post-1992 universities, UCLan includes dentistry, pharmacy and astrophysics in a surprisingly wide portfolio of subjects.

There are 230 undergraduate programmes in all, and now medicine is being offered to international students, on a five-year MBBS programme costing £36,600 a year, in line with the overseas fees at other medical schools. The Dental School was one of the few to open in 100 years, while the architecture degree was the first for a decade. UCLan also has campuses in Cyprus and Mauritius, and was the first of its peer group to appear in the QS World University Rankings. A separate rating of teaching, research and facilities by QS gave the university four out of five stars.

Closer to home, the university has another campus in Burnley, giving local students the opportunity to gain qualifications without leaving home. The campus hosts a collaboration with Cisco Systems for advanced manufacturing, incorporating robotics, computer vision, non-destructive testing and component assembly.

UCLan has long been a leader in widening participation, with 45 per cent of its undergraduates coming from the four lowest socio-economic classes, many of them local people in their twenties. Large numbers take external programmes delivered in further education colleges, which have been praised for their quality by assessors. Four-year Foundation Entry Honours degrees are available in most subjects, providing a route into university

Preston
Lancashire PR1 2HE

01772 892400 (course enquiries)
uadmissions@uclan.ac.uk
www.uclan.ac.uk
www.uclansu.co.uk
Affiliation: none

The Times and Sunday Times **Rankings**

Overall Ranking: **=101** (last year: 92)

Teaching quality:	=84	79.7%
Student experience:	=89	82.3%
Research quality:	=85	5.6%
Entry standards:	=71	323
Student–staff ratio:	=72	16.7
Services & facilities/student:	=52	£2,067
Expected completion rate:	116	78.1%
Good honours:	110	62%
Graduate prospects:	98	64.5%

for people without traditional qualifications or those returning to education.

The university's roots stretch back to 1828 and it has established partnerships with a variety of high-profile organisations. UCLan academics work with NASA on solar dynamics, with the Department of Health on sector-leading stroke research, and with the Bill and Melinda Gates Foundation on nutritional science. There are also collaborations with the Football Association, Professional Golfers' Association and International Olympic Committee on sport and exercise science research.

There was some world-leading research in all 16 subject areas that were assessed in the 2014 Research Excellence Framework. The Undergraduate Research Internship Scheme enables students to work on research projects for up to ten weeks.

UCLan has a strong focus on entrepreneurship and has established a range of business incubation facilities for its students and graduates. UCLan is consistently in the UK's top three for the number of graduate start-ups, with 77 per cent still trading after two years. The university works with a wide variety of industrial partners and many undergraduate programmes are directly linked to them. All students can take advantage of work placements and other opportunities to enhance their employability. Travel bursaries are available for study or work experience abroad, and there is free tuition in a variety of languages, including Arabic, Chinese, Japanese and Russian. The Confucius Institute, at Preston, supports the development of Chinese culture in the area. More than 500 students have been helped to visit China.

The university is in the top 30 for environmental performance in the People and Planet Green League and was the first in the UK to install solar trackers. The sports facilities were used as official training venues for the 2012 Olympics and the 2013 Rugby League World Cup. UCLan has nearly 50 teams in the British Universities and Colleges Sport (BUCS) league.

Compared with Manchester or Liverpool, the security risks and cost of living are both low, yet Preston is only 50 minutes away from both cities. The students' union offers a range of sporting clubs, societies and a "Give it a Go" programme.

Tuition fees

» Fees for UK/EU students 2017–18 £9,250
  Degree courses at partner colleges £6,000–£9,250
  Placement year £1,000
» UK fees are expected to increase by the rate of inflation from 2018–19 onwards.
» Fees for international students 2017–18 £11,950–£17,500
  Medicine £36,600
» Check the university's website for the latest information on fees, scholarships, bursaries and other forms of student support.

Students

Undergraduates:	16,375	(4,835)
Postgraduates:	1,015	(3,435)
Mature students:	32.7%	
International students:	8.5%	
Applications per place:	5.9	
From state-sector schools:	98.2%	
From working-class homes:	45.1%	
Satisfaction with students' union	71%	

For detailed information about sports facilities:
www.uclansu.co.uk/teamuclan

Accommodation

Number of places and costs refer to 2016–17
University-provided places: around 2,200
Percentage catered: 0%
Self-catered costs: £79.03 – £83.02 (standard);
£97.37 – £ 99.54 (en suite); £86.87 – £107.80 (self-contained flats) a week.
The Accommodation Service assists first years to find suitable housing.
International students: as above.
www.uclan.ac.uk/accommodation

University of Chester

It has been a time of unprecedented physical expansion for the University of Chester, which opened the first undergraduate base in Shrewsbury in 2015 to add to its campuses in Warrington and Thornton, on the Wirral, and four others in its home city. The latest addition, also in 2015, was the Queen's Park Campus in Chester, the wartime headquarters of the army's Western Command, which now houses the Faculty of Business and Management.

The university had opened the UK's first new engineering faculty for two decades in 2014, when it welcomed the first students to the former Shell research facility at Thornton Science Park campus near Ellesmere Port. Applications declined in 2015, but the university still almost matched the previous year's record enrolment.

Chester's parent institution was established in 1839 as the first purpose-built college for the training of teachers. William Gladstone was among the founders of the Church of England college, which pre-dated all the English universities apart from Oxford, Cambridge, London and Durham. The link with the Church remains, as does the teacher training provision, which has been rated "outstanding" by Ofsted. But there was already a much broader range of courses by the time university status arrived in 2005. Degrees have been designed to support the practical and vocational demands of the professions, with many including an extended period of work experience. There is also a range of Foundation degrees, mainly in health subjects.

The Parkgate Road Campus, the original headquarters, is only a short walk from the centre of Chester, a 32-acre site boasting manicured gardens and a number of new developments. White's Dining Hall has been refurbished, £4.8 million is being spent overhauling the main learning resources centre, and improved sports facilities have cost another £1 million. The adjacent Riverside Innovation Centre provides facilities and support for new and growing businesses, including those run by entrepreneurial students and graduates.

Kingsway Campus, which also has a new learning resources centre, is home to the Faculty of Arts and Media, and the faculties of Health and Social Care and Education and Children's Services are based Chester's historic County Hall. The newly developed Institute of Medicine has a portfolio of postgraduate programmes which have already enrolled their first research students.

The Warrington Campus, which has eight halls of residence, focuses on the creative industries and public services. It has high-quality production facilities and the university has links with the BBC in

---

Parkgate Road
Chester CH1 4BJ

01244 511000 (enquiries)
enquiries@chester.ac.uk
www.chester.ac.uk
www.chestersu.com
Affiliation: Cathedrals
Group

The Times and Sunday Times **Rankings**

Overall Ranking: **81** (last year: 87)

Teaching quality:	=27	82.9%
Student experience:	=99	81.6%
Research quality:	=100	4.1%
Entry standards:	96	304
Student–staff ratio:	=31	14
Services & facilities/student:	42	£2,148
Expected completion rate:	105	80.4%
Good honours:	103	63.8%
Graduate prospects:	99	64.3%

Salford, which opens up new employment opportunities for graduates. The library has been tripled in size, and a business centre opened for students and local firms. There is also a venue which regularly attracts up-and-coming acts.

Around a fifth of the undergraduates are 21 or more on entry and two-thirds are female. Nearly all are state educated, and more than a third have working-class roots. Progression agreements guarantee interviews to students at a number of local colleges, subject to certain conditions, but there is no reduction in entry requirements. Completion rates had been improving, but have now slipped back above the national average for Chester's courses and entry qualifications.

The university more than doubled the number of submissions made to the 2014 Research Excellent Framework compared with the 2008 assessments. Some research was judged to be world-leading in all but one of the 15 subject areas, but in spite of above-average student satisfaction, Chester has recovered only some of the ground lost in last year's league table.

A student contract of the type that is becoming universal in higher education sets out clear conditions on the offer of a place, as well as detailing the university's responsibilities. Students promise to "study diligently, and to attend promptly and participate appropriately at lectures, courses, classes, seminars, tutorials, work placements and other activities which form part of the programme". The university undertakes to deliver the student's programme, but leaves itself considerable leeway beyond that.

There are extensive sports facilities at Warrington and especially on the Parkgate Road Campus, where new tennis courts, a 100-metre sprint track and a floodlit 3G multi-use sports pitch have been added.

A new hall of residence there has added more than 200 rooms and another 160 places have been added through the purchase of a former Travelodge, allowing most first-years to be offered university accommodation. In keeping with the University's Christian foundation, there are chapels on two campuses and a number of other faith spaces. Students' union facilities form the basis of the social scene, but the picturesque city of Chester also has a lot to offer.

Tuition fees

» Fees for UK/EU students 2017–18 £9,250
  Foundation degree £7,650
  Foundation degree at partner colleges £5,135–£7,650
  Placement year £1,385
» UK fees are expected to increase by the rate of inflation from 2018–19 onwards.
» Fees for international students 2017–18 £11,800
» Check the university's website for the latest information on fees, scholarships, bursaries and other forms of student support.

Students

Undergraduates:	8,845	(2,035)
Postgraduates:	1,595	(2,650)
Mature students:	19.7%	
International students:	5.4%	
Applications per place:	7.7	
From state-sector schools:	96.7%	
From working-class homes:	33.9%	
Satisfaction with students' union	77%	

For detailed information about sports facilities:
www.chestersu.com/sports-societies

Accommodation

Number of places and costs refer to 2016–17
University-provided places: 1,442
Percentage catered: 38% (including semi-catered)
Catered costs: £128.10 – £157.50 a week.
Self-catered costs: £82.60 – £165.00 a week.
First years cannot be guaranteed accommodation.
International students: guaranteed accommodation if they apply by the advertised date.
www.chester.ac.uk/accommodation
accommodation@chester.ac.uk

University of Chichester

Chichester is planning to almost double the number of students at its Bognor Regis campus, making space to offer at least 30 more degrees in engineering, digital technology and media subjects.

The university, which currently has fewer than 6,000 students, will remain among the smallest in the UK, but is upgrading the facilities at both of its seaside locations. A new academic block on the Chichester campus will be open before those starting courses in 2017 arrive. The building will include a multi-use space that may be used for dance or as a cinema or theatre, as well as additional teaching space, IT facilities and a bigger, more modern students' union shop. A three-storey music centre providing high-quality learning and rehearsal space is also under construction.

The university traces its history back to 1839, when the college that subsequently bore his name was founded in memory of William Otter, the education-minded Bishop of Chichester. It became a teacher training college for women, who still account for two-thirds of the places, and eventually merged with the nearby Bognor Regis College of Education. The Chichester campus – which will remain the larger of two – continues to carry the Bishop Otter name, signifying a continuing link with

the Church of England. The chapel was refurbished and its surroundings landscaped in 2013.

Chichester has a proud record in the National Student Survey, always ranking highly for both teaching quality and the wider student experience. It wins our University of the Year for Student Retention award for the second time this year, having lifted the title previously in 2013. About half the national average for its courses and entry qualifications – just 6 per cent – drop out before completing their degrees. Nine out of ten students made the university their first choice.

Chichester is aiming to be internationally recognised as a "beacon of good practice for high-quality, student-centred higher education" by 2020 and is clearly making good progress. An £8-million grant will fund the new Engineering and Digital Technology Park on the Bognor Regis Campus, serving local business as well as students. Other developments in Bognor have seen the Dome transformed into a business and research centre and a new learning resources centre established.

The second phase of the university's investment plan aims to bring facilities on the Bishop Otter Campus up to the same standard as those in Bognor Regis. The learning resources centre has been overhauled and a coffee shop added. The Alexandra Theatre in Bognor is used as a

College Lane
Chichester
W. Sussex PO19 6PE

01243 816000 (admissions)
admissions@chi.ac.uk
www.chi.ac.uk
www.ucsu.org
Affiliations: GuildHE;
Cathedrals Group

The Times and Sunday Times **Rankings**

Overall Ranking: **82** (last year: =69)

Teaching quality:	=27	82.9%
Student experience:	=40	84.9%
Research quality:	81	6.4%
Entry standards:	=92	305
Student–staff ratio:	=61	16
Services & facilities/student:	121	£1,255
Expected completion rate:	=43	89.1%
Good honours:	=74	69%
Graduate prospects:	117	58.5%

base for the musical theatre programme and there are links, too, with the Chichester Festival Theatre. The Mathematics Centre, at Bognor, has an international reputation, working with over 30 countries as well as teaching the university's own students. It has become a focal point for curriculum development in Britain and elsewhere.

The current portfolio of some 300 courses ranges from adventure education to humanistic counselling, fine art and the psychology of sport and exercise. The PE teacher training course is one of the largest in the country and is highly rated by Ofsted.

Chichester achieved university status as one of a new band of institutions that were expected to focus on teaching rather than research. But it was given the power to award research degrees in 2014 and entered a quarter of its eligible staff for the Research Excellence Framework. There were good results in music, drama and performing arts, English and sport.

Residential places are roughly equally divided between the two campuses, enabling Chichester to guarantee accommodation to anyone making the university a firm choice before the January UCAS deadline. There is a university bus service linking the two and there are students' union bars at each.

Sports facilities are good and the university was chosen to provide training facilities before the 2012 Olympic Games. Since then, a sports dome has been added to the existing tennis courts to provide an all-weather, multi-sport facility, and a new running track has been installed. The Tudor Hale Centre for Sport includes state-of-the-art laboratories, a refurbished fitness suite, sport injury clinic and teaching clinic. The university also runs a Gifted Athlete Programme, which has supported a Commonwealth judo champion and a potential 2016 Olympic sailor, among others.

The small cathedral city of Chichester is best known as a yachting venue, and Bognor is said to have the longest stretch of coastline in the south, where all types of water sports are available.

Both campuses offer a good supply of private housing and some student-oriented bars. Much of the surrounding countryside has been designated an area of outstanding natural beauty.

Tuition fees

» Fees for UK/EU students 2017–18   £9,250
  Placement year   £1,850
» UK fees are expected to increase by the rate of inflation from 2018–19 onwards.
» Fees for international students 2016–17   £10,620–£12,240
» Check the university's website for the latest information on fees, scholarships, bursaries and other forms of student support.

Students

Undergraduates:	4,225	(425)
Postgraduates:	360	(440)
Mature students:	14.1%	
International students:	2.4%	
Applications per place:	5.2	
From state-sector schools:	96.9%	
From working-class homes:	31.9%	
Satisfaction with students' union	75%	

For detailed information about sports facilities:
www.ucsu.org/activities/sport

Accommodation

Number of places and costs refer to 2016–17
University-provided places: 751
Percentage catered: 58%
Catered costs: £128.03 (single) – £162.05 (single, en suite).
Self-catered costs: £99.05 (single) – £135.03 (en suite).
First years are guaranteed accommodation if conditions are met.
International students: as above.
www.chi.ac.uk/study-us/accommodation

City, University of London

City changed its name in September 2016 to City, University of London, making it quite clear to prospective students and academic or business partners that it is now part of the capital's world-renowned federal university.

Applications were already growing – by 8 per cent in 2015 – but Professor Sir Paul Curran, the Vice-Chancellor, believes that the new status will strengthen City's international profile and expand its research and education capabilities. As one of the University of London's 18 autonomous colleges, City will continue to set its own entrance requirements and award its own degrees.

Once a college of advanced technology, the university now has more than a quarter of its students taking business courses, and nearly as many taking health and community subjects, with the remainder studying law, computing, mathematics, engineering, journalism and the arts.

The university has also been recruiting strongly to improve its research performance, although it entered little more than half of its eligible academics in the 2014 assessments. Three-quarters of its submission to the 2014 Research Excellence Framework was rated as world-leading or internationally excellent, with music and business producing the best results.

Cass Business School is one of City's great strengths, ranking among the top 50 business schools in the world.

Based in the heart of the financial district, it has built up an impressive cadre of visiting practitioner lecturers who find it easy and convenient to visit. The City Law School was the first in London to offer a "one-stop shop" for legal training, from undergraduate to professional courses.

The Department of Journalism, within the School of Arts and Social Sciences, is also highly regarded and has benefited from new facilities costing £12 million. There is a flourishing short course programme which ranges from sitcom writing to e-business.

City's Northampton Square Campus has been rejuvenated and another £130 million of refurbishment and new developments are planned over the next four years. The library has been renovated at a cost of £2.3 million, giving students more space, upgraded technology and better support.

The Student Centre and Careers Centre have been refurbished and a new common room added. The City Law School has been upgraded and the School of Health Sciences has moved to the main campus with new facilities, including a new biomedical and clinical skills centre.

The students' union is popular and the Student Centre, which provides advice on a range of topics, is the only one in the UK to receive the Service Mark Quality Standard

Northampton Square
London EC1V 0HB

020 7040 5060
enquiries@city.ac.uk
www.city.ac.uk
www.culsu.co.uk
Affiliation: none

The Times and Sunday Times **Rankings**		
Overall Ranking: **50** (last year: =41)		
Teaching quality:	=72	80.1%
Student experience:	55	84.3%
Research quality:	53	21.4%
Entry standards:	=43	375
Student–staff ratio:	71	16.6
Services & facilities/student:	26	£2,469
Expected completion rate:	68	85.4%
Good honours:	60	71.8%
Graduate prospects:	=15	82.6%

from the Institute of Customer Service.

City has been rising up our league table, with good levels of graduate employment and some of the highest rates of student satisfaction in London, where many institutions continue to register low scores. The university attracts international students from more than 150 countries. It has links with 50 European universities and many more further afield. Many students spend a year of their course abroad. There is a range of scholarships worth up to £3,000 a year for students who achieve exceptional grades at A level, International Baccalaureate or other qualifications.

There are over 18,000 students, 46 per cent of them postgraduates – one of the highest proportions in the UK. City also remains among the most popular universities at undergraduate level, with about ten applications for each place. The university has also increased its part-time numbers, against the national trend, with many students taking short courses that do not lead to a formal qualification.

City has a better record than most of its peer group for widening participation in higher education, with 46 per cent of its undergraduates coming from low-income groups – well ahead of the national average (35 per cent) for its courses and entry qualifications.

The university has strong links with business and the professions, and reaps the benefits with consistently good graduate employment figures. Courses have a practical edge, and many of the staff hold professional, as well as academic, qualifications. Three interdisciplinary centres have been launched to increase collaborative teaching and research, as well as to build stronger links between industry and academia.

The redeveloped sports centre, between the campus and the business school, is now the largest university sports facility in central London. The 3,000 square metres of floor space at CitySport is available to students, staff and the local community. At its heart is the Saddlers Sport Hall, which meets Sport England standards and has seating for up to 400 spectators, and the centre also has a separate fitness area.

Tuition fees

» Fees for UK/EU students 2017–18 £9,250
   Franchised course provision £8,000–£9,000
   Year abroad £1,385
   Placement year £1,850
» UK fees are expected to increase by the rate of inflation from 2018–19 onwards.
» Fees for international students 2017–18 £14,000–£16,500
» Check the university's website for the latest information on fees, scholarships, bursaries and other forms of student support.

Students

Undergraduates:	8,280	(1,415)
Postgraduates:	6,280	(2,305)
Mature students:	18.6%	
International students:	35.3%	
Applications per place:	10.1	
From state-sector schools:	90.5%	
From working-class homes:	46%	
Satisfaction with students' union	59%	

For detailed information about sports facilities:
www.city.ac.uk/sport-and-leisure

Accommodation

Number of places and costs refer to 2016–17
University-provided places: 1,291 through private providers
Percentage catered: 0%
Self-catered costs: £140.00 – £267.50 a week.
Accommodation is guaranteed for first-year undergraduates if conditions are met. Residential restrictions apply.
International students: housing guaranteed if conditions are met.
accomm@city.ac.uk
www.city.ac.uk/study/undergraduate/accommodation

Coventry University

Coventry's rapid rise has been the sensation of UK rankings over the last few years, and the university is capitalising on its greatly enhanced profile by embarking on the largest and most significant development in its history. Planned additions in the city centre will cost £125 million and include a new headquarters, an international student centre and business incubation unit. They will bring total spending on capital projects to more than £350 million by 2021. The region's only Confucius Institute, fostering links between the West Midlands and China, is already open, and a £60-million science and health building will be ready for entrants in 2017.

There is even a new campus in Scarborough, which will take its first students in September 2016. Such is the belief in the university's brand presently, the campus on the North Yorkshire coast is taking the name Coventry University. The university also has students at two joint ventures in Turkey and China, and 29 partners in 17 countries also teach Coventry's courses.

Three years ago, Coventry achieved the highest ever position in our league table by a post-1992 university, and it remains ahead of its peer group. It was *The Times and Sunday Times* Modern University of

the Year in 2014, 2015 and 2016 and was also named University of the Year by *Times Higher Education* in 2015. Much of its success is due to student satisfaction ratings that are among the highest in the country, but it has shown ambition in a number of areas. It was among the first provincial universities to offer courses in London, and took its rivals by surprise by opening its own no-frills university college when £9,000 fees were introduced in 2012. The college is on the main Coventry campus and caters for students who do not require the full range of services. Its courses lead to Coventry degrees or diplomas, but fees in 2017 will be significantly reduced. The London campus, which opened in 2013, is business-oriented and mainly for international students.

Applications rose for the seventh year in a row in 2015 and the size of its undergraduate intake increased by almost 1,000 students. Undergraduates like the guaranteed return of marked work within ten days and the opportunity to make their own assessments of academics, who receive awards for excellent teaching. The Centre for Academic Writing offers advice on essays and theses, while the Maths Support Centre includes a statistics advisory service and specialist support service for dyslexics.

Coventry halved the number of degree programmes it offers in order to focus on the most popular, successful courses and produce a well-designed and coherent

Priory Street
Coventry CV1 5FB

024 7765 2222 (admissions)
studentenquiries@coventry.ac.uk
www.coventry.ac.uk
www.cusu.org
Affiliation: University
Alliance

The Times and Sunday Times Rankings

Overall Ranking: **47** (last year: 47)

Teaching quality:	4	87.6%
Student experience:	=4	89.8%
Research quality:	=107	3.8%
Entry standards:	83	317
Student–staff ratio:	=35	14.6
Services & facilities/student:	48	£2,116
Expected completion rate:	=74	84.4%
Good honours:	=69	70.1%
Graduate prospects:	30	79.9%

portfolio. It has embraced computer-assisted learning, supported by an expanded computer network, and prioritised employability through the Add+vantage scheme. Its modules cover a wide range of skills and help students gain work-related knowledge and prepare for a career. The International Centre for Transformational Entrepreneurship helps students and small firms to start up and grow a business.

The university traces its origins back to 1843, and has already made significant progress rejuvenating its 33-acre campus close to the city centre. Much of the ten-year programme involves student facilities such as the showcase turreted library, which cost £20 million. A £55-million engineering and computing building includes a dedicated ethical hacking lab, an ex-RAF Harrier Jump Jet and a wind-tunnel built by the Mercedes F1 team, all of which are used by undergraduates. The Hub contains the students' union, a music venue, plenty of informal study space, shops and restaurants. Other recent projects have included more residential accommodation, an arts centre and a sports centre.

The Institute for Advanced Manufacturing and Engineering has a bespoke "Faculty on the Factory Floor" unit at Unipart's Coventry manufacturing site. Undergraduate and postgraduate programmes in manufacturing engineering have been designed to provide students with an academic learning environment blended with access to real industry projects.

Coventry is also investing £100 million to increase its research capacity and performance, with new centres focusing on areas of strength. Results in the 2014 Research Excellence Framework were in sharp contrast to those for student satisfaction: placing the university in the bottom ten, having entered only 13 per cent of its eligible academics for assessment. Over 60 per cent of their work was considered world-leading or internationally excellent, with health subjects producing 94 per cent at this level.

Student residences are within walking distance of the campus and city centre. Students in Coventry welcome the relatively low cost of living there, and the city is not short of student-oriented nightlife.

Tuition fees

» Fees for UK/EU students 2017–18: £9,250
  Foundation degree £5,736
  Courses at Coventry University College
  and Scarborough Campus £6,009–£7,102
» UK fees are expected to increase by the rate of inflation from 2018–19 onwards.
» Fees for international students 2016–17 £11,359–£13,476
» Check the university's website for the latest information on fees, scholarships, bursaries and other forms of student support.

Students

Undergraduates:	18,460	(3,065)
Postgraduates:	3,810	(2,265)
Mature students:	18.3%	
International students:	27.1%	
Applications per place:	6.9	
From state-sector schools:	96.7%	
From working-class homes:	41.7%	
Satisfaction with students' union	79%	

For detailed information about sports facilities: www.coventry.ac.uk/life-on-campus/student-life/sport-coventry

Accommodation

Number of places and costs refer to 2016–17
University-provided places: 3,675 (includes 1,876 beds on Nomination Agreements)
Percentage catered: 12%
Catered costs: £142 (38 weeks).
Self-catered costs: £110 – £149 (40–44 weeks).
First years are guaranteed housing if conditions are met.
International students: as above.
www.coventry.ac.uk/study-at-coventry/student-support/accommodation

University for the Creative Arts (UCA)

The demand for places at the University for the Creative Arts (UCA) is taking longer to recover from the introduction of £9,000 fees than at other arts-based institutions. Although the numbers starting degrees increased slightly in 2015, applications were still 50 per cent lower than in the boom years immediately before the fees went up. It has been good news for applicants, however – almost two-thirds of them received offers in 2015, compared with fewer than half in 2011.

The university offers four-year degrees, incorporating a Foundation year, as well as the three-year format, and two-year Foundation degrees, which can be topped up to produce an Honours degree. Professor Simon Ofield-Kerr, the Vice-Chancellor, plans to increase international student numbers, while also maintaining UCA's local roots. All the students are encouraged to develop international perspectives, understanding and ambitions so that they are able to practise across the world. Collaboration between courses is also encouraged, so that students benefit from exposure to a range of disciplines.

Many staff are practitioners as well as academics, and the founding colleges have produced a string of famous graduates, such as Tracey Emin, Karen Millen and Zandra Rhodes – who has now become the university's Chancellor. Other high-profile alumni include the luxury jeweller Stephen Webster, Oscar-winning animators Michael Dudok de Wit and Suzie Templeton, artists Humphrey Ocean and Tacita Dean, and textile designer Roger Oates. UCA was named in the world's top 20 universities for studying fashion in the Business of Fashion Global School Rankings, which are based on surveys of fashion students, alumni and industry professionals.

The four campuses are spread across Kent and Surrey, where two well-established art colleges came together to form the university. The constituent colleges date back to Victorian times.

The largest campus is in Farnham, in Surrey, which was declared a Craft Town in 2013, with active support from the university. More than 2,000 students take a wide range of subjects from advertising, animation and computer games technology to film production, journalism, music composition and technology. A new acting and performance course has been launched with Farnham Maltings, where students have access to a network of theatre professionals, as well as performance and rehearsal spaces, and a screening room. A purpose-built student village in the centre of town has 350 rooms and there are two galleries

UCA Canterbury
New Dover Road
Canterbury
CT1 3AN

01252 892883 (enquiries)
enquiries@ucreative.ac.uk
www.uca.ac.uk
http://ucasu.com
Affiliation: GuildHE

The Times and Sunday Times Rankings

Overall Ranking: **53** (last year: =62)

Teaching quality:	14	84.4%
Student experience:	70	83.5%
Research quality:	111	3.4%
Entry standards:	=76	321
Student–staff ratio:	14	12.1
Services & facilities/student:	18	£2,647
Expected completion rate:	=71	84.9%
Good honours:	104	63.4%
Graduate prospects:	126	53.6%

on campus, as well as teaching space, and a library and learning centre. The campus includes research centres for crafts, textiles, and sustainable design. Additional facilities have been provided for the growing computer games courses, which now have a dedicated studio room with specialist computers.

The second Surrey-based campus is in Epsom, and specialises in fashion, graphics and music courses, although it also offers general art, design and media courses at further education level. Degrees include music journalism, fashion promotion imaging and graphic design. There is a modern library and learning resource centre for more than 1,200 students, a bar and café on campus, and three halls of residence. A new £5.9-million teaching block includes learning and resource facilities, a 200-seat auditorium and a digital media centre.

The largest of the two Kent campuses, at Rochester, offers a full range of art and design courses, covering fashion, photography, computer animation and jewellery making. The purpose-built campus is set on a hillside overlooking the city centre and the River Medway. Halls of residence with 214 places are close to the campus, which has studio spaces, a library and learning resource centre, and a gallery. Students taking UCA's popular television production course are based at Maidstone TV Studios – the largest independent studio complex in the UK – and also have access the facilities of the Rochester campus.

At Canterbury, the accent is on architecture, but there are also degrees in fine art, interior design, graphic design, and illustration and animation. The modern site is close to the city centre and contains purpose-built studios, workshops and lecture theatres. The Canterbury School of Architecture is the only such school to remain within a specialist art and design institution, encouraging collaboration between student architects, designers and fine artists.

UCA's courses are also taught in six partner colleges, including one in India. Results in the National Student Survey have been improving, particularly in relation to teaching quality.

Almost two-thirds of the university's small submission to the Research Excellence Framework was rated world-leading or internationally excellent and 90 per cent was placed in the top two categories for its impact.

Tuition fees

» Fees for UK/EU students 2017–18 £9,250
» UK fees are expected to increase by the rate of inflation from 2018–19 onwards.
» Fees for international students 2017–18 £12,350
» Check the university's website for the latest information on fees, scholarships, bursaries and other forms of student support.

Students

Undergraduates:	4,450	(30)
Postgraduates:	165	(160)
Mature students:	15.6%	
International students:	11.7%	
Applications per place:	5.1	
From state-sector schools:	97.6%	
From working-class homes:	39%	
Satisfaction with students' union	52%	

For detailed information about sports facilities:
http://clubs.ucasu.com/go

Accommodation

Places and costs refer to 2016–17
University-provided places: 969
Percentage catered: 0%
Self-catered costs: £68.44 (twin); £100.65 – £143.23 (single); £120.32 – £155.00 (en suite) a week (39 weeks).
Priority is given to disabled students (new and returning) and new full-time students by distance.
International students: guaranteed housing if application received by mid June.
www.uca.ac.uk/life-at-uca/accommodation

University of Cumbria

Cumbria is upgrading its largest campus, in Lancaster, in time for the new intake in 2017. There will be 2,500 square metres of new teaching space to complement the £9.2-million Gateway development for student services, the modern library and sports complex added in recent years. The university is spending more than £25 million in all to cater for the 4,500 students at the former St Martin's College campus, which is a ten-minute walk from Lancaster town centre and now includes a gymnastics centre and fitness suite, as well as extensive residential accommodation.

The university also operates on five sites in Cumbria itself. There are two campuses in Carlisle and one in Workington, as well as a university centre at Furness College, in Barrow.

It has also reopened one of the UK's most attractive campuses, in the Lake District setting of Ambleside, mainly as the base for conservation and forestry degrees and the country's largest programme of outdoor education courses. The former college site, which now has improved student accommodation, had been mothballed as a result of financial difficulties that have now been overcome. It has been refurbished and new amenities provided in conjunction with the Lake District National Park Authority.

The Institute for Leadership and Sustainability (IFLAS), which is part of the business school, is developing a portfolio of activities that make the best use of its unique setting. The transfer of courses from Newton Rigg, near Penrith, is part of a ten-year estates plan.

Cumbria's focus since its establishment in 2007 has been on attracting more students from a region of unusually low participation in higher education, as well as on serving the social and economic needs of the county.

Almost all the undergraduates are state educated, four in ten are from working-class homes and the proportion from areas without a tradition of higher education is one of the highest in England, at one in five. However, both applications and enrolments were down slightly in 2015.

The university has been developing new degrees in science, technology, engineering and mathematics (STEM) subjects and a high-spec laboratory in Carlisle because there was no provision at this level within Cumbria.

It is a partner in both the National College for Nuclear and the new Project Academy for Sellafield, which will help provide specialist education and training in delivering decommissioning, reprocessing and nuclear waste management.

The university's headquarters are in Carlisle, where the larger of the two sites

---

Fusehill Street
Carlisle, Cumbria CA1 2HH

0845 606 1144 (enquiries)
enquirycentre@cumbria.ac.uk
www.cumbria.ac.uk
www.ucsu.me
Affiliations: MillionPlus;
 Cathedrals Group

The Times and Sunday Times Rankings

Overall Ranking: **119** (last year: 119)

Teaching quality:	=76	80%
Student experience:	123	78.8%
Research quality:	122	1.2%
Entry standards:	=109	292
Student–staff ratio:	113	19.7
Services & facilities/student:	=114	£1,349
Expected completion rate:	=77	84.3%
Good honours:	111	61.6%
Graduate prospects:	=92	66.3%

is in a parkland setting close to the River Eden. The second campus, closer to the city centre, boasts a new Learning Gateway, an innovative multimedia learning resource centre, and a sports centre with a four-court sports hall and well-equipped fitness room.

The former Cumbria Institute of the Arts can trace its history in Carlisle back to 1822, eventually becoming the only specialist institute of the arts in the North West, and one of only a small number of such institutions in the country.

The creative arts are one of the main areas earmarked for development and produced by far the best results in the 2014 Research Excellence Framework (REF), with 90 per cent of the submission judged to have world-leading or internationally excellent impact. Overall, Cumbria is just two places off the bottom of our research ranking, having entered only 27 academics for the REF, 8 per cent of those eligible. Almost 30 per cent of their work was placed in the top two categories.

Nearly a third of the first-year students are 21 or over, and only a quarter come from Cumbria itself. There are partnerships with the four further education colleges in the county to provide higher education locally.

The university was finally established after a series of false starts, formed by the amalgamation of a former teacher training college and an arts institute, with the addition of two campuses acquired from the University of Central Lancashire.

Cumbria is one of the largest teacher training providers in England, and has relaunched its business school with an emphasis on programmes in areas of particular strength, such as small- and medium-sized enterprises, ethics and leadership, and sustainability. Business interaction centres in Carlisle and Ambleside support business development and student entrepreneurship.

There is a London campus on a new site on the doorstep of Canary Wharf, which opened in 2013. The Education Faculty has been helping schools and training teachers in East London – and broadening the experience of its trainees – for more than 15 years.

Tuition fees

- » Fees for UK/EU students 2017–18   £9,250
-     Foundation degree   £9,250
- » UK fees are expected to increase by the rate of inflation from 2018–19 onwards.
- » Fees for international students 2017–18   £10,500
- » Check the university's website for the latest information on fees, scholarships, bursaries and other forms of student support.

Students

Undergraduates:	5,260	(1,695)
Postgraduates:	1,065	(1,050)
Mature students:	30.3%	
International students:	1.5%	
Applications per place:	5.4	
From state-sector schools:	97%	
From working-class homes:	41.9%	
Satisfaction with students' union	58%	

For detailed information about sports facilities:
www.cumbria.ac.uk/student-life/facilities/sports

Accommodation

Number of places and costs refer to 2016–17
University-provided places: 1,000
Percentage catered: 20%
Catered costs: £74.10 – £115.00 a week (plus catering plan).
Self-catered costs: £64.65 – £115.00 a week.
First year are guaranteed halls accommodation if Cumbria is first choice.
International students: guaranteed halls accommodation if conditions are met.
www.cumbria.ac.uk/student-life/accommodation

De Montfort University

Notwithstanding this year's 14-place fall in our table, prompted by a dip in student satisfaction scores in the latest National Student Survey, De Montfort is around 20 places ahead of where it stood in our table three years ago, and has seen the number of students starting degrees surge by more than 1,000 over the same period.

Perhaps believing that success breeds success, DMU has even become the "official higher education partner" of Premier League champions Leicester City, having worked with the club for several years. There are also partnerships with Leicester Tigers rugby club, Leicestershire cricket and Leicester Ladies hockey club.

Work has begun on striking new buildings for some of DMU's best-known schools and departments – fashion and textiles, arts, design and architecture. The £136-million "campus transformation project" will include an upgraded students' union, improved catering facilities, and a "green lung" at the heart of the campus, producing more outdoor social space. The centrepiece will be the impressive Vijay Patel Building, with sector-leading art and design facilities.

The work has been partly funded through one of the first investment bonds issued to a modern university.

DMU has already spent more than £140 million concentrating all its activities on its Leicester headquarters, when once it stretched from Bedford to Lincoln via Milton Keynes.

The university is aiming to provide the most comprehensive programme of overseas study at any UK university in order to expand its students' cultural horizons and make them employable across the world. Since 2015, every undergraduate course has included at least one module that offers an international experience through a network of overseas universities and businesses. The #DMUglobal programme is aiming to give 11,000 students – more than half of the current total – courses, internships or fieldwork overseas by 2020. More than 2,600 students took advantage of the scheme in its first year, visiting over 40 different countries.

The university also offers students the opportunity to participate in the award-winning Square Mile programme, which uses DMU's academic expertise and a network of student volunteers to offer valuable services to the local community, as well as national and international projects.

Almost 60 per cent of the university's research was judged to be world-leading or internationally excellent in the 2014 Research Excellence Framework.

Home to more than 60 specialist research groups and institutes, DMU focuses on "real world" research such as

The Gateway
Leicester LE1 9BH

0116 250 6070 (enquiries)
contact via website
www.dmu.ac.uk
www.demontfortsu.com
Affiliation: none

The Times and Sunday Times **Rankings**

Overall Ranking: **67** (last year: 53)

Teaching quality:	=80	79.9%
Student experience:	=81	83.1%
Research quality:	=67	8.9%
Entry standards:	=106	293
Student–staff ratio:	=103	18.6
Services & facilities/student:	50	£2,101
Expected completion rate:	57	86.6%
Good honours:	=69	70.1%
Graduate prospects:	47	75.5%

hospital infection control, housing policy research and participation in the £1-billion EU project to simulate a human brain. The OASYS project, which provides solar power for thousands of villagers in remote parts of South Asia, won the International Green Gown Award 2015 for community innovation.

There are already strong links with business and industry, such as the partnerships with Hewlett-Packard and Deloitte, which support innovative educational programmes as well as research collaborations. DMU has done well, too, in the National Teaching Fellowships – only five universities have won more than its total of 18. A Performance Arts Centre for Excellence allows the university to deliver innovative teaching for students of dance, drama and music technology, while £5.4 million has been spent transforming the former sports centre into The Venue@DMU events centre with is a full range of high-tech audio and visual equipment.

Four further education colleges across the East Midlands are linked into the university's IT network and offer its Foundation degrees and other courses. DMU has a proud record for widening access to higher education, with more than 40 per cent of undergraduates coming from working-class homes. It was one of the first to set up an employment agency to help students find part-time work as well as find careers upon graduation. De Montfort also has a strong reputation for the support it gives to disabled students. The dropout rate has improved consistently: at less than 10 per cent, it is now significantly lower than the national average for the university's courses and entry grades.

Sports facilities are excellent: an £8-million leisure centre includes a 25-metre swimming pool and an eight-court sports hall, while the new £1-million venue, The Watershed, also hosts indoor sport as well as activities for DMU's 100-plus societies. The university is now adding high-quality football pitches at nearby Beaumont Park for use by students and the local community.

The city of Leicester has become a more vibrant location, and has benefited from a £3-billion regeneration project. Rents in the private sector are low and the university has 2,500 rooms in halls within walking distance of the city centre.

Tuition fees

» Fees for UK/EU students 2017–18 — £9,250
  Foundation degree — £6,000
  Placement year / Year abroad — £650
  Degree courses at partner colleges — £6,000–£7,950
» UK fees are expected to increase by the rate of inflation from 2018–19 onwards.
» Fees for international students 2016–17 — £11,750–£12,250
» Check the university's website for the latest information on fees, scholarships, bursaries and other forms of student support.

Students

Undergraduates:	14,270	(1,745)
Postgraduates:	1,060	(2,570)
Mature students:	16.0%	
International students:	10.8%	
Applications per place:	5.4	
From state-sector schools:	97.2%	
From working-class homes:	43.1%	
Satisfaction with students' union	76%	

For information about sports facilities:
www.demontfortsu.com/activities/sportsclubs

Accommodation

Number of places and costs refer to 2016–17
University-provided places: around 2,500
Percentage catered: 0%
Self-catered costs: £92 (standard) – £162 (studio) a week (38–43 weeks).
First years cannot be guaranteed accommodation.
International students: new students are guaranteed accommodation (subject to the terms and conditions).
www.dmu.ac.uk/study/undergraduate-study/accommodation

University of Derby

There may be more than 80 universities ahead of Derby in our overall league table, but it is in the top 20 for teaching quality, as measured in the National Student Survey. The university guarantees that 85 per cent of its classes contain fewer than 30 students and that undergraduates can have access to their personal tutor whenever they need it. In an age when contact hours and staff feedback are hot topics, both are significant. The university has student representatives on all its senior management committees – another aspect of its focus on student needs.

The Institute for Learning Enhancement and Innovation works with academic staff to ensure that students receive the best possible learning experience. Derby's emphasis on "real-world learning" is underlined by facilities that include a simulated hospital and working radiography suite, new facilities for replica crime scenes, industry-standard kitchens and a fine dining restaurant, computer games suites, a commercial spa and salon, a law court and a 58-acre Outdoor Leadership Centre.

The university has invested £150 million on its campuses in ten years – £27 million in 2015 alone – creating a University Quarter for the city of Derby. A striking copper office block that has been vacant since it was completed in 2013 now houses

the law school. By 2017, there will also be a £12-million building nearby for science, technology, engineering and maths, financed partly through a funding council grant.

The Markeaton Street site, which was refurbished in 2016, hosts arts, design, engineering and technology courses, while courses in health and social care are based at Britannia Mill, ten minutes' walk away.

The university's main campus is two miles from the city centre, and caters for most of the other subjects including business, computing, science, humanities and education. The students' union, multi-faith centre and main sports facilities are on this site, which also houses clinical skills facilities, including a purpose-built iDXA suite. The university also owns and runs the 550-seat Derby Theatre in the city centre, which houses theatre arts programmes as well as continuing as a producing theatre.

The three bases are linked by free shuttle buses and the UniBus service, which also connects with the train station and city centre.

Beyond its home city, the university teaches nursing in Chesterfield and has a campus in Buxton that is based in the former Devonshire Royal Hospital and offers courses in spa, outdoor recreation and hospitality management, as well as further education programmes. The landmark building houses a training restaurant, a beauty salon and a health spa, as well as

Kedleston Road
Derby DE22 1GB

01332 591167 (enquiries)
askadmissions@derby.ac.uk
www.derby.ac.uk
www.udsu.co.uk
Affiliation: none

The Times and Sunday Times Rankings

Overall Ranking: **83** (last year: 84)

Teaching quality:	=19	83.5%
Student experience:	=62	83.9%
Research quality:	115	2.5%
Entry standards:	=92	305
Student–staff ratio:	=41	14.8
Services & facilities/student:	77	£1,798
Expected completion rate:	96	81.8%
Good honours:	89	66.1%
Graduate prospects:	101	64%

more conventional teaching facilities. A Foundation degree in spa management is also taught in London, at the London School of Beauty and Make-up. A new sports centre opened in Buxton in 2012 and almost £9 million is now being spent on a new campus in Chesterfield for nursing, engineering, IT and business innovation.

The university entered only 19 per cent of its eligible academics for the 2014 Research Excellence Framework, when almost 30 per cent of its submission reached one of the top two categories.

Business engagement is a higher priority. The Institute for Innovation in Sustainable Engineering, for example, supports advanced manufacturing with 3-D printing and advanced testing with industrial partners such as Rolls-Royce. A University Technical College for students aged between 14 and 19 has a focus on manufacturing, with Rolls-Royce again among the partners.

Apprenticeship provision at the university grew by 75 per cent in 2015 and Derby is among the leaders in the development of higher and degree apprenticeships, which are already available in mineral products technology, health and social care and advanced manufacturing engineering. Derby is also working with Sage and two accountancy bodies to offer a higher apprenticeship degree as a route to a professional accounting qualification.

Foundation degrees are available in a variety of subjects, allowing students to start a course at a partner college before transferring to the university.

The "Skillbuilder" career development programme covers a range of transferable skills to assist graduates in the employment market. Derby is also at the forefront of developing a Higher Education Achievement Record that students can make available electronically to prospective employers.

The university has spent £30 million in five years to maintain its guarantee of accommodation for all first years, with another 350 residential places on the way in the city centre.

A new £10.5-million sports centre opened on the main campus in 2015. The facilities include fitness and cycling studios, climbing wall, squash and badminton courts plus an indoor sprint track and sand pit.

Tuition fees

- » Fees for UK/EU students 2017–18 £9,250
  Placement year £1,000
- » UK fees are expected to increase by the rate of inflation from 2018–19 onwards.
- » Fees for international students 2017–18 £11,750–£12,250
- » Check the university's website for the latest information on fees, scholarships, bursaries and other forms of student support.

Students

Undergraduates:	9,905	(3,250)
Postgraduates:	855	(1,925)
Mature students:	20.6%	
International students:	8.0%	
Applications per place:	6.9	
From state-sector schools:	98%	
From working-class homes:	38.6%	
Satisfaction with students' union	64%	

For detailed information about sports facilities:
www.teamderby.com

Accommodation

Number of places and costs refer to 2016–17
University-provided places: 2,906
Percentage catered: 0%
Self-catered costs: £98.56 (standard) – £121.45 (premium en suite).
First-year students are guaranteed accommodation if they apply before 31 July.
Policy for international students: as above.
studentliving-housingteam@derby.ac.uk
www.derby.ac.uk/campus/accommodation

University of Dundee

Dundee – our Scottish University of the Year for a second successive year and shortlisted for the wider UK title – has a "big goal" that it admits could take 25 years to achieve: to be Scotland's leading university, celebrated internationally for the quality of its graduates and the impact of its research.

In some areas – particularly in the life sciences – it could claim to be there already. Dundee was the top university for biological sciences in the 2014 Research Excellence Framework (REF) and has opened the £50-million Discovery Centre to encourage interaction between different disciplines. Dundee had already received a Queen's Anniversary Prize for the achievements of its Centre for Anatomy and Human Identification. But the university's successes are not confined to the life sciences: it went up 17 places in our league table in the past two years to an all-time high UK ranking of 28. Its latest success is underpinned by a UK ranking of seventh for both student satisfaction with teaching quality and the wider student experience, as measured in the annual National Student Survey. *Times Higher Education* magazine rates it among the top 20 universities in the world founded in the last 50 years.

The university has completed a £200-million campus redevelopment designed by the leading architect, Sir Terry Farrell. Among the buildings added in recent years are those for clinical research, interdisciplinary research and applied computing. There have been extensions to the library and the sports centre, while almost £40 million was spent on wireless-networked student residences.

The IT facilities include superfast broadband, allowing the latest technologies to be used to enhance teaching. Dundee claims that its online learning environments are among the most advanced in the UK, available via the internet and mobiles, supporting all courses and providing specialist academic search tools.

The university attracted record numbers of applications and enrolments in 2015, having seen increases of more than 10 per cent in both. There are now over 15,000 students, including a healthy number from overseas.

Flagship work in the life sciences and medicine is led by research into cancer and diabetes. The new Discovery Centre is an annexe of the College of Life Sciences, which already benefits from the £13-million Wellcome Trust Building and the Sir James Black Centre, which cost £21 million. Its academics were the first in Britain to be invited to take part in Japan's Human Frontier science programme and are now the most-quoted researchers in their field.

Nethergate
Dundee DD1 4HN

01382 383838 (enquiries)
contact via website
www.dundee.ac.uk
www.dusa.co.uk
Affiliation: none

The Times and Sunday Times Rankings

Overall Ranking: **28** (last year: 37)

Teaching quality:	7	85.9%
Student experience:	7	88.8%
Research quality:	41	31.2%
Entry standards:	30	413
Student–staff ratio:	16	12.6
Services & facilities/student:	87	£1,705
Expected completion rate:	=59	86.4%
Good honours:	=35	77.8%
Graduate prospects:	24	80.9%

Set in 20 acres of parkland, the medical school is the one of the few components of the university outside the compact city-centre campus – some of the nursing and midwifery students are 35 miles away in Kirkcaldy. Other successes in the REF assessments included civil engineering, which came in the top three in the UK, and maths and general engineering, which were both in the top ten.

The university leads one of four "knowledge exchange hubs for the creative economy", tasked with bringing academics together with business and charities, and raising public awareness of the creative industries. The highly rated design courses are taught at the Duncan of Jordanstone College of Art. The university is a key participant in the Dundee-based V&A project to improve design in Scotland.

Dundee produces consistently strong graduate employment results. and claims to send more graduates into the professions than any other institution in Scotland. Most degrees include a career planning module and an internship option, and students have their own personal development website. The Enterprise Gym gives students the chance to improve their self-reliance and employability. They can also take the Scottish Internship Graduate Certificate, an eight-month programme combining a six-month internship with career management learning. A global equivalent lasts seven months with an internship in India or China.

Two-thirds of Dundee's students are from Scotland and nearly one in ten from Northern Ireland. More than one undergraduate in five comes from an area with little tradition of higher education, and almost three in ten are from working-class homes.

Applicants have access to MyDundee, an online portal giving further information during the application process. There is also a new Enquiry Centre providing a single point of contact for students needing support in a variety of areas. The city is benefiting from regeneration programmes, and enjoys a cost of living that is among the lowest at any UK university city. Spectacular mountain and coastal scenery is close at hand and the city offers lively nightlife, but social life tends to be concentrated on one of Scotland's most active students' unions.

Tuition fees

» Fees for Scottish and EU students 2017–18   No fee
» Fees for non-Scottish UK (RUK) students 2017–18   £9,250
  capped at £27,750 for four-year courses; MEng and MSci capped at £37,000; no cap for architecture, dentistry and medicine.
» Fees for international students 2017–18   £14,950–£17,950
      Medicine   £21,300–£35,000
      Dentistry   £28,600–£40,000
» There are particular support schemes for RUK students.
» Check the university's website for the latest information on fees, scholarships, bursaries and student support.

Students

Undergraduates:	8,770	(1,430)
Postgraduates:	1,665	(3,315)
Mature students:	28.1%	
International students:	13.9%	
Applications per place:	8.4	
From state-sector schools:	89.7%	
From working-class homes:	29.1%	
Satisfaction with students' union	88%	

For detailed information about sports facilities:
www.dundee.ac.uk/ise

Accommodation

Number of places and costs refer to 2016–17
University-provided places: 1,587
Percentage catered: 0%
Self-catered costs: £118.51 – £139.86 a week.
First-year students are guaranteed accommodation if conditions are met. No residential restrictions.
International students are guaranteed accommodation if conditions are met.
residences@dundee.ac.uk
www.dundee.ac.uk/accommodation

Durham University

Durham is transferring its medical courses to Newcastle University for the second time in little more than 50 years, with the School of Medicine, Pharmacy and Health vacating the Queen's Campus in Stockton-on-Tees as part of a fresh university strategy adopted after the arrival of a new vice-chancellor. Newcastle was Durham's medical school until becoming a university in its own right in 1963. Durham re-established a medical school at the start of the millennium, its students spending their first two years on the purpose-built campus in Stockton, concentrating on community medicine, before moving to Newcastle to complete their training.

The transfer is likely to take place as the new entrants arrive in 2017, with the Stockton campus being "repurposed" to house an international foundation college, running courses to prepare overseas students for degree-level study. The overall strategy is designed to focus resources on areas where Durham can make the greatest impact and improve the student experience.

The university is widely seen as the north of England's nearest equivalent to Oxbridge, with a collegiate structure and high standards that have made it a permanent fixture in our top ten, this year rising to its highest ever position of fourth in our league table. The university is rated in the top 100 in the world both by *Times Higher Education* magazine and QS. The demand for places has been even stronger since Durham joined the Russell Group of in 2012. Applications were up by another 5 per cent in 2015, although there was only a small rise in the numbers awarded places.

Undergraduates apply to one of 15 colleges, all of which are mixed. Colleges range in size from 300 to 1,300 students and are the focal point of social life, although all teaching is undertaken in central academic departments. There are significant differences in atmosphere and student profile, ranging from the historic University College, in Durham Castle, to modern buildings on the city's outskirts.

Investment continues on the Mountjoy Site for the sciences, with improved student facilities and an extension of the Bill Bryson Library (named after Durham's former Chancellor). There is a new law school and a £16.6-million extension of the Business School is now complete. A new physics research centre designed by the world-renowned architectural practice Studio Daniel Libeskind has recently opened, but the main development has been the Palatine Centre, a £50-million hub at the heart of the university that brings together the main student services.

Durham is the third-oldest university in England, and holds on to its academic

---

The Palatine Centre
Stockton Road
Durham DH1 3LE

0191 334 6128 (admissions)
admissions@durham.ac.uk
www.dur.ac.uk
www.durhamsu.com
Affiliation: Russell Group

The Times and Sunday Times Rankings

Overall Ranking: **4** (last year: 5)

Teaching quality:	=41	82.1%
Student experience:	=24	86.4%
Research quality:	16	39%
Entry standards:	5	526
Student–staff ratio:	=38	14.7
Services & facilities/student:	15	£2,683
Expected completion rate:	8	95.6%
Good honours:	4	89.4%
Graduate prospects:	=12	83.3%

traditions. Wherever possible, teaching takes place in small groups and most assessment is by written examination.

Four-fifths of the work assessed for the 2014 Research Excellence Framework was rated as internationally excellent or world-leading. Areas of particular strength include anthropology, archaeology, chemistry, classics, education, English, law, music, physics and theology.

The university attracts a largely middle class student body, with more than a third of undergraduates coming from independent schools. But a scheme that targets able pupils from schools in the North East, Cumbria and West Yorkshire has helped to bring in more applicants from non-traditional backgrounds. In addition to the normal open days, all those who receive an offer are invited to a special visit day to see if Durham is for them. Around 90 per cent come from outside the northeast of England and many are visiting the region for the first time.

Sports facilities are excellent and Durham is among the premier universities in national competitions. Its student performance programme covers 16 sports and there are national centres in cricket, fencing, lacrosse, rowing, rugby union and tennis. Three-quarters of all students take part in sport on a regular basis, and Durham's College Sport programme is one of the largest intramural competitions in the UK. Some 550 teams regularly compete across 18 sports. In 2015 Durham was named "Sports University of the Year" by *The Times and The Sunday Times* and has been ranked second in the British Universities and Colleges Sport (BUCS) league table since 2012.

The university dominates the small cathedral city of Durham and adds considerably to the local economy.

The university has introduced new safety measures for those socialising in Durham since three students drowned in the River Wear after nights out in the city in the space of 14 months. A programme praised by the Royal Society for the Prevention of Accidents includes improvements to riverside lighting and barriers, safety information, late-night taxis and a revised alcohol policy.

For those looking for nightlife, or just a change of scene, Newcastle is a short train journey away.

Tuition fees

» Fees for UK/EU students 2017–18 .... £9,250
   Year abroad £1,385
   Placement year £1,850
» UK fees are expected to increase by the rate of inflation from 2018–19 onwards.
» Fees for international students 2017–18 £17,400–£22,000
» Check the university's website for the latest information on fees, scholarships, bursaries and other forms of student support.

Students

Undergraduates:	12,675	(195)
Postgraduates:	3,400	(1,325)
Mature students:	6.2%	
International students:	17.2%	
Applications per place:	6.8	
From state-sector schools:	63.1%	
From working-class homes:	14.2%	
Satisfaction with students' union	35%	

For detailed information about sports facilities:
www.teamdurham.com

Accommodation

Number of places and costs refer to 2016–17
University-provided places: 4,413
Percentage catered: 70%
Catered costs: £178.54 – £237.34 a week (29–38 weeks).
Self-catered costs: £124.08 – £143.79 a week (38 weeks).
First-year undergraduates become members of a university college or society and are offered university housing.
International students: all first-year undergraduates are offered university accommodation.
www.dur.ac.uk/undergraduate/live/colleges

University of East Anglia

The University of East Anglia (UEA) is planning to grow over the next few years, capitalising on its position as an established top-20 university. It increased the size of its undergraduate intake by more than 900 students in 2015, when applications were up by more than 14 per cent. To help accommodate the extra students, two new residential buildings opened in September 2016, the first stage in a development that will add 915 places to UEA's already substantial stock.

The project is part of an ambitious building and refurbishment programme on the university's 320-acre campus on the outskirts of Norwich. Other recent developments include the opening of a £19-million medical education and research building named after Bob Champion, the Grand National-winning jockey whose cancer trust was the biggest donor, on the Norwich Research Park.

The students' union has been refurbished and the Law School has new premises on the Earlham Hall complex, while a Gymnastics Centre has been added to UEA's community Sportspark. There is also a new Enterprise Centre to develop students' entrepreneurial skills in an age when self-employment is increasingly common for new graduates.

A new online platform (#AskUEA) gives prospective students the chance to pose their own questions about university life, one of a number of improvements to the university's web services.

UEA invariably produces some of the best scores in the National Student Survey and had even stolen a march on its rivals by opening a "nap nook". Based on a development at James Madison University in the United States, it offers students a room with comfortable furniture and blackout curtains where they can have 40 minutes' sleep between lectures – eyeshades and anti-microbial pillows provided. The idea is to provide respite after an all-night session in the library, or elsewhere, aiding concentration and promoting good health.

The base in the City of London for international students that UEA shared with a private company has closed, as the university streamlines its portfolio of courses and concentrates its activities on Norwich. But the university has opened an office in Kuala Lumpur, and overseas students are expected to account for much of the coming expansion.

UEA celebrated its 50th anniversary in 2013, still offering some of the highly regarded broad subject combinations that it pioneered in its early days.

Environmental science is traditionally the flagship school – another international ranking placed UEA in the top 30 in the

---

Norwich Research Park
Norwich NR4 7TJ

01603 591515 (admissions office)
admissions@uea.ac.uk
www.uea.ac.uk
www.uea.su
Affiliation: none

Edinburgh
Belfast
NORWICH
London
Cardiff

The Times and Sunday Times Rankings

Overall Ranking: **15** (last year: 18)

Teaching quality:	=24	83%
Student experience:	16	87.4%
Research quality:	32	35.8%
Entry standards:	25	423
Student–staff ratio:	=20	13.2
Services & facilities/student:	17	£2,653
Expected completion rate:	=28	92.2%
Good honours:	=15	83.4%
Graduate prospects:	51	74.2%

world for the impact of its research in this field. The Climatic Research Unit and the Government-funded Tyndall Centre for Climate Change Research, which has a hub in Shanghai, are among the leaders in the investigation of climate change. But social work and pharmacy produced even better results in the 2014 Research Excellence Framework, when 82 per cent of all the work submitted by the university was placed in one of the top two categories.

Art history has the benefit of the Sainsbury Centre for the Visual Arts, perhaps the greatest resource of its type on any British campus. The refurbished and extended centre houses a priceless collection of modern and tribal art in a building designed by Norman Foster.

Creative writing is another of UEA's best-known features and the recipient of a Diamond Jubilee Queen's Anniversary Prize, while health studies have been among UEA's fastest-developing areas in recent years. The £81-million Quadram Institute, a new centre for food and health research, will open on the Norwich Research Park in 2018.

Throughout the university, students can bring any inquiries to four learning and teaching "hubs", one for postgraduates, another for nursing and two for undergraduates in the other 25 schools.

Nine out of ten undergraduates come from state schools or colleges, although only a quarter have a working-class background.

Most undergraduates have the opportunity of work experience as part of their course. An academic adviser guides all students on their options under the modular course system and monitors their progress through to graduation.

The university has sharpened its focus on employability with a strategy that promotes the development of the academic and wider skills that employers demand through the curriculum. In addition, a Graduate Intern Programme enables recent graduates to work for between four and twelve weeks at a business in the eastern region.

The university itself is situated in parkland, with easy access to Norwich, voted one of the best small cities in the world. The Sportspark is impressive, and the university was chosen as the base for the English Institute of Sport in the East.

Tuition fees

» Fees for UK/EU students 2017–18 £9,250
Courses at partner colleges £7,500–£8,500
Year abroad £1,385
Placement year £1,385

» UK fees are expected to increase by the rate of inflation from 2018–19 onwards.

» Fees for international students 2017–18 £14,800–£18,200
Medicine £30,000

» Check the university's website for the latest information on fees, scholarships, bursaries and other forms of student support.

Students		
Undergraduates:	10,840	(605)
Postgraduates:	2,900	(1,920)
Mature students:	15.3%	
International students:	20.2%	
Applications per place:	6.3	
From state-sector schools:	90.4%	
From working-class homes:	25%	
Satisfaction with students' union	68%	
For detailed information about sports facilities:		
www.ueasport.co.uk		

Accommodation
Number of places and costs refer to 2016–17
University-provided places: 4,372
Percentage catered: 0%
Self-catered costs: £73.15 – £148.82 (38 weeks).
First years are guaranteed housing if conditions are met.
International students (non EU) cannot be guaranteed accommodation.
accom@uea.ac.uk
https://portal.uea.ac.uk/accommodation

University of East London

Sharply improved scores for student satisfaction this year have lifted the University of East London (UEL) off the foot of our league table. The annual National Student Survey led to a 42-place improvement in ranking for students' satisfaction with teaching quality with a 33-place improvement for satisfaction with their wider student experience in our table.

There was a 10 per cent decline in both applications and enrolments in 2015 but the university chose not to drop its standards to fill up places – more than a third of the 16,000 applicants did not receive offers, a much higher rate than at most similar institutions.

Barely more than half of first years arrive with A levels and a similar proportion are 21 or older on entry – many choosing to start courses in February rather than in the autumn. Over half of the undergraduates come from working-class homes, many from the area's large ethnic minority populations. A successful mentoring scheme for black and Asian students has become a model for other institutions, while a guidance unit advises local people considering returning to education.

UEL's strategic vision prioritises engagement with the local community, encouraging students to use their knowledge and skills to improve the lives of others. The Legal Advice Centre provides pro bono advice, while students and graduates working in the not-for-profit Civic Architecture Office have supported projects ranging from local school expansions to prison rehabilitation initiatives. Staff and students are actively encouraged to undertake short and longer-term projects as part of study, research or volunteering.

Every undergraduate at UEL receives a free Samsung tablet, pre-loaded with core e-textbooks, as part of the university's efforts to cater for a student population where more than half are the first in their family to experience higher education. The initiative costs £2 million and another £3 million has been invested in new centralised "helpdesks" in the Student Support hubs at both Docklands and Stratford campuses. The student charter urges undergraduates to adopt the "35-hour attitude", which means studying for at least 35 hours a week, making good use of the Learning Resources Centre and handing work in on time.

There was a creditable showing in the 2014 Research Excellence Framework. The amount of world-leading research doubled, compared with the 2008 assessments, and 62 per cent of the work submitted was placed in the top two categories. The university was ranked equal first in England for the impact of its psychology research, all of which reached the top grade.

Stratford Campus,
Water Lane
London E15 4LZ
Docklands Campus
University Way
London E16 2RD
020 8223 3333 (admissions)
study@uel.ac.uk
www.uel.ac.uk
www.uelunion.org
Affiliation: MillionPlus

The Times and Sunday Times **Rankings**

Overall Ranking: **123** (last year: 127)

Teaching quality:	=80	79.9%
Student experience:	86	82.6%
Research quality:	76	7.2%
Entry standards:	120	278
Student–staff ratio:	=116	20
Services & facilities/student:	67	£1,933
Expected completion rate:	124	73.3%
Good honours:	=117	59.1%
Graduate prospects:	127	52.3%

The university is building on the legacy of the London 2012 Olympics, when it hosted the United States team at its new £21-million sports and academic centre at the Docklands Campus, called the Sports Dock. The prize-winning waterside campus, was the first new campus in London for 50 years. New developments include the London Design and Engineering University Technical College, which opened in 2016 on land adjacent to the Docklands Campus.

Recent projects have been centred mainly on nearby Stratford, the original headquarters in UEL's days as a pioneering polytechnic. A joint venture with Birkbeck, University of London, opened there in 2013. The £33-million University Square development offers a range of subjects including law, performing arts, dance, music and information technology as daytime or evening courses.

Elsewhere in Stratford, the Great Hall in University House now boasts a high-tech, 230-seat fully retractable lecture theatre, while the health and bioscience laboratories have been refurbished. The Cass School of Education has opened and a prize-winning new library, opened in 2013, has extensive digital resources and a 24-hour café.

The Noon Centre for Equality and Diversity in Business gives extra help to black, Asian, and minority ethnic students to prepare for a successful career in business. UEL is also strong on provision for disabled students and houses the Rix Centre for Innovation and Learning Disability. Almost 1,000 businesses are involved in mentoring programmes and/or a work-based learning initiative which offers accredited placements. The Centre for Clinical Education is London's only provider of clinical facilities and training in podiatry.

University housing is not plentiful, although there are now 1,200 bed spaces and the rents are good value for London. Social life for many students revolves around the Docklands Campus, although Stratford has more to offer since its post-Olympics transformation. Sports facilities and new students' union premises have been added at both campuses. UEL's high performing sports programme featuring £2 million in scholarships and bursaries is attracting talented young athletes. UEL students won six medals at the 2014 Commonwealth Games, and both students and graduates were selected for the Rio Olympics.

Tuition fees

» Fees for UK/EU students 2017–18 £9,250
  Year abroad £1,385
  Placement year £1,000
» UK fees are expected to increase by the rate of inflation from 2018–19 onwards.
» Fees for international students 2017–18 £11,440
» Check the university's website for the latest information on fees, scholarships, bursaries and other forms of student support.

Students

Undergraduates:	10,205	(1,470)
Postgraduates:	1,880	(2,295)
Mature students:	47.0%	
International students:	6.9%	
Applications per place:	7.5	
From state-sector schools:	97.7%	
From working-class homes:	54.7%	
Satisfaction with students' union	61%	

For detailed information about sports facilities:
www.uel.ac.uk/sport

Accommodation

Number of places and costs refer to 2016–17
University provided places: 1,200
Percentage catered: 0%
Self-catered costs: £125.84 (single en-suite) – £165.82 (en-suite studio) a week (37 weeks).
First years are guaranteed accommodation if conditions are met; priority given to disabled students.
International students: same as above.
dlres@uel.ac.uk
www.uel.ac.uk/Accommodation

Edge Hill University

The numbers starting degrees at Edge Hill have risen for three years in a row and reached record levels in 2015, the increased numbers drawn by Edge Hill's growing reputation, backed up by a move into the top 10 modern universities in our league table this year. The 10-place rise in our rankings has come off the back of outstanding scores in the annual National Student Survey.

A raft of new developments opened in 2016 to cater for them – a new £13-million technology hub will house the Department of Computing, the Geosciences building has been extended to providing more laboratory space, and new halls of residence will provide 168 new en-suite bedrooms, bringing the total number of students that can live on campus to 2,259.

A £30-million sports centre has already opened, with facilities that include an eight-court sports hall, a 25-metre swimming pool, an 80-station fitness suite, aerobics studio, health suite with sauna and steam rooms, a café and lounge area. The outdoor facilities include one of the largest running tracks in Europe, rugby, hockey and football pitches, an athletics field, netball and tennis courts and a "trim trail" with exercise stations. This has enabled Edge Hill to introduce a range of new undergraduate degree programmes, including sports coaching and development for 2017.

The university has spent more than £250 million in ten years improving and extending the 160-acre campus at Ormskirk, in West Lancashire. Edge Hill was in the top three for its facilities and campus environment in *Times Higher Education* magazine's 2016 student experience survey. The university's flagship building, Creative Edge, houses industry-standard equipment and resources for students on media, film, animation, advertising and computing degrees.

The complex is also home to the Institute for Creative Enterprise, which acts as an interface between academic research and the creative industries, giving students the opportunity to work on live TV and secure work placements without leaving the campus. The Label Recordings, Edge Hill's own record label, also gives students the chance to work in an industry setting on everything from talent spotting and recording, to creating music videos, and PR and marketing campaigns.

Although university status arrived only in 2005, Edge Hill moved to its landscaped campus in the 1930s and has been training teachers since the 19th century. It has long since expanded into other subjects, but remains the UK's largest provider of secondary teacher training and courses for classroom assistants. The university also won

---

St Helens Road
Ormskirk
Lancashire L39 4QP

01695 657000 (enquiries)
contact via website
www.edgehill.ac.uk
www.edgehillsu.org.uk
Affiliation: none

The Times and Sunday Times **Rankings**

Overall Ranking: **58** (last year: 68)

Teaching quality:	=10	85%
Student experience:	=28	86%
Research quality:	=92	4.9%
Entry standards:	65	328
Student–staff ratio:	=41	14.8
Services & facilities/student:	62	£1,968
Expected completion rate:	73	84.6%
Good honours:	72	69.8%
Graduate prospects:	66	71.5%

the lion's share of funding to deliver further training for qualified secondary school teachers. A range of new education degrees are planned for 2017, as well as two in computer science and one in biotechnology.

Psychology, criminology and policing, English, sport and media produced the best results in the 2014 Research Excellence Framework. Scores for all six areas in which the university submitted work showed improvement compared with the last assessments.

Beyond Ormskirk, there are seven satellite campuses in Liverpool, Manchester and other parts of the North West to enable students to live at home. In addition, a number of further education colleges in the region teach the university's Foundation degrees.

Edge Hill has one of the highest proportions of state-educated students in England – 99 per cent – and just under 40 per cent of undergraduates have a working-class background. The projected dropout rate has improved markedly and, at less than 9 per cent, is much better than the university's benchmark. An award-winning student finance support package rewards achievement, as well as encouraging students to complete their studies, rather than simply offering incentives for enrolling.

Since 2014, all undergraduates on arts and science programmes have the opportunity to undertake a sandwich year in industry or a year studying abroad to enhance their learning and boost their employability. All students have a personal tutor, as well as access to counsellors and financial advice.

The SOLSTICE e-learning centre is recognised officially as a national centre of excellence in teaching and learning. It has a particular focus on learning in the workplace, but is involved with curriculum development and delivery in all three of the university's faculties. Three-quarters of all graduates leave with professional accreditation.

There are plans for significant expansion following the purchase of land adjoining the campus. The university's healthy surplus has seen it rated as one of most financially stable in the UK. The spacious Student Hub building houses the students' union and also contains shopping and dining facilities, open access computers and social space.

Tuition fees

» Fees for UK/EU students 2017–18   £9,250
   Foundation degree   £6,165
   Year abroad   £1,385
   Placement year   £1,850
» UK fees are expected to increase by the rate of inflation from 2018–19 onwards.
» Fees for international students 2017–18   £11,575
» Check the university's website for the latest information on fees, scholarships, bursaries and other forms of student support.

Students

Undergraduates:	9,620	(2,495)
Postgraduates:	1,240	(2,820)
Mature students:	24.3%	
International students:	1.4%	
Applications per place:	5.7	
From state-sector schools:	99.1%	
From working-class homes:	39.1%	
Satisfaction with students' union	72%	

For detailed information about sports facilities:
www.edgehill.ac.uk/edgehillsport

Accommodation

Number of places and costs refer to 2016–17
University provided places: 2,259
Percentage catered: 17.6%
Catered costs: £105 a week (40 weeks).
Self-catered costs: £82 – £115 a week (40 weeks).
First years cannot be guaranteed housing. Residential restrictions apply. Students designated overseas for fees are guaranteed accommodation if conditions are met.
www.edgehill.ac.uk/undergraduate/accommodation

University of Edinburgh

Edinburgh is planning to invest £1.5 billion over the next decade on new buildings and campus improvements at a time when it is facing cuts of up to £14 million in its Scottish Government funding. The university's strategic vision stresses that investment is needed now in order to produce a "highly satisfied student body with a strong sense of community", where all undergraduates develop as student researchers and are offered the opportunity to draw on expertise outside their core discipline.

Student satisfaction has been a problem in recent years, with stubbornly low scores in the National Student Survey (NSS) keeping Edinburgh outside our top 20, and this year depressing its overall ranking. Just 10 institutions have a lower score for student satisfaction with their university experience, and Edinburgh ranks next to bottom for student ratings for the quality of the teaching they receive, with scores for assessment and feedback especially low. The university is addressing this with a new personal tutor system and a peer support scheme, among other measures.

The demand for places is higher than ever, with the volume of applications growing by almost 50 per cent in four years. The university has responded by increasing the intake by 1,200 places, but it remains one of the few to make offers to fewer than half of its applicants.

Edinburgh produced Scotland's best performance in the 2014 Research Excellence Framework (REF). Although behind St Andrews overall in our league table, the university retains a special status north of the border, where it is regarded as on a par with Oxbridge. More than 80 per cent of the research submitted for the REF was judged to be world-leading or internationally excellent. Sociology, earth systems and environmental sciences, including geography, and computer science and informatics were among the UK leaders.

The current research star is Professor Peter Higgs, who was awarded the 2013 Nobel Prize for physics for predicting the existence of the Higgs Boson, the so-called "God particle". Professor Higgs' success will boost Edinburgh's performance in at least one of the international rankings that currently give the most positive view of the university: it is rated just inside the top 20 in the world by QS.

The university is one of the two most expensive in the UK for British undergraduates from outside Scotland, who will pay £9,250 for the full four years of their degree in 2017. But there is a range of bursaries for English, Welsh or Northern Irish students. More than a quarter of the undergraduates come from outside the UK, while 2.5 million learners worldwide have

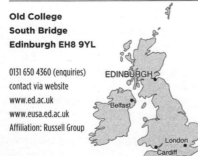

Old College
South Bridge
Edinburgh EH8 9YL

0131 650 4360 (enquiries)
contact via website
www.ed.ac.uk
www.eusa.ed.ac.uk
Affiliation: Russell Group

The Times and Sunday Times **Rankings**

Overall Ranking: **=37** (last year: 22)

Teaching quality:	127	71.8%
Student experience:	118	79.6%
Research quality:	10	43.8%
Entry standards:	9	487
Student–staff ratio:	=12	12
Services & facilities/student:	=52	£2,067
Expected completion rate:	36	91.3%
Good honours:	=12	84.5%
Graduate prospects:	58	73%

sampled Edinburgh's MOOCs (Massive Open Online Courses).

The university has always attracted a high proportion of middle-class candidates – many from England – and is a favourite in independent schools, whose students take about three places in ten. Measures to broaden the intake include an eight-week summer school for local teenagers and support for students in the transition to higher education. Selection guidelines aim to look beyond grades to consider candidates' potential, giving particular weight to references and personal statements.

The university's buildings are spread around the city, but most border the historic Old Town. These include the university's main library, which has been redeveloped at a cost of £60 million. The science and engineering campus is two miles to the south. Recent improvements include a new informatics building and the development of a "BioQuarter", a ground-breaking collaboration between the university and public bodies to consolidate Scotland's reputation as a world leader in biomedical science. A new library opened in 2014 on the science and engineering campus, while the Business School has relocated to the main campus. A research centre has been established for the study of Islamic civilisation and issues relating to Islam in Britain.

The Edinburgh Centre for Robotics, a collaboration with Heriot-Watt University, opened in 2015, bringing together scientists and engineers from both universities, as well as about 40 partners from industry. Planned projects include a new home for the School of Biological Sciences, the creation of a Data Technology Institute and a refurbishment of the historic School of Law at Old College. The plan also includes a redevelopment of the McEwan Hall – transforming the iconic home of university graduation ceremonies into a combined ceremonial and conferencing facility.

Sports facilities are impressive, and considerable sums have been spent making the university more accessible to disabled students. The students' union operates on several sites and there is a regular bus link between the science areas and the main university. The city itself is a treasure-trove of opportunities for its student population.

Tuition fees

» Fees for Scottish and EU students 2017–18   No fee
» Fees for non-Scottish UK (RUK) students 2017–18   £9,250 year, for up to 4 years (total £37,000).
» Fees for international students 2017–18   £17,700–£23,200
     Medicine   £32,100–£49,900
     Veterinary medicine   £30,200
» There are particular support schemes for RUK students.
» Check the university's website for the latest information on fees, scholarships, bursaries and other forms of student support.

Students

Undergraduates:	19,315	(780)
Postgraduates:	6,655	(2,125)
Mature students:	13.6%	
International students:	28.0%	
Applications per place:	10.2	
From state-sector schools:	68.5%	
From working-class homes:	18.7%	
Satisfaction with students' union	59%	

For detailed information about sports facilities:
www.ed.ac.uk/sport-exercise

Accommodation

Number of places and costs refer to 2016–17
University-provided places: about 6,020
Percentage catered: 23%
Catered costs: £125.58 – £256.83 a week.
Self-catered costs: £61.69 – £161.63 a week.
First years are guaranteed an offer of accommodation if conditions are met. Residential restrictions apply.
International students: accommodation guaranteed if conditions are met.
accom.allocations@ed.ac.uk; www.accom.ed.ac.uk

Edinburgh Napier University

If Scotland's first purpose-built studio complex on the outskirts of Edinburgh can get planning permission for its greenbelt site, there may be an opportunity for Edinburgh Napier to establish its own film academy as part of the development, giving students hands-on experience of film-making. The university already runs Screen Academy Scotland in partnership with Edinburgh College of Art (now part of the University of Edinburgh), reflecting the university's strong reputation in film education.

There are courses in writing, directing, producing and animation, and the creative arts produced the most successful of Edinburgh Napier's entries for the 2014 Research Excellence Framework.

The courses are currently based on Napier's Merchiston campus, which has seen much of the £100 million plus investment that has taken place at the university in recent years.

Computing, engineering and the built environment are also based on the campus, where there is a new student hub and reception area, as well as fully soundproofed music studios and a new broadcast journalism newsroom. Edinburgh Napier Students' Association is also based on the campus, as well as a refurbished library.

Other recent developments include two new student residences in the city centre with another under construction. The demand for places at Edinburgh Napier has been buoyant, despite rising entry requirements. The 13,000 students on the Edinburgh campuses include almost 4,000 international students, while another 4,000 take courses delivered with partners in Switzerland and several Asian countries, including China and India. The university is the largest UK provider of higher education in Hong Kong.

Once Scotland's first and largest polytechnic, Edinburgh Napier is named after the inventor of logarithms, John Napier.

The revamped Sighthill campus is home to the schools of Nursing, Midwifery and Social Care, and Life, Sport and Social Sciences. It has a five-storey learning resource centre, an environmental chamber and biomechanics laboratory, and a large simulation and clinical skills centre with mock hospital wards and a high dependency unit simulator suite. Integrated sports facilities feature a well-equipped fitness centre and a sports hall, as well as the BT Sport Scottish Rugby Academy.

The Craiglockhart campus houses the business school, which features a glass atrium with a cyber café and lecture theatres. Once a hydropathic hotel and then a hospital to treat shell-shocked soldiers

Craiglockhart Campus
Edinburgh EH14 1DJ

0333 900 6040 (enquiries)
contact via website
www.napier.ac.uk
www.napierstudents.com
Affiliation: MillionPlus

EDINBURGH

Belfast

London
Cardiff

The Times and Sunday Times **Rankings**

Overall Ranking: **=93** (last year: 93)

Teaching quality:	=72	80.1%
Student experience:	=73	83.3%
Research quality:	=94	4.6%
Entry standards:	52	350
Student–staff ratio:	118	20.1
Services & facilities/student:	120	£1,290
Expected completion rate:	90	82.5%
Good honours:	53	73.9%
Graduate prospects:	61	72.3%

during World War I, the architecture blends history and modernity. The campus also houses the War Poets Collection, an exhibition displaying the work of Siegfried Sassoon and Wilfred Owen. The Craiglockhart studio has been refurbished and offers an assortment of fitness classes.

Students have access to online lecture notes and study aids via Moodle, the university's Virtual Learning Environment. The web-based system supports learning, teaching and assessment via the student portal and is accessible from smart phones and tablet computers. There are fully networked libraries on each campus and a multimedia language laboratory and adaptive learning centre for students with special needs. The modular system allows movement between courses at all levels, and the option of starting courses in January, rather than September.

A model for other universities trying to reduce non-completion rates, Edinburgh Napier uses its students to mentor newcomers, runs bridging programmes and offers pre-term introductions to staff and information on facilities, as well as running summer top-up courses and teaching employability skills and personal development. The latest projected dropout rate of 9 per cent betters the UK average for the subjects on offer. Widening participation is high on the university's list of priorities, and more than 30 per cent of undergraduate places go to students from working-class homes. More than 2,000 students enter through "articulation routes", using their college qualifications to gain direct entry into year two or three of a Napier degree.

Many courses include a work placement, while the Confident Futures programme is said to be unique in higher education, using workshops to improve students' confidence and help them to develop skills, attributes and attitudes that will enhance their chances of being successful both while at university and in their careers. For the growing numbers choosing to start their own businesses, Bright Red Triangle (BRT), the university's student enterprise service, offers free office space and advice to students and alumni. It has helped about 300 companies to launch, more than half of which are still active. BRT also runs a commercial consulting practice, which employs students to work on commercial projects.

Tuition fees

» Fees for Scottish and EU students 2017–18   No fee
» Fees for non-Scottish UK (RUK) students 2017–18   £9,000 capped at £27,000 for 4-year courses and £36,000 for 5-year courses.
» Fees for international students 2017–18   £11,950–£13,900
» There are particular support schemes for RUK students.
» Check the university's website for the latest information on fees, scholarships, bursaries and other forms of student support.

Students

Undergraduates:	**9,310**	**(1,495)**
Postgraduates:	**1,150**	**(1,170)**
Mature students:	**40.9%**	
International students:	**16.6%**	
Applications per place:	**7.7**	
From state-sector schools:	**93.9%**	
From working-class homes:	**31.1%**	
Satisfaction with students' union	**64%**	

For detailed information about sports facilities:
www.napierstudents.com/teamnapiersports

Accommodation

Number of places and costs refer to 2016–17
University-provided places: around 1,500
Percentage catered: 0%
Self-catered costs: £90 (twin en suite); £135 – £140 (single en suite); £150 (studio) a week (38, 43 and 50 weeks).
First years and direct entrant undergraduates are guaranteed a place provided requirements are met.
International students: as above.
www.napier.ac.uk/study-with-us/undergraduate/accommodation

University of Essex

A record number of students started degrees at Essex in 2015, as the university made gradual progress towards its goal of growing by 50 per cent over five years. Its popularity with applicants continued to increase in 2016, following a 15 per cent rise in the demand for places – seven times the national average – in 2015.

To support its expansion while improving staffing levels, Essex announced the largest recruitment of academics in its history, with 57 new posts. It has also been upgrading and expanding its facilities, refurbishing its 1960s buildings and adding new developments like the £21-million "zero carbon" Essex Business School, which includes the Bloomberg Financial Market Lab, dedicated student services desk, study pods and innovation booths.

The Albert Sloman Library has expanded by 30 per cent and the new Silberrad Student Centre opened in 2015, providing a central point for student services, plus a 24-hour learning hub, new IT facilities, a media centre and 250 study spaces.

The new developments, costing more than £200 million, include a £1.4-million gym, renovation of the students' union bar, a café with adjoining learning space and shared IT workspace.

Future projects include a £10-million science, technology, engineering and mathematics building and a new teaching centre.

The main campus is set in 200 acres of parkland two miles from Colchester. Wivenhoe House, the original centrepiece, has been converted into a four-star hotel, home to and run by the Edge Hotel School.

Having spent many years trying to live it down, Essex has been embracing its radical past, telling prospective applicants that it welcomes independent thinkers and "rebels with a cause". The university, which celebrated its 50th anniversary in 2014, has also set itself the target of reaching the top 25 in our league table, with every subject in the top 20 per cent of its discipline. That first target is not so far off being achieved: Essex's overall ranking has improved from 39 to 30 over the past three years.

The social sciences are its greatest strength, featuring among the top 100 universities in the world in both the QS and *Times Higher Education* rankings. Essex received the only Regius professorship, in political science, in the awards to mark the Queen's Diamond Jubilee.

It achieved the best results in the 2014 Research Excellence Framework (REF) in politics and was in the top ten for economics and art history. The REF results as a whole represented a big improvement on an already successful set of assessments in 2008.

Wivenhoe Park
Colchester
Essex CO4 3SQ

01206 873666 (enquiries)
admit@essex.ac.uk
www.essex.ac.uk
www.essexstudent.com
Affiliation: none

The Times and Sunday Times Rankings

Overall Ranking: **30** (last year: 35)

Teaching quality:	=38	82.4%
Student experience:	18	87.2%
Research quality:	25	37.2%
Entry standards:	86	313
Student–staff ratio:	=69	16.5
Services & facilities/student:	5	£2,945
Expected completion rate:	51	88.3%
Good honours:	=51	74.3%
Graduate prospects:	=55	73.4%

The university moved into the top 25 in our research ranking, with almost 80 per cent of a large submission rated world-leading or internationally excellent.

The incorporation of the East 15 Acting School, in Loughton, as a department of the university was Essex's first venture beyond Colchester.

There has since been heavy investment in a third site in the centre of Southend – a modern multi-faculty campus offering courses in business, health and the arts. There is an accommodation complex which also houses a gym and fitness studio, while The Forum comprises a public and academic library, learning facilities, café and gallery, as well as having a floor reserved for student use.

The student population is unusually diverse for a pre-1992 university, with high proportions of mature and overseas students. More than a third of undergraduates are from working-class homes and 96 per cent went to state schools or colleges.

The university's employability initiatives were praised by the Quality Assurance Agency. The award-winning Frontrunners scheme, established by the university and students' union, arranges on-campus, paid work experience for students.

There is also an extensive internship programme and many courses offer work placement opportunities. The Big Essex

Award recognises students' extracurricular activities, volunteering and work experience, while Essex Abroad supports students studying, working or volunteering overseas. Language tuition is free, and the university also does not charge fees for a full year abroad or a placement year.

Social and sporting facilities are good, with an active students' union and some 40 acres of land on campus devoted to sports facilities. The number of student sports club members has doubled to 4,000 in recent years, while another 2,400 students take part in drop-in sessions.

All new first years are guaranteed a place in university accommodation, which has been voted some of the best in the UK. Some ground-floor flats have been adapted for disabled students. A £23-million development opened on campus in 2013 and another 1,000 places are planned. All the campuses are within easy access of London

Tuition fees

» Fees for UK/EU students 2017–18   £9,250
  Placement year / Year abroad   no fee

» UK fees are expected to increase by the rate of inflation from 2018–19 onwards.

» Fees for international students 2017–18   £13,350–£15,450

» Check the university's website for the latest information on fees, scholarships, bursaries and other forms of student support.

Students

Undergraduates:	**9,770**	**(1,315)**
Postgraduates:	**2,415**	**(935)**
Mature students:	**16.4%**	
International students:	**30.2%**	
Applications per place:	**6.8**	
From state-sector schools:	**96%**	
From working-class homes:	**38.3%**	
Satisfaction with students' union	**77%**	

For detailed information about sports facilities:
www.essex.ac.uk/sport

Accommodation

Number of places and costs refer to 2016–17
University-provided places: 4,692
Percentage catered: 0%
Self-catered costs: Colchester: £76.93 (South Towers) – £140.98 (Meadows en suite) a week; Southend: £135.24 (en suite) – £166.81 (studio flat).
New first years are guaranteed accommodation if conditions are met.
International students: new students, as above.
accom@essex.ac.uk; www.essex.ac.uk/accommodation

University of Exeter

Nine out of ten students who applied to Exeter in 2015 received a conditional offer of a place, one of the highest rates in the UK. Part of the reason is that since joining the Russell Group in 2012, the university has been attracting better-qualified applicants, as well as expanding rapidly. The undergraduate intake was 40 per cent bigger in 2015 than three years earlier, adding more than 1,700 places.

Firmly established in our top 10, Exeter is also among the top 130 universities in the *Times Higher Education* world rankings. It has invested £380 million on the main Streatham Campus, close to the centre of Exeter, one of the most attractive settings at any university.

The Living Systems Building opened in autumn 2016, and future development plans are centred on the St Luke's Campus, a mile from the main campus, which houses the medical school, as well as the highly rated Department of Sport and Health Sciences and the Graduate School of Education.

The £10.5-million South Cloisters development will provide research, teaching and student study space for the medical school, complementing a £27.5-million health education and research centre at the Royal Devon and Exeter Hospital. The school grew out of the former Peninsular College of Medicine and Dentistry, which was established in association with Plymouth University in 2006. The partners have gone their separate ways, with Plymouth taking dentistry and Exeter offering a BSc in medical sciences in addition to the established Bachelor of Medicine, Bachelor of Surgery (BMBS).

The university's other base is the £100-million Penryn Campus in Cornwall, which has helped boost applications in recent years. Shared with Falmouth University, the campus offers Exeter degrees in biosciences, geography, geology, clean energy, English, history, politics and mining engineering. A £30-million Environment and Sustainability Institute has opened on the campus and there is a new base there for the Business School. A £5.5-million science and engineering research support facility opened in autumn 2016.

Developments on the Streatham Campus have included student residences costing £130 million and impressive new sports facilities, which include a well-equipped fitness centre. There has been substantial investment in the Exeter Business School, a new Mood Disorders Centre and new facilities for biosciences and the Law School.

But the jewel in the crown of the new developments is the Forum, a £50-million complex which creates a central hub and features an extended library, new student services centre, technology-rich learning

---

Northcote House
The Queen's Drive
Exeter EX4 4QJ

0300 555 6060 (UK admissions)
ug-ad@exeter.ac.uk
www.exeter.ac.uk
www.exeterguild.org
Affiliation: Russell Group

The Times and Sunday Times **Rankings**

Overall Ranking: **=9** (last year: 7)

Teaching quality:	22	83.3%
Student experience:	=10	87.9%
Research quality:	18	38%
Entry standards:	14	471
Student–staff ratio:	59	15.8
Services & facilities/student:	23	£2,537
Expected completion rate:	6	96%
Good honours:	11	84.8%
Graduate prospects:	29	80.2%

spaces, a new auditorium and additional social and retail facilities. The Exchange, a £10-million learning, teaching and research building at Penryn Campus, created in conjunction with students, is to Penryn as the Forum is to Streatham.

Always among the leading universities in the National Student Survey, Exeter also recorded much-improved results in the 2014 assessments of research. More than 80 per cent of a large submission to the Research Excellence Framework was rated as world-leading or internationally excellent, with clinical medicine, psychology and education producing particularly good results.

The university has also been introducing a raft of new degrees, including several undergraduate Masters courses and five new pathways in the medical sciences. A legal practice course taught by the University of Law for graduates who want to become solicitors was added in 2016.

Almost a third of Exeter's undergraduates come from independent schools – a much higher proportion than the national average for the university's subjects and entry qualifications, although this figure has been coming down gradually. The share of places taken by students from the four poorest socio-economic groups, at less than 16 per cent, is among the lowest in the UK. However, the dropout rate of less than 4 per cent is also among the lowest.

Exeter's longstanding international focus is exemplified by a growing range of four-year programmes "with international study". All students are offered tuition in foreign languages and even some three-year degrees include the option of a year abroad. Career management skills are built in and students have a wide range of work experience opportunities.

The Career Zone has been expanded to increase career support and internships, while the university's Exeter Award provides official recognition of extracurricular activities. The number of student volunteers is among the highest at any university.

Over £20 million has been invested in first-class sports facilities in the last few years. Exeter is one of only nine UK universities to have indoor tennis facilities to national competition standards. Although the city is relatively small, there is no shortage of student-oriented bars and clubs.

Tuition fees

» Fees for UK/EU students 2017–18		£9,250
Year abroad		£1,385
Placement year		£1,850
» UK fees are expected to increase by the rate of inflation from 2018–19 onwards.		
» Fees for international students 2017–18		£16,500–£21,000
Medicine		£29,500
» Check the university's website for the latest information on fees, scholarships, bursaries and other forms of student support.		

Students

Undergraduates:	16,095	(75)
Postgraduates:	3,270	(1,110)
Mature students:	7.1%	
International students:	21.2%	
Applications per place:	7.2	
From state-sector schools:	68%	
From working-class homes:	15.5%	
Satisfaction with students' union	79%	

For detailed information about sports facilities:
http://sport.exeter.ac.uk

Accommodation

Number of places and costs refer to 2016–17
University-provided places: 5,471
Percentage catered: 24%
Catered costs: £153.50 (shared); £165.25 – £231.72 a week.
Self-catered costs: £100.18 – £166.48 a week (40, 42, 44 weeks).
Unaccompanied first years are guaranteed accommodation provided conditions are met.
International students: as above.
sid@exeter.ac.uk; www.exeter.ac.uk/accommodation

University of Falmouth

Falmouth heads a clutch of arts universities that are challenging the leading post-1992 institutions, ranking fifth this year among all modern universities in our league table.

Applications have continued to rise following a 30 per cent increase which was the biggest at any university in 2014. This surge in popularity has enabled Falmouth to increase the size of its undergraduate intake for three years in a row, despite offering places to only half of those applying. Most courses demand between 104 and 120 points on the new UCAS tariff system, but portfolios or auditions are as important as A levels on many courses. Some degrees hold out the possibility of unconditional offers for promising applicants.

There are still fewer than 5,000 students taking a range of subjects including architecture, digital media and creative writing, as well as graphic design and fashion. The university still regards itself as a specialist institution, but degrees now include acting, business entrepreneurship and marketing.

Founded in 1902 as Falmouth School of Art, the institution merged in 2008 with Dartington College of Arts in south Devon, thereby adding a variety of performance-related courses to its portfolio. The former Dartington courses have relocated to the purpose-built Academy of Music and Theatre Arts (AMATA) on the Penryn Campus, which Falmouth has shared with the University of Exeter since 2002. The unique joint students' union, FXU, serves all Falmouth students and those attending Exeter's Cornish outpost.

The university has invested more than £100 million on its two campuses over the past decade. Among the new facilities are a design centre, art studios, TV studio, 117-seat cinema, motion capture studio, video editing suites, specialist animation software, audio suites, professional-standard photography studios, darkrooms, photography store and AMATA, which has fully sprung Harlequin dance floors, rehearsal studios, practice rooms and flexible theatre space.

The Exchange, on the Penryn Campus, contains teaching and library space as well as study areas, while an Academy for Innovation and Research focuses particularly on the digital economy and sustainable design. A 54-place nursery and a new £4-million Sports Centre opened before the start of the 2016 academic year.

The original Falmouth campus, near the town centre, boasts subtropical gardens and an outdoor sculpture canopy, as well as studios, library and catering facilities. There is an impressive Graphic Design Building, opened in 2014, which houses the School of Communication Design. It has open-plan graphic design studios, a 150-seater lecture

Woodlane
Falmouth
Cornwall TR11 4RH

01326 213 730 (admissions)
contact through website
www.falmouth.ac.uk
www.fxu.org.uk
Affiliation: GuildHE

The Times and Sunday Times Rankings

Overall Ranking: **52** (last year: 56)

Teaching quality:	=17	83.6%
Student experience:	=67	83.7%
Research quality:	=94	4.6%
Entry standards:	=80	318
Student–staff ratio:	106	18.9
Services & facilities/student:	108	£1,434
Expected completion rate:	=46	88.6%
Good honours:	48	74.8%
Graduate prospects:	34	79.3%

theatre, design labs and photography spaces.

About 60 per cent of the undergraduates are female, although men are marginally more likely to receive an offer. The university has an internal teaching qualification for staff to ensure high standards in teaching, learning and assessment. The university offers each new arrival a student mentor for a year to support them during their transition to university life.

Most of the 36 degrees offered in 2016 are single Honours. The university has introduced new "externally facing" courses, including programmes that enable students to set up a business while studying. The BA in business entrepreneurship uses the successful Team Academy model for teaching, prioritising practical experience and mentoring. There are new degrees in digital games and computing for games.

Falmouth Launchpad, launched in 2014, is a graduate entrepreneurship programme with an emphasis on building technology companies. There is also a focus on the "learning and leisure" market, making use of Cornwall's tourist attractions, businesses and landmarks.

An extended Media Centre on the Penryn Campus, with new computers, a 3-D printer and stereoscopic projector, houses the Photographic Centre. Falmouth has been awarded Skillset Academy status for its media courses. The animation and visual effects department has become part of the Cross Channel Film Lab, which aims to develop innovative visual effects for use in low-budget feature film production, working on films alongside experts within the industry.

Glasney Student Village, on the Penryn Campus, was extended in 2012. There are also residential places in Falmouth, enabling the university to guarantee all full-time first years accommodation in their 1,800 university-provided places as long as they apply by the published deadline. A private company is planning to provide another 900 rooms in the town for Falmouth and Exeter students.

The Sports Centre has a gymnasium, exercise studio and multi-use games area. As befits the seaside location, there are many water sports activities. Students make full use of Cornwall's coastline and rugged moors, but there are good transport links to London and Europe. Plenty of tourist-related work is available and there is lively nightlife during the holiday season.

Tuition fees

» Fees for UK/EU students 2017–18   £9,250
» UK fees are expected to increase by the rate of inflation from 2018–19 onwards.
» Fees for international students 2017–18   £15,000
» Check the university's website for the latest information on fees, scholarships, bursaries and other forms of student support.

Students

Undergraduates:	3,955	(60)
Postgraduates:	120	(150)
Mature students:	13.7%	
International students:	6.7%	
Applications per place:	3.9	
From state-sector schools:	94.9%	
From working-class homes:	27.5%	
Satisfaction with students' union	77%	

For detailed information about sports facilities:
www.fxu.org.uk/sport_soc

Accommodation

Places and costs refer to 2016–17
University-provided places: approx. 1,800
Percentage catered: 0%
Self-catered costs: £77.28 (shared) – £128.80 (single en suite); standard rooms: £111.79 – £130.06; studios: £152.37 – £172.27 (42 weeks).
First years are guaranteed housing if conditions are met.
International students: non-EU students, as above.
www.falmouth.ac.uk/facilities/university-accommodation

University of Glasgow

Glasgow has embarked on plans to reshape its estate to an extent that it describes as the "third major staging point" in its 560-year history. The acquisition of the 14-acre Western Infirmary site will allow the university to expand as it invests £1 billion over five years on new buildings and refurbishment.

Work begins in 2017 on a learning and teaching hub on University Avenue with space for 3,000 students. There will also be new buildings for arts, social sciences, the Institute of Health and Wellbeing, and the College of Science and Engineering, as well as a research and innovation hub housing large-scale, inter-disciplinary projects and incubator space for spin-out collaborations with industry.

The university also hopes to extend its global reach, having opened a joint graduate school with China's Nankai University, and set up new partnerships with institutions in Canada, Hong Kong and the United States. It has had a branch in Singapore for five years, working with the Singapore Institute of Technology (SIT) to deliver joint engineering and mechatronics degree programmes.

More than a fifth of the undergraduates in Glasgow are from outside the UK. They seem to enjoy the experience, having voted Glasgow sixth in the UK and eighth in the world for overall satisfaction in i–graduate's independent International Student Barometer. However, almost two-thirds of the students come from Scotland — many from Glasgow and the surrounding area.

Glasgow moved into the top dozen universities in the UK for research after a much-improved performance in the 2014 assessments, although the university remains just behind Edinburgh and St Andrews for research in our table. It ranked in the UK top ten in 18 subject areas, the best results coming in architecture, agriculture, veterinary science and chemistry.

The Institute for Gravitational Research has since shared global recognition for the world's first official detection of gravitational waves.

Glasgow also led the university sector in responding to the refugee crisis, offering fee waivers and extending eligibility for scholarships, as well as taking in Syrian academics to study for PhDs. The political awareness of its students had already been highlighted when Mhairi Black won a seat at the 2015 general election when still a Glasgow undergraduate.

The university enjoys the rare distinction of having been established by Papal Bull, beginning its existence in the chapterhouse of Glasgow Cathedral in 1451. Since 1871 it has been based on the Gilmorehill Campus in the city's fashionable West End. The

University Avenue
Glasgow G12 8QQ

0141 330 2000 (switchboard)
www.gla.ac.uk/about/contact
www.gla.ac.uk
www.guu.co.uk
www.qmunion.org.uk
Affiliation: Russell Group

GLASGOW
Edinburgh
Belfast
London
Cardiff

The Times and Sunday Times Rankings

Overall Ranking: **29** (last year: 26)

Teaching quality:	89	79.4%
Student experience:	34	85.6%
Research quality:	12	39.9%
Entry standards:	12	478
Student–staff ratio:	=33	14.5
Services & facilities/student:	29	£2,292
Expected completion rate:	50	88.4%
Good honours:	30	79.3%
Graduate prospects:	20	81.8%

Veterinary School and outdoor sports facilities are located at Garscube, four miles away, undergraduate medical degree students are now undertaking clinical training in the new £25-million Teaching and Learning Centre at the new Queen Elizabeth University Hospital, and there is also a campus at Dumfries, which is taking liberal arts and teacher education degrees to southwest Scotland. More than £13 million has been invested in improved sporting and social facilities there.

In addition, £35 million has been spent to create teaching and learning facilities at the redeveloped Kelvin Hall, which gave improved access to the collections of the university's art gallery and museum, The Hunterian, from late 2016.

Glasgow is no stranger to innovation: it was the first university in Britain to have a school of engineering, and the first in Scotland to have a computer. More recently, it appointed Scotland's first Gaelic language officer and the country's first chair of Gaelic. The £20-million Stratified Medicine Scotland Innovation Centre involves a consortium of universities, NHS Scotland and industry partners.

Almost half of the university's applications are for arts or sciences degrees, rather than specific subjects, reflecting the popularity of a flexible system that allows students to delay choosing a specialism until the end of their second year.

The university operates a number of access initiatives, including the Top Up programme, which has been working with schools in the West of Scotland since 1999, and Talent Scholarships, which are worth £1,000 a year to 60 academically able Scots who could face financial difficulties in taking up a place. The Internship Hub facilitates more than 350 paid opportunities each year, including 150 on-campus internships.

Most students like the combination of campus and vibrant city, with the added bonus that Glasgow has been rated among the most cost-effective locations in which to study. There is a choice of two students' unions, plus a sports union supporting more than 40 clubs and activities. New union facilities, including a nightclub and four café-bars, opened in 2015.

Tuition fees

» Fees for Scottish and EU students 2017–18   No fee
» Fees for non-Scottish UK (RUK) students 2017–18   £9,250 a year, capped at £27,750 for most courses; MEng, MSci courses capped at £37,000; no cap for dentistry, medicine and veterinary medicine.
» Fees for international students 2017–18   £16,000–£19,500
   Medicine   £42,000
   Dentistry   £39,000
   Veterinary medicine   £26,750
» There are particular support schemes for RUK students.
» Check the university's website for the latest information on fees, scholarships, bursaries and other forms of student support.

Students		
Undergraduates:	16,985	(2,180)
Postgraduates:	5,725	(1,930)
Mature students:	22.5%	
International students:	20.8%	
Applications per place:	6.9	
From state-sector schools:	84.5%	
From working-class homes:	21.4%	
Satisfaction with students' union	76%	
For detailed information about sports facilities:		
www.gla.ac.uk/services/sport		

Accommodation

Number of places and costs refer to 2016–17
University-provided places: 3,448
Percentage catered: 7%
Catered costs: £161.28 – £178.36 a week.
Self-catered costs: £90.37 (twin) – £147.42 (large single en suite) a week.
First years are guaranteed housing if conditions are met.
International students: first years are guaranteed accommodation if conditions are met.
www.gla.ac.uk/undergraduate/accommodation

Glasgow Caledonian University

Glasgow Caledonian (GCU) describes itself as the "University for the Common Good" and has become the first in Scotland to be named as one of Ashoka's global network of Changemaker Campuses committed to social enterprise and innovation. Its aim over the next four years is to establish a global reputation for delivering social benefit and impact through education, research and social innovation.

GCU is already highly international. In 2014 it became the first UK university to open a campus in New York and previous overseas ventures had seen it co-found the Grameen Caledonian College of Nursing in Bangladesh, set up an affiliation with an engineering college in Oman, and partner with universities and colleges in China, India and South America. Now the university has helped to found the African Leadership College in Mauritius, where the first students will begin GCU degrees in January 2017.

The university was also the first Scottish university to open a London campus which, like the one in New York, has fashion at its heart. GCU's British School of Fashion has partnerships with firms such as House of Fraser and Marks and Spencer, which has a design studio in GCU London and funds a scholarship programme. There are also courses in fashion business creation, luxury brand marketing and management, and international fashion marketing. Across the university, more than half of the undergraduate programmes are accredited by professional bodies and include work placement opportunities.

GCU is one of the largest providers of graduates to the NHS in Scotland. As the only Scottish university delivering optometry degrees, it trains 90 per cent of the country's eye care specialists. The School of Engineering and Built Environment teaches three-quarters of Scotland's part-time construction students, while Glasgow School for Business and Society pioneered subjects such as entrepreneurial studies and risk management and offers highly specialist degrees, such as tourism management and consumer protection.

In Glasgow, more than £70 million has been invested to create a single campus that does justice to a thriving institution of 17,000 students. The centrepiece is the £30-million Heart of the Campus development, which was completed in 2016. It features a striking new glass reception area and atrium, a 500-seat teaching and conference facility, and a new eating mall. The £1.2-million Doble Innovation Centre for On-line Systems will create new research and student placement opportunities in the

---

Cowcaddens Road
Glasgow G4 0BA

0141 331 8630 (enquiries)
studentenquiries@gcu.ac.uk
www.gcu.ac.uk
www.gcustudents.co.uk
Affiliation: none

GLASGOW
Edinburgh
Belfast
London
Cardiff

The Times and Sunday Times Rankings

Overall Ranking: **99** (last year: 94)

Teaching quality:	120	75.7%
Student experience:	=96	81.8%
Research quality:	=77	7%
Entry standards:	40	387
Student–staff ratio:	123	21.1
Services & facilities/student:	105	£1,523
Expected completion rate:	86	83.3%
Good honours:	=56	73%
Graduate prospects:	=69	71.2%

engineering sector. The campus includes the only INTO centre in Scotland, running preparatory courses for international students. The health building brings together teaching and research facilities, including a virtual hospital.

Health was one of the university's strengths in the 2014 Research Excellence Framework, which placed half of GCU's submission in the top two categories. It was in the top 20 in the UK for allied health research and did well in social work and social policy, and the built environment.

However, student satisfaction levels have failed to keep pace with rises elsewhere, and falls in our rankings for both student satisfaction with teaching quality and the wider student experience have brought GCU close to slipping out of our top 100 institutions.

Other learning resources include multi-media studios, a Fashion Factory and an eye clinic equipped with latest technologies for teaching and research. Student facilities include the Arc sports centre, 24-hour computer labs, an employability centre and Students' Association building. GCU was among the top ten universities in the 2015 People and Planet Green League of environmental and ethical performance. It was also the first university in Scotland to achieve EcoCampus Platinum status for sustainability.

Widening participation in higher education has always been one of the university's main aims, and some famous names are supporting its efforts. Professor Muhammad Yunus, the Nobel Laureate and anti-poverty campaigner, is the Chancellor, while Sir Alex Ferguson has pledged £500,000 to a bursary programme. The Caledonian Club works with children and their families in Glasgow and London.

More than a third of the undergraduates are from working-class homes and about three-quarters are the first in their family to attend university. The Advanced Higher Hub offers students in their final year at schools across Glasgow specialist teaching, access to GCU's facilities and preparation for university life. The university has introduced a series of measures – such as better academic, social and financial support – for those at risk of dropping out. The projected dropout rate of less than 8 per cent is now the lowest among Scotland's post 1992 universities.

Glasgow is a lively and affordable city with a large student population.

Tuition fees

- » Fees for Scottish and EU students 2017–18   No fee
- » Fees for non-Scottish UK (RUK) students 2017–18   £9,000 a year, capped at £27,000 for 4-year courses.
- » Fees for international students 2017–18   £11,500
- » There are particular support schemes for RUK students
- » Check the university's website for the latest information on fees, scholarships, and other forms of student support.

Students

Undergraduates:	11,910	(2,185)
Postgraduates:	1,645	(1,195)
Mature students:	41.1%	
International students:	8.1%	
Applications per place:	7.6	
From state-sector schools:	97.2%	
From working-class homes:	34.7%	
Satisfaction with students' union	68%	

For detailed information about sports facilities:
www.gcustudents.co.uk/sport

Accommodation

Number of places and costs refer to 2016–17
University-provided places: 660
Percentage catered: 0%
Self-catered costs: £99.79 (standard) or £113.09 (en suite) a week (39 weeks).
All students are entitled to apply, but priority will be based on age, distance from the university and, if international students, residing in a country outside the EU.
accommodation@gcu.ac.uk
www.gcu.ac.uk/study/undergraduate/accommodation

University of Gloucestershire

A £38-million student village is due to open in Cheltenham by the time new entrants to Gloucestershire arrive in September 2017. It will provide accommodation for nearly 800 students at a time of record enrolments – the numbers starting degrees rose by almost 25 per cent in two years to 2015. The university opened a £1-million technology suite and a £1.8-million Performing Arts and Events Centre that September.

It is now hoping to redevelop its campus in Gloucester to house a new Business School, student accommodation, and upgraded sports facilities. There are also plans for a Cyber Security Training and Conference Centre, funded by the Local Enterprise Partnership (LEP), as a joint initiative with a further education college. With only 8,000 students, the university is planning further gradual growth to ensure financial stability without sacrificing a community feel that is popular with students.

Gloucestershire was the first university for more than a century to have formal links with the Church of England when it achieved full university status in 2001. The three campuses are only seven miles apart, so students are not as isolated as they are in some split-site institutions. The main Park Campus is on the attractive site of the former College of St Paul and St Mary, a mile from the centre of Cheltenham, and houses the Faculty of Business, Education and Professional Studies. Art and design, and the Institute of Education and Public Services are closer to the town centre, at Francis Close Hall. The Oxstalls Campus, in Gloucester, was purpose-built a year after university status arrived and caters for sport and exercise sciences, leisure, tourism, hospitality and event management.

Oxstalls also houses the Countryside and Community Research Institute, the largest rural research centre in the UK, which produced much the best results in the 2014 Research Excellence Framework. Overall, 44 per cent of Gloucestershire's submission was rated as world-leading or internationally excellent, but fewer than 20 per cent of the eligible staff took part.

The university claims to offer undergraduates more time with academics than almost any other in the UK. It rose 17 places this year in our overall table, largely because of outstanding scores in the National Student Survey. In most subjects, students are said to spend at least a quarter of their time in lectures, seminars or other supervised activities. Most teaching groups are relatively small and 16 of the staff have been recognised as National Teaching Fellows by the Higher Education Academy.

The Park Campus
The Park
Cheltenham GL50 2RH

01242 714845 (admissions)
admissions@glos.ac.uk
www.glos.ac.uk
www.yourstudentsunion.com
Affiliation: Cathedrals
Group

The Times and Sunday Times Rankings

Overall Ranking: **71** (last year: 88)

Teaching quality:	=27	82.9%
Student experience:	=40	84.9%
Research quality:	=107	3.8%
Entry standards:	=67	326
Student–staff ratio:	=96	18.3
Services & facilities/student:	=78	£1,789
Expected completion rate:	=59	86.4%
Good honours:	=74	69%
Graduate prospects:	102	63.9%

Originally a teacher training college founded in 1847, the university's primary training courses are still rated as outstanding by Ofsted. There is a good range of work placements for other students, which are undertaken by a third of all undergraduates. The Degreeplus initiative combines internships with additional training to improve students' future employment prospects. One in three stays in the county after graduating, many working in local schools after training to be teachers.

Gloucestershire's work with local business and initiatives which integrate employability and sustainability into the curriculum were among the features commended by the Quality Assurance Agency in a 2015 review of the university. Gloucestershire Growth Hub, launched in association with the LEP, for example, gives students more opportunities to work on "real life" business projects.

Gloucestershire has a longstanding focus on green issues, and again finished in the top six in the People and Planet Green League of universities' environmental performance for 2015. There are allotments for students, diplomas in environmentalism and an International Research Institute in Sustainability that brings together researchers from around the world.

In addition to its conventional degrees, the university is offering a range of two-year "fast track" degrees, in subjects such as biology, events management and law.

The university's intake is diverse, with nearly all the undergraduates coming from state schools and more than a third from working-class homes. There is also a joint venture with INTO providing preparatory programmes for international students. The projected dropout rate has improved dramatically over recent years, and the latest figure of 6 per cent is well below the national average for the university's subjects and entry qualifications.

Gloucestershire has a strong sporting tradition and is the only university to have a professional rugby league team. Three students were selected for the Great Britain rugby union sevens teams at the Rio Olympics. The sports facilities include a sports hall, gym and tennis courts. All first-year applicants have priority for housing if they make Gloucestershire their first choice and apply by the required deadline.

Tuition fees

» Fees for UK/EU students 2017–18 £9,250
  Foundation degrees at partner colleges £6,000–£7,500
  Placement year £1,000
» UK fees are expected to increase by the rate of inflation from 2018–19 onwards.
» Fees for international students 2016–17 £11,750
» Check the university's website for the latest information on fees, scholarships, bursaries and other forms of student support.

Students

Undergraduates:	5,940	(590)
Postgraduates:	520	(805)
Mature students:	19.1%	
International students:	3.7%	
Applications per place:	4.2	
From state-sector schools:	97.1%	
From working-class homes:	36.4%	
Satisfaction with students' union	67%	

For detailed information about sports facilities:
www.glos.ac.uk/life/sport

Accommodation

Number of places and costs refer to 2016–17
University-provided places: about 1,460
Percentage catered: 0%
Self-catered costs: £91 – £186 a week (40 weeks).
First-year undergraduates have priority for halls.
International students: first-year undergraduates are guaranteed accommodation if conditions are met.
accommodation@glos.ac.uk
www.glos.ac.uk/life/accommodation

Goldsmiths, University of London

Goldsmiths, like other arts-dominated institutions and many of those based in London, struggles in the National Student Survey – it was in the bottom four for the student experience and the bottom 25 for teaching quality, despite small improvements in both this year.

Applications and enrolments have been buoyant, however. The numbers starting degree courses have risen for the last three years, as Goldsmiths' strengths in the creative arts have been supplemented by new courses in subjects such as clinical psychology, management and entrepreneurship, and politics, philosophy and economics (PPE).

With fewer than 9,000 students, Goldsmiths remains small for a multi-faculty university and intends to grow further in the next few years. New courses in curating, data science, economics, marketing, drama and politics are helping to make progress on that objective.

Goldsmiths is based on a single campus in south-east London that has a mixture of traditional and modern buildings. The Professor Stuart Hall Building contains purpose-built media facilities such as radio and TV studios, the Ben Pimlott Building boasts state-of-the-art research facilities and studio space for art students, while the flagship Richard Hoggart Building has been refurbished and its surroundings re-landscaped to create a space for outdoor arts and events.

The refurbishment is part of a £6-million programme of investment in the campus that also includes a new recording studio and a new Fairtrade coffee shop and social learning space in the Library building. A 19th-century church on campus has been transformed into a space for teaching, exhibitions, performances and studios, and there are plans to create an art gallery elsewhere on campus. There are also excellent computing facilities, including Oculus Rift and motion capture facilities, and sophisticated psychology labs.

Alumni such as Damien Hirst and Antony Gormley are at the top of their fields. In recent years, director Steve McQueen won the Best Picture Oscar for *12 Years A Slave*, James Blake won the Mercury Prize for his album *Overgrown*, and Laure Prouvost was named winner of the Turner Prize, making her the seventh former Goldsmiths student to receive the award. The £10,000 Goldsmiths Prize, launched in 2013, has cemented Goldsmiths' position in the field of creative writing, a subject offered at both undergraduate and postgraduate level, and former students have won awards including *The Sunday*

New Cross
London SE14 6NW

020 7078 5300 (enquiries)
course-info@gold.ac.uk
www.gold.ac.uk
www.goldsmithssu.org
Affiliation: none

The Times and Sunday Times Rankings

Overall Ranking: **=54** (last year: 66)

Teaching quality:	=108	77.4%
Student experience:	125	76.8%
Research quality:	36	33.4%
Entry standards:	49	358
Student–staff ratio:	=28	13.8
Services & facilities/student:	68	£1,895
Expected completion rate:	=81	84%
Good honours:	=22	80.6%
Graduate prospects:	113	59.8%

Times Young Writer of the Year Award and the Dylan Thomas Award, while two MA creative and life writing graduates were named in *Granta*'s 2013 Best of Young British Novelists list.

Of the work submitted for the 2014 Research Excellence Framework, 70 per cent was considered world-leading or internationally excellent, placing Goldsmiths just outside the top 20 universities on this measure. The best results came in communication and media studies, and the college did particularly well in the new assessments of research impact. The entire submission in music was considered world-leading in this respect. The QS rankings place Goldsmiths among the world's top 30 universities for communication and only just outside the top ten for art and design.

Goldsmiths is committed to increasing recruitment from the surrounding boroughs, offering bursaries of up to £9,000 a year to Lewisham students from low-income families and other awards for those living nearby. Around a quarter of new undergraduates are 21 or over on entry, and there is a growing cohort of international students. Almost nine out of ten UK undergraduates are state educated, and three in ten come from the four poorest socio-economic groups.

There are integrated work placements on many degrees and workshops help students to develop entrepreneurial skills.

Goldsmiths also places great emphasis on equipping students with creative thinking skills. The Gold Award encourages students to develop the skills and experience that employers are looking for, while the Higher Education Achievement Report recognises students' co-curricular achievements.

There is a thriving music scene; a varied events programme includes music recitals, exhibitions, public lectures and readings.

The students' union has a strong tradition in volunteering and in recent years it has won several awards for its campaigning on ethical and environmental issues.

There are over 1,400 rooms available in halls of residence, many of which are in New Cross, and all are within a 30-minute commute of the campus. Priority for places is given to international students and new undergraduates from outside the London area. There is a well-equipped and affordable gym on campus, but the sports pitches are 30 minutes away.

Tuition fees

» Fees for UK/EU students 2017–18 — £9,250
   Year abroad — £1,385
» UK fees are expected to increase by the rate of inflation from 2018–19 onwards.
» Fees for international students 2017–18 — £13,500–£19,990
» Check the university's website for the latest information on fees, scholarships, bursaries and other forms of student support.

Students

Undergraduates:	5,035	(200)
Postgraduates:	1,945	(985)
Mature students:	26.5%	
International students:	19.8%	
Applications per place:	6.3	
From state-sector schools:	89.1%	
From working-class homes:	30.8%	
Satisfaction with students' union	49%	

For detailed information about sports facilities:
www.gold.ac.uk/sports

Accommodation

Number of places and costs refer to 2016–17
University-provided places: over 1,400 (on- and off-campus halls of residence managed by Goldsmiths or private providers).
Percentage catered: 0%
Self-catered costs: £109 – £255 a week.
Priority is given to new full-time students that meet the conditions of their offer; distance restrictions apply.
International students will be given priority.
www.gold.ac.uk/accommodation

University of Greenwich

Greenwich claims (fairly) that its main campus is "one of the grandest university settings in the world" – a World Heritage site on the banks of the Thames with buildings designed by Sir Christopher Wren. The university is spending £25 million to upgrade its facilities, turning the Dreadnought Building into a student centre. Due to open early in 2018, it will have new teaching and learning space and enhanced computing facilities, as well as student services, a café, gym and the students' union.

Elsewhere in Greenwich, the prize-winning Stockwell Street development, which includes 14 landscaped roof terraces, was designed partly by the university's own specialists in architecture. There is a large architecture studio, a model-making workshop, TV and sound studios, as well as the main library and other facilities. A new hall of residence has opened nearby, while two other halls are being refurbished.

A new student hub also opened in September 2016 in Chatham at the Medway Campus, which Greenwich shares with the University of Kent. A listed building has been transformed into a student centre, with entertainment and social spaces. The campus houses the schools of pharmacy, science and engineering, the Natural Resources Institute, nursing and some business courses.

Education, health and the social sciences are situated at Avery Hill, a Victorian mansion on the outskirts of southeast London, which boasts a £14-million sports and teaching centre with a café, sports hall and 220-seat lecture theatre. There are also laboratories for health courses that replicate NHS wards. The campus contains a student village of 1,300 rooms, alongside teaching accommodation.

Average entry grades at Greenwich have increased by the equivalent of more than five grades at A level in six years, reaching AAB in 2015. The rise is reflected in the university's highest-ever proportion of students achieving good Honours degrees.

Since 2011, the number of staff with an accredited teaching qualification has increased by 40 per cent and the number with a doctorate by 20 per cent. Greenwich has a special programme to encourage innovation in its teaching and learning, designed to produce graduates who not only have good academic knowledge but also the skills sought by employers, such as a high level of digital literacy, familiarity with new technology and expertise in social media.

There are now over 21,000 Greenwich students in the UK, while another 15,500 are taking the university's courses in 29 other countries.

The university has a longstanding commitment to extend access to higher education: over half the undergraduates

Old Royal Naval College
Park Row
Greenwich
London SE10 9LS

020 8331 9000 (course enquiries)
courseinfo@gre.ac.uk
www.gre.ac.uk
www.suug.co.uk
Affiliation: University
 Alliance

The Times and Sunday Times Rankings

Overall Ranking: **107** (last year: 106)

Teaching quality:	=110	77.3%
Student experience:	113	80.4%
Research quality:	=92	4.9%
Entry standards:	62	337
Student–staff ratio:	=103	18.6
Services & facilities/student:	83	£1,763
Expected completion rate:	87	83.2%
Good honours:	=97	65%
Graduate prospects:	95	66%

come from the four poorest socio-economic groups – one of the biggest proportions in the UK. Many of the 5,000 international students are postgrads or research students.

More than half of Greenwich's students take professionally accredited degree programmes and a similar proportion undertake a substantial work placement as part of their studies. Greenwich is the only university in the country to have an on-campus strategic relationship with a recruitment firm. It has invested more than £1 million in the service, launched in 2013, which aims to place final-year students or recent graduates in full-time, graduate-level jobs that are suited to their skills, as well as finding them high-quality internships and other opportunities along the way.

The university is also increasing the number of research-active staff as part of an ambitious programme of investment in research. The £18-million annual income from research and consultancy is among the largest proportion at any former polytechnic.

More than 200 academics entered the 2014 Research Excellence Framework – a considerable increase on 2008 – and 42 per cent of their work was placed in the top two categories. The university won a Queen's Anniversary Prize for Further and Higher Education in 2015 for its work on improving crop production and boosting the incomes of rural farming communities in Africa.

Greenwich was also in the top 20 in the 2015 People and Planet Green League of universities' environmental performance. True to a longstanding commitment to cut carbon emissions, a combined heat and power plant is being built to provide the Medway campus's electricity and hot water. The scheme is part of a €6-million international project led by the university's Faculty of Engineering and Science to investigate sustainable sources of energy for the future.

Sports facilities are improving, with a £1.7-million project under way to add two new all-weather pitches and changing rooms to the facilities at the Avery Hill campus. Record numbers are engaging with sports clubs and societies, which enjoyed a record 38 per cent increase in memberships last year.

Tuition fees

» Fees for UK/EU students 2017–18	£9,250
Partner colleges degree	£8,630–£9,250
Foundation degree	£6,165
Year abroad	£1,385
Placement year	£1,000

» UK fees are expected to increase by the rate of inflation from 2018–19 onwards.

» Fees for international students 2017–18   £11,500

» Check the university's website for the latest information on fees, scholarships, bursaries and other forms of student support.

Students

Undergraduates:	12,945	(3,160)
Postgraduates:	2,480	(2,710)
Mature students:	33.9%	
International students:	14.9%	
Applications per place:	8.6	
From state-sector schools:	97.8%	
From working-class homes:	54%	
Satisfaction with students' union	63%	

For detailed information about sports facilities:
www2.gre.ac.uk/about/campus/facilities/sport

Accommodation

Number of places and costs refer to 2016–17
University-provided places: 2,400
Percentage catered: 0%
Self-catered costs: £115.99 – £191.94 a week.
First years are guaranteed a place. Conditions apply.
International students: new students get priority.
www.gre.ac.uk/accommodation
ah.accommodation@gre.ac.uk (Avery Hill Campus)
gr.accommodation@gre.ac.uk (Greenwich Campus)
me.accommodation@gre.ac.uk (Medway Campus)

Harper Adams University

Harper Adams is our Modern University of the Year, having risen to 36th in this year's league table, the highest position yet secured by a university created since 1992.

Students now rank the quality of teaching they receive here in the top 10 in the UK after a significant rise in ranking on this measure, recorded in the latest National Student Survey (NSS). It also finished in the top five in our analysis of the sections of the NSS devoted to the student experience, continuing a stellar record that began before university status was conferred in 2012.

The higher-placed of two universities in our table devoted predominantly to agriculture-related courses, Harper Adams also features in the top 10 in our agriculture and forestry subject table.

There are now more than 4,500 students, but little more than half are on campus at any one time. The rest are on placement years or accredited part-time programmes in industry. They include a growing number of international students and there are links with four agricultural universities in China.

Based on a single campus in the Shropshire countryside, the university offers degrees in business, veterinary nursing and physiotherapy, land and property management, engineering and food studies, as well as agriculture. New degrees in food science, automotive and mechanical engineering, and geography were launched in 2016. Contrary to the stereotypes associated with its agricultural specialisms, the majority of entrants to degree courses are female. About one undergraduate in six went to an independent school, but almost half have a working-class background.

Almost every course includes work placements, provided by a network of 500 employers, some of whom also endow student scholarships. The projected dropout rate of less than 6 per cent is barely half the national average for the university's courses and entry qualifications.

Harper Adams has been upgrading its teaching and research facilities, and also investing in new academic appointments. The Agricultural Engineering Innovation Centre opened in 2014 and a Veterinary Services Centre followed a year later, as a response to rising demand for courses in veterinary nursing, clinical animal behaviour and veterinary physiotherapy. The latest development has seen the opening of the £4-million Dairy Crest Innovation Centre on campus, providing a unique resource for collaboration, including student research projects and industrial placements.

The university is one of a small number of locations where the Government is funding Centres for Innovation as part of its national strategy for agricultural technology. Construction of the Harper Adams hub is

---

Newport
Shropshire TF10 8NB

01952 815000 (admissions)
admissions@harper-adams.ac.uk
www.harper-adams.ac.uk
www.harpersu.com
Affiliation: GuildHE

The Times and Sunday Times Rankings

Overall Ranking: **36** (last year: 49)

Teaching quality:	=8	85.1%
Student experience:	=4	89.8%
Research quality:	84	5.7%
Entry standards:	59	342
Student–staff ratio:	=49	15.4
Services & facilities/student:	6	£2,877
Expected completion rate:	=46	88.6%
Good honours:	105	63.2%
Graduate prospects:	59	72.8%

already under way and its opening is set for early 2017. New laboratories costing £2 million opened at the end of 2016 and a glasshouses complex for the Crops and Environment Research Centre and a new aquaculture centre are planned.

The university is already a centre of excellence for entomology teaching and research in the UK, and has launched the industry-led Soil and Water Management Centre. Harper Adams entered only 17 staff for the 2014 Research Excellence Framework – two fewer than in 2008 – but more than half of their work was considered to be internationally excellent or world-leading.

The students' union, careers service and café are all under one roof at the heart of the campus, where open access computers allow students to work and socialise in the same area. The Main Building, which dates from the opening of the institution in 1901, was once the centre of all campus activities with bedrooms, teaching rooms and even a shooting gallery. The Bamford Library is one of the largest specialist land-based collections in the UK, but the new university's most prized feature is its 640-hectare commercial farm, which has been undergoing a multimillion-pound development, including expanded dairy, pig and poultry units. At its heart, Ancellor Yard is a redevelopment of the original farm courtyard, the former home of Thomas

Harper Adams after whom the university is named. It houses the Frank Parkinson Farm Education Centre and the Frontier Crops Centre. The £2-million dairy unit serves 400 cows.

There are more than 800 residential places on campus and first years take priority in the allocation of places. A shuttle bus runs three times a day for students living in nearby Newport to get to the campus and there is free parking for students. Sports facilities include a gymnasium, shooting ground, heated outdoor swimming pool, rugby, cricket, football and hockey pitches, tennis courts and an all-weather sports pitch. There is a dance/fitness studio and even a 4x4 club, as well as a rowing club which operates from nearby Shrewsbury. Although rural, the social scene at Harper Adam is strong, with recent students' union events including a live BBC Radio 1 broadcast by Scott Mills and Chris Stark, with an impromptu visit by music superstar Ed Sheeran.

Tuition fees

» Fees for UK/EU students for 2017–18 £9,250
  Placement year £1,850
» UK fees are expected to increase by the rate of inflation from 2018–19 onwards.
» Fees for international students 2017–18 £10,200
» Check the university's website for the latest information on fees, scholarships, bursaries and other forms of student support.

Students

Undergraduates:	2,265	(2,125)
Postgraduates:	100	(555)
Mature students:	4.7%	
International students:	5.1%	
Applications per place:	4.7	
From state-sector schools:	84.6%	
From working-class homes:	44.4%	
Satisfaction with students' union	85%	

For detailed information about sports facilities:
www.harper-adams.ac.uk/facilities/sports.cfm

Accommodation

Places and costs refer to 2016–17
University-provided places: 805
Percentage catered: 52%
Catered costs: £111.00 – £173.00 a week (36 weeks).
Self-catered costs: £114.00 – £123.75 a week (36 weeks).
Priority is given to new full-time students on a first come first served basis. Provision for students with disabilities.
International students: entitled to housing for first year of study.
www.harper-adams.ac.uk/accommodation

Heriot-Watt University

Heriot-Watt's new Go Global scheme encourages students to take advantage of the university's highly international nature and transfer between its five campuses during their degrees. They have their choice of Dubai and Malaysia, as well as the three Scottish campuses, with other options available through the Erasmus+ and other exchange schemes. About 100 have signed up for a semester or a full academic year abroad in the first year of the scheme.

Over a fifth of the students in Edinburgh, Orkney and Galashiels are from outside the UK and 20,000 students are taking Heriot-Watt courses in 140 other countries. The university is responsible for almost half of all Scottish degrees awarded to people studying overseas.

Heriot-Watt celebrated its 50th anniversary as a university in 2016, but it traces its history back to 1821, when it became the world's first Mechanics Institute. Its name honours George Heriot and James Watt – two giants of commerce and industry – indicating a commitment to practical, applied learning. The approach has produced consistently good rates of graduate employment. Now a research-led university, it specialises in science and engineering, business and management, languages and design.

More than 80 per cent of the work submitted for the 2014 Research Excellence Framework was rated as world-leading or internationally excellent, and Heriot-Watt was among the leaders in the UK in mathematics, general engineering, and architecture, planning and the built environment, where it made joint submissions with Edinburgh. The university did particularly well in the new assessments of the impact of research and features in the top 30 of our research ranking.

The main campus has an attractive parkland setting in the Edinburgh suburb of Riccarton, and there are two smaller Scottish bases in Orkney and at the Scottish Borders campus in Galashiels.

New residences have opened recently in Galashiels and Edinburgh, where another 450 rooms were added in 2016.

ORIAM (formerly the National Performance Centre for Sport) also opened on the Edinburgh campus in 2016, with high-quality sports facilities that can be used by students. The £33-million centre features an indoor replica of the Hampden Park football pitch, outdoor synthetic and grass pitches, a nine-court sports hall, a 3G indoor pitch and a fitness suite, as well as world-class facilities for sports science and medicine.

In addition, the £20-million Lyell Centre opened in the same year. It is a major research centre for geological,

Edinburgh Campus
Edinburgh EH14 4AS

0131 451 3376 (admissions)
ugadmissions@hw.ac.uk
www.hw.ac.uk
www.hwunion.com
Affiliation: none

The Times and Sunday Times Rankings

Overall Ranking: **=37** (last year: =38)

Teaching quality:	=76	80%
Student experience:	38	85.3%
Research quality:	28	36.7%
Entry standards:	33	407
Student–staff ratio:	=53	15.6
Services & facilities/student:	27	£2,375
Expected completion rate:	=74	84.4%
Good honours:	45	75.5%
Graduate prospects:	32	79.7%

petroleum and marine sciences, staffed by the university and the British Geological Survey, which has its Scottish headquarters there.

A new programme to provide additional and upgraded teaching, learning and study space started in 2016.

The Scottish Borders Campus, 35 miles south of Edinburgh, specialises in textiles, fashion and design. It offers one of the few degrees in the world in menswear and the only course in Scotland in fashion communication. Heriot-Watt and Borders College share the merged campus to deliver higher and further education in a region that has been historically underprovided.

The campus at Stromness in Orkney is for postgraduates, and specialises in renewable energy.

The Dubai Campus opened in 2005 and now has 3,800 students taking business, engineering, science and technology, or textiles and design courses. Numbers in the Gulf state are expected to rise further.

The purpose-built Malaysian Campus, which had its first intake in 2014, has space for up to 4,000 students to take degrees in science, engineering, business, mathematics and design. The £35-million campus has a spectacular lakeside location in the administrative capital of Putrajaya, close to Kuala Lumpur.

More than half of the UK-based students are from Scotland and 15 per cent from other parts of Britain and Northern Ireland. Nine out of ten are from state schools and colleges, while more than a quarter come from working-class homes. The projected dropout rate of 7 per cent is better than the UK average for the university's courses and entry qualifications.

The Edinburgh halls of residence are conveniently placed and house more than 2,000 students. Built in the grounds of a former country house, the landscaped campus boasts a loch and a sunken garden.

Regular bus services link the campus to the city centre and its wide range of nightlife and cultural events. The university has a programme of sports scholarships, and representative teams do well.

Music also thrives: there is a professional Director of Music and a number of music scholarships, as well as a varied programme of events.

Tuition fees

» Fees for Scottish and EU students 2017–18   No fee
» Fees for non-Scottish UK (RUK) students 2017–18   £9,250
» Fees for international students 2017–18   £13,770–£17,440
» There are particular support schemes for RUK students.
» Check the university's website for the latest information on fees, scholarships, bursaries and other forms of student support.

Students

Undergraduates:	6,595	(450)
Postgraduates:	2,105	(1,560)
Mature students:	18.0%	
International students:	20.3%	
Applications per place:	8.3	
From state-sector schools:	89.8%	
From working-class homes:	26.1%	
Satisfaction with students' union	58%	

For detailed information about sports facilities:
www.hw.ac.uk/sports.htm

Accommodation

Number of places and costs refer to 2016–17
University places provided: 2,042
Percentage catered: 0%
Self-catered costs: £105.84 (standard) – £159.74 (en suite) a week.
All new first years are guaranteed housing provided conditions are met and applications in place by noon on 25 August.
International students: as above.
www.hw.ac.uk/student-life/campus-life.htm

University of Hertfordshire

The addition of 2,500 residential places since 2015 and the refurbishment of 500 more represent another significant step in Hertfordshire's ten-year plan to provide a "distinctive campus experience for students, staff and visitors, in which the dynamism of the university is embodied in its physical estate".

In 2016, an impressive new science building was opened, which will bring all science teaching under one roof, with high-tech laboratories and areas for informal learning and socialising. Still to come by 2020 are a new engineering building, more teaching accommodation and a conference centre. At the same time, the university has been developing academically, adding pharmacy and postgraduate medicine in 2015 and architecture in 2016.

The university has three sites, including a purpose-built £120-million campus, close to the original Hatfield headquarters, which boasts some outstanding facilities. The de Havilland and College Lane sites are linked by cycle ways, footpaths and free shuttle buses.

The de Havilland Campus, named after the aircraft manufacturer, has a learning resources centre, £15-million sports complex and 1,600 networked, en-suite residential places. The £10-million Law School includes a fully functioning court room with a public gallery, mediation centre and law clinic.

The new Hutton Hub, on the College Lane Campus, brings together a counselling centre, students' union, pharmacy, bank and a juice bar. Also on the campus, as well as the new accommodation, is the Forum, a £38-million venue with three entertainment spaces, a restaurant, a café and multiple bars.

The third site is the Bayfordbury Campus, home to one of the UK's largest teaching observatories, as well as a field centre for life and medical sciences. Bayfordbury Observatory is equipped with seven individually housed large optical telescopes, four radio telescopes and a high definition planetarium.

Hertfordshire has built a reputation as perhaps the leading "business-facing university" in the UK and has now set out to make the same mark internationally.

The university plays an important role in the regional economy and runs several subsidiary companies including a regional bus service, as well as offering work placements and study abroad on most courses.

Health subjects account for the largest share of places. An innovative degree in paramedic science was Britain's first, its students using the UK's largest medical simulation centre to learn how to treat patients in emergency situations. Last year saw the launch of a new four-year

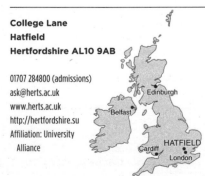

College Lane
Hatfield
Hertfordshire AL10 9AB

01707 284800 (admissions)
ask@herts.ac.uk
www.herts.ac.uk
http://hertfordshire.su
Affiliation: University
Alliance

The Times and Sunday Times Rankings
Overall Ranking: **91** (last year: 76)

Teaching quality:	=103	78.2%
Student experience:	=96	81.8%
Research quality:	=85	5.6%
Entry standards:	=100	301
Student–staff ratio:	91	17.5
Services & facilities/student:	44	£2,142
Expected completion rate:	=94	82.1%
Good honours:	=97	65%
Graduate prospects:	=39	77.5%

undergraduate Master of Optometry programme.

The creative arts have also been growing, with the addition of a £10-million media centre on College Lane Campus boasting the latest technology for the teaching of music, animation, film, television and multimedia. It includes one of the region's largest art galleries.

An Automotive Centre has upgraded the teaching facilities for that branch of engineering, as well as boosting interaction with industry – an impressive number of British Formula One teams have at least one Hertfordshire graduate.

The student intake is diverse, with 42 per cent of undergraduates from lower socio-economic groups and 97 per cent state-educated. However, the projected dropout rate has risen to 14 per cent – higher than the national average for the university's subjects and entry grades. The Careers and Employment Service offers students support during their time at Hertfordshire as well as for two years after they graduate. The Enterprise Team helps to turn business or social enterprise ideas into successful ventures.

In the 2014 Research Excellence Framework, more than half of Hertfordshire's work was placed in one of the top two categories. The best results were in history, where 45 per cent of the submission was judged to be world-leading and all of it was given the top grade for its external impact. Nursing, philosophy and astronomy were also highly rated.

The Learning and Resource Centres on the two main campuses are open 24/7, providing 3,000 study places, 1,200 computer workstations and Wi-Fi. Students can use the StudyNet information system for study, revision or communication, as well as to access university information. Over 400 different software applications are available for student use, including a Microsoft Office 365 account for students.

The £15-million Hertfordshire Sports Village includes a 110-station health and fitness centre, 25-metre pool, physiotherapy and sports injury clinic and a large, multi-purpose sports hall. The Sports Village is the home of Hertfordshire Mavericks netball team and has supported alumni who have gone on to play for a variety of teams at a professional level.

Tuition fees

» Fees for UK/EU students 2017–18 £9,250
  Foundation degrees at partner colleges £6,000
  Placement year no fee
» UK fees are expected to increase by the rate of inflation from 2018–19 onwards.
» Fees for international students 2017–18 £11,350–£11,850
» Check the university's website for the latest information on fees, scholarships, bursaries and other forms of student support.

Students

Undergraduates:	15,405	(3,815)
Postgraduates:	1,955	(3,710)
Mature students:	19.2%	
International students:	14.0%	
Applications per place:	7.5	
From state-sector schools:	97.3%	
From working-class homes:	42.5%	
Satisfaction with students' union	74%	

For detailed information about sports facilities:
www.uhsport.co.uk

Accommodation

Number of places and costs refer to 2016–17.
University provided places: 4,709
Percentage Catered: 0%
Self-catered costs: £87.29 (twin); £133.21 – £150.01 (single en suite); £171.99 (studio) a week.
First years are guaranteed accommodation if applications are made before given deadlines.
International students: as above.
accommodation@herts.ac.uk
www.herts.ac.uk/university-life/student-accommodation

University of the Highlands and Islands

The University of the Highlands and Islands describes itself as "the UK's leading integrated university encompassing both further and higher education". It is also by far the most dispersed university in our tables, a federation of 13 colleges and research institutions spread across hundreds of miles in the north and west of Scotland, with 70 local learning centres.

As such, it fits uneasily into our league table – it proved impossible to calculate a meaningful staff/student ratio from the unique mix of part-time and full-time staff and students – and this year it has fallen to the foot of our rankings for the first time. It has become a huge asset to the regional economy, however, helping to create and sustain businesses, as well as championing local culture and the environment.

With so many courses tailored to regional economic and social needs, the demand for places has been growing by leaps and bounds. Applications have risen for seven years in a row, and the total in 2015 was twice that in 2012. The university took time to adapt to its growing popularity, but the undergraduate intake was up by a third last year.

A new campus at Inverness and further developments at both its Shetland College and at its West Highland College, at Portree on the Isle of Skye, as well as the opening of the £6.5-million Alexander Graham Bell Life Science Centre at its Moray College, will enable it to take even more students in future. The university has signed a £44-million agreement with specialist student residences developer Cityheart to build and operate student residences, with a block of 40 en-suite rooms already completed in Fort William.

The students are predominantly mature and part-time, drawn largely from the Highlands and Islands. But the university has begun to recruit more young entrants – taking a record number in 2015 – as well as attracting greater numbers from the rest of Scotland, other parts of the UK and overseas.

Students take a broad range of qualifications, from Higher national certificates and diplomas to degrees and professional development awards. Teaching is increasingly through "blended" learning, combining online and face-to-face teaching, with small class sizes and extensive use of video conferencing. The university offered its first accelerated degree in 2015, with geography available at Inverness or at Lews Castle College, on Lewis, over three years rather than the usual four. It launched degrees in contemporary film making in the Highlands and Islands in 2016 and

Executive Office
12b Ness Walk
Inverness IV3 5QS

0845 272 3600 (course enquiries)
contact via website
www.uhi.ac.uk
www.hisa.uhi.ac.uk
Affiliation: MillionPlus

The Times and Sunday Times Rankings

Overall Ranking: **128** (last year: 126)

Teaching quality:	=100	78.6%
Student experience:	126	74.1%
Research quality:	n/a	..
Entry standards:	=106	293
Student–staff ratio:	n/a	..
Services & facilities/student:	127	£543
Expected completion rate:	128	67.7%
Good honours:	122	55.1%
Graduate prospects:	128	51.1%

nursing in 2017, taking over the courses run by Stirling University in Inverness and Stornoway.

The university's colleges spread from Dunoon in the southwest to the village of Scalloway, in the Shetland Islands, in the north. The university's network of campuses is much wider, however. Argyll College, for example, has 13 sites on the mainland and on islands such as Arran, Islay and Mull.

Courses are also taught at more than 50 learning centres located throughout the Highlands and Islands, Moray and Perthshire. Some colleges are relatively large and located in the urban centres such as Perth, Elgin and Inverness. Others are smaller institutions, including some whose primary focus is research. The university insists, however, that all have a student-centred culture and an individual approach.

Several of the colleges are in spectacular locations. Lews Castle College in Stornoway in the Outer Hebrides, for example, is set in 600 acres of parkland. It claims "possibly the UK's most attractive location to study art" for its harbour-side Lochmaddy campus in North Uist. Sabhal Mòr Ostaig is the only Gaelic-medium college in the world, set in breath-taking scenery on the Isle of Skye, while the Highland Theological College is in Dingwall. West Highland College does not even have a central campus, although its degree in adventure tourism management is taught in Fort

William, close to Ben Nevis. North Highland College has an equestrian centre in Caithness, six miles from the main campus in Thurso, with international-sized outdoor and indoor arenas.

The UHI Millennium Institute was established in 2001 – more than a decade after it was proposed – and university status arrived ten years later. There are now 8,300 students taking more than 100 undergraduate courses, some completely online and many offering the opportunity to study entirely through Gaelic.

There are a dozen specialist research centres and a new enterprise and research centre on the Inverness Campus. They helped to produce some extremely good results in the 2014 Research Excellence Framework. Almost 70 per cent of the research submitted for review was classified as world leading or internationally excellent, but the large proportion of part-time staff made it impossible to compile an accurate score for research quality in our table.

Tuition fees

» Fees for Scottish and EU students 2016–17   No fee
    Online courses   £5,400-£6,120
» Fees for non-Scottish UK (RUK) students 2016–17 £8,000-£9,000, capped at £24,000 for 4-year courses.
» Fees for international students 2016–17   £10,000-£11,000
» There are particular support schemes for RUK students.
» Check the university's website for the latest information on fees, bursaries and other forms of student support.

Students

Undergraduates:	5,020	(2,395)
Postgraduates:	100	(335)
Mature students:	46.0%	
International students:	3.9%	
Applications per place:	4.0	
From state-sector schools:	99.2%	
From working-class homes:	46.2%	
Satisfaction with students' union	40%	

Sports provision for each campus is through local community facilities.

Accommodation

On-site halls of residence are available at five of the partner colleges.

The other colleges provide lists of local lodgings or private rented accommodation. Some international students prefer to stay with host families. Contact each college via the website:

www.uhi.ac.uk/en/studying-at-uhi/first-steps/accommodation

University of Huddersfield

A number of universities film lectures so that students can revisit the content later online. But Huddersfield is going one step further, in response to requests from the students' union, by filming tutorials as well. Academics, many of whom are opposed to the scheme, will be allowed to opt out. This year's top 20 ranking for student satisfaction with teaching quality suggests staff have little to fear from so-called "lecture capture" but many worry that it will negatively affect student attendance and participation in a key part of the academic experience.

The university has been a leader in measures to improve teaching and learning, enrolling all academics the Higher Education Academy, the professional body devoted to raising teaching standards, for example. Huddersfield staff have won 15 National Teaching Fellowships since the scheme began.

It is also focusing on graduate employment, students' other great concern. Every undergraduate does some work experience as part of their degree course and a third take extended placements in business or industry. Many students now develop their own businesses for the work placement component of their course, taking advantage of the advice and facilities available at the university's Duke of York Young Entrepreneur Centre. With 70 per cent of graduates emerging with a professional qualification, Huddersfield is just outside the top 50 for graduate prospects and attracted a string of awards for entrepreneurship and its overall performance.

Huddersfield is investing £58 million on teaching and research facilities, and has brought the university together on one town-centre campus with a combination of new builds and imaginative conversions.

The 19th-century Ramsden Building, the historical heart of the university, has been refurbished and there are ultra-modern facilities behind its carefully preserved exterior. Canalside, a refurbished mill complex, provided extra space for computing, and education occupies another mill site. The university has created "pocket parks" and a landscaped area along the reopened Narrow Canal to provide additional green space.

Recent developments include a striking creative arts building and a business school. The £22.5-million Student Central opened in 2014, bringing together library, computing, sport, leisure, catering, social and meeting facilities, as well as providing a new home for the students' union. Alongside it, the university has been creating a new community space. The University Square project revamps the main access points to the Queensgate campus and will be used

Queensgate
Huddersfield
HD1 3DH

01484 473 969 (admissions)
admissionsandrecords@hud.ac.uk
www.hud.ac.uk
www.huddersfield.su
Affiliation: University
Alliance

The Times and Sunday Times Rankings

Overall Ranking: **77**(last year: =69)

Teaching quality:	=17	83.6%
Student experience:	=42	84.8%
Research quality:	61	9.4%
Entry standards:	64	332
Student–staff ratio:	120	20.6
Services & facilities/student:	=78	£1,789
Expected completion rate:	97	81.7%
Good honours:	96	65.1%
Graduate prospects:	=55	73.4%

for events such as film nights, concerts and Christmas markets for the whole town as well as students. The £1.5-million Heritage Quay archive centre already serves both students and public, and includes a Holocaust Heritage and Learning Centre, a major resource for the region. The next big project is the £27.5-million Oastler Building for the Law School and the School of Music, Humanities and Media, opening in 2017.

The university has always been strong on widening participation in higher education. Over 46 per cent of full-time undergraduates are from working-class homes – far more than the national average for the university's courses and entry qualifications – and many come from areas without a tradition of higher education. The dropout rate has improved, and the latest projection of less than 13 per cent is better than the national benchmark.

A tradition of vocational education dates back to 1841, and the university has a long-established reputation in areas such as textile design and engineering. Many arts and social science courses have a vocational slant, too – for example, politics features a work placement module, which often takes students to the House of Commons.

Some of the most successful areas in the 2014 Research Excellence Framework were in the arts and social sciences. Huddersfield did well overall, entering almost a third of its academics for assessment and still seeing nearly 60 per cent of its work rated world-leading or internationally excellent. There were particularly good results in music, drama and performing arts, as well as in English, social work and social policy.

Recent research initiatives include the establishment of a Centre for Evolutionary Genomics, an £8-million Centre for Innovative Manufacturing in Advanced Metrology, a Turbocharger Research Institute and new facilities for the Institute of Railway Research, which is set to conduct research on HS2. The Medium Energy Ion Scattering Accelerator, relocated from Daresbury Laboratories, is one of only ten of its type in the world, and the university's materials research will be bolstered by a new £3.5-million electron microscope.

Most residential accommodation is concentrated in the Storthes Hall Park student village, but additional housing is available at Ashenhurst, just over a mile from the campus. Students tend to base their social life around the students' union.

Tuition fees

» Fees for UK/EU students 2017–18 £9,250
Placement year £900
» UK fees are expected to increase by the rate of inflation from 2018–19 onwards.
» Fees for international students 2017–18 £13,000–£14,000
» Check the university's website for the latest information on fees, scholarships, bursaries and other forms of student support.

Students

Undergraduates:	13,280	(1,805)
Postgraduates:	1,915	(2,620)
Mature students:	20.7%	
International students:	14.2%	
Applications per place:	6.0	
From state-sector schools:	97.9%	
From working-class homes:	46.2%	
Satisfaction with students' union	71%	

For detailed information about sports facilities:
www.hud.ac.uk/sport-fitness-health

Accommodation

Number of places and costs refer to 2016–17
University-provided places: 1,666 in privately owned halls
Percentage catered: 0%
Self-catered costs: £75 – £111 a week.
First years are housed on a first come, first served basis provided conditions are met.
International students: as above.
huddersfield@digstudent.co.uk; hudlets@hud.ac.uk
www.hud.ac.uk/uni-life/accommodation

University of Hull

Students starting courses at Hull in 2017 will be arriving in the UK City of Culture, with their university as a principal partner in the year of activities. Students will be at the heart of the action as volunteers, performers and patrons, and the campus will host many of the events. A £9.5-million performance and concert venue was completed in time for the celebrations, featuring ambisonic studio, ensemble practice room and top-quality recording facilities.

It is part of a £200-million programme to upgrade the 94-acre main campus, less than three miles from the centre of Hull. The award-winning Brynmor Jones Library, with its striking new atrium and revamped exterior, has become the centrepiece of the campus.

Hull has been focusing on improvements to the student experience after traditionally high levels of satisfaction have slipped in recent years. Some £2 million has been spent remodelling University House, which accommodates student services and a refurbished students' union, The Lawns halls of residence, on the Cottingham Campus, have also been refurbished and a £30-million development, The Courtyard, accommodating another 560 students, opened there in autumn 2016. The main campus has already seen new buildings

for languages and chemistry, a Graduate Research Institute and a state-of-the-art sport, health and exercise science laboratory in recent years.

The adjoining West Campus contains the Business School, a new Enterprise Centre to support local firms and the medical school, which is run jointly with the University of York. The Allam Medical Building will form the centrepiece of a new £28-milllion Health Hub in 2017. As well as the medical school, it will include the Faculty of Health and Social Care, and Sport, Health and Exercise Science.

A recent audit by the Quality Assurance Agency made Hull one of only three universities in the latest round of reviews to receive a commendation for enhancing student learning opportunities. An Institute for Learning encourages academics to put research findings into practice, developing training courses and developing the university's interest in lifelong learning. The university also received 5-star ratings for teaching, employability, internationalisation and facilities in an assessment by QS, the publishers of global university rankings.

Applications were down by more than 10 per cent in 2015 after two years of increases, but a significantly higher proportion of those who were made offers chose Hull, and the numbers starting courses actually rose. Merit scholarships of £2,000 for applicants achieving at least

---

Cottingham Road
Hull HU6 7RX

01482 466100 (admissions)
admissions@hull.ac.uk
www.hull.ac.uk
www.hyms.ac.uk
www.hullstudent.com
Affiliation: none

The Times and Sunday Times Rankings

Overall Ranking =65 (last year: 67)

Teaching quality:	96	78.9%
Student experience:	=56	84.1%
Research quality:	54	16.7%
Entry standards:	=57	344
Student–staff ratio:	=64	16.2
Services & facilities/student:	60	£1,971
Expected completion rate:	=81	84%
Good honours:	=66	70.4%
Graduate prospects:	60	72.7%

BBB at A level, or the equivalent, are one obvious attraction. Those with A*AA receive £1,000 in subsequent years as well.

More than 60 per cent of the work entered for the 2014 Research Excellence Framework was rated as world-leading or internationally excellent, although Hull made a relatively small submission for a pre-1992 university. The best results were in the allied health category, where 87 per cent of the research was awarded three or four stars, while geography and computer science also did well. Hull won a Queen's Anniversary Prize for its research into slavery and played a major role in shaping the UK's Modern Slavery Act.

A longstanding focus on Europe shows in the wide range of languages available at degree level, with the purpose-built Language Institute heavily used by students regardless of subject. Strength in politics is reflected in a steady flow of graduates into the House of Commons. The Westminster Hull Internship Programme (WHIP) offers a year-long placement and month-long internships for British politics and legislative studies students. The Legal Advice Centre, staffed by law students, provides guidance and advice to the public.

There is also a focus on employability, which includes the option of a 20-credit module on career management skills. The careers service approaches undergraduates early in their time at Hull and sets up meetings with potential employers. The Enterprise Centre has a successful record with those who would rather start their own businesses – 86 of the 137 start-ups nurtured there were active five years later, 23 of them still as tenants.

The university is winding down its Scarborough campus, transferring all its undergraduate provision to Hull so that teaching can be better aligned with research. Coventry University has stepped into the breach with an operation of their own to maintain a higher education presence in the North Yorkshire town.

The university and the city of Hull have always commanded loyalty among students, who appreciate the modest cost of living and ready availability of accommodation, as well as the quality of courses. By focusing all its activities back on Hull, the university will hope to draw on these strengths and recover some of the lost ground that has left it stuck in the middle reaches of tables such as ours.

Tuition fees

» Fees for UK/EU students 2017–18 £9,250
Foundation degree £7,195
» UK fees are expected to increase by the rate of inflation from 2018–19 onwards.
» Fees for international students 2017–18 £12,800–£15,300
Medicine £29,400
» Check the university's website for the latest information on fees, scholarships, bursaries and other forms of student support.

Students

Undergraduates:	11,290	(2,110)
Postgraduates:	2,135	(1,480)
Mature students:	26.2%	
International students:	9.6%	
Applications per place:	5.0	
From state-sector schools:	94.1%	
From working-class homes:	33.2%	
Satisfaction with students' union	79%	

For detailed information about sports facilities:
www2.hull.ac.uk/student/sportscentre1.aspx

Accommodation

Number of places and costs refer to 2016–17
University-provided places: 2,760 (owned stock); 297 (leased/associated stock)
Percentage catered: 44%
Catered costs: £94.10 – £149.10 (37 weeks).
Self-catered costs: £72.95 – £175.00 (34–51 weeks).
New, unaccompanied first years are guaranteed accommodation until 1 September if conditions are met.
International students: as above.
www2.hull.ac.uk/student/accommodation-new.aspx

Imperial College of Science, Technology and Medicine

Imperial describes itself as the only university in the UK to focus exclusively on science, medicine, engineering and business, and it is also among the leading institutions in the world with that combination of specialisms. Never out of the top five in our overall league table, Imperial also features in the top ten of both the QS and *Times Higher Education* world rankings.

Only Oxford and Cambridge have higher entry standards and fewer than half of those applying receive an offer. Nevertheless, applications have risen by more than 20 per cent in three years and there was a small increase in the numbers accepted in 2015. Those who do win a place will be encouraged to learn that Imperial's graduates have the best employment rate in the UK of any multi-faculty university and the second-highest average starting salaries. Its two-place fall in this year's league table is wholly attributable to some poor scores in this year's National Student Survey, particularly on teaching quality.

Imperial's research was found to have greater impact on the economy and society than any other university's when this was assessed for the first time in the 2014 Research Excellence Framework. It had the best impact results in the country in 8 of the 14 areas in which it submitted work and 90 per cent of its research was rated as world-leading or internationally excellent. Four "global challenges" have been adopted for future research: discovery and the natural world; engineering novel solutions; health and well-being; and leading the data revolution. The opening of the Dyson School of Design Engineering, funded through a £12-million donation from the James Dyson Foundation, should help.

Imperial is unique in the UK for providing teaching and research in the full range of engineering disciplines. An even bigger donation – £40 million from Michael Uren, an industrialist and Imperial graduate – is helping Imperial to develop a 25-acre site near the former BBC Television Centre in West London. The gift will fund a biomedical engineering centre at the heart of the White City Campus. The full development will cost a total of £3 billion and will also feature a Research and Translation Hub, bringing together the academic and business communities.

Imperial now has nine sites in London, due mainly to the expansion of its activities in medicine in the 1990s, but undergraduates in most other subjects will continue to be based at the original South Kensington Campus.

More than a third of the undergraduates are from independent schools – one of the

---

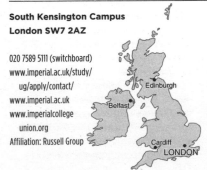

South Kensington Campus
London SW7 2AZ

020 7589 5111 (switchboard)
www.imperial.ac.uk/study/
ug/apply/contact/
www.imperial.ac.uk
www.imperialcollege
union.org
Affiliation: Russell Group

The Times and Sunday Times **Rankings**

Overall Ranking: **5** (last year: 3)

Teaching quality:	124	74.8%
Student experience:	=77	83.2%
Research quality:	2	56.2%
Entry standards:	3	567
Student–staff ratio:	=5	11.1
Services & facilities/student:	2	£3,170
Expected completion rate:	4	96.4%
Good honours:	8	86.5%
Graduate prospects:	2	90.5%

highest proportions at any university and considerably more than the benchmark calculated by the Higher Education Statistics Agency. The Imperial Horizons programme, designed to give students an edge in their future career, provides opportunities to debate global challenges such as climate change, drawing on expertise from across the university. Many degrees offer a work placement or year abroad, and students are actively encouraged to seek summer internships. The Undergraduate Research Opportunities Programme offers "hands-on" research experience.

The Faculty of Medicine is one of Europe's largest in terms of its staff and student numbers, as well as its research income. There are teaching bases attached to a number of hospitals in central and west London, while the UK's first Academic Health Science Centre (AHSC), run in partnership with Imperial College Healthcare NHS Trust, aims to translate research advances into patient care. The centre is one of only five in the country, denoting international excellence in biomedical research, education and patient care.

In its first overseas venture, Imperial is also a partner in a new medical school in Singapore, run jointly with Nanyang Technological University. The growing business school is Imperial's main venture beyond the world of science and technology.

It is highly rated and is accredited by the three largest and most influential business school accreditation associations worldwide. There is also an environmental research campus at Silwood Park, 25 miles west of London.

A university in its own right since leaving the University of London in 2007, Imperial continues to upgrade and expand its South Kensington campus facilities A second residential complex and refurbishments to the central library were followed by improvements to the students' union bar and nightclub. Further library improvements are being phased in over several years to minimise disruption. The students' union claims to have the largest selection of clubs and societies in the country. Outdoor sports facilities are remote, but a new and well-equipped sports centre on the South Kensington campus offers students free gym and swimming facilities, on payment of an initial joining fee.

Tuition fees

- » Fees for UK/EU students 2017–18 £9,250
  Placement year £925 or £1,850
- » UK fees are expected to increase by the rate of inflation from 2018–19 onwards.
- » Fees for international students 2017–18 £25,000–£28,000
  Medicine £38,500
- » Check the university's website for the latest information on fees, scholarships, bursaries and other forms of student support.

Students

Undergraduates:	9,010	(5)
Postgraduates:	6,260	(1,335)
Mature students:	2.1%	
International students:	41.4%	
Applications per place:	6.9	
From state-sector schools:	64.8%	
From working-class homes:	16.2%	
Satisfaction with students' union	71%	

For detailed information about sports facilities:
www.imperial.ac.uk/sport

Accommodation

Number of places and costs refer to 2016–17
University-provided places: 2,531
Percentage catered: 0%
Self-catered costs: £98 – £267 a week (39, 39 weeks).
First-year undergraduates are guaranteed accommodation if application received by 31 July.
International students: as above.
accommodation@imperial.ac.uk
www.imperial.ac.uk/study/campus-life/accommodation

Keele University

Keele boasts the largest campus in the country, 600 acres of parkland in the heart of England, near Stoke. The university is ensuring that even more of the 10,000 students will be able to live as well as work there in future by building two new halls close to the centre of the campus. The first development of 453 new bedrooms is set for completion in autumn 2017, with almost another 1,000 rooms to follow, as well as an upgrade of all the existing campus accommodation.

A third of all undergraduates, as well as many postgraduates and even some staff, live on a campus which includes an arboretum and has won a clutch of environmental awards. Students can grow their own fruit and vegetables on campus, and all undergraduates can take a module in sustainability or environmental studies.

The university is aiming to grow by a third over five years, with postgraduates accounting for many of the new places. The numbers starting first degrees rose by 400 in 2015, despite a small decline in applications. More than £115 million has been spent on the campus since the turn of the century.

The latest phase has transformed the heart of the campus, reconfiguring the Union Square plaza and providing a social hub for both informal and formal events.

A new development to meet student demand for courses in the life sciences will provide two teaching laboratories, capable of hosting 120 students. There will also be two additional research laboratories and offices to support extra staff and postgraduate research students.

Keele has consistently excellent results in the annual National Student Survey (NSS) and ranks in the top five on both measures (teaching quality and student experience) in our analysis of the NSS outcomes. It wins our University of the Year for Student Experience award.

As well as responding to student feedback on campus services, the university does more than most universities to help its graduates in the employment market. The distinctive Keele Curriculum, introduced as the university celebrated its 50th anniversary in 2012, covers voluntary and sporting activities as well as the academic core. It is the only one in the UK that can lead to accreditation by the Institute of Leadership and Management.

The student charter identifies ten "graduate attributes" that include independent thinking, synthesising information, creative problem solving, communicating clearly, and appreciating the social, environmental and global implications of all studies and activities. The university has also been at the forefront of moves to record in more detail what

---

Keele

Staffordshire ST5 5BG

01782 734 010 (admissions)
admissions@keele.ac.uk
www.keele.ac.uk
http://keelesu.com
Affiliation: none

The Times and Sunday Times **Rankings**

Overall Ranking: **42** (last year: 43)

Teaching quality:	5	87.2%
Student experience:	3	90.4%
Research quality:	52	22.1%
Entry standards:	=50	352
Student–staff ratio:	=20	13.2
Services & facilities/student:	86	£1,740
Expected completion rate:	=43	89.1%
Good honours:	83	67.2%
Graduate prospects:	33	79.5%

graduates have achieved through a Higher Education Annual Report.

The academic year is divided into two 15-week semesters, with breaks at Christmas and Easter. Nearly all undergraduates have the option of spending a semester abroad at one of the university's partner universities.

Nine out of ten undergraduates are state educated and almost one in three come from working-class homes. The university has been trying to broaden its intake further by offering special projects and masterclasses in local schools and hosting a summer school. The projected dropout rate of less than 6 per cent is well below the national average for the university's subjects and entry qualifications.

Health subjects have been the main focus of development in recent years. First degrees in physiotherapy and nursing and midwifery were added to the well-established postgraduate medical school. Keele also offers a five-year undergraduate medical course taught in new facilities on the Keele campus and nearby teaching hospitals. Facilities for pharmacy and the natural sciences have also been improved.

Keele's results in the 2014 Research Excellence Framework showed considerable improvement on the 2008 assessments. Over 70 per cent of the work submitted was placed in the top two categories, with researchers in primary care and health sciences, pharmacy, chemistry, science and technology, the life sciences and history scoring particularly well.

The university is within an hour's drive of Manchester and Birmingham. Crime statistics suggest that Keele is the safest university campus in the West Midlands.

For those who live off campus, the cost of living in the Potteries and the surrounding area is relatively low. The highly rated students' union, which has undergone a £2.7 million renovation, offers entertainment on campus every night of the week during term. It has won the Best Bar None Gold Award, for responsible drinking and a safe environment, for five years in a row.

A new £1.7-million improvement and upgrade of the sports facilities opened in 2016. It includes the creation of a full-size 3G football pitch suitable for all-weather play in a variety of sports to supplement the indoor facilities.

Tuition fees

» Fees for UK/EU students 2017–18 £9,250
   Year abroad £1,385
   Placement year £500
» UK fees are expected to increase by the rate of inflation from 2018–19 onwards.
» Fees for international students 2017–18 £13,000–£16,000
   Medicine £27,800
» Check the university's website for the latest information on fees, scholarships, bursaries and other forms of student support.

Students

Undergraduates:	6,670	(655)
Postgraduates:	755	(1,555)
Mature students:	12.2%	
International students:	15.7%	
Applications per place:	8.8	
From state-sector schools:	93.8%	
From working-class homes:	32.1%	
Satisfaction with students' union	84%	

For detailed information about sports facilities:
www.keele.ac.uk/sport

Accommodation

Number of places and costs refer to 2016–17
University-provided places: 3,200
Percentage catered: 5%
Catered costs: £141.21 – £161.44 a week (37 weeks).
Self-catered costs: £61.59 – £140.00 a week (34–51 weeks).
First years are guaranteed accommodation on campus if Keele is first or firm choice university.
International students: guaranteed accommodation for the duration of their course. Deadlines apply.
www.keele.ac.uk/studyatkeele/accommodation

University of Kent

Kent was among the first universities to announce that it would raise its fees for new students to the maximum of £9,250 in 2017 if Parliament passed the necessary legislation. The university said it had published the higher fee to ensure that both potential and existing students had as much notice as possible and to comply with consumer protection guidelines.

The numbers starting degrees have risen gradually for three years in succession, with applications back to the levels seen before the last fee increase.

Kent opened its first new college for undergraduates in 45 years in 2015. Turing College has 800 study bedrooms and a hub building with social and study areas, catering facilities and a launderette. The development allowed Kent to maintain its position as one of the best-provided universities for accommodation, with nearly 5,400 places in Canterbury alone for 15,000 full-time students there. Every student is attached to college, although they do not select it themselves. The colleges act as the focus of social life – especially in the first year – and include academic as well as residential facilities.

The university celebrated its 50th anniversary in 2015 after achieving outstanding results in the latest official assessments of university research. Almost three-quarters of the work submitted for the Research Excellence Framework was judged world-leading or internationally excellent. The successes, led by social work and social policy, music and drama, and modern languages, helped Kent to maintain its highest-ever position in our league table and gain a shortlisting for our University of the Year award.

The university was already a perennial high-performer in the National Student Survey and is also in the top 20 for staffing levels. Kent encourages all its academics to take a Postgraduate Certificate in Higher Education. Its staff have been awarded National Teaching Fellowships in five of the last seven years.

Capitalising on its location, Kent is also perhaps the UK's most active in Europe, both in terms of its participation in EU programmes and in its continental ventures. Styling itself "the UK's European university", Kent now has postgraduate sites in Brussels, Paris, Athens and Rome, as well as giving many undergraduates the option of a year abroad. There are partnerships with over 100 European universities.

Kent's original low-rise campus is set in 300 acres of parkland overlooking Canterbury. Recent developments include the prize-winning Colyer-Fergusson Music Building and Kent School of Architecture's new Crit Building. A media centre opened

The Registry
Canterbury
Kent CT2 7NZ

01227 827272 (admissions)
information@kent.ac.uk
www.kent.ac.uk
www.kentunion.co.uk
Affiliation: none

***The Times and Sunday Times* Rankings**

Overall Ranking: **23** (last year: =23)

Teaching quality:	=59	80.9%
Student experience:	31	85.9%
Research quality:	33	35.2%
Entry standards:	48	361
Student–staff ratio:	17	12.7
Services & facilities/student:	94	£1,666
Expected completion rate:	=33	91.6%
Good honours:	=26	80.1%
Graduate prospects:	25	80.6%

in 2014 and the redevelopment and extension of the library will be complete well before new students arrive in 2017. The student centre has a nightclub large enough to attract big-name bands, as well as a theatre, cinema and bars.

Two further developments are a new law clinic, with a dedicated mooting chamber, competed in 2016, and a £26-million building, scheduled for 2017, for Kent Business School and the School of Mathematics, Statistics and Actuarial Science, allowing two of the university's most successful departments to expand.

The university also has a Medway Campus, at the old Chatham naval base, which is shared with Greenwich and Canterbury Christ Church universities. The School of Pharmacy, is the main feature of a £50-million development which now has more than 2,000 Kent students, including those in the School of Music and Fine Art. There are more than 1,000 residential places and Grade 2 listed former swimming baths have been converted into a student hub, incorporating facilities for the students' union, bar and other social spaces, for the 2016 academic year.

The university also has a base in Tonbridge serving 3,000 part-time students, who are mainly taught in associate colleges.

Entry grades have been rising in most subjects. Offers are pitched according to the UCAS points tariff, although those taking

A levels are expected to pass at least three subjects (one of which may be general studies). Kent awards scholarships of £2,000 a year, renewable annually, to candidates who achieved at least three As at A level, or the equivalent. Where one subject is maths or a modern foreign language, the threshold is AAB. Graduates fare well in the employment market – the university regularly features among the top 20 for graduate starting salaries.

Some students find both Canterbury and Medway limited in social terms, but campus security is good and the sports facilities have improved considerably following an investment of £4.8 million in a fitness suite that includes an extensive range of free weights, as well as four Olympic power-lifting platforms. There is also a multipurpose fitness and dance studio, and an indoor tennis centre has been added alongside the sports centre.

Tuition fees

»	Fees for UK/EU students 2017–18	£9,250
	Courses at partner colleges	£6,000–£9,250
	Year abroad	£1,385
	Placement year	£1,385

» UK fees are expected to increase by the rate of inflation from 2018–19 onwards.

» Fees for international students 2017–18   £13,810–£16,480

» Check the university's website for the latest information on fees, scholarships, bursaries and other forms of student support.

Students

Undergraduates:	14,555	(495)
Postgraduates:	2,690	(1,250)
Mature students:	11.8%	
International students:	20.4%	
Applications per place:	6.6	
From state-sector schools:	92.3%	
From working-class homes:	32.5%	
Satisfaction with students' union	73%	

For detailed information about sports facilities:
www.kent.ac.uk/sports

Accommodation

Number of places and costs refer to 2016–17
University-provided places: 5,381
Percentage catered: 12%
Catered costs: £128 – £232 a week.
Self-catered costs: £109 – £168 a week.
First years are guaranteed accommodation provided applications received before 31 July.
International students: as above.
hospitality-enquiry@kent.ac.uk
www.kent.ac.uk/accommodation

King's College London

The proportion of applicants receiving offers from King's has leapt from under half to two-thirds, as the university has taken the opportunity to expand following the lifting of restrictions on undergraduate recruitment. It added 1,500 places to the undergraduate intake between 2011 and 2015, as applications rose sharply.

Partly in order to make room for the new arrivals, King's will occupy Bush House, the former headquarters of the BBC World Service, opposite its Strand campus, on a phased basis from September 2016. The addition of Bush House and its four neighbouring buildings will enable King's to upgrade its teaching facilities. It had already expanded into the East Wing of Somerset House, providing impressive new premises for The Dickson Poon School of Law, and earmarked £140 million of further campus developments. Libraries on all the main campuses have been upgraded – part of a £60-million programme of improvements to student facilities.

Once known primarily for science, King's now has a distinguished reputation across eight schools, including humanities, law and social sciences, which includes war studies. Its research strength has established it in the top 25 of the QS World University Rankings, although low satisfaction scores in the National Student Survey keep it out of the top 25 in our league table. In common with a number of other elite Russell Group universities, King's occupies a position in the bottom 20 for student satisfaction with both teaching quality and their wider student experience.

In the 2014 Research Excellence Framework, 85 per cent of the university's submission was judged to be world-leading or internationally excellent, placing it in the top ten on this measure. Law, education, clinical medicine and philosophy all ranked in the top three in the country and there were good results in general engineering, history, psychology and communication and media studies. The results produced the biggest increase in research funding of any university.

Today's researchers follow in a tradition that has seen King's play a part in many of the advances that shape modern life, including the discovery of DNA and the development of radar. Twelve alumni or academics have won Nobel Prizes. It is Europe's largest centre for the education of doctors, dentists and other healthcare professionals, and home to six Medical Research Council centres. King's Health Partners Academic Health Sciences Centre represents a pioneering collaboration between the university and three NHS foundation trusts.

In 2016, King's also formed a new

Strand
London WC2R 2LS

020 7848 7000 (enquiries)
contact via website
www.kcl.ac.uk
www.kclsu.org
Affiliation: Russell Group

The Times and Sunday Times Rankings

Overall Ranking: **27** (last year: 27)

Teaching quality:	123	74.9%
Student experience:	114	80.3%
Research quality:	9	44%
Entry standards:	15	464
Student–staff ratio:	9	11.7
Services & facilities/student:	46	£2,127
Expected completion rate:	17	94%
Good honours:	=15	83.4%
Graduate prospects:	4	88%

research and teaching alliance with Arizona State University and the University of New South Wales that includes degrees in sustainability, global health, community health, whole person care, business and global logistics management.

King's is one of the oldest and largest of the University of London's colleges, describing itself as "the most central university in London" with four of its five campuses within a single square mile around the banks of the Thames. The fifth is not far away at Denmark Hill in south London. The original Strand site and the Waterloo Campus house most of the non-medical departments. Nursing and midwifery and some biomedical subjects are also based at Waterloo, while medicine and dentistry are mainly at Guy's Hospital, near London Bridge, and in the St Thomas' Hospital Campus, across the river from the Houses of Parliament.

The Denmark Hill Campus is home to the Institute of Psychiatry, Psychology and Neuroscience, as well as more medicine and dentistry subjects.

About one student in five is from outside the European Union, many of them among the 10,000 postgraduates. An institutional audit by the Quality Assurance Agency gave King's the highest mark, stressing the excellence of the student support services. Graduates enjoy among the best employment rates in the UK and typically also earn some of the highest starting salaries. King's location means students are in an enviable position for accessing opportunities for work experience.

More than a quarter of the undergraduates come from independent schools, but a similar proportion are from low-income families – significantly better than average for the courses and entry qualifications. The Access to Medicine course, which attracts talented students from generally low-performing schools into medical degrees, has now been replicated for dentistry, with the Enhanced Support Dentistry Programme.

Accommodation at King's is plentiful and spread over a variety of residences. Some of the outdoor sports facilities are a long train ride from the campuses, but there are facilities for all the main sports, as well as rifle ranges, gyms and a swimming pool.

Tuition fees

» Fees for UK/EU students 2017–18		£9,250
Year abroad		£1,350
Placement year		£1,350

» UK fees are expected to increase by the rate of inflation from 2018–19 onwards.

» Fees for international students 2017–18	£17,050–£22,800
Medicine		£33,000
Dentistry		£39,200

» Check the university's website for the latest information on fees, scholarships, bursaries and other forms of student support.

Students

Undergraduates:	14,195	(3,415)
Postgraduates:	6,580	(4,545)
Mature students:	17.8%	
International students:	26.2%	
Applications per place:	8.2	
From state-sector schools:	74.9%	
From working-class homes:	26.2%	
Satisfaction with students' union	65%	

For detailed information about sports facilities:
www.kcl.ac.uk/campuslife/sport

Accommodation

Number of places and costs refer to 2016–17

University-provided places: 4,840; 420 Intercollegiate.

Percentage catered: 9% (all Intercollegiate)

Catered costs: £139.55 (standard single) – £263.50 (studio).

Self-catered costs: £155 (standard single) – £369 (studio) a week (40 weeks).

New full-time undergraduate students and international postgraduates are guaranteed the offer of one year in accommodation if specific conditions are met.
www.kcl.ac.uk/study/ug/residences

Kingston University

Kingston is number one in the UK for graduate start-up companies and has been among the top two universities for this for seven years in succession. There were 371 of these in 2014–15 and the combined turnover of all the university's start-ups came close to £30 million. The Enterprise Department was established more than a decade ago to give advice to would-be entrepreneurs in any subject and the possibility of financial support with start-ups.

A career focus runs through all Kingston's courses. The university has the third largest engineering faculty in London, for example, with its own Learjet and a flight simulator to support its highly regarded aeronautical engineering courses.

Given this success, it is surprising that Kingston does not rank higher in our league table for graduate prospects and that it has fallen into the bottom ten in our overall ranking this year, following a decline in rankings across all eight of our performance indicators where there is new data.

The university is working hard to improve its offer to students, however. The first stage of a £6.8-million project to create sophisticated new science, technology, engineering and maths (STEM) facilities on the Penrhyn Road campus opened in autumn 2016. Alongside the new laboratories is an innovative new outreach space where the public can explore how cutting-edge technologies are making an impact on people's daily lives.

The university has already spent £20 million on the John Galsworthy Building on the campus, which incorporates lecture theatres, flexible teaching space and information technology suites as well as a "Knowledge Centre" for students to do coursework. Another £50-million building is due to open in 2019, which will include a resources centre, auditorium and two cafés. The projects are part of a £123-million programme to revitalise the university's entire estate.

A new learning resources centre is part of an £11-million programme of improvements at the university's Knights Park campus, which has included the refurbishment of studio space, an upgraded reception and gallery area and external landscaping. Library facilities on each campus have been upgraded, bringing together library, computing and multimedia facilities to encourage interactive and group learning. The learning resources centres have received government recognition for excellent customer service. The main centres are open 24 hours a day during term-time weekdays, while a high-tech self-issue system has speeded up borrowing.

The School of Art, which is rated in the top 100 in the world by QS, has been

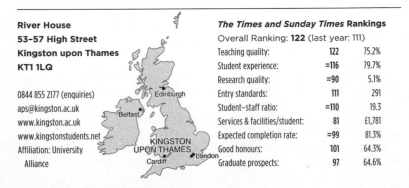

River House
53–57 High Street
Kingston upon Thames
KT1 1LQ

0844 855 2177 (enquiries)
aps@kingston.ac.uk
www.kingston.ac.uk
www.kingstonstudents.net
Affiliation: University
Alliance

The Times and Sunday Times Rankings

Overall Ranking: **122** (last year: 111)

Teaching quality:	122	75.2%
Student experience:	=116	79.7%
Research quality:	=90	5.1%
Entry standards:	111	291
Student–staff ratio:	=110	19.3
Services & facilities/student:	81	£1,781
Expected completion rate:	=99	81.3%
Good honours:	101	64.3%
Graduate prospects:	97	64.6%

celebrating its 140th anniversary and achieved among the best results in the 2014 Research Excellence Framework (REF), together with history and English, where the whole submission was given the top grade for its external impact. The university entered relatively few academics for the REF – only 16 per cent of the eligible staff – but 60 per cent of the submission reached the top two categories and there was some world-leading research in each of the nine areas in which it was assessed.

Kingston is to head the largest project in a new Government-funded programme to boost postgraduate study. Its aim is to encourage students who might not normally become postgraduates to continue on to Master's courses in science, technology, engineering and mathematics and then track how they progress.

The Faculty of Health, Social Care and Education (run jointly with St George's, University of London) now has more than 7,000 students and has won two major NHS London contracts, which will increase numbers in nursing and physiotherapy. There is a link with the Royal Marsden School of Cancer Nursing and Rehabilitation, enabling some students to spend up to half of their course on clinical placements working in hospital, primary care and community settings.

The university markets itself as in "lively, leafy London", making a virtue of its suburban, riverside location southwest of central London as well as its proximity to the bright lights. Two of its four campuses are close to Kingston town centre; another is at Kingston Hill, two miles away; the fourth is in Roehampton Vale, where a former aerospace factory site now contains a new technology block. The campuses are joined by a free university bus service.

Kingston has one of the most ethnically mixed student populations of any UK university, and many undergraduates are also the first in their family to experience higher education. Nearly a third of Kingston's places go to mature students and approaching half to those from working-class families. Most students like the university's location, although they complain about the high cost of living. More than £20 million has been spent on halls of residence and Kingston's sports facilities have improved with the addition of a £2.65-million sports pavilion and upgraded sports ground.

Tuition fees

» Fees for UK/EU students 2017–18 £9,250
  Foundation degree £5,050–£6,165
» UK fees are expected to increase by the rate of inflation from 2018–19 onwards.
» Fees for international students 2017–18 £12,000–£14,500
» Check the university's website for the latest information on fees, scholarships, bursaries and other forms of student support.

Students

Undergraduates:	15,500	(1,475)
Postgraduates:	2,160	(2,775)
Mature students:	32.5%	
International students:	14.5%	
Applications per place:	8.6	
From state-sector schools:	96%	
From working-class homes:	47.3%	
Satisfaction with students' union	62%	

For detailed information about sports facilities:
www.kingston.ac.uk/sport

Accommodation

Number of places and costs refer to 2016–17
University-provided places: 2,574; private hall: 208
Percentage catered: 0%
Self-catered costs: £115 – £145 a week (university provided; 40 weeks); £212.50 – £298.00 (private hall; 50 weeks).
Self-catering accommodation is offered to most first years who make Kingston their firm choice through UCAS.
International students: as above, offered places if conditions met, subject to availability.
www.kingston.ac.uk/accommodation

Lancaster University

Lancaster has been the top university in our league table from the northwest of England for more than a decade, and has this year achieved its target of a place in our top ten – a position it last held five years ago. In the longer term, it is committed to becoming a "global player" in both teaching and research, with a place among the top 100 universities in the world.

It is moving in the right direction, now being inside the top 130 in the QS global ranking. Lancaster is the only UK university with a presence in sub-Saharan Africa, having opened a branch campus in Ghana. There are also partnerships with universities in India, Pakistan, Malaysia and China that mean as many students are taking a Lancaster degree overseas as in the UK. Hundreds of Lancaster students also spend part of their courses in America, Asia, Australia or Europe.

The university's research grades improved substantially in the 2014 assessments, when 83 per cent of its work was considered world-leading or internationally excellent. There were particularly good results in business and management, sociology, English, and maths and statistics, and a strong performance across the board. Lancaster was the only university in the region to receive an increase in funding because of the quality and volume of its submission. It has since received a Queen's Anniversary Prize for corpus linguistics, that is analysing the main world languages as used in print, speech and social media.

Lancaster is more successful than most research universities in widening participation among under-represented groups. Nine out of ten undergraduates are state educated and almost a quarter come from the four lowest socio-economic classes. Outreach activity includes summer schools for 600 sixth-formers and college students, masterclasses for 2,000 and mentoring for 250 students.

Still a relatively small university, Lancaster has 13,000 students on a 360-acre parkland campus. Undergraduates join one of eight residential colleges on campus, which become the centre of most students' social life. Most house between 800 and 900 students in self-catering accommodation, and each has its own bar and social facilities.

The historic city of Lancaster is a ten-minute bus ride away. Both the campus and city have been rated among the safest in the UK. The campus has had a £500-million makeover, with much of the money going on eco-friendly student residences and an impressive new library with high speed Wi-Fi, 27 bookable group study rooms, loanable laptops and print, scan and copy facilities on every floor. Lancaster has been in the

---

Bailrigg
Lancaster LA1 4YW

01524 592028 (admissions)
ugadmissions@lancaster.ac.uk
www.lancaster.ac.uk
http://lusu.co.uk
Affiliation: none

LANCASTER

The Times and Sunday Times Rankings

Overall Ranking: **=9** (last year: 11)

Teaching quality:	40	82.3%
Student experience:	=12	87.8%
Research quality:	15	39.1%
Entry standards:	26	421
Student–staff ratio:	=23	13.4
Services & facilities/student:	8	£2,827
Expected completion rate:	25	92.8%
Good honours:	39	76.8%
Graduate prospects:	17	82.5%

top three in the National Student Housing Survey for the best university halls since 2010, taking the award six times, and is one of only five UK universities to be awarded an International Accommodation Quality Mark, indicating over 90 per cent positive feedback from international students.

The university is set to spend millions more on refreshing the campus walkways and developing its Management School. A 24-hour student learning space provides flexible learning environments and social space with up-to-date technology. Other recent developments include a leadership centre for the highly rated Management School, which has helped 4,700 students to find work placements in the micro-business and start-up sector.

An award-winning building for engineering has seen undergraduate numbers double. The university has also brought together art, design and theatre studies with the university's public art gallery, concerts and theatre, invested heavily in design and established a Confucius Institute as a hub for Chinese language teaching and culture.

Lancaster has been the most successful university at reducing carbon emissions, winning particular praise for its innovative wind turbine project, which generates approximately 15 per cent of its annual electricity consumption. The university has won a string of environmental awards for its residences and other facilities.

The university has always championed a flexible degree structure, in which most undergraduates make their final choice of degree only at the end of the first year. The degree portfolio now includes medicine.

The university has established a new department of chemistry, which offers an undergraduate degree in the subject, and there is a new Centre for Organisational Health and Wellbeing.

Some of England's most unspoilt countryside is on the university's doorstep, including the Lake District and the Forest of Bowland.

The university hosts a thriving live arts scene for the campus, the city and the region, with professional theatre, dance, exhibitions and concerts.

Sports facilities are good and convenient, with £20-million sports centre on campus. Road and rail communications are good, but Lancaster is inevitably more limited for off-campus nightlife.

Tuition fees

» Fees for UK/EU students 2017–18 £9,250
» UK fees are expected to increase by the rate of inflation from 2018–19 onwards.
» Fees for international students 2016–17 £14,500–£17,470
  Medicine £28,050
» Check the university's website for the latest information on fees, scholarships, bursaries and other forms of student support.

Students

Undergraduates:	9,160	(70)
Postgraduates:	2,290	(1,445)
Mature students:	5.6%	
International students:	29.6%	
Applications per place:	7.1	
From state-sector schools:	90.1%	
From working-class homes:	23.9%	
Satisfaction with students' union	62%	

For detailed information about sports facilities:
www.lancaster.ac.uk/sport

Accommodation

Number of places and costs refer to 2016–17
University-provided places: 6,600 (plus about 900 places in university-managed houses)
Percentage catered: 5%
Catered costs: £173.32 – £179.90 a week (31 weeks).
Self-catered costs: £85.40 (standard) – £151.55 (studio) a week (40 weeks).
All first years are normally housed if conditions are met.
International students: as above.
www.lancaster.ac.uk/facilities/accommodation

University of Leeds

The big civic universities generally do well at attracting applicants, but find it difficult to match the satisfaction levels at the smaller campus institutions. Leeds is the exception to this rule: it remains among the most popular universities, but few of its peer group comes close to matching its performance in the National Student Survey. Strong results in the NSS – despite a slight dip this year – have helped Leeds to three successive rises in our league table to reach its highest-ever position, and earn our University of the Year award this year after two years of being shortlisted.

Last year it was the only Russell Group university to feature in the top 20 in the survey for both teaching quality and the broader student experience. Leeds is also in the top 100 in the QS World University Rankings, and in the top 50 for English, education, communication and media studies, geography, and earth sciences.

More than 80 per cent of the research assessed in the 2014 Research Excellence Framework was considered world-leading or internationally excellent, placing Leeds in the top ten in the UK in 30 per cent of its subject areas.

The university is truly cosmopolitan, with 5,000 international students from 141 countries among a total of more than 31,000.

Leeds has one of the largest Study Abroad programmes in the country, with nearly 200 options ranging from Spain to Singapore.

The university occupies a 98-acre site within walking distance of the city centre. A five-year capital programme costing £520 million has seen the opening of a new undergraduate library, with 1,000 seats, flexible facilities and on-site academic skills support. There is also a new £42-million Enterprise and Innovation Centre, which will assist students with start-up plans and accelerate business creation and growth across the city.

Another major development has linked the engineering buildings with those for physical sciences. Previous improvements included a new home for the Institute of Communications Studies with 41 edit suites, TV and radio studios, newsroom and 60-seat cinema, a £12.5-million Energy Research building and the refurbishment of the Leeds Dental Institute. The already large students' union, famous for its long bar and big-name rock concerts, is being extended and refurbished for completion in spring 2017. In the next phase of the plan, the North East Quarter development will bring together physics, computing and imaging science.

There are more than 560 undergraduate programmes, with students encouraged to take courses outside their main subject. The distinctive Leeds Curriculum requires undergraduates to undertake a research

---

Leeds
LS2 9JT

0113 343 2336 (enquiries)
study@leeds.ac.uk
www.leeds.ac.uk
www.luu.org.uk
Affiliation: Russell Group

The Times and Sunday Times Rankings		
Overall Ranking: **13** (last year: 14)		
Teaching quality:	=34	82.7%
Student experience:	=12	87.8%
Research quality:	27	36.8%
Entry standards:	18	436
Student–staff ratio:	=25	13.5
Services & facilities/student:	19	£2,604
Expected completion rate:	22	93.5%
Good honours:	17	83.3%
Graduate prospects:	21	81.4%

project in their final year, which is intended to be seen as the "pinnacle of their academic achievement" and is weighted accordingly.

Leeds was commended by the Quality Assurance Agency for its enhancement of the student learning experience. The Student Education Service provides support from the point of application to beyond graduation, and the university is establishing a new Institute for Teaching Excellence and Innovation. Leeds has been awarded more National Teaching Fellowships (22) than any other university in England. It has invested over £2 million in a new lecture capture and multimedia management system – one of the largest in Europe. Students can access video and audio recordings of many lectures and other teaching activities, through the university's Virtual Learning Environment, allowing them to study at their own pace.

The university has devoted one of the largest amounts of any institution to financial support for students, and has continued to do so in 2016, when up to a third of UK and EU undergraduates are expected to benefit. The LeedsforLife service provides students with academic and careers advice, as well as help to identify work placements and volunteering opportunities. It is available for five years after graduation. The award-winning Careers Centre hosts some of the world's biggest employers at the university, as well as advising those who choose to set up on their own. Leeds has more market listed spin-outs than any other university.

The rise of Leeds as a shopping and clubbing centre has added to the attractions of the university. Over 2,500 students volunteer in the local community and 400 students are trained as mentors and tutors supporting schools in the region.

In recent years there has been an increase in students living in purpose-built student accommodation close to campus and the city centre.

Sports and social facilities are first rate, and Leeds teams regularly excel in competition. The university hosts one of six centres of cricketing excellence. It has more playing field space than any other, while The Edge sports centre includes a 25-metre swimming pool and a huge fitness suite.

Tuition fees

- » Fees for UK/EU students 2017–18   £9,250
  Year abroad   £1,385
  Placement year   £1,385
- » UK fees are expected to increase by the rate of inflation from 2018–19 onwards.
- » Fees for international students 2017–18   £15,750–£19,750
  Medicine   £29,750
  Dentistry   £32,750
- » Check the university's website for the latest information on fees, scholarships, bursaries and other forms of student support.

Students

Undergraduates:	22,270	(735)
Postgraduates:	5,455	(2,570)
Mature students:	8.5%	
International students:	11.8%	
Applications per place:	8.0	
From state-sector schools:	80.9%	
From working-class homes:	22.5%	
Satisfaction with students' union	92%	

For detailed information about sports facilities:
http://sport.leeds.ac.uk

Accommodation

Number of places and costs refer to 2016–17
University-provided places: 7,900
Percentage catered: 23%
Catered costs £141 – £194 a week (39 weeks).
Self-catered costs: £83 – £165 a week (42–51 weeks).
Single first years are guaranteed a place if conditions are met.
International students: guaranteed to full free-paying undergraduates if conditions are met.
www.accommodation.leeds.ac.uk

Leeds Beckett University

There are some challenging targets in a new strategic plan for Leeds Beckett following the arrival of Professor Peter Slee as Vice-Chancellor. They include substantial improvements in some areas that have caused the university to slip in our league table, such as halving the drop-out rate within five years and ensuring that almost nine out of ten students are satisfied with the standard of teaching.

The demand for places had started to recover from two disastrous years in which applications fell by almost 30 per cent when the former Leeds Metropolitan University changed its name to Leeds Beckett. But there was a further drop of more than 11 per cent in 2015.

Professor Slee hopes to capitalise on the city's central position in the Government's Northern Powerhouse plans to revive the university's fortunes. Leeds Beckett has Customer Service Excellence accreditation for the entire university, one of only two in the UK to do so. It also holds the Gold Investors in People standard, and is the only university to achieve both of these independent standards. There have also been good scores in the International Barometer, a global survey of international students, in which Leeds Beckett came top in the world for the technology used by students, second for virtual learning and third for its laboratories.

There are two bases in Leeds: the City Campus, in the heart of the city centre, and the Headingley Campus, three miles away in 100 acres of park and woodland.

The latter boasts outstanding sports facilities, including a sports arena and multi-use sports pitches. The sports centre offers a variety of options for performance and participation sport, alongside the £2-million Carnegie Regional Tennis Centre and teaching accommodation for education, informatics, law and business.

Over 7,000 students take part in some form of sporting activity, and there is a range of sports scholarships. The Athletic Union hosts 48 clubs and the 80 university teams are among the most successful in national competition. Several recent alumni and others who use the university as their training base took part in the Rio Olympics. An annual pass for both the Headingley and City campus facilities currently costs £125.

In the first developments of their kind, a new stand was built at the Headingley rugby ground, with classrooms, coaching facilities and social space for use by the university and the two professional clubs, and a

City Campus
Leeds
LS1 3HE

0113 812 3113 (enquiries)
admissionsenquiries@
  leedsbeckett.ac.uk
www.leedsbeckett.ac.uk
www.leedsbeckettsu.co.uk
Affiliation: none

The Times and Sunday Times Rankings

Overall Ranking: =112 (last year: 114)

Teaching quality:	93	79.2%
Student experience:	=65	83.8%
Research quality:	=100	4.1%
Entry standards:	=109	292
Student–staff ratio:	121	20.7
Services & facilities/student:	106	£1,522
Expected completion rate:	=113	78.7%
Good honours:	94	65.3%
Graduate prospects:	94	66.1%

pavilion at the adjacent Test and County Cricket ground has similar multi-use facilities.

Little more than half of all undergraduates are taking conventional full-time degrees, such is the popularity of sandwich and part-time courses. It is intended that all Leeds Beckett students should leave the university with three graduate attributes: to be enterprising, digitally literate and have a global outlook. All undergraduate courses have been redesigned with these qualities in mind and all include at least two weeks work-related learning a year.

The university has a longstanding reputation for widening participation in higher education and runs a wide range of summer schools, attended by more than 24,000 young people a year.

The City Campus has seen a £100-million transformation and is still being improved. The futuristic Rose Bowl lecture theatre complex houses the business school, while Broadcasting Place is home to the Faculty of Arts and Society. The former BBC building next door has reopened as Old Broadcasting House and hosts the Enterprise Office, which helps identify opportunities to generate commercial income and support bids for funding and contracts.

Recent campus developments include a £1-million clinical skills suite and cutting-edge biomedical sciences laboratories, and the library has been refurbished. A growing emphasis on educational technology is enhanced by 24-hour libraries, which have achieved the Customer Service Excellence standard for ten years in a row.

The university almost doubled the number of academics it entered for the 2014 Research Excellence Framework compared with the 2008 assessments. Just over a third of their work was rated as world-leading or internationally excellent, with architecture and sports studies producing much the best results. Leeds Beckett's reputation is mainly for applied research: three interdisciplinary research institutes focus on health, sport and sustainability, and there are ten centres in more specialist fields.

Leeds Beckett is benefiting from the city's growing reputation for nightlife, but it is making its own contribution with a famously lively entertainments scene. Those who accept places before Clearing are guaranteed university accommodation.

Tuition fees

- » Fees for UK/EU students 2017–18 £9,250
  Placement year no fee
- » UK fees are expected to increase by the rate of inflation from 2018–19 onwards.
- » Fees for international students 2017–18 £10,500
- » Check the university's website for the latest information on fees, scholarships, bursaries and other forms of student support.

Students

Undergraduates:	17,330	(4,230)
Postgraduates:	1,510	(2,950)
Mature students:	12.3%	
International students:	5.7%	
Applications per place:	5.1	
From state-sector schools:	95.4%	
From working-class homes:	35.4%	
Satisfaction with students' union	70%	

For detailed information about sports facilities:
www.leedsbeckett.ac.uk/sport

Accommodation

Number of places and costs refer to 2016–17
University-provided places: 4,500
Percentage catered: 0%
Self-catered costs: £90 – £175 a week (40–45 weeks).
First years with Conditional Firm or Unconditional Firm offers guaranteed accommodation if they book before the booking deadline.
International students: guaranteed accommodation if conditions are met.
www.leedsbeckett.ac.uk/accommodation

Leeds Trinity University

Leeds Trinity has a new strategy for teaching and learning centring on student-led enquiry, which places more onus on students to develop and lead their own learning in order to be more employable when they graduate. To guide them from induction to beyond graduation, the university has introduced a programme of personalised support, which was shortlisted in the *Times Higher Education* Awards.

The schemes are in the hands of a newly launched Learning Hub, a department dedicated to personalised, academic skills development and mentoring. This proactive approach bore fruit in last year's National Student Survey when Leeds Trinity ranked in the top 20 for teaching quality. However, this year's results led to the university dropping 65 places on this measure in our league table, a sign of considerable volatility.

The university has been increasing the variety of degrees and is planning three new dual honours politics degrees, three more with English and a degree in public health and wellbeing in 2017. The university already offers accelerated two-year degrees in education and sport, and tourism and leisure management. Like all the undergraduate programmes, they include full-time professional work placements.

Leeds Trinity is one of two institutions given university status in 2012 that are Catholic foundations. It "promotes dialogue and teaching of the Catholic Church", but is not controlled by the Church and welcomes students of all faiths and none. The university grew out of two Catholic teacher training colleges established in the 1960s. Education is still the biggest subject – a new Institute for Childhood and Education will pool the expertise of its acclaimed departments of Primary Education, Secondary Education and Children, Young People and Families – but there are also schools of Arts and Communication and Health and Social Sciences. There are still little more than 3,000 students, despite recent growth.

The university's campus is in Horsforth, 20 minutes northwest of Leeds city centre. Some £15 million has been invested in campus improvements and there are plans to spend another £25 million to cater for 1,000 more students over the next five years.

New halls opened in autumn 2016 saw 800 student bedrooms on campus. An extension to the library will be ready for the start of the academic year in 2017, providing additional teaching and learning space.

A previous development upgraded the Media Centre, which is now fully digital for video and audio operations, and students are able to shoot in HD following the purchase of broadcast-quality portable cameras. A new range of computers and studio cameras

Brownberrie Lane
Horsforth
Leeds LS18 5HD

0113 283 7123 (admissions)
admissions@leedstrinity.ac.uk
www.leedstrinity.ac.uk
www.ltsu.co.uk
Affiliations: GuildHE,
  Cathedrals Group
MillionPlus

The Times and Sunday Times Rankings

Overall Ranking: **96** (last year: 91)

Teaching quality:	=84	79.7%
Student experience:	=116	79.7%
Research quality:	119	2%
Entry standards:	=115	287
Student–staff ratio:	125	21.6
Services & facilities/student:	99	£1,630
Expected completion rate:	70	85%
Good honours:	49	74.7%
Graduate prospects:	73	70.6%

have been installed to meet the demands of journalism and media production courses. The Centre for Journalism has developed two additional multimedia newsrooms with easy access to studios, equipment and editing suites.

The three-year Digital Campus project involves the investment of £1.2 million to provide a seamless, resilient and flexible ICT environment, accessible from off campus. The launch of a self-service system for borrowers at the library has already doubled usage figures.

The students' union was re-launched in 2013, when it relocated to the main campus building and restructured itself to have a greater focus on academic representation and meeting the needs of a diverse range of students. Extra social space for students and staff has been developed at the same time. The student bar and venue has been revamped and given a new location.

In 2015 the university opened the Trinity Enterprise Centre to help students launch their own businesses. Its advice and facilities are available to local businesses as well as students.

Only 20 academics were entered for the 2014 Research Excellence Framework, but there were good results in communication, cultural and media studies, and library and information management. The flagship research centre, the Leeds Centre for Victorian Studies, celebrated its 20th anniversary in 2014.

Nearly two-thirds of the students are female and almost as many are the first in their family to attend university. Leeds Trinity exceeds all its national benchmarks for widening participation in higher education: more than 40 per cent of undergraduates come from working-class homes, while nearly a quarter are from areas with little tradition of sending students to university — one of the highest proportions in the country. The projected dropout rate has improved considerably and is now lower than the national average for Leeds Trinity's courses and entry qualifications. Among the outreach activities is a new Children's University, based on the campus, which offers high-quality, exciting and innovative learning activities outside normal school hours to children aged 7 to 14.

Sports facilities are good and include a 3G pitch and new changing facilities. The city is one of the most popular with students, although the campus is not central.

Tuition fees

- » Fees for UK/EU students 2017–18 £9,250
  Foundation degree £5,000
- » UK fees are expected to increase by the rate of inflation from 2018–19 onwards.
- » Fees for international students 2017–18 £11,250
- » Check the university's website for the latest information on fees, scholarships, bursaries and other forms of student support.

Students

Undergraduates:	2,710	(80)
Postgraduates:	280	(435)
Mature students:	11.8%	
International students:	0.7%	
Applications per place:	7.7	
From state-sector schools:	98.1%	
From working-class homes:	42.3%	
Satisfaction with students' union	62%	

For detailed information about sports facilities:
www.leedstrinity.ac.uk/student-life/trinity-sport

Accommodation

Places and costs refer to 2016–17
University-provided places: 800
Percentage catered: 25%
Catered costs: £116 – £126 a week (41 weeks).
Self-catered costs: £91 – £120 a week (41 weeks).
Priority is given to first-year students.
International students: same as above.
accommodation@leedstrinity.ac.uk
www.leedstrinity.ac.uk/student-life/accommodation

University of Leicester

Leicester attracted record applications in 2015 after three successive years of growth in the demand for places. The discovery of the remains of Richard III by its archaeologists in 2012 placed the university in the global spotlight. It will be hoping that Leicester City's surprise Premier League win will also help to make it a more fashionable student destination.

The numbers starting degrees have grown by 20 per cent since 2012, as the university has implemented a £1-billion development plan. The new £42-million Centre for Medicine is now open, providing teaching and learning facilities for the College of Medicine, Biological Sciences and Psychology. The £32-million library has doubled the available space and brought the total number of workspaces to 1,500. The university is continuing to invest £6 million a year in its resources and facilities.

New degree options were introduced in 2016, with the aim of providing the most flexible curriculum in the UK. Undergraduates can choose single, joint or major/minor courses. The move follows research by the university which revealed strong demand among current students and prospective applicants for more flexibility in degree options. Those choosing a major/minor programme will have the flexibility to combine a wide range of subjects, including new areas such as global studies. They will be able to spend 75 per cent of their time studying their principal subject and 25 per cent on the minor element. Many existing subjects are available as majors and minors, with more coming on stream in later years.

The university has also introduced a number of employability initiatives, including a new undergraduate internship programme which promises to make up to 500 paid internships available each year. The Career Development Service won an award from the Association of Graduate Recruiters for the best overall strategy for preparing students for work in 2015.

Leicester believes in blending teaching and research. Three-quarters of the work submitted to the 2014 Research Excellence Framework was rated as world-leading or internationally excellent, with the School of Museum Studies producing the best results, as it did in 2008. The results, which were also good in clinical medicine, biology, earth science and general engineering, brought a substantial increase in research funding.

Leicester also has a long-established reputation in space science, with Europe's largest university-based space research facility, including the £52-million National Space Centre.

The Department of Genetics, where DNA fingerprinting was discovered, is another star feature. Four new research

University Road
Leicester LE1 7RH

0116 252 5281 (admissions)
admissions@le.ac.uk
https://le.ac.uk
www.leicesterunion.com
Affiliation: none

The Times and Sunday Times Rankings

Overall Ranking: **25** (last year: =28)

Teaching quality:	=65	80.5%
Student experience:	32	85.8%
Research quality:	=37	31.8%
Entry standards:	38	390
Student–staff ratio:	19	12.9
Services & facilities/student:	10	£2,742
Expected completion rate:	31	91.8%
Good honours:	38	77.2%
Graduate prospects:	49	75.3%

institutes, established in 2016, focus on precision medicine, structural and chemical biology, space and earth observation science, and cultural and media economies.

The university was founded as a memorial to the fallen of the First World War and it has been playing a full part in the commemoration of the war's centenary.

Clinical medicine is taught at the city's three hospitals, but all other teaching and much of the residential accommodation is concentrated in a leafy suburb a mile from the city centre. Little more than 10,000 full-time undergraduates are based on the main campus, but substantial postgraduate and distance learning programmes bring Leicester close to the size of other big city universities.

The undergraduate population is among the most socially diverse of any university in our top 30. More than nine out of ten undergraduates come from state schools and 27 per cent came from low-income families in 2014–15.

Leicester has nearly 4,200 student bed spaces, so first years are guaranteed a residential place. New facilities at Oadby Student Village include group study areas, social spaces, cinema room and a refurbished bar. Many second- and third-year students also live in hall, although the majority choose to live in the reasonably priced private accommodation available nearby.

The main sports facilities are conveniently located: currently, students will pay a basic membership fee of £123 a year to use them.

Its ethnic diversity means that the city of Leicester offers a rich cultural experience, and in term time 12 per cent of the population are students. According to HSBC, it is the most affordable destination in the UK for first- and second-year students. Leicester is big enough to provide all the normal sports and entertainment opportunities, but also offers events such as the biggest Diwali celebrations outside India. The Demos Bohemian index rated Leicester the second most creative city in Britain behind London, and Birmingham is also easily accessible via public transport. The award-winning students' union has been refurbished and is the only union in the country to contain an O2 Academy.

Tuition fees

» Fees for UK/EU students 2017–18   £9,250
   Year abroad   £1,250
   Placement year   £1,000
» UK fees are expected to increase by the rate of inflation from 2018–19 onwards.
» Fees for international students 2017–18   £15,290–£18,855
   Medicine   £18,855–£35,170
» Check the university's website for the latest information on fees, scholarships, bursaries and other forms of student support.

Students

Undergraduates:	10,290	(740)
Postgraduates:	4,990	(1,975)
Mature students:	10.8%	
International students:	22.2%	
Applications per place:	8.2	
From state-sector schools:	91.2%	
From working-class homes:	26.9%	
Satisfaction with students' union	74%	

For detailed information about sports facilities:
www2.le.ac.uk/offices/sports

Accommodation

Number of places and costs refer to 2016–17
University-provided places: 4,173
Percentage catered: 18%
Catered costs: £124.60 – £192.50 a week (39 weeks).
Self-catered costs: £85.40 – £174.30 (39–42 weeks).
First-year students are guaranteed accommodation if conditions are met.
International students: as above.
accommodation@le.ac.uk
www2.le.ac.uk/offices/accommodation

University of Lincoln

Lincoln's £7-million Engineering Hub, built in collaboration with Siemens and former East Midlands Development Agency, was the UK's first purpose-built engineering school in 25 years, and won an award for collaboration with business and industry. It is already being expanded to create the Isaac Newton Building – a major new research and teaching facility which will be home to the university's new School of Mathematics and Physics, as well as the Schools of Engineering and Computer Science. A cutting from the apple tree that is said to have inspired Sir Isaac at his Lincolnshire birthplace at Woolsthorpe Manor will be planted next to the new facility. The second phase, including a spectacular 500-seat lecture theatre, opens in spring 2017.

The development epitomises the collaborative, locally focused, high-quality approach that has seen Lincoln make its mark since the university moved from Hull 20 years ago. It is now among the top five post-1992 universities in our table and close to the top 50 overall.

The university has invested £200 million in its purpose-built campus next to a marina in the centre of the city and expects to spend another £130 million over the next decade. The funding includes a £48-million loan from the European Investment Bank, and will provide new teaching and research facilities, as well as on-campus accommodation for another 440 students.

The accent will be on science and health subjects, with major new developments in both areas by 2017. The Boole Technology Centre will open then, providing offices, laboratories and technical workshops for more than 20 local businesses. A new building for the University's School of Psychology and School of Health and Social Care is also due to open in early 2017. The most recent addition is the new £14-million Science and Innovation Park, launched in collaboration with Lincolnshire Co-operative. Its first major building, the Joseph Banks Laboratories, opened in 2014 as the new base for the university's schools of chemistry, life sciences and pharmacy.

Lincoln has won national recognition for its collaboration with business and industry, most notably with Siemens, which named the university one of its Global Principal Partners, together with Cambridge, Manchester and Newcastle. Another example of its successful work with employers is the National Centre for Food Manufacturing, based in Holbeach, which specialises in new food manufacturing technologies.

In the 2014 Research Excellence Framework (REF), Lincoln's research in the Agriculture, Veterinary and Food Science

---

Brayford Pool
Lincoln LN6 7TS

01522 886644 (enquiries)
contact via website
www.lincoln.ac.uk
http://lincolnsu.com
Affiliation: University
Alliance

***The Times and Sunday Times* Rankings**

Overall Ranking: **51** (last year: =62)

Teaching quality:	=8	85.1%
Student experience:	9	88.5%
Research quality:	58	10.3%
Entry standards:	60	340
Student–staff ratio:	=56	15.7
Services & facilities/student:	84	£1,755
Expected completion rate:	42	89.3%
Good honours:	=79	67.7%
Graduate prospects:	=63	71.9%

subject area was rated second in the UK for quality of outputs. There was a good performance more broadly in the REF, when more than half of a large submission was considered internationally excellent or world leading. The university is committed to research-engaged teaching across its curriculum, and encourages undergraduates to work with postgraduates and academic staff on research projects. Several degrees can be taken as work-based programmes, with credit awarded for relevant aspects of the jobs.

Lincoln was the first university to win a Charter Mark for exceptional service. In its most recent Quality Assurance Agency review, the university was commended for the innovative ways in which it gives its students a voice. This translated into exceptional results in the annual National Student Survey (NSS). The university ranks in the top 10 in our table this year for student satisfaction with both the quality of the teaching and their wider student experience.

There are now more than 13,000 students, with the numbers starting full-time degrees growing by almost 10 per cent in 2015. A one-stop-shop provides them with careers advice, enhances their CVs, helps them to gain work experience and find jobs, as well as supporting graduates who are setting up their own businesses. The university has expanded its graduate internship scheme and runs a popular summer placement programme.

It is also working to increase its international profile, launching a Foundation programme to prepare overseas students before joining the first year of an undergraduate degree. Science provision has already expanded considerably, with pharmacy, chemistry and physics among recent additions. The popular School of Psychology now has more than 900 students, while the new School of Mathematics and Physics welcomed its first students in September 2014.

The city is adapting to its student population with new bars and clubs, and in 2014 the students' union was named Union of the Year by the National Union of Students. The campus also has a £6-million performing arts centre, which contains a 450-seat theatre and three large studio spaces, and there is a popular entertainment venue in a former railway engine shed. University and private accommodation jointly provide more than 4,000 bedspaces.

Tuition fees

» Fees for UK/EU students 2017–18   £9,250
    Placement year / Year abroad   no fee
» UK fees are expected to increase by the rate of inflation from 2018–19 onwards.
» Fees for international students 2017–18   £12,800–£14,500
» Check the university's website for the latest information on fees, scholarships and other forms of student support.

Students

Undergraduates:	9,465	(1,615)
Postgraduates:	1,040	(1,140)
Mature students:	12.6%	
International students:	9.4%	
Applications per place:	4.8	
From state-sector schools:	97.7%	
From working-class homes:	37.1%	
Satisfaction with students' union	73%	

For detailed information about sports facilities:
www.lincoln.ac.uk/home/campuslife/sportatlincoln

Accommodation

Number of places and costs refer to 2016–17
University-provided places: 1,600
Percentage catered: 0%
Self-catered costs: £102 – £132 a week.
Student accommodation prioritised by distance within application date.
International students are given detailed information and assistance.
accommodation@lincoln.ac.uk
www.lincoln.ac.uk/home/accommodation

University of Liverpool

A 28 per cent increase in applications to Liverpool was by far the largest at any university in 2015, as the demand for places grew for the third year in a row. The university's response was to add another 800 places to the undergraduate intake. Liverpool is investing £600 million in its city-centre campus to make room for the extra students and upgrade its facilities in a number of areas.

A 10-year development plan has already provided new and improved teaching and research accommodation, as well as new leisure facilities and more student accommodation. New teaching laboratories for the sciences are said to be Europe's most advanced. The university is also spending £70 million on interdisciplinary research facilities for the health and life sciences that will bring together more than 600 scientists to focus on the major health challenges of the 21st century. The management school has been extended, and the Guild of Students building refurbished, while the new Materials Innovation Factory is intended to make Liverpool a world leader in computer-aided material science by 2020.

Other developments include the award-winning £28.6-million Central Teaching Hub, which provides world-class facilities for the teaching of physical sciences, additional student social space and a £4-million investment in sports facilities. The library now offers 24-hour access following a £17-million redevelopment.

Most students have the opportunity to spend a year studying in China, where Liverpool has a campus in the historic city of Suzhou, run in partnership with Xi'an Jiaotong University. The university, which featured in the latest QS ranking of higher education in the five BRICS countries, is expected to have 10,000 students next year. There is also a postgraduate site in the City of London for professional courses.

Liverpool is involved in collaborations with universities in Chile, Mexico and Spain that will allow students to complete part of their degree at one or more of these institutions via a range of options such as projects or placements. The university intends not only to increase the number of students who study abroad, but also to expand the availability of courses for those who may not be able to travel. It is already the largest provider of online postgraduate courses in Europe, with some 10,000 students taking Liverpool degrees all around the world.

The proportion of undergraduates from working-class homes is among the highest in the Russell Group, although still slightly less than the national average for the courses and entry qualifications. The university has committed nearly 30 per cent

---

Liverpool L69 3BX

0151 794 5927 (enquiries)
irro@liverpool.ac.uk
www.liverpool.ac.uk
www.liverpoolguild.org
Affiliation: Russell Group

The Times and Sunday Times Rankings

Overall Ranking: **39** (last year: =38)

Teaching quality:	=84	79.7%
Student experience:	=50	84.4%
Research quality:	40	31.5%
Entry standards:	36	395
Student–staff ratio:	10	11.8
Services & facilities/student:	33	£2,237
Expected completion rate:	30	91.9%
Good honours:	43	75.8%
Graduate prospects:	=44	76.9%

of its additional fee income to support for students from lower-income backgrounds and enhanced measures to prevent students from dropping out. More than a quarter of new undergraduates qualify for support. The projected dropout rate has been improving and is now below 5 per cent. In the humanities, the Honours Select programme allows students to follow major/minor and joint Honours models of study in an extremely wide range of areas.

Liverpool entered a relatively low proportion of its eligible academics for a Russell Group university in the 2014 Research Excellence Framework, which held it back in our research ranking even though 70 per cent of the work was judged to be world-leading or internationally excellent. Chemistry produced spectacular results, with more than half of its research considered world-leading and only 1 per cent not in the top two categories. Computer science and general engineering also scored particularly well.

Liverpool also has one of Europe's largest facilities for training dentists and there has been substantial investment in new educational technology.

But by far the biggest spending programme, totalling some £250 million, is devoted to student accommodation. More than 2,000 study bedrooms were added on the campus in two years and the university's off-campus accommodation is being refurbished. New residences will also be built at the Greenbank site, at suburban Mossley Hill, to provide a self-contained student village.

The Guild of Students is the centre of campus social activity on campus, but the city is famously lively. The indoor and outdoor sports facilities have been refurbished and a new gym has opened at the Greenbank Halls site. A 25-metre swimming pool is open to the public as well as students.

The university has one of the largest careers resources centres in the UK and has introduced an innovative programme of "boot camps" giving new graduates opportunities for networking with employers while developing employability skills. More than £2 million is being invested in student and graduate internships, most of them paid and lasting for substantial periods.

Tuition fees

» Fees for UK/EU students 2017–18   £9,250
   Year abroad   £1,385
   Placement year   £1,850
» UK fees are expected to increase by the rate of inflation from 2018–19 onwards.
» Fees for international students 2017–18   £13,400–£16,800
   Medicine, dentistry and veterinary medicine   £30,850
» Check the university's website for the latest information on fees, scholarships, bursaries and other forms of student support.

Students

Undergraduates:	17,325	(525)
Postgraduates:	3,035	(1,830)
Mature students:	9.8%	
International students:	27.0%	
Applications per place:	8.5	
From state-sector schools:	87.7%	
From working-class homes:	25.9%	
Satisfaction with students' union	70%	

For detailed information about sports facilities:
www.liverpool.ac.uk/sports

Accommodation

Number of places and costs refer to 2016–17
University-provided places: 4,452
Percentage catered: 42%
Catered costs: £141.40 – £194.60 a week (39 weeks).
Self-catered costs: £124.60 – £153.65 a week (39 weeks).
First-year undergraduate students are guaranteed accommodation if requirements are met.
International postgraduate students: as above.
www.liverpool.ac.uk/accommodation
accommodation@liv.ac.uk

Liverpool Hope University

Undergraduates at Liverpool Hope are guaranteed small group tutorials with a named tutor each week, and that all the teaching they receive should be informed by research. Students obviously appreciate the approach since they voted the university into the top two for teaching quality in the 2016 National Student Survey, having been fifth in 2015. A further rise in overall satisfaction and in graduate employment has helped to propel Liverpool Hope up our table this year.

The university boycotted league tables for several years after finishing bottom on its first appearance. But, in its second year back, it has climbed into our top 50 and is third highest of institutions founded after 1992. Both applications and enrolments are rising after a dip when £9,000 fees were introduced.

Hope was formed from the merger of two Catholic and one Church of England teacher training colleges in 1980, and now sponsors an academy with the same dual-faith character. A university since 2005, it describes itself as "teaching led, research informed and mission focused". The university's top priorities are student satisfaction and employability, although it includes "taking faith seriously" among its five key values. It is in the top 20 of all universities for the percentage of academic staff with doctorates.

More than half of the eligible staff were entered for the 2014 Research Excellence Framework – far more than at most post-1992 universities – and there were good results in education and theology. There are research-led seminars in the final year of degree courses to introduce undergraduates to a research culture, and all students produce a dissertation or advanced research project.

The university has moved away from modular degrees to an integrated curriculum, with a "disciplinary core" in each subject to ensure that all students, whether taking single or combined honours, have a similar experience and get a more rounded view of their subject. Most opt for combined subject degrees, choosing after the first year whether to give them equal weight or to go for a major/minor arrangement.

The university has increased its national recruitment profile, with nearly 60 per cent of students now coming from beyond Merseyside. Undergraduates can register for the Service and Leadership Award, which is credit rated and runs alongside their degree work. Students can volunteer locally, within the region or internationally as part of Global Hope, the university's award winning overseas charity. The university has links with a number of overseas institutions which share its mission and values.

Hope Park
Liverpool L16 9JD

0151 291 3111 (enquiries)
enquiry@hope.ac.uk
www.hope.ac.uk
www.hopesu.com
Affiliation: Cathedrals
 Group

The Times and Sunday Times Rankings

Overall Ranking: **49** (last year: =79)

Teaching quality:	2	89.9%
Student experience:	6	89.6%
Research quality:	=62	9.2%
Entry standards:	=92	305
Student–staff ratio:	=64	16.2
Services & facilities/student:	72	£1,856
Expected completion rate:	110	79.6%
Good honours:	88	66.2%
Graduate prospects:	38	78%

Nearly 20 per cent of the undergraduates are over 20 on entry and female students outnumber their male counterparts by more than two to one. Hope comfortably exceeds all the official benchmarks for widening participation in higher education. Almost all the undergraduates are state educated, over 40 per cent are from working-class families and more than one in five is from an area with little tradition of higher education – one of the highest proportions in England. The Network of Hope brings university courses to sixth-form colleges across the northwest of England, in areas where there is limited higher education.

The university is concentrated on two sites in Liverpool, and there is a residential outdoor education centre in Snowdonia, North Wales. The main campus – Hope Park – is three miles from the city centre in the suburb of Childwall, while the creative and performing arts are based at the more central Creative Campus in Everton, where a performance centre houses one of only three Steinway Schools in England, as well as practice rooms, recording spaces and a theatre.

The £5-million main library, on the Hope campus, has 700 study spaces and electronic access from other sites. Recent campus developments have included a Centre for Education and Enterprise, which supports local business and hosts the Faculty of Education.

There is a new food court and a library and reading room on the Creative Campus, with a Renaissance-style garden which includes an outdoor performance area. An £8.5-million Health Sciences building opened in 2016, housing specialist laboratories for nutrition, genomics, cell biology and psychology, along with facilities for sport and exercise science, including a 25-metre biomechanics sprint track. Phase two of the development, a £5.5-million sports complex, opened in late 2016, with a sports hall, gym, strength and conditioning suite, squash courts, café, lecture theatres and retractable tiered spectator seating.

The 1,160 residential places are enough to guarantee accommodation for new entrants who apply before Clearing. Liverpool is a popular student city and the university has partnerships with the Royal Liverpool Philharmonic Orchestra, Liverpool Tate, the National Museums Liverpool and Liverpool Sound City to develop cultural programmes.

Tuition fees

- » Fees for UK/EU students 2017–18 £9,250
- » UK fees are expected to increase by the rate of inflation from 2018–19 onwards.
- » Fees for international students 2016–17 £10,800
- » Check the university's website for the latest information on fees, scholarships, bursaries and other forms of student support.

Students

Undergraduates:	3,745	(175)
Postgraduates:	575	(1,055)
Mature students:	18.1%	
International students:	1.9%	
Applications per place:	6.8	
From state-sector schools:	98.2%	
From working-class homes:	43.2%	
Satisfaction with students' union	72%	

For detailed information about sports facilities:
www.hope.ac.uk/hopeparksports

Accommodation

Number of places and costs refer to 2016–17
University-provided places: 1,160
Percentage catered: 0% (catering packages available)
Self-catered costs: £77 – £87 (shared); £100 – £123 (en suite) a week (36 weeks).
First years are guaranteed accommodation if Liverpool Hope is their first choice and they apply before Clearing.
International students: rooms are available at specific locations, depending on course.
www.hope.ac.uk/halls

Liverpool John Moores University (LJMU)

Liverpool John Moores (LJMU) was one of the pioneers of the employment-focused curriculum that has since been introduced in a number of universities. The prizewinning World of Work (WoW) initiative, which involves leading companies and business organisations, encourages all undergraduates to become expert in eight transferable skills, applicable to a wide range of careers. All students are offered extensive work-related learning opportunities, both paid and voluntary, and some located overseas. The Centre for Entrepreneurship supports students and graduates who want to start up in business, become self-employed or work freelance, as well as helping to embed enterprise education in the curriculum.

But the university has been making improvements to the student experience more broadly. A new Teaching and Learning Academy was launched in 2015, offering assistance from the transition from school, through university and into the workplace. The university's virtual learning environment, Blackboard, enables students to access most teaching materials and a range of other support features online. There is a library on each of the three campuses, two of which are open 24 hours a day, seven days a week during semesters.

LJMU has also begun work on its "connected university campus village" that will locate all students and staff in the city centre. The university currently has three campuses, one of which is four miles outside the city, but the new £100-million development is due for completion at the start of the academic year in 2018. The main building will span seven floors with additional use of the roof for sports and leisure.

Investments totalling £180 million over the last ten years have transformed the existing facilities. Developments include the award-winning John Lennon Art and Design Building and the £25.5-million life sciences building, where the world-class facilities include an indoor 70-metre running track and labs for testing cardiovascular ability, motor skills and biomechanics functions. The £37.6-million Redmonds Building houses Liverpool Screen School, with its industry-standard TV and radio studios, the Liverpool Business School and the School of Law. A £5-million grant will see teaching accommodation for science, technology, engineering and maths dramatically upgraded in a joint venture with the University of Liverpool. It aims to create 1,000 jobs and house 300 new businesses over a ten year period in a spacious bespoke building.

Kingsway House
Hatton Garden
Liverpool L3 2AJ

0151 231 5090 (course enquiries)
courses@ljmu.ac.uk (enquiries)
www.ljmu.ac.uk
www.liverpoolsu.com
Affiliation: University Alliance

The Times and Sunday Times **Rankings**

Overall Ranking: **=86** (last year: 74)

Teaching quality:	=65	80.5%
Student experience:	=56	84.1%
Research quality:	=67	8.9%
Entry standards:	56	345
Student–staff ratio:	95	18.1
Services & facilities/student:	112	£1,374
Expected completion rate:	=74	84.4%
Good honours:	=56	73%
Graduate prospects:	88	67%

Named after a football pools millionaire, LJMU has never been afraid to innovate. Early examples included the original student charter and the first degrees in sports science and criminal justice, as well as the first distance learning degree in astronomy.

The university again attracted near-record applications in 2015 and now has more than 20,000 students in its home city and another 4,500 taking LJMU courses overseas. Most are based in an area between Liverpool's two cathedrals, while the suburban IM Marsh Campus specialises in education and community studies.

More than 40 per cent of the students are drawn from the Merseyside area. The university's efforts to extend access to higher education are successful: almost all the undergraduates are state-educated and 40 per cent come from the four poorest socio-economic groups. A wide range of scholarships and bursaries include the John Lennon Imagine Awards, match-funded through a gift of £260,000 from Yoko Ono, which help students who have either been in local authority care or who are estranged from their parents. The university has a number of disability support services, and an improved dropout rate is much better than the national average for the university's courses and entry grades.

A growing research reputation is a source of particular pride. More than 60 per cent of the work submitted for the Research Excellence Framework was rated world-leading or internationally excellent, with the proportion topping 80 per cent in physics. The university was ranked second in the UK for sports science and fourth among post-1992 universities for law and education. The physics results covered astronomy, in which researchers and students use the university's own robotic telescope in the Canary Islands.

Liverpool was ranked in the ten best cities in the world to visit in 2014 by Rough Guides and is one of the most affordable, as well as enjoyable, student cities in the UK. Student facilities have been improving and there are discounts on theatre tickets and free access to art exhibitions and orchestral performances. Sports facilities include an Olympic-sized swimming pool, two golf courses, fitness suites and weights rooms and all-weather football pitches. Students also have free off-peak access to 11 Lifestyles Fitness Centres across the city.

Tuition fees

» Fees for UK/EU students 2017–18	£9,250
STEM Foundation year	£7,700
Year abroad	no fee
Placement year	£1,007

» UK fees are expected to increase by the rate of inflation from 2018–19 onwards.

» Fees for international students 2017–18   £11,630–£12,660

» Check the university's website for the latest information on fees, scholarships and other forms of student support.

Students

Undergraduates:	16,535	(1,300)
Postgraduates:	1,230	(1,570)
Mature students:	17.5%	
International students:	4.7%	
Applications per place:	6.3	
From state-sector schools:	96.6%	
From working-class homes:	39.6%	
Satisfaction with students' union	50%	

For detailed information about sports facilities:
www.ljmu.ac.uk/sport

Accommodation

Number of places and costs refer to 2016–17
University-provided places: 3,800 plus 15,000 through Liverpool Student Homes.
Percentage catered: 0%
Self-catered costs: £89 – £137 a week.
All new students are guaranteed a place in university approved housing, even if applying through Clearing.
International students: as above.
accommodation@ljmu.ac.uk
www.ljmu.ac.uk/accommodation

London Metropolitan University

London Met has announced plans to invest £125 million to create a single campus in Islington, bringing all of its faculties together in one location for the first time.

The visual arts, architecture, business and law courses will start to move from their current buildings at Aldgate and Moorgate in 2017. Two-thirds of London Met students said they would prefer a single campus to produce more of a community and enhance the opportunities for collaboration. The move will take place over several years and will be accompanied by a curriculum review and significant investment in IT and other facilities.

A new Programme for Improved Student Outcomes already guarantees an accredited, work-related learning opportunity for all students to provide real-world experience in preparation for the graduate jobs market.

There are £1,000 bursaries for all students who qualify for a full maintenance loan, and every course will have a presence on the university's virtual learning environment, giving more opportunities for students to learn remotely, at times and in locations that suit them.

Despite the improvements, however, applications have dropped for five years in a row and the intake is about half the size it was at its peak. Professor John Raftery, the Vice-Chancellor, says the revamp, which will also cut the staff by almost 400, will "effectively create a new higher education offering in London, with a structure fit to meet the needs of its time."

London Met was the product of the 2002 merger of London Guildhall and North London universities, although its origins date back to the mid 19th century. The existing buildings on Holloway Road include a Graduate Centre designed by Daniel Libeskind.

The university has strong business links, especially in London's "Tech City", where it has a business accelerator which has been ranked in the top five in Europe. It provides regular workshops, bootcamps and an incubator programme for students thinking of setting up their own businesses, as well as offering 40 new graduates internships and additional training.

The university has always catered particularly for groups who are under-represented at traditional universities. More than a third of the students are from ethnic minorities, and the proportion of mature students is among the highest in England. More than half of the UK undergraduates come from low-income families – far above the average for the courses and entry qualifications. The projected dropout rate had been improving, but is among the

166–220 Holloway Road
London N7 8DB

020 7133 4200 (enquiries)
admissions@londonmet.ac.uk
www.londonmet.ac.uk
www.londonmetsu.org.uk
Affiliation: MillionPlus

The Times and Sunday Times Rankings

Overall Ranking: **127** (last year: 125)

Teaching quality:	=110	77.3%
Student experience:	104	81.4%
Research quality:	110	3.5%
Entry standards:	126	251
Student–staff ratio:	=86	17.4
Services & facilities/student:	123	£1,210
Expected completion rate:	126	71.1%
Good honours:	126	52.6%
Graduate prospects:	114	59.2%

highest in the UK in the latest survey, at more than 28 per cent.

Student support services have been remodelled and a new Peer Assisted Student Support (PASS) scheme sees successful second- and third-year students coach first years on their course. This extra support has been known to improve progression and attainment by up to 10 per cent.

Undergraduates take year-long modules consisting of 30 weeks of timetabled teaching. Over a year, students will typically study four modules and receive a minimum of 60 teaching hours per module. The university is in the top ten for the amount of supervised teaching time and expects first-year students to have 12 hours of teaching a week, giving the maximum possible opportunity for development and guidance.

Overall satisfaction has improved by 9 percentage points in three years, helping the university to move away from the bottom of the National Student Survey as a whole.

Languages are a strength: London Met is one of only 22 universities globally to be members of the UN Language Careers Network

There has already been increased investment in the campus and the university has also been working hard to reduce its carbon footprint and was the top university on this measure in 2015. The refurbished library on the Holloway Road has more computers and informal learning spaces, as well as a café, while the £30-million Science Centre features one of the largest teaching laboratories in Europe, with 280 workstations, specialist laboratories and a nuclear magnetic resonance room.

However, London Met entered far fewer academics for the 2014 Research Excellence Framework than it did in the 2008 assessments, only 15 per cent of those eligible. As a result, it has slipped down our research ranking, even though half of its submission was rated as world-leading or internationally excellent and there were particularly good scores in English and health subjects.

The residential accommodation is limited, but many of London Met's students live at home.

There are nine fitness centres, as well as other sports facilities. The competitive teams are successful and the social scene is lively in north London.

Tuition fees

» Fees for UK/EU students 2017–18 £9,250
  Foundation degrees £6,000–£9,250
» UK fees are expected to increase by the rate of inflation from 2018–19 onwards.
» Fees for international students 2017–18 £11,400
» Check the university's website for the latest information on fees, scholarships, bursaries and other forms of student support.

Students

Undergraduates:	9,385	(1,645)
Postgraduates:	1,445	(1,610)
Mature students:	57.5%	
International students:	12.4%	
Applications per place:	9.1	
From state-sector schools:	97.3%	
From working-class homes:	51.4%	
Satisfaction with students' union	64%	

For detailed information about sports facilities:
www.londonmet.ac.uk/about/sport-and-fitness

Accommodation

Number of places and costs refer to 2016–17
University-provided places: Students have access to accommodation in a wide range of halls of residences provided by specialist student accommodation providers.
Percentage catered: 0%
Self-catered costs: Single rooms from £139 – £355 a week.
The university cannot guarantee a place in halls.
International students: as above.
www.londonmet.ac.uk/about/studentservices/
advice-and-well-being/accommodation

London School of Economics and Political Science (LSE)

Universities in London tend to struggle in the National Student Survey (NSS), but none has as much trouble as the LSE, which is bottom this year both for the sections relating to teaching quality and those for the wider student experience. The School's strength in other areas ensures that it is still in the top ten overall in our league table, but its NSS scores have contributed to a drop of five places in two years.

There have been no such difficulties in international rankings, which are based largely on research. The LSE remains in the top 25 in the *Times Higher Education* rankings, while QS placed it in the top five in the world in eight different subjects.

Its reputation as one of the top universities in the world for the social sciences attracts the highest proportion of international students at any publicly funded university.

There are more than 10 applicants for every place, fewer than three of whom receive an offer. The School is planning to "grow steadily over time" and to refine its admissions system so that those with the greatest potential (and not just the highest grades) gain entry. But it is likely to remain one of the most selective institution in our table in terms of applications per place.

The LSE has been hemmed in by its cramped estate around London's Aldwych, which is being developed as the School also expands into nearby buildings. It opened its first new building for more than 40 years in 2014, the Saw Swee Hock Student Centre (SAW), which houses the students' union, the careers and accommodation services and a multi-faith prayer centre.

Now the school is spending £120 million on its central buildings redevelopment, which will replace a number of existing buildings.

Areas of study range more broadly than the School's name suggests: the 250 undergraduate courses include management, mathematics and environmental policy.

The LSE was among the top universities in the 2014 Research Excellence Framework, with more "world-leading" research than any university in our table. It was the clear leader in the social sciences, with particularly good results in social work and social policy, and communication and media studies. A £10-million donation from alumnus Firoz Lalji has since created a new academic centre focused on Africa.

The School has a long history of political involvement, from its foundation by Beatrice and Sidney Webb, pioneers of the Fabian movement, to the 31 alumni and former staff who are MPs and 42 current members of the House of Lords.

Houghton Street
London WC2A 2AE

020 7955 7125 (admissions)
contact via website
www.lse.ac.uk
www.lsesu.com
Affiliation: Russell Group

The Times and Sunday Times Rankings

Overall Ranking: **8** (last year: 9)

Teaching quality:	128	68.5%
Student experience:	128	73.1%
Research quality:	4	52.8%
Entry standards:	4	540
Student–staff ratio:	=7	11.6
Services & facilities/student:	7	£2,858
Expected completion rate:	3	97.6%
Good honours:	7	86.6%
Graduate prospects:	10	84.6%

The tradition lives on, not only among the academics, but in a students' union which claims to be the only one in Britain to hold weekly general meetings at which every student may attend and vote.

More than 30 past or present heads of state have either been LSE students or academics, as have 16 Nobel prizewinners in economics, literature and peace – including George Bernard Shaw, Bertrand Russell, Friedrich von Hayek and Amartya Sen.

Its international character not only gives the LSE global prestige, but also an unusual degree of financial independence: only a small proportion of its funding comes from Government sources.

More than 30 per cent of the British undergraduates are from independent schools, one of the highest proportions in England. Substantial efforts are being made to attract a broader intake: the school is spending half of its additional fee income on student support and other activities to widen participation – a bigger proportion than any other university.

The Norman Foster-designed redevelopment of the Lionel Robbins Building houses a much-improved library. The number of books borrowed by LSE students is more than four times the national average, according to one survey.

More than £5 million has been invested in LSE LIFE, an academic, personal and professional development centre housed in the library. Routes between many of the buildings have been pedestrianised, in keeping with a commitment to green issues that regularly sees the School near the top of the People and Planet Green League of universities' environmental performance.

London's top nightspots are on the doorstep for those who can afford them and discounted student nights are easy to find. There are also 190 national student societies.

With nearly 4,000 residential places for fewer than 10,000 full-time students, there is a good chance of avoiding central London's notoriously high private-sector rents; there are spaces in hall for all first-year undergraduates who want them.

Tuition fees

» Fees for UK/EU students 2017–18 £9,250
Year abroad £1,385
» UK fees are expected to increase by the rate of inflation from 2018–19 onwards.
» Fees for international students 2017–18 £18,408
» Check the university's website for the latest information on fees, scholarships, bursaries and other forms of student support.

Students

Undergraduates:	4,330	(80)
Postgraduates:	5,770	(420)
Mature students:	2.7%	
International students:	46.8%	
Applications per place:	10.7	
From state-sector schools:	69%	
From working-class homes:	21.1%	
Satisfaction with students' union	55%	

For detailed information about sports facilities:
www.lsesu.com/join-in/sports

Accommodation

Number of places and costs refer to 2016–17
University-provided places: 3,658; 240 intercollegiate
Percentage catered: about 38%
Catered costs: £100.80 – £266.80 a week.
Self-catered costs: £124.25 – £349.17 a week.
First-year undergraduates are guaranteed an offer of accommodation.
International students: new undergraduates are guaranteed an offer.
www.lse.ac.uk/lifeAtLSE/accommodation

London South Bank University

London South Bank has almost 7,000 sponsored students, more than one in three, and one of the reasons that it features among the top 15 universities for graduates' starting salaries. The average of almost £23,600 in 2015 was £3,000 higher than the national average. The university has 1,000 employer partners and has been among the first to embrace degree apprenticeships, where students divide their time between workplace training and higher education.

London South Bank has adopted three "core principles" – student success, real world impact and access to opportunity – in its quest to be "an enterprising civic university that addresses real world challenges". Three-quarters of the students are from the capital and 40 per cent are drawn from ethnic minorities. Many of the 13,000 undergraduates take sandwich courses, but Vice-Chancellor Professor David Phoenix would like even more to spend part of their course in industry. He also plans to create more of a campus feel by knitting together the university's various buildings with more green spaces. London South Bank has invested over £50 million in modern teaching facilities, and developments costing another £38 million

are in the pipeline. The university hopes to benefit from the £3-billion regeneration of the Elephant and Castle area on its doorstep. The £4-million Elephant Studios @LSBU media centre opened in 2016, with advanced technology facilities and an industry-standard theatre and rehearsal suite.

The main campus is in Southwark, not far from the South Bank arts complex. It includes the Centre for Efficient and Renewable Energy in Buildings, a unique teaching, research and demonstration resource for low-carbon technologies, and the UK's first inner-city green technology research centre. The £10-million Clarence Centre for Enterprise and Innovation opened in 2014 to support students' start-up businesses and provide a gateway for the local community to access the university's expertise. London South Bank is one of the top universities for "knowledge transfer partnerships" and has been shortlisted for the Duke of York Award for University Entrepreneurship in the 2016 Lloyds Bank National Business Awards.

The university entered more academics for the 2014 Research Excellence Framework than for previous assessments and scored well on the external impact of its research, with almost three-quarters of the submission placed in the top two categories on this measure.

Some health students are based on

103 Borough Road
London SE1 0AA

0800 923 8888 (course enquiries)
course.enquiry@lsbu.ac.uk
www.lsbu.ac.uk
www.lsbsu.org
Affiliation: MillionPlus

The Times and Sunday Times Rankings

Overall Ranking: **120** (last year: 120)

Teaching quality:	115	77.1%
Student experience:	=107	81.2%
Research quality:	=64	9%
Entry standards:	125	256
Student–staff ratio:	82	17.2
Services & facilities/student:	58	£1,995
Expected completion rate:	125	73.2%
Good honours:	114	60.4%
Graduate prospects:	48	75.4%

the other side of London, in hospitals in Romford and Leytonstone, where there is a smaller satellite campus in Havering to supplement that in Southwark. The university now trains 40 per cent of London's nurses and has well-regarded courses in occupational therapy and radiography. London South Bank degrees are also taught at a network of overseas colleges that stretches from China to the Caribbean.

New courses for 2017 include BAs in international relations with sociology, politics or criminology, heritage tourism and attractions management, and human geography with planning, housing or tourism development.

London South Bank has always given a high priority to widening participation in higher education and takes more than half of its students from the lowest socio-economic groups – far more than other universities with similar courses and entry qualifications. The diversity of the intake is encouraged by initiatives such as the summer school for local people to upgrade their qualifications. The courses start at the end of June and are limited to 15 hours a week so as not to affect benefit entitlements.

However, the projected dropout rate for undergraduates is among the highest in the country and the university has struggled in the National Student Survey. London South Bank is targeting much of its fee income

on providing support to help more students complete their studies in the expected time, including scholarships, bursaries, student advice, skills workshops, drop-in sessions, language assistance, and health and wellbeing support.

A new student centre has brought the students' union and many support services together to make them more convenient and accessible. London South Bank is the first university to receive four accreditations from the Institute of Customer Service for excellent service across its accommodation service, library and learning resources, Student Life Centre and Academy of Sport. London South Bank is one of the few universities in central London to have its halls of residence close by: all are less than ten-minutes' walk away. A new-look sports centre opened in 2014 after a £1-million makeover, with a multipurpose sports hall, therapy services and facilities that include a 40-station fitness suite and sports injury clinic. The university provides a comprehensive sports scholarship scheme.

Tuition fees

» Fees for UK/EU students 2017–18 £9,250
Placement year no fee

» UK fees are expected to increase by the rate of inflation from 2018–19 onwards.

» Fees for international students 2016–17 £11,600

» Check the university's website for the latest information on fees, scholarships, and other forms of student support.

Students

Undergraduates:	8,830	(4,190)
Postgraduates:	1,655	(3,060)
Mature students:	47.6%	
International students:	9.1%	
Applications per place:	10.1	
From state-sector schools:	97.8%	
From working-class homes:	50.7%	
Satisfaction with students' union	65%	

For detailed information about sports facilities:
www.lsbu.ac.uk/academy-of-sport

Accommodation

Number of places and costs refer to 2016–17
University-provided places: 1,300
Percentage catered: 0%
Self-catered costs: £118.50 (standard) – £143.20 (en suite) a week.
First-year UK students are not guaranteed accommodation, but priority is given to those living outside Greater London.
International students: first years are guaranteed accommodation if conditions are met.
www.lsbu.ac.uk/student-life/accommodation

Loughborough University

Loughborough has climbed another two places in our table to the verge of the top ten, despite a decline in student satisfaction, one of its perennial strengths. The university's growing popularity, with applications up by more than 20 per cent in three years, has brought increased entry qualifications and there has been further progress in completion rates, which are now among the best in the UK.

Loughborough is best known for its illustrious sporting pedigree, but its academic reputation has been growing rapidly in recent years. Loughborough earns another shortlisting this year as our University of the Year after climbing two places in our league table and in recognition of its contribution to Great Britain's Olympic effort. There was no rival for our Sports University of the Year award, a second victory in four years.

Only eight universities entered such a high proportion of their eligible staff – 88 per cent – for the 2014 Research Excellence Framework (REF). Almost three-quarters of their research was judged to be world-leading or internationally excellent, with sport and exercise sciences producing the best results in the UK and six other subject areas featuring in the top ten. The university was also awarded five stars in the QS global rating of its facilities and performance in teaching, research, employability and internationalisation.

The university's 216-acre campus in the East Midlands has seen a series of developments in recent years. The West Park Teaching Hub opened in February 2016, with five-tiered lecture theatres, two seminar rooms, and a central learning and exhibition zone. Work has begun on STEMLab, which will house science and engineering laboratories, workshops, computer-aided design and rapid prototyping facilities and a design studio, enabling Loughborough to develop a suite of teaching programmes in bio-science and bio-engineering. The building will be operational in 2017. Loughborough has also opened a London campus for postgraduates in the Queen Elizabeth Olympic Park, which will focus on research and innovation.

Most subjects are available either as three-year full-time or longer sandwich degrees, which include a year in industry and help Loughborough to a place in the top ten for graduate prospects. The university is a leader in the use of computer-assisted assessment, offering students the chance to gauge their own progress online.

However, despite high spending on student support and outreach activities, Loughborough misses all its access benchmarks: fewer than a quarter of the undergraduates are from working-class

Epinal Way
Loughborough
Leicestershire LE11 3TU

01509 223522 (admissions)
admissions@lboro.ac.uk
www.lboro.ac.uk
www.lsu.co.uk
Affiliation: none

The Times and Sunday Times Rankings
Overall Ranking: **11** (last year: 13)

Teaching quality:	=44	81.9%
Student experience:	=10	87.9%
Research quality:	=30	36.3%
Entry standards:	31	411
Student–staff ratio:	=35	14.6
Services & facilities/student:	21	£2,582
Expected completion rate:	=11	94.9%
Good honours:	19	81.7%
Graduate prospects:	=8	85.3%

homes and only 6 per cent are from areas of low participation in higher education.

The Office for Standards in Education rates Loughborough in its top category for teacher training in physical education, design and science. Loughborough is also a leader in art and design and remains a major centre of engineering, with more than 2,800 students in a £20-million integrated engineering complex. Civil, aeronautical and automotive engineering are particularly strong. The university's Science and Enterprise Park includes the £59-million BAE-sponsored Systems Engineering Innovation Centre. Loughborough has now been awarded almost £10 million from the Government towards the establishment of the new National Centre of Excellence in Gas Turbine Combustion System Aerodynamics, which will position it as a leader in aerospace engineering and technology.

Sports facilities that were already among the best in the country improved still further with the opening of a £5.6-million health and fitness centre. Loughborough is the official Innovation Partner of the International Hockey Federation and was chosen as one of two national centres for British swimming to prepare for the Rio 2016 and Tokyo 2020 Olympic Games. The university also hosts a £10-million National Sport and Exercise Medicine Centre of Excellence, one of three in the UK.

The campus boasts a 50-metre swimming pool, national academies for cricket and tennis, a gymnastics centre and a high-performance training centre for athletics. The university also hosts the UK's only centre for disability sport and has spent £15-million on its Sports Technology Institute. The programme of sports scholarships is the largest at any university. At the 2014 Commonwealth Games, the university's athletes claimed 35 medals in seven sports and over 50 athletes with Loughborough connections took part in the 2016 Olympic and Paralympic games, with 18 athletes winning Olympic medals across 11 events.

Almost £70 million is being spent on new student accommodation, with 5,000 rooms in the first phase and another 1,300 to come in four new halls. Social activity is concentrated on a prize-winning students' union which is among the most popular in the country with its members. The town of Loughborough is a mile away, with Leicester and Nottingham within easy reach.

Tuition fees

» Fees for UK/EU students 2017–18   £9,250
» UK fees are expected to increase by the rate of inflation from 2018–19 onwards.
» Fees for international students 2017–18   £16,000–£19,900
» Check the university's website for the latest information on fees, scholarships, bursaries and other forms of student support

Students

Undergraduates:	11,935	(205)
Postgraduates:	2,090	(1,360)
Mature students:	2.8%	
International students:	10.0%	
Applications per place:	6.6	
From state-sector schools:	82.7%	
From working-class homes:	21.9%	
Satisfaction with students' union	90%	

For detailed information about sports facilities:
http://loughboroughsport.com

Accommodation

Number of places and costs refer to 2016–17
University-provided places: 5,662
Percentage catered: 42.5%
Catered costs: £130.93 – £176.85 (39-week contract)
Self-catered costs: £84.49 – £163.71 (39-week contract)
Undergraduate first-year first-choice students are guaranteed accommodation if they apply prior to 1 August.
International students: guaranteed housing in same residence for two years.
www.lboro.ac.uk/services/campus-living/accommodation

University of Manchester

Manchester is mid-way through a £1-billion, ten-year plan to create a single campus that the university hopes will help to secure a place among the top 25 research universities in the world. It has only four places to go in the QS World University Rankings, although a little more in other international exercises.

In our league table, however, with its focus on undergraduate study, Manchester has slipped out of the top 30 this year, largely due to a decline in student satisfaction, which has been its nemesis in previous editions. It is not in the top 100 in the sections of the National Student Survey relating to teaching, feedback and learning resources, although it is in the top 20 for research, entry standards and graduate prospects.

More than 80 per cent the work submitted to the 2014 Research Excellence Framework was considered world-leading or internationally excellent, although the university entered a lower proportion of its academics than many of its peers in the Russell Group.

The first projects in the campus masterplan opened in 2015. They were the Manchester Cancer Research Centre and the National Graphene Institute, together with the Whitworth art gallery, which has been refurbished and has won several awards, including the Art Fund's Museum of the Year. The initial phase of the plan is due to be complete by 2019, and includes the £350-million Manchester Engineering Campus Development (MEDC), new facilities for the Alliance Manchester Business School and a student village which will eventually have 3,000 rooms. The MECD alone will be one of the largest single construction projects ever undertaken by a UK university, housing Manchester's four engineering schools and two research institutes. The university is also spending several million pounds to bring benefits to the local area, capitalising on improvements due to be made to Oxford Road.

In the second phase, the University of Manchester library will be refurbished and a bigger and better students' union added. The overriding aims of the campus improvements are to improve the student experience and reduce carbon emissions.

Outstanding teaching is one of the three goals in the university's strategy. The £24-million Alan Gilbert Learning Commons provides more than 1,000 flexible learning spaces, high-quality IT facilities, and a hub for student-centred activities and learning support services. A new teaching block helps to cater for 2,000 undergraduates following a problem-based curriculum in the medical school. The Learning Through Research Initiative funds undergraduates to work with researchers.

Oxford Road
Manchester M13 9PL

0161 275 2077 (admissions)
ug-admissions@manchester.ac.uk
www.manchester.ac.uk
http://manchesterstudents
union.com
Affiliation: Russell Group

Edinburgh
Belfast
MANCHESTER
London
Cardiff

***The Times and Sunday Times* Rankings**

Overall Ranking: **32** (last year: =28)

Teaching quality:	=110	77.3%
Student experience:	=71	83.4%
Research quality:	13	39.8%
Entry standards:	17	439
Student–staff ratio:	=23	13.4
Services & facilities/student:	30	£2,283
Expected completion rate:	24	92.9%
Good honours:	40	76.2%
Graduate prospects:	19	82.2%

There are three Nobel prizewinners on the staff. Sir John Sulston, who chairs the Institute of Science, Ethics and Innovation, won the prize for physiology or medicine in 2002. Professors Andre Geim and Kostya Novoselov brought the all-time complement of laureates to 25 when they took the physics prize in 2010 for the isolation of graphene's properties. In addition to the National Graphene Institute, a £60-million Graphene Engineering Innovation Centre is planned, as is the Sir Henry Royce Institute for Advanced Materials Research, a £235-million project that is a major part of the Government's 'Northern Powerhouse' initiative. Manchester was awarded a Regius professorship in materials to celebrate the Queen's 90th birthday.

The 2004 merger of the Victoria University of Manchester with the neighbouring University of Manchester Institute of Science and Technology (UMIST) created the biggest conventional university in the UK outside the federal University of London. Manchester remains the most popular university in the country in terms of total applications.

It also has more international students than any other university, drawn from 160 countries, and has 129 nationalities among its workforce. The university has been trying to broaden its intake, with a particular focus on increasing recruitment from the city and its surrounding area. It admits more low-income students than most of the other universities in the Russell Group and is now close to the national benchmarks for widening participation.

The Manchester Leadership Programme and the University College for Interdisciplinary Learning encourage students to think beyond academia and towards their impact as citizens. Employers in *The Times'* top 100 companies named Manchester as their favourite recruiting ground in 2015 – an important accolade when some firms limit their recruiting visits – and they also rate the careers service highly.

Manchester's famed youth culture and the university's position at the heart of a huge student population help to ensure keen competition for places, and hence high entry standards, in most subjects. There are first-rate sports facilities and the university's teams frequently rank near the top of the British Universities and Colleges Sport (BUCS) league.

Tuition fees

» Fees for UK/EU students 2017–18 £9,250
» UK fees are expected to increase by the rate of inflation from 2018–19 onwards.
» Fees for international students 2017–18 £17,000–£21,000
   Medicine and dentistry £21,000–£38,000
» Check the university's website for the latest information on fees, scholarships, bursaries and other forms of student support.

Students

Undergraduates:	26,145	(585)
Postgraduates:	8,420	(3,445)
Mature students:	9.8%	
International students:	25.0%	
Applications per place:	7.9	
From state-sector schools:	82.4%	
From working-class homes:	21.5%	
Satisfaction with students' union	75%	

For detailed information about sports facilities:
www.sport.manchester.ac.uk

Accommodation

Number of places and costs refer to 2016–17
University-owned/managed places: 8,030
Percentage catered: approx 27%
Catered costs: £91.95 – £179.67 a week (40 weeks).
Self-catered costs: £71.62 – £160.90 a week (40 weeks).
First years are guaranteed housing if conditions are met.
International non-EU students are guaranteed accommodation for the duration of their stay if conditions are met.
www.accommodation.manchester.ac.uk

Manchester Metropolitan University

Manchester Metropolitan (MMU) has jumped 30 places in three years in our league table, after slipping well below its accustomed ranking early in the decade. It is now at its highest position for 13 years. Progress on this scale is not easy when the university has the second-largest number of undergraduates of any university in our table and added nearly 800 undergraduates to its intake in 2015. Entry standards are still higher than at most post-1992 universities.

More than 1,000 courses are offered in over 70 subjects, more of them professionally accredited than at any other university and many involving work placements. The business school was awarded the prestigious international AACSB accreditation in 2016, a distinction conferred on only 5 per cent of business schools in the world.

The university has launched a new £200-million plan which will deliver a new arts and culture centre, as well as improvements to the campus environment. The five sites in Manchester have now been reduced to two linked campuses as part of a £350-million investment programme which was completed in 2014. Much of this has been devoted to learning resources rather than buildings. The prize-winning EQAL programme, for example, recast undergraduate courses in line with student feedback and integrated them with the Moodle virtual learning environment. The new buildings have been winning prizes, however. The Brooks Building, which hosts the education and health faculties, won an award for regeneration, while the new Manchester School of Art and the £10-million students' union building featured in the RIBA national awards. The university also finished in the top three of the People and Planet Green League of environmental performance for the second time in a row in 2015.

The Birley Fields Campus, which includes the Brooks Building, is one of the most environmentally sustainable in the UK. It is close to the original All Saints Campus, on the university's border with Hulme and Moss Side. New science and engineering buildings at All Saints cost £42 million, while the £75-million business school headquarters is next to the Mancunian Way.

A third campus, the Cheshire Campus, at Crewe, 35 miles south of Manchester, serves 800 trainee teachers and 3,000 other students taking contemporary arts and sports science. The university, which has launched a Centre for Urban Education, trains more teachers than any other and its courses are rated as outstanding by Ofsted.

All Saints Building
All Saints
Manchester M15 6BH

0161 247 6969 (general enquiries)
contact via website
www.mmu.ac.uk
www.theunionmmu.org
Affiliation: University
Alliance

The Times and Sunday Times Rankings

Overall Ranking: **=72** (last year: 77)

Teaching quality:	=76	80%
Student experience:	85	82.7%
Research quality:	75	7.5%
Entry standards:	54	348
Student–staff ratio:	=53	15.6
Services & facilities/student:	85	£1,741
Expected completion rate:	85	83.6%
Good honours:	=66	70.4%
Graduate prospects:	90	66.5%

The campus occupies an area now known as the University Quadrant, which features a drama, music and dance centre, and a £30-million student village, business school and £10-million Sport Science Centre. Over £5 million has been invested in the five-storey library that is open 24/7, even during Easter and Christmas vacations.

There is a longstanding commitment to extending access to higher education: more than 40 per cent of the undergraduates come from working-class homes, many from areas of low participation.

The university's overseas links have expanded rapidly in recent years, with MMU offering exchange opportunities in Europe and further afield, as well as establishing teaching bases abroad. MMU is also planning a new independent, international medical school in partnership with Manchester and Salford universities.

Academics are encouraged to take a three-year MA in teaching, but less than a quarter were entered for the 2014 Research Excellence Framework. Almost two-thirds of the work submitted was rated world-leading or internationally excellent, with health, art and design, and English producing the best results. The Poet Laureate, Professor Carol Ann Duffy, is Creative Director of the Writing School in the English department.

More than half of the students come from the Manchester area, easing the pressure on housing in a city of nearly 90,000 university students. MMU plays an important role in the region's economy, not least because almost two-thirds of graduates stay and work in the North West. The university employs 50 of its own graduates on paid internships for up to 12 months.

All first years who request accommodation can be housed; priority goes to disabled students and those who live furthest away. The university's sports facilities are good and there is an innovative partnership with Manchester City Women's Football Club, promising bespoke education programmes and matchday access for events management students.

The city's attractions do no harm to recruitment levels, but much depends on where the course is based. For those at Crewe there is an active students' union on campus. Some applicants are daunted by the size of the university, but individual courses and sites usually provide a social circle.

Tuition fees

- » Fees for UK/EU students 2017–18   £9,250
  Foundation year   £6,165
  Placement year / Year abroad   £680
- » UK fees are expected to increase by the rate of inflation from 2018–19 onwards.
- » Fees for international students 2017–18   £12,720–£14,100
- » Check the university's website for the latest information on fees, scholarships, bursaries and other forms of student support.

Students

Undergraduates:	23,955	(1,855)
Postgraduates:	2,220	(3,325)
Mature students:	15.8%	
International students:	5.8%	
Applications per place:	6.7	
From state-sector schools:	96.9%	
From working-class homes:	41.5%	
Satisfaction with students' union	78%	
For detailed information about sports facilities:		
www2.mmu.ac.uk/sport		

Accommodation

Number of places and costs refer to 2016–17
University provided places: 5,237
Percentage catered: 0%
Self-catered costs: Manchester: £94 – £199; Cheshire: £95 a week.
All new full-time students will be housed if applications are received by 15 August and requirements are met.
International students: as above.
accommodation@mmu.ac.uk
www2.mmu.ac.uk/accommodation

Middlesex University

Middlesex took a record number of undergraduates in 2015, increasing its intake by more than a third despite falling applications. The university had already increased its average entry qualifications and improved staffing levels, helping it to an 11-place rise in this year's league table.

The growing population on its north London campus is outnumbered by those taking Middlesex courses outside the UK. There are branch campuses in Mauritius, Dubai and Malta, and partner colleges on five continents. Middlesex is the first overseas university in Malta and is opening a new campus in Mauritius in 2017, while the longer-established Dubai campus now has 2,500 students.

Altogether, the university has 38,000 students, including more than 1,200 undergraduates in London from other EU countries, the product of a longstanding focus on Europe. But three-quarters of the full-time students on the main campus are from London, many of them returning to education after a period at work.

A long-running reorganisation programme has reduced the seven campuses which used to straggle around north London to one impressive base at Hendon. The university has invested more than £200 million bringing about the transformation and attracting 150 new academics.

The campus boasts a new library, well-equipped biomedical and technology labs, modern classrooms and lecture theatres, a high-end TV production studio and art and design workshop spaces.

The latest addition has top-level green credentials, with four living walls and a living roof. The £14-million Ritterman building, which was completed in 2016, provides specialist teaching rooms for the Schools of Science and Technology, Art and Design, and Media and Performing Arts.

The last phase of the programme saw nursing and the other health subjects move to Hendon, where The Grove, the £80-million centre for art, design and media, has won a string of accolades. It includes Sony-designed, equipped and built TV studios and newsroom, and flexible performance and exhibition spaces centred around an atrium.

Earlier developments included the roofing over of the main quadrangle to provide social space. This was followed by the opening of the Forum for student services and facilities that include the students' union, catering and event space. The campus even boasts one of the country's few Real Tennis courts.

Only one institution outside Oxbridge reports higher spending than Middlesex. It is £1,000 per student ahead of many of its peers. ICT facilities have been updated with

---

The Burroughs
Hendon
London NW4 4BT

020 8411 5555 (enquiries)
contact through website
www.mdx.ac.uk
www.mdxsu.com
Affiliation: MillionPlus

The Times and Sunday Times Rankings

Overall Ranking: **74** (last year: =85)

Teaching quality:	=90	79.3%
Student experience:	=89	82.3%
Research quality:	60	9.7%
Entry standards:	=100	301
Student–staff ratio:	=66	16.3
Services & facilities/student:	4	£3,049
Expected completion rate:	122	74.7%
Good honours:	=107	62.2%
Graduate prospects:	75	70.3%

wireless access throughout the campus and students are sent a free e-book at the start of every module, which the university says will save them £450.

The highly flexible course system allows students to start some courses in January if they prefer not to wait until autumn, and offers the option of an extra five-week session in the summer to try out new subjects or add to their credits. There is a range of work-based courses that allow participants to gain recognition and academic credit for learning in the workplace. The conventional degrees are also focused on future employment, many including work placements or the option of a sandwich year.

The university has reorganised into six schools to focus on its strengths in business, computing and the arts. More than a third of the eligible staff were entered for the 2014 Research Excellence Framework, and 58 per cent of their work was placed in one of the top two categories. Art and design produced the best results, with three-quarters of the research assessed as world-leading or internationally excellent.

Almost all of the British students are state educated, more than half of them coming from the four poorest socio-economic groups. Middlesex does not offer bursaries, believing that outreach and retention activities are more effective means of broadening the intake and improving completion rates. The projected dropout rate has improved, but is still higher than the national average for the courses and entry qualifications.

There are more than 1,600 residential places on or near the campus, with more to come in the next few years. Nearly 700 places were added in September 2016 in a £31-million development on Wembley's Olympic Way. Priority in their allocation is given to international students and other first years whose first choice is Middlesex and who live outside London.

Sports facilities have been improving and now include a well-equipped "fitness pod" at Hendon with a gym and multipurpose outdoor courts. The Sports Development Team at Middlesex is the largest provider of coaching courses in North London. Beyond Hendon, the West End and London's other attractions are only a tube ride away.

Tuition fees

» Fees for UK/EU students 2017–18 £9,250
　Year abroad £1,385
　Placement year £1,385
» UK fees are expected to increase by the rate of inflation from 2018–19 onwards.
» Fees for international students 2017–18 £11,500–£12,500
» Check the university's website for the latest information on fees, scholarships, bursaries and other forms of student support.

Students

Undergraduates:	12,010	(1,665)
Postgraduates:	1,895	(1,910)
Mature students:	28.3%	
International students:	20.7%	
Applications per place:	7.3	
From state-sector schools:	98.1%	
From working-class homes:	56.3%	
Satisfaction with students' union	67%	

For detailed information about sports facilities:
www.mdx.ac.uk/life-at-middlesex/sport

Accommodation

Number of places and costs refer to 2016–17
University-provided places: 1,639
Percentage catered: 0%
Self-catered costs: £135 – £250 a week (40 weeks).
Full-year first-year students are guaranteed accommodation if conditions are met.
International students are allocated a room on first come, first served basis provided application is received by the deadline.
www.mdx.ac.uk/life-at-middlesex/accommodation

Newcastle University

For those applying straight from school, Newcastle represented the best chance of securing an offer from a Russell Group university in 2015. Offers were made to more than nine out of ten 18-year-olds – a significantly higher proportion than in previous years, although the numbers eventually taking up places went up by little more than 6 per cent.

That may change in 2017, as 2,000 students and staff transfer into the university from Durham's School of Medicine, Pharmacy and Health. Until now, there has been a joint arrangement for medicine, in which 99 students spent their first two years on Durham's Stockton campus before joining Newcastle's 244 medics for the rest of their course. In future, all training will take place in Newcastle and those taking pharmacy and other health subjects will also transfer – probably from September 2017.

The move will make Newcastle one of the few universities to offer medicine, dentistry, biomedical sciences, psychology and pharmacy.

It was also the first UK university to open an overseas medical school – the first cohort in Johor, Malaysia, graduated in 2014 – while Newcastle University International Singapore offers a range of engineering degrees in association with the Singapore Institute of Technology.

The university's home campus is in the heart of a city that is frequently rated top for student life. Newcastle plans to spend almost £100 million on improvements over the next four years. New buildings have already opened for physics, music and medicine. Science and engineering laboratories have been upgraded and disabled access improved. The refurbished library, which is open 24 hours a day during term time, is the only one in the UK to have been awarded five Charter Marks in a row for excellent customer service.

The biggest development is the £250-million Science Central project, run in partnership with the city council. One of the largest developments of its kind, it brings together academia, the public sector, business and industry to create a global centre for urban innovation on a 24-acre city-centre site. The first phase opened in 2015, with the Core Building, which houses the Cloud Innovation Centre – part of the School of Computing Science – and the Centre for Professional and Executive Development. The Key Building houses world-leading research on fabric structures and the £58 million Urban Sciences Centre will be added in 2017.

A third campus, on the site of the former Newcastle General Hospital, focuses on research into ageing and is another element

Newcastle upon Tyne
NE1 7RU

0191 208 6000 (enquiries)
contact via website
www.ncl.ac.uk
www.nusu.co.uk
Affiliation: Russell Group

Edinburgh
Belfast
NEWCASTLE UPON TYNE
London
Cardiff

The Times and Sunday Times Rankings

Overall Ranking: **22** (last year: =23)

Teaching quality:	=27	82.9%
Student experience:	=12	87.8%
Research quality:	=21	37.7%
Entry standards:	20	432
Student–staff ratio:	=51	15.5
Services & facilities/student:	69	£1,894
Expected completion rate:	=11	94.9%
Good honours:	20	81.3%
Graduate prospects:	=15	82.6%

of the university's lead role in turning Newcastle into one of the six officially designated science cities.

The university also has a campus in London in partnership with INTO, the company which runs a teaching and accommodation complex on the Newcastle campus to prepare international students for undergraduate and graduate courses. Newcastle University London offers courses from the triple-accredited business school for the international market.

Newcastle has a number of unusual features for a traditional university, such as a fine art degree with intense competition for places, and a longstanding reputation for agriculture, which benefits from two farms in Northumberland. The award-winning ncl+ initiative encourages all students to develop employability skills through extra-curricular activities. Students commit to at least 70 hours of activity, and the award will appear on their Higher Education Achievement Report.

The university is in the top 15 for graduate prospects and is one of those most targeted by leading employers. It also registers high levels of satisfaction, finishing in the top 30 for teaching quality and the top 15 for the broader student experience in the National Student Survey. Almost 80 per cent of the research entered for the 2014 Research Excellence Framework was judged to be world-leading or internationally excellent. Neuroscience, English and computing science rated as leading departments in the UK.

Newcastle is popular with students from independent schools, who took more than a quarter of the places in 2014, but the university was among the first in its peer group to mount substantial programmes to attract more students from non-traditional backgrounds. It leads a national scheme to promote fair access to higher education and won a *Times Higher Education* award for its provision for autistic students in 2015.

The students' union has been refurbished and a Student Forum created alongside it as a central outdoor social space. The campus also hosts an independent theatre, museum and art gallery. University accommodation is plentiful, and a £75-million project will replace much of the existing stock and add 350 places by 2018, as well as extending the sports centre.

Tuition fees

- » Fees for UK/EU students 2017–18 £9,250
  Year abroad £1,385
  Placement year £1,850
- » UK fees are expected to increase by the rate of inflation from 2018–19 onwards.
- » Fees for international students 2017–18 £13,980–£17,935
  Medicine and dentistry £17,935–£33,190
- » Check the university's website for the latest information on fees, scholarships, bursaries and other forms of student support.

Students

Undergraduates:	16,800	(50)
Postgraduates:	4,700	(1,560)
Mature students:	7.6%	
International students:	19.6%	
Applications per place:	6.5	
From state-sector schools:	74.5%	
From working-class homes:	20.3%	
Satisfaction with students' union	80%	

For detailed information about sports facilities: www.ncl.ac.uk/sport

Accommodation

Number of places and costs refer to 2016–17
University-provided places: 4,502
Percentage catered: 14.5%
Catered costs: £135.38 a week.
Self-catered costs: £83.30 – £155.19 a week.
All single undergraduates are guaranteed a room in university-managed accommodation provided requirements are met.
International students: as above.
www.ncl.ac.uk/enquiries; www.ncl.ac.uk/accommodation

Newman University

Newman has announced the latest phase of a £70-million development programme, investing £22 million in new student accommodation and teaching space. The campus has already seen the opening in 2013 of a new library and entrance building. Work has now begun on a 100-bed hall of residence, a 10,000 square metre extension to a teaching building and the refurbishment of four others. The developments will enable Newman to continue expanding – the undergraduate intake has grown by 40 per cent since university status was awarded in 2012.

The university has arrested a two-year fall in our league table in spite of a sharp decline in previously excellent student satisfaction. Much-improved scores for graduate prospects, completion and staffing have ensured a rise of three places, although still not into the top 100.

Newman is one of three Catholic foundations among the crop of institutions that were upgraded in 2013 and 2014.

It takes its name from John Henry Newman, the author of *The Idea of the University* and a Catholic cardinal in the 19th century. His vision of a community of scholars guides the university, which was established in 1968 as a teacher training college, but now has a wider portfolio of degrees, mainly in the social sciences and humanities. The influence of John Henry Newman is evident in the small class sizes and interactive teaching style adopted by the university.

The university stresses its Catholic affiliation, but also its commitment to be inclusive in its recruitment and subsequent activities. It says it is proud to welcome staff and students of all religions and backgrounds, adding that, "In line with Newman's view of a university, we focus on a formative education, developing the whole student into independent thinkers who have the ability to question, evaluate and develop creative solutions to problems rather than just retain knowledge about their subject."

Based in Bartley Green, eight miles southwest of Birmingham city centre, the campus is in a quiet residential area with views over the Bartley Reservoir and the Worcestershire countryside beyond.

The modern buildings are arranged around a series of inner quadrangles of lawns and trees. All full-time degrees include work placements, some of which are abroad, and undergraduates can opt to study at a partner university in Europe or further afield to broaden their horizons and boost their CVs.

There is also a range of part-time courses and Foundation degrees, most of which are taught at Newman, rather than partner colleges. The university received one of

Genners Lane
Bartley Green
Birmingham B32 3NT

0121 476 1181 (admissions)
admissions@newman.ac.uk
www.newman.ac.uk
www.newmansu.org
Affiliation: GuildHE,
Cathedrals Group

The Times and Sunday Times Rankings

Overall Ranking: =112 (last year: =115.)		
Teaching quality:	=59	80.9%
Student experience:	110	80.9%
Research quality:	114	2.8%
Entry standards:	=102	300
Student–staff ratio:	=76	16.9
Services & facilities/student:	100	£1,561
Expected completion rate:	111	79.3%
Good honours:	=117	59.1%
Graduate prospects:	86	67.7%

eight national awards to effect change in the strategic approach to technology in learning and teaching. The successful bid drew on a project designed to improve the university's own students' digital literacy, part of a larger initiative called "Newman in the Digital Age".

The university offers some of the most generous scholarships at any university: £10,000 over three years for British degree students in subjects other than teacher training who make the university their first choice and achieve at least BBB or ABC at A level. There is no need to make an application – the university will contact eligible students in August – but the recipients will need to pass all their modules first time and average at least 60 per cent to qualify for the following year's payment.

The awards are part of a range of scholarships and bursaries, which include £2,000 awards for teacher training students and £12,000 awards for those from the Newman University Catholic Higher Education Network of schools. Newman was shortlisted for the *Times Higher Education* award for Outstanding Student Support in 2015.

Only 23 academics were entered for the latest research assessments, but that was twice as many as in 2008. Education and history produced the best results, but less than a third of the university's research was placed in the top two categories.

Newman does not employ staff for research alone in order to ensure that students have regular contact with active researchers in their area.

Three-quarters of the undergraduates are female, almost all of them state-educated, and more than half come from working-class homes.

Halls of residence currently provide single study-bedrooms for 200 students, close to the teaching areas and library. First-year students take priority in their allocation, but those entering through Clearing may have to live off campus.

The refurbished fitness suite and performance room have improved sports facilities that already included an artificial sports pitch, sports hall, gymnasium and squash courts. Birmingham city centre, with its abundance of cultural venues and student-oriented nightlife, is about 20 minutes away.

Tuition fees

» Fees for UK/EU students 2017–18 £9,250
» UK fees are expected to increase by the rate of inflation from 2018–19 onwards.
» Fees for international students 2017–18 £11,100
» Check the university's website for the latest information on fees, scholarships, bursaries and other forms of student support.

Students

Undergraduates:	1,720	(505)
Postgraduates:	255	(245)
Mature students:	30.1%	
International students:	0%	
Applications per place:	6.2	
From state-sector schools:	99.6%	
From working-class homes:	56.2%	
Satisfaction with students' union	56%	

For detailed information about sports facilities:
www.newman.ac.uk/sport

Accommodation

Places and costs refer to 2016–17
University-provided places: 200
Percentage catered: 0%
Self-catered costs: around £97.50 (standard) – £125.00 (en suite) a week (40 weeks).
Priority, but no guarantee, is given to new first-year students.
International students: guaranteed housing.
www.newman.ac.uk/accommodation

University of Northampton

Northampton suffered its first major reverse in our league table last year, after jumping more than 40 places in the early years of the decade. Its decline has continued in the new edition, with a drop of 15 places, due mainly to lower student satisfaction and a poor year for graduate employment. There should be better times ahead, however, as the university prepares to move to a new, purpose-built campus in the heart of the town in 2018.

Waterside Campus will provide academic facilities for 15,000 students, residential accommodation for 1,200 and leisure facilities open to the community, transforming a 58-acre brownfield site. The development of the campus has been funded through a £231.5-million bond which has been guaranteed by the Treasury – the first time the Government has made such a guarantee. Another £60 million will come through partnerships with the county and borough councils. The two existing sites will be sold for housing when the move takes place. The new campus will give the university scope to expand, as well as providing improved facilities, although applications were down by more than 10 per cent in 2015.

The project typifies the ambitious nature of a university which was the first in the UK to be named a "Changemaker Campus" by the Ashoka global network of social entrepreneurs and has since been ranked top in the country for social enterprise. Every student has the opportunity to work in a social enterprise as part of their course, developing new entrepreneurial skills to make them more employable. This may involve a work placement, volunteering or building sustainable social and economic partnerships which would, in turn, be supported by the university.

Although it was awarded university status only in 2005, Northampton can trace its history back to the 13th century. Henry III dissolved the original institution, allegedly because his bishops thought it posed a threat to Oxford. The modern university originated in an amalgamation of the town's colleges of education, nursing, technology and art. It has a particular focus on training for public services in the region, with students combining their studies with work placements in the community.

Business is the university's most popular area, but teacher training and health subjects are not far behind – the university is the region's largest provider of teachers and healthcare professionals.

Northampton takes its mission to widen participation in higher education seriously: almost all the undergraduates are state educated and four out of ten come from working class homes – more than the

Park Campus
Boughton Green Road
Northampton NN2 7AL

0800 358 2232 (courses freephone)
study@northampton.ac.uk
www.northampton.ac.uk
www.northamptonunion.
com
Affiliation: none

The Times and Sunday Times **Rankings**

Overall Ranking: **97** (last year: =82)

Teaching quality:	=68	80.4%
Student experience:	=92	82.1%
Research quality:	112	3.2%
Entry standards:	118	281
Student–staff ratio:	=103	18.6
Services & facilities/student:	32	£2,250
Expected completion rate:	=63	85.8%
Good honours:	87	66.3%
Graduate prospects:	=123	56.8%

national average for the university's courses and entry qualifications.

The university entered a quarter of its eligible staff for the 2014 Research Excellence Framework. Only 30 per cent of its research was placed in the top two categories, but there was an outstanding result in history, where two-thirds of the work was considered world-leading or internationally excellent. There are now 11 research centres, focusing on everything from contemporary fiction to anomalous psychological processes and transitional economics in China.

Of the two existing sites, Park Campus is on the edge of Northampton, while the smaller Avenue Campus is more central. They are linked by a regular and free weekday bus service, as well as by "Boris bikes". Park Campus is set in 80 acres of open green parkland, with accommodation, a sports hall, students' union centre and nightclub. Two of the main buildings have been refurbished and expanded as part of a programme of improvements, which included an extension to the business school.

Avenue Campus, the centre for art, design, science and technology, and the performing arts, hosts frequent theatre performances and exhibitions in its own art gallery. A former school houses a technology and research centre with NVision and a 3-D immersive technology and visualisation facility.

The university also backs the iCon building in Daventry, which provides a base for green businesses and sponsors a university technical college in the town, as it does at the nearby Silverstone motor racing circuit.

There are more than 2,100 residential places, including a choice of mixed and single-sex halls. The latest development added 475 rooms in the centre of Northampton.

Sports enthusiasts are well catered for, with rugby union, football, first-class cricket and Silverstone on the doorstep. The sports facilities include a gym, sports hall and outdoor pitches on the Park Campus.

The town has a number of student-oriented bars, but the two campuses' union bars remain the hub of the social scene. Both London and Birmingham are about an hour away by train.

Tuition fees

- » Fees for UK/EU students 2017–18 £9,250
  Year abroad £1,350
  Placement year £875
  Foundation degree £8,750
- » UK fees are expected to increase by the rate of inflation from 2018–19 onwards.
- » Fees for international students 2016–17 £10,900–£11,900
- » Check the university's website for the latest information on fees, scholarships, bursaries and other forms of student support.

Students

Undergraduates:	8,975	(1,970)
Postgraduates:	640	(1,705)
Mature students:	26.9%	
International students:	9.6%	
Applications per place:	6.0	
From state-sector schools:	97.6%	
From working-class homes:	40.2%	
Satisfaction with students' union	68%	

For information about sports facilities:
www.northamptonunion.com/activities/sports

Accommodation

Number of places and costs refer to 2016–17
University-provided places: 2,114
Percentage catered: 0%
Self-catered costs: £61.50 (small twin) – £150.00 (single studio) a week (42 weeks).
New first years have priority, on first come, first served basis, provided requirements are met.
International students: As above.
accommodation@northampton.ac.uk
www.northampton.ac.uk/study/student-life/accommodation

Northumbria University

Having invested £200 million in award-winning campus facilities over the last decade, Northumbria is going to spend another £52 million over the next two years to help create a "new type of excellent university" with a focus on business and the professions, as well as academic excellence and research.

A Student Central Zone will bring all student-facing services together in one area and there will new buildings for computing and architecture, as well as major renovations of the central Ellison and Lipman buildings. A number of Northumbria's graduates who now work in leading architecture and construction firms will be involved in the development. The university hopes that one impact will be on student satisfaction, which dipped slightly this year, stalling its progress towards its goal of a place in the top 30.

Northumbria is the biggest university in northeast England, with almost 34,000 students at all levels from 131 countries. It has been raising entry standards rather than expanding further. An £18-million staffing plan brought in more academics and enhanced the university's research capability. Northumbria more than doubled the numbers entered for the 2014 Research Excellence Framework compared with the 2008 assessments while improving the results. Sixty per cent of the work was judged to be world-leading or internationally excellent, attracting one of the biggest increases in research funding at any university.

Most subjects are based on the main campus, with health, education and community programmes located at the Coach Lane campus, less than two miles away, where £20 million has been spent upgrading facilities. There is a learning resources centre there, as well as new sports facilities and a clinical skills centre, where students learn in simulated hospital environments.

Northumbria also opened a campus in the City of London in 2014, with an initial focus on business courses. Business and accounting programmes are both accredited by the Association to Advance Collegiate Schools of Business, making Newcastle Business School the only institution in Europe to achieve double accreditation and helping it to the title of Business School of the Year in *Times Higher Education*'s 2015 awards.

On the main campus, an expansion of the library in response to student feedback added 100 IT spaces, more social learning and informal space, a dedicated Language Zone and a completely refurbished basement.

Around half of the students are from the

Sutherland Building
Ellison Place
Newcastle upon Tyne
NE1 8ST

0191 349 5600 (course enquiries)
er.admissions@
  northumbria.ac.uk
www.northumbria.ac.uk
www.mynsu.co.uk
Affiliation: none

The Times and Sunday Times Rankings

Overall Ranking: **=65** (last year: =64)

Teaching quality:	=54	81.2%
Student experience:	=65	83.8%
Research quality:	=64	9%
Entry standards:	47	364
Student–staff ratio:	=80	17.1
Services & facilities/student:	102	£1,543
Expected completion rate:	52	87.5%
Good honours:	73	69.7%
Graduate prospects:	=63	71.9%

North East, but numbers drawn from other parts of the UK have been rising.

There are almost 2,500 international students on campus and another 3,600 taking Northumbria courses overseas. A school of design is being established in Jakarta, Indonesia, jointly with BINUS International University.

More than a third of the British undergraduates are from the four lowest socio-economic classes. Free one-day taster courses run throughout the year to give prospective students an idea of what university life would be like. There are £1,000 bursaries for applicants from the poorest homes and 100 others, worth £2,750, to encourage those graduating to stay on for selected Masters courses.

More than 560 employers sponsor undergraduate programmes – one of the highest rates in the UK – and accreditation comes from almost 50 professional bodies. The post-registration nursing programmes were the first to receive accreditation from the Royal College of Nursing and have been voted the best in the UK for three successive years. All Northumbria's teacher training programmes have been rated as outstanding by Ofsted for 14 years in a row. The Student Law Office, which offers legal advice under professional supervision as part of a degree, won a Queen's Anniversary Prize in 2013. Northumbria is also ranked third in the UK for graduate start-ups based on both estimated turnover and number of jobs created, having supported the development of more than 130 graduate companies since 2009.

Sports facilities are good and Northumbria has been in the top ten of the British Universities and Colleges Sport league table since 2013–14. A £30-million sports centre includes a swimming pool, multiple laboratories, a climbing wall and a 3,000-seat indoor arena for professional sport and other events. There is also a generous sport scholarship scheme.

Most first years are offered places in university accommodation that was placed in the top three in the 2014 Student Housing Survey. There are now 5,000 rooms available, and there is a plentiful supply of privately rented housing in Newcastle, a location that has become a major attraction to students. Northumbria finished joint top with Newcastle University for having the best student nightlife in a *Which?* university survey published in July 2016.

Tuition fees

» Fees for UK/EU students 2017–18 £9,250
   Placement year £1,000–£1,850
» UK fees are expected to increase by the rate of inflation from 2018–19 onwards.
» Fees for international students 2017–18 £12,500–£14,500
» Check the university's website for the latest information on fees, scholarships, bursaries and other forms of student support.

Students

Undergraduates:	18,865	(3,835)
Postgraduates:	2,200	(2,170)
Mature students:	16.9%	
International students:	10.5%	
Applications per place:	5.6	
From state-sector schools:	94.2%	
From working-class homes:	37.2%	
Satisfaction with students' union	77%	

For detailed information about sports facilities:
https://northumbriasport.com

Accommodation

Number of places and costs refer to 2016–17
University-provided places: 5,000
Percentage catered: 5%
Catered costs: £110.25 a week.
Self-catered costs: £73.50 (single) – £128.00 (en suite).
First years who need accommodation can be offered places.
International students: first years are guaranteed accommodation if requirements met.
www.northumbria.ac.uk/study-at-northumbria/accommodation

Norwich University of the Arts (NUA)

NUA is still finding its level in our league table, as it makes only its second appearance. A sharp decline in student satisfaction and a poor year for graduate employment have resulted in a drop of 27 places, but the university started from a high base, having entered the ranking in the top half, just outside the top 60.

NUA received university status in 2012, but was too specialist to qualify for the table until the restrictions were relaxed last year. Still among the smallest institutions in the *Guide*, it plans to double in size over the next few years. NUA added more than 20 per cent to the undergraduate intake in its first three years as a university, but the process will be gradual so as not to place too much strain on its facilities.

Developments such as the opening of a new building for the School of Architecture has allowed for a larger intake. The school moved to the Grade II-listed Boardman House, in the city centre, which includes new studios for media students and was purchased as the first stage of a £10-million development plan. The building won an award from the Royal Institute of British Architects, while the architecture degree has been prescribed by the Architects

Registration Board, exempting graduates from the professional exams that are the first step to becoming an architect.

Unlike the other arts universities, NUA makes a virtue of focusing entirely on the arts, design and media, rather than venturing into business or the humanities and social sciences. The university traces its history back to 1845, when the Norwich School of Design was established by the artists and followers of the Norwich School of Painters, the only provincial British group with an international reputation for landscape painting. Former tutors include Lucian Freud, Michael Andrews and Lesley Davenport.

The campus is concentrated on the pedestrianised centre of Norwich, from the 13th-century Garth, which is now the photography centre, to the Monastery Media Lab and St Georges, where the traditional high ceilings and huge windows make it an ideal setting for Fine Art. The university's public art gallery enables students to showcase their work and gain experience curating and organising exhibitions, while the library houses the largest specialist art, design and media collection in the eastern region. An Ideas Factory, incorporating a digital start-up incubation hub, was added in 2015.

There are only 18 BA degrees and fewer than 2,000 students, 62 per cent of whom are female. Approaching 40 per cent of the

---

Francis House
3-7 Redwell Street
Norwich
NR2 4SN

01603 610561 (enquiries)
studentrecruitment@
nua.ac.uk
www.nua.ac.uk
www.nuasu.co.uk
Affiliation: GuildHE

Edinburgh
Belfast
NORWICH
London
Cardiff

The Times and Sunday Times Rankings

Overall Ranking: **88** (last year: 61)

Teaching quality:	=90	79.3%
Student experience:	122	79.1%
Research quality:	=85	5.6%
Entry standards:	41	378
Student–staff ratio:	93	17.8
Services & facilities/student:	=114	£1,349
Expected completion rate:	49	88.5%
Good honours:	=77	67.9%
Graduate prospects:	120	57.7%

undergraduates come from working-class homes and the projected dropout rate of less than 8 per cent is much better the national average for its courses and entry qualifications. Most courses include units of self-managed learning and exploration that allow students to concentrate on areas of particular interest. Agreements with tutors focus on personal study and help students negotiate individual pathways through their courses.

More than half of the work submitted to the 2014 Research Excellence Framework was judged to be world leading or internationally excellent, with 90 per cent placed in the top two categories for its impact on the broader cultural and economic landscape.

NUA has invested significantly in hardware and software that is professionally relevant and suitable for its diverse range of academic requirements. IT resources can be accessed in the workshops, library, computer-teaching rooms, seminar rooms, and at numerous terminals available throughout the campus. NUA has its own art materials shop, which sells basic and specialist art supplies at discounted prices.

Individual studio space is provided for all full-time students in the faculties of art and design, while students in the media faculty have access to digital media workstations. Workshops for everything from digital video editing to laser cutting provide specialised

resources and are staffed by experienced professionals, including graduates and practising artists.

A new residential development in the city centre opened in 2015, more than doubling the number of rooms managed by the university. The new cluster flats have brought the total to almost 350 rooms, with priority going to international students and first years living furthest away from the university.

NUA does not have its own sports facilities, but its students have access to the University of East Anglia's Sportspark, which boasts some of the best facilities in the higher education system, including an Olympic-sized swimming pool.

The city of Norwich is attractive and popular with students whilst consistently rated one of the safest and "greenest" cities in the UK.

Tuition fees

» Fees for UK/EU students 2017–18   £9,250
» UK fees are expected to increase by the rate of inflation from 2018–19 onwards.
» Fees for international students 2016–17   £13,000
» Check the university's website for the latest information on fees, scholarships, bursaries and other forms of student support.

Students

Undergraduates:	1,820	(0)
Postgraduates:	20	(40)
Mature students:	12.0%	
International students:	4.9%	
Applications per place:	4.2	
From state-sector schools:	98.2%	
From working-class homes:	37.6%	
Satisfaction with students' union	47%	

For detailed information about sports facilities: www.nua.ac.uk/norwich/sport

Accommodation

Number of places and costs refer to 2016–17
University-provided places: 345
Percentage catered: 0%
Self-catered costs: £95 – £155 a week (46 weeks).
First years cannot be guaranteed housing. Distance restrictions apply.
International students: as above
accommodation@nua.ac.uk
www.nua.ac.uk/study/accommodation

University of Nottingham

Nottingham is back in our top 20 after a rise of five places, due mainly to a significant increase in student satisfaction. It is the biggest rise among the leading group and enough to earn a nomination as *The Sunday Times* University of the Year.

A member of the Russell Group, Nottingham has award-winning campuses in China and Malaysia as well as 330 acres of parkland in its home city that is one of the most attractive university settings in the UK. With undergraduates encouraged to transfer between campuses and over 8,000 international students in Nottingham, the university markets itself as a global institution. It is in the top 75 universities in the world in the QS rankings, with 21 subjects in the top 100.

One of the two universities (the other is Manchester) most targeted by major UK employers for the recruitment of graduates for the past three years, it wins our award for University of the Year for Graduate Employment.

University Park has been named as the most sustainable campus in the world for the last four years. A £40-million sports complex opened in September 2016, with a host of facilities including a 60-metre indoor sprint track, hydrotherapy pool and 200-station fitness suite, while an expanded engineering and science library opened earlier in summer 2016.

The building programme also includes a new teaching building, the redevelopment of the Portland Building and more space for the students' union. A mile away is the 30-acre Jubilee Campus, which houses the schools of management and finance, computer science and education, as well as 750 residential places. New sports facilities, research laboratories, teaching space and student accommodation have all been added in recent years.

The latest addition is the Centre for Sustainable Chemistry, part-funded by GlaxoSmithKline, which will be housed in a carbon-neutral building that is the first of its kind in the UK. The Medical School is also close to University Park, with a £4.5-million facility for nursing located at Derby Hospital.

The biosciences and veterinary schools are at Sutton Bonington, 12 miles south of the city in a rural setting. A £9-million amenities building opened in 2015 providing a 500-seat dining hall, student common rooms and staff lounge, as well as a graduate centre, faith room and facilities for the student guild.

The university's purpose-built campuses in China and Malaysia both have echoes of Nottingham's distinctive clock tower and are centres of research as well as teaching. With 6,000 students at Ningbo, in China, and

---

University Park
Nottingham NG7 2RD

0115 951 5559 (enquiries)
undergraduate-enquiries@
nottingham.ac.uk
www.nottingham.ac.uk
www.su.nottingham.ac.uk
Affiliation: Russell Group

The Times and Sunday Times **Rankings**

Overall Ranking: **20** (last year: 25)

Teaching quality:	=54	81.2%
Student experience:	=28	86%
Research quality:	20	37.8%
Entry standards:	23	425
Student–staff ratio:	=20	13.2
Services & facilities/student:	36	£2,180
Expected completion rate:	=20	93.7%
Good honours:	=24	80.5%
Graduate prospects:	14	82.7%

almost 5,000 half an hour's drive from Kuala Lumpur, both are well established. They bring Nottingham's total student population to more than 44,000, making it one of the largest UK institutions.

The university has shown its strength in research with two Nobel prizes since the millennium for work carried out at Nottingham. More than 80 per cent of the work entered for the 2014 Research Excellence Framework was rated as world-leading or internationally excellent. The university was in the UK's top ten in half of the 32 subject areas in which it made submissions, with pharmacy, chemistry and physics producing particularly good results.

Nottingham has succeeded in broadening its UK intake, but still has more independent school students and fewer from working-class homes than the national average for the subjects it offers. Summer schools and master classes provide support for teenagers from backgrounds without a history of progressing to selective universities and the university is a member of the Sutton Trust's Pathways to Law access programme. Once in, students tend to stay the course – the dropout rate of less than five per cent is among the best in the country.

The Nottingham Advantage Award offers extra-curricular modules, as well as providing scores of internships for graduates, who enjoy lifetime access to the careers service, which has teams in each faculty.

The two main campuses in Nottingham are within three miles of the city centre, which has a good selection of student-friendly clubs. University Park and the medical school are now linked to the centre by tram. However, halls of residence and the students' union tend to be the centre of social life for students, especially in the first year. New bars, café facilities and a nightclub were included in a £1-million makeover of union facilities.

Even before the new sports village, sports provision was excellent and includes a water-based hockey pitch and 25-metre pool. Team performances have improved so much that Nottingham made the top four in the BUCS leagues in 2016, and a number of students and alumni took part in the Rio Olympics.

Tuition fees

» Fees for UK/EU students 2017–18 £9,250
  Year abroad £1,350
  Placement year £1,800
» UK fees are expected to increase by the rate of inflation from 2018–19 onwards.
» Fees for international students 2017–18 £15,570–£20,070
  Veterinary medicine £29,730
  Medicine £21,120–£35,010
» Check the university's website for the latest information on fees, scholarships, bursaries and other forms of student support.

Students

Undergraduates:	22,665	(1,150)
Postgraduates:	5,475	(2,620)
Mature students:	12.0%	
International students:	18.2%	
Applications per place:	7.4	
From state-sector schools:	77.8%	
From working-class homes:	20.3%	
Satisfaction with students' union	70%	

For detailed information about sports facilities:
www.nottingham.ac.uk/sport

Accommodation

Number of places and costs refer to 2016–17
University-provided places: 7,500
Percentage catered: 33.3%
Catered costs: £151.22 – £207.37 a week (31 or 51 weeks).
Self-catered costs: £98.00 – £163.15 a week (44 or 51 weeks).
First years are guaranteed accommodation if conditions are met.
International undergraduates: as above.
www.nottingham.ac.uk/accommodation

Nottingham Trent University

Nottingham Trent (NTU) is the biggest university in our top 20 for teaching quality, a part of the National Student Survey normally dominated by much smaller institutions. Only five universities recruited more undergraduates in 2015, and there are now 27,000 students in all, including 3,000 from outside the UK.

NTU is also in the top ten for the number of students on year-long work placements, a format that the university is doubly keen to promote since establishing that it greatly improves the job prospects of students from poor backgrounds. Nearly nine out of ten disadvantaged students find professional jobs six months after graduation – virtually the same proportion as those from more affluent families – compared with 57 per cent who take three-year degrees.

A third of the undergraduates come from working-class homes and more than nine out of ten were state educated. From 2017–18, most courses will include a work placement of at least four weeks. NTU is also aiming to offer all its students an "international learning experience", which may involve a study or work placement abroad, learning a foreign language or studying another culture or country.

In little over a decade, Nottingham Trent has invested £421 million in buildings and equipment. Recent projects have seen the redevelopment of the Clifton Campus, five miles from the centre of Nottingham, with a new central pavilion building and teaching suite, as well as a modernised and upgraded refectory and library. The development, which includes a "superlab" for 200 science students and a new teaching and learning building, opened in 2015.

The university is to invest £10 million more on its facilities for science, technology, engineering and mathematics (STEM) disciplines.

It had already opened a new students' union and 500 student bedrooms, bars and other social space on the main city site in 2014. Other projects on the campus have included the upgrading of art and design facilities, as well as new lecture theatres, laboratories, student services areas and restaurants.

Art and design, architecture, law, business and the social sciences are taught at the City site, while science and technology, education, and the humanities are based at Clifton, which has seen the addition of six new blocks of high-quality student accommodation that will form part of a student village. The Brackenhurst Campus, 14 miles outside Nottingham, is devoted to animal, rural and environmental studies. It includes one of the region's best-equipped equestrian centres, with a purpose-built

---

Burton Street
Nottingham NG1 4BU

0115 848 4200 (admissions)
contact via website
www.ntu.ac.uk
www.trentstudents.org
Affiliation: University
   Alliance

The Times and Sunday Times Rankings

Overall Ranking: **57** (last year: 54)

Teaching quality:	13	84.6%
Student experience:	33	85.7%
Research quality:	80	6.5%
Entry standards:	=89	306
Student–staff ratio:	=72	16.7
Services & facilities/student:	70	£1,891
Expected completion rate:	=63	85.8%
Good honours:	61	71.4%
Graduate prospects:	57	73.1%

indoor riding area, as well as 340 residential places. Some £20 million has been spent there on a new animal unit and veterinary nursing centre, and an eco-friendly library opened in 2013.

Best known for fashion and other creative arts, the university also boasts one of the UK's biggest law schools, offering legal practice courses both for solicitors and barristers, as well as degrees. Many courses are sponsored by employers. A Trailblazer Apprenticeship in management, for example, gives students a degree and CIMA qualification in four years instead of the usual seven, with fees and salary paid by a company. NTU is also building on a long and distinguished history in teacher education with the launch of the Nottingham Institute of Education, a new centre of excellence that is intended to align teaching and research expertise more effectively from the early years to higher education.

An extensive research programme attracted an £8-million donation – thought to be the largest to a post-1992 university – to advance the university's work in cancer diagnosis and therapy. Researchers at the purpose-built facility on the Clifton campus work with leading cancer research institutions in the USA, Europe and Asia. More than half of the research submitted to the 2014 Research Excellence Framework was considered world-leading or internationally excellent, but NTU still slipped down our research ranking. The best results were in health subjects and general engineering, where more than 80 per cent of the work was placed in the top two categories. The university has since won a Queen's Anniversary Prize for new technologies for food safety and security, and aviation security.

NTU has a strong sporting reputation, frequently reaching the top 20 in the BUCS leagues. The Lee Westwood Sports Centre, which includes a 100-station gym, sports halls, studios, and a nutrition training centre, is on the Clifton Campus, where the outdoor facilities include an Olympic-standard hockey pitch.

Social life varies between campuses, but all have access to the city's lively cultural and clubbing scene. A bus service links the main campuses and the city's tram system serves the university.

Tuition fees

» Fees for UK/EU students 2017–18	£9,250
Foundation degree	£9,250
Year abroad	£1,380
Placement year	£1,380

» UK fees are expected to increase by the rate of inflation from 2018–19 onwards.

» Fees for international students 2017–18	£12,900

» Check the university's website for the latest information on fees, scholarships, bursaries and other forms of student support.

Students

Undergraduates:	20,305	(1,555)
Postgraduates:	2,230	(2,800)
Mature students:	11.4%	
International students:	6.6%	
Applications per place:	6.0	
From state-sector schools:	93.7%	
From working-class homes:	33.1%	
Satisfaction with students' union	85%	

For detailed information about sports facilities:
www4.ntu.ac.uk/sport

Accommodation

Number of places and costs refer to 2016–17
University-provided places: 4,764
Percentage catered: 0%
Self-catered costs: £83.93 – £163.03 (44–51 weeks).
First years and new students are guaranteed accommodation if booked by 31 July.
International students: guaranteed accommodation as above.
accommodation@ntu.ac.uk
www.ntu.ac.uk/accommodation

The Open University (OU)

The national collapse in part-time higher education has hit the Open University hard: it has lost a third of its students in five years and gone from healthy surpluses to a £7-million deficit in 2014–15. Peter Horrocks, who moved from the BBC World Service to become Vice-Chancellor in 2015, has won agreement to close seven regional offices and shed a number of posts, while calling for the OU to become more agile and innovative. Although still much the largest university in the UK and the choice of 60 per cent of all part-time students, the OU now has fewer than 175,000 students, compared with 260,000 at the start of the decade.

However, Mr Horrocks has promised "unprecedented" investment in research and continued substantial spending on massive open online courses (MOOCs) that are free to students. The university is hosting FutureLearn, a consortium of leading universities and cultural organisations such as the British Museum and the British Council, offering MOOCs of varying lengths in a growing range of subjects. Some MOOCs now offer academic credits towards OU degrees.

The OU remains one of the world's most highly regarded distance learning institutions, a model for universities on every continent. It does not appear in our league table because the absence of on-campus undergraduates makes the OU unsuitable for comparison with conventional universities on some of the measures used. It offers curriculum resources free via its OpenLearn website and was the first UK university to extend free learning to the social media site Bibblio. Its size has not prevented it ranking near the top of the National Student Survey every year, although it slipped out of the top 20 for overall satisfaction in 2016.

Undergraduate fees are £5,572 for the equivalent of full-time study in 2016–17 and the cheapest at any university. The OU provides fee waivers for students from poor backgrounds through its Widening Access and Success programme. Three in ten students are under 25 years old and three-quarters work either full- or part-time while studying. Over 60 per cent of undergraduates are female and most live in the UK, but there are now 15,000 students in other countries. The OU offers special support for disabled students and currently has more than 20,000 students with disabilities.

The university's headquarters are at Milton Keynes, Buckinghamshire, but it has 350 study centres and regional centres in each of its 13 regions around the UK, as well as offices and exam centres abroad. The open access principle that was a cornerstone

---

Walton Hall
Milton Keynes MK7 6AA

0300 303 5303 (enquiries)
contact via website
www.open.ac.uk
www.open.ac.uk/ousa
Affiliation:
University Alliance

***The Times and Sunday Times* Rankings**
The available data do not match the data used to rank the other full-time universities, so the Open University could not be included in the league table this year.

of its foundation remains in place: no formal qualifications are required to study on most undergraduate programmes.

In addition to degrees in a named subject, the OU also awards "Open" Bachelor degrees, where the syllabus is designed by the students combining a number of modules. Assessment is by both continual assessment and examination or, for some modules, a major assignment. Except in fast-moving areas such as computing, there is no limit on the time taken to complete a degree. The OU also intends to become a major provider of degree apprenticeships, with students progressing towards a full degree while working for their employer, who pays their tuition fees in full.

Almost 6,000 part-time associate lecturers (tutors) guide students through degrees. The OU's "Supported Open Learning" system allows students to work where they choose – at home, in the workplace or at a library or study centre. They have contact with fellow students at tutorials, day schools or through online conferencing and electronic forums, social networks and informal study groups.

An increasing amount of material is delivered online, and can be accessed on mobile devices as well as computers. The university was awarded £2.7 million to create online laboratories for science and engineering that are available 24 hours a day for students worldwide to set up and participate in remote-controlled experiments.

The OU now produces mainstream television and radio programming aimed at bringing learning to a wider audience. The OU also leads the universities placing material on the iTunes U site and was one of the first to make e-books available there.

In the 2014 Research Excellence Framework 72 per cent of the OU's submission was considered world-leading or internationally excellent. There was an outstanding result in music, and good performances in art and design and electronic engineering.

Tuition fees

» Fees vary depending upon the type of course, on where you live and the number of credits you plan to study. In 2016–17, in England a course of 120 credits of study (a year's full-time study) is £5,572, which can be covered by a tuition fee loan. Access Curriculum year 0 30-credit course reduced to £675.
» In Scotland, Wales and Northern Ireland, a course of 120 credits is £1,786, and there may be government assistance in paying the fee.
» For international students, a course of 120 credits is £5,572.
» The costs of all courses are given in the course descriptions: **www.open.ac.uk/courses**
» Various forms of financial help are available: **www.open.ac.uk/courses/fees-and-funding**

Students

Undergraduates:	n/a	(122,805)
Postgraduates:	225	(9,335)
Satisfaction with students' union	62%	

Accommodation

As the courses provided are part time, the university does not provide accommodation.

Residential summer schools form part of many courses. These are normally held at traditional universities during the summer vacation.

University of Oxford

Fewer than a quarter of 18-year-olds applying to Oxford in 2015 received an offer – the lowest proportion in the UK and significantly less than at Cambridge. In part, the reason is that Oxford has succeeded in increasing the number of applications it attracts by more than 40 per cent in the last decade, reaching record levels, but there are no more places for undergraduates.

According to official figures, it is the wealthiest UK university, with a surplus of £191 million – more than all Scotland's universities combined – and there is considerable development taking place. But any expansion is likely to be in postgraduate places. Some subjects now demand two A* grades and another A at A level and 99 per cent of successful candidates achieve at least three As at A level, or their equivalent.

Applications must be made by mid-October – a month earlier if you wish to be interviewed overseas – and it is not possible to apply to both Oxford and Cambridge. There are written tests for some subjects and you may be asked to submit samples of work. The prize is a place at the oldest and probably the most famous university in the world, with 26 Nobel prize-winners and 27 British prime ministers among its alumni and former academics.

Oxford remains second in our table,

but moved to top place in *Times Higher Education* magazine's global ranking, which puts a heavier emphasis on research.

Ironically, it slipped off the top of our table last year after falling behind Cambridge in research following our analysis of the 2014 Research Excellence Framework. Oxford achieved the best results in the UK in nine subject areas and 87 per cent of its submission was rated as world-leading or internationally excellent, but it entered 87 per cent of eligible staff, compared with 95 per cent at Cambridge. Oxford has since won a Queen's Anniversary Prize for collaborations between engineering and medical technology.

Professor Louise Richardson, a leading scholar on global terrorism, became Oxford's first female vice-chancellor in more than 900 years of existence when she arrived from St Andrews University in 2015. She is overseeing a programme of improvement and expansion of teaching facilities with the aid of the largest ever European Investment Bank loan to a university, at £200 million. The money has been allocated to both planned buildings and some that have already been completed. In the Science Area, existing buildings are being refurbished and modernised.

Among the many recent projects was the opening of a new building at the Botnar Research Centre for research on arthritis,

University Offices
Wellington Square
Oxford OX1 2JD

01865 288000 (admissions)
contact via website
www.ox.ac.uk
https://ousu.org
Affiliation: Russell Group

The Times and Sunday Times Rankings

Overall Ranking: **2** (last year: 2)

Teaching quality:	43	82%
Student experience:	23	86.5%
Research quality:	3	53.1%
Entry standards:	2	577
Student–staff ratio:	3	10.5
Services & facilities/student:	3	£3,130
Expected completion rate:	2	97.7%
Good honours:	1	92.4%
Graduate prospects:	11	84.3%

osteoporosis and other bone and joint diseases.

Oxford's biggest capital development for more than a century, on the site of the old Radcliffe Infirmary, has seen more student accommodation for neighbouring Somerville College, a new Mathematical Institute building and a new building for the humanities added. The £75-million Blavatnik School of Government opened on the site in 2015.

The £110-million Precision Cancer Medicine Institute, supported by a £35-million Government grant, is perhaps the most ambitious single project currently planned.

Oxford continues to try to broaden its intake, mounting 3,000 outreach events involving 72 per cent of all UK schools with a sixth form, but it still admits the lowest proportion of undergraduates from the bottom four socio-economic groups – just ten per cent – and the most from independent schools.

The university also offers the most generous financial support in UK higher education for students from poor backgrounds. A £75-million donation helps to provide bursaries and fee waivers worth up to £7,500 a year for those whose family income is less than £16,000.

Selection is in the hands of the 30 undergraduate colleges, which vary considerably in their approach to this issue and others. Sound advice on colleges' academic strengths and social factors is essential for applicants to give themselves the best chance of winning a place and finding a setting in which they can thrive.

A minority of candidates opt to go straight into the admissions pool without expressing a preference for a particular college. The choice is particularly important for arts and social science students, whose tuition is based in college. Science and technology are taught mainly in central facilities.

All subjects operate on eight-week terms and assess students entirely on final examinations – a system some find too pressurised. Student satisfaction rates have declined this year, particularly in the sections of the National Student Survey relating to teaching, feedback and academic support, but Oxford's drop-out rate is the second lowest in the country.

Tuition fees

» Fees for UK/EU students 2017–18 £9,250
  Year abroad £1,385
» UK fees are expected to increase by the rate of inflation from 2018–19 onwards.
» Fees for international students (including college fees of £7,350) 2017–18 £23,105–£30,540
  Medicine £25,430–£34,956
» Check the university's website for the latest information on fees, scholarships, bursaries and other forms of student support..

Students

Undergraduates:	11,425	(5,160)
Postgraduates:	7,620	(1,800)
Mature students:	3.7%	
International students:	16.8%	
Applications per place:	5.9	
From state-sector schools:	55.7%	
From working-class homes:	10%	
Satisfaction with students' union	34%	

For detailed information about sports facilities:
www.sport.ox.ac.uk

Accommodation

www.ox.ac.uk/students/life/accommodation
www.ox.ac.uk/admissions/undergraduate/colleges/college-listing

Also see chapter 13 for information about individual colleges.

Oxford Brookes University

Oxford Brookes has dropped 14 places in our league table this year, largely as a result of a fall in student satisfaction and lower spending on facilities. More than 80 per cent of final-year undergraduates were satisfied both with the quality of teaching and the broader student experience but, in a highly competitive environment, a decline of less than 2 percentage points meant the loss of at least 25 places on this measure.

For many years the highest-placed post-1992 university in our table, Brookes is no longer in the top 15 of this group and is only just in the top 70 overall. But it remains a highly popular choice for applicants: the numbers starting degrees were at record levels in 2015 after an increase of 13 per cent on the previous year.

The university also has a strong international profile, notably through a global partnership with the Association of Chartered Certified Accountants, which gives Brookes far more students than any other UK university – over 200,000 – taking its qualifications in other countries.

In 2015, the university celebrated the 150th anniversary of its establishment as the Oxford School of Art. There is a tradition of innovation that dates back to its time as a polytechnic, when it pioneered the modular degree system that has swept British higher education. The latest example is the grade point average (GPA) system that it introduced to give its students a more accurate assessment of their work on graduation. Students still receive the traditional British Honours degree classification as well, but all their marks from the first year onwards now count towards their GPA, which has strong recognition overseas.

The main campus at Headington is almost unrecognisable even from five years ago. The award-winning Abercrombie Building opened in 2013 for architecture students and the £132-million John Henry Brookes Building followed a year later and was rated among the top 15 new buildings in the UK that year. It brings together the library and teaching space with the students' union and support services.

The university is spending £13 million a year on refurbishment across all campuses and additional building at Headington and the Harcourt Hill Campus, which houses the School of Education. The Faculty of Business is expected to move from the Wheatley Campus into modernised facilities in Headington in 2017. Wheatley will close completely by 2022, but continues to be the base for engineering and technology for now. The university is a Government-designated regional centre for motorsport and high-performance engineering, with graduates in all F1 teams.

Headington Campus
Gypsy Lane
Oxford OX3 0BP

01865 741111 (enquiries)
query@brookes.ac.uk
www.brookes.ac.uk
www.brookesunion.org.uk
Affiliation: University
Alliance

***The Times and Sunday Times* Rankings**

Overall Ranking: **69** (last year: 55)

Teaching quality:	53	81.3%
Student experience:	=59	84%
Research quality:	57	11.4%
Entry standards:	61	338
Student–staff ratio:	=96	18.3
Services & facilities/student:	119	£1,301
Expected completion rate:	=41	90%
Good honours:	47	74.9%
Graduate prospects:	71	70.9%

Brookes moved its activities in Swindon to a new, larger site in autumn 2016 after seven years delivering nursing and healthcare courses in the town. The new Swindon Campus, featuring a library, teaching spaces and skills labs, offers the potential for further growth and development, as well as upgrading the facilities. Brookes partners with Swindon College to deliver Foundation and degree courses and is also a co-sponsor of the town's university technical college (UTC Swindon) for 14–19 year olds.

The university excelled in the 2014 Research Excellence Framework, when it entered more academics than most of its peer group and still saw almost 60 per cent of its work rated as world-leading or internationally excellent. There were particularly good results in architecture, English and history. The overall performance produced a 41 per cent rise in research funding, among the top ten increases in England.

There have been accolades, too, in teaching. Ofsted rates the primary teacher training as outstanding and nine Brookes academics now have National Teaching Fellowships.

The university's Oxford location is an advantage in student recruitment. It is particularly popular with independent schools, which provide almost a quarter of the undergraduates – much the highest proportion among the post-1992 non-specialist universities and twice the national average for the university's subjects and entry grades. Brookes has been trying to attract more students from state schools and has targeted areas in Oxfordshire and the wider region.

The impressive sports facilities include a 25-metre swimming pool and 9-hole golf course. Brookes is home to the top university squad for young rowers aiming to get into Team GB, and Katherine Grainger, the rowing silver-medallist at the Rio Olympics following her gold in London, became Chancellor of the university in 2015. The cricketers combine with Oxford University to take on county teams.

The students' union runs one of the biggest entertainment venues in Oxford, a city that can be expensive, but which offers enough to satisfy most students.

Tuition fees

» Fees for UK/EU students 2017–18 — £9,250
  Foundation degrees at partner colleges — £6,160–£7,200
  Bachelor degrees at partner colleges — £7,200
  Placement year / Year abroad — £1,380
» UK fees are expected to increase by the rate of inflation from 2018–19 onwards.
» Fees for international students 2017–18 — £12,640–£13,730
» Check the university's website for the latest information on fees, scholarships, bursaries and other forms of student support.

Students

Undergraduates:	11,505	(2,030)
Postgraduates:	1,845	(2,080)
Mature students:	25.0%	
International students:	15.3%	
Applications per place:	6.6	
From state-sector schools:	75.9%	
From working-class homes:	27.9%	
Satisfaction with students' union	43%	

For detailed information about sports facilities:
www.brookes.ac.uk/brookes-sport

Accommodation

Number of places and costs refer to 2016–17
University-provided places: 4,700
Percentage catered: 3%
Catered cost: £147.46 a week (38 weeks).
Self-catered cost: £107.59 – £170.32; £187.00 – £200.57 (studio).
First years selecting Oxford Brookes as their Firm choice and meeting all the deadlines are given preference for housing.
International students: as above.
www.brookes.ac.uk/students/accommodation

Plymouth University

Plymouth has moved up five places in the latest edition of our league table – a welcome recovery after dropping more than 25 places in four years. Professor Judith Petts, who became Vice-Chancellor in 2016 after moving from Southampton, will be hoping to restore the university's fortunes after a turbulent period in which her predecessor was suspended and later replaced without explanation.

Plymouth has not been without recent successes: only two post-1992 universities produced better results in the 2014 Research Excellence Framework (REF) and *Times Higher Education* magazine ranks it among the 60 leading universities in the world that are under 50 years old.

Plymouth entered a far larger proportion of its academics for the REF than most of its peer group and still saw nearly two-thirds of its research judged world-leading or internationally excellent. The university also topped the People and Planet Green League of environmental performance in 2015.

Over £200 million has been spent on the main city campus. The library has been extended and upgraded and the students' union refurbished. There have been new buildings for the Faculty of Health and Human Sciences and the Plymouth Institute of Education, as well as a £35-million arts complex. The £1-million Immersive Vision Theatre is thought to be the first of its kind at a UK university, giving the feeling of being "in", rather than just observing, different types of image. The £19-million Marine Building contains the country's most advanced wave tanks, a navigation centre with ship simulator, and business incubation space for companies in the marine renewables sector. A new Marine Station opened in 2014, with facilities for scientific diver training, as did a £7-million centre for the performing arts, which has teaching and research facilities, a 250-seat venue and unparalleled disabled access for students.

Plymouth is the only post-1992 university with its own medical school since ending its partnership with Exeter University in the management of the former Peninsula College of Medicine and Dentistry. The school had an initial entry of only 75 students taking medicine, although Plymouth kept all 50 of Peninsula's places in dentistry. It has already expanded to more than 300 students through an increase in core numbers and the addition of degrees in biomedical and healthcare sciences. The university is the largest provider of nursing, midwifery and health professional education and training in the region. Research facilities for the medical school costing £15 million will open in 2017.

With some 26,000 students, Plymouth

Drake Circus
Plymouth
PL4 8AA
01752 585858 (enquiries)
admissions@plymouth.ac.uk
www.plymouth.ac.uk
www.upsu.com
Affiliation: University
   Alliance

The Times and Sunday Times Rankings

Overall Ranking: **80** (last year: =85)

Teaching quality:	58	81.1%
Student experience:	=77	83.2%
Research quality:	56	15.9%
Entry standards:	85	314
Student–staff ratio:	68	16.4
Services & facilities/student:	101	£1,555
Expected completion rate:	=71	84.9%
Good honours:	71	69.9%
Graduate prospects:	78	69.8%

is the region's largest higher education institution and was the first university to be awarded Regional Growth Fund money to promote economic development. It has one of the country's top ten business incubation facilities – part of its managed portfolio of £100 million worth of incubation and innovation assets. In 2013, it became the first university in the world to be awarded the Social Enterprise Mark, the only independent accreditation of social enterprise. Plymouth was awarded national teaching centres in health and social care, experiential learning in environmental and natural sciences, institutional partnerships, and education for sustainable development – all of which have now been brought into the university's core activities. Its academics have won 20 National Teaching Fellowships, one of the best performances of any university.

Plymouth is a partner in the Combined Universities in Cornwall, which is boosting further and higher education in the county. The university has a unique relationship with its 18 partner colleges, which constitute a faculty of the university, and have shared £3.5 million in capital investment. They spread from Cornwall to Somerset, taking in Jersey, and have 10,000 students studying university courses. The intake reflects Plymouth's position as the working-class hub of the South West, with over 94 per cent of students state-educated and around a third from the poorest social classes. Some 12,000 students undertake work-based learning or placements with employability skills embedded throughout the curriculum, while the Plymouth Award recognises extra-curricular achievements.

Student facilities include a new £3-million Health and Wellbeing Centre and a 1,300-bed student village costing £15 million.

Upgraded facilities for water sports and an £850,000 fitness centre have added to the sports facilities, while a range of sports scholarships and bursaries support high-fliers. The university has a partnership with Plymouth Albion Rugby Club to promote and support sport in the city and it invested £2.5 million in the £45-million Plymouth Life Centre. There are sessions exclusively for students at the city's international-standard swimming and diving centre, and the city centre is not short of student-oriented nightlife.

Tuition fees

- » Fees for UK/EU students 2017–18 £9,250
  Placement year £1,230
- » UK fees are expected to increase by the rate of inflation from 2018–19 onwards.
- » Fees for international students 2016–17 £12,250–£12,500
  Medicine £17,800–£33,000
- » Check the university's website for the latest information on fees, scholarships, bursaries and other forms of student support.

Students

Undergraduates:	19,390	(3,335)
Postgraduates:	1,460	(1,715)
Mature students:	25.1%	
International students:	7.9%	
Applications per place:	5.2	
From state-sector schools:	94.1%	
From working-class homes:	31.9%	
Satisfaction with students' union	82%	

For detailed information about sports facilities: www.upsu.com/sports/clubs

Accommodation

Number of places and costs refer to 2016–17
University-provided places: 2,821
Percentage catered: 0%
Self-catered costs: £97.30 – £165.00 a week (40–41 weeks).
First years are guaranteed university if conditions are met.
International students: Apply in the same way as UK students.
residencelife@plymouth.ac.uk
www.plymouth.ac.uk/student-life/services/accommodation

University of Portsmouth

Portsmouth is the most affordable city in the UK for students, according to the annual survey by NatWest bank. Portsmouth students pay slightly more rent than the UK average, but work the most hours and have the highest income from part-time jobs during term-time. They still have time to socialise since Portsmouth was also third in the survey as the most sociable place to study.

But there is more to Portsmouth than affordability – it is among the top ten post-1992 universities in our league table, with good rates of student satisfaction even after a slight decline on last year's stellar scores in the National Student Survey. A number of subjects now offer common first years, with specialisation in later years, allowing students to select final degree programmes that suit their skills and interests.

Teaching in all subjects is concentrated on the Guildhall campus in the centre of Portsmouth, with most residential accommodation nearby. The campus has undergone extensive redevelopment. A £14-million wing on the Eldon Building created an additional 3,000 square metres of space and provided the Faculty of Creative and Cultural Industries with purpose-built facilities, including a 200-seat screening room, exhibition space and a range of studios and seminar rooms. Students in the faculty also benefit from a partnership with the New Theatre Royal, which enables them to use the facilities in a £10-million building that opened in 2015 alongside the original theatre.

Provision in engineering and science will be expanded after the opening of an £11-million Future Technology Centre in 2017. The centre will include simulation, visualisation, modelling and prototyping facilities, particularly to encourage more female students to take science and technology courses. Already there are 8,500 undergraduates taking STEM (science, technology, engineering and maths) subjects, as Portsmouth's intake has hit record levels.

The university has a growing reputation in health subjects. The £9-million Dental Academy trains student dentists in their final year at King's College London in a team-based setting with dental therapists and hygienists. More than 600 radiographers, paramedics, medical technologists, pharmacists, and social workers graduate each year. New courses have been announced to address regional shortages in nursing and in optometry, with a degree in adult nursing taking its first students in February 2017.

Health subjects led the way to a good performance in the 2014 Research Excellence Framework. Almost two-thirds of the research was rated as world-leading

University House
Winston Churchill Avenue
Portsmouth
Hampshire PO1 2UP

023 9284 5566 (admissions)
admissions@port.ac.uk
www.port.ac.uk
www.upsu.net
Affiliation: University Alliance

The Times and Sunday Times Rankings

Overall Ranking: **59** (last year: 59)

Teaching quality:	=34	82.7%
Student experience:	=36	85.4%
Research quality:	70	8.6%
Entry standards:	=71	323
Student–staff ratio:	=49	15.4
Services & facilities/student:	63	£1,952
Expected completion rate:	=63	85.8%
Good honours:	63	71.2%
Graduate prospects:	62	72%

or internationally excellent. The best results were in dentistry, nursing and pharmacy, and in physics, with around 90 per cent of the submission reaching the top two categories. A Forensic Innovation Centre opened in 2015, with students and researchers working alongside police forensic scientists and digital crime-fighters in the UK's first operational police forensic research facility to be based on a university campus.

Portsmouth also has one of the largest language departments in the country, teaching six languages to degree level and offering free language courses to all students. About 1,000 students go abroad for part of their course, and at least as many come from the continent. The university is an official centre of teaching and research about the EU, and also has 3,000 international students from further afield.

Employability skills and training are embedded throughout 250 degree programmes. High-quality simulated learning environments, such as a mock courtroom, pharmacy, journalism newsroom, forensic suite and dental wards provide real-life professional skills.

Almost a third of undergraduates come from the four lowest socio-economic groups, well below the national average for the university's subjects and entry qualifications. Much of the extra income from £9,250 fees is being spent on initiatives to broaden the intake. Unlike many other universities,

Portsmouth is also maintaining its spending on bursaries, believing that most of the recipients would have struggled to stay on their courses without financial support.

A £6.5-million student centre caters for the multicultural population of the university and includes alcohol-free areas. The university library has more than 1,400 study spaces, a mix of silent, group or social study areas.

Modernised sport, exercise and fitness facilities include gyms, dance studios and a sports hall. The university's seafront location provides an excellent base for water sports, and nearly £1 million has been invested in an all-weather 3G pitch, suitable for football, rugby, lacrosse and American football.

From 2017, two new halls of residence will open in the centre of Portsmouth, ensuring that university accommodation is available to all who apply in time and make Portsmouth their firm choice.

Tuition fees

» Fees for UK/EU students 2017–18 £9,250
Courses at partner colleges £6,165
Placement year / Year abroad £925
» UK fees are expected to increase by the rate of inflation from 2018–19 onwards.
» Fees for international students 2017–18 £12,600–£14,400
» Check the university's website for the latest information on fees, scholarships, bursaries and other forms of student support.

Students

Undergraduates:	16,455	(1,860)
Postgraduates:	1,540	(1,770)
Mature students:	13.3%	
International students:	16.6%	
Applications per place:	6.0	
From state-sector schools:	95.9%	
From working-class homes:	32.9%	
Satisfaction with students' union	79%	

For detailed information about sports facilities:
www.sportportsmouth.co.uk

Accommodation

Number of places and costs refer to 2016–17
University-provided places: 3,700
Percentage catered: 20%
Catered costs: £110 – £155 a week (40 weeks)
Self-catered costs: £87 – £146 (40 weeks)
Most UK/EU first years are offered university accommodation if conditions are met.
International students: guaranteed housing for first year of study if conditions are met.
www.port.ac.uk/why-portsmouth/accommodation

Queen Margaret University

Queen Margaret (QMU) is working towards including a work placement and/or an industrial partner for every programme as part of a focus on employability. Graduate prospects is one of the measures that has held the university back in our league table, but there are partnerships with a growing number of organisations, including Ryder Cup Europe, and a highly successful Employer Mentoring Scheme. The programme matches third- and fourth-year students with experienced professionals who have relevant industry experience.

Academically, QMU is focusing on its strengths and channelling investment into three flagship areas: health and rehabilitation, sustainable business, and culture and creativity. It expects to add others, such as the area of food and drink, in the next few years.

It has already launched the Scottish Centre for Food Development and Innovation and has a partnership with the Edinburgh New Town Cookery School, run by a former graduate of QMU, to support students on the international hospitality management degree.

Named after Saint Margaret, the 11th-century Queen of Scotland, the institution dates back to 1875 and was originally a school of cookery for women. The university moved into an impressive, modern campus designed in consultation with the students in the seaside town of Musselburgh, to the southeast of Edinburgh, when it was awarded university status in 2007. The campus, which has won a string of awards, is one of the most environmentally sustainable in the UK, exceeding current standards. QMU has made sustainability a top priority in the curriculum as well as in the way it operates.

Specialist laboratories and clinics are well equipped. The nursing simulation lab, for example, is set out like a hospital ward, helping to instil students with the confidence to move on easily to a work placement or career in the NHS or private practice. A high-quality learning resource centre, parts of which are open 24 hours a day, offers a variety of study spaces.

There are now more than 6,000 students at all levels, three-quarters of them female, divided between two schools: Arts, Social Sciences and Management, and Health Sciences. The university promises "inter-professional" teaching and research to encourage the professions to work better together.

Health is an area of particular strength: QMU has the broadest range of allied health courses in Scotland, from dietetics, podiatry and audiology, to art therapy, music therapy and health psychology. Courses in international health attract students from all

Queen Margaret University Drive
Musselburgh EH21 6UU

0131 474 0000 (enquiries)
admissions@qmu.ac.uk
www.qmu.ac.uk
www.qmusu.org.uk
Affiliation: none

The Times and Sunday Times Rankings

Overall Ranking: **=101** (last year: 96)

Teaching quality:	64	80.6%
Student experience:	=73	83.3%
Research quality:	79	6.6%
Entry standards:	=50	352
Student–staff ratio:	=96	18.3
Services & facilities/student:	110	£1,399
Expected completion rate:	=108	79.7%
Good honours:	55	73.2%
Graduate prospects:	119	57.8%

over the world.

The interdisciplinary drama and performance degree draws together the university's established strengths in acting, screen work, community theatre, contemporary performance and playwriting to reflect the current needs of a changing profession. QMU also offers a degree in costume design and construction.

Research ratings improved considerably in the 2014 Research Excellence Framework. Although only 22 per cent of the eligible staff were entered, almost 60 per cent of their work was considered world-leading or internationally excellent. Renowned for its research in speech and language sciences, QMU saw 92 per cent of its work in this area rated in the top two categories, placing the university second in the UK and first in Scotland.

In 2016, QMU launched new centres for research and knowledge exchange, which place academics in direct contact with individuals in business, industry and the health profession. One aim is to inform teaching practice and ensure that students' learning is current and relevant.

QMU operates an innovative Associate Student scheme with three local colleges. Associate Students are fully enrolled Queen Margaret University students from day one – and can even live there – but for the first one or two years they are based at the college on a linked certificate or diploma course before transferring to the university.

The campus is located next to Musselburgh train station, from where Edinburgh city centre is only a six-minute journey. There is also a frequent bus service from the campus to the city centre. The campus features include a students' union building, indoor and outdoor sports facilities, a variety of catering outlets and landscaped gardens with a range of environmental features.

There are 800 residential places on the campus, about 300 of them larger, premier rooms with double beds and more space. As part of its accommodation service, QMU offers a Residence Life Programme (ResLife) run in partnership with the sports centre and students' union that includes a range of social, educational, recreational and cultural activities both on and off campus. The aim is to help students settle in and feel welcomed and supported, as well as teaching them new skills.

Tuition fees

» Fees for Scottish and EU students 2017–18   No fee
» Fees for non-Scottish UK (RUK) students 2017–18   £7,000
» Fees for international students 2017–18   £11,250–£12,500
» There are particular support schemes for RUK students.
» Check the university's website for the latest information on fees, scholarships, bursaries and other forms of student support.

Students

Undergraduates:	3,030	(565)
Postgraduates:	495	(1,175)
Mature students:	27.3%	
International students:	18.3%	
Applications per place:	8.1	
From state-sector schools:	94.7%	
From working-class homes:	34.4%	
Satisfaction with students' union	44%	

For detailed information about sports facilities:
www.qmu.ac.uk/sports

Accommodation

Number of places and costs refer to 2016–17
University-provided places: 800
Percentage catered: 0%
Self-catered costs: £99 – £118 a week (40 or 50 week contract).
First years are guaranteed accommodation. Residential and age restrictions apply.
International students: guaranteed housing.
accommodation@qmu.ac.uk
www.qmu.ac.uk/accommodation

Queen Mary, University of London

Queen Mary (QMUL) appears to have succumbed to the "London effect" in the National Student Survey, dropping into the bottom 20 on both of our measures of student satisfaction and falling six places in *The Times and Sunday Times* league table as a result. In previous years, QMUL had maintained higher rates of satisfaction than most of its peers in the capital, which tend to struggle on this measure.

It does not suffer from the dispersed nature of other London institutions, with most of its undergraduates both taught and housed on a self-contained campus in the increasingly fashionable East End of London. Even the large medical school, Barts and the London School of Medicine and Dentistry, is based in nearby Whitechapel. Both applications and enrolments have risen by a third since the college joined the Russell Group of leading research universities in 2012.

Improvements in the Mile End campus that have cost £98 million over five years are continuing. The latest development will be a new Graduate Centre, opening in early 2017, for QMUL's growing population of postgraduates, which will also provide new premises for the School of Economics and Finance. The physics laboratories have been upgraded and refurbishment of the engineering and mathematics buildings will be complete before the start of the 2017 academic year.

The historic People's Palace, which brought education to the Victorian masses, is still Queen Mary's most recognisable feature, and has been restored to host cultural events for the institution and the local community. The campus includes an impressive learning resource centre and one of the largest residential complexes at any London university. The £21-million ArtsTwo building features a drama studio and lecture theatre. There is even room on campus for the second-oldest Jewish cemetery in England, dating from the 18th century.

The medical school, which is rated in the top 100 in the world by QS, is based in the £45-million Blizard Building. Its Institute of Dentistry moved into the first new dental school to be built in the UK for 40 years, when it occupied its new facilities costing £78 million in the Royal London Hospital in 2014.

Also on the Whitechapel campus are the Queen Mary BioEnterprises Innovation Centre for science companies and the Centre of the Cell, the first science education centre in the world to be located within working biomedical research laboratories. QMUL has launched a life sciences initiative, bringing together

---

Mile End Road
London E1 4NS

020 7882 5511 (admissions)
admissions@qmul.ac.uk
www.qmul.ac.uk
www.qmsu.org
Affiliation: Russell Group

Edinburgh
Belfast
Cardiff
LONDON

The Times and Sunday Times Rankings

Overall Ranking: **40** (last year: 34)

Teaching quality:	117	76.7%
Student experience:	112	80.7%
Research quality:	19	37.9%
Entry standards:	=28	417
Student–staff ratio:	11	11.9
Services & facilities/student:	25	£2,512
Expected completion rate:	38	90.5%
Good honours:	=51	74.3%
Graduate prospects:	31	79.8%

the faculties of science and engineering, humanities and social sciences, and Barts and the London School of Medicine and Dentistry to work together on personalised healthcare and to address major public health issues both locally and worldwide.

Queen Mary is also opening a new medical school in Malta. The Medicine MBBS Malta programme will be taught and delivered by QMUL staff on the islands of Malta and Gozo. It will closely match the London programme, with first students arriving in September 2017.

Medicine and the other health subjects did well in the 2014 Research Excellence Framework, but the best results came in the humanities. Around 95 per cent of the research in linguistics and in music, drama and the performing arts was rated as world-leading or internationally excellent. Over 85 per cent of QMUL's entire submission reached the top two categories, with chemistry, medicine, computer science and engineering doing particularly well.

Most lectures are filmed and made available online to allow students to go back over parts that they may not have understood.

Queen Mary has by far the highest proportion of undergraduates from working-class homes in the Russell Group – more than a third. Many come from London's ethnic minority groups and QMUL also attracts 20 per cent of its students from 155 countries outside the UK. There is a flourishing exchange programme, which includes universities in the USA, Australia, New Zealand and Japan, as well as Europe, while more than 2,000 students are in Beijing taking joint degrees from QMUL and the Beijing University of Posts and Telecommunications.

For Mile End students, social life centres on the campus, which features a refurbished students' union with a new bar. A subsidised health and fitness centre has helped improve the sports facilities.

Students welcome the relatively low prices (for the capital) in east London, and their proximity to the lively youth culture of Spitalfields, Shoreditch and Brick Lane. Queen Mary students can use the sports facilities at the Queen Elizabeth Olympic Park, including the Copper Box indoor arena and the Aquatic Centre's swimming pool.

Tuition fees

» Fees for UK/EU students 2017–18 £9,250
  Year abroad £1,385
  Placement year £1,850
» UK fees are expected to increase by the rate of inflation from 2018–19 onwards.
» Fees for international students 2017–18 £14,500–£19,550
  Medicine and dentistry £31,800
» Check the university's website for the latest information on fees, scholarships, bursaries and other forms of student support.

Students

Undergraduates:	11,375	(15)
Postgraduates:	3,540	(1,030)
Mature students:	9.8%	
International students:	23.3%	
Applications per place:	9.2	
From state-sector schools:	87.9%	
From working-class homes:	37%	
Satisfaction with students' union	71%	

For detailed information about sports facilities: www.qmsu.org/sportandfitness

Accommodation

Number of places and costs refer to 2016–17
University-provided places: 2,490
Percentage catered: 0%
Self-catered costs: £127 – £179 a week for a single room.
First years giving Queen Mary as first choice get priority, if terms and deadline conditions are met.
International students: all new applicants meeting the criteria are judged equally with home students living outside Greater London.
www.residences.qmul.ac.uk

Queen's University, Belfast

Queen's has returned to the top 30 in our league table after an absence of three years, with a rise of five places that (jointly with Nottingham) is the biggest in the leading group. Higher rates of student satisfaction, particularly in the sections of the National Student Survey relating to teaching, feedback and academic support, are mainly responsible.

The university was already in the top 15 for research after entering 95 per cent of its academics for the 2014 Research Excellence Framework, a proportion matched only by Cambridge. Despite the large submission, 77 per cent of the research was considered world-leading or internationally excellent and 14 subject areas were ranked in the UK's top 20.

The university has since won a Queen's Anniversary Prize for research and technology transfer in cyber security, and established of four Global Research Institutes in Food Security; Health Sciences; Electronics, Communications and Information Technology; and Global Peace, Security and Justice. Queen's claims to be the UK's top university for the commercialisation of intellectual property and the establishment of knowledge transfer partnerships, of which it has 350.

A member of the Russell Group, Queen's is recognised as Northern Ireland's premier university, with graduates in senior positions in 80 of the province's top 100 companies. Strictly non-denominational teaching is enshrined in a charter which has guaranteed student representation and equal rights for women since 1908. Queen's was one of four university colleges for the whole of Ireland in the nineteenth century, and still draws students from all over the island. However, the majority come from Northern Ireland, and Queen's suffers in the comparison of entry grades because relatively few sixth-formers in the province take four A levels.

The university is based in an attractive part of South Belfast, incorporating a significant part of the Victorian suburb which grew up around the iconic Lanyon building. Queen's has invested £350 million over the last decade enhancing the campus and the surrounding conservation areas – of the university's 250 buildings, 97 are listed – while providing cutting-edge facilities for education and research. The university plans to spend as much again over the next ten years.

Recent developments have seen the opening of the Wellcome-Wolfson Institute for Experimental Medicine, part of the £175-million Institute for Health Sciences; the refurbishment of the Ashby Building to create an engineering complex, and the opening of a Graduate School in the

---

University Road
Belfast BT7 1NN

028 9097 3838 (admissions)
admissions@qub.ac.uk
www.qub.ac.uk
www.qubsu.org
Affiliation: Russell Group

The Times and Sunday Times **Rankings**

Overall Ranking: **26** (last year: 31)

Teaching quality:	33	82.8%
Student experience:	8	88.7%
Research quality:	14	39.7%
Entry standards:	39	388
Student–staff ratio:	46	15.1
Services & facilities/student:	41	£2,151
Expected completion rate:	=26	92.6%
Good honours:	32	78.3%
Graduate prospects:	28	80.3%

historic Lynn Building, which includes an imposing central open-plan, vaulted space with masonry gothic arches. Further developments include new buildings for computer science and for law, where there is a moot courtroom allowing students to hone their advocacy skills. Both are now completed.

Fees for students from Northern Ireland have been less than half those charged to students from the rest of the UK, but serious cuts in Government funding may force the university to raise them to between £5,200 and £6,300 for those starting in 2017. Queen's already plans to reduce the undergraduate intake by 1,000 over three years to cope with an £8-million cut in its grant.

The university has 1,700 international students and is a favourite destination for American Fulbright Scholars. It is also among the top ten universities in Europe for the number of students who go on work placements abroad as part of the Erasmus scheme. Undergraduates are encouraged to take language programmes from a "virtual" language laboratory, which provides online tuition from any computer in the university.

IT facilities are good: Queen's was the first institution to meet the national target of providing at least one computer workstation for every five undergraduate students. A new £2-million wireless service has been rolled out to all areas of the campus in 2016.

Queen's boasts the only full-time university cinema in the UK, as well as an art gallery and theatre, all of which are open to students and the wider community alike. The much-improved city centre is not short of nightlife, but the social scene is still concentrated on the students' union and the surrounding area.

Sports facilities, which include a university cottage in the Mourne mountains, have seen a £20-million programme of investment. The Upper Malone playing fields feature an arena pitch which can host football, rugby or Gaelic sport, another 14 pitches, a 3-km recreational trail and conference facilities. The Physical Education Centre provides physiotherapy, sports massage and podiatry, and there is a new £1.2-million boathouse on the River Lagan. An Elite Athlete programme offers up to £8,000 of support for leading performers.

Tuition fees

- » Fees for NI/EU students 2017–18 — £4,030
- » Fees for English, Scottish, Welsh (RUK) students — £9,000
- » Fees for international students 2017–18 — £15,100–£18,800
  Medicine — £19,000–£35,900
  Dentistry — £29,140
- » There are particular support schemes for RUK students.
- » Check the university's website for the latest information on fees, scholarships, bursaries and other forms of student support.

Students

Undergraduates:	14,945	(3,915)
Postgraduates:	2,785	(2,210)
Mature students:	18.1%	
International students:	8.7%	
Applications per place:	7.2	
From state-sector schools:	98.5%	
From working-class homes:	31.9%	
Satisfaction with students' union	80%	

For detailed information about sports facilities:
www.queenssport.com

Accommodation

Number of places and costs refer to 2016–17
University-provided places: around 2,000
Percentage catered: 0%
Self-catered costs: £71 – £123 a week.
First-year students are guaranteed accommodation if conditions are met.
International students: as above.
accommodation@qub.ac.uk
www.stayatqueens.com

University of Reading

Reading has announced a £200-million capital investment programme to redevelop its campus facilities in order to become a "larger, vibrant and more sustainable institution" by the university's centenary year of 2026. Some of the projects are already under way and stem directly from student feedback, such as the need for extra study space and better technical resources. They include the redevelopments of the library and URS Building, the creation of the Chancellor's Building and the newly formed School of Architecture, the refurbishment of the Van Emden lecture theatre and the redevelopment of residential accommodation.

Funding has also been approved for two new developments – a Health and Life Sciences Building and an extension of teaching space at Henley Business School. The university is also planning further development of its Thames Valley Science Park, which will eventually provide 800,000 square feet of flexible laboratory and office space in a campus-style setting with a pedestrianised central concourse.

Reading has expanded its intake of undergraduates by more than 25 per cent since 2012 and is likely to grow further in 2016. The attractive main campus, which won four Green Gown environmental awards in a row, is set in 320 acres of parkland on the outskirts of Reading. The £4.4-million renovation of the 'old library' has now been completed, with the addition of a 3-D printer and 24-hour opening. The main library will be renovated and refurbished over the next three years.

Other recent improvements include an extension to the students' union, a refurbished sports centre and two new pavilions, a student services centre and business school, and £100 million on new and redeveloped halls of residence. The £17-million Hopkins Building added laboratories and teaching space for pharmacy and cardiovascular research, and there is a now a world-class Chemical Analysis Facility and an Enterprise Centre which brings together academic expertise with local and international technology-based businesses.

Originally Oxford University's extension college, Reading was one of only two universities established between the two world wars. As well as its two sites in Reading, the university also owns 2,000 acres of farmland at nearby Sonning and Shinfield, where the renowned Centre for Dairy Research (CEDAR) is located.

Around a fifth of undergraduates now come from outside the UK, many of them attracted by Reading's global reputation for courses and research in agriculture and development. The former

---

Whiteknights
PO Box 217
Reading RG6 6AH

0118 378 8372
ugadmissions@reading.ac.uk
www.reading.ac.uk
www.rusu.co.uk
Affiliation: none

***The Times and Sunday Times* Rankings**

Overall Ranking: **31** (last year: 32)

Teaching quality:	=70	80.2%
Student experience:	=42	84.8%
Research quality:	29	36.5%
Entry standards:	45	372
Student–staff ratio:	=38	14.7
Services & facilities/student:	38	£2,175
Expected completion rate:	=28	92.2%
Good honours:	=22	80.6%
Graduate prospects:	54	73.6%

Henley Management College became the university's business school in 2008. The college's attractive site, on the banks of the river at Henley-on-Thames, houses postgraduate and executive programmes, while undergraduates are taught on the main Whiteknights campus.

Reading has also opened a campus in Malaysia focusing on psychology, real estate, quantity surveying, pharmacy, and finance and business management. The campus for 3,000 students, at Edu-City on the Iskandar peninsular, on the southern tip of Malaysia, is shared with Newcastle and Southampton universities, which specialise in different disciplines.

Reading remains just outside the top 30 in our league table despite a strong performance in the 2014 Research Excellence Framework (REF), in which real estate, planning and construction management were among the leading players. The new School of Architecture will help the university to capitalise on a strong reputation in the built environment. Reading entered more academics for assessment in the REF than most of its peers and still saw almost 80 per cent of its research rated as world-leading or internationally excellent.

All undergraduates also have the opportunity to take work placements as part of their course, as well as taking career management skills modules that contribute five credits towards their degree classification. The online system, which has 200 web pages of advice, exercises and information, has been bought by 30 other universities and colleges. Sessions are delivered jointly by academics and careers advisors, with input from alumni and leading employers.

The halls of residence are either on or within easy walking distance of campus and the large students' union has been voted among the best in Britain.

There are over 50 sports clubs and representative teams have a good record in inter-university competitions. Water sports are strong, with off-campus boathouses on the Thames and a sailing and canoeing club nearby.

Reading has plenty of nightlife and an award-winning shopping centre. Students who live off campus can make use of the free bus service to take them back into the town centre. London is easily accessible, but the cost of living is on a par with the capital.

Tuition fees

» Fees for UK/EU students 2017–18   £9,250
    Placement year / Year abroad   £1,385
» UK fees are expected to increase by the rate of inflation from 2018–19 onwards.
» Fees for international students 2017–18   £15,300–£18,860
» Check the university's website for the latest information on fees, scholarships, bursaries and other forms of student support.

Students

Undergraduates:	9,575	(90)
Postgraduates:	3,020	(1,645)
Mature students:	8.5%	
International students:	18.9%	
Applications per place:	7.3	
From state-sector schools:	85.7%	
From working-class homes:	27.3%	
Satisfaction with students' union	83%	

For detailed information about sports facilities:
www.sport.reading.ac.uk

Accommodation

Number of places and costs refer to 2016–17
University-provided places: about 5,000.
Percentage catered: 18%
Catered costs: £139.82 – £178.25 (40 weeks, catering during terms).
Self-catered costs: £101.01 – £161.70 (40–51 weeks).
First-years are guaranteed a place if conditions are met.
International students: new students guaranteed housing if conditions are met.
www.reading.ac.uk/ready-to-study/accommodation

Robert Gordon University

Robert Gordon University (RGU) has suffered one of the biggest falls in this year's table – 18 places – largely because of lower student satisfaction and a drop in its traditionally stellar graduate employment rate. The university is still in the top 40 for graduate prospects, but it was in the top 20 in the 2016 *Guide* – and for many years before that.

As an institution with close ties to the North Sea oil industry, Robert Gordon has been hit hard by the drop in the price of oil and the impact on employers in the Aberdeen area. Even international student recruitment has been affected, although the overall numbers starting degrees have remained steady. At the start of the decade RGU was the leading post-1992 university in our table and on the verge of the top 50; it is now more than 30 places lower.

Named after an 18th-century philanthropist, Robert Gordon University has a pedigree in education that goes back 250 years. The university now offers about 300 courses and there is also a partnership with North East Scotland College, which allows students to progress from a college-based Higher National Diploma to the third year of an RGU degree course.

The university has invested heavily in research, but it has been reviewing its strategy after making a relatively small submission to the 2014 Research Excellence Framework and slipping down our ranking on this measure. More than 40 per cent of the work assessed was placed in the top two categories, with the best results coming in health subjects and communication and media studies.

A £135-million capital programme was completed in 2016, bringing the university together on one site for the first time. All teaching now takes place on the Garthdee campus, on the south side of Aberdeen, overlooking the River Dee.

A new building for the Scott Sutherland School of Architecture and Built Environment was the last piece of the jigsaw, although there will be further improvements following the sale of part of the university's historic city centre site.

The schools of engineering, computing science and digital media, pharmacy and life sciences moved from the Schoolhill site in the city centre in 2013. A striking green glass library tower with spectacular views over the river and city has become a landmark at the heart of the campus.

Previous developments included specialist facilities for the Faculty of Health and Social Care. The Aberdeen Business School, designed by Norman Foster, has been upgraded with new teaching and student learning spaces and an open plan area with IT access, group study areas,

Garthdee House
Garthdee Road
Aberdeen AB10 7QB

01224 262728 (enquiries)
ugoffice@rgu.ac.uk
www.rgu.ac.uk
www.rguunion.co.uk
Affiliation: none

The Times and Sunday Times Rankings

Overall Ranking: **=86** (last year: =69)

Teaching quality:	=97	78.8%
Student experience:	=89	82.3%
Research quality:	=103	4%
Entry standards:	37	392
Student–staff ratio:	99	18.4
Services & facilities/student:	111	£1,396
Expected completion rate:	88	83.1%
Good honours:	65	70.5%
Graduate prospects:	=39	77.5%

exhibition and seminar space.

With nursing and health sciences now accounting for 40 per cent of the places, RGU gives itself the soubriquet of the Professional University. Work placements lasting up to a year have become the norm on all the university's courses.

The creative industries are a growth area and there is a full portfolio of courses in business, design and engineering. But the university is still best known for its links with the offshore industries. The RGU Oil and Gas Institute has a DART (Drilling and Advanced Rig Training) simulator, providing a full-scale reproduction of an offshore platform or land rig.

Like many modern universities, Robert Gordon recruits most of its students locally, with large numbers taking part-time courses. Efforts to extend access beyond the normal higher education catchment have produced a diverse student population, with almost a third of undergraduates coming from working-class homes and 93 per cent from state schools or colleges.

There is a strong focus on new technology. An award-winning virtual campus was launched with an online course in e-business for postgraduates. The Moodle system is used by both on-campus and distance learning students, providing teaching, notes, online forums for discussion and electronic submission options.

Aberdeen sometimes seems to be a long way to go for students from other parts of the UK, but train and air links are excellent, and the city regularly features in the top ten for quality of life.

There is a £12-million sports and leisure centre, which includes a centre of excellence for the region in hockey, as well as a 25-metre swimming pool, three gyms, a climbing wall and bouldering room, a café bar, three exercise studios and a large sports hall. Sports scholarships are available to budding athletes, with Olympic swimmer Hannah Miley among the recipients.

Although private sector accommodation can be expensive, there are enough residential places to guarantee housing to first years from outside the locality and all first years are eligible to apply for a place in halls.

Tuition fees

» Fees for Scottish and EU students 2017–18   No fee
» Fees for non-Scottish UK (RUK) students 2017–18

                 £5,000–£6,750

    Pharmacy   £8,820
» Fees for international students 2017–18   £12,000–£15,300
» There are particular support schemes for RUK students.
» Check the university's website for the latest information on fees, scholarships, bursaries and other forms of student support.

Students

Undergraduates:	7,530	(1,575)
Postgraduates:	1,650	(2,490)
Mature students:	28.2%	
International students:	14.9%	
Applications per place:	5.4	
From state-sector schools:	93.4%	
From working-class homes:	32%	
Satisfaction with students' union	50%	

For detailed information about sports facilities:
www.rgu.ac.uk/student-life/campus-life/rgu-sport

Accommodation

Number of places and costs refer to 2016-17
University-provided places: 1,750
Percentage catered: 0%
Self-catered costs: £103 (single) – £200.00 (flat) a week.
All first-year students are eligible to apply for student accommodation.
International students: as above.
accommodation@rgu.ac.uk
www.rgu.ac.uk/student-life/accommodation

Roehampton University

A four-storey library adding 300 study spaces and costing £34 million will be open to the public as well as students. The centrepiece of an £80-million development programme for Roehampton's attractive main campus in south-west London should be ready in time for new students in 2017.

The programme is also expanding and improving the university's student accommodation. The Grade II-listed Downshire House is being refurbished and three new buildings erected in its grounds to create 210 new student bedrooms. Another 360 new bedrooms have been added for 2016 on the Digby Stuart site, which is being landscaped and pedestrianised. Another residential development, 20 minutes from the main campus by public transport, at Vauxhall, includes a swimming pool.

The university is also investing in new teaching facilities, including performance spaces for drama programmes, and media facilities for film and photography.

Although an independent university only since 2004, Roehampton has a distinguished history dating back to the mid-19th century. Whitelands College celebrated its 175th anniversary in 2016 and claims to have been the first in the country to open higher education to women. The university is a collegiate institution with four distinctive colleges, which still maintain some of the traditional ethos of their religious foundations: the Anglican Whitelands, the Roman Catholic Digby Stuart, the Methodist Southlands, and the Froebel, which follows the humanist teachings of Friedrich Froebel. Students need not follow any of these denominations to enrol in the colleges, whose leisure facilities and bars are open to all members of the university. Roehampton also has a Jewish resource centre and Muslim prayer rooms.

All four colleges are based on a single campus, with stunning parkland and lakes, on or adjacent to Roehampton Lane. The Growhampton scheme provides opportunities for students to learn about sustainability, as well as teamwork and leadership skills, through allotments, beehives and an orchard.

Roehampton outperformed all post-1992 universities in the 2014 Research Excellence Framework, entering two-thirds of its eligible academics for assessment and still seeing 66 per cent of its work rated as world-leading or internationally excellent. The university had the most highly rated dance department in the UK, with 94 per cent of research placed in the top two categories, while the results in education and English were among the best in London. Its successes produced a 40 per cent increase in funding for research.

While maintaining its historic strength in

Erasmus House
Roehampton Lane
London SW15 5PU

020 8392 3000
enquiries@roehampton.ac.uk
www.roehampton.ac.uk
www.roehampton
student.com
Affiliation: Cathedrals
Group

The Times and Sunday Times Rankings

Overall Ranking: **78** (last year: 78)

Teaching quality:	=108	77.4%
Student experience:	115	79.8%
Research quality:	50	24.5%
Entry standards:	=121	276
Student–staff ratio:	=43	14.9
Services & facilities/student:	39	£2,171
Expected completion rate:	=113	78.7%
Good honours:	68	70.3%
Graduate prospects:	100	64.2%

education, which still accounts for a quarter of the students, Roehampton has diversified into business, the arts and humanities, social sciences, and the human and life sciences. The School of Law welcomed its first students in 2015 and operates a legal advice clinic for the local community.

The university has also embraced the School Direct system of teacher training, operating in partnership with schools as well as running its own postgraduate and undergraduate training programmes.

An additional attraction on the main campus is the Glion Institute of Higher Education, a Swiss hospitality management college offering undergraduate and postgraduate programmes in its first overseas venture. The university is in partnership with Laureate, Glion's owners, to offer courses online. Roehampton now has 7,000 online students in business, education and psychology, and is adding programmes in public administration, public health and theology. International partnerships include an agreement with the EU Business School to offer Roehampton-accredited degrees to students across the continent.

The Quality Assurance Agency complimented Roehampton on the accessibility of academic staff to students and the positive ways in which they responded to student needs. Graduates are offered mentoring from alumni and internships, while a Santander Internship Scheme provides paid placements for students in local businesses and the chance to study abroad.

Almost all of the undergraduates were state educated, 43 per cent coming from working-class homes. The university does not offer bursaries to students from poor backgrounds, so only those winning scholarships will receive financial support.

Most first years who want a hall place are offered one. While rents are not cheap for those who prefer the private sector, students like the proximity of central London and the attractive suburbs around Roehampton.

The sports facilities on campus have been enhanced, with a new gym, two football pitches, running track and a multi-use games area. The sport performance and rehabilitation centre provides state-of-the-art laboratory facilities and performance coaching. The university is a high-performance centre for British fencing and sitting volleyball.

Tuition fees

- » Fees for UK/EU students 2017–18 £9,250
  Foundation degree £8,150
- » UK fees are expected to increase by the rate of inflation from 2018–19 onwards.
- » Fees for international students 2016–17 £12,500
- » Check the university's website for the latest information on fees, scholarships, bursaries and other forms of student support.

Students

Undergraduates:	5,810	(175)
Postgraduates:	935	(730)
Mature students:	17.9%	
International students:	9.5%	
Applications per place:	5.1	
From state-sector schools:	97%	
From working-class homes:	43%	
Satisfaction with students' union	71%	

For detailed information about sports facilities:
www.roehampton.ac.uk/student-life/sport-at-roehampton

Accommodation

Number of places and costs refer to 2016–17
University-provided places: 2,067
Percentage catered: 0%
Self-catered costs: £109.20 – £128.10 (standard);
£145.95 – £169.05 (en suite) a week.
First years are given priority if conditions are met.
International students: housing is guaranteed for the first year.
accommodation@roehampton.ac.uk
www.roehampton.ac.uk/Accommodation

Royal Agricultural University

The Royal Agricultural University (RAU) is said to be known as the "Oxbridge of the countryside" because of its privileged intake and beautiful campus near Cirencester, in the Cotswolds. Every monarch since Queen Victoria has visited it.

Certainly, the RAU has a global reputation in its field, although its size prevented it from becoming a university until 2013. As the Royal Agricultural College, it was the first institution of its type in the English-speaking world when it was established in 1845 on the initiative of the Fairford and Cirencester Farmers' Club, which was concerned at the lack of government support for education, particularly in relation to agriculture. It now educates students up to PhD level and also delivers degree courses in Hong Kong and China.

Like the other new entrant to our table last year (Norwich University of the Arts), the RAU is still finding its level. Having made its debut on the verge of the top 50, it has dropped 12 places in the new edition, mainly due to a fall in student satisfaction. It is still in the top ten for spending on student facilities and in the top 20 for completion – it was our University of the Year for Student Retention last year.

However, it has one of the lowest scores for research. Only 12 staff were entered for the 2014 Research Excellence Framework – a quarter of those with research contracts – and just 7 per cent of their work was placed in the top two categories.

The number of undergraduates has grown by about 20 per cent since university status was awarded, but the RAU is still the smallest publicly funded university in the UK. There are only ten degrees and three top-up courses for students who have completed Foundation degrees, as well as a growing portfolio of Master's courses.

A new School of Equine Management and Science was established in 2014, joining those focused on agriculture, food and the environment; business and entrepreneurship; and real estate and land management.

The institution embarked on its biggest-ever campus development programme in the run-up to university status. A new teaching block opened with seven well-equipped teaching rooms; a biomass heating system has been installed as part of the university's green agenda, but also as a teaching resource; a postgraduate study centre has been added; and a new accommodation block has opened with 50 en-suite rooms.

The two university farms, both close to the campus, cover a total of 1,200 acres. Coates Manor Farm focuses on arable farming, while Harnhill Farm is an example

Stroud Road
Cirencester
Gloucestershire
GL7 6JS
01285 652 531
admissions@rau.ac.uk
www.rau.ac.uk
www.rau.ac.uk/university
-life/social/student-union
Affiliation: GuildHE

The Times and Sunday Times Rankings		
Overall Ranking: **63** (last year: 51)		
Teaching quality:	=113	77.2%
Student experience:	=62	83.9%
Research quality:	123	1.1%
Entry standards:	=97	303
Student–staff ratio:	122	20.8
Services & facilities/student:	9	£2,811
Expected completion rate:	=18	93.8%
Good honours:	=107	62.2%
Graduate prospects:	50	74.7%

of an integrated livestock and cropping system. In addition, there is an equestrian centre providing stabling and livery facilities, and students also have access to a large dairy complex. All are run as commercial enterprises.

In 2014, the RAU added a Rural Innovation Centre, focusing on research translation, innovation and agri-technologies.

The RAU has always had a reputation for attracting well-heeled students: almost 40 per cent of the undergraduates come from independent schools – a much lower figure than last year, but still the same proportion as Cambridge. Yet almost one in three comes from the four poorest socio-economic groups, contributing to a unique student population.

The number of female students has been rising and has almost reached parity with the men, while 15 per cent are from outside the UK.

All business, equine and agriculture courses include a 20-week work placement. There is an extensive network of student placement sponsors in the UK and overseas, and part-time work is available both in the university and in nearby Cirencester. The university has been rated within the top ten UK universities and colleges for its enterprise activities.

On campus, there is a well-stocked library and computer suites, as well as specialist laboratories. The virtual learning environment ensures that all teaching materials are available online 24 hours a day.

The small numbers and countryside setting encourage a collegiate atmosphere. The campus is the centre of social activities, including four balls each year.

There are eight halls of residence on campus for undergraduates with 320 rooms enough for most first years to be offered a place. Private rentals are available in Cirencester and the surrounding area.

Sport plays an important part in student life and, in addition to the normal range, there are clubs for polo, clay pigeon shooting, beagling and team chasing (a cross-country equestrian sport). There are ample opportunities to explore the Cotswold countryside and London is only 90 minutes away by train.

Tuition fees

» Fees for UK/EU students 2017–18 £9,250
» UK fees are expected to increase by the rate of inflation from 2018–19 onwards.
» Fees for international students 2017–18 £10,000
» Check the university's website for the latest information on fees, scholarships, bursaries and other forms of student support.

Students

Undergraduates:	905	(45)
Postgraduates:	225	(10)
Mature students:	13.3%	
International students:	7.2%	
Applications per place:	3.7	
From state-sector schools:	57.6%	
From working-class homes:	29.9%	
Satisfaction with students' union	62%%	

For detailed information about sports facilities:
www.rau.ac.uk/university-life/social/sports

Accommodation

Number of places and costs refer to 2016–17
University-provided places: 320
Percentage catered: 20%
Catered costs: £123.69 – £201.23 (fully catered);
£98.77 – £176.31 (dinner, bed and breakfast) for 39 weeks.
Self-catered costs: £128.05 for 39 weeks.
First years cannot be guaranteed accommodation.
International students: as above.
accommodation@rau.ac.uk
www.rau.ac.uk/university-life/accommodation

Royal Holloway, University of London

Royal Holloway is aiming for a place among the top 20 UK universities as part of its strategic plan, and has moved two places in that direction this year. It is already in the top 20 for completion and outperforms all its peers in the University of London on student satisfaction. The university will hope that a £150-million estate plan – its most ambitious since the completion of its iconic Founder's Building in 1886 – will help make further progress.

The aim is to add new study, teaching and residential spaces while maintaining the character of one of the UK's most attractive and historic campuses. The centrepiece will be a new library and student centre in the heart of campus, which will open in 2017. Open 24 hours a day, the new building will also house the careers centre and other student services, a shop and café. Extensive use of glass will frame and reflect the Founder's Building, which was modelled on a French chateau and opened by Queen Victoria. Other elements in the plan include 600 new study bedrooms and the refurbishment of many more, additional teaching and performance space for media and arts students. A new science building opening in 2017 will have an emphasis on

attracting more female students into the science and engineering

The University of London's "Campus in the Country", as Royal Holloway is often known, has already seen investment of around £100 million during this decade. This included refurbishment of the 450 student rooms in the Founder's Building, which dominates the 135-acre woodland campus between Windsor Castle and Heathrow.

Other recent projects have included extensions to the School of Management and the existing main library, as well as more student residences. The students' union was upgraded and a new studio theatre added alongside the listed building that houses the drama and theatre department.

Both Bedford College and Royal Holloway, which amalgamated to form the existing college in 1985, were founded for women only, their legacy commemorated in the Bedford Centre for the History of Women. However, the gender balance is now roughly equal.

Although still best known for the arts, Royal Holloway has a broad portfolio of subjects. Applications are running at record levels – almost 50 per cent up on a decade ago – but, despite gradual increases in enrolments, there are still fewer than 10,000 students. This mark will be passed as the new buildings open. A wide portfolio of scholarships and bursaries includes some for postgraduates so that students who graduate

---

Egham
Surrey TW20 0EX

01784 414944 (admissions)
study@royalholloway.ac.uk
www.royalholloway.ac.uk
www.su.rhul.ac.uk
Affiliation: none

The Times and Sunday Times Rankings

Overall Ranking: **34** (last year: 36)

Teaching quality:	=44	81.9%
Student experience:	=62	83.9%
Research quality:	=30	36.3%
Entry standards:	35	400
Student–staff ratio:	=47	15.3
Services & facilities/student:	65	£1,941
Expected completion rate:	=18	93.8%
Good honours:	44	75.6%
Graduate prospects:	79	69.3%

with large debts are not deterred from continuing their studies.

More than 80 per cent of the work assessed in the 2014 Research Excellence Framework was judged to be world-leading or internationally excellent, placing Royal Holloway in the top 25 per cent of UK universities. It would have been higher still if a higher proportion of the academics had been entered. Geography achieved the best results in England, while earth sciences, psychology, mathematics, music, media arts and drama and theatre were all in their respective top tens.

Royal Holloway was chosen as an Academic Centre of Excellence in Cyber Security Research by the UK Government – one of only eight such awards nationwide.

Almost 15 per cent of the undergraduates come from independent schools, but the proportion coming from working-class homes is close to the national average for its courses and entry qualifications.

The Royal Holloway Passport, which is intended to enhance graduates' employability, recognises the additional skills that students gain from many extracurricular activities. An Advanced Skills Programme, covering information technology, communication skills and foreign languages, further encourages breadth of study. The university offers a number of e-degrees and promotes numerous opportunities to study abroad, building on the international flavour of the campus and its links with institutions such as New York, Sydney and Yale universities.

The college's green belt location at Egham, Surrey, ensures that social and cultural life is concentrated on the campus. However, the centre of London is only 35 minutes away by rail for those determined to seek the high life.

Sports facilities are good – Royal Holloway claims to be "the University of London's best sporting college". It has had considerable success with its "student talented athlete award scheme" (STARS). A thriving Community Action programme involves over 1,000 students volunteering with various local organisations and charities.

Many students come from London and the Home Counties, and go home at the weekend, but the lively students' union puts on entertainment and activities seven days a week.

Tuition fees

- » Fees for UK/EU students 2017–18 £9,250
  Year abroad £1,385
  Placement year £1,850
- » UK fees are expected to increase by the rate of inflation from 2018–19 onwards.
- » Fees for international students 2017–18 £14,000–£15,600
- » Check the university's website for the latest information on fees, scholarships, bursaries and other forms of student support.

Students

Undergraduates:	6,820	(350)
Postgraduates:	1,965	(780)
Mature students:	7.2%	
International students:	27.4%	
Applications per place:	7.2	
From state-sector schools:	84.1%	
From working-class homes:	28.4%	
Satisfaction with students' union	62%	

For detailed information about sports facilities:
www.royalholloway.ac.uk/sports

Accommodation

Number of places and costs refer to 2016–17
University-provided places: 2,931
Percentage catered: 37%
Catered costs: £78 – £173 a week (30–38 weeks).
Self-catered costs: £128 – £173 a week (30–38 weeks).
First year UK, EU and International undergraduates are guaranteed accommodation provided conditions are met.
studentaccommodation@royalholloway.ac.uk
www.royalholloway.ac.uk/studyhere/accommodation

University of St Andrews

St Andrews is our University of the Year for Teaching Quality and runner-up for UK University of the Year. It rose to third in our overall ranking this year, matching its highest position, after reversing an unexpected dip in student satisfaction last year. The university is back into the top three in the National Student Survey both for teaching quality and the broader student experience, and is now Scotland's only representative in the overall top 25.

There are fewer than 10,000 students and barely more than half of all applicants received offers in 2015, when the university cut the undergraduate intake by 20 per cent.

Forty per cent of successful candidates are international students, much the largest group coming from the United States, often on study abroad programmes. Another 30 per cent come from south of the border, even though – together with Edinburgh – St Andrews has the highest fees in the UK for undergraduates from England, Wales or Northern Ireland. It charges them £9,250 a year for the full four years of a degree, although there are bursaries for students from low-income families. Scots and other EU students continue to pay nothing.

The university celebrated its 600th anniversary in 2013 and is Scotland's oldest higher education institution and the third oldest in the English-speaking world.

Its reputation has always rested mainly on the humanities: St Andrews boasts Europe's first Centre for Syrian Studies, an Institute of Iranian Studies and a Centre for Peace and Conflict Studies. It has the UK's largest mediaeval history department and has now added film studies and sustainable development. It has also taken over the running of the town's Byre Theatre, which is used as teaching space by day while continuing to offer productions in the evenings and at weekends.

St Andrews has also been investing heavily in the sciences, which produced some of the best results in the 2014 Research Excellence Framework (REF), when over 70 per cent of its submission reached the top two categories. Classics and history of art scored particularly well, but more than 90 per cent of two joint submissions with Edinburgh in chemistry and physics was rated world-leading or internationally excellent.

A £3.7-million physics facility which opened in 2015 will put St Andrews at the forefront of research into superconductors and light-emitting materials, while an ultra-low vibration laboratory is the most advanced in the UK and one of a handful worldwide.

The £45-million Medical and Biological Sciences Building was one of the first in the

---

College Gate
St Andrews
Fife KY16 9AJ

01334 462150
(admissions)
student.recruitment@
st-andrews.ac.uk
www.st-andrews.ac.uk
www.yourunion.net
Affiliation: none

The Times and Sunday Times Rankings

Overall Ranking: **3** (last year: 4)

Teaching quality:	3	88.4%
Student experience:	2	91%
Research quality:	11	40.4%
Entry standards:	6	524
Student–staff ratio:	=7	11.6
Services & facilities/student:	16	£2,671
Expected completion rate:	9	95.5%
Good honours:	3	90.7%
Graduate prospects:	=12	83.3%

UK to integrate research facilities for the medical school with the other sciences.

St Andrews is now planning a £10-million research building and a "smart" aquarium that will be the most technologically advanced in the UK and make St Andrews one of the top marine institutes in the world. The university has the largest optical telescope in Britain. It is aiming to achieve zero waste by 2020 and set itself the target of becoming the first carbon neutral university in the UK, helped by the Guardbridge Energy Centre, a £25-million biomass project that will provide district heating for the university from 2017.

The town of St Andrews is steeped in history, as well as being the centre of the golfing world. The university accounts for more than half of its 18,000 inhabitants. Everything is within walking distance, but bicycles are common.

Among the many traditions are academic families, in which third- or fourth-year students help new undergraduates ("bejants" and "bejantines") adjust to university life. Undergraduates are encouraged to wear distinctive academic dress – the famous red gown signifies the artists and scientists of the United College and the black gown with its purple saltire identifies the divinity students of St Mary's College.

More than 40 per cent of the UK undergraduates come from independent schools. The university is in the middle of a £100-million fundraising campaign, £13 million of which is to support bright students who would otherwise be unable to attend St Andrews.

Students do not come to St Andrews for the nightclubs, but there are no shortage of parties in a tight-knit community. A £12-million extension and redevelopment of the Students' Association building was completed in 2015.

The university is also planning a £14-million transformation of its sports facilities, with a new sports hall, larger and better-equipped fitness suite, and an indoor tennis centre.

Nearly half of students live in university owned accommodation, with first-year undergraduates guaranteed a hall place provided they apply by the end of June. Investment of over £70 million in student housing has been sanctioned in a move which will provide 900 additional bed spaces and refurbish large areas of its existing residences.

Tuition fees

- » Fees for Scottish and EU students 2017–18   No fee
- » Fees for non-Scottish UK (RUK) students 2017–18   £9,250
- » Fees for international students 2017–18   £20,570
  Pre-clinical medicine   £28,200
- » There are particular support schemes for RUK students.
- » Check the university's website for the latest information on fees, scholarships and other forms of student support.

Students

Undergraduates:	7,020	(910)
Postgraduates:	2,400	(330)
Mature students:	3.1%	
International students:	40.4%	
Applications per place:	10.0	
From state-sector schools:	58.9%	
From working-class homes:	14.2%	
Satisfaction with students' union	77%	

For detailed information about sports facilities:
www.st-andrews.ac.uk/sport

Accommodation

Number of places and costs refer to 2016–17
University-provided places: 3,821
Percentage catered: 59%
Catered costs: £142 – £219 (33 or 38 weeks).
Self-catered costs: £98.95 – £206.84 a week (38 weeks).
Single first-year undergraduates are guaranteed accommodation if they apply by 30 June in year of entry.
Policy for international students: as above.
accommodation@st-andrews.ac.uk
www.st-andrews.ac.uk/accommodation/ug

St George's, University of London

St George's hit the headlines this summer by becoming the first university to advertise in advance that it would have places in medicine available in Clearing. The medical school was not short of candidates – only half of those applying in 2015 received offers – but it said going into Clearing was the "fairest way for us to get high-quality students".

St George's has done more than many medical schools to widen the intake into the profession. There is a shadowing scheme which offers sixth formers from Wandsworth and Merton state schools the opportunity to accompany a doctor or other healthcare professional at St George's or Queen Mary's Hospital. The school also runs taster days and spring and summer schools for aspiring doctors, as well as providing a package of financial support worth £2,000 for students with a household income of less than £25,000. Three out of ten undergraduates come from low-income households – well above average for the courses and entry qualifications.

St George's is the only free-standing medical school in the University of London and the only one in our table. It made a spectacular entrance to the table last year,

finishing in the top 50, after restrictions on specialist institutions were relaxed. But a sharp decline in student satisfaction – into the bottom six for both our teaching quality and student experience measures –has led to a drop of 22 places this year.

Courses cover the full range of biomedical and healthcare sciences, and not just medicine. With more than 5,500 students, it is one of the biggest medical schools in the country and has increased its intake of undergraduates for the last three years in succession.

The growth has come mainly in areas other than medicine, where numbers are centrally controlled. There is a joint provision with Kingston University in nursing, physiotherapy and radiology, as well as degrees in biomedical sciences and anatomy. This subject range helps St George's finish first in our performance indicator for graduate prospects.

The school was founded in central London, on Hyde Park Corner, where Edward Jenner was a student before performing the first smallpox vaccination. The hide of the cow he used in the original experiment remains at St George's, which moved to Tooting, in south London, in the 1970s. The medical school shares a clinical environment with St George's Hospital, one of the busiest in London. It also works closely with healthcare providers throughout south London to ensure that its

---

Cranmer Terrace
Tooting
London SW17 0RE

020 8725 2333 (enquiries)
study@sgul.ac.uk
www.sgul.ac.uk
www.sgsu.org.uk
Affiliation: none

The Times and Sunday Times Rankings

Overall Ranking: **70** (last year: 48)

Teaching quality:	126	72.7%
Student experience:	124	77.2%
Research quality:	51	22.2%
Entry standards:	19	435
Student–staff ratio:	18	12.8
Services & facilities/student:	11	£2,733
Expected completion rate:	=14	94.8%
Good honours:	50	74.4%
Graduate prospects:	1	95.1%

courses reflect latest clinical practices and that the students have diverse placement opportunities.

St George's has a strong research record, which includes the invention of the first endocardial cardiac pacemaker and pioneering work on in vitro fertilisation. It currently has important studies into dementia, malaria and antibiotic resistance. Only Imperial College London scored more highly for the external impact of its work in the 2014 Research Excellence Framework (REF). Overall, 70 per cent of the work submitted for the REF was considered world-leading or internationally excellent.

Three research institutes focus on biomedical and scientific discovery, advancing the prevention and treatment of disease in the fields of population health, heart disease and infection – three of the greatest challenges to global health in the 21st century.

The Tooting campus includes a preparatory centre for international students that is run jointly by St George's and the INTO foundation. Most students are taking English language courses or developing other necessary skills through the International foundation programme before joining medical degrees. St George's also offers a four-year graduate entry Bachelor of Surgery degree in Cyprus, at the University of Nicosia, where the first students graduated in 2015.

St George's was the first UK institution to launch the MBBS Graduate Entry Programme (GEP), a four-year fast-track medical degree course open to graduates in any discipline and which has become an increasingly popular route into the medical profession.

A £1-million refurbishment of the library took place in 2012 and three laboratories have been upgraded since then. There are 250 workstations in five IT suites, two of which are available 24 hours a day. The most recent addition, opening in 2015, was a virtual reality facility to give lifelike scenarios in an interactive environment to train paramedics about situations they might face in the real world.

There are almost 500 residential places, with priority for first years. The sports centre is on campus and competitive teams play in regional and national competitions. The West End is less than half an hour by tube for shopping and nightlife excursions.

Tuition fees

» Fees for UK/EU students 2017–18 £9,250
   Foundation degree £9,250
» UK fees are expected to increase by the rate of inflation from 2018–19 onwards.
» Fees for international students 2017–18 £15,170–£15,970
   Medicine £31,960
» Check the university's website for the latest information on fees, scholarships, bursaries and other forms of student support.

Students

Undergraduates:	2,615	(1,960)
Postgraduates:	195	(735)
Mature students:	30.5%	
International students:	9.4%	
Applications per place:	13.0	
From state-sector schools:	82.2%	
From working-class homes:	30.4%	
Satisfaction with students' union	65%	

For detailed information about sports facilities:
www.sgsu.org.uk/club-soc/sports-clubs

Accommodation

Places and costs refer to 2016–17
University-provided places: 486
Percentage catered: 0%
Self-catered costs: £156 (standard) – £166 (premium) for 42 weeks.
Undergraduates are prioritised for housing in their first year.
International students: as above.
accommodation@sgul.ac.uk
www.sgul.ac.uk/study/accommodation

University of St Mark and St John

St Mark and St John (Marjon) enjoys one of the biggest rises in our new league table, having fallen perilously close to the bottom after dropping more than 50 places in two years. Unusually large increases in student satisfaction were the main factor behind the university's rise of 18 places, but there was also a big rise in spending on student facilities.

Marjon's decline was due partly to its decision not to take part in the 2014 Research Excellence Framework (REF), which gives it no score in our table for research quality. It was the only publicly funded university for more than 20 years to submit no work for the official assessments of research. A new research strategy has already reversed the policy.

Marjon puts its newfound success in the National Student Survey down to an approach that "puts students' personal development front and centre of their experience". Every course includes core personal development training, where students work in small tutorial groups and have individual coaching. There was 100 per cent overall satisfaction in acting, secondary education with PE, sport development with PE, and sport journalism.

Marjon was also placed top of an index of social mobility produced by a former vice-chancellor for the graduate-level jobs secured by students recruited from poorer backgrounds. Nearly all the undergraduates are state educated and approaching 40 per cent come from the four lowest socio-economic groups.

The Plymouth-based university plans to double in size over the next decade, but will still have only about 5,000 students when the programme is complete. The aim is to develop a "credible and critical mass" in each area, to make economies of scale and invest in development. The cost will be relatively modest because the spacious greenfield campus has spare capacity following investment in buildings and sports facilities totalling £20 million in recent years.

But the university has promised to increase staffing levels in line with student numbers to maintain the small class sizes that are one of its selling points. There will be more students from overseas, but most will still come from Devon and Cornwall.

Established in 1840 as a Church of England teacher training college in London, with the son of poet Samuel Taylor Coleridge as its first principal, the university describes itself as "arguably the third oldest higher education institution in England". The College of St Mark and St John only moved to Plymouth in 1973. Still officially a Church of England Voluntary Institution,

---

Derriford Road
Plymouth
Devon PL6 8BH

01752 636890 (admissions)
admissions@marjon.ac.uk
www.marjon.ac.uk
www.marjonsu.com
Affiliations: GuildHE;
Cathedrals Group

***The Times and Sunday Times* Rankings**

Overall Ranking: **105** (last year: =123)

Teaching quality:	=27	82.9%
Student experience:	=36	85.4%
Research quality:	n/a	n/a
Entry standards:	=112	290
Student–staff ratio:	124	21.5
Services & facilities/student:	74	£1,814
Expected completion rate:	=94	82.1%
Good honours:	113	60.6%
Graduate prospects:	103	63%

it was one of several religious foundations among the universities awarded that status in 2013. The attractive modern Chaplaincy Centre is at the heart of the campus, but there is less emphasis on religion in the new university's promotional material than at some of its counterparts.

The university lists sport at the top of its list of specialisms, followed by education, languages, journalism and the creative arts. The Elite Sport Scholarship programme produced a Gold medallist at the 2014 Commonwealth Games in swimmer Ben Proud, who then broke the British 50-metre freestyle record at the 2016 Rio Olympics but narrowly missed a medal.

Recent campus developments have included extensive refurbishment of the library to provide a new social learning space. There has also been a new sports centre, refurbished student housing and a new entrance and student centre. New sports science labs include climate chamber, bod pod and an anti-gravity treadmill.

The university has also opened Plymouth Studio School on its campus for 14–19 year olds focusing on careers in sport, sport coaching, and development or sport management. The Journalism and Media Centre opened in 2013, conceived and designed by the lecturers. Teacher training remains strong, with Ofsted giving an outstanding rating for the leadership and management of courses that run in six counties, as well as in Cyprus and Germany.

The university is located on the expanding north side of Plymouth, close to the Dartmoor National Park and within easy reach of the sea. The green agenda extends to an on-campus duck pond and nature trail.

Sports facilities are extremely good: there is a floodlit 3G pitch, climbing wall, 25-metre indoor swimming pool and well-equipped gym, as well as a rehabilitation clinic and sports science lab.

There are residential places on campus for 456 students in seven halls of residence and 38 village houses; rents compare favourably with most universities. First-year students are guaranteed places and encouraged to take one up while they make the transition to higher education.

Those living on campus may only bring a car in exceptional circumstances, but the lively city centre is a short bus ride from the campus.

Tuition fees

- » Fees for UK/EU students 2017–18 £9,000
  Foundation degree £6,000–£9,000
- » UK fees are expected to increase by the rate of inflation from 2018–19 onwards.
- » Fees for international students 2017–18 £10,500–£11,250
- » Check the university's website for the latest information on fees, scholarships, bursaries and other forms of student support.

Students

Undergraduates:	1,875	(160)
Postgraduates:	95	(285)
Mature students:	33.3%	
International students:	1.6%	
Applications per place:	3.8	
From state-sector schools:	97.6%	
From working-class homes:	37%	
Satisfaction with students' union	63%	

For detailed information about sports facilities:
www.marjon.ac.uk/marjon-sport

Accommodation

Places and costs refer to 2016–17
University-provided places: 456
Percentage catered: 65%
Catered and self-catered costs: £85 (small), £90 – £95 (standard), £110 (en suite). All first years participate in the Dining-In-Scheme.
First years are guaranteed accommodation.
International students: guaranteed campus or homestay housing.
www.marjon.ac.uk/student-life/accommodation

St Mary's University, Twickenham

St Mary's has fewer than 6,000 students, but its athletes at the Rio Olympics would have finished 25th on the medal table, ahead of countries such as South Africa and Poland. The 22 current students and alumni brought home six medals, including three Golds. They were led by Mo Farah, a graduate of St Mary's, who has a scholarship programme for promising young athletes at the university.

The £8.5-million sports centre is good enough to have attracted the New Zealand, Australia and South Africa teams during the 2015 Rugby World Cup, and paralympian David Weir trains regularly at the university.

St Mary's focus is not confined to sports, however. It is the largest Catholic university in the UK, one of three created in recent years, with a long history in teacher training and growing numbers taking health and management courses.

The university has appointed a series of high-profile visiting professors, including Dr Mary McAleese, the former President of Ireland; Sir Vince Cable, the former Business Secretary; Cherie Blair in law; and Sir Clive Woodward, who coached England to the 2003 Rugby World Cup, in sport and business. Ruth Kelly, Education Secretary under Tony Blair, has become Pro Vice-Chancellor of Research and Enterprise.

The numbers starting degrees have grown for three years in a row, with applications rising by almost 10 per cent in 2015. But St Mary's has dropped 16 places in our latest league table, particularly due to falls in student satisfaction, completion and degree classifications.

Founded in Hammersmith in 1850 by the Catholic Poor Schools Committee to meet the need for teachers for the growing numbers of poor Catholic children, St Mary's moved along the river to Twickenham in 1925.

The spectacular Strawberry Hill House has been its centrepiece ever since. The house was designed as a Gothic fantasy between 1747 and 1792 by Horace Walpole, the son of Britain's first Prime Minister. Leased from the university by a trust, the building has now been restored and is open to the public.

The campus occupies 35 acres of gardens and parkland close to the Thames, with a variety of modern teaching and residential accommodation. Additional sports facilities are located in neighbouring Teddington. A new library, costing £6 million, is now fully open, as is the upgraded student television studio. There is also a new computer suite with the latest Apple MacPro workstations, offering students 24-hour access to professional-grade creative technologies.

Waldegrave Road
Strawberry Hill
Twickenham
London TW1 4SX

020 8240 4029 (admissions)
admit@stmarys.ac.uk
www.stmarys.ac.uk
www.stmaryssu.co.uk
Affiliations: GuildHE;
Cathedrals Group

The Times and Sunday Times Rankings

Overall Ranking: **116** (last year: =100)

Teaching quality:	=94	79%
Student experience:	=73	83.3%
Research quality:	=103	4%
Entry standards:	=106	293
Student–staff ratio:	119	20.2
Services & facilities/student:	124	£1,175
Expected completion rate:	=99	81.3%
Good honours:	115	59.4%
Graduate prospects:	76	70.1%

Only a third of today's students are training to be teachers and there are growing numbers taking sport, drama, theology and business-related degrees. Sixty per cent of the students are female and over 4 per cent of undergraduates come from outside the UK. The university has joined the US-based Common Application System, used by 500 universities around the world, to attract more.

There are nearly 500 undergraduate degree combinations, including a range of Foundation degrees, across four academic schools covering sport, health and applied science; education, theology and leadership; management and social sciences; and the arts and humanities. Although fees for degree courses are £9,250 in 2017, entrants to Foundation degrees will pay no more than £6,750 a year.

Nearly 40 per cent of the UK undergraduates are from working-class homes and the university has a number of outreach schemes designed to broaden the intake further. The E-Mentoring scheme, in which current students help selected groups of school pupils throughout the academic year, has received excellent feedback from participants. Other initiatives provide academic support and monitor the progress of under-represented groups once they begin courses.

St Mary's missed out on university status when a dozen other colleges were promoted in 2012, but succeeded in 2014. The university appointed Francis Campbell, a career diplomat and one-time private secretary to Tony Blair, as its first vice-chancellor. A former ambassador to the Vatican, he helped to secure a Papal visit to St Mary's in 2010.

St Mary's has a continuing commitment to training teachers for Catholic and other Christian schools, although it admits students of all faiths and none. Its first stated objective is "To be a distinctive institution within UK higher education, providing a unique experience for our students and staff by virtue of our values and identity as a Catholic university." Cardinal Vincent Nichols, President of the Catholic Bishops' Conference of England and Wales, became the university's chancellor in 2015.

Students like the combination of an attractive setting in southwest London that is only half an hour from Waterloo station by train.

Tuition fees

» Fees for UK/EU students 2017–18   £9,250
    Foundation degree   up to £6,750
» UK fees are expected to increase by the rate of inflation from 2018–19 onwards.
» Fees for international students 2016–17   £11,000
» Check the university's website for the latest information on fees, scholarships, bursaries and other forms of student support.

Students		
Undergraduates:	3,485	(420)
Postgraduates:	515	(915)
Mature students:	18.6%	
International students:	4.2%	
Applications per place:	4.8	
From state-sector schools:	95.7%	
From working-class homes:	38.8%	
Satisfaction with students' union	67%	

For detailed information about sports facilities:
www.stmarys.ac.uk/sport

Accommodation

Number of places and costs refer to 2016–17
University-provided places: approx 700
Percentage catered: 100%
Catered costs: £125.09 (small twin) – £209.37 (single en suite) inclusive of meal plan (37 weeks).
The university endeavours to provide accommodation to all new applicants who require it and apply by the deadline.
International students: some rooms reserved for new students.

www.stmarys.ac.uk/student-life/accommodation

University of Salford

Salford has been narrowing the range of subjects it offers to focus on its strengths in media, business, technology, science, engineering and health. The strategy has proved successful, with applications rising by 25 per cent in two years and the numbers starting degrees increasing by a similar amount.

Now the university is ready for a new phase of expansion, with a branch campus in Bahrain and plans for a private medical school in partnership with Manchester and Manchester Metropolitan universities. From September 2017, Salford will be the first UK university to have a campus in Bahrain, offering degrees in engineering, quantity surveying and computer science under the rubric of the British College of Bahrain. It will join the University of Salford Abu Dhabi, which already offers courses, mainly online, in that Gulf state.

The medical school, which will cater for international students, is a long-term project and part of Salford's plans for "considerable growth" over next five years.

However, the university continues to struggle in our league table, where it is held back particularly by low levels of completion and only moderate graduate prospects. It is the lowest ranked pre-1992 institution, coming just inside the top 100.

Significant improvements to the main campus will greet new entrants in 2017. The new £81-million Peel Park Quarter, with 1,367 residential places and impressive student facilities, is already open.

It will be followed early in 2017 by the New Adelphi, a flagship building at the gateway to the campus, which will be the main social hub and also the teaching centre for art, performance, and design and technology students. It will include a 350-seat theatre, industry-standard TV, radio and music studios, as well as exhibition space and café and bar areas. The university also has a £30-million development in MediaCityUK, in Salford Quays, where there are exceptional opportunities to work with BBC staff and other media professionals using the latest equipment, studios and laboratories.

There are three campuses, all of them, apart from Salford Quays, clustered around the River Irwell and within walking distance of Manchester city centre. University House, where students go for advice and support, has seen a £3-millon upgrade, while a 1960s teaching building has been remodelled and extended to accommodate six lecture theatres equipped with large-screen displays, a series of learning and breakout spaces, plus a café.

A £22-million headquarters for the Faculty of Health and Social Care is on the third site, with practice clinics, hospital

The Crescent
Salford
M5 4WT

0161 295 4545 (enquiries)
www.salford.ac.uk/contact-us
www.salford.ac.uk
www.salfordstudents.com
Affiliation: University
Alliance

The Times and Sunday Times Rankings

Overall Ranking: **98** (last year: 98)

Teaching quality:	=70	80.2%
Student experience:	=99	81.6%
Research quality:	71	8.3%
Entry standards:	63	335
Student–staff ratio:	=72	16.7
Services & facilities/student:	98	£1,641
Expected completion rate:	107	79.8%
Good honours:	62	71.3%
Graduate prospects:	106	61.5%

ward facilities and a human performance laboratory. There are now 5,000 students across the two health schools. The School of Nursing, Midwifery, Social Work and Social Sciences received outstanding ratings from its regulatory body and has a patient simulation lab, which has been accredited as a centre of teaching excellence, while the School of Health Sciences has an international reputation for the treatment of sports injuries.

Engineering is the university's traditional strength, attracting many of the 3,000 overseas students, and QS ranks Salford in the top 50 in the world for architecture. However, Salford Business School has been the main point of growth, as well as winning awards for innovation and the delivery of its courses via a mix of traditional teaching and business innovation projects.

Two-thirds of Salford's courses – and all of them in the business school – offer work placements, some of which are abroad and almost all counting towards degree classifications. The university has partnerships which provide research and work experience with the BBC, Adobe, international research institutions and the Salford China partnership programme among others. The Enterprise Academy scheme was commended by the EU for the success of student start-up businesses. Salford led the way in formally recognising interaction with business and industry as of equal importance to teaching and research.

The university entered only a third of its eligible academics for the 2014 Research Excellence Framework, but more than half of their work was found to be world-leading or internationally excellent.

The university does well on the Government's access measures: 42 per cent of the undergraduates come from working-class homes and there is a high proportion from areas sending few students to higher education. The dropout rate has been improving but, at almost 16 per cent, is still higher than the national average for the subjects and students' qualifications.

Salford's location is one of its main selling points, with Manchester a prime draw for students. In 2016 there were around 2,400 residential places within ten minutes' walk of the main campus, owned either by the university or a partner organisation.

Tuition fees

- » Fees for UK/EU students 2017–18 £9,250
  Year abroad £1,350
  Placement year no fee
- » UK fees are expected to increase by the rate of inflation from 2018–19 onwards.
- » Fees for international students 2016–17 £11,500–£13,300
- » Check the university's website for the latest information on fees, scholarships, bursaries and other forms of student support

Students

Undergraduates:	13,850	(1,045)
Postgraduates:	2,350	(1,675)
Mature students:	28.6%	
International students:	11.1%	
Applications per place:	6.1	
From state-sector schools:	97.9%	
From working-class homes:	42.2%	
Satisfaction with students' union	69%	

For detailed information about sports facilities:
www.salfordstudents.com/sport

Accommodation

Number of places and costs refer to 2016–17
University-provided places: over 2,400
Percentage catered: 0%
Self-catered costs: £79 (standard) – £139 (en suite);
£81 – £102 (flat) for 42 or 52 weeks.
First years are guaranteed accommodation (terms and conditions apply).
International students: as above.
salford@clvuk.com (Salford Student Village)
www.salford.ac.uk/study/life-at-salford/accommodation

University of Sheffield

The proportion of applicants receiving offers from Sheffield has been growing year by year as the university has increased the size of its undergraduate intake. It reached 85 per cent in 2015, compared with only 71 per cent in 2010, and the numbers starting degrees rose for the third year in a row.

A striking £81-million engineering building – the university's biggest single development – opened last year to cater for the additional students in one of Sheffield's key strengths. The aluminium-clad Diamond has 19 specialist laboratories and 1,000 study spaces for students across the university. The highly rated Faculty of Engineering, which has 4,000 students, had already opened the £21-million Pam Liversidge Building, named after one of UK's leading female engineers. There is also a technology park centred on an advanced manufacturing research centre, in which Boeing is the senior partner. Sheffield is the lead institution for systems engineering, smart materials and stem-cell technology in a research network of European, American and Chinese universities.

The main university precinct now stretches into an almost unbroken mile-long "campus" that ends not far from the city centre. Previous developments have seen the conversion of the former Jessop Hospital into a new centre for the arts and humanities and the renovation of the original University Library and the Arts Tower, which remains the tallest university building in the country after more than 40 years. The £23-million Information Commons operates 24 hours a day throughout the year, providing 1,300 study spaces and 500 computers linked to the campus network, as well as more than 100,000 books and periodicals. The university has spent £1.5 million refurbishing a purpose-built student skills centre, which offers support in a variety of areas.

The university is comfortably inside the top 20 favourite recruiting grounds for *The Times* 100 leading employers, according to High Fliers' 2016 graduate market survey. A new employability strategy includes two internship schemes offering 75 placements within the university.

Sheffield has dropped three places in the new league table, however, despite a big improvement in graduate prospects. Sheffield has been in the top three in *Times Higher Education* (*THE*) magazine's student experience survey for the last six years and its students' union has been the most popular in the National Student Survey (NSS) in all five years that unions have been assessed. But it does not replicate those successes in the section of the survey concerned with teaching quality, where it

Western Bank
Sheffield S10 2TN

0114 222 8030 (enquiries)
shefapply@sheffield.ac.uk
www.sheffield.ac.uk
http://su.sheffield.ac.uk
Affiliation: Russell Group

The Times and Sunday Times Rankings

Overall Ranking: **24** (last year: 21)

Teaching quality:	=62	80.7%
Student experience:	22	86.7%
Research quality:	23	37.6%
Entry standards:	27	420
Student–staff ratio:	=35	14.6
Services & facilities/student:	45	£2,142
Expected completion rate:	16	94.4%
Good honours:	29	79.5%
Graduate prospects:	22	81.3%

remains stubbornly ranked around mid-table, albeit considerably higher than many other Russell Group universities.

It is just outside the top 20 for research under our analysis of the 2014 Research Excellence Framework (REF), with 85 per cent of the research submitted considered world-leading or internationally excellent, with biomedical sciences, control and systems engineering, history and politics all in the top three in the UK. But the university entered a smaller proportion of its academics than most of its peers in the Russell Group.

Sheffield is in the top 100 in the world, according to the QS rankings, and attracts more than 6,000 international students. The student population is more diverse than in most Russell Group universities: over 86 per cent of the undergraduates come from state schools or colleges and 21 per cent are from working-class homes.

Most university flats and halls of residence are within walking distance, in the suburbs on the affluent west side of Sheffield. Residential accommodation is plentiful and was voted the best in the country for three years in a row in *THE*'s survey. Private housing is reasonably priced in student areas close to the university. The Endcliffe student village caters for 3,500 students in a mix of refurbished Victorian houses and new flats, while the Ranmoor Village houses over 1,000 students in self-catering apartments, which include some family apartments and studios.

The excellent sports facilities close to the main university precinct include five floodlit synthetic pitches, a large and well-equipped fitness centre, swimming pool with sauna and steam rooms, sports hall, fitness studio, multipurpose activity room, four squash courts and a bouldering wall. The 45 acres of grass pitches for football, rugby and cricket are a bus ride away. Sheffield has one of the biggest programmes of internal leagues at any university and elite sport is thriving. Alumnae brought home three Gold or Silver medals from the Rio Olympics.

The famously lively social scene is based on the recently extended students' union. The city has plenty of student-oriented bars and clubs, and town–gown relations are much better than in most major university centres. Crime statistics identify Sheffield as the safest big city in England.

Tuition fees

» Fees for UK/EU students 2017–18   £9,250
    Year abroad   £1,385
    Placement year   £1,230 or £1,850

» UK fees are expected to increase by the rate of inflation from 2018–19 onwards.

» Fees for international students 2017–18   £16,000–£20,470
    Medicine   £20,470–£35,500

» Check the university's website for the latest information on fees, scholarships, bursaries and other forms of student support.

Students

Undergraduates:	17,995	(980)
Postgraduates:	6,290	(1,930)
Mature students:	8.9%	
International students:	21.5%	
Applications per place:	6.9	
From state-sector schools:	86.5%	
From working-class homes:	21.2%	
Satisfaction with students' union	96%	

For detailed information about sports facilities:
www.sport-sheffield.com

Accommodation

Number of places and costs refer to 2016–17
University-provided places: 6,232
Percentage catered: 6%
Catered costs: £137.62 – £162.40 (42 weeks; 31 weeks of catering).
Self-catered costs: £98.35 – £193.29 (42–51 weeks).
First years are guaranteed accommodation if conditions are met.
International students: as above.
www.sheffield.ac.uk/accommodation

Sheffield Hallam University

Only the two big Manchester universities took more undergraduates than Sheffield Hallam in 2015. The university now has close to 37,000 students at all levels, and it was its scale that attracted Professor Chris Husbands away from the directorship of University College London's Institute of Education to become the Vice-Chancellor in 2016.

He is also chairing the group piloting the Government's new Teaching Excellence Framework, so will have the inside track on a programme that will be crucial to Hallam's (and other universities') future funding.

He has taken over a university that has dropped seven places in this year's table, mainly because of declining scores in student satisfaction and entry standards, but which has other strengths. The careers and employability centre, for example, secured the top rating of 96 per cent satisfaction in the 2015 National Centre for Universities and Business student employability index.

The university traces its origins in art and design back to the 1840s and has been training teachers for more than 100 years.

Business and industry are closely involved in the development of courses and more than half of the undergraduates take work placements. The university gives a full fee waiver for those who take a complete year out. More than 200 "specialist flexible courses" mix part-time study, distance learning and work-based learning. A "virtual campus" enables all students to access the growing volume of online teaching, assignments and discussion groups even when they are at home or on work placements.

Hallam is now one of the growing number of universities to make unconditional offers to the most promising students. Achievement Awards were offered in 2016 for the first time in a range of full-time courses.

The university exceeds all of its access benchmarks and the projected dropout rate of 9 per cent is lower than average for its courses and entry qualifications.

The university also has a growing international dimension, with large cohorts taught in partner institutions in Malaysia and other Asian countries, as well as almost 4,000 who come to Sheffield from outside the EU.

Hallam has completed a £110-million development plan, with the conversion of one of the most prominent locations in the city centre as a new home for the Sheffield Institute of Arts. All art and design courses, including fine art, fashion, product design, metalwork and jewellery, are now taught in the listed former Sheffield Head Post Office.

A £30-million development at the City Campus now houses the Sheffield Institute

City Campus
Howard Street
Sheffield S1 1WB

0114 225 5555 (enquiries)
enquiries@shu.ac.uk
www.shu.ac.uk
www.hallamstudentsunion.com
Affiliation: University
   Alliance

The Times and Sunday Times Rankings		
Overall Ranking: **79** (last year: 72)		
Teaching quality:	=76	80%
Student experience:	=71	83.4%
Research quality:	=88	5.4%
Entry standards:	=89	306
Student–staff ratio:	=69	16.5
Services & facilities/student:	51	£2,068
Expected completion rate:	61	86.3%
Good honours:	90	66%
Graduate prospects:	82	68.6%

of Education, training the majority of the region's new teachers, and the Heart of the Campus building at Collegiate Crescent campus opened in 2014 and has since won an award from the Royal Institute of British Architects.

The university is also upgrading its science and technology facilities after winning a £10-million grant from the funding council and is a partner in the development of the new Advanced Wellbeing Research Centre, which will be a key part of Sheffield's Olympic Legacy Park. The Health and Wellbeing faculty is one of the biggest providers of health and social care training in the UK and offers the widest range of sports courses. A new BSc course in sport and exercise technology will be available from September 2017.

Previous developments focused mainly on the City Campus, near the railway station and Sheffield's central shopping area. The Sheffield Business School brought together business, finance, management and languages, with several of the university's other specialisms to become the biggest at any post-1992 university. Business and management courses, which account for easily the biggest share of places, have their own city-centre headquarters, as does the students' union, which took over the spectacular, but ill-fated, National Centre for Popular Music.

Unlike many big post-1992 universities,

Hallam now guarantees accommodation for first years, although the large local intake means that many live at home. Transport in the city is excellent, with both well-run bus and tram services.

Sports facilities are supplemented by those provided by the city for the World Student Games. The impressive swimming complex, for example, is on the university's doorstep. The university has taken over the management of Sheffield's only athletics stadium, which will be among the facilities used for the BUCS Nationals, university and college students' annual games, for the next three years. The redeveloped facility is available to community groups, schools and local clubs, as well as students.

The university partnered with the Tour de France to offer volunteering opportunities for students when the 2014 race started in Yorkshire.

Tuition fees

» Fees for UK/EU students 2017–18   £9,250
    Placement year   no fee
» UK fees are expected to increase by the rate of inflation from 2018–19 onwards.
» Fees for international students 2017–18   £12,250–£12,750
» Check the university's website for the latest information on fees, scholarships, bursaries and other forms of student support.

Students

Undergraduates:	21,495	(3,150)
Postgraduates:	3,035	(3,850)
Mature students:	19.4%	
International students:	5.9%	
Applications per place:	5.7	
From state-sector schools:	96.4%	
From working-class homes:	40.8%	
Satisfaction with students' union	57%	

For detailed information about sports facilities:
www.shu.ac.uk/current-students/sport

Accommodation

Number of places and costs refer to 2016–17
University-provided places: 5,600
Percentage catered: 0%
Self-catered costs: £82.74 (standard single) – £210.00 (flat) a week (43 or 44 weeks).
All first years offered university allocated place if conditions met.
International students: as above.
accommodation@shu.ac.uk
www.shu.ac.uk/accommodation

SOAS, University of London

Big increases in student satisfaction have helped SOAS to a rise of nine places in this year's table, bringing it closer to the ranking it has enjoyed in previous years.

This progress comes as the school celebrates its centenary by coming together on a single campus for the first time in many years. It is taking over the North Block of Senate House, the headquarters of the University of London, which is at the western end of the SOAS precinct and will provide space for a new student hub including accommodation, course registration, student finance, careers and enterprise services, as well as additional teaching facilities.

The development will enable SOAS to capitalise on its growing popularity – applications grew by more than a quarter in two years, but there are still only 5,400 students on campus.

The only higher education institution in the UK specialising in the study of Africa, Asia and the Middle East, SOAS has dropped its full title (School of Oriental and African Studies) and promotes itself as SOAS University of London. It is led by Baroness Valerie Amos, who was the UK's first black woman Cabinet minister and has now become the first black woman to lead a British university.

The school has a global reputation in subjects relating to two-thirds of the world's population and that excellence will be enhanced by a £20-million gift from a graduate with a passion for South-East Asian art. The donation was worth more than a quarter of SOAS's annual income and will fund new posts, building development and scholarships for Asian students to come to London.

More than 3,000 students, most of them outside the UK, take SOAS's distance learning programmes. The transfer of University of London postgraduate programmes previously taught by Imperial College has made SOAS one of the world's largest providers of distance learning at this level.

The students in London come from more than 130 countries, but two-thirds are from Britain and the rest of the EU. Almost a fifth of the British undergraduates come from independent schools, but more than one in three are from the four poorest socio-economic groups. The school almost doubled its investment in student support with the switch to higher fees, as well as increasing its outreach activities.

The centrepiece of the Bloomsbury precinct is an airy, modern building with gallery space as well as teaching accommodation, a gift from the Sultan of Brunei.

The library is one of just five National

Thornhaugh Street
Russell Square
London WC1H 0XG

020 7898 4700 (enquiries)
study@soas.ac.uk
www.soas.ac.uk
https://soasunion.org
Affiliation: none

The Times and Sunday Times Rankings

Overall Ranking: **35** (last year: 44)

Teaching quality:	88	79.5%
Student experience:	=81	83.1%
Research quality:	46	27.9%
Entry standards:	32	410
Student–staff ratio:	=5	11.1
Services & facilities/student:	35	£2,206
Expected completion rate:	=77	84.3%
Good honours:	28	79.9%
Graduate prospects:	72	70.8%

Research Libraries in the country, holding 1.5 million volumes, periodicals and audiovisual materials in 400 languages, and attracts scholars from around the world.

More than 40 per cent of degree programmes offer the opportunity to spend a year at one of the school's many partner universities in Africa or Asia.

The school has a much wider portfolio of courses than its name would suggest, offering more than 400 degree combinations and 100 postgraduate programmes. Degrees are available in familiar subjects such as law, music, history and the social sciences, but with a different emphasis. There is also a more limited portfolio of Foundation programmes and language courses.

Approximately 45 per cent of undergraduates take a language as part of their degree and the school has now introduced a Language Entitlement programme which offers one term of a non-accredited SOAS Language Centre course free of charge. The £6.5 million Library Transformation Project has added more language laboratories, music studios, discussion and research rooms, and gallery space.

SOAS is in the top 80 in the QS World Rankings for the arts and humanities, which led the way in the 2014 Research Excellence Framework. Music, drama and the performing arts produced the best results in a submission in which two-thirds of the work was rated as world-leading or internationally excellent.

There is no separate students' union building, although the students do have their own recently refurbished bar, social space and catering facilities. The former University of London Union – now a student centre – is close at hand, with swimming pool, gym and bars. The West End is also on the doorstep.

Nearly 900 residential places are available within 20 minutes' walk of the school. However, the school has few of its own sports facilities and the outdoor pitches are remote, with no time set aside from lectures.

Students tend to be highly committed and often politically active – not surprising since many will return to positions of influence in their own country – and the variety of cultures makes for lively debate.

Tuition fees

» Fees for UK/EU students 2017–18 £9,250
Year abroad £1,385

» UK fees are expected to increase by the rate of inflation from 2018–19 onwards.

» Fees for international students 2016–17 £16,250

» Check the university's website for the latest information on fees, scholarships, bursaries and other forms of student support.

Students

Undergraduates:	2,955	(65)
Postgraduates:	1,945	(950)
Mature students:	16.4%	
International students:	38.6%	
Applications per place:	6.5	
From state-sector schools:	81%	
From working-class homes:	35.7%	
Satisfaction with students' union	72%	

For detailed information about sports facilities:
https://soasunion.org/activities/sports

Accommodation

Number of places and costs refer to 2016–17
University-provided places: 772 (Sanctuary Students) 105 (Intercollegiate Halls)
Percentage catered: 16%
Catered costs: £136.50 – £347.55 a week.
Self-catered costs: £151.43 – £428.23 a week.
Priority is given to new students on a first come, first served basis. Residential restrictions apply.
International students: as above, although a high priority.
www.soas.ac.uk/students/accommodation

University of South Wales

The University of South Wales (USW) has moved out of one of its five campuses and opening an extension to another, as it implements a controversial "realignment plan". The campus at Carleon, near Newport, closed because the 2013 merger of Glamorgan and Newport universities left too many buildings for the number of students.

Instead, investment has been focused on the £60-million Newport Knowledge Quarter and the ATRiuM Campus, in the centre of Cardiff, where a new building will add to the already extensive facilities for creative industries students. The reorganisation, which includes a two-phase expansion of the city-centre campus in Newport, is intended to help USW become the university of choice for vocationally focused education and applied research. The university also closed its London centre only a year after it opened, claiming that tougher visa restrictions had prevented it from attracting the international students it needed to make the venture economic.

USW is one of Wales's two largest universities, with almost 30,000 students at all levels, and the University of South Wales Group spreads its net much more widely. It includes the Royal Welsh College of Music and Drama and Merthyr Tydfil College, while a strategic alliance brings in further education colleges throughout southeast Wales. The alliance covers 38 campuses, providing 98,000 learners with advice and structured progression routes from further education to university.

About half of USW's own students are full-time undergraduates and of these, a quarter are at least 21 years old on entry. Three-quarters are from Wales and receive grants to reduce the cost of tuition.

A focus on employability extends to a variety of simulated learning facilities, including a moot court room, TV studios, stock exchange trading room, hospital wards, and scene-of-crime house. Aircraft maintenance and engineering students benefit from two on-campus working aircraft hangars complete with aircraft. USW is the only UK university to have a partnership with British Airways which enables students to graduate with an EASA licence as well as a degree.

There was a relatively small submission for the 2014 Research Excellence Framework, but half of the work was considered world-leading or internationally excellent. The best results came in a joint submission with Cardiff Metropolitan and Trinity St David universities in art and design, and in sport and exercise science, and social work and social policy.

The university has ranked outside the top 100 in our institutional table in the three

---

Pontypridd CF37 1DL

08456 76 77 78 (enquiries)
contact via website
www.southwales.ac.uk
www.uswsu.com
Affiliation: University
Alliance

The Times and Sunday Times **Rankings**		
Overall Ranking: **115** (last year: =112)		
Teaching quality:	102	78.4%
Student experience:	=120	79.4%
Research quality:	=103	4%
Entry standards:	=76	321
Student–staff ratio:	=86	17.4
Services & facilities/student:	96	£1,661
Expected completion rate:	=91	82.3%
Good honours:	99	64.9%
Graduate prospects:	125	56.4%

years that it has appeared. It is held back by low scores for student experience in the annual National Student Survey and weak graduate prospects.

The largest campus is in Pontypridd, where two sites cater mainly for science, engineering and health subjects. Recent developments there have included a new Law School and upgraded laboratories, as well as a £6-million Learning Resource Centre. Leisure facilities have been improving, with a modern recreation centre and a new students' union.

USW is also a significant player in the arts at its Cardiff Campus, notably through its internationally acclaimed film school, with industry-standard animation facilities and one of the UK's oldest photography schools. The new ATRiuM 2B will include facilities for advertising, TV and film set design and fashion, as well as dance studios, rehearsal spaces and photographic studios. The original ATRiuM building, next to the new BBC headquarters, hosts law and accounting and finance courses, as well as the Cardiff School of Creative and Cultural Industries.

Other recent developments include a £15-million upgrading of facilities for health, science and sport, as well as new halls of residence. The high-quality sports facilities, used by Olympians and All Blacks, have continued to improve: the university hosts one of six centres of excellence in cricket. USW has a good record in student competitions, especially in rugby, football and golf. Sports scholarships are available.

The award-winning Newport City Campus opened in 2011 and expansion is planned. It is the USW's home for professional and executive courses, early years, counselling and associated therapies, teacher training, and part-time business and accounting courses. Based at the heart of the new Knowledge Quarter, part of its remit is to attract inward investment and strengthen the local economy. Newport was rated the top university in Wales for enterprise education by the Knowledge Exploitation Fund for three years in a row.

The city is undergoing a £2-billion regeneration programme and has plenty of clubs and venues, including the multi-million pound Friars Walk entertainment and retail complex. Students in search of serious culture or clubbing gravitate to Cardiff.

Tuition fees

» Fees for UK/EU students 2017–18   £9,000
    Foundation degree   £8,000
» Welsh Assembly non-means-tested grant to pay fees above £4,046 for Welsh students. Tuition fee grant under review from 2018.
» Fees for international students 2017–18   £11,900
» Check the university's website for the latest information on fees, scholarships, bursaries and other forms of student support.

Students

Undergraduates:	15,110	(7,685)
Postgraduates:	1,940	(2,980)
Mature students:	27.6%	
International students:	11.8%	
Applications per place:	4.5	
From state-sector schools:	97.1%	
From working-class homes:	42%	
Satisfaction with students' union	60%	

For detailed information about sports facilities:
http://sport.southwales.ac.uk

Accommodation

Number of places and costs refer to 2016–17
University-provided places: 1,867
Percentage catered: 0% but catering package available.
Self-catered accommodation: £83 – £175 a week (40–51 weeks).
First-year students are offered accommodation. Local restrictions apply.
International students are guaranteed housing.
accom@southwales.ac.uk
www.southwales.ac.uk/accommodation

Southampton University

Southampton has dropped out of our top 20 this year after a fall of five places due mainly to a dip in student satisfaction.

The university had been moving up the table, benefiting from a strong performance in the 2014 Research Excellence Framework. It remains in the top seven for research quality after entering nine out of ten eligible academics for assessment and seeing more than 80 per cent of their work rated as world-leading or internationally excellent. The best results came in health subjects, environmental science, psychology, physics, chemistry, electronic engineering, and music, drama and performing arts.

Southampton is also in the top 15 for staffing levels but, like a number of Russell Group universities, it struggles on the sections of the National Student Survey concerned with teaching, feedback and academic support, barely reaching the top 100 on this measure.

The university invested £250-million programme upgrading its facilities in Southampton and Winchester, as well as opening a campus in Malaysia dedicated to engineering. The main Highfield Campus is in an attractive green location two miles from the city centre. The students' union has been refurbished and a purpose-built student services centre added to bring together learning support and other advisory facilities. The library has been greatly extended and includes social learning space designed by students. The striking £55-million Mountbatten Building for electronics and computer science, the Optoelectronics Research Centre and the £50-million Life Sciences Building have been added in recent years.

The latest developments added almost 1,500 rooms to the already substantial residential stock in two new accommodation complexes.

The nearby Avenue Campus is home to most of the humanities departments, while clinical medicine is based at Southampton General Hospital, where the university plans to open a £25-million cancer immunology centre in 2017. Winchester School of Art, which has been part of the university since 1996, has also enjoyed significant investment. Other sites include the National Oceanography Centre Southampton, based in the revitalised dock area.

The £116-million Boldrewood Innovation Campus has been developed with Lloyd's Register and is one of the largest university/business partnerships in the world. The campus is home to the Southampton Marine and Maritime Institute, which combines the university's expertise in ship science with other disciplines such as ocean science, law and business. Southampton was awarded one of the 12 Regius professorships to

University Road
Southampton SO17 1BJ

023 8059 4732 (admissions)
admissions@southampton.ac.uk
www.southampton.ac.uk
www.unionsouthampton
.org
Affiliation: Russell Group

The Times and Sunday Times **Rankings**

Overall Ranking: **21** (last year: 16)

Teaching quality:	=97	78.8%
Student experience:	=46	84.7%
Research quality:	7	44.9%
Entry standards:	=28	417
Student–staff ratio:	=12	12
Services & facilities/student:	31	£2,268
Expected completion rate:	32	91.7%
Good honours:	=26	80.1%
Graduate prospects:	=44	76.9%

celebrate the Queen's 90th birthday, in ocean sciences.

There are also particular strengths in computer science, where Sir Tim Berners-Lee, inventor of the Worldwide Web, is a professor. Southampton was a natural choice as one of the Government's eight academic centres of excellence in cyber security research. Southampton is in the top 100 in the QS global rankings and the proportion of income derived from research is among the highest in Britain.

The university's branch campus is at the Iksandar Education City development in Malaysia. Undergraduates can study astronautics and aeronautics, mechanical engineering, or electronics and electrical engineering for two years before finishing their degree in Southampton. The university has 8,000 international students and a growing number of those from the UK spend time at one of the partner institutions in 54 countries.

There is also a new Year in Employment programme giving students the choice of a role aligned to their degree or the chance explore a new working environment. Southampton is in the top 20 universities targeted for recruitment by firms in *The Times* Top 100 graduate employers, according to High Fliers' 2016 graduate market report. The university has introduced a more flexible curriculum at undergraduate level, with some subjects offering a "major/minor" structure that allows students to spend 25 per cent of their time on a subject other than their original degree choice. There are also interdisciplinary modules, such as intercultural communications, or sustainability in local and global environments, that are designed to give students a broader perspective.

Over 86 per cent of the students were state educated – one of the highest proportions in the Russell Group. Students act as ambassadors, associates and mentors in local schools and colleges, as part of the university's efforts to broaden its intake further.

Sports facilities are first class, with an indoor sports complex next to the students' union and a 25-metre pool. Sport and Wellbeing membership provides access to nine gyms – six on campus and three more across the city – while the outdoor sports complex has 20 grass and synthetic pitches.

Tuition fees

- » Fees for UK/EU students 2017–18 £9,250
  Year abroad £1,385
  Placement year £1,850
- » UK fees are expected to Increase by the rate of inflation from 2018–19 onwards.
- » Fees for international students 2017–18 £16,054–£19,725
  Medicine £19,725–£40,230
- » Check the university's website for the latest information on fees, scholarships, bursaries and other forms of student support.

Students

Undergraduates:	15,850	(305)
Postgraduates:	5,910	(1,735)
Mature students:	11.5%	
International students:	18.3%	
Applications per place:	7.0	
From state-sector schools:	84.8%	
From working-class homes:	23.1%	
Satisfaction with students' union	66%	

For detailed information about sports facilities:
www.southampton.ac.uk/sportandwellbeing

Accommodation

Number of places and costs refer to 2016–17
University-provided places: 7,000
Percentage catered: 8%
Catered costs: £133 – £179 a week.
Self-catered costs: £93 – £155 a week.
All full-time first years are guaranteed an offer of accommodation. Conditions apply.
International students: All non-EU students are guaranteed accommodation. Conditions apply.
www.southampton.ac.uk/uni-life/accommodation.page

Southampton Solent University

Southampton Solent has been in the top 25 universities for graduate start-ups for the last three years, helping to establish 46 companies in 2014–15, more than twice the sector average. Students wishing to set up their own businesses or become freelancers are offered rent-free offices and are supported by the Solent Entrepreneur Programme. They have access to the university's creative agency, Solent Creatives, and Re:So store – the first fully student-operated retail outlet in a UK shopping centre.

The university's support for students, which includes a Graduate Associate Scheme providing employment for 50 recent graduates, was identified as an example of best practice by the Quality Assurance Agency. Although the initiatives have yet to take Solent out of the bottom 10 for graduate prospects, the university has moved up five places in our table overall. Staffing levels have improved and the proportion of first-class and 2:1 degrees has risen by almost a third. The university won *Times Higher Education*'s award for the most improved student experience, although this did not translate into higher scores in the much larger National Student Survey.

Applications are running at record levels, with particularly strong demand for places in marine and maritime-based courses, which benefit from a world-renowned training and research facility for the superyacht, shipping and offshore oil industries.

Solent has capitalised on its strength in these areas by launching an innovative China Centre Maritime to focus on China's role as a major world maritime nation and promote collaboration in teaching, research and exchanges with Chinese universities in a variety of disciplines.

The university is UK higher education's premier yachting institution, with a world champion student team that has won the national championships four times in six years and alumni that have gone on to win Olympic and Paralympic Gold medals. Three new boats support courses at the purpose-built Watersports Centre, where some activities are targeted towards disadvantaged young people.

The industry-focused Solent Curriculum embraces a wide range of disciplines, however, including business, technology, the creative industries and sport. Students have the opportunity to work on projects for external clients and there is a strong representation of "non-traditional" disciplines, such as yacht and powercraft design, computer and video games, and music journalism and performance.

East Park Terrace
Southampton SO14 0YN

023 8201 5066 (admissions)
admissions@solent.ac.uk
www.solent.ac.uk
www.solentsu.co.uk
Affiliations: GuildHE;
    MillionPlus

The Times and Sunday Times Rankings

Overall Ranking: =110 (last year: =115)		
Teaching quality:	=90	79.3%
Student experience:	=96	81.8%
Research quality:	124	0.5%
Entry standards:	119	279
Student–staff ratio:	=76	16.9
Services & facilities/student:	88	£1,695
Expected completion rate:	115	78.5%
Good honours:	=79	67.7%
Graduate prospects:	121	57%

Creative Arts and Society courses now attract almost as many students as the consistently popular business school. The Centre for Professional Development in Broadcasting and Multimedia Production includes an online editing suite, digital television studio and gallery, for use by undergraduates as well as community groups and professionals. The university is a Skillset-accredited centre of excellence in television production, broadcast journalism, screenwriting and performance, with expertise in live event broadcast, studio and post-production. Solent TV is an award-winning entertainment and documentary web channel and students are part of the official Glastonbury festival filming team.

Programmes range from further education courses to doctorates. There is an extensive range of "top-up" and extended degrees as well as multiple start dates for courses. Solent recruits mainly in London and the south of England, a quarter of the HE students coming from Hampshire, but about 1,500 come from outside the UK.

A Research and Innovation Office has been established recently, but the university finished bottom of those that entered the 2014 Research Excellence Framework. It entered the lowest proportion of eligible academics, at only 7 per cent, and none of its research was placed in the top two categories for its external impact.

A £33-million teaching and learning building opened in 2016, expanding the city-centre campus. It is the latest project in a £100-million development programme, which will also see the business school relocate to refurbished premises at the heart of the campus before the end of 2016. Other recent developments include a ship-handling centre, a media academy, a new site for the Southampton School of Art and Design and FA-accredited football facilities costing £1 million used by the city's Premier League team. The Lawrie McMenemy Centre for Football Research is helping to cement the university's reputation for academic study of the sport and Solent has also become the country's largest provider of coaching education.

Students like the university's location, close to the city centre's shopping area and growing complement of bars and nightclubs. There are more than 2,300 hall places, most of which are allocated to first years. Sports facilities include a sports hall and fitness suite on campus and outdoor pitches, tennis and netball courts four miles away.

Tuition fees

» Fees for UK/EU students 2017–18 £9,250
» UK fees are expected to increase by the rate of inflation from 2018–19 onwards.
» Fees for international students 2017–18 £11,000
» Check the university's website for the latest information on fees, scholarships, bursaries and other forms of student support.

Students

Undergraduates:	9,770	(1,185)
Postgraduates:	110	(240)
Mature students:	18.0%	
International students:	13.3%	
Applications per place:	5.4	
From state-sector schools:	97.1%	
From working-class homes:	43.8%	
Satisfaction with students' union	62%	

For detailed information about sports facilities:
www.solent.ac.uk/solent-sport

Accommodation

Number of places and costs refer to 2016–17
University-provided places: more than 2,300
Percentage catered: 0%
Self-catered costs: £86.24 – £140.42 a week (41 weeks).
First years are allocated 90% of rooms.
International students: some accommodation is set aside.
accommodation@solent.ac.uk
www.solent.ac.uk/studying-at-solent/accommodation

Staffordshire University

Staffordshire is playing a leading role in the delivery of degree and higher apprenticeships, claiming the largest number of higher apprentices at any university. It is offering 180 higher apprenticeships, working with employers such as Vodafone and the NHS, and is finding that they are increasingly popular with young people.

The work-based qualifications are likely to play a growing part in the new Vice-Chancellor's vision of a "connected university". Professor Liz Barnes wants Staffordshire to be connected to the needs of students, businesses and industry and society. She arrived as the university was about to concentrate all its teaching, except in health and some education programmes, on the university's main campus in Stoke-on-Trent. The principal campus in Stafford is being sold, although the highly rated nursing and midwifery degrees and other health-related programmes are transferring to a £4-million centre of excellence in the town.

As well as saving money, the aim was to improve the student experience and create an award-winning, teaching-led university, with a focus on employability, enterprise and entrepreneurialism by 2017.

The main campus is at the heart of Stoke's University Quarter project, which encourages greater participation in higher education and forms a gateway to Stoke-on-Trent for anyone arriving at the city's main train station. An £80-million investment programme is upgrading a number of buildings, expanding the university library, extending student accommodation and improving the public spaces.

Some improvements had already been made on the Stoke campus. A £30-million science block opened in 2012 and another £12 million was spent on dedicated student spaces, exhibition areas, cafés and landscaping to create a more attractive study environment. There are modern halls of residence, a sports centre and lively students' union, as well as a 25-acre nature reserve – part of the university's sustained green commitment.

The university and its predecessors have occupied the College Road site for more than 100 years, and there have been celebrations in 2016 to mark 50 years of computing at degree level. Staffordshire was among the first institutions to offer a BSc in computer science and, more recently, has been a pioneer of two-year fast-track degrees, which are available in accounting and finance, business management, English and law.

Two satellite campuses have survived the reorganisation. Primary teacher training programmes are based at Lichfield, where there is an integrated further and higher education centre, developed in partnership

---

College Road
Stoke-on-Trent ST4 2DE

01782 294400 (enquiries)
enquiries@staffs.ac.uk
www.staffs.ac.uk
www.staffsunion.com
Affiliation: MillionPlus

The Times and Sunday Times **Rankings**
Overall Ranking: **92** (last year: 95)

Teaching quality:	=36	82.5%
Student experience:	=77	83.2%
Research quality:	55	16.5%
Entry standards:	117	284
Student–staff ratio:	=56	15.7
Services & facilities/student:	95	£1,663
Expected completion rate:	117	77.4%
Good honours:	82	67.3%
Graduate prospects:	122	56.9%

with South Staffordshire College, as well as business start-up units. The other site is in Shrewsbury, where nursing and midwifery students are based in the Royal Shrewsbury Hospital.

There are also 15,000 students taking Staffordshire courses outside the UK, almost half of them located around the Pacific Rim. They now make up more than a third of the university's intake, adding to a growing cohort of international students on the university's UK campuses.

With almost all of its undergraduates state-educated and 48 per cent coming from working-class homes, Staffordshire exceeds all the benchmarks for the breadth of its intake. There is good provision for students with disabilities and more than one undergraduate in five comes from areas with little participation in higher education, one of the biggest proportions in the country. The downside is the projected dropout rate, which remains above 20 per cent in the latest survey – well above the national average for the university's courses and entry qualifications.

Staffordshire increased the size and scope of its submission to the 2014 Research Excellence Framework, compared with previous research assessments, but still entered only 91 academics. The best results were in sport and exercise sciences, although all of the university's research in psychology was placed in the top two categories for its external impact. Applied research is Staffordshire's strong suit: its work has led to new products in markets as diverse as medical technology and recycling. Overall, the university is up three places in our league table, thanks mainly to rising student satisfaction.

The Stoke campus is within easy reach of the city centre and has a lively and active students' union. The University Quarter is attracting more social and leisure facilities.

Sports facilities are good and will see more investment as numbers on the Stoke campus rise. Good coaching has helped attract some outstanding athletes, who have access to sports science facilities to help with training schedules, psychological support and dietary assessments. The university has launched Team Staffs Sports Elite scholarships and spent £1.25-million refurbishing the sports centre, adding new studio spaces and tripling the capacity of the gym.

Tuition fees

- » Fees for UK/EU students 2017–18 £9,250
  Placement year no fee
  Courses at partner colleges £5,500–£7,601
- » UK fees are expected to increase by the rate of inflation from 2018–19 onwards.
- » Fees for international students 2017–18 £10,900
- » Check the university's website for the latest information on fees, scholarships, bursaries and other forms of student support.

Students

Undergraduates:	9,125	(5,645)
Postgraduates:	1,040	(1,925)
Mature students:	32.2%	
International students:	3.0%	
Applications per place:	5.5	
From state-sector schools:	99.3%	
From working-class homes:	47.6%	
Satisfaction with students' union	70%	

For detailed information about sports facilities:
www.staffs.ac.uk/teamstaffs

Accommodation

Number of places and costs refer to 2016–17
University-provided places: 1,041 (Stoke); 605 (Stafford)
Percentage catered: 0%
Self-catered accommodation: £95 – £118 a week (39 or 44 weeks).
First years have priority, if conditions are met.
International students: have priority, if conditions are met.
accommodation_stoke@staffs.ac.uk
accommodation_stafford@staffs.ac.uk
www.staffs.ac.uk/support_depts/accommodation

University of Stirling

Stirling is aiming to be in the top 25 universities in the UK by 2021, under a new strategy adopted in 2016. It has made a good start, with a seven-place rise in our new table, but has another 18 places to go.

This year's progress is down to increased student satisfaction and one of the biggest rises at any university in recent years in the percentage awarded good honours – up from 68 per cent to 83.7 per cent in 12 months. Stirling is also aiming to increase its income by £50 million and double its research profile.

Almost three-quarters of the work submitted to the 2014 Research Excellence Framework was judged to be world-leading or internationally excellent. The best results were in agriculture, veterinary and food science, where Stirling was ranked fourth in the UK. It was also top in Scotland for health sciences and third for psychology.

Applications are at record levels, but Stirling has not increased the size of its intake since 2013. It remains small, with only 11,000 students, and has one of the most beautiful campuses in the UK, set in 330 acres of parkland around a loch at the foot of the Ochil Hills. Students appear to like the community feel and easy access to improved facilities.

Stirling is particularly well provided with sports facilities, having been designated Scotland's University for Sporting Excellence. The campus is home to national swimming and tennis centres, as well as a golf course and a football academy. The sports centre has been refurbished and has a central gym, two strength and conditioning areas with weightlifting platforms and a cycle studio. A new High Performance Sports Science and Sports Medicine Facility opened in 2012. The university runs an international sports scholarship programme and manages Winning Students, the national sport scholarship programme for students across Scotland. Stirling student Duncan Scott won two silver medals in the pool at the 2016 Rio Olympics,

Stirling was awarded the maximum five stars in the QS global rating system, which covers teaching, graduate employability, internationalisation and inclusiveness. Academic facilities include a modernised library, a dedicated study zone and more than 700 computers for student use, many available 24 hours a day.

The university also has a purpose-built faith centre/chaplaincy which is open to students and staff of all faiths.

Preparatory courses for international students are available on campus and in London through a joint venture with INTO University Partnerships.

Its two nursing campuses at Inverness and Stornoway are transferring to the

---

Stirling Campus
Stirling FK9 4LA

01786 467044 (admissions)
admissions@stir.ac.uk
www.stir.ac.uk
www.stirlingstudentsunion.com
Affiliation: none

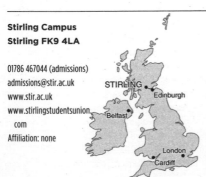

The Times and Sunday Times **Rankings**

Overall Ranking: **43** (last year: 50)

Teaching quality:	=68	80.4%
Student experience:	=67	83.7%
Research quality:	42	30.5%
Entry standards:	42	377
Student–staff ratio:	=43	14.9
Services & facilities/student:	75	£1,811
Expected completion rate:	62	86.1%
Good honours:	14	83.7%
Graduate prospects:	=39	77.5%

University of the Highlands and Islands in 2017.

Stirling was the British pioneer of the semester system, which has now become so popular throughout higher education. The academic year is divided into two blocks of 15 weeks with short mid-semester breaks. Students have the option of starting courses in January, rather than September, and can choose subjects from across all five faculties.

Undergraduates can switch the whole direction of their studies, in consultation with their academic adviser, as their interests develop. They can also speed up their progress on a Summer Academic Programme, which squeezes a full semester's teaching into July and August. Full-time students are not allowed to use the programme to reduce the length of their course, but part-timers can use it to make rapid progress.

Two-thirds of the students are from Scotland, but the remainder come from more than 100 different countries. International exchanges are common, with many of Stirling's students going to American, Asian and European universities each year.

Students appreciate the individual attention that a small campus university can offer, although some find the atmosphere claustrophobic.

A new centralised Student Hub team assists with all enquiries and provides student support services. A £38-million expansion of student accommodation was completed in 2015.

Stirling is not the top choice of night-clubbers, but there is a lively social scene based on the students' union. A new multipurpose social space has been developed in the union, to be used generally as a social study space, but also transformable into a nightclub venue, or space for society meetings or study groups. The Macrobert Arts Centre offers a full programme of cultural activities, while the surrounding countryside offers its own attractions for walkers and climbers.

The campus has been described by police as one of the safest in Britain and there is a Safe Taxi Scheme. A counselling and wellbeing service offers support for mental and emotional health, while the disability service supports a full range of student needs.

Tuition fees

» Fees for Scottish and EU students 2017–18   No fee
» Fees for non-Scottish UK (RUK) students 2017–18   £6,750
» Fees for international students 2017–18   £11,845–£14,105
» There are particular support schemes for RUK students.
» Check the university's website for the latest information on fees, scholarships, bursaries and other forms of student support.

Students

Undergraduates:	7,370	(625)
Postgraduates:	1,885	(1,220)
Mature students:	25.3%	
International students:	11.8%	
Applications per place:	8.4	
From state-sector schools:	96.4%	
From working-class homes:	32.1%	
Satisfaction with students' union	60%	

For detailed information about sports facilities:
www.stir.ac.uk/sport-at-stirling

Accommodation

Number of places and costs refer to 2016–17
University-provided places: 2,800
Percentage catered: 0%
Self-catered costs: £85 – £141 a week; £159 (studio flat) for 38–51 weeks (dependant on course).
All first-year undergraduate students are prioritised for suitable housing arranged by the university.
International students: as above.
accommodation@stir.ac.uk
www.stir.ac.uk/campus-life/accommodation

University of Strathclyde

The demand for places at Strathclyde was far higher in 2015 than at any time in the university's history. Applications were up by 27 per cent on the previous year, and the numbers starting courses grew by 900, even after a significant cut in the offer rate. Most of the increase came from mature students, who account for more than a quarter of undergraduates, attracted perhaps by Strathclyde's traditional strength in graduate employment.

The university frequently stresses the mission it has had since its establishment in 1796 – to be a "place of useful learning" – and is now aiming to be one of the world's leading technological universities. It has slipped two places in our table this year, after cutting spending on facilities and staffing, but is still in the top 50, with entry standards only just outside the top ten when the mix of subjects is taken into consideration.

Strathclyde also achieved spectacular results in the 2014 Research Excellence Framework, which took the university close to the top 20 in our research ranking. Almost 80 per cent of an exceptionally large submission was rated world-leading or internationally excellent. The university was top in the UK for physics and top in Scotland for business, among a clutch of eye-catching performances. It is the European partner for South Korea's global research and commercialisation programme and is the UK headquarters of Fraunhofer Gesellschaft, Europe's largest contract research organisation.

Strathclyde, which now adds Glasgow to its name, has been carrying out an ambitious £350-million development programme. The £89-million Technology and Innovation Centre, the largest in the UK at 25,000 square metres – the equivalent of 100 tennis courts – represents the most striking project.

All courses are taught on the city-centre John Anderson Campus, with the Faculty of Humanities and Social Sciences at its heart, enabling staff to work more closely with colleagues in research and teaching. The developments feature new and improved teaching areas, study space and facilities for students tailored to their specific subjects.

Away from the campus, the Advanced Forming Research Centre, a research partnership with international engineering firms, has opened near Glasgow Airport.

The university is the third largest in Scotland, with more than 22,000 students, and actively promotes wider access, comfortably exceeding the UK average for state-educated students. The university has endorsed an international movement to establish "Age-Friendly" universities; its Learning in Later Life programme has established itself as one of Scotland's most

---

16 Richmond Street
Glasgow G1 1XQ

0141 548 2913
ugenquiries@strath.ac.uk
www.strath.ac.uk
www.strathstudents.com
Affiliation: none

GLASGOW
Edinburgh
Belfast
London
Cardiff

The Times and Sunday Times **Rankings**

Overall Ranking: **48** (last year: 46)

Teaching quality:	119	76.3%
Student experience:	=46	84.7%
Research quality:	=21	37.7%
Entry standards:	13	476
Student–staff ratio:	112	19.4
Services & facilities/student:	73	£1,846
Expected completion rate:	=54	87.2%
Good honours:	=35	77.8%
Graduate prospects:	42	77.2%

successful routes to education for older people.

The business school, which is rated among the top 40 in Europe by the *Financial Times,* is normally considered Strathclyde's greatest strength. It is among the largest in Europe and one of only 68 in the world to be "triple accredited" by the main international bodies. The School has eight well-established international centres in Europe, the Gulf and South East Asia.

The engineering faculty is the largest in Scotland, and home to the biggest university electrical power engineering and energy research grouping in Europe. Strathclyde Enterprise Pathway allows students to develop, enhance and test their transferable skills, while alumni and businesses in the Strathclyde 100 network support the university's emerging entrepreneurs. Spin-out companies established at the university employ more than 800 people, making annual sales of £800 million. Only four universities in the UK have launched more spin-outs in the last ten years.

There is a student village on the main campus with around 1,400 rooms and 700 residential places are nearby in the Merchant City. The ten-floor union building attracts students from all over Glasgow. There are numerous cultural and political clubs and societies, plus over 40 sporting clubs and university teams.

Proximity to Glasgow's vibrant and celebrated music scene is a plus, and for those with more sophisticated tastes, there are numerous theatres and arts organisations, as well as standout museums such as the Kelvingrove Art Gallery, one of Scotland's top attractions, while Glasgow's medieval cathedral is next to the campus.

On the sporting side, Strathclyde was the only training venue in Scotland for the London 2012 Olympics, and the university's students and alumni made up 5 per cent of Team Scotland in the 2014 Commonwealth Games, when the campus formed part of the cycling road race route.

Plans have been approved for a £33-million Sport, Health and Wellbeing complex in the centre of Glasgow. It will include a six-lane swimming pool, a large gym and specialist academic space for teaching and research, and is expected to open in the summer of 2018.

Tuition fees

- » Fees for Scottish and EU students 2017–18 — No fee
- » Fees for non-Scottish UK (RUK) students 2016–17 £9,250 a year, capped at £27,750 for most courses.
  Placement year (RUK) £4,500
- » Fees for international students 2017–18 £13,500–£19,100
- » There are particular support schemes for RUK students.
- » Check the university's website for the latest information on fees, scholarships, bursaries and other forms of student support.

Students

Undergraduates:	12,205	(2,460)
Postgraduates:	3,965	(2,575)
Mature students:	29.7%	
International students:	13.2%	
Applications per place:	6.4	
From state-sector schools:	91.1%	
From working-class homes:	25.9%	
Satisfaction with students' union	73%	

For detailed information about sports facilities:
www.strathsports.co.uk

Accommodation

Number of places and costs refer to 2016–17
University-provided places: 2,155
Percentage catered: 0%
Self-catered costs: £99 – £133 a week (39 weeks).
First years are offered accommodation if they live further than 25 miles from the university.
International students: as above.
student.accommodation@strath.ac.uk
www.strath.ac.uk/studywithus/accommodation

University of Suffolk

Suffolk is the only newcomer to this year's *Guide*, having secured university status in August 2016. The Ipswich-based institution was the product of a unique collaboration between the universities of East Anglia and Essex, along with a network of local colleges, to bring higher education to one of the few counties without a university.

Founded in 2007 as University Campus Suffolk, it was expected to take 20 years to become an independent university, but was granted the power to award degrees in November 2015 and the Privy Council agreed to confer the full university title shortly afterwards. The two original partners will continue to work with the new university, but Suffolk will be fully independent, receiving direct Government funding for the first time.

Over the next five years, Suffolk aims to develop a broader base, raise its academic standing and remain financially sustainable. It hopes to be a distinctive "Community Impact" university, with a much larger student population, not only drawn from the region, but also nationally and internationally. Richard Lister, the Vice-Chancellor, expects the change in status to provide a £30-million annual boost to the local economy by 2020, as the university increases its undergraduate numbers from 4,600 to around 7,000.

The curriculum will focus more on science, technology, engineering and mathematics, and there will be greater partnership with local employers, such as BT and Ipswich Hospital. The university's initial strategy includes creating a more international community, developing significant research strengths and making further improvements to its Waterfront Campus.

Suffolk enters our table in the bottom three, but all the data refers to the period before it had become a university in its own right. It did not enter the 2014 Research Excellence Framework and it has not been possible to compile a score for spending on student facilities.

Student satisfaction has been high in previous years, but dropped sharply in the latest survey, which was also carried out before university status arrived. Overall satisfaction fell by 6 percentage points and Suffolk was in the bottom five for the sections of the National Student Survey that focus on the organisation of courses, learning resources and personal development.

The campus in Ipswich has four modern teaching buildings and has seen a £2.5-million renovation of the library. There are university centres, too, at Bury St Edmunds, at West Suffolk College; at Otley, on the site of Easton and Otley College;

Waterfront Building
Neptune Quay
Ipswich IP4 1QJ

01473 338833 (courses)
www.uos.ac.uk/forms/
  ask-us-question
www.uos.ac.uk
www.uosunion.org
Affiliation: GuildHE

The Times and Sunday Times Rankings

Overall Ranking: **126** (last year: n/a)

Teaching quality:	106	77.8%
Student experience:	=120	79.4%
Research quality:	n/a	n/a
Entry standards:	87	309
Student–staff ratio:	=116	20
Services & facilities/student:	n/a	n/a
Expected completion rate:	120	76.2%
Good honours:	127	51.6%
Graduate prospects:	=110	61%

at Suffolk New College, in the Education Quarter of Ipswich; and at Lowestoft and Great Yarmouth colleges. There are also Leap Centres in smaller premises from Newmarket to Felixstowe, and even smaller Leap Points in libraries and children's centres, all with access to Suffolk's facilities.

The students are spread across seven departments within two faculties – arts, business and applied social science, and health and science. Courses are tailored to the labour market and include a range of Foundation degrees. There are more than 100 undergraduate course options, with offerings in business, computing, engineering health care, psychology and sport. Four out of ten students are over 25 when they start their courses, most of them coming from the region. Almost three-quarters of the students are full-timers and two-thirds are female. Many students live at home, but there is a privately operated hall of residence for 590 students close to the campus in Ipswich. The university accredits other accommodation in the town and in its other locations.

A partnership with Ipswich Town Football Club is typical of the approach to community partnership of this small but growing institution. A suite of football sports science and coaching courses has been launched as part of a formal partnership with the Championship team. Expanding the university's existing sports science provision, the five new MSci degrees available from 2016 will cover football coaching, performance analysis, sports performance physiology, sports psychology, and strength and conditioning. The four-year Masters courses include placements at Ipswich Town, and students will need 120 new-style UCAS tariff points to get a place in 2017.

The proportion of students from working class homes, at 45 per cent, is higher than average for the university's courses and entry grades, while the percentage from areas of low participation in higher education is among the highest in the country, at 26 per cent. Suffolk has been devoting a larger-than-average share of its fee income to student support, more than half of its spending going on cash bursaries for students from under-represented backgrounds. However, a projected dropout rate of 17.5 per cent is high, even allowing for the diverse intake.

Tuition fees

» Fees for UK/EU students 2017–18 £9,250
  Foundation degree £8,220
  Placement year £1,850
» UK fees are expected to increase by the rate of inflation from 2018–19 onwards.
» Fees for international students 2017–18 £10,080–£11,580
» Check the university's website for the latest information on fees, scholarships, bursaries and other forms of student support.

Students

Undergraduates:	3,465	(1,220)
Postgraduates:	65	(310)
Mature students:	54.2%	
International students:	2.5%	
Applications per place:	3.9	
From state-sector schools:	97%	
From working-class homes:	44.8%	
Satisfaction with students' union	66%	

For detailed information about sports facilities: www.uosunion.org/sports

Accommodation

Number of places and costs refer to 2016–17
University-provided places: 590
Percentage catered: 0%
Self-catered costs: £116 – £128 (single en suite); £157 (studio) a week (42 weeks).
First-years are advised to apply for accommodation before 30 June; advice available regarding off-campus housing.
International students: as above.
www.uos.ac.uk/content/accommodation

University of Sunderland

Sunderland is one of the few universities to rise in our table despite falling levels of student satisfaction. Much-improved staffing levels and increased spending on student facilities have helped it to move up four places.

The demand for places has never fully recovered from the coalition Government's decision to raise fees, however. Despite generous financial support for students from poor backgrounds, applications have dropped for four years in a row and were 30 per cent lower in 2015 than 2011.

With the offer rate rising over the same period, the decline in the numbers actually starting courses has been less severe, but almost 60 per cent of the students have a household income of less than £25,000 a year. Surveys of first-year undergraduates found that 38 per cent of them had been influenced in their choice of university by Sunderland's package of support, which includes £600 towards public transport costs or university rents, as well as a Sunderland Scholarship of £1,000 in their first two years if they are among the 75 per cent whose household income is less than £42,620.

The university has launched a number of new degrees in subjects from cosmetic science to manufacturing engineering. A new School of Nursing is opening, taking its first students in 2017. Its three-year degree will be the first in the UK to be linked directly to a School of Pharmacy. The school will be located in the new Sciences Complex development, which will be completed by September 2017 and will include a new paramedic practice programme and the Northern Centre for Photography. The Faculty of Applied Sciences is one of the largest in the UK, with over 4,000 students.

The university's original City Campus also features the £12-million CitySpace, which has improved the sports and social facilities, a £12-million student village, a one-stop shop for student services, an outdoor performance area and a design centre.

There are two other campuses, one in Sunderland and the other in London, near Canary Wharf, which offers business, tourism and nursing degrees, as well as postgraduate programmes.

Within Sunderland, the Sir Tom Cowie Campus, at St Peter's, occupies 24 acres on the banks of the River Wear. It is built around a 7th-century abbey described as one of Britain's first universities and incorporates the National Glass Centre, a heritage centre for the glass industry, and exhibition space.

The campus also houses the business school and the faculties of applied sciences, law, and arts, design and media. The media centre provides students with excellent television and video production facilities.

City Campus
Chester Road
Sunderland SR1 3SD

0191 515 3000 (course helpline)
student.helpline@
 sunderland.ac.uk
www.sunderland.ac.uk
www.sunderlandsu.co.uk
Affiliation: MillionPlus

The Times and Sunday Times Rankings

Overall Ranking: **100** (last year: 104)

Teaching quality:	=65	80.5%
Student experience:	=81	83.1%
Research quality:	=82	5.8%
Entry standards:	=112	290
Student–staff ratio:	=66	16.3
Services & facilities/student:	82	£1,770
Expected completion rate:	106	80.3%
Good honours:	125	54.6%
Graduate prospects:	89	66.8%

The popular media courses now include magazine, fashion, broadcast and sports journalism, while the LLB degree includes space law, the first module of its kind in the UK.

Sunderland now has more than 19,000 students at all levels, around a third of them from outside the UK. Almost 30 per cent of the UK undergraduates come from areas of low participation – the highest proportion at any university. A pioneering access scheme offers places to mature students without A levels, as long as they reach the required levels of literacy, numeracy and other basic skills.

Provision for disabled students is excellent, with trained support staff in the libraries and in every academic school, and special modules to help dyslexics. The main campus houses the North East Regional Assessment Centre, which assesses the requirements of students with disabilities and specific learning difficulties. There is special provision at the five halls of residence.

Many students take work placements with multinational companies that have been attracted to the North East and now have links with the university. The Institute for Automotive and Manufacturing Advanced Practice has a team of 40 researchers and consultants working with local businesses, while nearby Nissan helped to design a course in mechanical engineering.

Less than a third of the work submitted for the 2014 Research Excellence Framework reached the top two categories, but the university entered almost 40 per cent of the eligible academics, a much higher proportion than most of its peers. There was some world-leading research in 10 of the 13 subjects in which it submitted work.

The city of Sunderland is fiercely proud of its identity and has the advantage of a riverside and coastal location.

The leisure facilities are good: the city has the North East's only 50-metre swimming pool and dry ski slope, as well as Europe's biggest climbing wall and a theatre showing West End productions. The attractions of Newcastle are less than half an hour away by Metro or bus.

Tuition fees

» Fees for UK/EU students 2017–18   £9,250
    Foundation degree   £7,965
    Placement year   £500
» UK fees are expected to increase by the rate of inflation from 2018–19 onwards.
» Fees for international students 2017–18   £10,750
» Check the university's website for the latest information on fees, scholarships, bursaries and other forms of student support.

Students

Undergraduates:	9,360	(1,535)
Postgraduates:	1,860	(940)
Mature students:	27.6%	
International students:	25.1%	
Applications per place:	5.5	
From state-sector schools:	97.2%	
From working-class homes:	44.9%	
Satisfaction with students' union	60%	

For detailed information about sports facilities:
www.unisportsunderland.com

Accommodation

Number of places and costs refer to 2016–17
University provided places: 1,135 beds (halls), 548 (The Forge).
Percentage catered: 0%
Self-catered costs: £77.54 (standard room) – £97.30 (en suite) for 40 weeks.
New first years are guaranteed accommodation in accordance with the university's allocation policy.
International students: as above.
http://services.sunderland.ac.uk/facilities/accommodation

University of Surrey

Surrey has dropped out of our top ten after only one year because of a decline in the measure that was most associated with its rise. The university is still well inside the top 20 in the National Student Survey both for teaching quality and the broader student experience, but it was in the top four for both last year. The dip of three percentage points has cost it six places in the overall table. Surrey, which was our 2015 University of the Year, is still growing – the numbers starting courses were almost 70 per cent higher in 2015 than in 2013, despite rising entry standards.

In a transformative period, the university has extended its campus in Guildford, opened a £45-million veterinary school – only the second to be established in half a century – and also developed a joint venture in China. The 5G Innovation Centre, which received £58 million support from an international consortium, opened in 2016, bringing Surrey's researchers together with the major global players in mobile telecommunications, and a new building will open in 2017 with specialist facilities for a new portfolio of "engineering for health" degrees.

The university has been celebrating its 50th anniversary in 2016 with a new Vice-Chancellor, Professor Max Lu, the former Provost of the University of Queensland, who is keen to develop Surrey's international reputation. Surrey received the maximum five stars in the QS global rating of universities, which covers facilities, teaching, research, inclusiveness and internationalisation. All students are encouraged to take a free course in a European language alongside their degree, in a programme known as the Global Graduate Award.

The university has a high proportion of students from outside the UK – approaching a quarter – and over half of its research publications have an international partner. It is a founding member of the University Global Partnership Network (UGPN), involving North Carolina State University and the Universidad de São Paulo in Brazil.

There are over 100 strategic partnerships across the globe, but the biggest development has seen the opening of a campus in Dalian, China, with the Dongbei University of Finance and Economics.

Surrey's home campus is ten minutes' walk from the centre of Guildford and includes two lakes, playing fields and enough residential accommodation to enable all first years to live in. Developments since 2000 have cost £400 million and include a refurbished and extended library and learning centre, and the gleaming Duke of Kent Building, which houses the growing health and medical provision.

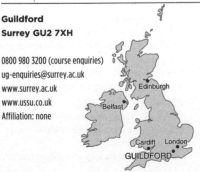

Guildford
Surrey GU2 7XH

0800 980 3200 (course enquiries)
ug-enquiries@surrey.ac.uk
www.surrey.ac.uk
www.ussu.co.uk
Affiliation: none

The Times and Sunday Times Rankings

Overall Ranking: **14** (last year: 8)

Teaching quality:	16	83.7%
Student experience:	17	87.3%
Research quality:	44	29.7%
Entry standards:	24	424
Student–staff ratio:	30	13.9
Services & facilities/student:	14	£2,697
Expected completion rate:	=33	91.6%
Good honours:	21	80.7%
Graduate prospects:	23	81.1%

The proportion of research income coming from private business and industry has grown to about 70 per cent. BP sponsored the Centre for Petroleum and Surface Chemistry, for example. The Surrey Research Park is one of the largest in the UK still to be owned, funded and managed by its host university.

Almost 80 per cent of the work submitted to the 2014 Research Excellence Framework was rated as world-leading or internationally excellent. The best results were in nursing and other health subjects.

Large numbers of students take engineering and science subjects. But the university has other strengths, notably in business and the sector-leading School of Hospitality and Tourism Management. It has also incorporated the Guildford School of Acting and opened the £4.5-million Ivy Arts Centre, with a 200-seat theatre and workshops.

SurreyLearn, the virtual learning environment, allows students to work with others on their courses online and to take part in discussions and blogs, as well as allowing lecturers to set coursework and interact with students.

Undergraduates in most subjects undertake work placements of one year, or several shorter periods, often abroad. As a result, most degrees last four years.

The dropout rate of less than 6 per cent is better than expected for a university with Surrey's subjects and entry qualifications.

The Manor Park Campus, which is effectively an extension of the university's Stag Hill headquarters, provides over 1,800 residential places for students and staff, as well as a reception building with café, bar and lounge areas.

The £36-million Surrey Sports Park has extensive indoor and outdoor facilities. The main campus is the centre of social life, and has new leisure facilities, including upgraded dining and social areas.

Guildford has plenty of retail, cultural and recreational facilities and the proximity of London (35 minutes by train) is an attraction to many students, although it also helps account for the high cost of renting in the private sector.

Tuition fees

» Fees for UK/EU students 2017–18 £9,250
Year abroad £1,350
Placement year £1,800
» UK fees are expected to increase by the rate of inflation from 2018–19 onwards.
» Fees for international students 2017–18 £15,000–£19,500
Veterinary medicine £30,000
» Check the university's website for the latest information on fees, scholarships, bursaries and other forms of student support.

Students

Undergraduates:	9,595	(995)
Postgraduates:	2,405	(1,310)
Mature students:	14.2%	
International students:	24.4%	
Applications per place:	9.4	
From state-sector schools:	91.9%	
From working-class homes:	28.6%	
Satisfaction with students' union	77%	

For detailed information about sports facilities:
www.surreysportspark.co.uk

Accommodation

Number of places and costs refer to 2016–17
University-provided places: 5,063
Percentage catered: 0%
Self-catered costs: £69 – £165 a week.
All first years are guaranteed a place if they apply by the deadline.
International non-EU students are guaranteed housing for the standard duration of their course. Remaining places are allocated to final-year students.
www.surrey.ac.uk/accommodation

University of Sussex

Sussex has entered a new phase of growth after adding more than 600 places to its intake of undergraduates in 2015 – an increase of 18 per cent on the previous year. Only one university in England had a higher offer rate than Sussex's 93 per cent. The aim is to increase the numbers starting degrees by 50 per cent by 2018 in order to provide opportunities for a more diverse range of students and achieve the "critical mass" that Sussex considers necessary to strengthen the interdisciplinary approach that has been its hallmark since the 1960s, to engage with partners and be internationally competitive in research.

The university remains in our top 20, and three-quarters of the work submitted for the Research Excellence Framework was judged to be world-leading or internationally excellent. Sussex was among the leaders in history, English, psychology and geography.

The campus, four miles from the centre of Brighton in the suburb of Falmer, is already serving a record number of students: 15,000, of whom 11,200 are undergraduates. The university has completed a £100-million campus development plan, refurbishing Sir Basil Spence's original buildings and adding new ones. The most recent addition is a £29-million academic building offering a mix of lecture theatres, study and teaching space, and a social centre. A significant redevelopment of the engineering facilities is in progress, including a £10-million investment in a Computing, Robotics, Electronics and Mechatronics Centre. The Attenborough Centre, reopened in 2015, has become an interdisciplinary arts hub for the university and the wider community.

The library, which has undergone a £6-million redevelopment and introduced 24-hour opening during term time, has seen a 50 per cent increase in use. An investment of £1.5 million in IT developments has doubled the number of computers available to students and installed higher-speed Wi-Fi in all the student residences.

Arts and social science students account for the biggest share of places, but the physical and life sciences are not far behind. Except in accredited courses, undergraduates are encouraged to study outside their core area. They can take a language or an elective in another subject, leading to a major/minor degree and opening up opportunities to study abroad.

There are two 12-week teaching periods, with a mid-year assessment period – a pattern that the university believes improves the way students learn and are assessed.

Sussex is in our top six for graduate prospects, improving on an already high employment rate. Student support includes a work-study programme to help students

---

Sussex House
Brighton BN1 9RH

01273 876787 (enquiries)
study@sussex.ac.uk
www.sussex.ac.uk
www.bsms.ac.uk
www.sussexstudent.com
Affiliation: none

The Times and Sunday Times **Rankings**

Overall Ranking: **18** (last year: 19)

Teaching quality:	=84	79.7%
Student experience:	=28	86%
Research quality:	=37	31.8%
Entry standards:	=43	375
Student–staff ratio:	=47	15.3
Services & facilities/student:	13	£2,722
Expected completion rate:	37	91.1%
Good honours:	31	79.1%
Graduate prospects:	6	86.2%

earn money, funded work placements and three years' aftercare for graduates to help them find a career that suits them. The Sussex Plus programme documents and credits students' extra-curricular skills, while a new initiative, Startup Sussex, supports students' creative business ideas and social projects.

Although little more than 50 years old, the university can count three Nobel prize winners among its former academics. The first fruits of a £50-million fundraising campaign have seen the opening of major research centres on adoption, corruption, Middle East studies and consciousness science. A successful joint medical school, shared with neighbouring Brighton University, is split between the Royal Sussex County Hospital and the two universities' Falmer campuses.

Sussex is committed to taking candidates with no family experience of higher education and has a prize-winning scheme to support them with rent reductions and scholarships. The share of places going to students from the four poorest socio-economic groups is still lower than the national average for the university's courses and entry qualifications. But black and ethnic minority students have been increasingly successful, almost 80 per cent achieving a First or 2:1, exceeding the average across the university.

A fifth of undergraduates come from outside the EU and the university has performed consistently well in the International Student Barometer, which gauges overseas students' satisfaction.

Together with other first years, they are guaranteed a place in university-managed accommodation that has been expanded and upgraded in recent years. There are now more than 5,000 residential places, and Sussex's plans for the future include a major housing development to replace old accommodation and add 2,000 more places. A new life sciences building is also planned to complement the highly rated Genome Research Centre.

The campus is located within the South Downs National Park, with excellent transport links into town. There is no shortage of social events on campus and Brighton has plenty to offer. Sports facilities were good enough to house pre-Olympic training. Sports scholarships are available to outstanding athletes, including four reserved for basketball and hockey players.

Tuition fees

» Fees for UK/EU students 2017–18 £9,250
» UK fees are expected to increase by the rate of inflation from 2018–19 onwards.
» Fees for international students 2017–18 £15,100–£18,750
  Medicine (2016–17) £28,000
» Check the university's website for the latest information on fees, scholarships, bursaries and other forms of student support.

Students

Undergraduates:	10,140	(10)
Postgraduates:	2,565	(825)
Mature students:	12.5%	
International students:	27.2%	
Applications per place:	5.4	
From state-sector schools:	86.7%	
From working-class homes:	22.5%	
Satisfaction with students' union	71%	

For detailed information about sports facilities:
www.sussex.ac.uk/sport

Accommodation

Number of places and costs refer to 2016–17
University-provided places: 5,030
Percentage catered: 0%
Self-catered costs: £86.82 – £151.00 (single) a week. Some shared rooms available.
First-year students are guaranteed accommodation if conditions are met.
International students: first-year students as above.
housing@sussex.ac.uk
www.sussex.ac.uk/study/accommodation

Swansea University

Swansea has become the top university in Wales in our table and wins our inaugural Welsh University of the Year title, having overtaken Cardiff for the first time in more than 20 years of publication. The feat comes as the university embarks on a £60-million upgrade of its main campus less than a year after opening a spectacular new one overlooking Swansea Bay.

The buzz around the university is such that applications rose by more than 60 per cent in three years and the intake of undergraduates was 1,600 higher.

The new capital programme, funded through a loan from the European Investment Bank, will improve the library and upgrade laboratories and other teaching facilities on the original Singleton Park campus. It will also enable work to begin on the second phase of the Bay Campus, which opened in 2015, adding a Computational Foundry which the university expects to make it a global destination for computer scientists.

The £450-million, 65-acre Bay Campus is the only one in the UK with direct access to a beach. It is home to the College of Engineering and School of Management and houses about 1,500 students in new halls of residence, relieving pressure on the original campus five miles along the coast.

Its focus will be on applied research with industry – the new Engineering Quarter houses two research institutes, where there are collaborations with Rolls-Royce, Ericsson, Sony and British Aerospace.

Swansea was the UK's first campus university when it opened in 1920, enjoying a prime position at the gateway to the Gower peninsula, the UK's first Area of Outstanding Natural Beauty. Some £72 million has already been invested in the Singleton Park Campus. Recent developments include the £1.2-million Richard Burton Archives and two Institute of Life Science buildings housing researchers in areas including health nano-technology and big data public health research. The nearby Swansea University Medical School, which celebrated its tenth anniversary in 2014, is one of the UK's fastest growing.

Swansea's strongest suit in our table is in graduate prospects, where it is well inside the top 30. The Employability Academy provides paid internships and coordinates a variety of career support activities. By the time of its centenary, the university's target is to be recognised among the top 200 universities in the world. Although it is still some way off that objective, it has been awarded the maximum five stars in QS's global rating system, which covers facilities, teaching, research and employability, as well as inclusiveness and internationalisation.

Singleton Park
Swansea SA2 8PP

01792 295111 (enquiries)
admissions@swansea.ac.uk
www.swansea.ac.uk
www.swansea-union.co.uk
Affiliation: none

The Times and Sunday Times Rankings

Overall Ranking: **=44** (last year: =41)		
Teaching quality:	=54	81.2%
Student experience:	48	84.6%
Research quality:	35	33.7%
Entry standards:	=67	326
Student–staff ratio:	=38	14.7
Services & facilities/student:	54	£2,055
Expected completion rate:	39	90.1%
Good honours:	41	76.1%
Graduate prospects:	26	80.5%

Four-fifths of the work submitted for the 2014 Research Excellence Framework was assessed as world-leading or internationally excellent, with health subjects, English and general engineering doing particularly well.

Undergraduates are encouraged to stray outside their specialist area in their first year. Many degrees include opportunities to work abroad or study at one of more than 100 partner institutions worldwide.

Only 28 per cent of undergraduates come from working-class homes – significantly less that the UK average for the university's subjects and entry grades – but the projected dropout rate of 6.6 per cent, by contrast, is significantly better than Swansea's benchmark figure. The department of adult and continuing education teaches mature students throughout the Valleys and elsewhere in South Wales, while the South West Wales Reaching Wider Partnership encourages students who would not usually aspire to attend university, to consider it.

Swansea has good provision for disabled students, whose needs are addressed through a £250,000 assessment and training centre.

The university has one of the best ratios of computers available for student use at any university and the two new halls have taken the number of residential places to about 4,000.

The £20-million International Sports Village was used as a training facility by the New Zealand and Canada squads during the 2015 Rugby World Cup. It has an athletics track, grass and all-weather pitches, squash and tennis courts plus the indoor athletics training centre and 80-station gym.

The adjacent Wales National Pool has 50- and 25-metre pools and is the Welsh National Performance Centre. The 360 Beach and Water Sports Centre is the only university-operated centre of its kind, while five miles away at Fairwood, the university also has grass and 3G pitches, built in partnership with Swansea City Football Club.

The Bay Campus has a sports hall plus two smaller gyms, but the Singleton Park Campus will remain the focal point of most students' leisure activities. The city has a good range of leisure facilities, and Cardiff is less than an hour away by train for those looking for a change of scene.

Tuition fees

- » Fees for UK/EU students 2017–18 £9,000
  Placement year £1,800
- » Welsh Assembly non-means-tested grant to pay fees above £4,046 for Welsh students. Tuition fee grant under review from 2018.
- » Fees for international students 2017–18 £12,900–£16,950
  Medicine £33,320
- » Check the university's website for the latest information on fees, scholarships, bursaries and other forms of student support.

Students

Undergraduates:	11,360	(2,105)
Postgraduates:	1,680	(870)
Mature students:	14.8%	
International students:	15.4%	
Applications per place:	5.7	
From state-sector schools:	91.8%	
From working-class homes:	27.9%	
Satisfaction with students' union	73%	

For detailed information about sports facilities:
www.swansea.ac.uk/sport

Accommodation

Number of places and costs refer to 2016–17
University-provided places: about 4,000
Percentage catered: 5%
Catered costs: £97 – £102 (standard rooms) a week.
Self-catered costs: £79.60 (twin) – £222.20 (flat) a week.
First-year students holding a firm offer are guaranteed accommodation if conditions are met.
International students: offered up to 3 years' housing.
accommodation@swansea.ac.uk
www.swansea.ac.uk/accommodation

Teesside University

Teesside's applications and enrolments had risen for three years in a row and were running at record levels in 2015. It has been a period of unprecedented growth for the university, which has invested £260 million to develop both at the main campus in Middlesbrough town centre and at a second site in Darlington, which now houses the National Biologics and Manufacturing Centre. Teesside's strategy up to 2020, under its new vice-chancellor Paul Croney, is for further growth and a focus on the student experience and "real-world impact".

The university is already in the top 25 for student satisfaction relating to teaching, feedback and academic support, and the top 50 for the broader student experience. Teesside is also ranked in the top three in the UK for overall satisfaction in the International Student Barometer, which is confined to overseas students. The university's personal tutors emerged as the best in the world.

Almost two-thirds of the 16,000 undergraduates are from the North East and over a third are 21 or over on entry. The university is well known for its commitment to widening access to higher education. Only one university in England has a higher proportion of undergraduates from areas of low participation in higher education, while the share of places going to students from working-class homes is significantly higher, at 46 per cent, than the national average for Teesside's courses and entry qualifications.

The new Campus Heart features a £20-million teaching building which opened in 2015, providing a mix of flexible modern teaching space and offices. Science and engineering facilities are being upgraded and there has been extensive landscaping. Another £10 million has been committed for further improvements to the library, students' union and catering facilities.

The university has also spent £10 million purchasing an apartment block and refurbishing the 75 four to eight-bedroom apartments. Other recent developments include a centre for creative technologies for computing, media and design.

But the biggest project has been DigitalCity Innovation, the university's centre for digital excellence and entrepreneurship, which has helped in the creation of hundreds of new businesses. Teesside was the first former polytechnic to win *Times Higher Education* magazine's University of the Year award and also has a Queen's Anniversary Prize for its services to business and enterprise.

The £13-million campus in Darlington has a focus on business services, professional education and training support. The Forge, the university's business engagement hub, is based there.

Middlesbrough TS1 3BA

01642 218121 (switchboard)
enquiries@tees.ac.uk
www.tees.ac.uk
www.tees-su.org.uk
Affiliation: University
Alliance

The Times and Sunday Times **Rankings**

Overall Ranking: **=101** (last year: 102)

Teaching quality:	23	83.1%
Student experience:	=42	84.8%
Research quality:	109	3.6%
Entry standards:	=89	306
Student–staff ratio:	=86	17.4
Services & facilities/student:	71	£1,863
Expected completion rate:	=103	80.6%
Good honours:	119	57.5%
Graduate prospects:	91	66.4%

Only 14 per cent of Teesside's eligible academics were entered for the 2014 Research Excellence Framework, but almost 60 per cent of their work was considered world-leading or internationally excellent – twice as much as in the previous research assessments. Social work and social policy, history and health subjects produced the best results. The 11,000 health students are by far the largest group in the university, while design and computer animation and gaming are generally regarded as the other main strengths.

The School of Computing was ranked as one of the top 20 places in the world to study animation by *3D World* magazine. Graduates have gone on to work at Pixar, DreamWorks, Framestore, Sega and Ubisoft. Teesside University Business School has been relaunched with a new look and a range of new undergraduate and postgraduate courses.

The university supports the career development of its graduates for a minimum of two years after graduation and is expanding paid work placements as part of a student's course. The Get Ahead scheme provides three-month paid internships and training for graduates, as well as helping to provide summer placements for second-year students.

The main campus has shops, bars, cafés and restaurants on the doorstep, and the students' union has been rated among the top ten in the country. The internationally renowned contemporary art gallery, mima (Middlesbrough Institute of Modern Art), a member of the Plus Tate Network, is now part of the university.

Beyond Middlesbrough there is a beautiful coastal fringe and the North York Moors are nearby. The cost of living is another attraction: both university rents and those in the private sector are amongst the cheapest in the UK.

Sports facilities include a new £3-million gym on campus and a water sports centre on the River Tees. The university supports elite athletes with scholarships, coaching and access to the latest sport science techniques. A £17-million sport and health sciences building has a hydrotherapy pool among its facilities. Although not part of the university, a new £21-million sports village offers an athletics stadium with indoor and outdoor tracks, gym and multi-sports court.

Tuition fees

» Fees for UK/EU students 2017–18	£9,250
Year 4 of integrated Master's degree	£4,625
Foundation degree	£6,150
Placement year / Year abroad	no fee
» UK fees are expected to increase by the rate of inflation from 2018–19 onwards.	
» Fees for international students 2016–17	£10,750
» Check the university's website for the latest information on fees, scholarships, bursaries and other forms of student support.	

Students

Undergraduates:	9,055	(6,825)
Postgraduates:	755	(1,280)
Mature students:	38.4%	
International students:	6.3%	
Applications per place:	4.3	
From state-sector schools:	99.3%	
From working-class homes:	45.7%	
Satisfaction with students' union	85%	

For detailed information about sports facilities:
www.tees.ac.uk/sport

Accommodation

Number of places and costs refer to 2016–17
University-provided places: 1,193
Percentage catered: 0%
Self-catered costs: £58 – £110 a week (40 weeks).
First years are guaranteed a place if conditions are met.
International students: guaranteed accommodation if conditions met.
accommodation@tees.ac.uk
www.tees.ac.uk/accommodation

Trinity Saint David, University of Wales

The first phase of a new £300-million Swansea Waterfront Innovation Quarter in the city's SA1 area is due to be ready when students join the University of Wales Trinity Saint David (UWTSD) in 2018. Work has started on the initial development, which will comprise the Faculty of Architecture, Computing and Engineering as well as a new library building and external public spaces. Teaching, learning, research and leisure facilities will be built around the Prince of Wales Dock.

The second phase, covering a further 18,000m² is due for completion in 2021 for academic and business use. Core student services, including student support and a students' union, will be located alongside sports and leisure facilities, and there will also be community and commercial amenities. The 19-acre campus will complement the university's existing £30-million investment in a Cultural Quarter for the city between the Dynevor Centre for Art, Design and Media and the soon-to-be-opened ALEX Design Exchange campus in the former Swansea Central Library.

Two mergers in three years created UWTSD, the second adding the former Swansea Metropolitan University. UWTSD does not appear in any of our league tables, having chosen not to release data. Swansea Met boycotted league tables throughout its brief existence as an independent university.

The old Trinity Saint David finished just outside the bottom ten on its last appearance in the table and the new version was in the bottom ten for overall satisfaction in the 2015 National Student Survey. But there was an improvement of 5 percentage points in overall satisfaction in 2016, bringing it up to the average for universities with the same subjects and entry scores.

UWTSD would have been in the bottom five of our research ranking after the Research Excellence Framework, however, where only 12 per cent of the eligible academics were entered for assessment. The best results were in theology, where 65 per cent of the submission was rated as world-leading or internationally excellent, compared to 46 per cent for the university as a whole.

The university offers students the choice of a rural or urban experience – from the green campuses of Lampeter and Carmarthen to the urban surroundings of Swansea. UWTSD markets itself as both old and new since in the whole of England and Wales, only Oxford and Cambridge were awarding degrees before St David's College, Lampeter. The college went on to become the smallest publicly funded

---

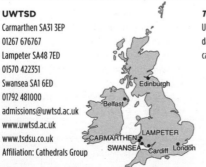

UWTSD
Carmarthen SA31 3EP
01267 676767
Lampeter SA48 7ED
01570 422351
Swansea SA1 6ED
01792 481000
admissions@uwtsd.ac.uk
www.uwtsd.ac.uk
www.tsdsu.co.uk
Affiliation: Cathedrals Group

The Times and Sunday Times **Rankings**
University of Wales Trinity Saint David blocked the release of data from the Higher Education Statistics Agency and so we cannot give any ranking information.

university in Europe before merging with Trinity University College, 23 miles away in Carmarthen, in 2010. The university also has a London campus, near the Oval cricket ground, for international students taking business, management and IT degrees. A group structure connects UWTSD with two large further education colleges in southwest Wales, Coleg Ceredigion and Coleg Sir Gâr, in Carmarthenshire.

The UWTSD Lampeter Campus continues to make a virtue of its size by stressing its friendly atmosphere and intimate teaching style. It remains a small, rural community that suits students who seek a close-knit campus experience. Based on an ancient castle and modelled on an Oxbridge college, St David's College was established to provide a liberal arts education. The original quadrangle remains, but there have been significant changes in recent years, notably the introduction of such subjects as anthropology, archaeology, Chinese, classics and philosophy.

The Carmarthen Campus was established in 1848. It has a long history of teacher training and has developed a reputation for education-related programmes including early childhood, social inclusion, and youth and community work. In addition, the university offers a range of programmes in the creative and performing arts, as well a growing portfolio within the School of Sport, Health and Outdoor Education,

which makes use of the natural resources of west Wales.

The Swansea Campus began life as a college of art in 1853, subsequently joined by education and technical colleges. Based in the centre of Wales's second city, Swansea Met became a university only in 2008 and became part of UWTSD in 2013. Its automotive engineering courses – especially those focused on motorsport – are its best-known feature, but there has been strong demand for places on a variety of vocationally oriented courses.

The university surpasses all its benchmarks for widening participation in higher education, although the dropout rate is higher than average for its courses and entry qualifications.

The university provides employability support that runs alongside academic programmes, with work placement schemes and internships to provide opportunities for students to build core skills to improve their career prospects.

Tuition fees

» Fees for UK/EU students 2017–18 £9,000
» Welsh Assembly non-means-tested grant to pay fees above £4,046 for Welsh students. Tuition fee grant under review from 2018.
» Fees for international students 2017–18 £10,400
» Check the university's website for the latest information on fees, scholarships, bursaries and other forms of student support.

Students

Undergraduates:	6,085	(2,575)
Postgraduates:	955	(805)
Satisfaction with students' union	58%	

For detailed information about sports facilities:
www.uwtsd.ac.uk/student-life/sport

Accommodation

Number of places and cost refer to 2016–17
L refers to Lampeter, CM to Carmarthen, S to Swansea
University-provided places: 623 (L), 631 (CM), 300 (S)
Percentage catered: 0% (L), 75% (CM); 0% (S)
Catered costs: £84.37 – £105.37 (CM) a week (38 weeks).
Self-catered costs: £68 – £88 (S & L) a week (38 weeks).
First years can normally be placed in university accommodation.
International students: guaranteed housing for first year.
www.uwtsd.ac.uk/accommodation

Ulster University

Ulster dropped 11 places in our table this year, but the university's bigger challenge is coping with cuts of £8.6 million in its Government grant. Having withdrawn a number of courses in film studies, history, computing and engineering, it has now announced the closure of the modern languages department, the ending of teaching in interior design, and "rationalisation" of computing, maths, business management and marine studies.

This may mean subjects transferring between the four campuses, which may become more specialist. Ulster expects to cut 1,200 places over three years, and last year's budget announcement appeared to have an instant effect since the university filled 740 fewer places despite making nearly 1,000 more offers than in 2014.

The university is still hoping to expand in the longer term, however. Plans were submitted in summer 2016 to increase the number of undergraduates at the Magee Campus in Derry/Londonderry by more than 2,500 to 6,000. An £11-million teaching block has been approved to prepare for the increased numbers. New teaching and arts blocks opened in 2015 on the Coleraine Campus, where a new £5.1-million Sports Centre opens in spring 2017.

There are even bigger plans for developments in Belfast's Cathedral Quarter, where the first phase of a £250-million campus opened in 2015. However, construction is behind schedule for the next phase and the 12,450 students on the university's Jordanstown site will not now move until September 2019.

The High Performance Sports Centre, which houses the Sports Institute for Northern Ireland, will remain in Jordanstown, historically Ulster's main teaching centre. Some £20 million has been invested in the sports facilities there, including outdoor and indoor sprint tracks, sports science and sports medicine facilities, which will remain available to students.

At present, Belfast concentrates on art and design, architecture, hospitality event management, photography and digital animation. Jordanstown, seven miles out of Belfast, will remain the location for courses starting in 2018 in business and management, the built environment, computing and engineering, health and sport sciences, and social sciences.

The third campus, at Coleraine, on Northern Ireland's north coast, offers environmental and life sciences, humanities, media, film and journalism, and tourism management. A new £6.5-million media centre there has been rated as one of the "most impressive in the UK" by the National Council for the Training of Journalists. It includes a HD television

Cromore Road
Coleraine
BT52 1SA
028 7012 3456
Jordanstown and Belfast:
registryjn@ulster.ac.uk
Coleraine and Magee:
registryce@ulster.ac.uk
www.ulster.ac.uk
http://uusu.org
Affiliation: none

The Times and Sunday Times Rankings

Overall Ranking: **68** (last year: 57)

Teaching quality:	50	81.5%
Student experience:	20	86.9%
Research quality:	=37	31.8%
Entry standards:	88	307
Student–staff ratio:	=80	17.1
Services & facilities/student:	76	£1,799
Expected completion rate:	101	81%
Good honours:	91	65.9%
Graduate prospects:	96	65.6%

studio, the largest multimedia newsroom on the island of Ireland, HD editing suites and five satellite feeds.

The BBC also has a studio on the campus, which is home to the £11-million Centre for Molecular Biosciences, whose academics produced the most highly rated work in the 2014 Research Excellence Framework. More than 70 per cent of the university's whole submission was considered world-leading or internationally excellent, with law and nursing and health science also producing outstanding results.

Magee has a focus on the creative and performing arts, nursing and social work, computing, business and management, and social sciences. Its expansion will focus on computer science, engineering and creative technologies. A £12-million Centre for Stratified Medicine has opened near the campus, at Altnagelvin Hospital.

Ulster also has branch campuses in London and Birmingham, where it offers courses in business, computing and engineering in partnership with QA Higher Education, a private organisation that also delivers apprenticeships and training programmes.

The university has a growing number of international students – about 1,800 from more than 100 different countries. The eLearning at Ulster programme provides an alternative mode of study, offering courses online to students all over the world.

The university has committed itself to becoming the leading provider of "professional education for professional life". Most courses now include the option of a year-long work placement.

The university, which features in *Times Higher Education* magazine's top 100 universities in the world that are under 50 years old, is the largest in Northern Ireland. It is in the top 20 in the sections of the National Student Survey relating to learning resources, personal development and the organisation of courses, and in the top 50 for the sections that focus on teaching, feedback and academic support. Nearly 100 per cent of undergraduates are from state schools and around 45 per cent come from working-class backgrounds.

The university's award-winning sports outreach programme has been particularly successful. Accommodation is guaranteed for all first-years students on all four campuses and the students' union is also active at every location. The social life inevitably varies according to campus.

Tuition fees

» Fees for NI/EU students 2017–18	£4,030
» Fees for English, Scottish and Welsh students	£9,000
» Year abroad / Placement year	£2,005
» Fees for international students 2016–17	£12,890
» Check the university's website for the latest information on fees, scholarships, bursaries and other forms of student support.	

Students

Undergraduates:	16,720	(3,855)
Postgraduates:	2,000	(3,510)
Mature students:	27.1%	
International students:	8.2%	
Applications per place:	6.8	
From state-sector schools:	99.9%	
From working-class homes:	44.6%	
Satisfaction with students' union	54%	

For detailed information about sports facilities:
http://uususport.org

Accommodation

Number of places and costs refer to 2016–17
University-provided places: 2,366 over three campuses.
Percentage catered: 0%
Self-catered costs: average £74.60 (standard) – £102.60 (en suite) a week (37 weeks).
First-year students are guaranteed accommodation if conditions are met.
International students: same as above.
accommodation@ulster.ac.uk
www.ulster.ac.uk/ulster-life/accommodation

University College London

UCL has reclaimed its accustomed place in our top six after a rise of four places this year. There have been marginal improvements in student satisfaction, although UCL is still in the bottom ten universities in the National Student Survey for teaching, feedback and academic support. This is far outweighed by top-five finishes for research, staffing levels, degree classifications and graduate prospects.

UCL is also in the top seven universities in the world in the QS rankings, which place more emphasis on research. Such was the quality and quantity of UCL's submission to the 2014 Research Excellence Framework that only Oxford received a higher research grant for the following academic year.

More than 90 per cent of the eligible academics were entered for assessment and over 80 per cent of their work was rated as world-leading or internationally excellent. UCL had the most world-leading research in medicine and the biological sciences, the largest volume of research in science, technology, engineering and maths, and the biggest share of top grades in the social sciences. Professor John O'Keefe's 2014 Nobel Prize in Physiology or Medicine brought the number of laureates associated with UCL to 29.

University College London is planning to invest £1.25 billion over ten years to implement its Transforming UCL programme, which includes a new campus in Stratford on the Queen Elizabeth Olympic Park, as well as developing its existing campuses. It is the largest capital investment programme UCL has undertaken since building its original Bloomsbury campus, and one of the biggest in UK higher education.

The funding includes a £280-million loan from the European Investment Bank, the largest sum ever lent by the bank to a university. UCL has more EU students than any English university.

Projects in Bloomsbury include the refurbishment and expansion of the highly rated Bartlett School of Architecture and the building of a new student centre. UCL East will bring together cross-disciplinary expertise in areas such as creativity and material culture, future global cities, experimental engineering, and education and research through public service, including the UCL Centre for Access to Justice.

With record applications coming in, UCL has expanded for four years in a row, adding 1,600 places to the undergraduate intake. The proportion of 18-year-olds receiving offers has gone up from 36 per cent to 61 per cent as a result.

Already comfortably the largest of the University of London's colleges, it now

---

Gower Street
London WC1E 6BT

020 7679 3000 (enquiries)
study@ucl.ac.uk
www.ucl.ac.uk
http://uclu.org
Affiliation: Russell Group

The Times and Sunday Times Rankings

Overall Ranking: **6** (last year: 10)

Teaching quality:	121	75.5%
Student experience:	=94	81.9%
Research quality:	5	51%
Entry standards:	7	506
Student–staff ratio:	2	10.2
Services & facilities/student:	12	£2,727
Expected completion rate:	7	95.7%
Good honours:	5	89%
Graduate prospects:	5	87.2%

has more than 36,000 students since the incorporation of the Institute of Education in December 2014.

All first-year students are helped to make the academic and social adjustment to university life through the Transition Programme, which includes peer mentoring and workshops. Concerted attempts are being made to broaden the undergraduate intake with summer schools, outreach activities and campus-based programmes. The share of places going to independent school students has been going down but, at almost 30 per cent, it remains among the highest in Britain.

UCL has a history of pioneering subjects that have become commonplace in higher education: modern languages, geography and fine arts among them. Students are required to have a foreign language GCSE at grade C or above, although they are allowed to reach this standard during their degree if they have not taken a language at school.

UCL is pioneering the idea of education for global citizenship, encouraging students to explore academic ideas from different cultural perspectives and to work on problems of international importance, as well as contributing to their local community and the university's social and cultural life. A quarter of all undergraduates spend part of their course at one of the 300 partner universities overseas.

The medical school, with 11 associated teaching hospitals, is a large and formidable unit. UCL is a founding partner in the new Francis Crick Institute that will undertake leading-edge research to advance understanding of health and disease. There is also an archaeology and conservation campus in Qatar. Nearer home, a new School of Management was established in 2015 and opened in Canary Wharf in 2016.

The academic pace can be frantic but, close to the West End and with its own theatre and recreational facilities, there is no shortage of leisure options. Students also have access to the facilities of the student centre in the former University of London Union building in Bloomsbury.

Residential accommodation is plentiful and of a good standard. Indoor sports and fitness facilities are close at hand, but the main outdoor pitches, though good enough to attract professional football clubs, are a (free) coach ride away in Hertfordshire.

Tuition fees

- » Fees for UK/EU students 2017–18 £9,250
  Year abroad £1,385
- » UK fees are expected to increase by the rate of inflation from 2018–19 onwards.
- » Fees for international students 2017–18 £17,710–£23,710
  Medicine £32,670
- » Check the university's website for the latest information on fees, scholarships, bursaries and other forms of student support.

Students

Undergraduates:	15,835	(990)
Postgraduates:	12,310	(6,475)
Mature students:	7.9%	
International students:	36.1%	
Applications per place:	7.6	
From state-sector schools:	70.4%	
From working-class homes:	19%	
Satisfaction with students' union	66%	

For detailed information about sports facilities:
http://uclu.org/services/sport

Accommodation

Number of places and costs refer to 2016–17
University provided spaces: 5,937 (including 1,128 intercollegiate places)
Percentage catered: 14%
Catered costs: £143.43 – £206.29 a week (39 weeks).
Self-catered costs: £135.59 (single) – £228.69 (en-suite single) a week (39 weeks).
First years are guaranteed a place if conditions are met.
International postgraduate students: as above.
www.ucl.ac.uk/prospective-students/accommodation

University of Warwick

Warwick is one of the Russell Group universities to have expanded most at undergraduate level since recruitment restrictions were relaxed. It added almost 1,000 students to its intake over the three years up to 2015, increasing the proportion of applicants who receive offers by more than a quarter. The university is still in the top ten for entry standards, however, and seventh in the table overall.

The most successful of the "plate glass" universities of the 1960s, Warwick has never been out of our top ten and is only just outside the top 50 in the QS World University Rankings. The university has a centre in Venice and a close partnership with Monash University, in Melbourne. The business school launched a London base in the Shard in 2015 and Warwick has received approval to become the first UK university to open a campus in California. The ambitious project involves a partnership with a non-profit-making trust to create a campus for 6,000 students near Sacramento, in the north of the state. The first postgraduates will arrive in 2018.

On the main campus, three miles south of Coventry, a £250-million investment programme is under way. A £20-million teaching and learning building, with 500- and 250-seat lecture theatres and social learning spaces, opens in 2017, as will the £150-million National Automotive Innovation Centre, where research engineers from car manufacturers will work closely with Warwick Manufacturing Group (WMG). The centre is part-funded by Government as well as by Jaguar Land Rover and Tata Motors. The Centre will include the world's most adaptable driving simulator for research on driverless cars. WMG is also planning a Cycling Innovation and Technology Hub to provide a "catalyst for business to accelerate technological innovation within the UK cycling industry".

The first phase of a £30-million extension to Warwick Business School has already opened, making it one of the largest business schools in the UK. The university is also planning new interdisciplinary research labs, a humanities building, and improved facilities for a number of other subjects.

The university has reconfigured its research around its "Global Research Priorities" programme, which focuses on key areas of international significance. Current themes include energy, connecting cultures, food security, global governance, individual behaviour and innovative manufacturing.

Almost 90 per cent of the work submitted for the 2014 Research Excellence Framework was rated as world-leading or internationally excellent, confirming Warwick's place among the top ten

Coventry CV4 7AL

024 7652 3723 (admissions)
ugadmissions@warwick.ac.uk
www.warwick.ac.uk
www.warwicksu.com
Affiliation: Russell Group

The Times and Sunday Times Rankings		
Overall Ranking: **7** (last year: 6)		
Teaching quality:	=72	80.1%
Student experience:	=50	84.4%
Research quality:	8	44.6%
Entry standards:	8	490
Student–staff ratio:	15	12.5
Services & facilities/student:	22	£2,566
Expected completion rate:	=11	94.9%
Good honours:	18	82.7%
Graduate prospects:	27	80.4%

universities for research. English and computer science produced the best results, but Warwick ranked in the UK's top ten in 14 different subject areas.

A new Cancer Research Unit is bringing together experts in maths, physics and engineering to research new treatments using digital technologies. The university has been awarded £14.5-million to establish an Advanced Steel Research Centre and is one of six Midlands universities sharing £60 million for energy research.

The university's mission statement also stresses community links and the extension of access to higher and continuing education. There is a smaller proportion of independent school students than at most leading universities – a quarter – although this does not translate into large numbers of working-class undergraduates. The dropout rate is among the lowest in Britain, at little more than 5 per cent, although even that is higher than in recent years.

The university will spend £2.4 million in 2016–17 on a "student lifecycle" approach to widening participation, helping non-traditional students from before the application stage through to employment or postgraduate study. The scheme will include bursaries of up to £3,000 a year for those from families with a combined income of less than £35,000.

Warwick is also one of the few leading universities to embrace 2+2 Foundation degrees, running courses in social studies and health and social policy, along with three-year Foundation degrees in early years and person-centred counselling and psychotherapy.

There is also a thriving graduate entry medical school, with over 2,000 students, which was extended in 2016.

The 750-acre campus has a wide range of residential accommodation and there is an off-campus study facility for the many students living in nearby Leamington Spa.

The campus sports facilities are both extensive and conveniently placed, and include a running track, an indoor climbing centre and an indoor tennis centre. Further investment is planned in its sports facilities and the already extensive Warwick Arts Centre.

Coventry has a growing range of student-oriented facilities and good travel links to London and other parts of the country.

Tuition fees

» Fees for UK/EU students 2017–18 £9,250
2+2 degree £6,935
Foundation degree £6,165
» UK fees are expected to increase by the rate of inflation from 2018–19 onwards.
» Fees for international students 2017–18 £17,460–£22,260
Medicine (graduate entry) £20,338–£35,520
» Check the university's website for the latest information on fees, scholarships, bursaries and other forms of student support.

Students

Undergraduates:	12,850	(1,910)
Postgraduates:	4,940	(3,985)
Mature students:	5.9%	
International students:	28.3%	
Applications per place:	7.4	
From state-sector schools:	75%	
From working-class homes:	19.3%	
Satisfaction with students' union	71%	

For detailed information about sports facilities:
www2.warwick.ac.uk/services/sport

Accommodation

Number of places and costs refer to 2016–17
University-provided places: 6,469 (on campus); 2,250 (head leasing) Percentage catered: 0%
Self-catered costs: £77 – £171 a week (34, 39, 40 and 51 weeks).
Warwick Accommodation plans to accommodate all first year undergraduates in campus accommodation (terms and conditions apply).
International students: undergraduates as above.
www2.warwick.ac.uk/services/accommodation

University of West London

West London enjoys the biggest rise of any university in this year's table, jumping 37 places from near the foot of the ranking to 84th place. It has gone up on almost every measure, but has gained most from big rises in student satisfaction following last year's opening of the £50-million Future Campus.

The first phase was called the Heartspace because of its central location on the university's Ealing campus, and provides a vibrant social area for students and staff.

The opening of the Paul Hamlyn Library followed in autumn 2015, stretching across all four floors of the campus. The 24-hour social learning area has a variety of study spaces, 40 PC desks and a Mac lab. Other new facilities include a concrete testing lab, an architecture studio, music practice rooms and a new performance space. The project has seen West London move into the top 20 for spending on student facilities

The campus had already seen significant investment, as the university opted for the narrower geographical focus implied when it dropped the title of Thames Valley University.

The campus in Slough closed and most activities were concentrated on the institution's original base, as UWL set about becoming the country's leading university for employer engagement, with an accent on the creative industries and entrepreneurship.

The university offers students guaranteed work placements, in-study financial support and employment prospects which improved considerably in the latest survey and compare favourably with its peer group. Undergraduates have access to an award-winning student portal, which combines academic study with social networking.

Many of the degrees include the option of a Foundation year and there is a portfolio of two-year Foundation degrees, which involve employers such as Compaq, Ealing Studios and the Savoy Hotel Group.

Reorganisation of the university has seen the pre-registration nursing courses that dominated the Slough Campus move to Reading, leaving just part-time business courses and some post-registration nursing at a different site in Slough.

The Reading Campus, which houses the Berkshire Institute of Health, is within walking distance of the station and focuses entirely on nursing and midwifery. The landmark Paragon Building in Brentford, not far from the Ealing campus, remains the headquarters of one of the largest healthcare faculties in Britain, with top-quality ratings for nursing and midwifery.

The university is ethnically diverse, with only 45 per cent of the undergraduates of white, UK origin. More than half of the students are 21 or more on entry, and about 60 per cent are female.

St Mary's Road
Ealing
London W5 5RF

0800 036 8888 (admissions)
courses@uwl.ac.uk
www.uwl.ac.uk
www.uwlsu.com
Affiliation: MillionPlus

The Times and Sunday Times Rankings

Overall Ranking: **84** (last year: 121)

Teaching quality:	=44	81.9%
Student experience:	=50	84.4%
Research quality:	120	1.6%
Entry standards:	=102	300
Student–staff ratio:	=53	15.6
Services & facilities/student:	20	£2,600
Expected completion rate:	121	74.9%
Good honours:	112	61.3%
Graduate prospects:	81	68.9%

Nearly 50 per cent of the undergraduates come from low-income families, but UWL's projected dropout rate of almost 19 per cent is significantly worse than the national average for its courses and entry qualifications.

There are means-tested scholarships and bursaries in 2016 and January 2017 to support full-time undergraduates whose household income is below £25,000, and fee waivers for part-time students where income is £42,875 or less.

The university has specialist scholarships and bursaries for each of the academic schools, funded by alumni. These are available for students with high academic entry grades or demonstrating outstanding applied skills.

Among UWL's strengths is the School of Hospitality and Tourism, which is recognised by the Académie Culinaire de France for its culinary arts programmes, while the London College of Music, which is part of the university, has some of the longest-established music technology courses in the country.

However, the university is in the bottom five of our research ranking after entering only 13 per cent of eligible academics for the 2014 Research Excellence Framework. A quarter of its submission was judged to be world-leading or internationally excellent, the best results coming in communication and media studies.

The town-centre sites in Ealing and Brentford are linked by a free bus service. The busy Ealing base is within easy reach of central London. Almost half of UWL's students are from London or Berkshire.

The Paragon has more than 800 residential places, including 100 that are reserved for students entering through Clearing – but 400 places were lost when agreement could not be reached on an extension of the lease for the Clayponds Student Village. Those relying on private housing find the cost of living high.

A refurbished students' union with a modern bar area, café and gym opened in 2013, alongside a new performance centre. The union has established links with local sports teams, ensuring that all the university's sports clubs have access to good facilities in the vicinity.

Tuition fees

» Fees for UK/EU students 2017–18	£9,250
Placement year	£1,230

» UK fees are expected to increase by the rate of inflation from 2018–19 onwards.

» Fees for international students 2016–17	£10,650

» Check the university's website for the latest information on fees, scholarships, bursaries and other forms of student support.

Students

Undergraduates:	7,010	(1,975)
Postgraduates:	585	(925)
Mature students:	50.4%	
International students:	17.2%	
Applications per place:	7.6	
From state-sector schools:	98.1%	
From working-class homes:	49.9%	
Satisfaction with students' union	76%	

For detailed information about sports facilities: www.uwlsu.com/groups

Accommodation

Number of places and costs refer to 2016–17
University-provided places: 1,279
Percentage catered: 0%
Self-catered costs: £146.90 (en suite); £257.00 (studio) a week (44 or 51 weeks).
First years are allocated housing on a first come, first served basis.
International students: same as above.
studentservices@uwl.ac.uk
www.uwl.ac.uk/students/undergraduate/accommodation

University of the West of England, Bristol (UWE)

UWE Bristol has regained its place among the top ten post-1992 universities in our table after a rise of 13 places this year. It is back in the top 60 after a big increase in student satisfaction and improved graduate prospects.

The university has also taken the unusual step of publishing its employment rate three years, rather than just the normal six months, after graduation. At 82 per cent in professional jobs, this was well ahead of the national average. The university attributes its success partly to the involvement on campus of employers such as Aardman Animations, BBC, Spike Island and the Watershed.

There is a partnership with Arnolfini, the centre for the contemporary arts, to base 300 creative arts students in its harbourside location. Another 100 students take the unique Team Entrepreneurship programme, where they learn by practice by setting up their own businesses, and UWE Bristol also has one of the largest internship programmes at any university.

Already the biggest higher education institution in the region, UWE Bristol has not followed the expansion route favoured by many universities in recent years.

A £250-million campus masterplan is intended to ensure that the university is competitive in teaching, research and student facilities, but has the option of taking more students in future.

A new students' union opened in 2015 on the main Frenchay Campus and the following year a University Enterprise Zone to foster greater collaboration between academics and small- and medium-sized businesses opened. A £55-million building for the Faculty of Business and Law will be ready in 2017 and £35 million is being invested in the Bower Ashton studios on the City Campus.

There has been investment, too, at the Glenside Campus with upgraded suites for radiotherapy and hospital wards. Eventually, there may even be a 20,000-seat stadium shared with Bristol Rovers on land bought by the university to extend the Frenchay campus.

The three sites in Bristol are mainly in the north of the city, with regional centres near hospitals in Gloucester and Bath that concentrate on nursing and allied health professions. The main campus, four miles from the city centre, has already doubled in size and seen a number of improvements, including the opening of the UK's largest robotic laboratory and the biggest exhibition and conference centre in the region. The main library is open around the clock during term time.

Frenchay Campus
Coldharbour Lane
Bristol BS16 1QY

0117 328 3333 (admissions)
admissions@uwe.ac.uk
www.uwe.ac.uk
www.thestudentsunion.co.uk
Affiliation: University
 Alliance

The Times and Sunday Times Rankings

Overall Ranking: **60** (last year: 73)

Teaching quality:	=24	83%
Student experience:	=26	86.2%
Research quality:	69	8.8%
Entry standards:	=69	324
Student–staff ratio:	=100	18.5
Services & facilities/student:	47	£2,118
Expected completion rate:	89	82.9%
Good honours:	54	73.3%
Graduate prospects:	46	76.4%

More than half of the students come from the West Country and the university has broadened its intake considerably in recent years. The proportion of independent school entrants has dropped below 6 per cent, while the share of places going to students from working-class homes is over 30 per cent. However, the projected dropout rate is still well above the national average for the university's subjects and entry qualifications, at 16 per cent.

Hartpury College, near Gloucester, is an associate faculty of the university, specialising in agriculture, equine studies and other land-based courses. The university's degrees are also taught in a growing number of institutions overseas. UWE Bristol's own international college, run in partnership with the Kaplan group, provides preparatory courses for students from outside the UK coming to Bristol.

More than 60 per cent of the work submitted for assessment in the 2014 Research Excellence Framework was rated as world-leading or internationally excellent. Health subjects and communication and media studies produced the best results.

Law received a commendation from the Legal Practice Board and UWE Bristol is one of just four universities recognised by the Forensic Science Society for the quality of courses in the subject. The careers and employment service was rated the best in the country in 2014, partly for an innovative web-based jobs and placement service it runs with the local chamber of commerce. The university also runs the UWE Bristol Futures Award to certificate extra-curricular activities and encourage students to acquire skills that will help in the employment market.

Bristol is a hugely popular student centre: an attractive and lively city, but not cheap. There are more than 4,500 places in university accommodation since the addition of 400 rooms to the student village on the Frenchay Campus in 2014. This includes accommodation for nearly 300 students on the Glenside Campus.

Another 561 rooms at Frenchay are being added in 2017. A £5.5-million sports complex there has a 70-station fitness suite, as well as outdoor facilities. The separate Wallscourt Farm gym is designed for elite athletes.

Tuition fees

» Fees for UK/EU students 2017–18 £9,250
   Courses at partner colleges £6,000–£9,250
   Year abroad £1,385
   Placement year £1,850
» UK fees are expected to increase by the rate of inflation from 2018–19 onwards.
» Fees for international students 2017–18 £11,750–£12,500
» Check the university's website for the latest information on fees, scholarships, bursaries and other forms of student support.

Students

Undergraduates:	18,355	(2,540)
Postgraduates:	2,035	(3,735)
Mature students:	25.1%	
International students:	11.6%	
Applications per place:	5.3	
From state-sector schools:	94.1%	
From working-class homes:	30.2%	
Satisfaction with students' union	72%	

For detailed information about sports facilities:
www.thestudentsunion.co.uk/opportunities/sports

Accommodation

Number of places and costs refer to 2016–17
University-provided places: about 4,598
Percentage catered: 0%
Self-catered costs: £88.12 – £197.28 (40 to 45 weeks).
First-year students are guaranteed housing in university-approved accommodation provided requirements are met.
International students: as above, and are offered housing where possible if they apply outside the deadline date.
accommodation@uwe.ac.uk
www1.uwe.ac.uk/students/accommodation

University of the West of Scotland (UWS)

UWS has moved up 12 places in our table this year, with much higher entry standards and a better completion rate, as well as improved student satisfaction. The university already did well in the National Student Survey and is now only just outside the top 40 in the sections relating to teaching, feedback and academic support.

Although still outside the top 100 overall, UWS is planning a brand new campus in Hamilton and has made improvements in Paisley and Ayr that could herald further progress in future. Applications have risen for six years in a row and are more than twice as high as when UWS welcomed its first intake in 2007, following the merger of the University of Paisley with Bell College, in Hamilton.

Now among the largest modern universities in Scotland, UWS has its headquarters in Paisley, where more than £30 million has been spent expanding the residential accommodation and improving student facilities. The Atrium, a flexible learning area with interactive technology, meeting spaces and a café that is open to staff, students and members of the public had its official opening in 2016.

Another £81 million was invested in a modern campus for 2,300 students in Ayr, and there is also a campus in Dumfries, which is operated in partnership with the University of Glasgow and Dumfries and Galloway College.

The university was planning to move out of Hamilton because it was unable to upgrade the former premises of Bell College, one of the partners in the merger that formed UWS. But it is now waiting to move to a new EcoCampus on the Hamilton International Technology Park, only two miles from the current campus. Relocation to the new campus, which will have teaching and learning facilities, residential accommodation, students' union and laboratory space, may begin in September 2017. UWS has also opened its first development outside Scotland with the establishment of a London Campus in Southwark. It is already home to over 150 students of business, enterprise and health, and a number of other disciplines are due to be added by 2017.

The university is based in an area of low participation in higher education, although it is within reach of nearly 40 per cent of the population of Scotland. Almost all UWS's students are state educated and 40 per cent are from working-class homes. The projected dropout rate has improved dramatically, but is still higher than the benchmark set according to the subject mix and entry qualifications.

Paisley Campus
Paisley
Renfrewshire PA1 2BE

0141 848 3000 (enquiries)
info@uws.ac.uk
contact via website
www.uws.ac.uk
www.sauws.org.uk
Affiliation: MillionPlus

The Times and Sunday Times Rankings

Overall Ranking: **106** (last year: 118)

Teaching quality:	=41	82.1%
Student experience:	69	83.6%
Research quality:	=97	4.3%
Entry standards:	66	327
Student–staff ratio:	=114	19.8
Services & facilities/student:	113	£1,365
Expected completion rate:	112	79%
Good honours:	93	65.5%
Graduate prospects:	77	69.9%

The university has set itself a series of challenging targets to achieve by 2020, including big increases in student satisfaction, completion rates and the proportion progressing to Honours degrees. The overall intention is to become Scotland's most "student-focused" university. UWS has signed a formal Student Partnership Agreement with the students' association, which won NUS Scotland's Higher Education Students' Association of the Year award for 2016.

There are almost 2,000 international students, mainly from other EU countries. The School of Health, Nursing and Midwifery is the largest north of the border, and for the second year in a row the university is seventh in the UK in our Education table.

Many students either take sandwich degrees or have work placements built into their courses. There are close links with business and industry and all students are offered hands-on computer training. UWS was the first UK university to be approved by Microsoft, Macromedia and Cisco, and has the status of Microsoft Academic Professional Development Centre. A games development laboratory, supported by Sony, was part of a £300,000 package of investment in multimedia and games facilities.

Health subjects produced much the best results in the 2014 Research Excellence Framework, when 44 per cent of its submission reached one of the top two categories.

The university's main Paisley Campus has a modern library and learning resource centre, a £5-million students' union building and upgraded sports facilities on the outskirts of the town. UWS is bringing more students into the town centre with the completion of a £17.6-million student accommodation development. A new Student Hub opened in 2016, bringing together frontline services for students.

The attractive Dumfries campus has 550 students, while the Ayr campus is shared with SRUC (Scotland's Rural College) and has a prize-winning library with flexible space. A £12-million investment in information technology across all campuses is being phased over three years.

Paisley is Scotland's largest town, while Hamilton ranks fifth. In both places, the university draws a high proportion of the students from the local area.

Tuition fees

- » Fees for Scottish and EU students 2017–18   No fee
- » Fees for non-Scottish UK (RUK) students 2017–18   £9,250 capped at £27,750 for all four-year courses
- » Fees for international students 2017–18   £12,300–£13,800
- » There are particular support schemes for RUK students.
- » Check the university's website for the latest information on fees, scholarships, bursaries and other forms of student support.

Students

Undergraduates:	9,855	(3,045)
Postgraduates:	835	(1,000)
Mature students:	54.6%	
International students:	5.2%	
Applications per place:	5.6	
From state-sector schools:	99.1%	
From working-class homes:	40.6%	
Satisfaction with students' union	51%	

Sports facilities: www.uws.ac.uk/study-at-uws/life-at-uws/sports-and-social

Accommodation

Number of places and costs refer to 2016–17
University-provided places: 859 (496 at Paisley; 200 at Ayr; 156 at Hamilton; 7 at Dumfries)
Percentage catered: 0%
Self-catered costs: £85 (Hamilton) £109.50 – £142.00 (other campuses) a week.
Undergraduates have priority (conditions apply).
International students: single students guaranteed accommodation if conditions are met.
www.uws.ac.uk/accommodation

University of Westminster

Westminster draws its students from more countries – 169 at the last count – than any university in the UK, if not the world. More than 8,000 international students include almost 1,500 undergraduates from the EU. Westminster's courses are also taught in nine overseas countries, from Sri Lanka to Uzbekistan, a characteristic which won the university a Queen's Award for Enterprise.

Expanding the opportunities for students to study or work abroad is one of the main planks of the university's Global Engagement Strategy. But there is also a strong local focus to Westminster's work – the number of part-time students has been rising, for example, at a time of catastrophic falls nationally. Overall applications dipped in 2015 but remained higher than at any point in the university's history before 2014.

Westminster promises a "dynamic synergy" between the creative arts and design, architecture and the built environment, science and technology, business, law, and the social sciences and humanities. Its ultimate aim is to be the leading "practice-informed" university. Westminster works with a network of over 3,000 companies and encourages all students to undertake a work placement which can form part of their degree.

All the university's courses were reviewed as part of its Learning Futures programme, which came into operation in 2016. The structure of undergraduate programmes has changed to promote deeper learning through year-long modules, weaving work-related skills into degrees. There will be new support for employability and international mobility, and awards for students' extra-curricular activities will recognise outstanding contributions of benefit to the public.

Almost half of the UK undergraduates are from the four poorest socio-economic groups and the numbers from ethnic minorities are among the highest at any university. The projected dropout rate has been improving and is now lower than average for Westminster's courses and entry qualifications.

Almost two-thirds of the work submitted for the 2014 Research Excellence Framework was judged to be world leading or university excellent, albeit with less than 30 per cent of the eligible staff entered. Westminster was again among the leading universities for communication and media studies, and there were even better results in art and design, as well as a good performance in English. The university has since established the Westminster Institute for Advanced Studies to foster interdisciplinary and independent critical thinking, supporting research in the sciences and humanities.

---

309 Regent Street
London W1B 2HW

020 7915 5511 (enquiries)
course-enquiries@
  westminster.ac.uk
www.westminster.ac.uk
www.uwsu.com
Affiliation: none

Edinburgh
Belfast
Cardiff
LONDON

The Times and Sunday Times Rankings

Overall Ranking: **117** (last year: =115)

Teaching quality:	125	73.5%
Student experience:	=105	81.3%
Research quality:	59	9.8%
Entry standards:	=80	318
Student–staff ratio:	=114	19.8
Services & facilities/student:	93	£1,675
Expected completion rate:	98	81.5%
Good honours:	76	68.6%
Graduate prospects:	118	58.1%

Westminster traces its history back to 1838, when it became the UK's first polytechnic. Last year it opened the newly restored Regent Street Cinema, which is considered to be the birthplace of British cinema as the first in the country to show moving pictures to a paying audience. The headquarters building, near the BBC's Broadcasting House, houses social sciences, humanities and languages.

Westminster offers one of the widest ranges of language teaching of any British university and partners SOAS, University of London, in leading the "Routes into Languages" programme to encourage more people to learn a language.

The university has continued to invest heavily in its buildings and facilities, with major refurbishment taking place at the Regent Campus and Little Titchfield site. A new fabrication laboratory and studios will reinforce the faculty's position as one of the UK's leading centres in architecture.

The Business School was selected as a Centre of Excellence by the Chartered Institute for Securities and Investment – one of only 12 centres worldwide. The Harrow site has been redeveloped with a new library and resource centres, multimedia newsroom, flexible performance areas and a café. The university has also invested £2 million on the Cavendish Campus modernising the life sciences laboratories.

But Westminster is perhaps best known for its Faculty of Media, Arts and Design. Westminster alumni won two Oscars in 2016: Asif Kapadia took the award for Best Documentary Feature, while Shan Christopher Ogilvie produced the Best Live Action Short Film.

Westminster has added considerably to its stock of residential accommodation in recent years. The latest development saw the opening of a student village for first years close to Wembley Stadium. The university had already added a £6-million block of halls in Harrow and refurbished its Marylebone halls, but there is no way round the capital's inflated housing market at some stage.

The Harrow Campus is lively socially, but those based on the other campuses tend to be spread around the capital. Sports facilities are also dispersed, with playing fields and a boathouse in Chiswick, west London, and a fully-equipped gym at the central Regent Campus.

Tuition fees

» Fees for UK/EU students 2017–18	£9,250
Foundation degree	£6,165
Placement year	£1,350

» UK fees are expected to increase by the rate of inflation from 2018–19 onwards.

» Fees for international students 2017–18	£12,500

» Check the university's website for the latest information on fees, scholarships, bursaries and other forms of student support.

Students

Undergraduates:	13,145	(3,000)
Postgraduates:	2,230	(2,095)
Mature students:	18.8%	
International students:	21.1%	
Applications per place:	7.2	
From state-sector schools:	96.2%	
From working-class homes:	49.3%	
Satisfaction with students' union	58%	

For detailed information about sports facilities:
www.uwsu.com/sports

Accommodation

Number of places and costs refer to 2016–17
University-provided places: 1,770
Percentage catered: 0%
Self-catered costs: £135.03 – £215.60 (38 week contracts).
First-year students have priority for 1,200 rooms. Residential restrictions apply.
International students: as above.
studentaccommodation@westminster.ac.uk
www.westminster.ac.uk/study/prospective-students/
student-accommodation

University of Winchester

Winchester is one of the small campus universities that have benefited from strong performances in the National Student Survey (NSS). It was in the top four for overall satisfaction last year and on the verge of the top ten for the quality of teaching and feedback provided by academics. That has come to at least a temporary halt this year, however, with a drop of more than 30 places on both our measures of student satisfaction – covering teaching quality and the wider student experience – costing the university nine places in our overall table. It is still in the top 50 for satisfaction with teaching. There were declines, too, in entry standards and staffing levels, although the completion rate has improved significantly. Winchester is one the few universities to have appointed its own ombudsman to handle complaints.

The numbers starting degrees have grown for five years in succession. The university now has over 7,000 students – twice as many as when university status was awarded in 2005. It is involved in a national initiative to promote social entrepreneurship and offers support to graduates who wish to start their own businesses.

Winchester has also been investing in research and held its own in the latest assessments. Almost 45 per cent of the work entered for the 2014 Research Excellence Framework was considered world-leading or internationally excellent, with communications and history producing the best results.

The university has since established a Centre for English Identity and Politics, run by John Denham, the former Labour Universities Secretary. A Centre for Animal Welfare has also opened in 2016 to follow the Sport and Exercise Research Centre, which opened with nine fully funded research studentships to celebrate the 175th anniversary of the original institution's foundation. It was then a Church of England foundation for teacher training and was known as King Alfred College until 2004.

The university is still best known for its education courses, which Ofsted rates as outstanding, although they no longer dominate in terms of student numbers. Other degrees span business, arts, humanities, health and social care, and social science. Undergraduates can take advantage of exchange schemes with a number of American universities, as well as others in Japan and across Europe.

The number of international students has trebled since 2010 and now accounts for almost 7 per cent of the places. Thirty per cent of British undergraduates are from low-income families and 96 per cent are state educated.

Sparkford Road
Winchester
Hampshire SO22 4NR

01962 827234 (enquiries)
course.enquiries@winchester.ac.uk
www.winchester.ac.uk
www.winchester
students.co.uk
Affiliations: GuildHE;
Cathedrals Group

The Times and Sunday Times Rankings

Overall Ranking: =72 (last year: =64)

Teaching quality:	48	81.7%
Student experience:	=73	83.3%
Research quality:	=82	5.8%
Entry standards:	105	295
Student–staff ratio:	=72	16.7
Services & facilities/student:	116	£1,344
Expected completion rate:	45	88.7%
Good honours:	37	77.3%
Graduate prospects:	=108	61.2%

The compact site is on a wooded hillside overlooking the cathedral city, a ten-minute walk away, with views of the surrounding countryside. The campus is well equipped, with theatrical performance spaces, sports hall and fitness suite supplemented by the £3.5-million Winchester Sports Stadium. Open to local people as well as students, the stadium has a 400-metre, eight-lane athletics track with supporting facilities for field events and a floodlit all-weather pitch. Six performing arts studios offer the latest technology for student productions.

An award-winning extension to the library added 450 study spaces and extra computers, while a modern Learning and Teaching Building significantly improved the facilities for lectures and independent study.

The University Centre houses the students' union, a nightclub, cinema, catering facilities, a bookshop and a supermarket.

A "learning café" creates an informal working space with networked PCs and wireless internet access. Building on the success of this development, the university has developed a second social learning space, with PC access, a café, informal seating areas and outside terracing. The students' union has achieved consistently good ratings in the NSS.

The West Downs Campus, which is only a short walk away, is the base for the business school and the location for a £12-million student village providing more than 700 residential places. There is also a gallery that is open to the public and a centre for research and knowledge exchange. Two other complexes adjacent to the King Alfred Campus provide self-catering accommodation for almost 900 students, while there are three catered halls of residence on the campus itself. The newest student village includes a large gym, available to local residents as well as students and staff. The new gym is part of a major investment by the university to enhance its sports facilities.

Students value the close-knit atmosphere and find the city is livelier than its staid image might suggest, with a number of bars catering to their tastes. Southampton is not far for those who hanker after the attractions of a bigger city, and London is only an hour away by train.

Tuition fees

» Fees for UK/EU students 2017–18   £9,250
    Foundation degree in childhood studies   £4,000
    Year abroad   £1,385
    Placement year   £1,385
» UK fees are expected to increase by the rate of inflation from 2018–19 onwards.
» Fees for international students 2017–18   £11,600
» Check the university's website for the latest information on fees, scholarships, bursaries and other forms of student support.

Students		
Undergraduates:	5,530	(380)
Postgraduates:	305	(1,275)
Mature students:	14.0%	
International students:	6.1%	
Applications per place:	4.5	
From state-sector schools:	96.1%	
From working-class homes:	30.4%	
Satisfaction with students' union	83%	

For detailed information about sports facilities:
www.winchester.ac.uk/campuscitylife/Sportsfacilities

Accommodation

Number of places and costs refer to 2016–17
University-provided places: approximately 1,700 on campus and 200 off campus.
Percentage catered: 5%
Catered costs: £149.80 (contract 28.2 weeks).
Self-catered costs: £85.14 – £236.49 (37–50 weeks).
All first-year full-time undergraduates who fulfil conditions are guaranteed housing.
www.winchester.ac.uk/Studyhere/
Student%20accommodation

University of Wolverhampton

Wolverhampton has declined to release any data for use in league tables since 2009, when it finished just outside the top 100. Its intake of undergraduates has dropped by more than 600 since then. The university is one of only three to maintain a boycott this year. A statement on its website says that tables such as ours disadvantage universities like Wolverhampton and do not represent a fair picture of their strengths. As a result, it is missing from the main ranking and all the subject tables.

The statement advises applicants to use publicly available data, such as results from the 2014 Research Excellence (REF), which it claims recognise the university's research as world-leading. In fact, 8 per cent of the Wolverhampton submission was awarded the 4* rating that signified world-leading research.

Scores have been rising in the National Student Survey, however. The 2016 survey showed an increase of 2 percentage points in overall satisfaction, taking Wolverhampton out of the bottom 40 universities.

Wolverhampton academics have been awarded six National Teaching Fellowships, while research mainly serves the needs of business and industry, as well as underpinning teaching. By far the best REF results were in information science, where almost 90 per cent of the research submitted was considered world-leading or internationally excellent.

Wolverhampton is halfway through a £250-million programme that promises the biggest investment in its history to drive economic growth for the benefit of students and the wider region. The five-year project will include new buildings and facilities, as well as investment in teaching, research and skills training.

An £18-million building for the business school opened in 2015 and impressive new engineering facilities are being provided in Telford and Wolverhampton. New courses are being offered in automotive and motorsport engineering, electronic and telecommunications engineering, chemical engineering and, most recently, aerospace engineering.

A new science centre, the Rosalind Franklin Building, opened fully in 2015. A bigger project will see the £65-million redevelopment of the derelict Springfield Brewery site in the city to create a new campus for construction and the built environment. The new West Midlands Construction University Technical College (UTC) is already open, an Elite Centre for Manufacturing Skills will follow in August, and the university's School of Architecture and the Built Environment

Wulfruna Street
Wolverhampton WV1 1LY

01902 321032 (course enquiries)
enquiries@wlv.ac.uk
www.wlv.ac.uk
www.wolvesunion.org
Affiliation: none

The Times and Sunday Times **Rankings**
Wolverhampton blocked the release of data from the Higher Education Statistics Agency and so we cannot give any ranking information.

will complete a range of provision that will provide skills and education from the age of 14 through to postgraduate courses and executive education. A second UTC in West Bromwich specialises in health sciences.

The university has three bases in the West Midlands: the original site in the centre of Wolverhampton, a campus in Walsall dedicated to sport and performance, as well as education and part of the School of Health and Wellbeing, and a purpose-built campus at Telford, Shropshire, which focuses on business and engineering.

In 2016, the university launched the Wolverhampton School of Art, a new vision for art and design in the city. The same year also saw the opening of University Centre Telford, a partnership with Telford College of Arts and Technology, offering short courses and professional development programmes in a prominent town centre location. The university also offers part-time courses at Stafford, but a branch campus in Mauritius was short-lived. Its closure was announced only four years after it opened, with only 140 students enrolled.

Wolverhampton's success in widening participation in higher education is such that only one university (Bradford) has a higher proportion of undergraduates coming from working-class homes. Almost all the students are from state schools and one in five comes from an area of low participation. The university draws two-thirds of its 19,000 students from the West Midlands. Over a third of the places are filled by mature students and about the same proportion come from the region's ethnic minorities. The university is leading a regional scheme to encourage young people to consider higher education.

Student facilities have been improved with the redevelopment of the students' union on the City Campus and the opening of a new union bar on the Walsall Campus. The Performance Hub, in Walsall, the university's centre for performing arts, has exceptional facilities for music, dance and drama. There is a 350-bed student village and sports facilities, including a Sports Science and Medicine Centre which was used to train Olympic contenders.

The city has a growing nightlife, and the university was voted the friendliest in the West Midlands by former students. The cost of living is reasonable, and Birmingham is only a metro tram ride away.

Tuition fees

» Fees for UK/EU students 2017–18 £9,250
  Foundation degree £8,250
  Foundation degree at partner colleges up to £6,165
  Placement year / Year abroad no fee
» UK fees are expected to increase by the rate of inflation from 2018–19 onwards.
» Fees for international students 2017–18 £11,475
» Check the university's website for the latest information on fees, scholarships, and other forms of student support.

Students

Undergraduates:	12,690	(3,535)
Postgraduates:	1,375	(1,465)
Satisfaction with students' union	64%	

For detailed information about sports facilities:
www.wlv.ac.uk/study-here/student-life/wlv-sport

Accommodation

Number of places and costs refer to 2016–17
University-provided places: 1,646
Percentage catered: 0%
Self-catered costs: £77 – £99 a week (37 weeks).
First-year students are offered accommodation provided requirements are met. Residential restrictions apply.
International students: same as above.
accommodationservices@wlv.ac.uk
www.wlv.ac.uk/study-here/accommodation

University of Worcester

Higher levels of satisfaction with teaching, feedback and academic support have helped Worcester to a rise of ten places in this year's table. The university has also done much better on graduate prospects and has awarded more good honours degrees. Worcester is now in the top 40 for teaching quality in the National Student Survey, although it slipped slightly in the sections relating to learning resources, course organisation and personal development.

Growth in the demand for places has resumed after a single year's dip – there were more than twice as many applications in 2015 as when Worcester became a university in 2006. As a result, the university has been able to continue growing – it increased the undergraduate intake by 16 per cent in 2015 – while raising entry standards.

Sport, education and business courses have been particularly popular, and there have been increases, too, in biochemistry, journalism, illustration, nursing and several other health subjects. In 2016, the university introduced law to its portfolio.

Worcester was also one of the most improved universities in the 2014 Research Excellence Framework compared with previous assessments: it went up 20 places in our research ranking, partly because it entered five times as many academics as in 2008. A third of the work was considered world leading or internationally excellent, with history and art and design achieving the best scores. The performance has produced a big increase in research funding.

The university has three campuses less than a mile from each other and all close to the city centre. The main St John's Campus occupies a parkland site 15 minutes' walk from the city centre. It includes science facilities, the National Pollen and Aerobiology Research Unit, the digital arts centre and drama studio, and an AstroTurf pitch.

The City Campus largely occupies the historic buildings of the former Worcester Royal Infirmary in the heart of the city. It includes teaching, residential and conference facilities and is the site of Worcester Business School. Further developments are taking place at the City Campus over the next two years following the acquisition of adjacent city centre buildings. Almost next door is the university's spectacular library and history centre, The Hive, which brings together many services from Worcestershire County Council, including archaeology and history, with those of the university. The Hive was the first joint public and university library to open in Britain, and has won several awards.

The other star facility is a 2,000-seat indoor sporting arena, opened in 2013,

---

Henwick Grove
Worcester WR2 6AJ

01905 855111 (admissions)
admissions@worc.ac.uk
www.worcester.ac.uk
www.worcsu.com
Affiliation: GuildHE

The Times and Sunday Times Rankings

Overall Ranking: **90** (last year: =100)

Teaching quality:	=36	82.5%
Student experience:	=56	84.1%
Research quality:	=97	4.3%
Entry standards:	=97	303
Student–staff ratio:	=83	17.3
Services & facilities/student:	118	£1,315
Expected completion rate:	66	85.7%
Good honours:	92	65.8%
Graduate prospects:	85	68%

which is one of only two specialist sports venues in the UK designed specifically for wheelchair athletes as well as the able-bodied. In 2015 it won a national award for Buildings that Inspire, and hosted the European Wheelchair Basketball Championships, as well as top-flight netball, basketball and martial arts events.

The Arena, on the Riverside Campus, is being developed as an International Centre for Inclusive Sport and Health, and will include a new cricket centre in partnership with Worcestershire County Cricket Club. The university has also purchased a plot of land on the outskirts of the city, which has sports pitches and a 10-acre lake, which will be adapted for a range of inclusive water sports and other outdoor activities.

The university's commitment to disability sports extends to the UK's first disability sport degree. Worcester's Vice-Chancellor, Professor David Green, spoke about sporting inclusion at a conference at the 2016 Paralympic Games in Rio.

First as a post-war emergency teacher training college and later as a university college, the institution has always been the only provider of higher education in Worcestershire. The university remains strong in education and also in nursing and midwifery. It is the partner university for the National Childbirth Trust, delivering all of the trust's antenatal training.

More than a third of the undergraduates come from working-class homes and the projected dropout rate is better than average for Worcester's subjects and entry standards. The university has long-established projects working with primary schools to try to broaden the intake further. There are excellent links with local businesses and students have access to an extensive "earn-as-you-learn" programme. An emphasis on employability was commended by the Quality Assurance Agency. A number of partner colleges, as well as less conventional study centres such as hospices and specialist national organisations, offer Worcester courses.

The cathedral city is not large, but is safer than many university locations, and has its share of pubs and clubs that cater for a growing student clientele. An active students' union acts as a social hub and the university has more than 1,000 residential places on the St John's and City campuses.

Tuition fees

- » Fees for UK/EU students 2017–18 £9,250
  Foundation degree £9,250
  Placement year £900
- » UK fees are expected to increase by the rate of inflation from 2018–19 onwards.
- » Fees for international students 2017–18 £11,700
- » Check the university's website for the latest information on fees, scholarships, bursaries and other forms of student support.

Students

Undergraduates:	7,110	(1,415)
Postgraduates:	600	(945)
Mature students:	34.0%	
International students:	5.6%	
Applications per place:	5.2	
From state-sector schools:	98%	
From working-class homes:	36.9%	
Satisfaction with students' union	68%	

For information about sports facilities:
www.worcester.ac.uk/your-home/sport-at-worcester.html

Accommodation

Number of places and costs refer to 2016–17
University-provided places: around 1,000
Percentage catered: 0%
Self-catered costs: £91 (standard) – £149 (en suite) a week.
First-year students are guaranteed accommodation, on a first come, first served basis, if conditions are met.
International students are accommodated if conditions are met.
accommodation@worc.ac.uk
www.worcester.ac.uk/your-home/living-in-halls.html

Wrexham Glyndŵr University

Applications to Wrexham Glyndŵr held up well in 2015 in spite of a decision to shut the London campus, which once accounted for almost a quarter of the university's total enrolment. However, the associated course closures resulted in a drop of 18 per cent in the numbers starting degrees. Ceasing recruitment to the London campus was a condition of the reinstatement of the university's licence to recruit international students after 200 students were judged by UK Visas and Immigration to have invalid English language qualifications. The remaining London students are being taught at a small site in Kingston, but in future all full-timers will be based in Wales.

The university has now added the town of Wrexham to its title to stress its location. It had already taken the name of the 15th-century Welsh prince Owain Glyndŵr (who championed the establishment of universities throughout Wales) when university status was awarded in 2008.

Wrexham Glyndŵr's main campus and a smaller base for the Art School are in Wrexham and there are two further sites at Northop, in Flintshire, and St Asaph, in Denbighshire. Total student numbers are down to 6,700, just over half of whom are full-time undergraduates. Almost half are 21 or more on entry. Nearly all the undergraduates are state-educated, approaching half of them coming from the four poorest socio-economic groups – far more than average for the university's subjects and entry grades. Wrexham Glyndŵr also has the largest proportion of disabled students in Wales and has a dedicated centre that assesses students' needs before they embark on a course.

Northop hosts the university's rural campus, specialising in courses on animal studies and biodiversity. Students have access to a small-animal unit containing a wide range of species from monkeys to snakes and scorpions, as well as an equine centre.

The St Asaph Campus is a research centre that brings together academia and industry, focusing on high-level opto-electronics technology, as well as hosting the headquarters of the university's commercial arm, Glyndŵr Innovations. There is also an Advanced Composite Training and Development Centre, at Broughton, in partnership with Airbus, which has a large plant nearby. Research carried out there will help to improve the efficiency of aircraft and feed into the university's undergraduate engineering courses, which are also developed in association with Airbus.

The university entered only 34 academics for the 2014 Research Excellence

Mold Road
Wrexham
LL11 2AW

01978 293439 (enquiries)
enquiries@glyndwr.ac.uk
www.glyndwr.ac.uk
www.wrexhamglyndwrsu.
org.uk
Affiliation: GuildHE

The Times and Sunday Times Rankings

Overall Ranking: **125** (last year: 122)

Teaching quality:	=19	83.5%
Student experience:	88	82.4%
Research quality:	117	2.3%
Entry standards:	127	250
Student–staff ratio:	126	22.1
Services & facilities/student:	103	£1,533
Expected completion rate:	123	74.2%
Good honours:	120	55.6%
Graduate prospects:	116	58.9%

Framework, but a third of their work was judged to internationally excellent, with some world-leading.

Most of its teaching and research takes place in Wrexham, however, where more study and social spaces were added in 2016. It is the only university to own an international football stadium – the oldest in the world – having bought the Racecourse Ground to safeguard the future of Wrexham FC and provide more facilities for its students.

The university already had a partnership with the club, whose land, next door to the university's Plas Coch site, hosts the 200-bed Wrexham Village. Part of the Plas Coch Hostel was transformed in 2013 into a library featuring more than 13,000 books collected by a New York scholar.

The campus also contains a modern sports centre that includes two floodlit artificial pitches, an international standard hockey pitch, a human performance laboratory and indoor facilities that contain a sports hall with a 1,000 square-metre sprung floor, dance studios and a gym.

Wrexham Glyndŵr has embarked on a series of academic developments, including two-year fast-track degrees and four-year Master's degrees in art and design, engineering and computing. The £2-million Centre for the Child, Family and Society, based on a Scandinavian concept, allows those working in the field of child development to hone their skills in both academic and practical activities.

The Centre for the Creative Industries has up-to-date TV, radio and online production studios, which are the regional home of BBC Cymru Wales as well as playing a key role in the university's television degree.

Other facilities include a recording studio that is available around the clock, a Chinese medicine clinic, crime scene labs, computer game development labs, flight simulator and supersonic wind tunnel.

A high proportion of the students are local, many living at home, which inevitably affects the social scene, but eases the pressure on residential accommodation.

Wrexham is not without nightlife, and there has been a £90,000 upgrade of the students' union, where the Centenary Club has become a popular venue. It has featured a stream of top comedians recently, while the stadium hosts the Focus Wales festival, in 2016 starring Stereophonics.

Tuition fees

- » Fees for UK/EU students 2017–18 £9,000
- » Fees for international students 2017–18 £11,500
- » Welsh Assembly non-means-tested grant to pay fees above £4,046 for Welsh students. Tuition fee grant under review from 2018.
- » Check the university's website for the latest information on fees, scholarships, bursaries and other forms of student support.

Students

Undergraduates:	3,455	(2,420)
Postgraduates:	390	(505)
Mature students:	49.7%	
International students:	23.0%	
Applications per place:	3.9	
From state-sector schools:	98.2%	
From working-class homes:	46.2%	
Satisfaction with students' union	70%	

For detailed information about sports facilities:
www.sport.glyndwr.ac.uk

Accommodation

Number of places and costs refer to 2016–17
University-provided places: 235
Percentage catered: 0%
Self-catered costs: £83.75 (single, shared kitchen and bathroom) – £96.50 (en suite) a week (37 weeks).
First-year full-time undergraduates are given priority in accordance with the university's allocation policy.
International students: guaranteed housing if conditions are met.
www.glyndwr.ac.uk/en/Accommodation

University of York

A big increase in student satisfaction with teaching, feedback and academic support has not been enough to prevent York dropping two places in our table, with lower scores on six of the other seven indicators.

It had already lost ground on some of its competitors in the 2014 Research Excellence Framework, when it submitted a lower proportion of its academics for assessment than most of the leading universities. Nevertheless, more than 80 per cent of the research was considered world leading or internationally excellent, and York was in the top ten for the impact of its research. Eight departments were ranked in the top five for their subject and the university remains in the top 20 both for research quality and overall.

The university is situated within walking distance of York's historic city centre, where archaeology and medieval studies are based in suitably ancient buildings. All students join one of the nine colleges – small, distinct communities based on the two linked campuses. They combine academic and social roles and provide a network of support, events and activities. Some departments have their headquarters in one of the colleges, but the student communities are a mix of disciplines, years and sexes.

York has invested £750 million on its estate since deciding that the university was too small to maximise its research capability and satisfy the growing demand for its places, increasing its student population by 50 per cent. Recent developments include teaching and research buildings for biology, chemistry and environmental studies, and a cross-departmental teaching and learning centre. This will be followed in September 2017 by the opening of the Piazza Learning Centre, which will feature a 350-seat auditorium and more than 30 flexible learning spaces.

York has launched a series of initiatives to help develop its students' transferable skills and enhance their employment prospects. Over 400 employers visit York each year to offer workshops, seminars and networking events, including many alumni working in senior positions from a diverse range of industries. The Student Internship Bureau (SIB) sources paid internships, and a number of courses include the option of an industrial placement.

Students also have the opportunity to work towards the York Award, the university's certificate of personal development, recognising their achievements in activities such as volunteering and work experience.

Over 2,000 York students volunteer each year, working in schools, environmental organisations and to support charities and social enterprises. York is also the first UK

Heslington
York YO10 5DD

01904 324000 (admissions)
ug-admissions@york.ac.uk
www.york.ac.uk
www.hyms.ac.uk
www.yusu.org
Affiliation: Russell Group

The Times and Sunday Times Rankings

Overall Ranking: **17** (last year: 15)

Teaching quality:	15	83.8%
Student experience:	15	87.5%
Research quality:	17	38.3%
Entry standards:	21	431
Student–staff ratio:	=33	14.5
Services & facilities/student:	43	£2,144
Expected completion rate:	23	93.3%
Good honours:	=24	80.5%
Graduate prospects:	43	77%

university to host a crowd-funding website helping students to fund their personal projects.

The latest figures for widening participation in higher education saw York meet its benchmarks for the first time for the recruitment of state school students and those from areas of low participation, but not for the proportion of undergraduates from low-income families. Every student has a supervisor responsible for their academic and personal welfare, and support for studies alongside the main curriculum includes access to foreign language tuition and Mathematics and Writing Study Skills Centres. Students can also access free university Wi-Fi in York city centre and a free laptop loan service in the main University Library and the King's Manor Library.

A member of the Russell Group since 2012, York is expanding the overseas opportunities open to students. There are "international study centres", or themed summer schools, at partner universities and the Centre for Global Programmes is helping to increase the range of exchanges and study abroad schemes. Participation in some form of international mobility increased in three years from less than 4 per cent to almost 10 per cent. The university provides a growing number of travel grants and scholarships to help students participate in overseas opportunities.

Social life on campus is lively. There are television and radio stations, as well as several student newspapers and magazines. The students' union runs over 180 societies, covering everything from juggling to jazz, and supports 63 student-led sports teams.

Sports facilities are good, and include four sports halls and a dance studio. The £12-million York Sports Village features a 25-metre pool, learner pool, 100-station gym, full-size 3G pitch and three further five-a-side pitches. The university has the only velodrome in Yorkshire, a 1-km cycling track and an athletics track. Tennis and squash facilities have been refurbished and £30,000 invested in coaching.

Cultural events abound on campus and in the city, which is also famous for a high concentration of pubs and its music scene. The free Festival of Ideas, run by the university, is the largest of its type in the UK.

Tuition fees

- » Fees for UK/EU students 2017–18 — £9,250
  Year abroad — £1,385
  Placement year — £1,850
- » UK fees are expected to increase by the rate of inflation from 2018–19 onwards.
- » Fees for international students 2017–18 — £16,290–£20,500
  Medicine — £29,400
- » Check the university's website for the latest information on fees, scholarships, bursaries and other forms of student support.

Students

Undergraduates:	11,710	(1,100)
Postgraduates:	3,205	(815)
Mature students:	10.2%	
International students:	14.7%	
Applications per place:	7.4	
From state-sector schools:	82.9%	
From working-class homes:	19.6%	
Satisfaction with students' union	60%	

For detailed information about sports facilities:
www.york.ac.uk/study/student-life/sport

Accommodation

Number of places and costs refer to 2016–17
University-provided places: 5,668
Percentage catered: 16%
Catered costs: £123 – £173 a week.
Self-catered costs: £106 – £150 a week.
First-year undergraduates are guaranteed accommodation if terms and conditions are met.
International students: as above.
accommodation@york.ac.uk
www.york.ac.uk/study/accommodation

York St John University

York St John is aiming to be "the best of England's small universities" – by which it means those with fewer than 8,000 students – by 2020. Among its targets are better course organisation, assessment and feedback to produce increased student satisfaction and higher completion rates, as well as better results in the next Research Excellence Framework (REF).

This year's table suggests that it is focusing on the right areas because a dramatic decline in the National Student Survey and lower scores for completion, good honours and graduate prospects have led to a drop of more than 20 places.

The university will continue to charge the lowest fees in England in 2017–18, only £3,500, on its Foundation degrees in education. But the courses are for a limited range of mature students without traditional qualifications; the fees for all Honours degrees will be £9,250.

The university is a Church of England foundation that dates back to 1841, when the Diocesan Training School opened with just one pupil on the register, in whose honour the students' union is named. Full university status finally arrived in 2006.

Divided between York and Ripon for most of its existence, the university now concentrates all its activities on York. The 11-acre campus faces York Minster across the city walls and is a five-minute walk from the city centre. It has seen £91 million of development in recent years and more is planned.

The Fountains Learning Centre, which provides a striking entrance to the university, has been refurbished. It has 530 computer workstations, multimedia group-work facilities, 24-hour access to enhanced self-service facilities and an enlarged book stock, as well an internet café and lecture theatre. Nearby, the prize-winning De Grey Court, which cost £15.5 million and serves the health and life sciences, links the university quarter with the city centre.

The university's mission statement says its provision is "shaped" by the York St John's church foundation, although it welcomes students of all beliefs. The Business School is the biggest faculty, having overtaken education and theology, as well as health and life sciences.

Almost two-thirds of the students are female and there is a growing cohort of international students. Almost 97 per cent of the UK undergraduates attended state schools or colleges, and more than a third come from one of the four poorest socio-economic groups. York St John was also one of only six universities to score full marks for its support of gay and lesbian in an annual guide published by equality charity Stonewall.

New Mayor's Walk
York YO31 7EX

01904 876598 (information hotline)
admissions@yorksj.ac.uk
www.yorksj.ac.uk
http://ysjsu.com
Affiliations: Cathedrals
   Group, GuildHE

The Times and Sunday Times Rankings

Overall Ranking: **=110** (last year: 89)

Teaching quality:	=80	79.9%
Student experience:	109	81.1%
Research quality:	=100	4.1%
Entry standards:	99	302
Student–staff ratio:	=100	18.5
Services & facilities/student:	107	£1,463
Expected completion rate:	56	86.9%
Good honours:	116	59.2%
Graduate prospects:	=104	61.7%

There are now 6,500 students, but the university plans to grow by 10 per cent over the next four years. The volume of applications has grown by almost 60 per cent since university status arrived, but four years of increases came to an end in 2014 and is yet to resume.

The faculty of arts has been one of the main points of expansion, especially in degree programmes such as film and television, media and American studies. Another music technology suite has been added and performance spaces include two dedicated TV studios, digital non-linear edit suites, digital imaging equipment and equipment for sound manipulation.

Psychology produced the best results in the 2014 REF, when the 30 per cent of research regarded as world-leading or internationally excellent represented a big improvement on the 2008 assessments.

Relatively high numbers of local mature students ease the pressure on residential accommodation. As a result, first years choosing York St John as their first choice and who want to live in university-owned accommodation are now guaranteed places. A new private development of shared flats and studio apartments opened in 2015.

On campus, there is a sports hall, climbing wall, basketball, netball, indoor football and cricket nets. The university's sports facility, Nestlé Rowntree Park, opened in 2015. Just under a mile from the campus, the 57-acre site includes a 3G pitch for rugby and football, a synthetic pitch for hockey and small-sided games, three netball courts and three tennis courts, as well as grass pitches, a sprint track and a bowling green. A new sports centre opened there the following year with a sports hall, gym, changing rooms and conference and teaching space.

The students' union won the NUS award for Small and Specialist Union of the Year in 2014, having doubled its number of societies and society members. York is popular as a student city with a growing range of clubs as well as, supposedly, a pub for every day of the year.

Tuition fees

» Fees for UK/EU students 2017–18 £9,250
   Foundation degree in education £3,500
» UK fees are expected to increase by the rate of inflation from 2018–19 onwards.
» Fees for international students 2017–18 £10,000–£11,500
» Check the university's website for the latest information on fees, scholarships, bursaries and other forms of student support.

Students

Undergraduates:	5,065	(655)
Postgraduates:	425	(405)
Mature students:	13.4%	
International students:	8.7%	
Applications per place:	6.0	
From state-sector schools:	96.5%	
From working-class homes:	34.9%	
Satisfaction with students' union	70%	

For detailed information about sports facilities:
www.yorksj.ac.uk/ysjactive

Accommodation

Number of places and costs refer to 2016–17
University-provided places: 1,650
Percentage catered: 9%
Catered costs: £122 – £148 a week (34 weeks).
Self-catered costs: £90 – £165 a week (44–48 weeks).
First years choosing university as first choice are guaranteed accommodation.
International students: guaranteed housing.
accommodation@yorksj.ac.uk
www.yorksj.ac.uk/study/accommodation

Specialist Institutions of Higher Education

1 Specialist colleges of the University of London

This listing gives contact details for specialist degree-awarding colleges within the University of London not listed elsewhere within the book. Those marked * are members of GuildHE (www.guildhe.ac.uk). Fees are given for UK/EU undergraduates for a single year of study.

Courtauld Institute of Art
Somerset House
Strand
London WC2R 0RN
020 7848 2645   **www.courtauld.ac.uk**
Fees 2017–18: £9,250

Heythrop College
Kensington Square
London W8 5HN
020 7795 6600   **www.heythrop.ac.uk**
postgraduate only

London Business School
Regent's Park
London NW1 4SA
020 7000 7000   **www.london.edu**
Postgraduate only

London School of Hygiene and Tropical Medicine
Keppel Street
London WC1E 7HT
020 7299 4646   **www.lshtm.ac.uk**
Postgraduate medical courses

Royal Academy of Music
Marylebone Road
London NW1 5HT
020 7873 7373   **www.ram.ac.uk**
Fees 2017–18: £9,250

Royal Central School of Speech and Drama*
Eton Avenue
London NW3 3HY
020 7722 8183   **www.cssd.ac.uk**
Fees 2017–18: £9,250

Royal Veterinary College
Royal College Street
London NW1 0TU
020 7468 5147   **www. rvc.ac.uk**
Fees 2017–18: £9,250

University of London Institute in Paris
9–11 rue de Constantine
75340 Paris Cedex 07, France
(+33) 1 44 11 73 83
http://ulip.london.ac.uk
Degrees offered in conjunction with Queen Mary and Royal Holloway colleges
Fees 2016–17: £9,000

2 Specialist colleges and private institutions

This listing gives contact details for other degree-awarding higher education institutions not mentioned elsewhere within the book. All the institutions listed below offer degree courses, some providing a wide range of courses while others are specialist colleges with a small intake. Those marked * are members of GuildHE (**www.guildhe.ac.uk**). Fees are given for UK/EU undergraduates for a single year of study.

BPP University
6th floor, Doulton House
Chorlton Street, Manchester M1 3HY
Campuses in Abingdon, Birmingham,
Bristol, Cambridge, Leeds, Liverpool,
London, Manchester.
03331 224 359 **www.bpp.com/bpp-university**
Fees 2017–18: £13,500 (two-year course);
£9,000 (three-year course)

Conservatoire for Dance and Drama
Comprised of
Bristol Old Vic Theatre School
Central School of Ballet
London Academy of Music and Dramatic
    Art (LAMDA)
London Contemporary Dance School
National Centre for Circus Arts
Northern School of Contemporary Dance
Rambert School of Ballet and
    Contemporary Dance
Royal Academy of Dramatic Art (RADA)
Tavistock House, Tavistock Square
London WC1H 9JJ
020 7387 5101 **www.cdd.ac.uk**
Fees 2017–18: £9,250

Glasgow School of Art
167 Renfrew Street, Glasgow G3 6RQ
0141 353 4500 **www.gsa.ac.uk**
Fees 2016–17: Scotland / EU, no fee
RUK £9,000

Guildhall School of Music and Drama
Silk Street, Barbican, London EC2Y 8DT
020 7628 2571 **www.gsmd.ac.uk**
Fees 2017–18: £9,250

The University of Law
Birmingham, Bristol, Chester, Exeter,
Guildford, Leeds, London (Bloomsbury and
Moorgate), Manchester
0800 289997 **www.law.ac.uk**
Fees 2016–17: £9,000 (two-year course)
£6,000 (three-year course)

Leeds College of Art*
Blenheim Walk, Leeds LS2 9AQ
0113 202 8000 **www.leeds-art.ac.uk**
Fees 2017–18: £9,250

Liverpool Institute for Performing Arts*
Mount Street, Liverpool L1 9HF
0151 330 3000 **www.lipa.ac.uk**
Fees 2017–18: £9,250

The London Institute of Banking and Finance
4–9 Burgate Lane
Canterbury, Kent CT1 2XJ
01227 818609
Student campus:
25 Lovat Lane, London EC3R 8EB
020 7337 6293 **www.libf.ac.uk**
Fees 2016–17: £6,000

New College of the Humanities
19 Bedford Square, London WC1B 3HH
020 7637 4550 **www.nchlondon.ac.uk**
Fees 2017–18: £12,000

Pearson College
80 Strand, London WC2R 0RL
0203 7334 456
www.pearsoncollegelondon.ac.uk
Fees 2017: £9,000

Plymouth College of Art*
Tavistock Place, Plymouth PL4 8AT
01752 203434   **www.plymouthart.ac.uk**
Fees 2017–18: £9,250

Ravensbourne*
6 Penrose Way, Greenwich Peninsula,
London SE10 0EW
020 3040 3040   **www.ravensbourne.ac.uk**
Fees 2017–18: £9,250

Regent's University London*
Inner Circle, Regent's Park,
London NW1 4NS
020 7487 7505   **www.regents.ac.uk**
Fees Autumn 2017: £16,400

**Rose Bruford College of Theatre and
Performance***
Lamorbey Park, Burnt Oak Lane,
Sidcup, Kent DA15 9DF
020 8308 2600   **www.bruford.ac.uk**
Fees 2017–18: £9,250

Royal College of Music
Prince Consort Road, London SW7 2BS
020 7591 4300   **www.rcm.ac.uk**
Fees 2017–18: £9,250

Royal Conservatoire of Scotland
100 Renfrew Street, Glasgow G2 3DB
0141 332 4101   **www.rcs.ac.uk**
Fees 2016–17: Scotland/EU, no fee;
RUK £9,000

Royal Northern College of Music
124 Oxford Road, Manchester M13 9RD
0161 907 5200   **www.rncm.ac.uk**
Fees 2017–18: £9,250

**Royal Welsh College of Music and
Drama**
Castle Grounds, Cathays Park,
Cardiff CF10 3ER
029 2034 2854   **www.rwcmd.ac.uk**
Fees 2017–18: £9,000

St Mary's University College*
191 Falls Road, Belfast BT12 6FE
028 9032 7678   **www.stmarys-belfast.ac.uk**
Fees 2016–17: £3,925; RUK £9,000

Scotland's Rural College
Campuses at Aberdeen, Ayr,
Cupar, Dumfries, Ecclesmachan, near
Broxburn, Edinburgh
0800 269453   **www.sruc.ac.uk**
Fees 2016–17: Scotland/EU, no fee;
RUK £5,600

Stranmillis University College
Stranmillis Road, Belfast BT9 5DY
028 9038 1271   **www.stran.ac.uk**
Fees 2016–17: £3,925; RUK £9,000

**Trinity Laban Conservatoire of Music
and Dance**
Music Faculty: King Charles Court
Old Royal Naval College,
Greenwich, London SE10 9JF
020 8305 4444
Dance Faculty: Laban Building, Creekside
London SE8 3DZ
020 8305 9400   **www.trinitylaban.ac.uk**
Fees 2017–18: £9,250

Writtle University College*
Lordship Lane, Writtle, Chelmsford, Essex
CM1 3RR
01245 424200   **www.writtle.ac.uk**
Fees 2017–18: £9,250

University Open Days 2017

The dates shown are for undergraduate Open Days that had been confirmed by the end of November 2016. For any universities not listed, please consult their websites as their Open Days had not been announced at that point. Also consult **www.opendays.com**.

Most Open Days will need to be booked well ahead of attendance. For multi-campus universities, different campuses often have different dates and you will need to ensure that you visit the correct campus for the course you are interested in.

Aberdeen: 26 August, 21 October

Aberystwyth: 12 July, 16 September, 14 October, 11 November

Anglia Ruskin: 7 June, 10 June

Bangor: 24 June, 1 July, 14 October, 28 October

Bath: 15 June, 16 June, 16 September

Bedfordshire: *Bedford* 15 February, 29 April, 5 July; *Luton* 29 April, 5 July);
    Milton Keynes 8 February, 15 March, 10 May

Birkbeck: 10 May, 22 June, 12 September, 22 November, 6 February 2018

Birmingham: 23 June, 24 June, 9 September, 14 October

Birmingham City: 10 June, 7 October, 11 November

Bishop Grosseteste: 3 June, 5 July, 18 August, 24 September, 15 October

Bournemouth: 10 June, 1 July; further dates to be announced

Bradford: 24 June, 6 October, 7 October, 4 November (am), 22 November (pm)

Brighton: *Grand Parade* 4 June, 10 June, 7 October, 11 November; *Moulsecoomb* 10 June,
    14 October; *Hillbrow, Eastbourne* 1 July, 28 October; *Falmer* 1 July, 4 November

Bristol: 16 June, 17 June, 9 September

Buckingham: 11 March, 1 July, 18 July, 19 August, 7 October, 2 November

Buckinghamshire New: 8 March, 29 April, 3 June, 19 August

Cambridge: 6 July, 7 July

Cardiff: 26 April, 7 July

Cardiff Metropolitan: *Health Sciences* 18 February, 22 April, 10 June;
    Art and Design 11 March; *Education* 4 February, 17 June; *Management* 18 February,
    8 April, 10 June

Chester: June, October (dates to be confirmed)

City, University of London: 23 June, 24 June, 16 September

Coventry: 17 June, 9 September, 14 October, 11 November; *London* 15 March;
    Scarborough 21 June

Creative Arts: 25 February; further dates to be announced

Cumbria: *All campuses* 18 August; *Lancaster and Brampton, Carlisle* 8 June;
    Fusehill, Carlisle 15 June; *Ambleside* 22 June

De Montfort: 18 February, 18 March; further dates in to be announced

Derby: *Chesterfield* 25 February, 17 June; *Derby and Buxton* 25 February, 10 June

Dundee: 28 August, 23 September

Durham: 26 June, 1 July, 23 September

East Anglia: 7 July, 8 July, 9 September, 21 October

East London: 4 March, 22 April, 26 April, 17 June, 19 July

Edge Hill: 17 June, 19 August

Essex: 17 June, 16 September, 21 October; *Southend* 28 October

Open Days cont

Exeter: 2 June, 3 June, 2 September; *Penryn* 10 June, 23 September

Falmouth: 20 May, 7 October, 28 October, 18 November

Glasgow: 15 June; further dates to be announced:

Goldsmiths: 15 February; further dates to be announced

Greenwich: 25 February; further dates to be announced

Hertfordshire: 18 March, 17 June

Highlands and Islands, Inverness: 1 March, 1 April, 30 May, 8 August

Huddersfield: 21 June, 22 June, 21 October, 8 November, 1 December

Hull: 8 July, 7 October, 21 October, 18 November

Imperial College: 28 June, 29 June, 16 September

Keele: 17 June, 20 August, 15 October, 2 December

Kent: 1 July, 7 October, 21 October; *Medway* 17 June, 15 October

King's College London: *Strand* 24 June, 9 September; *Guys* 10 June, 8 July

Kingston: 8 March, 21 June, 6 September

Leeds: 17 June, 22 June, 23 June, 9 September, 7 October

Leeds Beckett: 16 June, 7 October, 28 October, 25 November

Leicester: 7 July, 15 September, 16 September, 21 October

Lincoln: 7 July, 8 July, 23 September, 7 October, 21 October, 11 November, 25 November, 13 December

Liverpool: 23 June, 24 June, 23 September, 21 October

Liverpool Hope: 28 June, 8 July, 16 September, 21 October, 18 November

Liverpool John Moores: 23 June, 7 October, 21 October, 8 November

London Metropolitan: 1 July, 19 August, 2 September, 7 October, 4 November, 2 December

London School of Economics: 29 March; further dates to be announced

London South Bank: 17 June; further dates to be announced

Loughborough: 30 June, 1 July, 22 September, 23 September

Manchester: 23 June, 24 June, 30 September, 14 October

Manchester Metropolitan: 21 June; further dates to be announced

Middlesex: 11 February, 10 June

Newcastle: 30 June, 1 July, 16 September

Newman: 17 June, 8 July, 7 October, 10 November

Nottingham: 30 June, 1 July, 15 September, 16 September

Nottingham Trent: 22 March; further dates to be announced

Oxford: 28 June, 29 June, 15 September

Plymouth: 29 April, 28 June

Queen Mary, University of London: 23 June, 24 June, 7 October

Reading: 16 June, 17 June, 30 September, 7 October

Robert Gordon: 2 September, 11 October

Roehampton: 8 July; further dates to be announced

Royal Agricultural: 10 April

Royal Holloway: 14 June, 17 June

St Andrews: 8 March, 5 April, 12 April, 19 April; further dates to be announced

St Mark and St John: 10 June; further dates days to be announced

St Mary's, Twickenham: 14 June, 16 September, 25 October, 1 December

Sheffield: 21 June, 8 July, 9 September, 21 October

Sheffield Hallam: 9 June, 10 June, 1 October, 11 November, 2 December

SOAS, London: 14 June

Southampton Solent: 10 June; further dates to be announced

Staffordshire: *Stafford* 24 June; *Stoke* 10 June

Stirling: 17 June, 16 September (date may change), 28 October

Suffolk: 7 March, 22 April, 8 July

Sunderland: 10 June, 22 August

Surrey: 30 June, 1 July, 16 September, 14 October

Swansea: 17 June, 14 October, 28 October

Teesside: *part-time courses* 8 March, 12 July, 6 September; *full-time courses* to be announced

Trinity St David: *Carmarthen* 4 February, 24 June; *Lampeter* 1 July; *Swansea* 18 February, 1 July

University College London: 30 June, 1 July, 9 September

University College Birmingham: 13 March, 1 April

Warwick: 23 June, 24 June

West London: 25 March, 21 June, 1 July, 14 October, 11 November

West of England: *All campuses* 30 September, 4 November; *City* 3 June, 18 November; *Frenchay, Gloucester, Bristol Zoo* 17 June; *Glenside* 17 June, 18 November

West of Scotland: *Ayr* 30 September, 4 October; *Dumfries* 6 September, 4 November; *Hamilton* 20 September, 28 October; *Paisley* 27 September, 7 October

Westminster: 18 March, 21 June

Winchester: 9 June, 1 July, 8 September, 9 September, 30 September, 14 October, 28 October

Wolverhampton: 4 February, 17 June, 19 August

Worcester: 25 June

Wrexham Glyndŵr: 4 March, 10 June, 19 August

York: 30 June, 1 July, 16 September, 17 September

York St John: 3 July, 19 August, 28 October, 11 November

Index